Lecture Notes in Computer Science 16606

Founding Editors

Gerhard Goos
Juris Hartmanis

The series Lecture Notes in Computer Science (LNCS), including its subseries Lecture Notes in Artificial Intelligence (LNAI) and Lecture Notes in Bioinformatics (LNBI), has established itself as a medium for the publication of new developments in computer science and information technology research, teaching, and education.

LNCS enjoys close cooperation with the computer science R & D community, the series counts many renowned academics among its volume editors and paper authors, and collaborates with prestigious societies. Its mission is to serve this international community by providing an invaluable service, mainly focused on the publication of conference and workshop proceedings and postproceedings. LNCS commenced publication in 1973.

Jan vom Brocke · Leona Chandra Kruse ·
Alan Hevner · Michael Rosemann ·
Monica Chiarini Tremblay · Robert Winter
Editors

Design for Better Futures: Beyond the Science of the Artificial

Completed Research

21st International Conference on Design Science Research
in Information Systems and Technology, DESRIST 2026
Münster, Germany, June 8–10, 2026
Proceedings, Part II

 Springer

Editors
Jan vom Brocke
University of Münster
Münster, Germany

Alan Hevner
University of South Florida
Tampa, FL, USA

Monica Chiarini Tremblay
William & Mary School of Business
Williamsburg, VA, USA

Leona Chandra Kruse
University of Agder
Kristiansand, Norway

Michael Rosemann
Queensland University of Technology
Brisbane, QLD, Australia

Robert Winter
University of St.Gallen
St.Gallen, Switzerland

ISSN 0302-9743   ISSN 1611-3349 (electronic)
Lecture Notes in Computer Science
ISBN 978-3-032-28312-2   ISBN 978-3-032-28313-9 (eBook)
https://doi.org/10.1007/978-3-032-28313-9

This Springer imprint is published by the registered company Springer Nature Switzerland AG
The registered company address is: Gewerbestrasse 11, 6330 Cham, Switzerland

If disposing of this product, please recycle the paper.

Preface

Over the past two decades, as Design Science Research (DSR) has become a central paradigm in Information Systems, the Design Science Research in Information Systems and Technology (DESRIST) conference has provided a prominent forum for the most current state of DSR. The intellectual roots of this orientation lie in Herbert A. Simon's *The Sciences of the Artificial.* Simon drew a clear line between the natural sciences, which explain phenomena that occur in nature, and disciplines concerned with artifacts deliberately created by humans. Engineering, architecture, and management all belong to this second class of applied sciences. Information Systems joined them by studying how digital artifacts and socio-technical systems can be purposefully designed to achieve desired outcomes under constraints.

Fast forward to 2026 – the landscape in which DSR operates has changed profoundly both in the complex problems we engage and the cutting-edge technologies we apply. Contemporary digital technologies – artificial intelligence, digital platforms, data infrastructures, and cyber-physical systems – rarely appear as isolated artifacts. They exist within dense socio-technical arrangements of interacting technologies, human actors, organizational practices, and institutional rules. More importantly, many digital artifacts are no longer stable objects but evolve constantly. They learn from data, adapt through algorithmic updates, develop through platform ecosystems, and continuously reshape the application environments in which they operate. What we design today does not remain fixed tomorrow. It grows, mutates, and interacts with other systems and actors. This transformation raises a deep question for DSR. If the artificial is no longer a stable artifact but an evolving socio-technical presence in everyday life, what are we designing, how can we best perform design, how do we control the emergent artifact behaviors, and how do we measure design success? In other words, the role of meta-design is gaining significance.

The artifacts of Design Science Research are now omni-present, yet many of us wonder whether this is the future we once imagined. We see artificial systems safeguarding citizens and being deployed in zones of conflict. They assist medical practitioners, yet at times introduce new burdens of cognitive load and accountability. They guide learning in classrooms but can steal students' attention and erode their curiosity. Regulations aim to protect the rights tied to personal data yet often arrive after the fact. Often, the artificial moves first; human comprehension and behavior follows. And we, still living, still human, want improved agency and control over our own better futures.

What does it mean to design for better futures? And, more importantly, what ideas and thinking might lie beyond the science of the artificial? These questions inspire our conference theme, *"Design for Better Futures: Beyond the Science of the Artificial."* With this theme, our twenty-first edition of DESRIST extended the boundaries of what counts and could count as design science. We envisioned DESRIST 2026 as a space to reimagine Design Science Research as both the science and the practice cultivating futures that are not only smarter, more ethical, and sustainable, but alive: growing, adapting, and breathing with the worlds they take root in.

Thus, we invited researchers from the Design Science Research community and beyond to reflect critically and creatively on the role of design in envisioning the futures that are possible, plausible, and probable considering both exciting new opportunities and cautionary risks. Related questions DESRIST 2026 hoped to answer included among others: How can Design Science contribute to achieving desired futures?; How can anticipatory design help to increase the robustness of organizations considering uncertain futures?; and How does Design Science Research change when a future point of reference, and not a current problem, is the starting point? As designed systems become increasingly complex and intertwined with our social, ecological, and institutional worlds, we must design systems that are sensitive to the broader ecosystems, both human and non-human, in which our designs will take hold and impact critical decisions.

This year, the Conference Chairs and the Program Chairs worked in a particularly close alignment, very much in the spirit of our conference theme. We did begin with clearly defined roles but soon found ourselves gently adapting them—perhaps our own small experiment in moving beyond the artificial. We designed, coordinated, and improvised together, often without quite noticing where one role ended, and another began. What started as a neat division of responsibilities became a collective act of co-designing the conference. It therefore felt only natural to carry this spirit forward in jointly editing this volume.

We received 231 submissions (108 full research papers, 54 research-in-progress papers, 35 prototype papers, and 34 submissions to the doctoral consortium, student track, and startup and industry forum). Each full research and research-in-progress paper was reviewed in a double-blind process by a minimum of two referees, and each prototype paper, as well as the submissions to the doctoral consortium, student track, and startup and industry forum, was reviewed single-blind by a minimum of two referees. These Springer Volumes 1 and 2 contain 48 full research papers with an acceptance rate of 44%.

We extend our sincere thanks to the wonderful team of colleagues and friends whose contributions were essential to making DESRIST in Münster a reality. First and foremost, we would like to thank Timo Strohmann, our key Managing Co-Chair, who—together with Katrin Bergener, Armin Stein, and Fumi Kurihara—navigated the many organizational challenges of this conference with great skill and dedication. We also extend our sincere appreciation to Hans-Henning Näscher and Lea Kleinekathöfer for their outstanding support in organizing the conference. We are equally grateful for the rich exchange with our General Co-Chairs Samir Chatterjee, Shirley Gregor, and Gunjan Mansingh.

With 10 research tracks, each led by 3–4 co-track chairs representing all three strategic regions of the Association for Information Systems—Americas; Europe, the Middle East, and Africa; and Asia Pacific—DESRIST 2026 was truly global and diverse. We cordially thank all colleagues among our 35 track chairs: Ahmed Abbasi, Aleksi Aaltonen, Roman Beck, Eva Bittner, Hanna Buyssens, Michael Cahalane, Kieran Conboy, Dimo Dimov, Edona Elshan, Gilbert Fridgen, Asif Gill, Amir Haj-Bolouri, Dirk Hovorka, Sarah Hönigsberg, Timothy Hor, Kai R. Larsen, Christine Legner, Jan Marco Leimeister,

Olivia Liu Sheng, Roman Lukyanenko, Kadi Lubi, Matthew Mullarkey, Nadine Ostern, Sophie Petzolt, Shahper Richter, Thorsten Schoormann, Christoph Seckler, Matthias Söllner, Yenni Tim, Heikki Topi, Lauri Wessel, and Stefano Za.

We are also very grateful for the wonderful work of colleagues contributing to additional DESRIST formats, such as the Doctoral Consortium, Prototypes, the Impact Forum, the Startup and Industry Forum, and the Student Track: Pär Ågerfalk, Ann-Kristin Cordes, Brian Donnellan, Michael Gau, Asif Gill, Thomas Haskamp, Iris Junglas, Fumi Kurihara, Alexander Maedche, Stephanie Missonier, Oliver Müller, Isabel Ramos, Lisa Seymour, Timo Strohmann, and Stefan Thalmann.

Last but not least, we would like to express our gratitude to Gregor Kipping, who professionally managed the entire process of producing these proceedings together with our valued colleagues at Springer Nature – we would like to thank them for their consistent and outstanding support. Given the large number of high-quality contributions, the 2026 proceedings are published in three volumes: Volumes 1 and 2 include all accepted full papers, while Volume 3 contains prototypes and research-in-progress papers, edited by the General Chairs and the Publication Chair.

We deeply appreciate the dedication and thoughtful engagement of our track chairs and reviewers, as well as the many authors who entrusted us with their work. It is inspiring to see our community continue to grow and flourish. We were especially delighted to feature interdisciplinary and practice-oriented keynote speakers, whose perspectives inspire us to think differently about design for better futures. Finally, we are particularly grateful to the local organizing team at the University of Münster for making the conference a truly memorable experience for all participants.

June 2026

Jan vom Brocke
Leona Chandra Kruse
Alan Hevner
Michael Rosemann
Monica Chiarini Tremblay
Robert Winter

Organization

Conference Co-chairs

Jan vom Brocke	University of Münster, Germany
Leona Chandra Kruse	University of Agder, Norway
Alan Hevner	University of South Florida, USA

Program Co-chairs

Robert Winter	University of St. Gallen, Switzerland
Michael Rosemann	Queensland University of Technology, Australia
Monica Chiarini Tremblay	William & Mary School of Business, USA

General Co-chairs

Samir Chatterjee	Claremont Graduate University, USA
Gunjan Mansingh	University of the West Indies, Jamaica
Shirley Gregor	Australian National University, Australia

Doctoral Consortium Co-chairs

Lisa Seymour	University of Cape Town, South Africa
Alexander Maedche	Karlsruhe Institute of Technology, Germany
Pär Ågerfalk	Uppsala University, Sweden

Prototypes Co-chairs

Oliver Müller	Paderborn University, Germany
Michael Gau	University of Liechtenstein, Liechtenstein
Stephanie Missonier	HEC Lausanne, Switzerland

Impact Forum Co-chairs

Brian Donnellan   Maynooth University, Ireland
Asif Gill   University of Technology Sydney, Australia
Iris Junglas   College of Charleston, USA

Startup and Industry Forum Co-chairs

Timo Strohmann   University of Münster, Germany
Fumi Kurihara   University of Münster, Germany
Thomas Haskamp   University of Münster, Germany

Student Track Co-chairs

Ann-Kristin Cordes   University of Kiel, Germany
Isabel Ramos   Universidade do Minho, Portugal
Stefan Thalmann   University of Graz, Austria

Managing Co-chairs

Fumi Kurihara   University of Münster, Germany
Katrin Bergener   University of Münster, Germany
Timo Strohmann   University of Münster, Germany
Armin Stein   University of Münster, Germany

Springer Proceedings Chair

Gregor Kipping   University of Liechtenstein, Liechtenstein

Website and System Chair

Hans-Henning Näscher   University of Münster, Germany

Communication Chair

Lea Kleinekathöfer   University of Münster, Germany

Track Chairs

Theme Track – Design for Better Futures: Beyond the Science of the Artificial

Jan vom Brocke   University of Münster, Germany
Leona Chandra Kruse   University of Agder, Norway
Alan Hevner   University of South Florida, USA

General Track – "From Insight to Impact"

Jan Marco Leimeister   University of St. Gallen, Switzerland
Aleksi Aaltonen   Stevens Institute of Technology, USA
Eva Bittner   Hamburg University, Germany
Khushbu Tilvawala   University of Auckland, New Zealand

The Future of Financial Services

Gilbert Fridgen   University of Luxembourg, Luxembourg
Nadine Ostern   Queensland University of Technology, Australia
Roman Beck   Bentley University, USA

Future of Data-Driven and AI-Enabled Design

Hanna Buyssens   ESCP Business School, Germany
Michael Cahalane   University of New South Wales, Australia
Kieran Conboy   University of Galway, Ireland
Amir Haj-Bolouri   University West, Sweden

Future of Healthcare and Wellbeing

Lauri Wessel	European New School of Digital Studies, Germany
Ahmed Abbasi	University of Notre Dame, USA
Kadi Lubi	Tallinn University of Technology, Estonia

Future of Design and Entrepreneurship

Christoph Seckler	ESCP Business School, Germany
Dimo Dimov	University of Bath, UK
Timothy Hor	RMIT University, Australia
Sophie Petzolt	Fraunhofer IAO, Germany

Future of Responsible and Sustainable Design

Thorsten Schoormann	Roskilde University, Denmark
Yenni Tim	University of New South Wales, Australia
Olivia Liu Sheng	Arizona State University, USA
Sarah Hönigsberg	ICN Business School, France

Future of Design Science Education

Matthias Söllner	University of Kassel, Germany
Heikki Topi	Bentley University, USA
Shahper Richter	University of Auckland, New Zealand
Stefano Za	Gabriele d'Annunzio University Chieti-Pescara, Italy

Future of Design Science Methodology

Roman Lukyanenko	University of Virginia, USA
Christine Legner	HEC Lausanne, Switzerland
Dirk Hovorka	University of Sydney, Australia
Kai R. Larsen	University of Colorado Boulder, USA

Future of Ecosystems for Design Science Research

Matthew Mullarkey	University of South Florida, USA
Asif Gill	University of Technology Sydney, Australia
Edona Elshan	Vrije Universiteit Amsterdam, Netherlands

Reviewers

Aleksi Aaltonen	Stevens Institute of Technology, USA
Salar Abaspur	University of Cologne, Germany
Gemza Ademaj	University of Notre Dame, USA
Maike Althaus	Paderborn University, Germany
Yehia Alzoubi	American University of the Middle East, Kuwait
Jana Ammann	LMU Munich, Germany
Katazo Amunkete	Namibia University of Science and Technology, Namibia
Arnold F. Arz von Straussenburg	University of Koblenz, Germany
Tamara Babaian	Bentley University, USA
Dinko Bacic	Loyola University Chicago, USA
Charlotte Bahr	Friedrich-Alexander-Universität Erlangen-Nürnberg, Germany
Madhushi Bandara	University of Technology Sydney, Australia
Christian Bartelheimer	University of Göttingen, Germany
Richard Baskerville	Georgia State University, USA
Ingrid Bauer-Hänsel	University of St. Gallen, Switzerland
Ransome Bawack	Audencia Business School, France
Christian Beecks	FernUniversität in Hagen, Germany
Vincent Beermann	Hasso Plattner Institute, Germany
Daniel Beverungen	Paderborn University, Germany
Manuel Bieri	University of Bern, Switzerland
Grace Billiris	University of Technology Sydney, Australia
Annemarie Bloch	University of Duisburg-Essen, Germany
Mads Bødker	Copenhagen Business School, Denmark
Martin Böhmer	Martin Luther University Halle-Wittenberg, Germany
Marten Borchers	University of Hamburg, Germany
Nina Boulus-Rødje	Roskilde University, Denmark
Tobias Brandt	University of Münster, Germany
Katharina Breiter	University of Hohenheim, Germany
Michael Breitner	Leibniz University Hannover, Germany
Ulrich Bretschneider	University of Kassel, Germany
Constantin Brîncoveanu	Goethe University Frankfurt, Germany
Olivia Bruhin	University of St. Gallen, Switzerland

Lorenzo Matthias Burcheri	University of Luxembourg, Luxembourg
Hanna Buyssens	ESCP Business School, Germany
Michael Cahalane	University of New South Wales, Australia
Marcel Cahenzli	University of St. Gallen, Switzerland
Kevin Carillo	TBS Education, France
Riccardo Cerretani	Gabriele d'Annunzio University Chieti-Pescara, Italy
Samir Chatterjee	Claremont Graduate University, USA
Michele Cipriano	Università Cattolica del Sacro Cuore, Italy
Shannon Colville	Queensland University of Technology, Australia
André Coners	South Westphalia University of Applied Sciences, Germany
Ryan Cook	University of Notre Dame, USA
Marian Cooray	University of New South Wales, Australia
Clinton Daniel	University of South Florida, USA
Danielly de Paula	Hasso Plattner Institute, Germany
Laura Detels	University of Göttingen, Germany
Chedia Dhaoui	University of New South Wales, Australia
Ronja Dobler	University of Münster, Germany
Mateusz Dolata	Zeppelin University, Germany
Ronan Doyle	University of Galway, Ireland
Andreas Drechsler	Victoria University of Wellington, New Zealand
Hanyu Duan	Hong Kong University of Science and Technology, China
Henry Edison	Blekinge Institute of Technology, Sweden
Maarja-Liis Elland	Tallinn University of Technology, Estonia
Edona Elshan	Vrije Universiteit Amsterdam, Netherlands
Jan Enkmann	Hasso Plattner Institute, Germany
Jürgen Fleiß	University of Graz, Austria
Sandro Franzoi	University of Münster, Germany
Natalie Früholz	Fraunhofer IWU, Germany
Michael Gau	University of Liechtenstein, Liechtenstein
Maria George	University of New South Wales, Australia
Matt Germonprez	University of Nebraska Omaha, USA
Heiko Gewald	Neu-Ulm University of Applied Sciences, Germany
Ahmad Ghazawneh	Halmstad University, Sweden
Mona Ghazi	ESCP Business School, Germany
Soham Ghosh	Trinity College Dublin, Ireland
Karoline Glaser	TU Dresden, Germany
Rob Gleasure	Copenhagen Business School, Denmark
Sarah Götz	University of Kassel, Germany

Max Gräser	Leipzig University, Germany
Renate Griessel-Duminy	ESCP Business School, Germany
Nick Große	TU Dortmund University, Germany
Rahel Gubser	Freie Universität Berlin, Germany
Tan Gürpinar	Quinnipiac University, USA
Ram Prasad Gurung	LUT University, Finland
Amir Haj-Bolouri	University West, Sweden
Martin Hänel	University of Kassel, Germany
Thomas Haskamp	University of Münster, Germany
Andreas Hein	University of St. Gallen, Switzerland
Daniel Heinz	Karlsruhe Institute of Technology, Germany
Savindu Herath	ETH Zurich, Switzerland
Malte Högemann	Osnabrück University, Germany
Maike Holtkemper	FernUniversität in Hagen, Germany
Sarah Hönigsberg	ICN Business School, France
Timothy Hor	RMIT University, Australia
Flora Horn	TU Dresden, Germany
Dirk Hovorka	University of Sydney, Australia
Michal Hron	Ghent University, Belgium
Han-Fen Hu	University of Nevada, Las Vegas, USA
Anna Hupe	University of Kassel, Germany
Aida Huskic	Open University of the Netherlands, Netherlands
Jan-Paul Huttner	German Aerospace Center (DLR), Germany
Mirijana Irnich	Osnabrück University, Germany
Christian Janiesch	TU Dortmund University, Germany
Andreas Janson	University of St. Gallen, Switzerland
Alireza Jaribion	University of South Florida, USA
Jonna Järveläinen	University of Jyväskylä, Finland
Florian Johannsen	Schmalkalden University of Applied Sciences, Germany
Frederick K. Johnson	University of California, Berkeley, USA
George Joukhadar	University of New South Wales, Australia
Gustaf Juell-Skielse	University of Borås, Sweden
Jürgen Jung	Frankfurt University of Applied Sciences, Germany
Iris Junglas	College of Charleston, USA
Pieter Kamminga	Open University of the Netherlands, Netherlands
Marlon Kampmann	South Westphalia University of Applied Sciences, Germany
Jesse Katende	University West, Sweden
Matthias Keller	Vlerick Business School, Belgium
Bijan Khosrawi-Rad	Leuphana University Lüneburg, Germany

Theodore Kindong	Linköping University, Sweden
Samuel Kirshner	University of New South Wales, Australia
Hermann Klöckner	Anhalt University of Applied Sciences, Germany
Charlotte Knickrehm	Goethe University Frankfurt, Germany
Christoph Kollwitz	ICN Business School, France
Björn Konopka	TU Dortmund University, Germany
Huda Koulani	University of Kassel, Germany
Diana Kozachek	University of St. Gallen, Switzerland
Julia Maria Kraus	LMU Munich, Germany
Kristin Krebs	University of Wuppertal, Germany
Sylvana Kroop	FHWien der WKW, Austria
Fumi Kurihara	University of Münster, Germany
Jan Laufer	University of Duisburg-Essen, Germany
Seung Jong Lee	Arizona State University, USA
Amelia Li	University of New South Wales, Australia
Mahei Manhai Li	University of Kassel, Germany
Jonas Liebschner	Karlsruhe Institute of Technology, Germany
Eric T.K. Lim	University of New South Wales, Australia
Sebastian Lins	University of Kassel, Germany
Alexander Maedche	Karlsruhe Institute of Technology, Germany
Onkar Malgonde	North Carolina State University, USA
Munir Mandviwalla	University of South Florida, USA
Osama Mansour	Lund University, Sweden
Harry Martin	Open University of the Netherlands, Netherlands
Julian Marx	University of Melbourne, Australia
Secil Matasova	Tallinn University of Technology, Estonia
Martin Matzner	Friedrich-Alexander-Universität Erlangen-Nürnberg, Germany
Valentin Mayer	University of Bayreuth, Germany
Alexander Meier	University of St. Gallen, Switzerland
Christian Meske	Ruhr University Bochum, Germany
Sophia Meywirth	University of Kassel, Germany
Frederik Möller	TU Braunschweig, Germany
Stefan Morana	Saarland University, Germany
Roland M. Mueller	Berlin School of Economics and Law, Germany
Pavankumar Mulgund	University of Memphis, USA
Julian M. Müller	Friedrich-Alexander-Universität Erlangen-Nürnberg, Germany
Sanaz Nabavian	University of Niagara Falls, Canada
Martina Navratilova	South Westphalia University of Applied Sciences, Germany
Maximilian Nebel	TU Dortmund University, Germany

Nicolas Neis	University of Würzburg, Germany
Chloe Nguyen	University of New South Wales, Australia
Giang Tra Nguyen	ESCP Business School, Germany
Anastasija Nikiforova	University of Tartu, Estonia
Kerli Norak	Tallinn University of Technology, Estonia
David Nowak	University of Münster, Germany
Mairead O' Connor	University of New South Wales, Australia
Shawn Ogunseye	Bentley University, USA
Grant Oosterwyk	University of Cape Town, South Africa
Agnieszka Patecka	European University Viadrina, Germany
Asger Balle Pedersen	IT University of Copenhagen, Denmark
Haiat Perozzo	LIUC – Università Cattaneo, Italy
Per Persson	University of Gothenburg, Sweden
Christoph Peters	Bundeswehr University Munich, Germany
Louisa Peters	University of Göttingen, Germany
Dimitri Petrik	University of Stuttgart, Germany
Ralf Plattfaut	University of Duisburg-Essen, Germany
Nadia Pocher	University of Luxembourg, Luxembourg
Jens Pöppelbuß	Ruhr University Bochum, Germany
Matthias Pohl	German Aerospace Center (DLR), Germany
Merle Pohl	European University Viadrina, Germany
Katja Pott	Bern University of Applied Sciences, Switzerland
Nicolas Prat	ESSEC Business School, France
Jan Pries-Heje	Roskilde University, Denmark
Sandeep Purao	Bentley University, USA
Saima Qutab	University of Auckland, New Zealand
Jana-Rebecca Rehse	University of Mannheim, Germany
Alexander Richter	Victoria University of Wellington, New Zealand
Shahper Richter	University of Auckland, New Zealand
Dennis M. Riehle	University of Koblenz, Germany
Roman Rietsche	Bern University of Applied Sciences, Switzerland
Michael Rosemann	Queensland University of Technology, Australia
Kristina Rosenthal	Hochschule Niederrhein, Germany
Matti Rossi	Aalto University, Finland
Linda Sagnier Eckert	Karlsruhe Institute of Technology, Germany
Hannu Salmela	University of Turku, Finland
Alexander Schiller	University of Regensburg, Germany
Hannes Schlieter	TU Dresden, Germany
Tim Schmeckel	University of Agder, Norway
Sofia Schöbel	Osnabrück University, Germany
Dewan Scholtz	University of Galway, Ireland
Thorsten Schoormann	Roskilde University, Denmark

Anika Schröder	Copenhagen Business School, Denmark
Gerhard Schwabe	University of Zurich, Switzerland
Christoph Seckler	ESCP Business School, Germany
Julia Seitz	Karlsruhe Institute of Technology, Germany
Kristina Sen	Vlerick Business School, Belgium
Mike Seymour	University of Sydney, Australia
Shahban Shah	Graz University of Technology, Austria
Forough Shahpasandi	University of Jyväskylä, Finland
Dominik Siemon	LUT University, Finland
Janice Sipior	Villanova University, USA
Lisa Skrzyppek	Ruhr University Bochum, Germany
Marco Smacchia	Gabriele d'Annunzio University Chieti-Pescara, Italy
Balwinder Sodhi	Indian Institute of Technology Ropar, India
Matthias Söllner	University of Kassel, Germany
David Sonnabend	University of Kassel, Germany
Pauline Speckmann	TU Dortmund University, Germany
Fabian Stangl	University of Applied Sciences Upper Austria, Austria
Veda C. Storey	Georgia State University, USA
Gero Strobel	University of Duisburg-Essen, Germany
Timo Strohmann	University of Münster, Germany
Jens Strüker	University of Bayreuth, Germany
Rick Sullivan	HEC Montréal, Canada
Janina Sundermeier	Freie Universität Berlin, Germany
Sampsa Suvivuo	Aalto University, Finland
Sabina Szymoniak	Częstochowa University of Technology, Poland
Masoumeh Tavakoligargari	University of Koblenz, Germany
Katja Thoring	Technical University of Munich, Germany
Antonia Tolzin	University of Kassel, Germany
Evgenia Yvonni Tseloni	University of Luxembourg, Luxembourg
Tuure Tuunanen	University of Jyväskylä, Finland
Umair Ul Hassan	University of Galway, Ireland
Azka Umair	University of Galway, Ireland
Erdi Ünal	Ruhr University Bochum, Germany
Vamsi Vallurupalli	University of Galway, Ireland
Alexander van der Staay	TU Dortmund University, Germany
Christine Van Toorn	University of New South Wales, Australia
John Venable	Curtin University, Australia
Anthony Vigil	University of South Florida, USA
Anna Klara Vohrer	University of St. Gallen, Switzerland
Hendrik Wache	ICN Business School, France

James Wallace	Harvard Business School, USA
David Walter	University of Hildesheim, Germany
Annika Wambsganss	ESCP Business School, Germany
Belinda Wang	University of Sydney, Australia
Blair Wang	Curtin University, Australia
Jingyang Wang	University of Lausanne, Switzerland
Sofie Wass	University of Agder, Norway
Florian Weber	University of Kassel, Germany
Hans Weigand	Tilburg University, Netherlands
Anna Elisabeth Wenzel	TU Dortmund University, Germany
Pauline Weritz	University of Twente, Netherlands
Henning Werminghaus Nusch	South Westphalia University of Applied Sciences, Germany
Oliver Werth	OFFIS - Institute for Information Technology, Germany
Richard Wiebe	University of Würzburg, Germany
Martin Wiener	TU Dresden, Germany
Manuel Wiesche	TU Dortmund University, Germany
Jost Wiethölter	Münster University of Applied Sciences, Germany
Malin Wik	Karlstad University, Sweden
Axel Winkelmann	University of Würzburg, Germany
Anna Wolters	University of Koblenz, Germany
Hetiao Xie	University of Queensland, Australia
Jennifer Xu	Bentley University, USA
Jack Yang	University of New South Wales, Australia
Jongtae Yu	King Fahd University of Petroleum and Minerals, Saudi Arabia
Ryan Yurosko	University of South Florida, USA
Liudmila Zavolokina	University of Lausanne, Switzerland
Anna Zeitsev	University of Tampa, USA
Julian Zerbin	Paderborn University, Germany
Xinyuan Zhang	University of Notre Dame, USA
Xinyue Zhang	University of New South Wales, Australia
Lina Zhou	University of North Carolina at Charlotte, USA
Sandra Zilker	Friedrich-Alexander-Universität Erlangen-Nürnberg, Germany
Markus Zimmer	University of Agder, Norway
Zoe Zoepffel	University of Münster, Germany
Philipp zur Heiden	Paderborn University, Germany

Contents

Future of Design Science Education

Future of Design Science Methodology

Future of Ecosystems for Design Science Research

Future of Design and Entrepreneurship

Design Principles for Engaging with Desirable Future(s): A Study on Experiencing Entrepreneurial Action to Co-Create Common Future(s) Within Planetary Limits

Annemarie Bloch(✉)

University of Duisburg-Essen, 45127 Essen, Germany
`annemarie.bloch@icb.uni-due.de`

Abstract. In times of poly-crisis, imagining alternative future(s) and courses of action towards them have become a way to address challenges like climate change and social issues in both theory and practice. Research suggests that desirable futures require collective imagining and co-creating among different actors. However, a perceived lack to be able to influence future(s) with effective outcome may limit or even inhibit individuals to imagine and engage with future(s) in the first place. This study suggests that combining entrepreneurial action with imagining future(s) in practical learning experiences addresses this perceived lack. Based on empirical data from a course in entrepreneurship education, the study's findings show, how a sense of able-ness to engage with future(s) could be cultivated among students who had perceived future(s) as something abstract and non-influential prior to the course. The study draws on literature on entrepreneurial action in context of crisis and scholarship on future making to support and extend the findings. It contributes to scholarship on future making with design knowledge on how to cultivate *a sense of able-ness* to support individuals in co-creating common future(s), proposing entrepreneurial action as complementary approach to future making and entrepreneurship within planetary limits.

Keywords: Entrepreneurial action · desirable futures · planetary boundaries

1 Introduction

Throughout this course, my perspective on creating and designing futures has changed significantly. Before, I saw the future mostly as something abstract, something that simply 'happens' and that we adapt to. During the course, I learned that the future is not fixed, but something we can actively shape through ideas, creativity, and collaboration. (RP5)

The ability to imagine 'better' [1] or 'desirable' future(s) is regarded necessary to address grand challenges and create courses of action towards alternative future(s) in collective endeavors [2]. Research on entrepreneurial action as process towards novelty and innovation with imagination as essential driver thereof [3, 4] could provide valuable insights into addressing desirable future(s) and creating relevant courses of action.

J. vom Brocke et al. (Eds.): DESRIST 2026, LNCS 16606, pp. 3–20, 2026.
https://doi.org/10.1007/978-3-032-28313-9_1

Through creating novelty in imagining the not-yet and designing artifacts, entrepreneurs are considered to craft future(s) [5]. In the context of shared 'desirable' future(s), entrepreneurial action would then involve imaginations of 'what should be' [2, 6, 7] and could be explored as a way towards crafting imaginations of desirable future(s) into realized ones. However, what if actors are lacking the sense that they can imagine or shape future(s) at all? In times of poly-crisis, a context of simultaneously happening, interrelated political, societal and ecological challenges [8], actors may perceive they are inhibited to engage with future(s), limiting an aspired shaping of collective future(s) that are desirable for many.

The analytical insights from my course in entrepreneurship education show that the participating students felt that they could not influence future(s) prior to the course and that they would simply need to adapt to whatever comes. However, the students changed their perspectives on future(s) from being abstract and untouchable to something that could be actively shaped. A *sense of able-ness* to engage with future(s) was cultivated. Indeed, it was imagining future(s) together with practicing entrepreneurial action in teamwork while consciously contemplating on the planet's deteriorating health that instilled a sense of hope and eagerness to start engaging with future(s). I argue that a *sense of able-ness for engaging with future(s)* is required to join in future making in the first place [9, 10]. This sense of able-ness relates to an individual's perception of being able to influence future(s) and engage in future-oriented change. This perception can change over time and is highly subjective, rather than a sense of agency in a structured understanding. Through the course, I discovered that students in the course perceived that future(s) cannot be influenced, which led to this design science study. To examine this, I pose **the research question (RQ)**: *What are design principles that cultivate a sense of able-ness for engaging with desirable future(s) in the context of poly-crises?*

The **purpose of this paper** is to understand how actors can be supported in feeling able to start and continue engaging with future(s) as requirement to collectively create common future(s) and courses of action, specifically in the context of poly-crisis. It aims at equipping individuals collectively to perceive themselves as future makers. With this, I follow calls to engage with questions on desirable future(s) through (design science) research [2, 11, 12]. I primarily **contribute** with design knowledge on how we can cultivate *a sense of able-ness for engaging with future(s)* through entrepreneurial action as approach. The remainder of the paper is structured in the common way, including elements of a design science study in entrepreneurship. Hence, after describing the **methodological approach**, I illustrate the **problem analysis**, followed by **design requirements** and a detailed description of derived **design principles**.

2 Theoretical Background

Entrepreneurship is considered as "innovative process meant to actualize desired and believed-to-be-possible futures" [13, p. 274] under uncertainty. Imagining is a crucial element driving entrepreneurial action throughout its process [3]. However, studies have shown that Knightian uncertainty as mainstream assumption in entrepreneurship does not explain entrepreneurial action in the context of crisis sufficiently [14, 15]. Researchers argue that in the context of poly-crisis, base assumption in entrepreneurship research have to be reconsidered [16, 17]. During poly-crisis, conditions of uncertainty pass the economic realm, making uncertainty 'more'. Entrepreneurs face instability in political, societal and legal realms that threaten reliability, balance and steadiness of institutions like policies and even the state and its legitimacy as such, [17]. Entrepreneurs and other actors must deal and engage with uncertainty characterized by "several simultaneous crises with a complex set of vital, uncontrolled problems" [17, p. 5]. In such a context, inherent elements such as hope, courage and self-efficacy are emphasized next to the role of community as influential and important aspects in entrepreneurial action in crisis [14–17].

Similarly, organization studies are exploring different explanations for organizing in face of grand challenges in scholarship on future making [6, 9]. Arguments that conventional theorizing and methodological approaches are not sufficient anymore in light of interrelated crises are brought forward [2]. Instead of merely explaining what is going on based on data from the past, researchers call to look forward and turn to forms of prospective theorizing [18, 19] and engaging with novel approaches across disciplines to sufficiently address contemporary challenges that have massive implication for humanity's future(s), like ecological crises and the planetary emergency [12, 20, 21]. In exploring future(s) as temporal dimension in plurality, "planning as a way of producing and enacting future" [8, p. 1451] in managerial ways are not considered sufficient approaches anymore. Instead, scholars on future making propose to engage with practices [9] to theorize on future making, to take a prospective theorizing approach [18], or to consider future making as emancipatory process that has to be negotiated and collectively enacted through imagining [6]. Further, a close-ness of future making to entrepreneurship is pointed out [10]. As "unknowable and pluralistic" [10, p. 1447], 'the future' is experienced as problematic, while entrepreneurship appears to answer this perspective in its solution-oriented manner.

In entrepreneurship research, entrepreneurs view problems confidently as potential opportunities. In case of mainstream for-profit entrepreneurship opportunities improve "an individual's, team's, or organization's socioeconomic position" [13, p. 274]. However, such base assumptions and that we perceive individuals, and entrepreneurs specifically, as *able* to shape and indeed craft future(s) [10], may not be feasible anymore in times of economic crisis [22] or in context of poly-crisis [17, 23, 24]. Moreover, faced with planetary emergency and crises of ecological ecosystems [20, 21, 25], entrepreneurship may have to engage with more than just creating economic profit. Indeed, research on entrepreneurial action in context of crisis suggests that the behavior of successful entrepreneurs is linked to sustainability [26]. Ecological challenges, the loss of biodiversity and climate change, feed into the instability of societal institutions and present interrelated, simultaneous crises and are an essential part of poly-crisis [27]. However, mainstream entrepreneurship research has not yet picked up existing frameworks on planetary boundaries [28] or Earth systems as requirements to be included if humanity as a whole – entrepreneurship included – aims for our planet to remain a resilient habitat for humanity. Hence, this DSR study also addresses the need to consider entrepreneurial action within limits in its design knowledge.

Considering the different calls for alternative approaches to research on future(s) including designing 'better' or 'preferable' future(s) [1], abilities and capacities to imagine, shape and craft desired futures are therefore essential. Scholarship on future making calls to question the assumption that everyone can participate in crafting future(s) per se [2, 10], proposing inquiries for crafting future(s) in democratic ways that are desirable on a societal level and include specifically marginalized communities and groups [6]. I suggest that for this, a sense of able-ness to engage with future(s) is necessary first to inclusively participate in shaping and crafting future(s). In contrast, a perceived unable-ness to engage with future(s) would restrain efforts to engage actors and communities in imagining and co-creating desirable future(s) to democratically build courses of action crucial for socio-economic transitions. Scholarship in entrepreneurship is lacking insights into how future(s) and consequential action [29] can be imagined and engaged with if there is no perception of being able to influence future(s) in the first place, specifically in contemporary times of poly-crisis. Addressing these gaps, this DSR study illustrates through a course in entrepreneurship education how a sense of able-ness for imagining and engaging with future(s) can be cultivated in case of prior absence of such a perception. A sense of able-ness suggests an individual's perception of being able to imagine and engage with future(s) with influential outcome, gained through lived experience. Rather than an objective evaluation of abilities and capacities, or a structurally oriented conception of agency, a sense of able-ness refers to a subjective perception that is temporally situated and malleable, possible of changing over time. Based on this conceptual understanding, this research does not aim to contribute to debates on agency.

3   Method

For this study, I applied a design science research (DSR) approach, guided by Peffers et al.'s (2007) strategy on building design artifacts and taking further inspiration from DSR in entrepreneurship [11, 31]. The development of design knowledge for this study followed a bottom-up approach [32], using empirical data. The design implications were influenced by an instantiation of an artefact that was iteratively developed for another DSR study. In that study, I applied entrepreneurship as approach for designing sustainable futures in entrepreneurship education for both bachelor and master students. In the process of analyzing the coded data for that project, I discovered a 'new problem'. I had assumed unconsciously that the participating students would feel able to create and design future(s). However, when I engaged with the data collected during the course, I found that this perception had indeed been missing before the course. Hence, I re-engaged with a part of the data that would give me more insights, the students' reflection papers (RPs).

3.1   Research Context

The course is a part of entrepreneurship education at a university, designed to blend knowledge on planetary boundaries, sustainability and regeneration [33] with entrepreneurship in a hands-on, practice-based learning experience. Students learn and apply typical tools used in entrepreneurship education, like the business model canvas

(BMC). The students are required to develop a (business) idea, tackling present societal problems including a first physical or digital prototype. They thus experience typical elements of processes of entrepreneurial action with a strong focus on peer exchange and learning. Creative activities in relation to imagining future(s), reflection exercises and group discussions extend common activities in entrepreneurship education. As lecturer, I have been developing the course since 2022 with the last two iterations (beginning and end of 2025) conducted in the context of future(s). Framed under the theme of designing futures, I portrayed the students as future makers (FMs). As lecturer, I clarified that we believe that an entrepreneurial mindset can be learnt and that everyone can be entrepreneurial, while it does not necessarily need to lead into founding a start-up. With that, I framed entrepreneurial action in the course as approach for creating hands-on solutions for existing problems.

3.2 Research Approach

I followed Tuunanen et al.'s (2023) [34] proposal to 'decompose' DSR into echelons and concentrated on those addressing the problem, objectives and requirements as well as design and development. I worked iteratively, starting from the course data. The empirical data consists of field notes and teaching material as contextual data and the reflection papers (RPs) as main source of data. RPs from 20 students were analyzed, covering 78 pages. An analysis of the RPs provides insights into the students' needs, challenges and learnings with regards to imagining and engaging with future(s). The students were asked to illustrate their perspectives and learnings in relation to future(s) and designing future(s) at different points.

After discovering the problem of perceived unable-ness to shape future(s), I re-engaged in an open coding process with the data from the RPs [35]. I created first-order, informant-centric coding to understand 'what is going on' in reflection to the research question. Through the students' own evaluations on different points of time of their learning journey, they did not only reflect upon problems and challenges they had experienced prior and during the course ('Issues' Is1-6, Fig. 1). They also described their own development processes and reflected upon which course conditions helped and which did not ('design requirements' MR1 with DRs1-3 and MR2 with DR4, Fig. 1), what worked well ('design principles' DPs1-4, DP6, Fig. 1) and what they thought was required for continuing their endeavors towards imagined future(s) ('Issue' I7, 'design requirements' MR2 with DR5 and 'design principles' DP5, DPs7-8, Fig. 1). I aggregated the students' backward- and forward-looking reflections and allocated them to issues, DRs and DPs. I then consulted selected academic literature. The literature can be found in the theoretical background and as references in each DP. It was used to challenge and enrich the empirical findings, drawing from entrepreneurship and organization and management research with foci on imagination, crisis, and, respectively, recent debates on future making. Imagination is a crucial part for both entrepreneurship and future related scholarship. Literature on crisis was chosen to consider a context of poly-crisis. Debates on future making were chosen to evaluate the students' experiences and evaluations in relation to proposals on processes for desirable future(s) with a specific focus on theorizing by Comi and colleagues [6]. I derived at seven issues and related seven design requirements (MRs and DRs) to them, which are addressed through eight design principles (DPs) (Fig. 1).

4 Problem Analysis and Design Implications

The issues illustrated in Fig. 1 describe the students' perceived unable-ness to imagine and engage with future(s). They include experienced challenges during the course and those they could imagine constraining them when further engaging with crafting desirable future(s). The analysis of the students' reflection suggests that the environment and context they experienced and how they learnt about entrepreneurial action and engaging with future(s) was essential for cultivating a sense of able-ness. The DRs also address the students' anticipations of possible external challenges and constraining conditions along prospective timelines, depicted in Sect. 4.2.

4.1 Perceptions as Issues

An analysis of the students' reflection papers (RPs) revealed that a single future, "*the future*" (emphasis added), was the only, temporally distant and non-influential option on the horizon (I1). Experienced as abstract, the students could not imagine how to influence it or that it was shapable at all, or they simply did not engage with it. Alternative future(s) were unimaginable. It resulted into withdrawing into the personal realm and restricted them from joining a potential, collective space of imagining and engaging with future(s) together with others (I2). Assumptions on how future(s) would be made and the lack of ideas about how imagining alternatives and crafting courses of action towards them limited the students in engaging with future(s) (I3). Restricting beliefs and lack of knowledge therefore led to not engaging with imagining and crafting future(s) and action at all, not in the present nor as anticipations in a near future.

When the students were asked to imagine future(s) together to derive at shared ones in small groups, exchanging perspectives and ideas made them realize how their own experiences and knowledge could influence their future imagination(s). By listening to other students' future imaginations, they realized how their own imagination(s) were biased or limited (I4). During teamwork, conflicts among team members could constrain joint imagining and co-creating for shared future(s) (I5).

The data also indicates an overall belief among the students that they could not efficiently contribute to complex challenges such as climate change, which meant that no courses of action would materialize (I6). Generally, existing ideas about sustainability prior to the course had not allowed the students to fully comprehend the planet's state of health and humanity's contribution to it, revealing that systemic interrelations and interdependencies of ecological and social systems had not been recognized. Without awareness and understanding of systemic interrelations, complex problems such as climate change could not be understood well and courses of action would naturally be dismissed together with the ability and capacities for having impact at all.

4.2 Processual Change

The students' own processual evaluations of their experiences show that they recognized during the course, how present conditions could influence possible present action and, consequentially, possible future(s). The guiding questions in the reflection papers asked them to imagine potential external challenges along a temporal scale of future(s). They saw challenges partially rooted in present conditions, such as infrastructural barriers or restrictions in personal or collective spaces (I7).

Overall, the analysis on the students' learnings and development in the course shows that the perceived initial unableness was not a fixed state, suggesting that design interventions can influence a sense of able-ness for imagining and engaging with future(s). Further, gaining more understanding on ecological and social challenges and systems' interrelations did not restrict them further. Learning about the planet's state of health could have easily led to paralysis. Instead, gaining knowledge and applying it in entrepreneurial action served to increase the students' commitment towards the planet and people. They started to see challenges as spurring them further towards action for learning more about it and engaging, also in their private lives.

4.3 Design Requirements

The design requirements serve to prescribe what is needed to cultivate a sense of able-ness for imagining and engaging with future(s), especially when unableness is experienced beforehand. I derived at two meta-requirements (MRs) with three and two corresponding design requirements (DRs), respectively (Fig. 1). The MRs are overarching requirements, relating to overall goals. They address issues through the corresponding DRs. I was guided by Maedche et al. (2019) [36] in formulating the DRs (full table including requirements and goals upon request). They are described below, addressing MRs and DRs illustrated in Fig. 1.

The DRs can include different actors, depending on the context the design knowledge is applied in. Generally, actors include individuals as prospective FMs and facilitators of the activities. For instance, in entrepreneurship courses in higher education, MR2 would address lecturers, professors or, generally, educators. If used in community-based work, it may cover facilitators of workshops or community spaces, mentors, or actors that provide funding, for instance for infrastructure (DPs5-8). FMs describe individuals included for engaging in co-creating future(s). Overarchingly (MR1), FMs need to share and discuss their individual ideas about future(s) to co-create shared imagination(s) within planetary limits and needs. For this, they need space, time, tools and methods to create common imagination(s) of the futures. They need to develop shared meaning and understanding of what future(s) means to them individually and collectively, how future(s) can look like and evolve. FMs need to be able to relate future imagination(s) to present and future challenges that require solutions **(MR1)**. Further, FMs need an understanding of values and views of their co-future makers. They need to accept differences and be open for changing their own views and letting go of ideas or arguments. They need to find common ground, agreeing on fundamentals while some differences and contradictory perspectives may have to be accepted **(DR1)**. Each FM needs an open mindset for others' views, values and experiences. They need an understanding that learning does not end in life, and instead foster curiosity, an attitude towards life-long learning and the possibility to change perspectives in face of complexity or tensions. For understanding oneself and others, FMs need to develop emotional intelligence for listening well and empathising. Those aspiring or taking a leadership role require specifically well-honed abilities to communicate and an attitude to serve others instead of their own goals. FMs need a good balance between asserting own values and ideas and considering those of others (**DR2**).

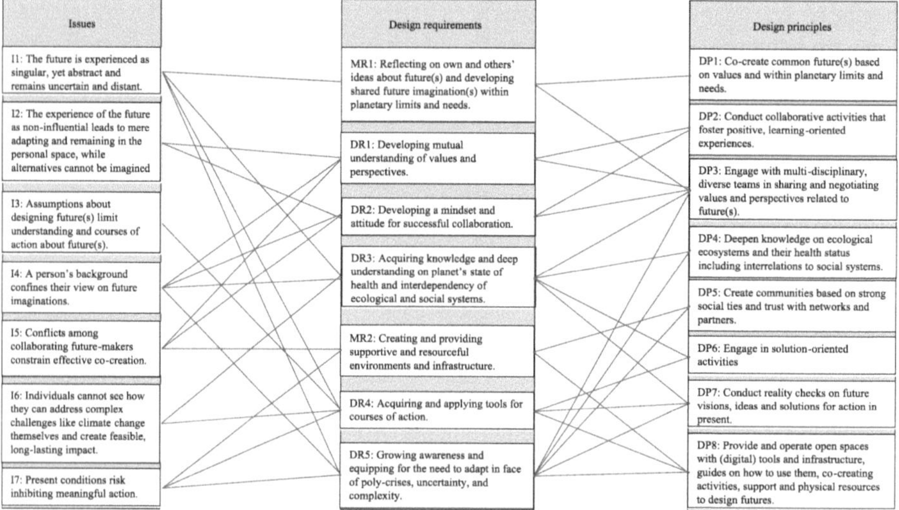

Fig. 1. Data structure: Issues, design requirements and design principles

They need to understand and relate to the systemic interrelations of ecological and social crises, challenges and positive influences. They need to have a sound understanding on the background and context of the planet's and societies' states of health and humanity's part in it. They need to understand the limits and needs of the planet in which humanity can safely live and act in (**DR3**). Overarchingly, FMs need safe spaces in which they can develop mutual understanding and common imagination(s) of the future(s). They need supportive environments for experimenting with ideas, creating solutions and testing and validating them (**MR2**). Furthermore, FMs need to know and experiment with tools, methods and resources to understand their usefulness and applicability. They need to learn and experience that sustainability and regeneration can be turned into practicality. They need to combine their skills, experiences, and knowledge to develop solutions for courses of action for realizing their future imagination(s) (**DR4**). Finally, FMs need awareness of themselves and others to adapt and correspond to global environments in the context of poly-crisis, including institutional uncertainty and complexity thereof. They need understanding of present and potential future challenges. They need relevant skills, a versatile and adaptive mindset, and relevant tools and resources to address and deal with changing and unpredictable conditions (**DR5**).

5   Design Principles

Eight design principles (DPs) are presented, while DP1 and DP5 address MR1 and MR2, functioning as higher principles to DPs2-4 and DPs6-8, respectively (see Fig. 1). The DPs describe mechanisms and aims, including exemplary activities that were conducted in the course that are inspired by design features and their role [32]. They serve as prescription to cultivate and maintain a sense of able-ness and to collectively engage with future(s).

5.1   DP1: Co-Create Common Future(s) Based on Values and Within Planetary Limits and Needs

DP1 may take place or be combined with DPs2-4 in the same activities. DP1 aims to *create common future(s) with shared meaning and a shared sense of purpose among FMs*. In the course, the students were asked to engage with their own and other students' ideas about future(s) to arrive at shared imagination(s) and to place them within planetary limits (MR1). Their imagination(s) were functioning as starting point for their (business) idea they had to develop in the course. The imaginations mirrored present problems they did not want to see in future times, picturing both utopias and dystopias. "This idea [i.e. the business idea] aligned with the forgotten vision we had drawn few hours earlier. So, in the end, the vision exercise actually helped us more than we expected" (RP14). The common future imaginations later served (unconsciously) as guidance in developing and recalibrating ideas and anticipated courses for action, strengthening a sense of able-ness. As literature proposes, dealing with desirable and undesirable future(s) confronted the students with their own values, present conditions and options for realizing goals as well as prevailing assumptions that they could thus challenge and scrutinize in light of future aspirations [2]. Literature suggests that values inherent in future(s) can serve as compass for future (entrepreneurial) endeavors [7].

5.2   DP2: Conduct Collaborative Activities that Foster Positive, Learning-Oriented Experiences.

DP2 suggests *conducting collaborative activities that foster positive and open learning-oriented experiences with regular exchanges and reflections*. It aims at mutual understanding and self-awareness among FMs (DR1), cultivating personal and collective growth, and building capacities in terms of skills, knowledge and experience on personal and collective levels (DR2). The experience of project-based teamwork was considered crucial for cultivating a sense of able-ness through imagining together and engaging in entrepreneurial action. As the students mostly did not know each other, developing a certain team spirit through activities was important for consecutive work. Teamwork that was perceived as engaging, effective and trustful allowed to share worries and hopes for future(s) (DP3). Practices and communication which considered and discussed values and encouraged mutual respect and openness (DR1) helped in cultivating positive teamwork in general and engaging with future(s) (DR2). As a student observed, "working with people I connected well with showed me how powerful collaboration can be when motivation, communication, and trust are present" (RP5). They were stressing abilities and skills to motivate and collaborate with others for creating change, also aiming for leadership skills. Their reflections mirror suggestions for democratic processes in creating desirable future(s) [6] and correspond with studies on successful, sustaining ventures in crisis-contexts [37]. Teams in which communication was not as open and not stressing listening and appreciating each other experienced challenges. Hence, FMs ideally embrace openness for learning through co-creative activities and the willingness to adapt accordingly (DRs1-2).

5.3 DP3: Engage with Multi-disciplinary, Diverse Teams in Sharing and Negotiating Values and Perspectives Related to Future(s)

DP3 *suggests suitable space, time and methods for sharing and negotiating values and perspectives with other FMs.* DP3 allows diverse perspectives, beliefs and values from FMs to be brought into imagining and engaging with future(s) (DR1). It addresses the need for creating jointly shared meaning about and of future(s) (MR1), feeding into common, value-based imagination(s) of future(s) within planetary limits (DR3). Discussing future(s) with others addresses the need for awareness and adaption in context of complexity and uncertainty (DR5). Guided questions posed by the lecturer throughout the courses made the students silently reflect on own perspectives and values, which could be shared openly in the course and in smaller groups afterwards (MR1 with DRs1-3). "Seeing how differently other teams imagined their futures showed me how powerful it can be to share ideas and learn from different viewpoints" (RP3). Joint reflection and introspective exercises are considered valuable for building preparedness (DR5) for dealing with crisis [38]. Through reflecting and discussing future(s) which they would like to see or, in case of dystopian imaginations, like to avoid, they created a pool of perspectives with similarities and differences and enhanced their understanding of each other (DP1). In that, they considered desirable future(s) "in a normative sense to denote collectively negotiated, value-laden judgements of what the future might and should be" [6, p. 2468] on the level of societies and including the ecological environment and the planet (DP1 and DP4).

5.4 DP4: Deepen Knowledge on Ecological Ecosystems and Their Health Status Including Interrelations to Social Systems

DP4 *deepens knowledge on planetary boundaries, ecological ecosystems and their state including impact factors and humans' dependence on the planet's systems in equilibrium.* It addresses the need to understand present challenges for ecological and social systems, their roots as well as interrelations and interdependencies (DR3). This allows to engage in profound problematization and problem understanding of present challenges. It aims to grow understanding of interrelations and workings of ecological and social systems to foster system thinking, addressing the need to grow awareness of challenges and complexity in the context of poly-crisis (DR5). The introduction to concepts and frameworks, like the Sustainable Development Goals by the United Nations, planetary boundaries and the 'Planetary Health Check' helped students to realize the state of global problems and planet's health as well as their interrelations.

I now see that sustainability goes beyond profit or longevity, it´s about creating systems that are socially and environmentally viable as well. True sustainability considers the people who are part of the ecosystem [...]. Each of these groups plays a [sic!] important role in shaping the future and designing for them requires empathy, inclusivity and responsibility. (RP10)

Literature supports the value of systems thinking [39] and calls for the integration of relevant concepts from natural science into business and management [20, 21]. Patterns in the data analysis illustrate that this knowledge led students to realize that holistic solutions were needed to be able to address local and global challenges [38]. Working with the concepts in practice-oriented projects was crucial to deepen understanding of complexities, specifically in the context of poly-crisis. It also instilled encouragement to address challenges and "embracing the future [by] combining hope with action. It is about believing that small steps matter and that one person can make a difference when they act with purpose" (RP8), although the grandness of challenges and their implication for the magnitude of solutions needed could have been demotivating. Literature similarly proposes "a deep reservoir of hope and courage [as] indispensable for navigating societal instability and institutional uncertainty" [17, p. 10]. Indeed, the shared experience of a dystopian outlook to future(s) may foster a sense of community [16].

5.5 DP5: Create Communities Based on Strong Social Ties and Trust with Networks and Partners

DP5 reflects MR2, addressing the need to create and provide supportive and resourceful environments. It is extended by DPs6-8 as related principles. They may take place within the same activities. In their reflections, the students valued the course's open atmosphere. An encouraging, positive facilitator was part of that and fostered a trustful environment (DP5), reflected by a student who "appreciated the overall welcoming course atmosphere and the collaborative group work, to achieve shared goals" (RP19). Building understanding and knowing of each other (DP2) strengthens personal ties for growing communities. In turn, social and community resources support resourcefulness, overall fostering innovation, specifically in context of crisis [16, 37]. Literature emphasizes the benefits of mutual encouragement and sense of belonging for building and maintaining resilience, hope and courage in the context of poly-crisis [16, 17]. At the same time, a shared sense of purpose was felt, as a student noticed,

everyone had similar concerns but expressed them differently. Some focused on pollution and recycling, others on inequality and education. During that discussion [i. e. sharing imaginations of future(s)] I felt strong [sic!] connection within our group because we all cared deeply about building a better future. (RP8)

Caring for 'building a better future' as a shared purpose can be the starting point for building communities with collective identities or shared meaning and emotional and social support, which are essential for performance and facing challenging [23, 38].

5.6 DP6: Engage in Solution-Oriented Processes for Courses of Action

DP6 proposes to *engage in solution-oriented activities and processes for developing solution-oriented artefacts in iterative and adaptable ways as form of engaging with imagined future(s), contributing to courses of action.* It addresses the need to acquire and apply tools (DR4) and the need to understand present problems deeply (DR3). DP6 suggests building artifacts iteratively as practice-oriented experience among FMs to cultivate a sense of able-ness for engaging with future(s). Artifacts can be physical or digital creations. Such a solution-oriented approach towards engaging with future(s) is also reflected in Comi et al.'s (2025) proposal for crafting future(s), in which "desirable futures take the form of imaginings. […] They are iteratively tested, stabilized and reified" [6, p. 2473], mirroring activities in entrepreneurial action. Imaginings themselves are an essential part throughout entrepreneurial action [3, 29]. They are necessary for entrepreneurs' imaginations of that which is not-yet [40] throughout the process of crafting artifacts as materialization of the not-yet-there in iterative processes [5].

It was inspiring to see how tangible it is to design a future when you have the right idea, the right team, and the right tools. It really feels like anything is possible. There are so many resources and ways to actually design a future. It was fascinating to see so many different ideas come to life. (RP4)

Experiencing 'ideas coming to life' portrays artifacts as essential materialization of imagining and engaging with future(s) [5, 6]. This materialization was also important for the students to grasp sustainable future(s) as something tangible and recognizing the need to turn imagination(s) into courses of action.

5.7 DP7: Conduct Reality Checks on Teams, Future Visions, Ideas and Artefacts

DP7 proposes to *conduct reality checks on teams, future visions, ideas and artefacts for courses of action in a continuously evolving present towards future(s).* It addresses the need to understand social and ecological challenges (DR3) and the requirement to experiment with tools, methods and resources to develop solutions for courses of action (DR4), while being aware of the complexity and dynamic character of a global world in context of poly-crisis (DR5). It aims at assessing and adapting artifacts and courses of action alongside imagined future(s) to cultivate a balance between do-able and imaginable future(s). It is recommended to conduct DP7 frequently and in iteration with DP6. Students emphasized the value of activities like feedback from the entire course, interviewing each other across teams and pitching their ideas for adapting and critically assessing their artefacts, also in relation to their imagined future(s). Literature stresses the need for iterative developing and adapting for feasible entrepreneurial action, specifically in context of crisis also in terms of organizing [16, 17, 23]. Sharing their creations made the students realize that imagined future(s) and courses of action would still need to find resonance among a broader collective to be able to have impact and consider external conditions. Yet, action may sometimes not be possible. "She [i. e. the lecturer] opened our eyes to the fact that even with strong intentions, political structures and the lack of governmental support can make meaningful action nearly impossible" (RP3). System thinking and knowing about local conditions and actors involved (DP4) was deemed necessary. These realizations mirrors theorizing on future making, where place, people and materials are considered co-creators of future(s) [6].

5.8 DP8: Provide and Operate Open Spaces with Tools and Infrastructure

DP8 suggests *providing and operating open spaces with (digital) tools and infrastructure, guides on how to use them, co-creating activities, support and physical resources to design futures.* It addresses the need to equip oneself and others to deal with changing and unpredictable conditions in context of poly-crisis (DR5) and the need to experiment with tools and methods (DR4) to increase translating future imagination(s) into courses of action. DP8 aims to support FMs in that by providing space and infrastructure for exploring courses of action in dialogue, creativity and trial-and-error approaches. In their anticipation of what they needed to craft future(s), the students emphasized the requirement for infrastructure and support to be able to follow courses of action towards desirable future(s) and turn them into actionable reality step by step. When reflecting about requirements for engaging with desirable future(s), the students saw need for an open space, in which ideas could be developed jointly, and experimenting and prototyping could take place without risk. They considered as "[important factor] the availability of institutions focused on helping people realize their creative ideas. Knowing that you are not alone and there are many people willing to support you is perhaps the most important factor" (RP7), which is also emphasized by literature [16].

Working alone has its limits. I've come to see how valuable it is to connect with others who are also committed to sustainability, education, or social justice. These networks offer not only inspiration but also practical support, whether through collaboration, feedback, or shared resources. (RP3)

The physical environment and the availability of infrastructure and people to support them with resources for experimenting and prototyping, feedback and experience-sharing was estimated as crucial for engaging with future(s) by the students.

6 Discussion

The analysis suggests that entrepreneurial action and imagining are crucial elements of an experienced process for cultivating a sense of able-ness for engaging with future(s). Entrepreneurial action is thereby considered as innovative process towards desirable futures. Further, co-creating desirable future(s) is regarded to need a suitable, supportive environment to develop and conduct courses of action from imagining towards realizing desirable future(s), all within planetary limits and needs [2]. In that, this DSR study is prescriptive in an ethical manner.

6.1 Design Knowledge to Cultivate Engaging with Common Future(s)

The study proposes that *a sense of able-ness* is an important perception required for engaging collectively in future making towards desirable future(s) [6]. A sense of able-ness critically questions assumptions that all individuals perceive themselves able to imagine or engage with future(s) per se. It promotes facilitating efforts designed to foster community, problem understanding, and creating solutions in collaboration (DPs) to cultivate a sense of able-ness in individuals prior or alongside efforts for future(s) making. A perceived unable-ness on the other hand may limit the potential of collective future making efforts. For cultivating such a sense, there are requirements in personal, collective and environmental dimensions as depicted in the DRs. The DPs (1–3) propose that sharing, discussing and creating future imagination(s) as well as reflecting upon them is essential for FMs to engage with the 'not yet' and to build the foundation for approaches towards imagined future(s). The experience of a plurality of future(s) through collaborating and developing a shared purpose contributed to cultivating a sense of able-ness. The learning on own and others' values through these experiences can further foster a sense of community by seeing what is shared with others and by recognizing what is important personally. The experience of community as shared source of connection and resources for jointly engaging with future(s) in turn cultivates a sense of able-ness (DPs5+8). These findings agree with literature on the power of communities in context of (poly-) crisis [14]. Further, knowledge on local conditions and problems as starting point for collaborating in creating solutions and seeing ideas materialize through different approaches cultivated a sense of able-ness by showing a plurality of solutions based on understanding problems systemically (DPs4, 6–7).

6.2   Entrepreneurial Action for Future Making

What looks in DRs and DPs like fostering an entrepreneurial mindset and infrastructures for building start-ups indeed reflects the students' experience of how engaging in processes of entrepreneurial action helped them to build a more positive outlook for future(s) and to cultivate the perception that they can contribute to shaping future(s). For scholarship on future making, these implications are relevant when aiming at engaging with future(s) as a form of democratically co-creating value-based desirable future(s), specifically when including marginalized communities and groups [6]. I suggest entrepreneurial action as a complementary approach together with imagining desirable future(s). This addresses existing proposals of literature on future making in iterative processes of 'testing, stabilizing and reifying' [6, p. 2473]. As complementary approach, entrepreneurship can be framed outside a business context, while entrepreneurial tools can assist in understanding problems, needs of stakeholders and actors involved. This suggestion relates to existing studies that reflect upon local organizing in the aftermaths of natural disasters, characterized by venture-like endeavors [37]. The role of imagining future(s) and materializations thereof in form of artifacts are crucial for cultivating a sense of able-ness by making the potential of future(s) visible and *experience-able* through interacting with them. Designing solution-oriented approaches and artifacts then become part of courses of action towards shared desirable future(s).

6.3   Entrepreneurial Action Within Limits

I further suggest that the needs and limits of ecological systems and the planet should be at the heart of 'better' futures to allow habitability for humanity and beyond. This suggestion links to calls in research [20, 21, 41]. It further supports proposals to consider entrepreneurship as "an intended solution to the crisis, not just coercively as a reaction to it" [17, p. 8]. For this, we all as potential future makers need to understand the needs and limits of planetary boundaries and ecological ecosystems (DP4). Future(s) are intricately linked to the planet's health and its systems in balance (DP1). Deep knowledge and understanding for a problematization of the status quo that challenges the planet's health are part of engaging with future(s). Problematizing the present time's status quo means raising awareness of potential future(s) following these present time(s) (DP7). A sense of able-ness therefore also includes knowing about present problems that have implications for future(s) while considering interrelations and interdependencies of ecological and social systems. Knowledge and awareness thereof are crucial not only for cultivating this perception. They are also crucial for courses of action in face of poly-crisis. So far, mainstream research on entrepreneurship has not acknowledged that planetary limits should be a requirement throughout entrepreneurial action. I therefore propose to consider the notion of entrepreneurial action within social and ecological limits and to engage more deeply with concepts from ecology and natural science, such as Earth System Boundaries and planetary boundaries [41], and systems thinking [39] in entrepreneurship research to allow for re-engaging with assumptions and relevant transfer into practice through (design science) research.

6.4   Limitations and Future Research

This study is based on insights from data collected from students in higher education. Different contexts and FMs with different backgrounds may mean that requirements and prescriptions must be adapted. Local context and societal conditions, including economic and political factors may be influential, too. There was one exception in the course which remained rather unoptimistic towards engaging with future(s) on a societal level with effective impact. Another student could participate only a few times and was lacking a sense of belonging and experience of change throughout the course. These two cases illustrate that cultivating a sense of able-ness may not work for everyone or only under certain circumstances. While the reflection papers as main source of data may suggest a tendency towards desirability bias, the guiding questions asked for critical evaluations and personal perspectives from the students. Talks with the students outside the course further confirmed the analytical insights from the data. While the proposed sense of able-ness appears close to self-efficacy, and data shows relations to hope and courage, this study does not theorize on these relations. It also does not explore, how the temporally situated sense of able-ness corresponds with self-efficacy as belief in the confidence of one's own abilities. Addressing the limitations of this study, I suggest conducting research in line with DSR as method and seeking exchange and integration of scholarship on future making, entrepreneurial action and design research for theorizing and researching desirable future(s) in form of engaged scholarship. First, research could explore different contexts and individuals with different backgrounds for including FMs in engaging with future(s). This should also investigate the experience of individuals mentioned in the limitations. Second, the effectiveness of DPs in similar and different contexts should be further evaluated and adapted accordingly. Third, this study can contribute to entrepreneurship in the context of crisis with practical and theoretical implications. For this, the interrelations of self-efficacy, hope and courage to a sense of able-ness and engaging with desirable future(s) through entrepreneurial action and community should be explored further in theory and in evaluating the artifact under these aspects for practice.

7 Conclusion

This study contributes with design knowledge on, *how we can cultivate a sense of ableness for engaging with desirable future(s) in the context of poly-crises* through eight design principles addressing individuals to collectively engage with desirable future. The proposed mechanisms combine activities of entrepreneurial action with imagining future(s) on a societal level for co-creating shared, desirable future(s) based on values and creating courses of action [6] within planetary limits. The study engages with scholarship on future making and entrepreneurial action as complementary approach for co-creating desirable future(s), suggesting more research at this disciplinary intersection, and on entrepreneurial action within limits to promote innovation that considers planetary needs and limits.

Acknowledgments. A heartfelt thanks to all students of the course 'Entrepreneurship with Purpose' at University Duisburg-Essen and at Freie Universität Berlin. Thanks for the joint learning.

Disclosure of Interests.   The author has no competing interests to declare that are relevant to the content of this article.

References

1. DESRIST Hompage 'Tracks'. https://desrist2026.org/tracks/. Accessed 17 Oct 2025
2. Gümüsay, A.A., Reinecke, J.: Researching for desirable futures: from real utopias to imagining alternatives. J. Manag. Stud. **59**, 236–242 (2022)
3. Elias, S.R.S.T.A., Chiles, T.H., Crawford, B.: Entrepreneurial imagining: how a small team of arts entrepreneurs created the world's largest traveling carillon. Organ. Stud. **43**, 203–226 (2022)
4. Wood, M.S., Bakker, R.M., Fisher, G.: Back to the future: a time-calibrated theory of entrepreneurial action. AMR **46**, 147–171 (2021)
5. Berglund, H., Dimov, D.: Visions of futures and futures of visions: entrepreneurs, artifacts, and worlds. J. Bus. Ventur. Insights **20**, e00411 (2023)
6. Comi, A., Mosca, L., Whyte, J.: Future making as emancipatory inquiry: a value-based exploration of desirable futures. J. Manag. Stud. **62** (6) (2025)
7. Dimov, D., Johnsen, C.G., Sørensen, B.M.: The future within: commitment, hope, and values in entrepreneurship. J. Bus. Ventur. Insights **23**, e00543 (2025)
8. Whiting, K., Park, H.: This is why "polycrisis" is a useful way of looking at the world right now. https://www.weforum.org/agenda/2023/03/polycrisis-adam-tooze-historian-explains/. Accessed 16 June 2024
9. Wenzel, M., Cabantous, L., Koch, J.: Future making: towards a practice perspective. J. Manag. Stud. **62**(6), joms.13222 (2025)
10. Wenzel, M., Krämer, H., Koch, J., Reckwitz, A.: Future and organization studies: on the rediscovery of a problematic temporal category in organizations. Organ. Stud. **41**, 1441–1455 (2020)
11. Dimov, D., Maula, M., Romme, A.G.L.: Crafting and assessing design science research for entrepreneurship. Entrep. Theory Pract. **47**, 1543–1567 (2023)
12. Romme, A.G.L., et al.: Open Letter About Design Science. https://bkilinc3.wixsite.com/open-letter-for-desi. Accessed 24 Jan 2026

13. Ramoglou, S., McMullen, J.S.: "What is an opportunity?": from theoretical mystification to everyday understanding. AMR **49**, 273–298 (2024)
14. Lee, Y., Kim, J., Mah, S., Karr, A.: Entrepreneurship in times of crisis: a comprehensive review with future directions. Entrep. Res. J. **14**, 905–950 (2024)
15. Sharma, G.D., Kraus, S., Liguori, E., Bamel, U.K., Chopra, R.: Entrepreneurial challenges of COVID-19: re-thinking entrepreneurship after the crisis. J. Small Bus. Manag. **62**, 824–846 (2024)
16. Audretsch, D.B., Kariv, D.: Entrepreneurship in the context of permanent crisis: the role of community support. Rev. Manag. Sci. **19**, 3143–3176 (2025)
17. Klyver, K., McMullen, J.S.: Rethinking entrepreneurship in causally entangled crises: a polycrisis perspective. J. Bus. Ventur. **40**(1) (2025)
18. Gümüsay, A.A., Reinecke, J.: Imagining desirable futures: a call for prospective theorizing with speculative rigour. Organ. Theory **5** (2024)
19. Muñoz, P., Dimov, D.: Facing the future through entrepreneurship theory: a prospective inquiry framework. J. Bus. Ventur. **38** (4) (2023)
20. (Tima) Bansal, P., Durand, R., Kreutzer, M., Kunisch, S., McGahan, A.M.: Strategy can no longer ignore planetary boundaries: a call for tackling strategy's ecological fallacy. J. Manag. Stud. **62** (2). joms.13088 (2024)
21. Williams, A., Whiteman, G.: A call for deep engagement for impact: addressing the planetary emergency. Strateg. Organ. **19**, 526–537 (2021)
22. Mühlböck, M., Warmuth, J.-R., Holienka, M., Kittel, B.: Desperate entrepreneurs: no opportunities, no skills. Int. Entrep. Manag. J. **14**, 975–997 (2018)
23. Giones, F., Brem, A., Pollack, J.M., Michaelis, T.L., Klyver, K., Brinckmann, J.: Revising entrepreneurial action in response to exogenous shocks: considering the COVID-19 pandemic. J. Bus. Ventur. Insights **14**, e00186 (2020)
24. Jiang, Y.D., Straub, C., Klyver, K., Mauer, R.: Unfolding refugee entrepreneurs' opportunity-production process — patterns and embeddedness. J. Bus. Ventur. **36**(5) (2021)
25. Potsdam Institute for Climate Impact Research: Seven of nine planetary boundaries now breached – ocean acidification joins the danger zone. https://www.pik-potsdam.de/en/news/latest-news/seven-of-nine-planetary-boundaries-now-breached-2013-ocean-acidification-joins-the-danger-zone. Accessed 12 Dec 2025
26. Korber, S., McNaughton, R.B.: Resilience and entrepreneurship: a systematic literature review. IJEBR **24**, 1129–1154 (2018)
27. IPCC: Summary for policymakers. In: Climate Change 2023: Synthesis Report. Contribution of Working Groups I, II and III to the Sixth Assessment Report of the Intergovernmental Panel on Climate Change, Geneva, Switzerland, pp. 1–34. IPCC (2023)
28. Rockström, J.: Planetary Boundaries. New Perspect. Q. **27**, 72–74 (2010)
29. Thompson, N.A., Byrne, O.: Imagining futures: theorizing the practical knowledge of future-making. Organ. Stud. **43**, 247–268 (2022)
30. Peffers, K., et al.: A design science research methodology for information systems research. J. Manag. Inf. Syst. **24**, 45–77 (2007)
31. Seckler, C., Mauer, R., Vom Brocke, J.: Design science in entrepreneurship: conceptual foundations and guiding principles. J. Bus. Ventur. Des. **1**(1–2) (2021)
32. Schoormann, T., Möller, F., Di Maria, M., Große, N.: Guiding design principle projects: a canvas for young design science researchers. J. Inf. Syst. Educ. **34**, 307–325 (2023)
33. Fischer, J., et al.: Mainstreaming regenerative dynamics for sustainability. Nat. Sustain. **7**, 964–972 (2024)
34. Tuunanen, T., Winter, R., Vom Brocke, J.: Dealing with complexity in design science research: using design Echelons. MISQ **48**(2), 427–458 (2024)

35. Corbin, J.M., Strauss, A.L.: Basics of Qualitative Research: Techniques and Procedures for Developing Grounded Theory. SAGE, Los Angeles, London, New Delhi, Singapore, Washington DC, Boston (2015)
36. Maedche, A., Gregor, S., Morana, S., Feine, J.: Conceptualization of the problem space in design science research. In: Tulu, B., Djamasbi, S., Leroy, G. (eds.) DESRIST 2019. LNCS, vol. 11491, pp. 18–31. Springer, Cham (2019). https://doi.org/10.1007/978-3-030-19504-5_2
37. Williams, T.A., Shepherd, D.A.: Building resilience or providing sustenance: different paths of emergent ventures in the aftermath of the Haiti earthquake. AMJ **59**, 2069–2102 (2016)
38. Muñoz, P., Kimmitt, J., Kibler, E., Farny, S.: Living on the slopes: entrepreneurial preparedness in a context under continuous threat. Entrep. Reg. Dev. **31**, 413–434 (2019)
39. Kimsey, M., Besharov, M., Casasnovas, G., Höllerer, M.A.: Thinking in systems: from ceremonial to meaningful use of systems perspectives in organization and management research. ANNALS **19**(2), 736–762 (2025)
40. Berglund, H., Glaser, V.L.: The artifacts of entrepreneurial practice. In: Research Handbook on Entrepreneurship as Practice, pp. 168–186. Edward Elgar Publishing (2022)
41. O'Neill, D.W., Fanning, A.L., Lamb, W.F., Steinberger, J.K.: A good life for all within planetary boundaries. Nat. Sustain. **1**, 88–95 (2018)

Designing AI-Based Entrepreneurial Coaching Systems

Jonas Liebschner(✉) ⓘ, Daniel Heinz ⓘ, and Gerhard Satzger ⓘ

Institute for Information Systems (WIN), Karlsruhe Institute of Technology,
Karlsruhe, Germany
{jonas.liebschner,daniel.heinz,gerhard.satzger}@kit.edu

Abstract. Startups innovate under extreme uncertainty and time pressure, creating a continual need for guidance across discovery, experimentation, and early product decisions. Human coaching can foster reflective learning and problem framing, but it is intermittent, capacity-constrained, and offers limited day-to-day visibility into venture work. Meanwhile, founders increasingly use LLM-based assistants, yet current tools are generic, overly affirmative, and poorly aligned with coaching goals because they lack persistent venture context, workflow continuity, and explicit agency boundaries. This paper contributes design-relevant knowledge of the problem space for AI-based entrepreneurial coaching systems. Drawing on interviews with startup founders and coaches in Germany, we explicate recurring breakdowns in current coaching and tool support and derive four empirically grounded design requirements: (1) task-oriented venture progression support, (2) structured venture building, (3) assumption-driven learning and validation, and (4) reflective and developmental support that preserves founder agency. We discuss design tensions, boundary conditions, and an agenda for evaluating AI coaching as scaffolding rather than substitution.

Keywords: Entrepreneurial coaching · virtual coaching systems · large language models · design requirements · design science research

1 Introduction

Startups operate under extreme uncertainty, scarce resources, and persistent time pressure. Founders must repeatedly make consequential choices while simultaneously constructing the information needed to decide – e.g., clarifying customer problems, testing value propositions, designing experiments, and translating evidence into product and business model iterations [1–3]. Especially first-time founders face unfamiliar tasks and must develop competence on demand, which creates a recurring need for guidance that supports learning rather than merely providing answers [4,5].

Entrepreneurship coaching addresses this need by fostering reflective learning, problem framing, and metacognitive capability under uncertainty [4,6]. In

© The Author(s), under exclusive license to Springer Nature Switzerland AG 2026
J. vom Brocke et al. (Eds.): DESRIST 2026, LNCS 16606, pp. 21–39, 2026.
https://doi.org/10.1007/978-3-032-28313-9_2

contrast to consulting or prescriptive education, coaching aims to strengthen founders' judgment and self-efficacy while retaining decision agency on the entrepreneur's side [4]. However, in many ecosystems, coaching remains episodic and capacity-constrained: access is uneven, continuity across sessions is limited, and coaches often lack visibility into founders' day-to-day decision situations [7]. As a result, founders frequently struggle to maintain coherent progress across heterogeneous activities (e.g., discovery, pitching, funding, prototyping), and coaching time is often spent on (re-)establishing context rather than on enabling deeper reflection and assumption testing.

At the same time, founders increasingly use LLM-based assistants for ideation, explanation, writing, and prototyping [8,9]. This creates an opportunity for more continuous, integrated support – yet also reveals a misfit: generic assistants are optimized for fluent, immediate responses, not for coaching outcomes. They often lack persistent venture context, provide overly affirmative feedback, and do not orchestrate multi-step innovation workflows or make agency boundaries explicit. In entrepreneurial settings, these limitations are critical: if an AI system primarily optimizes for plausible outputs, it can drift from *scaffolding* founders' learning toward *substituting* their judgment – undermining the developmental intent of coaching and risking overreliance in high-stakes decisions.

This paper, therefore, asks a design-oriented question: *What are the design requirements for AI-based entrepreneurial coaching systems?* We address this question within a design science research (DSR) program by contributing to the *problem space*: we explicate design-relevant shortcomings in current entrepreneurial coaching and current AI tool use, and we derive empirically grounded requirements for systems intended to function as coaching artifacts rather than generic assistants [10,11]. Empirically, we draw on semi-structured interviews with startup founders and coaches embedded in entrepreneurial support organizations in Germany to identify recurring breakdowns, unmet needs, and boundary conditions for AI-mediated coaching.

Our key contribution is a set of four design requirements that specify coaching-specific system demands: (DR-1) supporting task-oriented venture progression with continuity across iterations; (DR-2) enabling structured venture building by externalizing and refining venture logic into coherent representations; (DR-3) scaffolding assumption-driven learning and validation by making hypotheses explicit and integrating evidence; and (DR-4) providing reflective and developmental support that is constructively critical while preserving founder agency. We further discuss the scaffolding-substitution boundary as the central design tension and outline implications for designing and evaluating such systems.

2   Background and Related Work

2.1   Entrepreneurial Coaching

Entrepreneurial support organizations (ESOs), such as incubators and accelerators, have proliferated to improve entrepreneurs' prospects under uncertainty;

within many programs, entrepreneurial coaching is a core delivery mode of structuring learning and progress [12,13]. Across this context, coaching is typically framed as a *developmental* intervention: rather than providing "the right answer," it aims to strengthen founders' capacity for reflective learning, problem framing, and self-regulation under uncertainty [4,6]. This developmental orientation emphasizes building founders' self-sufficiency (e.g., self-awareness, skills, confidence) rather than dependence on an external "answer provider" [12,14]. Related work further highlights founder-level conditions such as *coachability* as consequential for whether coaching translates into learning and goal attainment [5,15].

A recurring theme is boundary work: coaching is commonly characterized by a facilitative role and retained decision-making authority on the founders' side, whereas mentoring emphasizes relationship-based guidance rooted in the mentor's experience, and consulting is more solution- and expertise-driven problem-solving [4,6]. Accordingly, entrepreneurial coaching is a collaborative relationship in which the coach helps founders surface and test assumptions, improve sensemaking, and translate insights into action – without assuming ownership of decisions [6,13]. This distinction is salient in accelerator settings, where rapid iteration can pull interactions toward prescriptive advice even though founders may benefit more from hypothesis-driven learning and deliberation over trade-offs [13].

Empirical research has begun to unpack what coaches do and which conditions shape effectiveness. Audet and Couteret [16] identify entrepreneurs' openness to change and commitment to the coaching relationship as decisive success conditions, enabled by process features such as a clear moral contract (shared goals, roles, and timetable), sustained meeting cadence, and sufficient trust/chemistry, and supported by program-level mechanisms such as careful matching and expectation setting. Complementing this, Ben Salem and Lakhal [17] propose and validate a measurement scale that specifies entrepreneurial coaching as three observable dimensions – enforcement of standards, empathy, and expectations for entrepreneurial performance – supporting more cumulative research on coaching quality. For digital and AI-mediated coaching, such specification matters because design requires translating coaching into observable activities, interaction patterns, and quality dimensions that systems can reliably enact.

Finally, coaching is not a monolithic service: it is shaped by founders' needs and by how ESOs configure provision. Evidence from university incubation suggests that value creation hinges on incubator-level coaching service design (e.g., roster breadth, accessibility, continuity) as well as interaction-level dimensions (e.g., content and rapport) within the coach-entrepreneur dyad [18]. Research further suggests gendered differences in how entrepreneurs experience and value coaching, implying that uniform coaching service designs may misfit some founder groups [18,19]. Taken together, this relational, developmental view implies a design challenge that is not simply "more coaching," but scalable support that scaffolds reflective, assumption-testing work and remains timely and tailored despite access and continuity constraints – making technology-mediated coaching attractive even though virtual delivery formats remain sparsely examined in the entrepreneurship coaching literature [12–14,18–20].

2.2 Virtual Coaching Systems

Virtual coaching systems (VCS) have emerged prominently in cyber-physical settings, particularly in healthcare and rehabilitation, where coaching is tightly coupled with sensing, monitoring, and timely feedback. Prior work shows that early VCS combined sensing technologies (e.g., wearables, ambient sensors) with system–user interaction components, yet often struggled to "close the loop" with sufficiently adaptive, real-time feedback and personalization [21]. Complementary rehabilitation research highlights that effectiveness hinges not only on algorithmic intelligence but also on interaction and integration design in everyday contexts, supported through iterative stakeholder involvement [22]. Together, these streams establish that VCS operate in dynamic environments that require context-aware adaptation and careful socio-technical design [21,22].

Recent work conceptualizes virtual coaches as partially to fully autonomous systems that aim to transform users' cognition, affect, and behavior toward a goal through repeated interaction [23]. This goal-oriented transformation differentiates coaches from generic virtual assistants that primarily optimize convenience: coaching systems are designed to stimulate developmental change by guiding effortful practice, reflection, and habit formation [23]. Ontologically, VCS intersect with (a) context-aware systems, because they tailor interventions to the user's situation, (b) behavior change support systems, because they employ persuasive and motivational mechanisms to support change without coercion, and (c) tutoring/educational agents, because they frequently scaffold learning and skill development [23,24]. Accordingly, VCS research draws on behavioral science and persuasive systems design to determine which interventions to deliver, when, and how to frame them to sustain engagement and outcomes [23,24].

Architecturally, VCS typically comprise (i) a user/context model capturing characteristics, goals, tasks, and situational signals [21,23], (ii) a decision core that determines *when*, *what*, and *how* to intervene [23], (iii) an interaction layer – often conversational or embodied – to support relational engagement and rapport [25,26], and (iv) learning/personalization capabilities that refine coaching strategies over time [21,27]. Evidence from healthcare conversational agent research also cautions that evaluations are frequently inconsistent, underscoring the need for clearer mechanism articulation and more rigorous assessment [28].

Design-oriented research has consolidated VCS insights into actionable guidance. For instance, Schlieter et al. [29] derive design principles for home rehabilitation coaching – adaptivity, coaching strategy, multi-user interface, and sustainable infrastructure – and demonstrate feasibility and acceptance in patient evaluations. As VCS interfaces move from scripted dialog to generative AI, additional challenges arise around safety, consistency, and goal alignment: generative coaching chatbots can change adoption and user experience outcomes, but they intensify the need for guardrails, transparency, and structured coaching workflows to prevent shallow affirmation and to maintain coherent coaching strategies over time [23, 30].

Entrepreneurship imposes distinct requirements that are only partially addressed in the general VCS literature. Compared to health behavior coaching with relatively stable targets and metrics, entrepreneurial work is open-ended, contextually idiosyncratic, and characterized by shifting goals, contested interpretations, and judgment under uncertainty. Consequently, entrepreneurial coaching systems must scaffold sensemaking, critical reflection, and iterative problem framing as ventures evolve, implying heightened requirements for persistent venture context (e.g., assumptions, experiments, evidence, decisions), orchestration of multi-step innovation workflows, and calibrated feedback that strengthens founders' self-efficacy rather than substituting their agency [23]. Moreover, entrepreneurial settings often involve multiple stakeholders, making coach-in-the-loop or hybrid arrangements – where AI provides continuous scaffolding and humans intervene at key moments – a salient design option, consistent with multi-user interface principles [29]. Overall, VCS research offers a mature conceptual and architectural basis, but entrepreneurial coaching amplifies the need for context persistence, structured reflective protocols, and agency-sensitive, constructively critical patterns – especially with LLM-enabled coaching interfaces [23, 29, 30].

3   Method

This study follows a design science research (DSR) approach [10, 11] and is positioned within the echeloned Design Science Research (eDSR) methodology proposed by Tuunanen et al. [31]. eDSR structures complex DSR programs into self-contained design echelons that each produce validated intermediate artifacts and corresponding design knowledge. Each echelon scopes a manageable sub-problem, specifies its own research activities and validation criteria, and yields an output artifact that serves as input for subsequent echelons. In line with eDSR, we report two echelons: (1) *problem analysis*, which produces an empirically grounded account of shortcomings in current entrepreneurial coaching and tool support, and (2) *objectives and requirements definition*, which yields design requirements for AI-based entrepreneurial coaching systems.

The empirical basis comprises semi-structured interviews [32] conducted in 2025 with stakeholders embedded in entrepreneurial coaching ecosystems in Germany. We conducted two interview rounds. In the first round, we interviewed 11 startup founders (S1–S11) about their current use of AI-based assistants in entrepreneurial work and their expectations of an ideal support tool. While founders expressed a strong interest in coaching-oriented AI support, they reported that such use cases were not yet routinely realized in practice. To investigate this gap in more depth, we conducted additional interviews with startup founders (S12–S19, n = 8) and startup coaches (C1–C8, n = 8), focusing on shortcomings in current coaching practice and requirements for potential AI-based solutions.

Table 1. Overview of conducted interviews.

ID	Round	Description	Length
S1	1	Predictive sales analytics for B2B wholesale/manufacturing	0:51 h
S2	1	Ticketing + cashless payments for clubs/associations	0:44 h
S3	1	AI-guided app framework for governed services/contracts and evergreen UIs	0:58 h
S4	1	Automated hotel pricing/RMS for independents	0:43 h
S5	1	Menopause support app with exercises, tips and tracking	0:33 h
S6	1	"Assortment Intelligence" for retail using public & enriched data	0:49 h
S7	1	Privacy-first AI for structured data, synthetic data, and automated dataflows	0:52 h
S8	1	AI-assisted matching platform for senior professionals	0:39 h
S9	1	Real-time AI translation for church services	0:47 h
S10	1	Conversational language-learning with AI partners	0:53 h
S11	1	School app for live classroom translation and inclusion	1:02 h
S12	2	Fine-wine investing as tokenized real-world assets	1:02 h
S13	2	Household coordination (tasks, expenses, lists, calendar, recipes)	0:51 h
S14	2	Low-cost tutoring marketplace (at home or online)	1:07 h
S15	2	Ticketing + cashless payments for clubs/associations	0:54 h
S16	2	AI-based social recruiting focusing on passive candidates	1:08 h
S17	2	AI-powered at-home swim training (smart tether + analytics)	1:36 h
S18	2	Smart ring to turn digital sheet-music pages hands-free	0:39 h
S19	2	AgTech robotics using computer vision to automate selective vegetable harvesting	0:57 h
C1	2	Startup coach at a university-wide central startup incubator	0:54 h
C2	2	Startup coach focused on coaching and matchmaking with corporate mentors	1:01 h
C3	2	Startup coach at a university-wide central startup incubator	0:55 h
C4	2	Lead of Startup Development at an IT-focused accelerator	0:51 h
C5	2	Startup coach at an academic venture creation/founding consultancy	0:56 h
C6	2	Startup coach at a university-wide central startup incubator	1:24 h
C7	2	Coach in a university startup program (early-stage venture support)	0:20 h
C8	2	Coach at an entrepreneurship research institute	0:20 h

We purposively sampled two stakeholder groups to capture complementary perspectives on entrepreneurial coaching: (1) startup founders as recipients and users of coaching, and (2) startup coaches, including professional coaches as well as actors affiliated with accelerator and university-based entrepreneurship programs. Coaches were particularly important for the problem analysis, as their cross-venture perspective and continuous exposure to diverse cases provided a wider view on recurring shortcomings of human- and technical tool-supported entrepreneurial coaching beyond individual founder experiences. The interview protocol elicited accounts of (i) current coaching practices, (ii) perceived challenges and limitations of existing coaching formats and digital tools, and (iii) expectations, concerns, and boundary conditions regarding AI-based systems in entrepreneurial coaching. All interviews were audio-recorded, transcribed verbatim, and anonymized prior to analysis. Table 1 provides an overview of the interviewees.

We analyzed the interview data using a Gioia-style coding procedure [33], adapted to problem analysis and requirements elicitation in DSR. Founder and coach transcripts were coded jointly, while distinguishing between problem-centered and solution-centered statements. In a first step, we assigned descriptive, informant-centric first-order codes to passages referring to shortcomings in current coaching and tool support, as well as to desired capabilities and envisioned use cases for AI-based coaching support. In a second step, we grouped related codes into second-order themes through comparison within and across founder and coach perspectives. In a third step, we synthesized these themes into aggregate dimensions. For the problem space, this yielded two aggregate dimensions; for the solution space, four, which were then translated into the design requirements.

Two researchers iteratively discussed coding, theme development, and clustering, resolving disagreements through deliberation until reaching a shared interpretation. Consistent with eDSR, we validated intermediate artifacts through structured author-team walkthroughs by reviewing emerging problem clusters and design requirements for (i) traceability to interview evidence, (ii) internal consistency and non-redundancy, and (iii) design actionability. We revised formulations when counterexamples or ambiguous mappings emerged. Throughout the analysis, we maintained analytical memos to document interpretive decisions and preserve traceability from empirical observations to themes to design requirements.

4 Current Shortcomings in Entrepreneurial Coaching

Our thematic analysis of the interviews converges on two recurring problem clusters that characterize shortcomings in contemporary entrepreneurial coaching. First, *human coaching* is constrained by limited capacity, heterogeneous founder readiness, and weak preparation at first contact. Second, *technical support* remains unsatisfactory: despite perceived promise, interviewees described substantial setup effort, prompt dependence, and ongoing verification as barriers to routine use.

4.1   Shortcomings in Human Coaching

Coaches repeatedly described **insufficient preparedness at first contact** as a recurring impediment to productive coaching. Founders often enter initial sessions without a clear articulation of their idea, core assumptions, or problem framing, which makes diagnosis and targeted developmental guidance difficult. As one coach noted, *"when people explain things in a fuzzy way, I find it difficult to really solve the issue, understand it, or build on it"* (C1). Another coach emphasized that *"the more we have as a basis, the more we can actually work through"* (C3). As a result, first meetings often remain superficial and end with *"homework"* to structure the concept and work through basic templates before coaching can become actionable: *"we say, look at these patterns and then we see each other again in maybe two months, once they've worked further on the concept"* (C6).

Beyond early encounters, **advisor capacity constraints** limit depth, continuity, and equitable tailoring. ESOs reported high consultation volumes and evaluative workloads that restrict how deeply coaches can challenge and accompany each venture. Interviewees referenced roughly 170 initial consultations by August (C1), and one coach stated, *"I look at 1,500+ pitch decks per year"* and have *"direct contact with over 500 startups annually"* (C4). Under such conditions, it becomes infeasible to *"support all with equal resources"* (C4). Capacity pressure pushes coaching toward a small set of *"core processes"* (C1), reinforcing episodic interaction and prioritization over sustained accompaniment.

Interviewees emphasized that **heterogeneous venture maturity** increases coordination overhead and reduces coaching fit, especially in first encounters. Entry points ranged from individuals with emerging ideas to teams arriving with pitch decks, prototypes, or incorporated ventures. As one coach put it, *"it ranges from people who just had an idea in the shower to teams that already come with pitch decks"* (C3). Another noted that first consultations occur *"on very different levels"* (C1). This variability increases early-session diagnostic work because coaches must first establish the team's stage and available artifacts before shifting toward reflective learning and higher-quality decision support.

Across interviews, a recurrent expectation was to **move basic structuring upstream** to improve coaching efficiency and quality. Several interviewees suggested that founders, especially those without prior experience, would benefit from structured guidance before meeting human coaches: *"for every second or third founder, it could definitely help to use [a dedicated tool] at the very beginning to sharpen the idea"* (C1). Others endorsed a division of labor in which founders work through fundamentals with an assistant and then bring more mature outputs to experts: *"in the best case, they already did this beforehand with the AI agent and then come to you with higher quality"* (C6). Interviewees also articulated a cost-of-change logic: *"if I challenge and sharpen the idea early, it costs much less later than rebuilding everything after months of work"* (C1). Some coaches envisioned structured early assessments using known criteria (e.g., from funding applications), arguing that *"a pre-evaluation based on these crite-*

ria would help advisors a lot" (C6) while providing an initial reality check for teams and ESOs.

4.2 Shortcomings of Technical Tool Support

Interviewees consistently described coaching work as individualized and experience-based, making **generic tools a poor fit**. Advisory work depends on the person, the team, and their context, requiring an understanding of personal needs to identify appropriate next support steps. As one interviewee explained, *"we work with everyone personally, look at their needs, and then find the right offer for them – so it completely depends on who comes to us"* (C7). Coaching was repeatedly described as *"highly customized"* (C3) and as requiring *"approaching the topic very individually"* (C1). This customization was not framed as a flaw of coaching, but it sets a high design bar for technical support: tools must accommodate heterogeneity without collapsing into generic advice.

Against this backdrop, current AI solutions were seen as promising but **not yet reliable or seamless enough for coaching practice**. Several interviewees reported using AI tools only experimentally; one coach stated that they do not currently use AI tools in consulting practice (C8). Others described running AI "alongside" human judgment while emphasizing the need for verification: *"we let the AI run alongside us and then check what it produces, but it's not 100%, so we still have to review whether it really fits"* (C4). This lack of reliability limits trust and discourages integration into time-sensitive routines, despite perceived demand: *"I definitely see a huge need for an AI tool that supports this"* (C6).

A central barrier is **prompt dependence**, which interviewees viewed as particularly misaligned with early-stage needs. One summarized: *"most of the time, once you can formulate the question, the answer is relatively trivial. The real challenge is finding the question that actually moves you forward."* Early-stage founders were described as arriving with vague starting points and asking questions such as *"where do I start?"* or *"what do I do with this idea now?"* (C7). Another interviewee captured the resulting limitation: *"AI is only as good as how precisely I formulate my question. And if I'm not good at asking a precise question, it doesn't help me"* (C8). In coaching settings, this creates a structural mismatch because prompt-dependent systems shift disproportionate effort onto novice founders precisely when guidance is most needed.

Even when AI tools are used, **high setup effort** limits their practicality as coaching aids. Interviewees described substantial manual work to make generic assistants coaching-relevant, including embedding domain knowledge, specifying criteria, and adding examples. One coach explained that *"here's a pitch deck, evaluate it"* does not work; instead, *"you have to feed in knowledge, adjust criteria, give examples. Only then you slowly get a usable baseline"* (C4). While such setups may support high-profile tasks, the effort to integrate them into everyday coaching was rarely seen as feasible. This reflects a broader tooling gap; as one coach put it, *"this classic entrepreneurship tool doesn't really exist yet, because these use cases just aren't covered"* (C1). As a result, despite experimentation and perceived potential, AI tools remain weakly embedded in routine coaching workflows because interaction overhead outweighs immediate benefits.

5   Design Requirements for AI-Based Entrepreneurial Coaching Systems

The design requirements below were derived from founders' and coaches' accounts of where they see potential for AI-based coaching support, complementing rather than following directly from the shortcomings in Sect. 4: the shortcomings describe *why* AI-based coaching support is needed and what interaction-level barriers it must overcome, while the design requirements specify *what* such a system should do – support venture progression (DR-1), structure venture building (DR-2), scaffold assumption-driven validation (DR-3), and provide reflective developmental feedback that preserves founder agency (DR-4).

The interviews depict entrepreneurial coaching as spanning diverse tasks (e.g., pitching, market research, idea development) while returning to a common core: founders must articulate their venture, surface and test assumptions, and advance through iterative learning cycles. Yet limited coaching capacity and low day-to-day visibility constrain continuous, individualized guidance. Participants therefore described a need for an AI-based coaching system that supports venture progress, helps refine venture logic, scaffolds assumption-driven validation, and provides developmental feedback (Fig. 1).

Across these design requirements, interviewees highlighted a boundary condition captured by a *scaffolding–substitution* tension. Continuous AI support is attractive, but entrepreneurial learning depends on engagement with external stakeholders (customers, investors, partners) and retained ownership on the founder's side. Accordingly, the system should not decide *for* founders; it should structure work, surface blind spots and inconsistencies, provoke evidence-seeking action, and maintain continuity across iterations. Technically, this implies interaction patterns that reduce prompt dependence through proactive clarification, guided onboarding, and artifact-centric workflows rather than assuming founders can formulate "the right prompt" from the outset.

DR-1: Task-Oriented Venture Progression Support. Founders and coaches emphasized that coaching creates value only when it produces concrete *progress on venture-relevant tasks*; advice without actionable next steps was described as frustrating. One founder expected structured guidance in response to early ideas: *"Here are my ideas, what do you think? Have you considered validating it? And then it gives you a plan of what you should do and that structure"* (S13). Progression support was framed less as content production than as turning ambiguous venture situations into actionable commitments.

A defining feature of coaching-oriented progression support is **continuity over time**. Venture work unfolds through many iterations, yet support interactions often "reset," prompting repeated context reconstruction and fragmented attention. Interviewees therefore valued persistent structures that keep open issues visible and make progress cumulative, whether as *"A checklist that stays,*

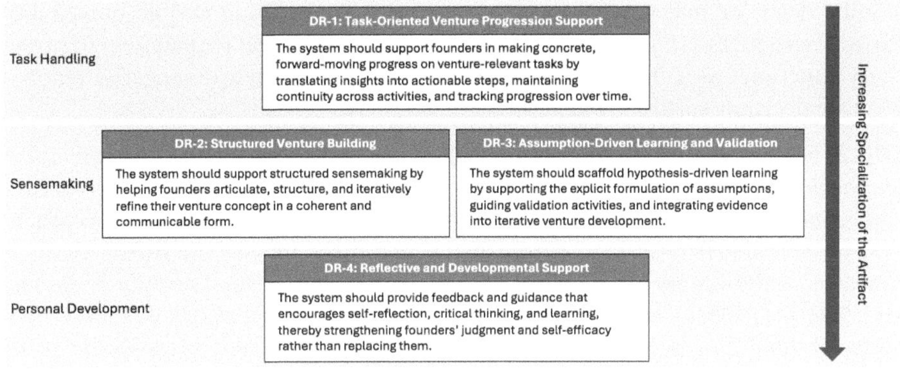

Fig. 1. Design requirements, positioned according to their focus and need for tool support.

so you know that these four things are still missing [...] so you don't come back completely new with different topics" (S16) or as an evolving roadmap: *"The idea ... that it can live a certain roadmap"* (S14). Persistence here is an intelligible, venture-specific trajectory that remains legible over time.

Progression support was also grounded in artifact-anchored feedback that directly enables action. Pitch decks were frequently cited because they operationalize venture logic for investors and reveal gaps: *"I would have simply wished that someone would look at my pitch deck [...] and tell me what investors want"* (S16). Given perceived variability in coaching quality (*"many people call themselves pitch coaches, but the quality varies strongly"* (S7)), interviewees saw value in scalable, structured critique. Founders likewise referenced other decision artifacts (e.g., pricing, go-to-market, marketing materials), including mentor-like benchmarking for pricing: *"it's really like a mentor"* (S17).

Finally, interviewees specified that "next steps" should reduce uncertainty rather than increase output volume and be supported by tracking that links hypotheses, evidence, and subsequent tasks. One founder envisioned an integrated loop: *"You have a list of hypotheses, you enter what you found out, and the model tells you which hypotheses you validated with which evidence, and what you still need to do"* (S15). Coaches reinforced this logic, noting that early-stage teams often over-invest in technical work while neglecting market learning and validation; accordingly, the system should redirect attention: *"It should already be a bit of a guide, showing where there is still a need for action and where you should sit down again and validate."* (C5). Thus, DR-1 requires sustaining venture progression through prioritized next steps, continuity, artifact-anchored critique, and traceable iteration.

Boundary Conditions. Progression support should not collapse into task completion: persistent action lists need to remain linked to the assumptions they address (DR-3) and the venture logic they refine (DR-2). It must preserve founder agency by treating priorities and next steps as proposals that founders can accept, modify, defer, or reject, with rationale recorded for learning and accountability. Proactive elements (e.g., reminders) should be optional and explainable so proactivity functions as a lightweight continuity aid rather than managerial enforcement or decision substitution.

DR-2: Structured Venture Building. A second theme concerns a *structured approach to venture building*: founders must continuously articulate, structure, and refine their venture concept to reason about it and communicate it to others. Coaches frequently described established frameworks such as the Business Model Canvas as scaffolds for articulation: *"If you have nothing, you basically go through the Business Model Canvas with questions and write things down. It's a good tool to understand how a company should be built and what actions come out of it"* (C3). Participants simultaneously stressed that such representations are means rather than ends: *"Often the problem is that people just fill out a canvas and think that's the goal. But that's not the idea; it's just a tool to help structure"* (C6). DR-2, therefore, concerns co-constructing coherent, revisable venture representations that make reasoning visible and discussable, not merely filling templates.

Founders already use AI to articulate and consolidate venture logic into formal artifacts (e.g., business plans, pitch narratives): *"I used AI to write business plans"* (S9). Coaches noted the institutional necessity of such artifacts, especially for funding: *"If you need funding, you need a business plan that you have to submit everywhere"* (C2). Interviewees also described a coaching-relevant workflow linking representation building to validation: *"We entered it into ChatGPT: what would a Business Model Canvas look like? And then we discussed it and thought, how can we validate it?"* (S15). Beyond documents, founders wanted orientation in the venture journey – *"Putting topics into clusters so that the chatbot tells you, you are actually operating here right now"* (S14) – while coaches emphasized convergence toward differentiation and positioning (e.g., *"USP is really a decisive criterion"* (C2)). This underscores a coaching-relevant distinction: the system should not merely produce representations, but help founders understand dependencies between elements and translate them into evidence-seeking activities.

Finally, interviewees emphasized that sensemaking must be incremental and non-overwhelming. Rather than generating exhaustive outputs, the system should guide focused, stepwise refinement through targeted questions and revisions: *"not overloading – but saying, okay, first work on these two questions; concretize this; send me a new version; then the machine can interact again"* (C1). In sum, DR-2 positions AI-based coaching as a sensemaking infrastructure that helps founders externalize, structure, and iteratively refine venture logic into coherent, communicable representations.

Boundary Conditions. The system must prevent "template theater," where form-filling creates an illusion of progress; representations should surface uncertainty, missing information, and dependencies on evidence (DR-3). Outputs should remain communicable and editable, prioritizing clarity and traceability to founder inputs so artifacts can be discussed with coaches, mentors, or investors without becoming opaque AI products. Persistence of venture context should be governed by the founder's control over what is stored, updated, and shared.

DR-3: Assumption-Driven Learning and Validation. A third design requirement concerns learning under uncertainty. Founders and coaches emphasized that ventures often fail not due to poor execution, but because consequential assumptions remain implicit or untested. Coaches described deliberate practices for making assumptions explicit and sequencing validation: *"I work a lot at the beginning with an assumptions map [...] and then you say: stop building the 25th feature and look at what is unvalidated"* (C5). Validation thus emerged as a primary engine of venture progress and a key differentiator from generic ideation assistance.

DR-3 requires the system to scaffold an *assumption–test–evidence chain*: help founders formulate falsifiable assumptions, prioritize them by impact and uncertainty, design appropriate validation activities (e.g., interviews, surveys, landing pages, experiments), and interpret evidence to update venture logic (DR-2) and subsequent actions (DR-1). Founders described AI support as valuable when it redirects attention toward validation: *"You haven't really done validation yet, maybe make sure you get a larger number of people in the survey"* (S13). They also used existing assistants to generate critical validation questions: *"I used ChatGPT or Gemini so that it simply asks me a few critical questions for validation"* (S16). Several interviewees envisioned closing the loop by feeding results back into the system: *"Imagine it tells you what you need to validate, then you put in the results, and then you get feedback on what that means."* (S15).

Interviewees emphasized focusing validation on what is consequential, including identifying critical risks and *"break points"* (S19). They also linked validation planning to stakeholder identification, such as recommending who to approach: *"especially a recommendation of which people you should maybe ask again"* (S18). In addition, participants described AI-based simulation and rehearsal (e.g., practicing customer interviews or investor conversations) as preparation before engaging external stakeholders; one coach suggested that *"an AI could probably do that really well, like a coach"* (C5). Across accounts, simulation was valued when it supports, rather than substitutes for, empirical validation.

Boundary Conditions. The system must prevent "validation-by-proxy" by treating desk research and simulation as preparation rather than evidentiary, and prompting external action: *"please don't go into your basement and build for three years. Ask people first. Only then may you start building something"* (S7). It should also communicate evidence quality and uncertainty by encouraging citation and explicit limits of inference; founders reported better outcomes when they *"actively ask for sources"* (S13). However, it must avoid false precision: while it can prioritize assumptions and propose tests, it should not overstate certainty or treat web-derived signals as conclusive proof.

DR-4: Reflective and Developmental Support. Finally, interviews underscored that entrepreneurial coaching is not only about tasks and structures, but about developing founders' judgment, critical thinking, and self-efficacy.

Founders valued feedback that is honest yet constructive: *"Criticism is good, but it has to be constructive and not destructive, so with suggestions or impulses on how to move forward"* (S13). Coaches similarly framed their role as providing reflective impulses rather than ready-made answers: *"The overarching idea is giving impulses – questions that make you reflect and think deeper"* (C4). This points to a coaching-specific interaction logic in which developmental support improves how founders reason and decide under uncertainty.

Participants valued dialogic support sustained over time – *"It's not like you ask a question, get an answer, and that's it. It's a process that keeps going"* (S9) – and stressed that coaching-aligned systems should not default to affirmation. One founder summarized the desired stance as being *"questioned critically"* (S18). Interviewees also wanted reflective questions to be justified, including brief explanations of relevance: *"Ask follow-up questions and give a reason why this question is being asked"* (S12). Several founders described pitch feedback as emotionally demanding and suggested that AI can lower defensiveness by being perceived as neutral: *"Pitch feedback is very emotional. It's much easier when it's a bot, because you know it doesn't want to harm you"* (S7). This neutrality was valued insofar as it supports deeper critique rather than smoothing over tensions.

Boundary Conditions. Founder agency must be preserved by separating critique, hypotheses, and suggestions from decisions so the system supports judgment formation rather than substituting it. Reflective depth should be paired with psychological safety by challenging ideas without demotivating founders and framing critique developmentally. Interaction should remain dialogic and context-sensitive; iterative follow-up questions are a core mechanism for reducing prompt dependence and strengthening coaching quality through clarification.

6   Discussion and Conclusion

This paper contributes design-relevant explanatory knowledge by clarifying what distinguishes *AI-based entrepreneurial coaching systems* from generic LLM assistance. Effective AI coaching, we argue, should be designed as *developmental infrastructure*: sociotechnical systems that institutionalize reflective, assumption-driven work and support judgment formation under uncertainty over time, rather than optimizing for fluent answers or short-term user satisfaction. This orientation aligns with coaching research that conceptualizes coaching as a developmental, non-prescriptive process rather than advice provision [4,12].

We articulate a design logic in which coaching value emerges when systems externalize venture logic into revisable representations, bind actions to assumptions and evidence, and introduce agency-preserving *developmental friction* through dialogic critique and justification. This logic directly targets the affirmative bias of current assistants, which tends toward uncritical validation and smooth completion [23,30]. Our contribution is therefore an account of *scaffolding without substitution*: accelerating progress while reducing the risk of premature closure, proxy validation, and responsibility drift.

More specifically, we contribute empirically grounded design requirements that distinguish AI-based entrepreneurial coaching systems from prior VCS work in health and rehabilitation [23,29], and LLM-based coaching for goal attainment and leadership [34,35]. Entrepreneurial coaching, however, involves distinct design demands – evolving open-ended goals, iterative revision of venture logic, assumption-driven validation cycles requiring external stakeholder engagement, and a high-stakes scaffolding–substitution boundary – that our design requirements make explicit and designable. This contribution is positioned independent of delivery mode: the design logic can be instantiated as either *AI-driven entrepreneurial coaching*, where the system enacts a standalone coaching stance, or *AI-augmented entrepreneurial coaching*, where the system complements human coaches and ESOs by providing continuity, structure, and reflective scaffolding between episodic encounters.

6.1 Implications for Research

This study links entrepreneurial coaching and VCS research by translating relational, developmental principles into designable sociotechnical mechanisms. Prior work emphasizes that coaching strengthens founders' judgment and self-efficacy while preserving decision agency [4,6]. We extend this view by arguing that core coaching functions can be partially *institutionalized* through persistent venture representations and interaction protocols that keep venture logic, assumptions, experiments, and evidence legible, revisable, and portable across time and hand-offs [12,13]. This reframes *continuity* as a theoretical construct and design variable: effectiveness depends less on uninterrupted interaction and more on maintaining a persistent venture state (revision history, commitments, and explicit links between actions, assumptions, and evidence) that reduces repeated context reconstruction.

Our findings also extend VCS research beyond behavioral adherence under relatively stable goals [21,24,29] toward *epistemic work* under goal ambiguity, where problem definitions and success criteria evolve as evidence accumulates [13]. Accordingly, AI-based entrepreneurial coaching systems should model context primarily as an evolving system of assumptions (DR-2/DR-3), not merely as user state. Distinguishing *AI-driven* and *AI-augmented* configurations clarifies boundary conditions for theorizing human–AI collaboration: in AI-driven coaching, the system must enact reflective questioning and calibrated critique while making uncertainty and agency boundaries explicit to avoid competence substitution; in AI-augmented coaching, the same mechanisms can operate as infrastructure that stabilizes venture state across sessions, improves boundary artifacts, and increases continuity under limited coach visibility. Finally, equity concerns [18,19] and LLM risks [23,30] imply that articulation and sensemaking should be treated as coached outcomes, with guardrails embedded into the design logic.

6.2   Design Implications: The Scaffolding–Substitution Boundary

Our findings elevate the scaffolding–substitution boundary from a cautionary note to a central design principle for AI-based entrepreneurial coaching systems. Founders valued efficiency and concrete direction, yet they and their coaches emphasized that entrepreneurial learning hinges on retained decision ownership and engagement with external stakeholders [12]. This creates a structural risk: systems optimized for convenience and short-term satisfaction tend to generate polished deliverables (plans, decks, strategies) that prematurely close inquiry, dampen evidence-seeking, and shift agency from founder to system.

We operationalize this boundary as *developmental friction*: calibrated reflection at decision-relevant moments while preserving forward momentum. Instead of seamless prompt–response loops, AI-based entrepreneurial coaching systems should implement *move-and-reflect* mechanisms that elicit assumptions, surface evidence gaps, check consistency against stored venture logic, and label outputs as provisional hypotheses contingent on validation. This implies an architecture with (1) a structured venture state model (logic, assumptions, experiments, decisions), (2) progression support that binds actions to assumptions and evidence to form a traceable learning trajectory, and (3) explicit agency protocols that require founders to accept, modify, defer, or reject recommendations with rationale to preserve responsibility boundaries and enable retrospective learning.

Given the legal and financial stakes of entrepreneurial guidance, guardrails are integral to this architecture. Minimum guardrails include uncertainty signaling, explicit differentiation between conjecture and evidence, escalation triggers for high-stakes domains, and auditability that links outputs to venture state and founder decisions.

6.3   Practical Implications for Entrepreneurial Support Organizations

For ESOs, AI-augmented entrepreneurial coaching systems enable a hybrid service design analogous to a flipped classroom: AI supports scalable structural work (onboarding, venture articulation, assumption mapping, experiment planning, pitch narrative structuring, readiness diagnostics), while humans focus on scarce, high-value functions (judgment under ambiguity, strategic trade-offs, accountability, founder psychology, and network brokering). This shifts human sessions away from reconstructing context and toward higher-order reflective work.

At the ecosystem level, such systems may improve scalability and equity by democratizing access to structured preparation that is unevenly available across founders and programs [18, 19]. However, this promise is conditional: if systems implicitly privilege dominant discourse styles or high prompt literacy, they may reproduce disparities. ESOs should therefore treat AI onboarding as capability building that helps founders articulate and reason. Credible deployment also requires governance for privacy, IP handling, liability boundaries, auditability, and coach onboarding for hybrid workflows, because these factors shape whether AI coaching can be integrated without eroding trust.

6.4   Limitations and Future Research

Our findings are shaped by contextual boundary conditions. The study is situated in largely university-embedded coaching settings in Germany and focuses on early-stage technology ventures amid rapidly evolving AI capabilities. Coaching norms, founder expectations, and acceptable AI roles may therefore differ across cultures, venture stages, and ecosystems. Accordingly, the derived design requirements should be treated as context-sensitive design starting points rather than universal prescriptions, requiring validation across diverse entrepreneurial settings.

Positioned within an eDSR approach [31], this paper contributes a problem-space analysis and a structured set of design requirements. Future research should build on this foundation in three directions. First, *solution-space instantiation* should translate the design requirements and scaffolding–substitution boundary into concrete architectures, design principles, and artifacts. Second, *empirical studies of coaching interaction* should examine how founders appropriate continuity structures and developmental friction in practice, including variation by founder experience, venture stage, and culture. Third, *ecosystem and longitudinal perspectives* should analyze AI-based entrepreneurial coaching within broader support infrastructures, assessing how persistent venture representations shape preparation and collaboration with coaches, mentors, and ESOs over time.

Whether the scaffolding–substitution boundary can be maintained at scale, and whether governance and safety mechanisms can prevent drift toward affirmative convenience, remain open questions and integral parts of a cumulative research agenda toward competence-enhancing AI coaching systems that strengthen entrepreneurial learning without substituting human judgment.

Acknowledgments. This work has been supported by the German Federal Ministry of Research, Technology and Space through the research project "SHAPE" under the grant reference 02K23A150.

Disclosure of Interests. The authors have no competing interests to declare.

References

1. Giardino, C., Unterkalmsteiner, M., Paternoster, N., Gorschek, T., Abrahamsson, P.: What do we know about software development in startups? Software IEEE **31**, 28–32 (2014)
2. Paternoster, N., Giardino, C., Unterkalmsteiner, M., Gorschek, T., Abrahamsson, P.: Software development in startup companies: a systematic mapping study. Inf. Softw. Technol. **56** (2014)
3. Upadhyay, N., Upadhyay, S., Dwivedi, Y.K.: Theorizing artificial intelligence acceptance and digital entrepreneurship model. Int. J. Entrep. Behav. Res. **28**(5), 1138–1166 (2021)
4. Klofsten, M., Öberg, S.: Coaching versus mentoring: are there any differences? In: Proceedings of the 16th Annual High Technology Small Firms Conference and Doctoral Workshop, University of Twente (2008)

5. Kuratko, D.F., Neubert, E., Marvel, M.R.: Insights on the mentorship and coachability of entrepreneurs. Bus. Horiz. **64**(2), 199–209 (2021)
6. Kotte, S., Diermann, I., Rosing, K., Möller, H.: Entrepreneurial coaching: a two-dimensional framework in context. Appl. Psychol. **70**(2), 518–555 (2021)
7. Raeisy, L., Salimi, G., Safavi, S.A.A., Mohammadi, M.: Influencing factors of incubators and accelerators' success in entrepreneurship development: an integrative review. J. Glob. Entrep. Res. **15**(1), 27 (2025)
8. Sammet, F., Gillig, H., Foo, M.D.: How do Startups use AI? A Q-methodology approach to understanding adoption patterns. In: European Conference on Innovation and Entrepreneurship, vol. 19, no. 1, pp. 950–959 (2024)
9. Rezazadeh, A., Kohns, M., Bohnsack, R., António, N., Rita, P.: Generative AI for growth hacking: how startups use generative AI in their growth strategies. J. Bus. Res. **192**, 115320 (2025)
10. Hevner, A.R., March, S.T., Park, J., Ram, S.: Design science in information systems research. MIS Q. **28**(1), 75–105 (2004)
11. Peffers, K., Tuunanen, T., Rothenberger, M., Chatterjee, S.: A design science research methodology for information systems research. J. Manag. Inf. Syst. **24**, 45–77 (2007)
12. Bergman, B.J., McMullen, J.S.: Helping entrepreneurs help themselves: a review and relational research agenda on entrepreneurial support organizations. Entrep. Theory Pract. **46**(3), 688–728 (2022)
13. Mansoori, Y., Karlsson, T., Lundqvist, M.: The influence of the lean startup methodology on entrepreneur-coach relationships in the context of a startup accelerator. Technovation **84–85**, 37–47 (2019)
14. Brinkley, M.L., Le Roux, I.: Coaching as a support function for potential entrepreneurs. South. Afr. J. Entrep. Small Bus. Manag. **10** (2018)
15. Kutzhanova, N., Lyons, T.S., Lichtenstein, G.A.: Skill-based development of entrepreneurs and the role of personal and peer group coaching in enterprise development. Econ. Dev. Q. **23**(3), 193–210 (2009)
16. Audet, J., Couteret, P.: Coaching the entrepreneur: features and success factors. J. Small Bus. Enterp. Dev. **19**(3), 515–531 (2012)
17. Ben Salem, A., Lakhal, L.: Entrepreneurial coaching: how to be modeled and measured? J. Manag. Dev. **37**(1), 88–100 (2018)
18. Nicholls-Nixon, C.L., Maxheimer, M.M.: How coaching services help early stage entrepreneurs: an exploration of gender differences. J. Small Bus. Enterp. Dev. **29**(5), 742–763 (2022)
19. Fielden, S., Hunt, C.: Online coaching: an alternative source of social support for female entrepreneurs during venture creation. Int. Small Bus. J. **29**, 345–359 (2011)
20. Marras, G., Opizzi, M., Loi, M.: Understanding the multifunctional role of entrepreneurial coaching through a systematic review of the literature. J. Manag. Psychol. **39** (2024)
21. Tsiouris, K.M., Tsakanikas, V.D., Gatsios, D., Fotiadis, D.I.: A review of virtual coaching systems in healthcare: closing the loop with real-time feedback. Front. Digit. Health **2** (2020)
22. Seregni, A., et al.: Virtual coaching for rehabilitation: the participatory design experience of the vCare project. Front. Public Health **9** (2021)
23. Weimann, T.G., Schlieter, H., Brendel, A.B.: Virtual coaches: background, theories, and future research directions. Bus. Inf. Syst. Eng. **64**(4), 515–528 (2022)
24. Oinas-Kukkonen, H.: Behavior change support systems: a research model and agenda. In: Ploug, T., Hasle, P., Oinas-Kukkonen, H. (eds.) Persuasive Technology, pp. 4–14. Springer, Heidelberg (2010)

25. Bickmore, T.W., Fernando, R., Ring, L., Schulman, D.: Empathic touch by relational agents. IEEE Trans. Affect. Comput. **1**(1), 60–71 (2010)
26. Bickmore, T.W., Picard, R.W.: Establishing and maintaining long-term human-computer relationships. ACM Trans. Comput.-Hum. Interact **12**(2), 293–327 (2005)
27. Kocaballi, A.B., et al.: The personalization of conversational agents in health care: systematic review. J. Med. Internet Res. **21**(11), e15360 (2019)
28. Laranjo, L., et al.: Conversational agents in healthcare: a systematic review. J. Am. Med. Inform. Assoc. JAMIA **25**(9), 1248–1258 (2018)
29. Schlieter, H., et al.: Designing virtual coaching solutions. Bus. Inf. Syst. Eng. **66**(3), 377–400 (2024)
30. Terblanche, N.H.D.: Smooth talking: generative versus scripted coaching chatbot adoption and efficacy comparison. Int. J. Hum.-Comput. Interact. **41**(14), 9109–9122 (2025)
31. Tuunanen, T., Winter, R., Brocke, J.V.: Dealing with complexity in design science research: a methodology using design echelons. MIS Q. **48**, 427–458 (2024)
32. Myers, M.D., Newman, M.: The qualitative interview in IS research: examining the craft. Inf. Organ. **17**(1), 2–26 (2007)
33. Gioia, D.A., Corley, K.G., Hamilton, A.L.: Seeking qualitative rigor in inductive research: notes on the Gioia methodology. Organ. Res. Methods **16**(1), 15–31 (2013)
34. Arakawa, R., Yakura, H.: Coaching copilot: blended form of an LLM-powered chatbot and a human coach to effectively support self-reflection for leadership growth. In: Proceedings of the 6th ACM Conference on Conversational User Interfaces, CUI 2024, pp. 1–14. Association for Computing Machinery, New York (2024)
35. Graßmann, C., Schermuly, C.C.: Coaching with artificial intelligence: concepts and capabilities. Hum. Resour. Dev. Rev. **20**(1), 106–126 (2021)

Future of Responsible and Sustainable Design

A Digital Twin-Based System to Support Urban Planners in Mitigating the Urban Heat Island Effect

Iresha Bandaranayake[✉] , Dominik Siemon , and Ram Gurung

LUT University, Lappeenranta, Finland
{iresha.himihami.mudiyanselage,dominik.siemon,ram.gurung}@lut.fi

Abstract. The urban heat island (UHI) effect describes elevated temperatures in urban areas relative to surrounding rural regions. Reductions in green spaces and natural cooling sources exacerbate this phenomenon, with prior studies demonstrating that urban modifications substantially contribute to UHI intensity. Therefore, designing a digital tool to identify and understand how new modifications affect temperature conditions plays a crucial role in optimized city planning. The digital twin (DT) concept can be considered as one approach to address this scenario. A DT is a digital platform that works as a one-to-one mapping between a digital simulation and a real-world environment. Our design science research project proposes a novel solution for this scenario using a DT system based on the city of Lahti, Finland. Our solution, a DT system, allows users to implement modifications, including trees, built-ups, and water bodies in the Lahti city area, to forecast their influence on land surface temperature (LST). The DT is combined with a machine learning (ML) model, which was trained to predict the LST, focusing on factors including geographical locations and spectral indices. The LST is forecasted, considering the changes that occurred after the modifications. Our solution is evaluated through a technical evaluation of the ML algorithm and a user evaluation with environmental specialists, urban planners, and students of sustainable urban planning studies.

Keywords: Digital Twin · UHI Effect · Land Surface Temperature · Spectral Indices · Forecasting · Urban Planning

1 Introduction

With rapid urbanization and industrialization, the world encounters numerous environmental challenges, including the urban heat island (UHI) effect. The UHI effect is a phenomenon where some city areas experience higher temperatures than nearby rural regions. The reduction of green spaces and natural cooling sources is a major cause of this problem. However, given current economic conditions and growing human needs, large construction and development projects have become unavoidable. Therefore, identifying sustainable strategies to minimize adverse effects, such as the UHI effect, is vital [1]. Elderly people and people

J. vom Brocke et al. (Eds.): DESRIST 2026, LNCS 16606, pp. 43–58, 2026.
https://doi.org/10.1007/978-3-032-28313-9_3

with heart and other chronic diseases are exposed to risk, and the heat-related mortalities depict a rapid increase with the influence of the UHI effect. Furthermore, the UHI effect contributes to increasing global warming, creating floods, storms, and diversely influences the ecosystems' energy flow, material flow, and biological habits [2–4].

Although previous studies identified significant reasons behind the UHI effect and proposed reasonable solutions and strategies to overcome the issue [5–7], tools that simulate and strongly predict the consequences of man-made changes are lacking. Many existing studies [5,6] focus on analysing historical data and proposing physical solutions to mitigate adverse effects. Therefore, designing a tool that operates as a one-to-one mapping between the real and virtual environment is important. Existing research has introduced approaches that communicate statistical results or environmental indicators through two-dimensional maps. However, these solutions largely remain descriptive and do not provide an interactive or simulated digital environment in which urban planners can easily explore and test potential interventions [8,9]. While a small number of studies are conceptually closer to our work, they typically address isolated components of the problem and lack an integrated end-to-end workflow [10,11]. In particular, prior work does not combine state-of-the-art predictive modeling with an explicit analytical framework for examining how different types of urban interventions influence outcomes, nor does it support intuitive, low-barrier use by planning practitioners. Although, previous studies identified significant drivers of the UHI effect and proposed mitigation strategies [5–7], existing approaches provide limited support for testing the likely effects of concrete interventions before implementation. Much of the prior work remains focused on analysing historical patterns, reporting environmental indicators, or presenting mitigation options in descriptive ways. As a result, urban planners still lack accessible tools for interactively exploring where particular interventions should be introduced and how alternative modifications may affect local land surface temperature (LST) in a specific urban context. Our work provides a digital platform for performing specific intervention tasks, including adding tree areas, water bodies, green roofs, and built-ups in a simulated 3D environment that mimics the physical structure of the city of Lahti. Therefore, this facilitates city planners to observe the LST changes that occur due to each intervention type.

Therefore, we propose a solution to overcome this scenario using a digital twin (DT) system based on the city of Lahti, Finland. A digital twin is a promising approach to address this gap because it connects urban data, predictive modelling, and a spatially explicit three-dimensional representation of the city in one environment. This makes it possible to examine intervention scenarios virtually and compare their likely thermal implications before changes are implemented in practice. Specifically, we propose a DT system that allows users (e.g., urban planners) to create modifications in the city area and forecast how they affect LST. Our system allows users to add modifications, including tree areas, buildings, green roofs, and water bodies, to locations in the city. It forecasts the potential changes in LST that occur due to the influence of modifications. The system uses a machine learning (ML) model pre-trained with satellite-based geospatial data for the forecasting process. The user interface of our system has been designed using a 3D visualization platform built with Cesium[1] Although this study is conducted, focusing only on the Lahti city area, it provides information on integrating similar solutions for other cities in Europe that face similar challenges. This work follows the design science research methodology and is guided by the following research question:

1. How can a DT system support urban planners in simulating and exploring the LST effects of urban heat mitigation interventions?

To address this question, the artifact was developed and assessed based on the following design goals and evaluation criteria:

- integration of environmental, spatial, and temperature data into a unified analysis pipeline,
- accurate forecasting of LST using spectral indices and bands,
- visualization of intervention-related temperature changes in a 3D city model, and
- evaluation of usability, reliability, and decision-support potential for intended users.

2   Background and Literature Review

Rapid urbanization and industrialization are found to be the main sources of the UHI effect. Several studies have been conducted to understand the factors influencing UHI. Many of them have considered LST as a proxy of UHI, since it measures the surface temperature that causes the UHI effect [12]. The factors affecting UHI can be divided into two categories: factors under human control and factors that are not controllable by humans [13]. Controllable factors include green areas, building materials, land use patterns, and building density, while uncontrollable factors include wind speed, cloud cover, and seasonal change. Understanding the controllable factors to intervene and create policies for designing urban areas is important for city planners and policymakers.

Remote sensing data is used to derive spectral indices such as Normalized Difference Vegetation Index (NDVI), Normalized Difference Water Index (NDWI), and Normalized Difference Built-up Index (NDBI). Spectral indices are mathematical relationships that combine different spectral bands of satellite imagery to identify specific surface features and distinguish between land cover types. NDVI is commonly used to identify vegetation, NDWI to detect water bodies, and NDBI to map built-up or urban areas. These indices provide a straightforward way to interpret satellite data for environmental and land-use analysis. Furthermore, prior studies highlighted that LST is highly linked to land use,

---

[1] Cesium is an open platform for software applications designed to use 3D geospatial data. https://cesium.com/.

vegetation cover, seasonal changes, population density, built-up areas, day-night temperature differences, and water bodies [4,14].

Recent studies indicate that despite their cool climate, mid-sized Nordic cities in high-latitude regions experience a significant heat island effect. In Lahti, the built-up areas tend to be warmer than the green or water areas during summer. However, water temperature distribution is correlated with atmospheric inversions rather than surface characteristics [15]. A microclimate analysis and future risk projections conducted to identify heat risk in Lahti reveal an increase in high-risk areas by 2040 if mitigation strategies are not implemented [6]. These findings underscore the importance of addressing these issues in mid-sized cities like Lahti through urban planning. To mitigate rising temperatures, it has been proposed to expand green areas by intensifying green infrastructure in the city plan [6].

Temperature prediction plays a crucial role in various fields, including agriculture, urban planning, tourism, airport weather forecasts, and for human beings. Identifying a suitable algorithm is always a challenge as traditional deterministic algorithms tend to fail in most complex real-world scenarios, and it is impossible to determine a universal algorithm that can perform similarly in all problems [16]. In recent decades, ML has become more popular among researchers in predicting temperature due to its ability to capture the nonlinear patterns of heat distributions in areas. ML-based temperature predictions using environment and weather data perform with higher accuracy than traditional statistical data analysis methods. Furthermore, ML models can provide sustainable solutions for monitoring and planning under varying climate conditions [17]. Researchers have used various ML models to predict temperature, including random forest, linear regression, support vector machine, and gradient boosting, to select the most accurate model. Many studies suggest that random forest performs higher accuracy than other ML algorithms for temperature predictions [18–20].

A DT is a virtual representation of a physical system (and its associated environment and processes) that is updated through the exchange of information between the physical and virtual systems [21]. The concept of DT is widely used in various domains, including urban planning, manufacturing, education, health, transportation, sports, business, and makes the processes smarter and more intelligent [23–25]. Applications of DTs span a wide range of scenarios in the context of urban city planning. For instance, they can be employed in traffic control, disaster management, and other areas related to climate change [26–28]. Therefore, implementing a DT is a well-suited solution for forecasting temperature changes, adhering to physical modifications.

3   Methodology

The main purpose of this study is to design and evaluate a DT-based artifact supporting urban planners to mitigate the UHI effect. Therefore, the study employs the design science research methodology as its primary research approach. In particular, the study adapts the echeloned design science research (^{e}DSR) model proposed by Tuunanen et al. (2024) to structure the research and validate the process [29].

The $^e DSR$ model consists of five echelons: problem analysis, objectives and requirement definitions, design and development, demonstration, and evaluation. Problem analysis, that is, the first echelon, was systematically validated across three approaches (see previous section). First, a literature review was conducted, and second, it was validated through a discussion with a domain expert (environmental specialist) from the city of Lahti. Thereafter, the historical LST data were analyzed. The validated problem statement was generated as design knowledge output in this echelon. In the next echelon, the design objectives and system requirements were defined and validated based on the problem analysis, by examining existing tools simulating the urban climate effects. The ideas of the domain experts were beneficial in ensuring the viability of the artifact. The proposed artifact was constructed during the design and development phase, adhering to the validated research objectives. Internal consistency, applicability, and design feasibility were confirmed by successfully implementing system components and iterative discussions among the research team. Then, in the demonstration echelon, the artifact was presented to domain experts, including an environment specialist from the city of Lahti. The artifact was refined, subjected to their feedback and suggestions. Eventually, the enhanced artifact was evaluated first with urban planners, an environmental specialist, and sustainable urban design students, in terms of usability, visualization clarity, potential usefulness, support in decision making, and trust in model accuracy. Feedback from domain experts was collected through scenario-based testing and analysed using qualitative and quantitative methods. Second, a technical evaluation of the ML prediction algorithm was conducted. Figure 1 shows the $^e DSR$ process followed in the study.

4   Problem Analysis and Objectives

Lahti is experiencing substantial increases in air temperature, consistent with Finland's overall warming trend. Furthermore, it has been identified that the urban area of the city of Lahti depicts a higher LST than rural areas. Additionally, it has been identified that urban areas will encounter a significant increase in the UHI effect in 2040. These factors negatively influence the current infrastructure, human beings, and the ecosystems. Hence, it is crucial to take necessary actions to mitigate the UHI effect [6]. These trends are not unique to the studied case but reflect broader patterns observed in cities across Europe, the world, and other urban regions facing comparable climatic, environmental, and urbanization dynamics.

Despite researchers having proposed various mitigation strategies, including expanding greenery areas and water bodies, adding seasonal shadings, and using reflective materials, there exists a lack of publicly available tools or interactive systems that facilitate predicting the UHI effect with man-made interventions.

To better understand UHI dynamics, ensure practical relevance, and validate the problem, a literature review was conducted to assess the current UHI

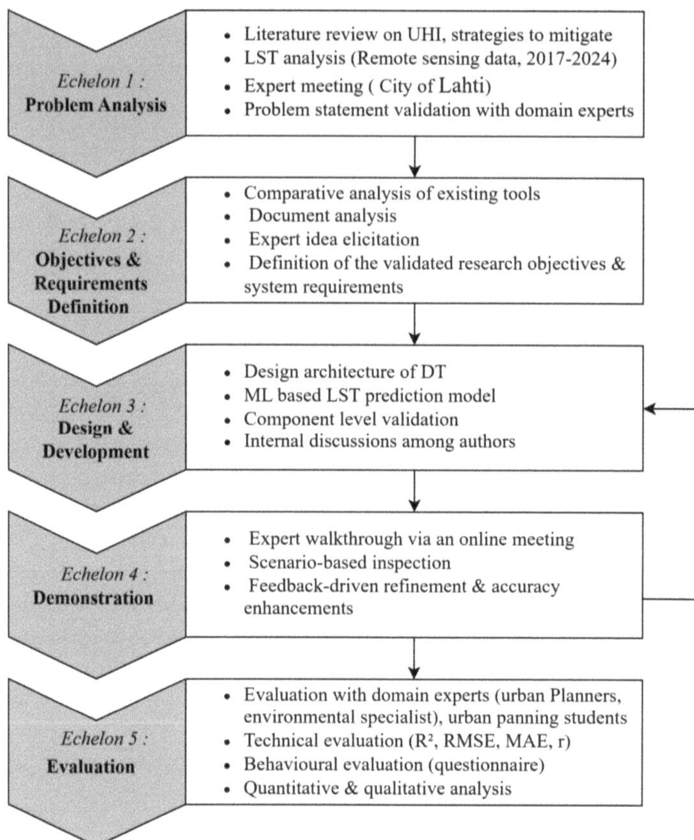

Fig. 1. Overview of the ^{e}DSR process

effect in the city of Lahti, its future impact, and mitigation strategies. Second, an online meeting with an environmental specialist in Lahti was held to obtain a better understanding of the UHI effect in Lahti, practical UHI challenges, and planning requirements. Third, an LST analysis was conducted for the summer months from 2017 to 2024 in Lahti using remote sensing data to gain a clear understanding of temperature changes during this period. Together, these activities confirmed both the presence of a growing UHI problem and the absence of interactive, intervention-oriented decision-support tools. Again, while these activities focus on the city of Lahti, the identified challenges and limitations are indicative of broader issues faced by many cities confronting rising UHI effects, increasing planning complexity, and a lack of accessible, intervention-oriented decision-support tools [1,2].

Based on the analysis, the following validated problem statement is formulated.

"City planners lack a tool that facilitates testing and forecasting temperature changes that tend to occur due to interventions (For instance, adding trees, buildings, or water bodies) in a simulated digital environment to mitigate the UHI effect."

To address this, the research pursues the following objectives.

1. To develop a DT mimicking the physical environment of the city of Lahti, integrated with environmental, spatial, and temperature data.
2. To implement an ML model that forecasts LST using accessible information, such as spectral indices and bands.
3. To present the LST changes that occur due to man-made interventions in the system.
4. To evaluate the usability, reliability, and usefulness of the proposed system with experts and researchers in the domain.

5   Design and Development of the Artefact

The artifact enables users to make interventions in the urban area in a simulated digital environment. Then, it forecasts the LST changes in the corresponding area using a pretrained ML model. This provides the ability to see the approximate changes in LST corresponding to the intervention type made by the user. Thus, city planners can analyze and make modifications to minimize the UHI effect caused by interventions.

5.1   Data Processing and Feature Extraction

Geospatial data for the city of Lahti for the summer season from 2021 to 2025 were collected from multiple sources using the Google Earth Engine platform. Sentinel-2 images were used to derive vegetation, built-up, water indices, including NDVI, NDBI, NDWI, and Enhanced Vegetation Index (EVI). While the indices NDVI and EVI both represent vegetation, EVI is more sensitive in dense vegetation areas than NDVI. Landsat 9 images were used to derive LST data. The predictor variables were derived from spectral bands (RED, GREEN, NIR, SWIR) as follows.

$$NDVI = \frac{NIR - RED}{NIR + RED} \tag{1}$$

$$NDWI = \frac{GREEN - NIR}{GREEN + NIR} \tag{2}$$

$$NDBI = \frac{SWIR - NIR}{SWIR + NIR} \tag{3}$$

Each data point contains spectral indices, geographic coordinates, and corresponding LST values in an area of $30\,\mathrm{m} \times 30\,\mathrm{m}$. The resultant data was randomly split into an 8:2 ratio for training and testing purposes.

5.2   ML Model

The LST values were forcasted using a random forest ML model. After data preprocessing, the feature engineering process was carried out to enhance the performance of the algorithm and the accuracy.

To avoid random bias and enhance the prediction reliability, a linear calibration model was fitted between model-predicted values and the actual observed LST values:

$$\text{LST}_{\text{corrected}} = m \cdot \text{LST}_{\text{predicted}} + c \tag{4}$$

where m and c are calibration parameters.

5.3   Intervention Modeling and Inference

The system facilitated the insertion of user-defined interventions, including tree areas, water bodies, buildings, and green roofs. Each intervention type (objects) had its own predefined spectral band reflectance (RED, GREEN, NIR, and SWIR), approximated using sample data collected from [22]. For an intervention made by the user, the intervention type and its location were captured before calculating the new spectral band mix of the corresponding area. The intervened area was captured using the nearest pixel identified using a KD-Tree structure. Then, the new spectral band mix of the required area was calculated using the following formula.

$$B_{\text{new}} = (1 - f)\, B_{\text{old}} + f\, B_{\text{object}} \tag{5}$$

where B_{new} is the new spectral band mix of the area, B_{old} is the old spectral band mix of the area, B_{object} is the band reflectance of the object and f is the intervention coverage fraction (proportion of the area covered by the intervened object).

Using the new spectral band values, corresponding spectral indices were computed. Thereafter, the new LST values were predicted by the ML model according to new predictor variables. The consequences of hypothetical interventions are simulated by modifying the input features assuming that the relationship between these features and the LST remains stable under these modifications.

$$\Delta\text{LST} = \text{LST}_{\text{new}} - \text{LST}_{\text{current}} \tag{6}$$

The 3D interactive city visualization was implemented using React.js with CesiumJS. The interactive web interface allows users to make interventions and receive temperature prediction results as a message via the front-end user interface.

5.4   Architectural Design

The artifact follows a three-layer architecture consisting of a data layer, a ML layer, and a visualization layer. This ensures modularity, scalability, and real-time interaction.

Within the artifact, the data layer provides data for model training. The ML layer consists of two components: model training component and model inference component. The model training component is an offline process responsible for preprocessing data, feature engineering, training the ML model, and model calibration to predict LST. The model inference component is responsible for recalculating predictor variables based on made interventions and calculating the change of temperature (ΔLST). The purpose of the design is not merely to predict the LST values but to facilitate making interventions in a virtual environment. However, unlike traditional DTs, this tool periodically updates the data instead of continuous bi-directional data exchange. This approach is consistent with its core intention, as this tool primarily focuses on simulating the scenarios for decision making rather than real-time control.

The visualization layer functions as a web-based approach developed using React.js with CesiumJS. It facilitates users to add interventions through an interactive interface. The user can add intervention objects, including vegetation, buildings, water bodies, and green roofs, in a 3D city model that mimics the real physical geo information of the city of Lahti. The user interface of the DT system is presented in Fig. 2. User interactions are sent to the backend as JSON requests that contain information related to the intervention type and the spatial coordinates. Thereafter, new temperature values are predicted using the pretrained ML model. The backend of the system was implemented using FastAPI. FastAPI is used to connect the web interface with the ML model, enabling real-time communication between user interactions and temperature prediction.

6   System Demonstration and Evaluation

The system evaluation and demonstration were conducted iteratively, and the artifact was refined according to expert feedback, following the ^{e}DSR process.

The DT artifact was demonstrated online to an environmental specialist after validating the architectural coherence and functional completeness. During this demonstration, a key suggestion was made regarding intervention logic. It was highlighted that, instead of relying on fixed parameters for each intervention type, considering other existing characteristics of the corresponding location is equally significant. To address this, the intervention logic was refined. Additionally, the ML model was retrained to improve accuracy, considering the geographical coordinates in addition to the other features and their derivatives. Thus, the accuracy and the credibility of the results were enhanced considering the local environmental characteristics.

Then, the complete DT workflow, from user intervention to presenting the forecasted temperature shift, was systematically tested and validated, ensuring the behavioral consistency of the system.

After addressing the requirements raised in the initial demonstration, the artifact was evaluated with domain experts. An environment specialist, two urban city planners, and two students specialized in sustainable city planning

Fig. 2. User Interface of the DT System

participated in the final evaluation. The participants examined the DT with different interaction options and observed the corresponding temperature changes accordingly. Their feedback was collected through an exploratory questionnaire which assessed several components: ease of use, visualization clarity, system usefulness, decision support, intention to use, accuracy, data trust, and overall user experience. Additionally, qualitative feedback was captured and analyzed thematically, while quantitative feedback was analyzed using standard statistical measures of central tendency and dispersion.

The technical evaluation phase mainly focused on examining the performance of the ML algorithm. The model was evaluated with standard metrics, including the coefficient of determination (R^2), the root mean square error ($RMSE$), the mean absolute error (MAE), and the Pearson correlation coefficient (r). The new optimized ML algorithm, trained with coordinate information and engineered features, depicted better performance than the initial model. The results depicted a higher accuracy than the initial model.

7   Results and Findings

In this section, a summary of the technical and behavioral evaluation of the DT is presented based on the feedback of the experts. The proposed artifact is evaluated in terms of predictive performance, usability, and value of the system for urban heat mitigation decision support.

7.1 Prediction Accuracy

Initially, a Random Forest ML model was evaluated with the metrics R^2, $RMSE$, MAE, and Pearson correlation coefficient (r). However, it depicted a comparatively weak performance. To address this, the model was trained recurrently with new engineered features along with spatial coordinates for summer data from 2021 to 2025. The new model depicted a higher prediction power, with $R^2 = 0.96$, $RMSE = 1.16\ °C$, MAE $= 0.85\ °C$, and $r = 0.98$.

7.2 Behavioural Results

Behavioral analysis of the artifact was conducted based on feedback provided by environmental specialists, urban planners, and students of sustainable urban planning studies. The evaluation was conducted based on a questionnaire to assess aspects including ease of use, visualization clarity, system usefulness, decision support, accuracy, trust, and overall experience.

Findings of Quantitative Analysis. Quantitative results, based on the closed-ended questions, suggest that the usability of the artifact is highly relevant in supporting urban planning and design decisions. The feedback emphasized that the artifact can be applied to compare alternative planning as well as to discuss the impact with stakeholders. Furthermore, the feedback on the visualization clarity is reasonably good. However, the trust in the prediction result was moderate. Although the participants agreed on the consistency of the results of the interventions with real-world expectations, it was suggested that improving the transparency of data sources and calculation methods. Although the quantitative analysis is based on a limited sample size, the participants were domain experts in urban and environmental planning, which supports the validity and relevance of the collected evaluations despite constraints on statistical generalization. The descriptive statistical results for the closed-ended questions are presented in Table 1.

Qualitative Findings and Design Implications. A qualitative analysis was conducted based on the feedback of open-ended questions. In their comments, our participants highlighted the usability of the artifact as a tool for taking urban planning decisions while mitigating the UHI effect. However, some suggestions, including color-based techniques to visualize temperature changes, area-based averaging, and further explanations of temperature predictions, were raised. Additionally, it was highlighted that adding more information regarding data sources and computation methods may improve the trust in the system. Thus, the analysis of the results suggests that the artifact has addressed the required intentions in a considerably successful manner. Furthermore, the results emphasize the usefulness of the system in urban city planning, optimizing environmental impacts.

Table 1. Descriptive statistical results for the closed-ended questions

Category	Category Mean	Category Median	Category Std
Ease of Use	3.92	4.0	0.42
Visualization Clarity	3.90	4.0	0.41
Usefulness	4.12	4.0	0.47
Decision Support and Intention to Use	3.95	4.0	0.56
Accuracy and Trust	3.70	4.0	0.50
Overall Reflection	4.33	4.0	0.48

8   Discussion and Implications

Our research has several implications and demonstrates how a DT can be operationalized as an intervention-oriented planning support system for mitigating the UHI effect by combining satellite-based environmental data, ML-based LST forecasting, and an interactive three-dimensional city interface. The findings position the work within existing research on UHI drivers and mitigation strategies [4–6], remote sensing approaches that use LST and spectral indices to capture urban heat patterns [12–14], and geographic IS-based UHI assessments that primarily support descriptive mapping and indicator communication [8,9]. While prior studies provide strong evidence on controllable contributors such as vegetation cover, built-up density, and land use patterns [4,13], they often do not provide an interactive environment in which urban planners can explore and compare alternative interventions in a low-barrier manner. The DT developed in our study contributes by translating these established relationships into an interactive workflow where users can implement specific modifications, such as adding trees, water bodies, buildings, and green roofs, and immediately observe predicted LST changes. This supports a shift from retrospective assessment toward prospective scenario comparison, which is central to planning practice when evaluating design alternatives under constraints [6]. In this sense, the contribution is not only the implementation of a prototype, but the demonstration that intervention-oriented UHI planning support benefits from combining predictive analytics with interactive and spatially explicit scenario exploration in a single environment.

From a DT perspective, prior research conceptualizes the DT as a virtual representation of a physical system that is updated through information exchange between physical and virtual counterparts [21]. In urban domains, DTs have been used to support planning and infrastructure contexts and are increasingly discussed as a means to address climate-related challenges [23,26–28]. Related work has also begun to connect urban DTs to UHI analysis [10,11]. Our study extends that emerging stream by demonstrating an end-to-end instantiation in which predictive modeling is embedded into the DT workflow and linked to explicit intervention logic. In particular, intervention effects are operationalized through spectral band mixing and subsequent recalculation of indices prior to prediction, using reflectance information derived from an established spectral library [22]. Theoretically, this illustrates how a DT can move beyond being primarily representational and become analytically useful for planning by coupling interactive manipulation with a prediction mechanism grounded in remote sensing features [12,14]. More specifically, our findings suggest that DTs for planning should not be designed merely as visualization platforms, but as environments in which user actions are translated into analytically meaningful consequences. For this class of systems, the crucial design issue is the explicit linkage between spatial intervention inputs and predictive logic, because without such linkage, the DT remains informative but not actionable for planning.

The ML results further position the contribution within research on data-driven temperature prediction. Prior work has shown that ML is well-suited for capturing nonlinear patterns in environmental temperature data [17] and that random forest models often provide strong performance in temperature-related forecasting tasks [18–20]. Consistent with this stream, the optimized random forest model achieved high predictive performance in our study. At the same time, the user evaluation indicates that trust in prediction results remained moderate even though participants perceived the intervention outcomes as consistent with real-world expectations and found the system usable for planning-related tasks. This pattern aligns with the broader implication that predictive performance alone does not ensure decision support value, particularly when users require transparency about inputs and computation to interpret model outputs in a planning context [21]. In our study, qualitative feedback specifically emphasized the need for clearer explanations of data sources and calculation methods, suggesting that transparency-oriented interface elements are an essential complement to predictive capability when DTs are applied to climate-related decision making [10,28]. This implies that the design of similar systems should treat explainability as a core requirement rather than a secondary feature. A system may achieve technically strong prediction accuracy, yet still face limitations in planning use if users cannot understand the basis on which simulated outcomes are produced.

Finally, our study contributes to the development of design knowledge by demonstrating the suitability of echeloned design science research for structuring a complex artifact that integrates heterogeneous data sources, predictive modeling, and interactive visualization [29]. The evaluation with domain experts provides evidence that the artifact supports comparing alternative planning scenarios and stakeholder discussions, while also identifying trust and transparency as central improvement targets. Taken together, our work complements existing descriptive UHI assessment approaches [8,9] and extends emerging research on UHI-oriented DTs [10,11] by providing an evaluated, intervention-focused system that links urban modifications to forecasted LST changes in an interactive planning environment. In this way, the study contributes both an instantiated artifact and a more general understanding of how intervention-oriented DTs for climate-sensitive urban planning can be designed to support exploration, comparison, and decision making before implementation in the physical city.

9   Conclusion and Future Work

In our research, we developed a DT-based planning support system that supports urban city planners to mitigate the UHI effect in city planning. Our system combines satellite-based environmental data, ML temperature predictions, and an interactive 3D web platform. DSR methodology was applied as the primary research methodology in this study. It guided the problem analysis, design, implementation of the artifact, and the evaluation process. Collected data were pre-processed, feature-engineered, and trained using random forest regressor to predict LST. Its performance depicted a significant accuracy and a strong correlation between predicted and actual values. The 3D city model was implemented using React.js with CesiumJS. FastAPI was used to implement the backend of the system. The interactive web interface of the DT allows users to make interventions such as adding tree areas, building blocks, water bodies, and green roofs, and receive prediction results as a message via the frontend user interface. To understand the system utility from the user's perspective, the system was evaluated by city professionals (urban city planners, environment specialists) and some students with a sustainable urban planning study background. The feedback was analysed using both qualitative and quantitative methods. Furthermore, the technical evaluation was conducted to measure the accuracy of the ML model using several evaluation metrics. Overall, the analysis results revealed that the system is easy to use, visuals are understandable and useful in exploring different planning scenarios and support sustainable urban planning and decision-making. The thematic analysis helped to understand the future improvements of the systems.

This study has considered four human interventions and their impact on LST, focusing on the standard spectral bands obtained by averaging sample data collected from ECOSTRESS Spectral Library - Version 1.0 – NASA. However, their impact can be changed according to building materials and tree types. In the future, the system can be developed to facilitate adding various tree types and different building materials. Furthermore, more features, such as roads and green corridors, can be added as modification options. Additionally, various strategies, including different shapes, can be introduced. Training an ML model for a city with noisy data patterns is challenging compared to a city like Barcelona. In this work, the ML models that forecasted LST with higher accuracy considered time or the coordinate points along with spectral indices. Therefore, training an ML model forecasting LST, solely depending on spectral indices, will lead to a significant improvement in system utility.

References

1. Yao, R., et al.: Urbanization effects on vegetation and surface urban heat islands in China's Yangtze River Basin. Remote Sensing **9**(6), 540 (2017). https://doi.org/10.3390/rs9060540
2. O'Malley, C., Piroozfar, P.A.E., Farr, E.R.P., Gates, J.: An investigation into minimizing urban heat island (UHI) effects: a UK perspective. Energy Procedia **62**, 72–80 (2014). https://doi.org/10.1016/j.egypro.2014.12.368
3. Yang, L.: Research on urban heat-island effect. Procedia Eng. **169**, 11–18 (2016). https://doi.org/10.1016/j.proeng.2016.10.002
4. Deilami, K., Kamruzzaman, M., Liu, Y.: Urban heat island effect: a systematic review of spatio-temporal factors, data, methods, and mitigation measures. Int. J. Appl. Earth Obs. Geoinf. **67**, 30–42 (2018). https://doi.org/10.1016/j.jag.2017.12.009
5. Mohajerani, A., Bakaric, J., Jeffrey-Bailey, T.: The urban heat island effect, its causes, and mitigation, with reference to the thermal properties of asphalt concrete. J. Environ. Manag **197**, 522–538 (2017). https://doi.org/10.1016/j.jenvman.2017.03.095
6. Negi, A., Emmanuel, R., Aarrevaara, E.: Planning for a warmer future: heat risk assessment and mitigation in Lahti, Finland. Atmosphere **16**(2), 146 (2025). https://doi.org/10.3390/atmos16020146
7. Esposito, A., et al.: Urban morphology and surface urban heat island relationship during heat waves: a study of Milan and Lecce (Italy). Remote Sens. **16**(23), 4496 (2024). https://doi.org/10.3390/rs16234496
8. Teo, Y.H., et al.: Urban heat island mitigation: GIS-based analysis for a tropical city Singapore. Int. J. Environ. Res. Public Health **19**(19), 11917 (2022). https://doi.org/10.3390/ijerph191911917
9. Cafaro, R., Cardone, B., D'Ambrosio, V., Di Martino, F., Miraglia, V.: A new GIS-based framework to detect urban heat islands and its application on the city of Naples (Italy). Land **13**(8), 1253 (2024). https://doi.org/10.3390/land13081253
10. Vitanova, L., Petrova-Antonova, D., Shirinyan, E.: Urban digital twin for assessing and understanding urban heat island impacts. Urban Clim. **62**, 102530 (2025). https://doi.org/10.1016/j.uclim.2025.102530
11. Koeva, M.: The role of digital twins in mitigating urban heat islands. GIM International. https://www.gim-international.com/content/article/the-role-of-digital-twins-in-mitigating-urban-heat-islands. Accessed 01 Dec 2025
12. Voogt, J.A., Oke, T.R.: Thermal remote sensing of urban climates. Remote Sens. Environ. **86**(3), 370–384 (2003). https://doi.org/10.1016/S0034-4257(03)00079-8
13. Memon, R.A., Leung, D.Y., Chunho, L.: A review on the generation, determination and mitigation of urban heat island. J. Environ. Sci. **20**(1), 120–128 (2008). https://doi.org/10.1016/S1001-0742(08)60019-4
14. Mansourmoghaddam, M., et al.: Modeling and estimating the land surface temperature (LST) using remote sensing and machine learning (Case study: Yazd, Iran). Remote Sens. **16**(3), 454 (2024). https://doi.org/10.3390/rs16030454
15. Suomi, J.: Extreme temperature differences in the city of Lahti, southern Finland: intensity, seasonality and environmental drivers. Weather Clim. Extremes **19**, 20–28 (2018). https://doi.org/10.1016/j.wace.2018.01.001
16. Wijerathne, H.M.C., Lanel, J., Perera, K., Wanigasekara, C.: On order degree problem for Moore bound. Axioms **14**(11), 802 (2025). https://doi.org/10.3390/axioms14110802

17. Srivastava, A., Maity, R.: Assessing the potential of AI–ML in urban climate change adaptation and sustainable development. Sustainability **15**(23), 16461 (2023). https://doi.org/10.3390/su152316461
18. Tsai, Y.-Z., et al.: Application of Random Forest and ICON models combined with weather forecasts to predict soil temperature and water content in a greenhouse. Water **12**(4), 1176 (2020). https://doi.org/10.3390/w12041176
19. Li, H., Li, J., Liu, L., Huang, L., Zhao, Q., Zhou, L.: Random Forest-based model for estimating weighted mean temperature in mainland China. Atmosphere **13**(9), 1368 (2022). https://doi.org/10.3390/atmos13091368
20. Singh, D.K., Rawat, N.: Machine learning for weather forecasting: XGBoost vs SVM vs Random Forest in predicting temperature for Visakhapatnam. Int. J. Intell. Syst. Appl. **15**(5), 57–69 (2023). https://doi.org/10.5815/ijisa.2023.05.05
21. Vanderhorn, E., Mahadevan, S.: Digital twin: generalization, characterization and implementation. Decis. Support Syst. **145**, 113524 (2021). https://doi.org/10.1016/j.dss.2021.113524
22. Jet Propulsion Laboratory (JPL), NASA: ECOSTRESS Spectral Library – Version 1.0. https://speclib.jpl.nasa.gov/. Accessed 23 Nov 2025
23. City of Helsinki: Helsinki 3D. https://www.hel.fi/en/decision-making/informationon-helsinki/maps-and-geospatial-data/helsinki-3d. Accessed 10 Nov 2025
24. Katsoulakis, E.: Digital twins for health: a scoping review. npj Digit. Med. (2024). https://doi.org/10.1038/s41746-024-01073-0
25. Department for Transport: Integrated network management digital twin: Economic benefits analysis (2024). https://www.gov.uk/government/publications/integrated-network-management-digital-twin-economic-benefits-analysis. Accessed 25 Nov 2025
26. Esri: 3D GIS helped Boston create a digital twin. Esri Blog (2018). https://www.esri.com/about/newsroom/blog/3d-gis-boston-digital-twin. Accessed 25 Nov 2025
27. Tokyo Metropolitan Government: Digital twin: A new solution for urban challenges in Tokyo (2024). https://www.english.metro.tokyo.lg.jp/w/110-101-005910. Accessed 25 Nov 2025
28. Bibri, S.E.: Synergistic integration of digital twins and zero energy buildings for climate change mitigation in sustainable smart cities: a systematic review and novel framework. Energy Build. **333**, 115484 (2025). https://doi.org/10.1016/j.enbuild.2025.115484
29. Tuunanen, T., Winter, R., vom Brocke, J.: Dealing with complexity in design science research: a methodology using design echelons. MIS Q. **48**(2), 427–458 (2024). https://doi.org/10.25300/MISQ/2023/16700

Design Principles for Ethical Automated Mental Workload Monitoring in the Industrial Internet of Things

Fatma Demircan⬛, Maximilian Nebel(✉)⬛, and Christian Janiesch⬛

TU Dortmund University, Dortmund, Germany
`{fatma.demircan,maximilian.nebel,`
`christian.janiesch}@tu-dortmund.de`

Abstract. The integration of humans-in-the-loop for decision-making in the Industrial Internet of Things (IIoT) has intensified workers' interaction with complex information systems. Tracking workers' mental workload, comparable to anomaly detection in IIoT, raises ethical questions requiring careful regulation. We contribute to mitigating these ethical risks with design principles drawing on responsibility-oriented ethical considerations, emphasizing precaution and the protection of long-term human well-being. Following design science research, design principles were derived based on literature to offer long-term ethical guidance rather than short-term solutions. While studies acknowledge ethical challenges related to workload monitoring, the practical problem remains how such insights can be translated into ethically responsible system design. The paper consolidates ethical concerns into actionable design principles fostering continuous ethical reflection throughout technology development. The proposed design principles were evaluated through qualitative interviews with practitioners to ensure relevance and incorporate their perspectives into refinement. The principles provide a foundation for developing ethically informed decision-making in IIoT, helping organizations align technological innovation with human-centric values.

Keywords: Design Principles · Ethics · IIoT · Mental Workload

1 Introduction

Technological progress and economic objectives expand the scope of human action and thereby increase the significance of technological decisions. This growing capacity to act entails a particular responsibility for the design and application of technical systems [13]. This view is prominently articulated by the philosopher Hans Jonas, who understands responsibility as a central ethical category in dealing with technological and economic progress [29]. Technology is therefore not value-neutral but requires a conscious ethical framing of its use in order to do justice to this responsibility.

Norbert Wiener approaches responsibility from a systems-theoretical perspective and argues that automation does not reduce human responsibility, but rather shifts it to higher levels of decision-making. As technical systems become increasingly powerful,

© The Author(s), under exclusive license to Springer Nature Switzerland AG 2026
J. vom Brocke et al. (Eds.): DESRIST 2026, LNCS 16606, pp. 59–76, 2026.
https://doi.org/10.1007/978-3-032-28313-9_4

potential consequences of their use also grow, while decisions are frequently based on the interpretation of complex automated processes. Since the consequences of such systems are not fully foreseeable, responsibility for their planning, organization, and control increases accordingly [47]. Wiener emphasizes that increases in productivity must not become an end in themselves but must serve human beings [47]. This understanding of responsibility remains relevant today as automation advances through data-driven technologies. The transformation of Industry 4.0 clearly illustrates this development, as a central goal is to increase productivity and efficiency through automation [25]. To achieve this, large volumes of operational data are collected, processed, and analyzed, improving processes or preventing unexpected production stops in real-time [33].

As a result, the decision-making of industrial workers has changed [25]. Decisions are data-driven, time-critical, and have far-reaching consequences [21]. This affects working conditions and the workers themselves. With the growing integration of humans-in-the-loop in industrial human-computer interaction, the risk of increased mental workload arises, which can impair workers' decision-making capabilities [41].

Industrial Internet of Things (IIoT) technologies, such as physiological sensors, offer the possibility of automatically capturing and analyzing mental workload in real-time to offer workers targeted support [10, 24]. Simultaneously, automated mental workload monitoring systems (Auto-MWMS) touch on sensitive domains such as privacy and power relations [37]. While these systems are designed to manage mental workload, they also carry the risk of enabling a form of surveillance and performance monitoring, thereby creating an ethical tension between promoting human well-being and safeguarding individual autonomy and privacy. To deploy Auto-MWMS in the IIoT in accordance with ethical responsibility, the development of a context-specific ethical framework is required. This framework must place the individual at its core and act preventively by addressing potential ethical challenges at an early stage. Furthermore, such a framework constitutes a prerequisite for ensuring that Auto-MWMS do not contribute to control or surveillance but instead support human decision-making capabilities in highly automated industrial systems. Although existing research addresses ethical challenges in the context of automated workload monitoring, it remains open how these can be translated into concrete design. In this context, design principles provide a suitable tool, as they enable the context-specific translation of ethical requirements into actionable design principles. Against this background, the following research question arises:

RQ: *Which design principles can guide the ethical development of Auto-MWMS to protect humans and address key ethical challenges within the IIoT?*

To answer, we present design principles enabling the ethical and responsible use of Auto-MWMS. The design is guided by the framework of Gregor et al. [16]. The remainder of the paper begins by outlining the ethical foundations, mental workload, and Auto-MWMS in IIoT contexts. Building on these foundations, our methodology for developing the design principles is described. The resulting design principles are then presented and subsequently evaluated through practitioner interviews to assess their relevance and applicability. Finally, the paper discusses key findings, derives implications for theory and practice, identifies limitations, and outlines directions for future research.

2 Background

2.1 Ethical Foundations

Our research can be situated within technology ethics because we focus on the normative evaluation and design of technological systems. The field of technology ethics examines the moral implications of technical artifacts, their development, and their use. Within technology ethics, the assumption that technological systems are value-neutral according to the neutrality thesis is discussed [13]. However, this perspective is critically questioned, as technical systems structure possibilities for action through the establishment of means-end relationships and are embedded in social as well as organizational contexts [13]. In this light, a particular form of technological responsibility emerges, which encompasses not only immediate usage situations but also indirect, long-term, and systemic effects [29]. Responsibility-oriented approaches in technology ethics emphasize that under such conditions, ethical requirements cannot be addressed only retrospectively, but must already be taken into account in the design of technical systems, as technological consequences are often characterized by uncertainty and may be irreversible [29]. Consequently, technology requires conscious normative framing to assume responsibility for the consequences of technical decisions.

2.2 Mental Workload

Ethical considerations particularly concern the effects of technology on the individuals operating them, making mental workload a key factor in responsible system design. In this section, cognitive load and task load are discussed as related constructs that contextualize the concept of mental workload. In the remainder of this paper, we use "mental workload" as an umbrella term encompassing both cognitive load and task load dimensions. This was done to avoid confusion during the qualitative evaluation process.

Cognitive Load. The cognitive load theory [42] distinguishes three types of load. Intrinsic load refers to the mental effort imposed by the inherent complexity of a task. Extraneous load describes the additional cognitive effort caused by the presentation of information. Germane load encompasses the cognitive resources needed for active processing, organization, and integration of new information with existing knowledge [41].

Understanding cognitive load is particularly important in human-machine interaction and industrial work contexts, as overload increases the risk of errors and leads to performance decrements due to fatigue [37]. This is especially relevant for data-intensive, AI-supported information systems in IIoT (e.g., anomaly dashboards). The increasing complexity and dynamic nature of production data substantially raises the cognitive demand placed on decision-makers [7, 41].

Task Load. Studies assessing workload consider cognitive load as well as task load, as they complement each other in explaining how individuals experience workload during task performance (e.g., [14, 41]). Task load captures both task-related and subject-related constructs. Task-related constructs are physical demand, mental demand, and temporal demand, each of which is linked to corresponding subject-related perceptions [17]. Physical demand reflects in the amount of effort required (e.g., when a person lifts heavy objects, the task becomes physically demanding). Mental demand is associated with frustration (e.g., when individuals have to comprehend complex information fulfilling a task). Temporal demand is related to performance (e.g., when a task must be completed within strict time limits) [17].

The task load constructs are commonly measured via the NASA-TLX questionnaire [17]. In addition to subjective measurements, objective indicators like physiological responses or performance metrics can provide complementary insights into task load and workload in general [9]. This aspect becomes particularly relevant in IIoT where sensor data enables real-time monitoring of decision-makers' states.

2.3   Automated Mental Workload Monitoring in the IIoT

Mental workload can be investigated through various approaches, including subjective self-monitoring (e.g., [17]), performance-based methods (e.g., [6]), and physiological (e.g., [6, 43]) or behavioral measurements (e.g., [41]). In this paper, we focus on physiological and behavioral indicators because they can be integrated into IIoT environments to monitor mental workload directly within the workspace.

Physiological signals such as heart rate provide insights into how people react physically to increasing mental workload [27, 34]. Changes in breathing patterns or skin conductance can also indicate stress or mental effort [26, 28]. These signals show how bodily reactions reflect rising demands during cognitive tasks. Behavioral measures complement these physiological indicators by capturing visible signs of attention and concentration. For instance, tracking eye movements can reveal focused visual behavior when cognitive demand increases [26]. Similarly, measuring brain activity helps to identify different levels of mental effort during task performance [26].

Together, these measurements provide a foundation for Auto-MWMS to help manage mental workload. In IIoT, sensors embedded in cyber-physical systems can continuously collect physiological and behavioral data from human decision-makers. Physiological sensors extend traditional machine monitoring by providing information about human states within these systems [24]. The resulting data streams enable real-time detection of overload situations and support adaptive interventions such as break recommendations or task adjustments. This integration aims to maintain human decision-making capability amid increasing automation and data intensity in IIoT. However, because these measurement approaches are intrusive and involve personal data collection, their use must be carefully regulated to ensure privacy and ethical handling.

3   Methodology

The overarching objective of our design science research is to develop design principles that generate actionable design knowledge guiding the development of Auto-MWMS in the IIoT, while being transferable to related artifacts. To achieve this, we structured our research into four phases based on Peffers et al. [36] (cf. Fig. 1). In the first phase, problem identification and motivation, we reviewed relevant literature and additional data as described in Sect. 3.1. During the second phase, we analyzed the collected literature using a concept matrix [46] to derive design requirements representing the goals that the artifact should fulfill. In the subsequent design phase, the requirements served as a foundation to develop design principles. Finally, in the demonstration and evaluation phase, we conducted expert interviews to assess both the design requirements and resulting design principles. Insights gained from the evaluation informed the refinement of our design principles. The following sections describe our data acquisition and development of design requirements and design principles in detail.

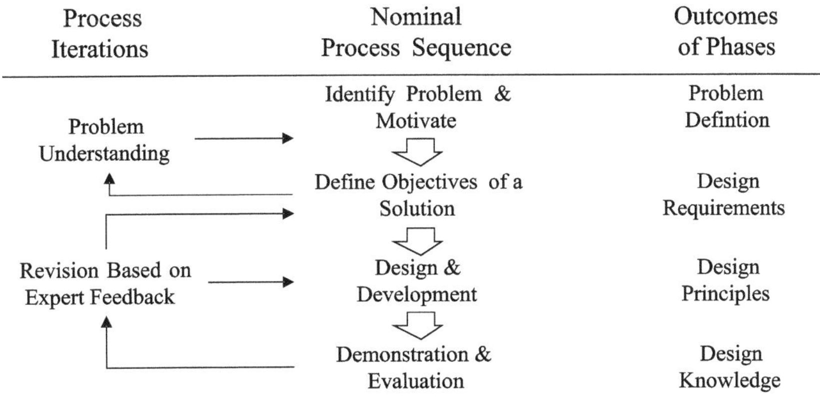

Fig. 1. Design phases, their outcomes, and process iterations during this research.

3.1 Data Collection

In our design science research, data collection aimed to identify ethical and value-related challenges that inform the development of design knowledge for Auto-MWMS in the IIoT. Recognizing that such systems raise not only technical but also ethical questions, we adopted a hermeneutic literature review approach following Boell and Cecez-Kecmanovic [4]. This method supports iterative exploration and interpretation, an essential feature for developing context-sensitive design knowledge when problem domains cannot be fully specified in advance [4].

The review was iterative to refine our understanding step by step. With each cycle, newly acquired insights informed subsequent searches and interpretations, allowing us to continuously adapt focus as our conceptual understanding of the underlying problem evolved. This interpretive process reflects the relevance and rigor cycles described in design science research literature, where past knowledge is built upon [18, 19].

Our keyword searches involved literature addressing "ethics", "monitoring", "Industrial Internet of Things", and "cognitive load". The search continued until saturation was reached after 61 added publications (i.e., no new ethical challenges or issues emerged). As inclusion criteria, we considered publications that address ethical issues in the context of IIoT, monitoring technologies, or mental workload and their implications for human decision-making, or that provide relevant conceptual, empirical, or normative insights. Additionally, foundational works in technology ethics as well as relevant legal frameworks were taken into account. Publications without a clear connection to ethical or human-centered aspects or to the application context of this study were excluded. The challenges and issues were documented in a concept matrix that provided a structured foundation for deriving design requirements (cf. Sect. 3.2).

To ensure completeness beyond academic discourse, we also included legal sources reflecting binding obligations within industrial contexts. Specifically, the General Data Protection Regulation (GDPR) [11] and the European Union Artificial Intelligence Act (EU AI Act) [12] were considered as key frameworks shaping responsible system behavior regarding sensitive personal data and automated decision-making processes.

Finally, we used the ACM Code of Ethics and Professional Conduct [1] as an established academic guideline to align our analysis with recognized professional values relevant to information systems. The code provides orientation for embedding ethical reflection into responsible design knowledge from a computer science perspective.

3.2 Development of Design Requirements and Design Principles

The development of our design requirements and principles is structured in three phases that were completed before final evaluation with domain experts. We first identified ethical challenges and issues related to Auto-MWMS through our literature review involving the concept matrix. To derive the design requirements from the challenges, we formulated preliminary requirements. Through iterative refinement guided by "why"-questions, they evolved into concrete design requirements aimed at capturing the underlying problems accurately. During evaluation, the requirements were compared with expert perspectives on essential system needs to ensure their practical relevance.

Building on the requirements, we developed corresponding design principles describing how an artifact should be implemented to fulfill them. The principles' structure follows Gregor et al.'s [16] template (*Implementer*, *Aim*, *User*, *Context*, *Mechanisms*, *Enactors*, and *Rationale*). Each principle should explicitly consider boundary conditions to clarify its contextual applicability limits so that other design studies can assess whether a design principle can be transferred or adapted to their specific context [16]. After the design requirements and principles were finalized, we evaluated them through direct discussions with domain experts who provided feedback for industrial settings.

3.3 Evaluation Approach

The design requirements and design principles were evaluated ex post [44]. We conducted three semi-structured interviews with experts from the fields of IT and industry to incorporate different perspectives on the application context as well as the associated ethical and organizational challenges [3]. The interviewees are referred to as I1–I3. I1 represents a strategic perspective as a managing director with a technical background in software development and experience in the development of data-driven systems, including applications with monitoring and tracking components. I2 provides a technical perspective as a full-stack developer involved in the development of data-driven systems. I3 contributes an operational perspective from an industrial context in which monitoring systems are already in use. The interviews and their subsequent analysis were structured into two halves. In the first half, interviewees were openly asked about their experiences, expectations, and perceived challenges related to Auto-MWMS in order to evaluate the previously developed design requirements based on the literature. To avoid influencing their responses, the design requirements were not disclosed at this stage. Instead, the interviewees were asked to independently identify relevant requirements and ethical issues based on their professional practice. The analysis of this half of the interviews was carried out using deductive qualitative content analysis, with the existing design requirements serving as coding categories. In the second half, the developed design principles were presented to the interviewees individually and discussed with regard to their clarity, appropriateness, and practical feasibility.

4 Results

4.1 Concept Matrix

The literature review resulted in 61 relevant studies that were documented in a concept matrix [46]. The purpose is to enable a structured identification of ethical challenges discussed in the publications and to provide an overview of their relative significance. Ethical challenges were iteratively organized within the matrix. As an initial point of orientation, core ethical principles such as *privacy protection, fairness*, and *transparency* were derived from the ACM Code of Ethics [1]. Building on this foundation, additional context-specific ethical challenges were identified through the literature. Conceptually related issues were grouped into overarching categories.

For each publication, we recorded the presence and relevance of an ethical challenge numerically: a value of "0" indicated that a challenge was not addressed. "1" signified that it was mentioned but not considered critical. "2" denoted that it was critically discussed or explicitly identified as problematic. This procedure allowed for both qualitative interpretation and quantitative comparison across studies. If new challenges emerged that did not fit existing categories, they were added to ensure completeness.

The resulting categories structure the problem space for ethical Auto-MWMS in the IIoT. The category *data protection and data security* addresses the handling of sensitive data concerning processing and storage [22]. Many publications emphasize anonymization or at least pseudonymization to prevent identification of individual employees [39]. *Consent and informed consent* refers to comprehensively informing employees about the purpose, scope, and implications of data collection to enable conscious participation [37]. Closely related is *transparency*, which supports trust and informed decision-making by ensuring traceability, access to information, and disclosure of data usage [22]. *Misuse and control of data* captures risks associated with repurposing collected information (e.g., performance monitoring for disciplinary measures) [22]. *Technological dependency* describes potential losses in autonomy due to reliance on IoT- or AI-based systems as well as insufficient human oversight over technical processes [5]. *Long-term effects on work environments* or individuals encompass personal consequences such as fear of surveillance alongside collective impacts on workplace climate and interpersonal relations [30, 37]. *Validity and interpretation of data* relates to inaccurate measurements or misinterpretations that may lead to unjust decisions [45].

Further categories include *ownership, access, and public/private boundaries*, addressing questions about data ownership rights; *manipulation and cybersecurity*, covering external attacks or internal tampering with data integrity [2]; *responsibility, law, and regulation*, concerning accountability frameworks within organizational contexts [22]; *fairness and discrimination*, referring to algorithmic bias or unequal treatment among individuals or groups [1]; and finally *sustainability*, which considers ecological aspects such as energy consumption or emissions linked to IIoT [31].

The categories do not represent strictly separated domains but rather clusters of inter-related ethical concerns. Many challenges overlap across multiple categories, indicating complex dependencies within sociotechnical systems.

Our conditional analysis based on numerical coding reveals substantial differences in how frequently specific categories are critically addressed (value "2"). *Data protection and data security* appear most prominently (n = 41), underscoring their central role in academic discourse on IIoT and Auto-MWMS-related ethics. *Responsibility, law, and regulation* also rank highly (n = 27), emphasizing strong connections between ethical concerns and legal obligations. *Manipulation and cybersecurity* (n = 27) and *long-term effects on work environments* (n = 24) form additional focal areas.

The prominence of *cybersecurity* shows the need to prevent data theft or sabotage [20]. By contrast, *transparency* and *consent* are often mentioned but rarely problematized independently. They tend to be treated as general preconditions for ethically sound system design rather than distinct critical issues. *Sustainability* receives limited attention (n = 46 for value "0"), suggesting that ecological considerations have so far played only a minor role in discussions surrounding Auto-MWMS within IIoT contexts.

4.2 Design Requirements

Based on the ethical challenges derived from the concept matrix, nine central design requirements for Auto-MWMS in the IIoT were identified. These requirements specify the fundamental conditions that such a system must fulfill to adequately address the identified ethical problem areas. In addition to the literature-based derivation, insights from interviews with industry stakeholders (I1-I3) were considered to evaluate practical perspectives on the relevance and applicability of these requirements.

DR1: Compliance with Legal Requirements. Auto-MWMS must comply with the GDPR, the EU AI Act, and other relevant labor law regulations. This reflects the high relevance of legal and regulatory aspects and the particular need to protect work-related and health-related data. This is also reflected in practice, where trust in legally compliant and responsible data handling is considered essential, for example, when stakeholders emphasize the importance of using "a cloud provider […] in whom one can trust beyond the legal framework that they handle the data responsibly" (I1).

DR2: Respect for Privacy, Ownership, and Individual Will. The privacy of employees, their data sovereignty, and their individual will must be respected at all times. The collection and use of workload data must not intrude into private spheres of life or restrict employees' personal autonomy [5]. Stakeholders particularly highlighted that employers should not have access to raw or overly detailed physiological data and that data sharing should be minimized: "to know […] when my employee's pulse was particularly high, but not how high. […] The relative values would […] suffice" (I1). They also noted that data should be "stored as locally as possible, […] shared with a minimal group of people, […] anonymized, and […] not traceable" (I1). Concerns were also raised about unintended inferences and sensitive secondary information: "The problem arises where secondary uses can emerge from these data [...]. As a result, I have [...] health data [...] that I perhaps should not have [...]" (I1).

DR3: Informed and Voluntary Consent. Workload monitoring may only be conducted on the basis of informed and voluntary consent. Employees must be able to understand which data are collected for which purposes and must be able to withdraw their consent at any time [37].

DR4: No Negative Consequences for Employees. The collection and use of workload data must not result in disadvantages for employees. In particular, such data must not be used for performance monitoring, behavioral control, or sanctioning [20]. Its use must be exclusively oriented toward the well-being of employees. In practice, stakeholders expressed strong concerns regarding function creep and disciplinary use, for example: "Do we really want [...] people to be punished [...] if they take a break that is two minutes too long?" (I1). They also questioned whether data might be repurposed for efficiency or personnel decisions: "Are these sensor data actually used only for the benefit of the employees [...] or are [...] statistics generated from which [...] efficiency data can be derived [...] for personnel decisions?" (I2). Additionally, permanent monitoring was perceived as potentially burdensome: "it is, of course, a form of control [...], and there may be employees who [...] feel uncomfortable because it is [...] a form of permanent monitoring" (I3).

DR5: Ensuring Honesty and Trust. The use of Auto-MWMS must be communicated transparently, comprehensibly, and honestly in order to foster trust among employees [20, 40]. Unclear objectives or opaque data practices jeopardize both acceptance and the ethical legitimacy of such systems. This concern was echoed by practitioners, for instance when questioning downstream data usage: "The data are there to begin with, and then the question is: Are they evaluated only in one direction, or does someone perhaps also look at them using a different filter?" (I2). Practitioners also stressed that employer access must be clearly limited and communicated: "the employer's access should [...] be restricted to the most essential aspects and [...] communicated [...], specifying which data can be accessed" (I2).

DR6: Support for Human-Centered Interaction. System design should consistently be oriented toward the needs of employees [32, 38]. Technologies must be ergonomic, as unobtrusive as possible, and easy to use, so that they do not impose additional burdens on work or impair employees' autonomy. From a practical perspective, usability and transparency toward employees were emphasized, for example: "That it is easy to use [...]. That employees are also able and allowed [...] to see [...] what their performance is like" (I3).

DR7: Compliance with current Security Standards. Workload data must be effectively protected against unauthorized access, manipulation, and cyberattacks [14]. The system must therefore comply with recognized and up-to-date security standards. Stakeholders explicitly highlighted this challenge: "the challenge of how to secure the system against access by third parties [...], how to implement this from a security perspective, and to whom access is granted" (I2).

DR8: Minimization of Errors. Errors in data collection, processing, and interpretation should be reduced as far as possible in order to avoid false conclusions and unjust decisions [45]. Otherwise, measurement errors, faulty sensors, or incorrect interpretations could be used as an erroneous basis for performance evaluations or disciplinary measures [45]. This not only undermines employees' trust in the system, but may also negatively affect their professional position and their personal situation [37, 45].

DR9: Sustainable System Design. The system should be designed to be maintainable, updatable, and usable over the long term in order to reduce resource consumption and enable a sustainable use of the deployed technologies [32]. This also includes energy-efficient system design and low-power operation, which support long-term usability and reduce maintenance effort as well as hardware replacement, contributing to ecological sustainability and system stability [32].

4.3 Design Principles

The design principles presented in this paper are derived from our previously defined design requirements (cf. Fig. 2) and were iteratively evaluated and refined through expert feedback. Their structure follows the schema proposed by Gregor et al. [16], with only slight modifications made to improve readability. In line with Chandra et al. [8], each principle explicitly considers boundary conditions (context) that define its applicability. General technological preconditions that are not explicitly stated in the requirements and principles, such as the appropriateness and functionality of measurement instruments and algorithms, are assumed to be fulfilled to enable Auto-MWMS at all.

While all principles address both human and technical aspects of the Auto-MWMS, DP2, DP3, and DP4 specifically represent design principles about user activity, focusing on how workers interact with the system [16]. The order of the design principles was chosen to guide a potential implementer chronologically.

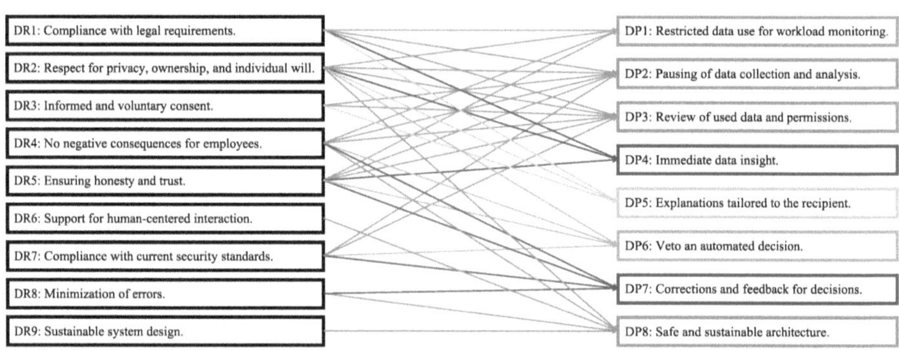

Fig. 2. Logical relations between design requirements and design principles.

DP1: For the Auto-MWMS to analyze workers' mental workload at the moment personal data is generated, the Auto-MWMS should employ privacy-preserving

methods that prevent identification, as well as performance measurements or supervision, because the system must comply with data protection regulations while still enabling valid mental workload monitoring. The monitoring of mental workload involves processing personal data. Employees may perceive this as an intrusion into their privacy and a potential threat to work morale [37]. There is also a risk that such data could be used for performance evaluations or other unfavorable decisions [37]. To address these concerns, system designs must systematically limit both identifiability and performance-related surveillance. Privacy-oriented architectures in IIoT-based wearable systems are described as suitable approaches to reduce these risks [32].

By implementing privacy-preserving methods, organizations can protect employees while ensuring the legally compliant use of Auto-MWMS. This aligns with the principles of data minimization and data protection by design ([11], Art. 5(1)(c), Art. 25). At the same time, such measures help mitigate risks for affected individuals as required for high-risk AI systems under the EU AI Act ([12], Art. 10, Art. 13).

DP2: For workers to be able to decide whether their data is analyzed at the moment mental workload data is generated, the Auto-MWMS must employ a mechanism to suspend data analysis, because individuals must have personal data sovereignty. The ability to temporarily pause the analysis of one's own data is essential to ensure that workers maintain effective control over the use of their personal information. Without such an option for intervention, data collection and analysis may be perceived as continuous and unavoidable, which can undermine employees' sense of autonomy in the workplace [23]. In addition, consent within hierarchical employment relationships can be structurally constrained if no practical possibility for temporary non-participation exists [37].

A technically implemented suspend mechanism therefore constitutes a concrete design solution to uphold informational self-determination during ongoing system operation. This aspect becomes particularly relevant in everyday work settings, where employees have emphasized the importance of being able to interrupt or suspend monitoring processes: "[…] without the possibility to intervene, this becomes a form of permanent monitoring that employees cannot escape from" (I3).

Such an approach aligns with the rights of data subjects to control and restrict the processing of personal data, including the right to withdraw consent at any time ([11], Art. 7(3)) and the right to object to processing ([11], Art. 21). Furthermore, enabling user control supports the requirement for human agency and oversight in high-risk AI systems as stipulated by the EU AI Act ([12], Art. 14).

DP3: For workers to be able to review their own data and manage given permissions without disclosing this information to anyone else, including supervisors, the Auto-MWMS must employ a mechanism that displays all data currently available and all configurable permissions, because individuals must have personal data sovereignty. A transparent presentation of available data and granted access rights enables informed and self-determined decisions regarding their use, thereby supporting the preservation of control and autonomy. At the same time, limiting access to the affected individual prevents unnecessary disclosure to supervisors or other third parties and reduces the risk of performance-related or purpose-inconsistent use [23, 37].

In the interviews, this aspect was frequently linked to questions of transparency and access control. One interviewee emphasized: "the employer's access should be restricted to the most essential aspects and clearly communicated, specifying which data can be accessed" (I2).

Such a transparency and disclosure mechanism aligns with the data subject rights established in the GDPR, particularly the right of access to personal data ([11], Art. 15) as well as the rights to rectification and restriction of processing ([11], Art. 16, Art. 18). It also supports the principle of purpose limitation ([11], Art. 5(1)(b)) by enabling individuals to understand which data are used for which purposes. Furthermore, this form of user-centered transparency contributes to fulfilling the transparency and traceability requirements for high-risk AI systems under the EU AI Act ([12], Art. 13), thereby strengthening informed human oversight.

DP4: For workers to have immediate insights into their own data in contexts where a screen can be used, the Auto-MWMS must employ a mechanism that streams the data in real-time to the workers' device, because individuals need to be able to assess which data are used and verify whether their current state is represented accurately. The ability to view one's own data in real time complements the transparency of stored information and access rights required in DP3 by adding a temporal dimension. It allows workers to immediately see which data are currently being collected and used and to verify whether their current state is accurately represented. This enhances individual control over the monitoring process and reduces the risk that erroneous or contextually inappropriate data remain unnoticed and are subsequently used in further analyses or decisions [23, 37]. Immediate access supports the data subject's right to transparent information about the processing of personal data ([11], Art. 12 and Art. 13) as well as the right of access ([11], Art. 15). Moreover, it facilitates early detection of incorrect or inaccurate data, thereby indirectly contributing to compliance with the principle of data accuracy ([11], Art. 5(1)(d)). In the context of AI-based systems, real-time feedback reinforces transparency and human oversight requirements for high-risk AI systems under the EU AI Act ([12], Art. 13, Art. 14), as it enables workers to understand and critically assess system-generated data during ongoing operation.

DP5: For the Auto-MWMS to explain decisions tailored to the recipients, the Auto-MWMS must employ a mechanism capable of interpreting and explaining these automated decisions, because individuals need to understand decisions that affect them, given that explanations are comprehensible and change based on the workers' literacy. For system-generated notifications and recommendations to be comprehensible and usable, explanations must match the user's level of digital and AI literacy. Natural language explanations in the preferred language help individuals with lower literacy interpret system outputs, for instance when an AI recommends taking a break due to high mental workload. This can help promote transparency and support trust in the system's functioning [5]. For users with high literacy or technical expertise, explainable AI methods can provide deeper insight into the system's reasoning. Adapting explanation formats accordingly promotes transparency and trust while operationalizing information rights under the GDPR ([11], Art. 12, 13; 22(3)) and fulfilling transparency obligations for high-risk AI systems under the EU AI Act ([12], Art. 13).

DP6: For the Auto-MWMS to enable workers to make final decisions themselves, given that there are alternative ways to perform the required action, the Auto-MWMS must employ a mechanism allowing affected workers to decline system-suggested decisions, because individuals should never be compelled by an automated system to act against their own will. Allowing workers to veto system-suggested actions ensures that automated recommendations do not become de facto binding and that human autonomy and decision-making responsibility are maintained. This prevents a transfer of control from individuals to the system and promotes a responsible and ethically sound use of AI-based technologies in the workplace [23].

Such functionality also operationalizes the right to obtain human intervention and to contest automated decisions as stipulated in the GDPR ([11], Art. 22(3)). Workers remain free to consciously reject system-generated recommendations without facing any disadvantage. At the same time, this reflects the requirement for effective human oversight in high-risk AI systems under the EU AI Act, which includes the ability to question or override system outputs ([12], Art. 14). In doing so, algorithmic recommendations are prevented from becoming implicitly binding or gradually replacing human decision-making authority.

DP7: For the Auto-MWMS to enable feedback and correction from affected workers, given that they can identify why a system decision was incorrect, the Auto-MWMS must employ a mechanism that improves future decisions based on user feedback, because individuals should have influence on decisions affecting them. The integration of feedback and corrections from affected workers ensures that automated decisions are not made unilaterally and that human influence remains preserved. This approach supports the correction of erroneous system assumptions, promotes the continuous improvement of future decisions, and fosters the responsible and ethically sound use of AI-based systems in the workplace [35].

Beyond purely technical correction mechanisms, the systematic inclusion of user feedback helps to operationalize existing rights related to data accuracy and participation. It gives practical effect to the right to rectification of inaccurate personal data under the GDPR ([11], Art. 16) as well as to the obligation to provide data subjects with effective means of influence in automated processing contexts ([11], Art. 22(3)). At the same time, it reflects the principle of appropriate human oversight for high-risk AI systems established by the EU AI Act ([12], Art. 14) and reinforces responsible use of automation in workplace environments.

DP8: For administrators to prevent negative consequences such as malfunctions, data leaks, or manipulations for the affected workers in the event of attacks or system failures, administrators must employ an updatable, secure, and sustainable system architecture compliant with appropriate security standards in order to comply with data protection regulations and increase user trust. A secure and regularly updatable system architecture is essential to protect personal data against unauthorized access, manipulation, and loss, while also limiting the impact of potential system failures. Such an approach supports compliance with data protection requirements and reduces risks for affected workers [2, 32].

This type of architecture operationalizes the obligations set out in the GDPR to ensure the security of processing, particularly regarding the confidentiality, integrity, and availability of personal data ([11], Art. 5(1)(f), Art. 32). At the same time, it aligns with the EU AI Act's requirements for adequate risk management as well as technical robustness and cybersecurity in high-risk AI systems ([12], Art. 9). Fulfilling these provisions strengthens legal compliance while enhancing system resilience against attacks and failures, contributing to long-term stability and user trust.

4.4 Evaluation

The evaluation results indicate that all previously defined design requirements are reflected in the interviewees' statements. In particular, aspects such as the protection of workers, the prevention of negative consequences as well as transparency and purpose limitation in data use were emphasized. Additional requirements, such as IT security, legal framework conditions, and human-centered system design, were also addressed, albeit with varying emphasis. No additional requirements were mentioned by the interviewees, suggesting that the derived design requirements comprehensively capture the central ethical and practical challenges of Auto-MWMS.

Regarding the design principles, all principles were assessed as understandable, relevant, and suitable for supporting system design. None of the principles were considered superfluous, and no additional principles were proposed. We used the qualitative feedback to refine and clarify the wording of the requirements and the associated design principles. Overall, the evaluation confirmed that the developed design principles adequately implement the identified requirements and provide an appropriate foundation for the ethically responsible design of Auto-MWMS.

5 Discussion

Against the background of our RQ, three central findings can be identified. First, the results show that ethical requirements for such systems can be systematically translated into concrete and implementable design principles. Second, our principles correspond to the ethical concerns articulated by practitioners and capture the central challenges of the application context. Third, the findings indicate that ethical responsibility in IIoT should not be understood as an individual attribute but as a distributed property of socio-technical system design. This distribution is reflected in the fact that essential protective mechanisms cannot be realized solely through the actions of individual actors but must be embedded in system architecture, interaction mechanisms, and organizational and employer-side decision structures.

This constitutes our theoretical contribution to bridging technology ethics and design science research by translating abstract normative concepts into concrete design mechanisms as design knowledge for Auto-MWMS in the IIoT. The empirical evaluation provides additional evidence for the conceptual robustness and practical applicability of this approach. Findings further specify responsibility as a structural characteristic of highly automated systems. In line with responsibility-oriented perspectives in technology ethics, responsibility emerges as a precautionary design principle, while Wiener's view of a shift of responsibility to higher system levels is confirmed. This extends the discourse on responsible automation by providing domain-specific design knowledge for

IIoT applications. The findings further highlight the ethical tension identified in the introduction between promoting human well-being through Auto-MWMS and safeguarding individual autonomy and privacy. While such monitoring systems can be understood as a form of responsible care for workers' well-being, they also entail the risk of inappropriate design or misuse, as technology is not value-neutral. As a result, a fundamentally beneficial approach may turn into an ethical regression if not carefully governed. The developed design principles demonstrate how this tension can be reduced through targeted design mechanisms and how both objectives can be systematically aligned. They further emphasize that ethical requirements must be integrated early in the system design process rather than being addressed retrospectively. In doing so, the results show how the ethical challenges identified in the introduction can be addressed and translated into practically applicable design solutions.

Additionally, the proposed design principles provide guidance for practitioners in the ethical design of Auto-MWMS in industrial contexts. For system designers, the principles translate ethical requirements and laws into actionable design knowledge. In this way, abstract values such as autonomy, transparency, and control are directly integrated into technical architectures and considered in early stages of system development, rather than being added retrospectively as corrective measures.

This reduces the risk of selectively addressing ethical aspects ("cherry picking") and of treating ethical issues purely ex post [15]. For organizations, the principles highlight that ethical responsibility also encompasses organizational decision-making and governance structures. They support the definition of clear purpose limitations, access policies, and responsibilities to prevent function creep and unintended performance surveillance, and to foster trust. The design principles further align stakeholder expectations, reducing incentives for strategic data manipulation. Furthermore, the evaluation indicates that while the proposed design principles effectively address key ethical challenges, their implementation may conflict with economic objectives. This points to a goal conflict in which ethically restrictive design decisions may compete with efficiency or functionality goals, highlighting that responsible system design requires not only technical but also organizational and economic considerations.

Our research has limitations. The evaluation is based on a limited number of interviews and could be extended by including additional stakeholder perspectives. Moreover, the design principles have not yet been implemented in real IIoT systems, requiring future work to investigate their technical realization and practical effects on acceptance, trust, and data quality. Finally, it remains unclear to what extent ethically restrictive system design can be reconciled with economic objectives in the long term, calling for further research on potential trade-offs and their organizational implications.

6 Conclusion

This study develops design principles for the ethical design of Auto-MWMS within the IIoT and shows how they can address key ethical challenges in this context. By integrating data protection and shared responsibility into system architecture, it provides a practical approach to balance efficiency and human well-being in industrial automation. Responsibility is thereby understood as a systemic design task rather than an individual burden, demonstrating that responsible automation can be achieved through deliberate technical and organizational choices. In this sense, the findings echo Wiener's insight that technological progress should not primarily be measured by productivity gains, but by the extent to which it serves human beings [47].

Acknowledgements. This research and development project is funded by the German Federal Ministry of Research, Technology and Space (BMFTR) within the "Zukunft der Wertschöpfung – Forschung zu Produktion, Dienstleistung und Arbeit" (Funding No. 02K23A070/02K23A071) and managed by Projektträger Karlsruhe (PTKA). The authors are responsible for the contents of this publication.

Disclosure of Interests. The authors have no competing interests to declare that are relevant to the content of this article.

References

1. Association for Computing Machinery (ACM): ACM Code of Ethics and Professional Conduct (2018). https://www.acm.org/code-of-ethics. Accessed 28 Jan 2026
2. Atlam, H.F., Wills, G.B.: IoT security, privacy, safety and ethics. In: Farsi, M., Daneshkhah, A., Hosseinian-Far, A., Jahankhani, H. (eds.) Digital Twin Technologies and Smart Cities. Internet of Things, pp. 123–149. Springer, Cham (2020).
3. Bell, E., Bryman, A., Harley, B.: Business Research Methods, 5th edn. Oxford University Press, Oxford (2019)
4. Boell, S.K., Cecez-Kecmanovic, D.: A hermeneutic approach for conducting literature reviews and literature searches. Commun. Assoc. Inf. Syst. **34** (2014)
5. Burr, C., Taddeo, M., Floridi, L.: The ethics of digital well-being: a thematic review. Sci. Eng. Ethics **26**(4), 2313–2343 (2020)
6. Byrne, A.: Measurement of mental workload in clinical medicine: a review study. Anesthesiol. Pain Med. **1**(2) (2011)
7. Cezar, B.G.D.S., Maçada, A.C.G.: Cognitive overload, anxiety, cognitive fatigue, avoidance behavior and data literacy in big data environments. Inf. Process. Manag. **60**(6), 103482 (2023)
8. Chandra, L., Seidel, S., Gregor, S.: Prescriptive knowledge in is research: conceptualizing design principles in terms of materiality, action, and boundary conditions. In: 2015 48th Hawaii International Conference on System Sciences, pp. 4039–4048. IEEE (2015)
9. Charles, R.L., Nixon, J.: Measuring mental workload using physiological measures: a systematic review. Appl. Ergon. **74**, 221–232 (2019)
10. Cranford, K.N., Tiettmeyer, J.M., Chuprinko, B.C., Jordan, S., Grove, N.P.: Measuring load on working memory: the use of heart rate as a means of measuring chemistry students' cognitive load. J. Chem. Educ. **91**(5), 641–647 (2014)
11. European Parliament and Council of the European Union: Regulation (EU) 16/679 GDPR (2016). https://eur-lex.europa.eu/eli/reg/2016/679/oj. Accessed 15 Jan 2026
12. European Parliament and Council of the European Union: Regulation (EU) 24/1689 AI Act (2024). https://eur-lex.europa.eu/eli/reg/2024/1689/oj. Accessed 15 Jan 2026
13. Fenner, D.: Einführung in die angewandte Ethik. francke Verlag (2010)
14. Galy, E., Cariou, M., Mélan, C.: What is the relationship between mental workload factors and cognitive load types? Int. J. Psychophysiol. **83**(3), 269–275 (2012)
15. Gogoll, J., Zuber, N., Kacianka, S., Greger, T., Pretschner, A., Nida-Rümelin, J.: Ethics in the software development process: from codes of conduct to ethical deliberation. Philos. Technol. **34**(4), 1085–1108 (2021)

16. Gregor, S., Chandra Kruse, L., Seidel, S.: Research perspectives: the anatomy of a design principle. Assoc. Inf. Syst. **21**(6) (2020)
17. Hart, S.G., Staveland, L.E.: Development of NASA-TLX (task load index): results of empirical and theoretical research. In: Advances in Psychology, vol. 52. pp. 139–183. Elsevier (1988)
18. Hevner, A.R.: A three cycle view of design science research. Scand. J. Inf. Syst. **19**(2) (2007)
19. Hinkelmann, K., Afonina, V., Montecchiari, D.: Visualizing argumentation for research problem and research design. In: Mandviwalla, M., Söllner, M., Tuunanen, T. (eds.) DESRIST 2024. LNCS, vol. 14621, pp. 168–181. Springer, Cham (2024).
20. Hinze, A., Bowen, J., König, J.L.: Wearable technology for hazardous remote environments: smart shirt and Rugged IoT network for forestry worker health. Smart Health. **23**, 100225 (2022)
21. Hsieh, R.-J., Chou, J., Ho, C.-H.: Unsupervised online anomaly detection on multivariate sensing time series data for smart manufacturing. In: 2019 IEEE 12th Conference on Service-Oriented Computing and Applications, pp. 90–97. IEEE (2019)
22. Karale, A.: The challenges of IoT addressing security, ethics, privacy, and laws. Internet Things **15**, 100420 (2021)
23. Keil, M., Vervier, L., Brauner, P., Ziefle, M.: Will you be watching me? A conjoint-based study on employee attitudes toward personal data usage in smart factories. Int. J. Hum. Comput. Interact. **41**(16), 10024–10044 (2024)
24. Kurebayashi, I., Maeda, K., Komuro, N., Hirai, K., Sekiya, H., Ichikawa, M.: Mental-state estimation model with time-series environmental data regarding cognitive function. Internet Things **22**, 100730 (2023)
25. Lasi, H., Fettke, P., Kemper, H.-G., Feld, T., Hoffmann, M.: Industry 4.0. Bus. Inf. Syst. Eng. **6**(4), 239–242 (2014)
26. Lucchese, A., Padovano, A., Facchini, F.: Comprehensive systematic literature review on cognitive workload: trends on methods, technologies and case studies. IET Collab. Intell. Manuf. **7**(1), e70025 (2025)
27. Macartney, M.J., et al.: Overnight sleeping heart rate variability of army recruits during a 12-week basic military training course. Eur. J. Appl. Physiol. **122**(9), 2135–2144 (2022)
28. Mahdavi, N., Tapak, L., Darvishi, E., Doosti-Irani, A., Shafiee Motlagh, M.: Unraveling the interplay between mental workload, occupational fatigue, physiological responses and cognitive performance in office workers. Sci. Rep. **14**(1), 17866 (2024)
29. Michelis, A.: Das Prinzip Verantwortung. Versuch einer Ethik für die technologische Zivilisation (1979). In: Bongardt, M., Burckhart, H., Gordon, J.-S., Nielsen-Sikora, J. (eds.) Hans Jonas-Handbuch, pp. 119–126. J.B. Metzler (2021)
30. Molè, M.: The quest for effective fundamental labour rights in the European post-pandemic scenario: introducing principles of explainability and understanding for surveillance through AI algorithms and IoT devices. In: 19th International Conference in Commemoration of Marco Biagi, p. 26 (2022)
31. Morales, M., Nousala, S., Ghobakhloo, M.: The complexity of sustainable innovation, transitional impacts of industry 4.0 to 5.0 for our societies: circular society exploring the systemic nexus of socioeconomic transitions. In: Nousala, S., Metcalf, G., Ing, D. (eds.) Industry 4.0 to Industry 5.0. Translational Systems Sciences, vol. 41, pp. 31–56. Springer, Singapore (2024).
32. Nguyen, T., Nguyen, D.H., Nguyen, QT., Tran, K.D., Tran, K.P.: Human-centered edge AI and wearable technology for workplace health and safety in industry 5.0. In: Tran, K.P. (eds.) Artificial Intelligence for Safety and Reliability Engineering. SSRE, pp. 171–183. Springer, Cham (2024).
33. Nunes, P., Santos, J., Rocha, E.: Challenges in predictive maintenance – a review. CIRP J. Manuf. Sci. Technol. **40**, 53–67 (2023)
34. O'Hara, R.B., Loftis, S.C., Rando, C.: Real-time biometric monitoring for cognitive workload detection: a narrative review of applications in high-demand professions (2025)

35. Paraman, P., Anamalah, S.: Ethical artificial intelligence framework for a good AI society: principles, opportunities and perils. AI Soc. **38**(2), 595–611 (2023)
36. Peffers, K., Tuunanen, T., Rothenberger, M.A., Chatterjee, S.: A design science research methodology for information systems research. J. Manag. Inf. Syst. **24**(3), 45–77 (2007)
37. Pütz, S., Rick, V., Mertens, A., Nitsch, V.: Using IoT devices for sensor-based monitoring of employees' mental workload: investigating managers' expectations and concerns. Appl. Ergon. **102**, 103739 (2022)
38. Reiman, A., Kaivo-oja, J., Parviainen, E., Takala, E.-P., Lauraeus, T.: Human work in the shift to Industry 4.0: a road map to the management of technological changes in manufacturing. Int. J. Prod. Res. **62**(16), 5613–5630 (2024)
39. Saifuzzaman, M., Ananna, T.N., Chowdhury, M.J.M., Ferdous, M.S., Chowdhury, F.: A systematic literature review on wearable health data publishing under differential privacy. Int. J. Inf. Secur. **21**(4), 847–872 (2022)
40. Segkouli, S., Giakoumis, D., Votis, K., Triantafyllidis, A., Paliokas, I., Tzovaras, D.: Smart Workplaces for older adults: coping 'ethically' with technology pervasiveness. Univ. Access Inf. Soc. **22**(1), 37–49 (2023)
41. Stahmann, P., Rodda, A., Nebel, M., van der Staay, A., Janiesch, C., Teuteberg, F.: Advanced analytics in real-time operational dashboards in smart manufacturing: effects on users' cognitive load and task load. J. Decis. Syst. **34**(1), 2593245 (2025)
42. Sweller, J.: Cognitive load during problem solving: effects on learning. Cogn. Sci. **12**(2), 257–285 (1988)
43. Traunwieser, S.: Neurodata-based headsets for the (digital) employee well-being – responsibilities between benefit and harm. Int. J. Ethics Syst. **41**(1), 64–87 (2024)
44. Venable, J., Pries-Heje, J., Baskerville, R.: FEDS: a framework for evaluation in design science research. Eur. J. Inf. Syst. **25**(1), 77–89 (2016)
45. Vermanen, M., Rantanen, M.M., Harkke, V.: Ethical framework for IoT deployment in SMEs: individual perspective. Internet Res. **32**(7), 185–201 (2022)
46. Webster, J., Watson, R.T.: Analyzing the past to prepare for the future: writing a literature review. MIS Q. **26**(2), xiii–xxiii (2002)
47. Wiener, N.: Man and the machine. Challenge **7**(9), 36–41 (1959)

Circular Transformation: A Design Science Approach to a Digital Assessment System for the Plastics Industry

Stephanos Filippakis[1]([envelope]) [iD], Ulvi Ibrahimli[2] [iD], Jonathan Lambers[3] [iD], Lisa Wolf[1], Heicke Gaedeke[3], Ulrich Müller-Steinfahrt[1] [iD], and Axel Winkelmann[2] [iD]

[1] Technical University of Applied Sciences Würzburg-Schweinfurt, 97070 Würzburg, Germany
stephanos.filippakis@thws.de
[2] University of Würzburg, 97070 Würzburg, Germany
ulvi.ibrahimli@uni-wuerzburg.de
[3] SKZ – German Plastics Center, 97076 Würzburg, Germany

Abstract. The transition toward a circular economy poses substantial challenges for manufacturers, who often lack actionable artifacts to assess their readiness and prioritize transformation efforts. While existing circular economy maturity models and digital sustainability tools offer conceptual guidance, they frequently remain generic or weakly connected to organizational decision-making. This study develops a Circular Transition Assessment Tool (CTAT) tailored to the plastics industry, which is notorious for its linear production philosophy. We adopt the design science research approach to develop a design theory: meta-requirements, design requirements, design principles, and design features for a circularity self-assessment system. Subsequently, we translate the design theory into an instantiated artifact. CTAT provides multicategorial, qualitative, and quantitative maturity feedback, contextual explanations, and actionable recommendations supported by transparent assessment logic and expert validation. The artifact is iteratively evaluated through workshops with plastics manufacturers and industry experts. The results indicate that CTAT helps organizations reflect on their current state of circularity, obtain credible assessments, and make informed decisions. The study contributes to the cumulative design knowledge of sociotechnical systems for sustainability and demonstrates how industry-specific assessment systems can support circular economy transitions in complex industrial contexts.

Keywords: Circular Economy · Design Science Research · Plastics Industry

1 Introduction

Plastics are widely used across sectors such as healthcare, mobility, electronics, and consumer goods. Yet their predominantly linear production and disposal patterns continue to raise sustainability concerns [4]. Rising waste volumes, persistent environmental leakage, and increasing regulatory requirements highlight the need for more resource-efficient and circular industry routines [14, 19]. Moving toward a circular economy (CE)

J. vom Brocke et al. (Eds.): DESRIST 2026, LNCS 16606, pp. 77–94, 2026.
https://doi.org/10.1007/978-3-032-28313-9_5

has therefore become a central policy and industry priority, particularly in sectors where material flows are large and technically complex [18, 27, 51]. For plastics manufacturers, adopting circular principles involves more than meeting regulatory thresholds. It requires revisiting product design choices, operational processes, and organizational capabilities [1, 3, 4]. Firms often struggle to evaluate their current circularity state, needs for transformation, and are challenged to develop prudent strategies for circularity [e.g., 14]. This challenge is compounded by the complexity of assessing circularity pathways accurately—managerial assumptions about a firm's circular readiness frequently prove incorrect, leading to misallocated resources, lost time, and competitive disadvantage [44]. This indicates that a structured, transparent method and actionable artifact can help organizations establish an accessible entry point in the circular transition.

In information systems (IS), a growing body of work examines how digital tools support circularity objectives [51]. Examples include sustainability dashboards, digital product passports, or lifecycle-based decision support [29, 30]. Recent studies further highlight the need for transparency, interpretability, and responsible system design when applying digital technologies in sustainability contexts [2, 9, 36]. Despite this progress, research often hesitates to go beyond the conceptual development [24, e.g., 36]. Firm-level actionable self-assessment systems—which help organizations understand their maturity, internal capabilities, and gaps—have received considerably less attention in information system research [7, 52]. Furthermore, there is a lack of research on how such instruments should be designed to provide transparent assessment logic, contextualized interpretation, and digital expert-aided guidance for users. This motivates the following research question (RQ):

RQ: How to design a digital self-assessment artifact that helps plastics manufacturers evaluate and advance their circular transition?

This question is relevant to information systems scholarship, as it examines how digital artifacts can support circular transitions in a domain with substantial environmental complexities [4, 52]. It also advances DSR discourse by formulating a design theory for sustainability-oriented self-assessment tools [e.g., 15]. To address this question, we have developed a Circular Transition Assessment Tool (CTAT) within our Germany-based research consortium, which comprises organizations focused on plastics. Following a design science research (DSR) methodology [22, 31], we derive meta-requirements, design requirements, and design principles that guide the artifact's development. Our aim is to craft a scientifically grounded, practical tool that supports firms in understanding their current position and identifying transformation priorities. The system provides a structured maturity assessment across five CE-relevant action areas, integrates established sustainability frameworks into operational indicators, and offers a transparent evaluation logic.

The study makes two contributions. First, it crafts general design knowledge for sustainability-oriented assessment systems that improve transparency, interpretability, and decision support in responsible digital tools. Second, it introduces a domain-specific digital circularity assessment method that translates the design knowledge into a tangible artifact. In this way, it demonstrates how design knowledge can be applied and generalized across various industry contexts.

The paper unfolds as follows: Introduction is followed by a brief review of the literature in Sect. 2. Section 3 outlines the methodology, and Sect. 4 presents the design theory, artifact instantiation, and the evaluation results. Section 5 discusses theoretical and practical implications, and Sect. 6 concludes the study.

2 Related Work

The German plastics industry remains largely linear, with new products containing, on average, only around 15% recyclate, i.e., material with a previous life cycle [11]. Cultivating circular practices, therefore, represents a substantial organizational challenge, as logistics, material processing, and manufacturing processes are historically shaped by linear production logics [28, 50]. The transformation toward circular processes, tasks, and business models further requires changes in organizational structures as well as in employees' mindsets and skillsets [25]. This complexity is exacerbated by managerial uncertainty, as many organizations lack clarity regarding their current state of circularity and how to systematically advance their existing efforts [e.g., 38]. These challenges underscore the need for structured and validated assessment approaches.

To substantiate this need, we conducted a structured literature review (see Sect. 3) of prior work on circular economy self-assessment and related approaches. Chirumalla et al. [10] propose a multi-level readiness framework grounded in an extensive literature review and validated through a case study. Although empirically well-founded and industry-agnostic, the framework is validated with a single company from the heavy-duty vehicle sector. This underscores the need for industry-specific assessments. Urain et al. [43] provide a comprehensive review of CE assessment literature, including scientific studies, standards, and existing diagnostic tools, and develop the Industrial Circular Economy Questionnaire (ICEQ). The 165-item instrument covers operational, strategic, and support processes but remains limited in sectoral representativeness, as several industries are represented by only one participating firm.

Pigosso et al. [32] present MATChE (Making the Transition to a Circular Economy), a co-developed self-assessment tool that has been applied by 330 manufacturing companies across 16 sectors. Although widely adopted, MATChE comprises only 30 questions across eight dimensions and thus offers a relatively high-level view of an organization's CE maturity. Baratsas et al. [3], on the other hand, propose a quantitative CE assessment framework for multiple business areas, based on a comprehensive catalog of indicators; however, the effort required to complete the assessment is considerable. Uhrenholt et al. [42] develop a conceptual model that distinguishes six organizational dimensions and six maturity levels of circularity. While theoretically valuable, the model lacks practical validation. Demko-Rihter et al. [13] introduce a CE readiness framework for companies in developing countries with the focus on products and business models. Despite its standardized structure, validation remains limited, as it has been applied to only one company.

Across the 15 analyzed studies, most assessment frameworks are implemented as questionnaire-based tools comprising between 30 [32] and 165 items [43]. Some approaches rely on external expert judgment, for example, through life-cycle analysis [7]. Methodologically, most studies begin with literature reviews—often incorporating scientific publications, standards, and existing tools—followed by the development of classification systems and corresponding assessment items. These are typically iterated with industry experts and evaluated through expert feedback, pilot applications, or broader rollouts. Validation approaches vary widely, ranging from theoretical expert discussions [42] to web-based tools applied within specific industries or across sectors, in some cases involving several hundred companies. Assessment outcomes are commonly expressed in five or six sequential maturity levels, with the goal of enabling organizations to identify their current state and gaps relative to higher levels of circularity. Several frameworks additionally report maturity scores per dimension, offering more granular insights into areas for action. However, only few studies provide concrete action recommendations or strategic guidance derived from assessment results. A comparison table of the aforementioned CE self-assessment tools is available in our supplementary material[1].

In summary, the literature presents a broad range of circular economy self-assessment frameworks, yet none explicitly address the specific conditions and challenges of the plastics industry—especially the underlying sociotechnical character of tool-based decision support. Multiple authors, therefore, call for industry-specific assessments to increase relevance and practical value [5, 10, 32, 43]. Responding to this gap, the present study introduces an industry-specific information system artifact; it focuses on the plastics industry, adopts multidimensional maturity scoring, and integrates individualized action recommendations and CE strategy suggestions. Given these gaps, a digital self-assessment information system emerges as the most suitable artifact type, as it can operationalize multi-dimensional maturity logic into an accessible format while embedding transparency, contextual guidance, and actionable recommendations—capabilities that purely conceptual frameworks or static questionnaires cannot adequately provide [22, 26, 49]. Beyond the general gaps, the plastics industry presents specific conditions not addressed by existing tools, including regulatory pressure around recyclate quotas and sector-specific action areas, such as a high variety of materials and additives, making substitution difficult and end-of-life logistics [4, 11].

3   Research Approach

We follow the design science research (DSR) methodology proposed by Peffers et al. [31] to develop design knowledge for circular transformation in the plastics economy. Adopting a problem-centered approach ensures that both the design theory and the resulting artifact directly address challenges faced by plastics processors (Fig. 2). The exploration of the problem space is presented in the introduction and related work sections. Building on this foundation, we iteratively developed our design theory and instantiated an artifact across two design cycles. The design objectives (DOs) guiding artifact development are: (DO1) enable structured circularity self-assessment tailored to plastics manufacturers; (DO2) provide transparent, multi-level maturity feedback with actionable recommendations; and (DO3) support credible, expert-validated decision-making in circular transformation contexts. These objectives directly informed the derivation of meta-requirements and design principles presented in Sect. 4.

---

[1] B2SHARE data repository: 10.23728/b2share.572bw-q9477.

First Design Cycle. We performed a systematic literature review (Fig. 1) following vom Brocke et al. [47] and used the existing academic literature as input to build a foundation for our initial design theory. We adopted a database-driven approach and searched academic publications from 2020 to 2025, as post-2019 regulatory momentum (European Green Deal) has substantially shaped firm-level CE assessment practice, and earlier foundational contributions are already well synthesized in existing reviews [43, 52]. The search strings are documented in Fig. 1.

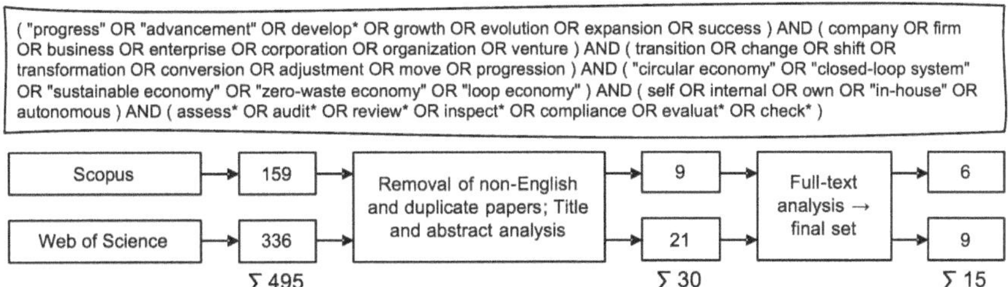

Fig. 1. Literature review process in line with vom Brocke et al. [47].

We used this input space to derive meta-design requirements and formulated design requirements, which are subsequently translated into design features. The initial design theory served as the basis for developing a design artifact—a digital self-assessment system. To ensure simplicity and user-friendliness, we opted for LimeSurvey and Microsoft Excel to configure the features. We then conducted three individual workshops with representatives from plastics-processing companies, plastics recycling companies, and a business association. This setup enabled us to capture perspectives from both core industry actors and a sector-wide, strategic viewpoint.

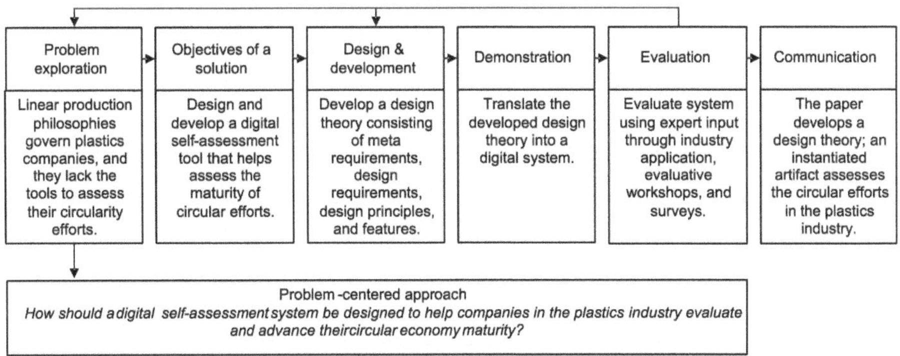

Fig. 2. Design Science Approach in line with Peffers et al. [31].

Second Design Cycle. In the second cycle, we systematically analyzed the qualitative feedback from the workshops and refined the design theory accordingly. This involved revising design requirements and principles, as well as adding, modifying, or removing specific features. The revised design theory was then re-instantiated in the artifact. A final evaluation round was conducted with a larger group of companies, combining qualitative feedback with quantitative assessments. For the quantitative evaluation, we applied the evaluation framework proposed by Sonnenberg and vom Brocke [39].

4 Designing a Self-assessment Artifact for Circular Economy

The meta-requirements and design requirements were derived through systematic coding of the SLR findings: recurring themes—such as the need for actionable performance insight, interpretive context, and transparent scoring—were inductively clustered and mapped to higher-order requirements (e.g., multiple studies noting the absence of concrete guidance [21, 31, 35] converged into MDR1). The resulting requirements were subsequently refined through ex-post analysis of the workshop interviews, which surfaced organizational nuances—such as the importance of stakeholder qualification and sector-specific customization—that anchored the design principles more firmly in practical decision-making contexts. The developed design theory is generalizable across assessment contexts; the domain-specificity is realized in the instantiation layer.

4.1 Meta-design-Requirements and Design Requirements

MDR1: Enable Actionable Performance Insight. Firm-level assessment platforms often aim to turn diagnostic information into a basis for prioritizing actions and planning transition pathways, rather than merely scoring current practice [32]. Similarly, recent work on sustainability performance measurement emphasizes that performance measurement systems and dashboards should provide "actionable insights" that support strategy execution and continuous improvement [12].

MDR2: Support User Decision Quality. Explanations and contextual information improve users' ability to understand system output and make better decisions, rather than simply accepting or rejecting recommendations [26]. User-centered studies on clinical and other decision support systems highlight that decision quality depends on aligning system outputs with domain knowledge, workflows, and users' cognitive needs [e.g., 40]. It implies that the artifact must be designed not as a static survey but as a decision aid that supports interpretation, prioritization, and trade-off evaluation.

MDR3: Ensure Transparent Assessment. Transparency and reliability are often identified as prerequisites for trust and adoption: users want to understand how results are produced, whether methods are robust, and where potential risks or biases lie [9, 20]. Analogously, circular economy self-assessment tools should make scoring logic, data use, expert involvement, and progress visible, so that firms can scrutinize and rely on the resulting maturity judgments.

The following design requirements translate the meta-requirements into operational conditions for more output-oriented design. *DR1: Provide multilevel performance feedback.* Company-level circular economy tools compare performance across multiple action areas or dimensions to reveal differentiated profiles rather than a single index [1]. The artifact, therefore, needs to deliver overall and action-area-specific feedback, enabling users to move seamlessly between aggregated and granular views.

DR2: Provide Interpretive and Comparative Context. Decision support research notes that users need contextualized information—such as reasons, definitions, and benchmarks—to calibrate their judgments [41]. Such corporate self-assessment tools typically include glossaries, example practices, and comparisons to peers or "best-in-class" organizations to help users situate their own performance [1, 49].

DR3: Provide Actionable Recommendations. It is useful that such assessment platforms go beyond diagnosis to suggest focus areas, improvement options, and transition paths, often via reports or workshop toolkits that link assessment results to concrete next steps [21, 36]. Accordingly, the self-assessment artifact should derive and communicate specific recommendations (e.g., priority action areas, suggested measures) from the performance profile, rather than leaving interpretation entirely to the user.

DR4: Maintain Transparency and Reliability. Recent work on trustworthy AI and digital decision support highlights that users' willingness to rely on system outputs is shaped by perceived technical reliability, transparency, and the availability of quality safeguards [8]. Translating this into the circular economy self-assessment context requires features that make progress and expert input visible, flag questionable response patterns, and provide traceability from scores back to underlying questions and data [33].

4.2 Design Principles, Features, and Design Theory

Design principles translate design requirements into prescriptive, solution-oriented guidance on how an artifact should be constructed [6, 45]. We discuss how a circular economy self-assessment tool should address the information, interpretation, decision-support, and transparency needs identified in the meta and design requirements. The final design theory is depicted in Fig. 3. The following four principles (and derived design features) structure the design space.

DP1: Integrate multi-level assessment visualization to address the need for differentiated, intelligible performance insight by structuring assessment output across multiple levels of granularity. Such visualization enables users to shift seamlessly between overall maturity and detailed action-area performance, thereby supporting diagnostic clarity and targeted decision-making (DF1: performance information on action areas; DF2: overall score; DF3: action-area-specific score).

DP2: Embed explanations and comparative context to enhance user understanding by pairing performance results with clarifying information, definitions, and reference points. Providing in-line explanations, terminology support, and benchmarking against best-in-class performers helps users interpret scores, understand underlying logic, and situate their performance within an external frame of reference (DF4: explanations of scores and rankings; DF5: analysis of strengths and weaknesses; DF7: best-in-class comparison; DF8: glossary for technical terms).

DP3: Enable intelligent support to produce recommendations that ensure that insights gained from the assessment translate into actionable guidance. By leveraging analytical or large language model (LLM)-based narrative synthesis, the system can process tailored improvement suggestions that help organizations prioritize actions and advance their circular economy performance in a structured manner (DF6: LLM-processed action recommendations).

DP 4: Provide contextualized feedback that reinforces assessment transparency and user orientation by making process status and progress continuously visible. Presenting real-time cues on completion, remaining steps, and assessment flow reduces uncertainty and strengthens user confidence in the reliability and structure of the assessment procedure (DF9: visual running feedback on progress).

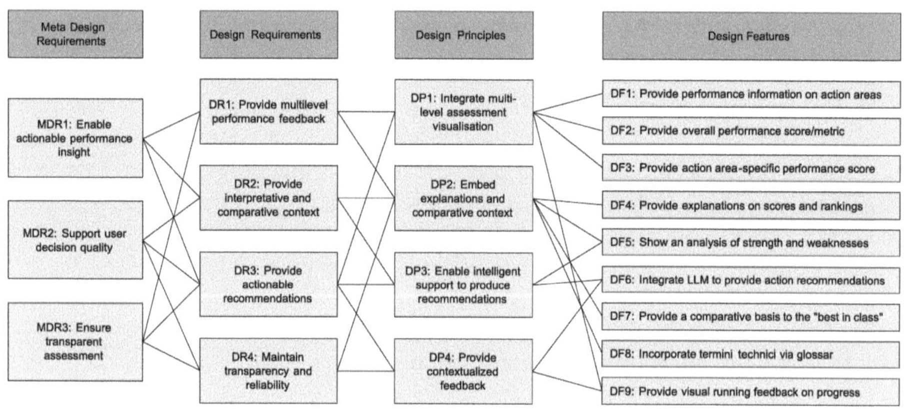

Fig. 3. Design theory for circular transition assessment systems.

4.3 Demonstration

This section describes the practical implementation of the Circular Transformation Assessment Tool (CTAT) and illustrates how the design features are integrated. Few parts of CTAT build on preliminary work by Filippakis and Müller-Steinfahrt [17]. The domain-specificity of CTAT is primarily embedded in its content layer—the action recommendations, maturity transitions, and feedback modules are grounded in plastics-industry-specific processes and material-flow logic— all of which were developed in close collaboration with plastics processors, recyclers, and industry associations.

CTAT guides users to a *Start* page that provides an introduction and collects basic company information. The assessment comprises five predefined action areas, each containing a fixed number of questions with corresponding answer options. A navigation bar continuously displays progress throughout the assessment (DF9). Figure 4 illustrates the beginning of the first action area (*Strategy and Planning*). Beneath the navigation bar, a bar chart visualizes the current score for the respective action area in real time

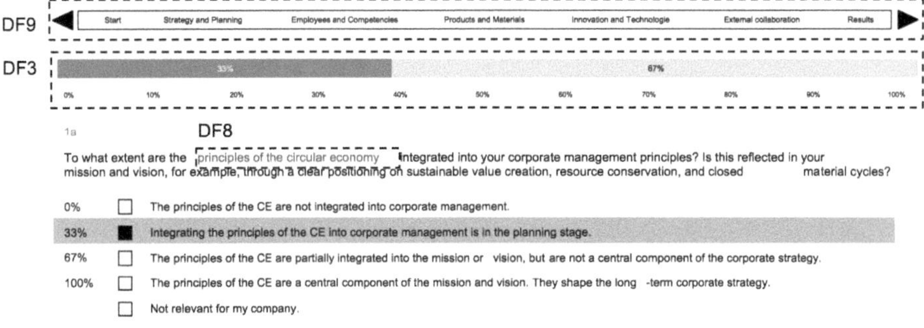

Fig. 4. CTAT navigation bar.

(DF3). Terminii technici used in the questionnaire are explained through a linked glossary (DF8).

The questionnaire follows a uniform structural logic. Three question types are employed: single-selection questions (22 items), multiple-selection questions (1 item), and question batteries (10 items)[2]. The breakdown of question types for each action area is as follows: Strategy and Planning: seven single-selection, one multiple-selection. Employees and Competencies: five batteries. Products and Materials: three batteries, seven single-selection. Innovation and Technology: two batteries. External Collaboration: eight single-selection. For each action area, a distinct focus on certain question types has emerged, which became apparent during development. The same applies to the number of questions.

Strategy and Planning	1c To what extent are the principles of circular economy implemented in goods production? (for each 11%)		
	Targets for maximum scrap rates	Targets for secondary material usage rates	Targets for the recycling of production waste, e.g., X% must be recycled and only 100-X% may be sent for thermal recovery
	Targets for the purity of collected production waste.	Targets for maximum non-production time of machines / minimum downtime of machines	Targets for information and data collection during production for the purpose of product traceability
	Targets for the proportion of renewable materials in production	Written corrective actions documented in quality management to eliminate raw material loss (granulate, film scraps, etc.).	Written preventive measures documented in quality management to counteract raw material loss (granulate, film scraps, etc.) during production.
	Not relevant to my company because…		

Employees and Competencies	2a To what extent do you provide training for employees on the following aspects of the circular economy? (Please indicate which of the four response options best applies to your company.)	Levels for each response in 2a
	Basic Understanding of Sustainability / Circular Economy and Global Interconnections*	No training on this topic.
	Circular Thinking and Systems Thinking (ISO 59004) (Examples: Business models/alternatives to the "Take, Make, Waste" model; Design for Circularity)*	No training on this topic, but it is being planned.
	Resource Efficiency Waste Management and Recycling, Proper Sorting	Individual employees from relevant departments receive training on this topic.
	Product Life Cycle Management / Life Cycle Thinking	All relevant employees receive training on this topic as needed.
	Sustainability Assessments	
	Digitalization and Automation	Not relevant to my company because…

Fig. 5. Extract from the assessment tool: first question from each action area.

In addition to the single-selection question example shown in Fig. 4, Fig. 5 illustrates examples of the other question types, including a question battery and a multiple-selection question. Regardless of question type, each item contributes a score between 0% and 100%. Action area-specific score is the average of all the question scores in the

---

[2] Complete list of question items is available as supplementary material over a public data repository B2SHARE-EUDAT: 10.23728/b2share.572bw-q9477.

respective action area. Respondents may also indicate that a question is "not relevant to my company," accompanied by a brief explanation. Such questions are excluded from the action area-specific score. After completing all action areas, users are directed to a *Results* tab, which presents action-area-specific scores (Fig. 6), the overall score, and the resulting maturity level using bar charts (DF2). The total score is calculated as the average of all areas of activity.

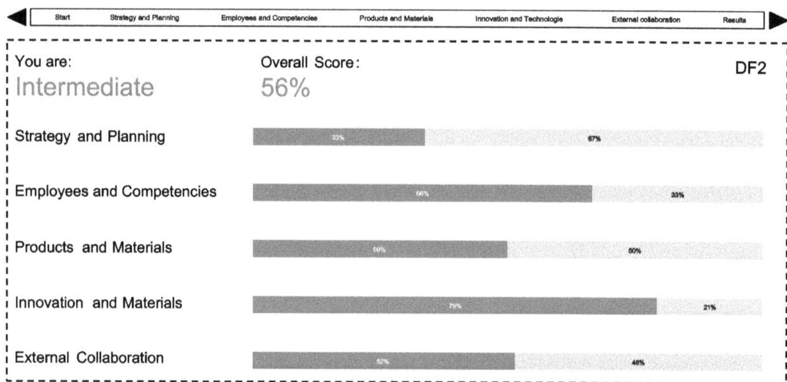

Fig. 6. Result page showing overall and multicategorical scoring, with action areas on the left.

This visualization enables users to quickly identify action areas with high or low improvement potential. To support targeted action planning, the tool derives individual, prescriptive action impulses that reflect the transition from a given answer to the next higher maturity level (e.g., beginner → intermediate → advanced → pioneer). CTAT operates at the organizational level, providing recommendations scoped to internal processes, capabilities, and strategic priorities. For this purpose, the research group developed custom action recommendations for each maturity-level transition (Fig. 7).

All responses from a completed CTAT are aggregated and assigned to one of four maturity levels or to "not relevant." Based on the assigned maturity level, the corresponding action recommendation is extracted for each question; no call to action is generated for questions marked as "not relevant" or already at the highest maturity level ("pioneer"). The extracted action recommendations are consolidated into a single text. To improve readability and consistency, this initially fragmented text is processed using a locally deployed large language model (LLM) with a fixed prompt (DF6): *"The following text contains action-oriented recommendations for a company. Summarize the text in 1,000 to 1,200 characters and address the reader with friendly imperatives, guiding them toward the recommended actions"*. As a final step, the system generates a two-page overview of the final assessment. The first page displays the overall score and action-area-specific scores, complemented by best-in-class comparisons shown in both tabular and spider-chart formats (DF7). In addition, predefined explanatory text modules clarify the scores within each action area (DF4). The second page highlights organizational strengths and weaknesses (DF5) and outlines initial action recommendations (DF1, DF6). An excerpt is shown in Fig. 7.

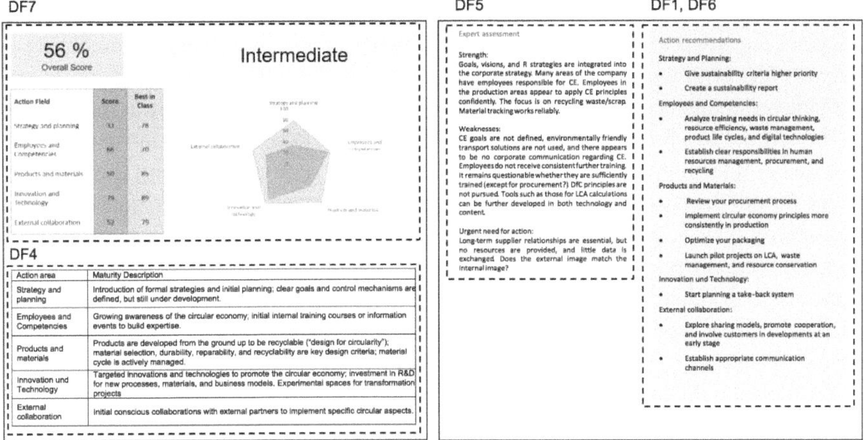

Fig. 7. Final assessment through digital two-page overview.

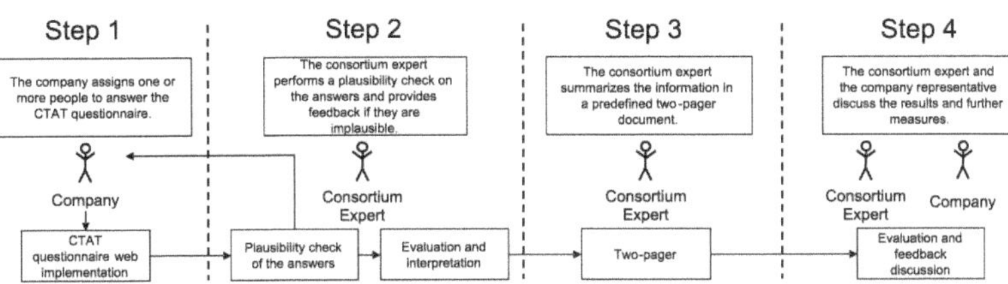

Fig. 8. High-level workflow demonstration.

To ensure alignment between scientific rigor and practical applicability, CTAT is embedded in a structured four-step process that combines quantitative assessment, qualitative expert review, and AI-supported synthesis. Figure 8 illustrates the workflow from questionnaire completion to the communication of expert-validated results. It is important to note that a company does not receive results immediately, but only after the research consortium's experts assess the plausibility of the provided responses and the tool-generated results. They enrich the tool results with their expert knowledge to ensure hallucination-free decision support. In the final step, experts and company representatives jointly discuss identified gaps in a feedback and evaluation session. This discussion serves as a starting point for developing customized transformation concepts.

4.4 Evaluation

We evaluated our artifact in two consecutive design cycles. The overarching goal was to explore whether the instantiated artifact adequately meets the identified meta-requirements and design principles, and whether it provides meaningful support for practitioners in the plastics industry.

First Design Cycle. In the first design cycle, we conducted application-oriented workshops with representatives from plastics-processing companies ($N_{companies} = 3$). We used our current research consortium to select companies and the individual participants. They were recruited through purposive (judgment) sampling because participating professionals had both a strong practical background and industry experience in materials and managerial science. The primary aim was to observe how potential users interact with the artifact in a realistic organizational setting and to collect qualitative feedback to refine theory and improve the artifact. Thereafter, we took notes during the workshops and employed thematic analysis to capture the main patterns in our qualitative data. Three central insights emerged: 1) the assessment should be completed by stakeholders with knowledge of relevant strategic and operational circularity processes, as selecting unqualified individuals may skew results; 2) some questionnaire items were irrelevant for the recycling sector but crucial for manufacturers, so customization for different industries is necessary; 3) contradictory answer choices were identified, suggesting that expert follow-up discussions are recommended alongside self-assessment.

Second Design Cycle. We refined our theory and the tool and initiated our second evaluation workshop ($N_{companies}$ = 5). This cycle focused on collecting further qualitative feedback and structured quantitative evaluations of the artifact's perceived quality and usefulness. Each workshop followed a standardized sequence. Participants first received an introduction to the final assessment logic, refined structure, and interface. Subsequently, they engaged in guided reflection sessions, during which they provided qualitative feedback on clarity, relevance, interpretability, expected usefulness, and limitations. Across participants, qualitative feedback indicated that the artifact supports structured reflection on the organization's current CE status and action areas (I1, I4, I5). Several participants described the assessment as a useful starting point for gaining an initial overview of their current position and identifying priority action areas[3]:

> *"It provides a nice, succinct digital overview that helps us directly see where we stand in our circularity efforts and expert-reviewed action impulses" (I2)*

Others noted that the results helped formalize and substantiate internally recognized challenges, thereby supporting managerial discussions and decision-making by providing an externally grounded and methodologically transparent reference point:

> *"While we know where our weaknesses lie, for top management to really initiate measures, such digital assessment systems help reexamine existing challenges and provide initial guidance in the form of action recommendations" (I3)*

In addition to qualitative input, participants completed a standardized questionnaire based on the evaluation criteria proposed by Sonnenberg and vom Brocke [39]. Overall, the quantitative feedback (N = 10) indicates a positive evaluation of the artifact across all assessed dimensions. Items related to ease of use, simplicity, understandability, and general applicability received the highest levels of agreement. This suggests that participants perceived the system as intuitive, accessible, and sufficiently flexible for use across different plastics-industry contexts. This insight also suggests that the survey completion demands an adequate cognitive burden. Perceived completeness and level of detail also received predominantly positive ratings, although a small number

---

[3] The quotes are reflection of the notes taken during the workshops and our memory protocols.

of respondents expressed reservations. This aligns with qualitative remarks concerning the breadth of indicators and the length of the questionnaire. The item on fidelity with real-world CE phenomena yielded the highest number of neutral responses. This pattern suggests that while participants generally recognized the relevance of the assessment logic, some were uncertain about how comprehensively the tool captures the complexity and heterogeneity of circularity-related processes in their specific context:

"It would be desirable to have better, [more realistic] comparability of materials [across sectors]; [for example] the life cycle of plastic products in the construction industry is significantly longer than in other sectors, such as the automotive industry."(I4)

Finally, responses regarding operational feasibility and expected positive impact indicate that participants believe the tool can be integrated into routine organizational practices and may add value to internal decision-making. Taken together, these results indicate that the artifact is perceived as usable, understandable, and practically meaningful, while also highlighting areas—particularly fidelity and perceived completeness—where iterative refinement may further strengthen its fit for diverse industrial settings.

5 Discussion

The findings indicate that digital self-assessment systems can effectively support transitions to the circular economy when designed as sociotechnical decision support rather than purely technical measurement tools. Participants valued the system's ability to digitally structure and substantiate already known circularity-related pain points, thereby creating a shared and transparent basis for internal discussion and prioritization (I2, I3). At the same time, the evaluation reveals a critical underlying dynamic: assessment results gain credibility and decision-relevance only when they are reviewed and contextualized by domain experts prior to dissemination (I3). This reinforces prior information systems research emphasizing that trust in sustainability-related decision support emerges from the interplay between automated analysis and human judgment—the sociotechnical view, rather than from automation alone [8, 21]. More precisely, the design principles and meta-requirements are intended to generalize across sustainability assessment contexts, while the action areas, benchmark definitions, and recommendation library represent domain-specific instantiations tied to the plastics industry and the consortium's expert base.

A second key insight concerns the tension between standardization and contextual fit. While users appreciated the transparent logic, multi-level feedback, and comparative views embedded in the artifact (I1, I14), they also highlighted limitations in capturing sector-specific and organizational nuances. This suggests that digital CE self-assessments should be designed to support structured reflection and contextual sense-making rather than to deliver definitive evaluations, echoing calls in sustainability and DSR literature for interpretive, responsible digital tools [35–37, 48]. Overall, the study shows that combining transparent digital assessment with human-in-the-loop validation is essential for producing credible, actionable, and responsible sustainability guidance in complex industrial settings.

5.1 Theoretical Contributions

It is worth distinguishing what this study inherits from prior maturity model practice and what it distinctly contributes to IS knowledge. Established CE assessment frameworks provide the structural foundation: questionnaire-based instruments, sequential maturity levels, and dimensional scoring [32, 43]. The IS contribution lies beyond this foundation—in the sociotechnical framing of assessment as decision support, the design principles for transparency and interpretability, and the integration of LLM-based narrative synthesis for user-friendly readability and actionable in organizational contexts [36].

This paper contributes to design science and information systems research [23] by developing a design theory for responsible, sustainability-oriented digital assessment systems [34, 46]. It specifies meta-requirements, design requirements, design principles, and prescriptive design features that show how transparency, interpretability, and actionable guidance can be systematically embedded into digital assessment artifacts. In doing so, the study advances DSR knowledge about how digital tools can be used to support organizational decision-making in sustainability transitions [36, 37]. Specifically, the design principles and method constitute a contribution to DSR and IS researchers seeking generalizable design knowledge, while the instantiated tool serves practitioners and industry stakeholders requiring an immediately applicable assessment instrument.

The paper further contributes to circular economy and sustainability literature by designing and evaluating a domain-specific Circular Transition Assessment Tool for the plastics industry. The artifact translates abstract circular thinking into industry-relevant indicators, maturity scoring, and actionable recommendations, enabling firms to diagnose their readiness and prioritize transformation efforts [10, 13]. This contribution demonstrates how scalable digital self-assessment tools can operationalize circular sensemaking in complex industrial contexts.

5.2 Practical Implications

For practitioners, this study provides CTAT as a scientifically grounded yet practically applicable self-assessment information system tailored to plastics-processing companies. Organizations in adjacent sectors should treat the design theory as a transferable blueprint while adapting the underlying indicators, benchmarks, and action recommendations to their specific industrial context. The system supports firms in establishing a clear starting point for their circular economy transformation by systematically identifying strengths, gaps, and priority areas for action, complemented by concrete recommendations. In the context of current European and German policy initiatives—such as the EU Clean Industrial Deal and the German National Circular Economy Strategy [16]—our study can support building the structured, transparent foundation for companies to navigate regulatory and strategic complexity and pursue circular transformation in a more focused, resilient manner. From a plastics research and industry-monitoring perspective, CTAT addresses the current lack of a systematic mechanism for tracking progress in the circular transition at the industry level. By scaling the tool's deployment, future work can establish industry benchmarks and calculate average maturity levels across the plastics industry. This can further support longitudinal analyses of transformation trajectories and help identify persistent and emerging challenges.

6　Conclusion

This study developed and evaluated a structured self-assessment method for the plastics industry using a design science research approach. By deriving a design theory and instantiating it in an information system artifact, the paper demonstrates how responsible, transparent, and actionable digital self-assessment systems can support organizational decision-making in circular transitions. The findings highlight the importance of combining structured digital assessment with interpretive support and expert validation to ensure credibility and practical relevance. The study has several limitations. First, the evaluation was conducted with a relatively small number of companies, which limits the generalizability of the empirical findings. Second, all participating organizations were based in Germany, and the assessment logic reflects the regulatory, institutional, and industry-specific conditions of the German plastics sector. Although the design knowledge is highly relevant and transferable, the system's transferability to other national or industrial contexts may be limited and will require careful adaptation. Future research can extend this work by evaluating and validating the artifact using larger, more diverse samples, including firms from other countries or institutional settings, and industrial sectors. Future research is also advised to explore how digital self-assessment systems can be integrated with longitudinal data to track temporal circular progress.

Acknowledgement. This work was carried out as part of the research and development project KARE, funded by the German Federal Ministry of Research, Technology, and Space (BMFTR) within the "The Future of Value Creation – Research on Production, Services and Work" program (funding number 02L22C200) and managed by the Project Management Agency Karlsruhe (PTKA). The authors are responsible for the content of this publication.

References

1. Bais, B., Molinaro, M., Orzes, G.: Assessing circular economy at company level: comparison of tools and methodological challenges. Sustain. Prod. Consum. **59**, 112–126 (2025)
2. Banerjee, G., Dhar, S., Roy, S., Syed, R., Das, A.: Explainability and transparency in designing responsible AI applications in the enterprise. In: Naik, N., Jenkins, P., Prajapat, S., Grace, P. (eds.) C3AI 2024. LNNS, vol. 884, pp. 420–431. Springer, Cham. https://doi.org/10.1007/978-3-031-74443-3_25
3. Baratsas, S.G., Pistikopoulos, E.N., Avraamidou, S.: A quantitative and holistic circular economy assessment framework at the micro level. Comput. Chem. Eng. **160**, 107697 (2022)
4. Barford, A., Ahmad, S.R.: Levers for a corporate transition to a plastics circular economy. Bus. Strategy Environ. **32**(4), 1203–1217 (2023)
5. Bashynska, I., et al.: Performance assessment of sustainable leadership of enterprise's circular economy-driven innovative activities. Sustainability **16**(2), 1–26 (2024)
6. Baskerville, R., Pries-Heje, J.: Projectability in design science research. J. Inf. Technol. Theory Appl. (JITTA) **20**(1) (2019)
7. Baumgartner, R.J., et al.: Exploring the role of companies in transitioning to a sustainable and circular future. In: Deutz, P., Vermeulen, W.J., Baumgartner, R.J., Ramos, T.B., Raggi, A. (eds.) Circular Economy Realities, pp. 64–95. Routledge, London (2024)

8. Bollaert, M., Augereau, O., Coppin, G.: Measuring and calibrating trust in artificial intelligence. In: Bramwell-Dicks, A., Evans, A., Winckler, M., Petrie, H., Abdelnour-Nocera, J. (eds.) INTERACT 2023. LNCS, vol. 14536, pp. 232–237. Springer, Cham (2024). https://doi.org/10.1007/978-3-031-61698-3_22

9. Cetinkaya, N.E., Krämer, N.: Between transparency and trust: identifying key factors in AI system perception. Behav. Inf. Technol., 1–15 (2025)

10. Chirumalla, K., Balestrucci, F., Sannö, A., Oghazi, P.: The transition from a linear to a circular economy through a multi-level readiness framework: an explorative study in the heavy-duty vehicle manufacturing industry. J. Innov. Knowl. **9**(4), 100539 (2024)

11. Conversio: Stoffstrombild Kunststoffe in Deutschland 2023 - Zahlen und Fakten zum Lebensweg von Kunststoffen (2024)

12. Dauerer, A.: A systematic literature review of performance measurement systems and the integration of ESG factors. Environ. Sustain. Indic. **27**, 100746 (2025)

13. Demko-Rihter, J., Sassanelli, C., Pantelic, M., Anisic, Z.: A framework to assess manufacturers' circular economy readiness level in developing countries: an application case in a Serbian packaging company. Sustainability **15**(8), 6982 (2023)

14. Domenech, T., Bahn-Walkowiak, B.: Transition towards a resource efficient circular economy in Europe: policy lessons from the EU and the member states. Ecol. Econ. **155**, 7–19 (2019)

15. Farmakis, T., Koukopoulos, A., Zois, G., Mourtos, I., Lounis, S., Kalaboukas, K.: Developing a circular and resilient information system: a design science approach. In: Thürer, M., Riedel, R., von Cieminski, G., Romero, D. (eds.) APMS 2024. IFIPAICT, vol. 728, pp. 64–79. Springer, Cham (2024). https://doi.org/10.1007/978-3-031-71622-5_5

16. Federal Ministry for the Environment, Climate Action, Nature Conservation and Nuclear Safety: The National Circular Economy Strategy (NCES) (2026). https://www.bundesumw eltministerium.de/en/topics/circular-economy/circular-economy-strategy

17. Filippakis, S., Müller-Steinfahrt, U.: Transformation gap detector for circular economy - a self-assessment approach for the plastic industry. In: Wehner, R., Akcaoglu, E. (eds.) Balancing Innovation and Resilience in International Business. Würzburg International Business Press (2025)

18. Geissdoerfer, M., Savaget, P., Bocken, N.M., Hultink, E.J.: The circular economy – a new sustainability paradigm? J. Clean. Prod. **143**, 757–768 (2017)

19. Geyer, R., Jambeck, J.R., Law, K.L.: Production, use, and fate of all plastics ever made. Am. Assoc. Adv. Sci. (2017)

20. Glassberg, I., Ilan, Y.B., Zwilling, M.: The key role of design and transparency in enhancing trust in AI-powered digital agents. J. Innov. Knowl. **10**(5), 100770 (2025)

21. Gregor, S., Hevner, A.R.: Positioning and presenting design science research for maximum impact. MIS Q. **37**(2), 337–355 (2013)

22. Hevner, A.R., March, S.T., Park, J., Ram, S.: Design science in information systems research. MIS Q. **28**(1), 75–106 (2004)

23. Ibrahimli, U., Hemmrich, S., Winkelmann, A.: Bridging systems theory and information systems: a framework for designing complex information systems. CAIS **58**(1), 37 (2026)

24. Ibrahimli, U., Hemmrich, S., Zauke, S., Winkelmann, A.: Overcoming lemon markets with business reputation ecosystem – a multi-agent simulation on monetary ratings. In: Wirtschaftsinformatik Proceedings (2024)

25. Kirchherr, J., Reike, D., Hekkert, M.: Conceptualizing the circular economy: an analysis of 114 definitions. Resour. Conserv. Recycl. **127**, 221–232 (2017)

26. Kolajo, T., Daramola, O.: Towards the design of explanation-aware decision support systems. In: Arai, K. (eds.) FTC 2024. LNNS, vol. 1154, pp. 89–105. Springer, Cham (2024). https://doi.org/10.1007/978-3-031-73110-5_7

27. Korhonen, J., Nuur, C., Feldmann, A., Birkie, S.E.: Circular economy as an essentially contested concept. J. Clean. Prod. **175**, 544–552 (2018)

28. Kraft, M.H.G., Christ, O., Scherer, L.: Management der Kreislaufwirtschaft. Springer Fachmedien Wiesbaden, Wiesbaden (2022)
29. Mboli, J.S., Thakker, D., Mishra, J.L.: An Internet of Things-enabled decision support system for circular economy business model. Softw. Pract. Exp. **52**(3), 772–787 (2022)
30. Melville, N.P.: Information systems innovation for environmental sustainability. MIS Q. **34**(1), 1–22 (2010)
31. Peffers, K., Tuunanen, T., Rothenberger, M.A., Chatterjee, S.: A design science research methodology for information systems research. J. Manag. Inf. Syst. **24**(3), 45–77 (2007)
32. Pigosso, D.C., McAloone, T.C.: Making the transition to a circular economy within manufacturing companies: the development and implementation of a self-assessment readiness tool. Sustain. Prod. Consum. **28**, 346–358 (2021)
33. Pu, P., Chen, L.: Trust building with explanation interfaces. In: Edmonds, E., Riecken, D., Paris, C.L., Sidner, C.L. (eds.) Proceedings of the 11th International Conference on Intelligent user Interfaces, New York, NY, USA, pp. 93–100. ACM. 01292006
34. Recker, J.: Designing information systems that support environmental sustainability: a framework-based review. In: Cooper, V.A., Kranz, J.J., Mathew, S.K., Watson, R.T. (eds.) Research Handbook on Information Systems and the Environment, pp. 114–148. Edward Elgar Publishing (2023)
35. Schoormann, T., Strobel, G., Möller, F., Petrik, D., Zschech, P.: Artificial intelligence for sustainability—a systematic review of information systems literature. CAIS **52**, 199–237 (2023)
36. Schrade-Grytsenko, L., Ibrahimli, U., Kappler, K.E., Bockshecker, A., Smolnik, S., Winkelmann, A.: Chatting for change: a design science study into crafting a chatbot system for corporate sustainability. In: Proceedings of the 59th Hawaii International Conference on System Sciences (2026)
37. Seidel, S., Jan, Pimmer, C., Brocke, J.: Enablers and barriers to the organizational adoption of sustainable business practices. In: AMCIS 2010 Proceedings (2010)
38. Seidel, S., Recker, J., vom Brocke, J.: Sensemaking and sustainable practicing: functional affordances of information systems in green transformations. MIS Q. **37**(4), 1275–1299 (2013)
39. Sonnenberg, C., vom Brocke, J.: Evaluations in the science of the artificial – reconsidering the build-evaluate pattern in design science research. In: Peffers, K., Rothenberger, M., Kuechler, B. (eds.) DESRIST 2012. LNCS, vol. 7286, pp. 381–397. Springer, Heidelberg (2012). https://doi.org/10.1007/978-3-642-29863-9_28
40. Spatscheck, N., Schaschek, M., Winkelmann, A.: The effects of generative AI's human-like competencies on clinical decision-making. J. Decis. Syst., 1–39 (2024)
41. Symons, V.J.: A review of information systems evaluation: content, context and process. Eur. J. Inf. Syst. **1**(3), 205–212 (1991)
42. Uhrenholt, J.N., Kristensen, J.H., Rincón, M.C., Adamsen, S., Jensen, S.F., Waehrens, B.V.: Maturity model as a driver for circular economy transformation. Sustainability **14**(12), 7483 (2022)
43. Urain, I., Eguren, J.A., Justel, D.: Development and validation of a tool for the integration of the circular economy in industrial companies: case study of 30 companies. J. Clean. Prod. **370**, 133318 (2022)
44. van Loon, P., van Wassenhove, L.N., Mihelic, A.: Designing a circular business strategy: 7 years of evolution at a large washing machine manufacturer. Bus. Strategy Environ. **31**(3), 1030–1041 (2022)
45. vom Brocke, J., Hevner, A., Maedche, A.: Introduction to design science research. In: vom Brocke, J., Hevner, A., Maedche, A. (eds.) Design Science Research. Cases. Progress in IS, pp. 1–13. Springer, Cham (2020). https://doi.org/10.1007/978-3-030-46781-4_1

46. vom Brocke, J., Seidel, S.: Environmental sustainability in design science research: direct and indirect effects of design artifacts. In: Peffers, K., Rothenberger, M., Kuechler, B. (eds.) DESRIST 2012. LNCS, vol. 7286, pp. 294–308. Springer, Heidelberg (2012). https://doi.org/10.1007/978-3-642-29863-9_22
47. vom Brocke, J., et al.: Reconstructing the giant: on the importance of rigour in documenting the literature search process, pp. 2206–2217 (2009)
48. vom Brocke, J., Watson, R.T., Dwyer, C., Elliot, S., Melville, N.: Green information systems: directives for the is discipline. CAIS **33** (2013)
49. Wiederhold, G.: Information systems that really support decision-making. J. Intell. Inf. Syst. **14**(2–3), 85–94 (2000)
50. Wilts, H.: Zirkuläre Wertschöpfung. Aufbruch in die Kreislaufwirtschaft. Friedrich-Ebert-Stiftung Abteilung Wirtschafts- und Sozialpolitik, Bonn (2021)
51. Zeiss, R., Ixmeier, A., Recker, J., Kranz, J.: Mobilising information systems scholarship for a circular economy: review, synthesis, and directions for future research. Inf. Syst. J. **31**(1), 148–183 (2021)

Green Lean Six Sigma – A Modeling Tool-Based Approach

Florian Johannsen[1]([envelope]) [iD] and Hans-Georg Fill[2] [iD]

[1] Hochschule Schmalkalden, Am Blechhammer 4-9, 98574 Schmalkalden, Germany
f.johannsen@hs-sm.de
[2] University of Fribourg, Bd de Pérolles 90, 1700 Fribourg, Switzerland
hans-georg.fill@unifr.ch

Abstract. Today, the imperative for organizations to optimize their processes for resource efficiency and environmental performance is driven not only by regulatory and compliance requirements, but also by evolving consumer expectations and the drive to implement sustainable information systems. In this context, Green Lean Six Sigma (GLSS) is receiving increasing attention as a means of redesigning business processes to achieve greater levels of environmental performance. However, there is no universally accepted GLSS standard, and it is not entirely clear how the quality techniques employed in such projects should be applied or potentially modified to align with environmental sustainability goals. To address this gap, this study proposes a modeling tool-based GLSS approach, based on quality techniques designed as model types, with the aim of providing practitioners with a useful means of undertaking GLSS initiatives. We evaluate the solution through illustrative scenarios, expert feedback and a usability study.

Keywords: Green Lean Six Sigma · Quality Technique · Metamodel

1 Motivation

Environmental sustainability is a high societal priority today, as reflected in political initiatives such as the United Nations' Sustainable Development Goals [1]. Companies are therefore increasingly obliged to subject their business processes to rigorous scrutiny and to redesign them in a manner that renders them more eco-friendly in order to meet the expectations of legislators and consumers alike [2]. In this context, entrepreneurial quality management (QM) represents a promising field of study with the potential to address environmental sustainability goals within companies, such as reducing air emissions or solid waste [3]. Various QM methods have been established over the years, e.g., Total Quality Management, Lean Management or Six Sigma just to mention a few. In recent times, further developments of these methods have been introduced to address the issue of environmental sustainability. Thereby, particularly the conjunction of Six Sigma and Lean Management with green principles (e.g., green manufacturing), a concept designated as 'Green Lean Six Sigma (GLSS)', receives great attention [4]. This can be explained by the popularity of the established DMAIC (Define, Measure, Analyze,

J. vom Brocke et al. (Eds.): DESRIST 2026, LNCS 16606, pp. 95–113, 2026.
https://doi.org/10.1007/978-3-032-28313-9_6

Improve, Control) cycle, which systematically structures GLSS projects along clearly defined phases. Furthermore, GLSS builds on techniques for data analysis, which is getting evermore important in times of Industry 4.0/5.0 [5]. However, due to the newness of the topic, there is no generally accepted GLSS standard yet [6]. Accordingly, it is unclear which quality techniques (e.g., Root-Cause-Analysis) are best suited for use in GLSS projects, or how established techniques can potentially be applied in a modified form to best achieve environmental sustainability goals. As a consequence companies often lack structured GLSS approaches that can be directly applied [7]. Likewise, there has been insufficient discussion of the appropriate codification and documentation of results in GLSS projects, an area where conceptual modeling can make a significant contribution. To address these gaps and to provide a means for the structured conduction of GLSS initiatives, we pose the following research question: *What might a modeling tool-based GLSS approach look like that offers quality techniques, designed as model types that support GLSS initiatives to achieve environmental sustainability goals?*

This study aims to design a GLSS approach based on conceptual model types and falls within the field of method engineering (ME) [8]. Generally ME and design science research (DSR) are closely linked [9], whereby ME focuses on the design, construction and adaption of methods, techniques and tools for IS development [8]. Transferring the idea of ME to GLSS, we implement our GLSS approach as a modeling tool prototype – an artifact we refer to as a modelling tool-based GLSS approach hereafter. Thereby, the GLSS approach itself represents a knowledge artifact, which gets instantiated through the prototype [9]. We refer to conceptual modeling because conceptual model types have proven to be highly valuable in QM for eliciting employees' process knowledge and documenting outcomes [10]. With this in mind, we propose a set of model types that systematically covers all stages of a GLSS initiative and refers to quality techniques from the traditional Six Sigma methodology [11]. We analyze how these quality techniques are used to promote environmental sustainability and whether they need to be modified to work accurately for GLSS. We use metamodels to highlight potential modifications and explain how they work in this particular context. These metamodels then form the basis for implementing the prototype. In line with *Goldkuhl and Karlsson* [9] we consider the metamodels and model types as method knowledge representations for our modeling tool-based GLSS approach. For process managers, this research provides a concrete, tool-based solution to conduct GLSS projects aimed at ensuring the environmental sustainability of business processes. From the perspectives of research and ME, this paper demonstrates what metamodels for selected quality techniques relating to environmental sustainability can look like and how they can be integrated into a holistic GLSS method.

The paper is structured as follows: First, foundations are explained before the research procedure is introduced. Then, the design and development of our solution are presented, followed by an evaluation using illustrative scenarios, expert feedback, and a usability study. The paper concludes with a discussion and an outlook.

2 Foundations

2.1 Green Quality and Green Lean Six Sigma (GLSS)

Enterprises are putting tremendous efforts into realizing environmentally sustainable work practices these days [12]. In this context, various approaches are discussed in the literature, including the use of information systems (IS) to support green transformation and concepts such as green manufacturing [13, 14]. Likewise the importance of QM to analyze as-is processes and convert these into eco-friendly should-be processes is widely recognized [4]. In view of this, it is surprising that the term 'green quality' has not yet been clearly defined. As a possible approach to give companies an idea of what 'green quality' is all about, *Gouda et al.* [15] propose a green quality framework that comprises the dimensions 'performance', 'reliability', 'conformance', 'durability', 'serviceability', 'traceability' and 'standardization'. Nevertheless, the project manager is currently particularly responsible for selecting the relevant quality dimensions and suitable quality techniques in accordance with the situation of the project [16]. An exemplary mapping of selected quality techniques to dimensions is shown in *Johannsen* [16] for instance. In this area, the GLSS method is based on the established 'Lean Six Sigma (LSS)' method, with a special focus on environmental quality objectives [7]. The term 'Lean' refers to the addition of Lean techniques [17] to 'Green Six Sigma' or 'Six Sigma'. Although there is no generally accepted GLSS standard, most projects are structured around the phases of the DMAIC cycle [6]. Therefore, the requirements of customers and stakeholders on a business process are specified in the Define-phase (D) and the project organization is set up. Process data is then collected and analyzed during the Measure-phase (M) to determine the level of goal achievement. Potential root cause problems for not reaching the project goals are subsequently identified in the Analyze-phase (A). Finally, improvement suggestions are developed in the Improve-Phase (I) and their effectiveness gets controlled during the Control-phase (C) [17]. Within all these phases, quality techniques are used to establish results (e.g., list of root cause problems) [11]. Thereby, a popular collection of 49 quality techniques in Lean Six Sigma is the so-called 7×7 toolbox, which contains 'management techniques', 'lean techniques' or 'design techniques' for instance [17]. However, some quality techniques undergo specific modifications when it comes to achieving environmental goals. For example, literature suggests to integrate environmental metrics (e.g., CO_2-emissions) into process flow diagrams to assess the carbon footprint of processed materials [18].

2.2 Conceptual Modeling and Environmental Sustainability

Conceptual modeling is a well-established technique in IS for supporting human communication and understanding as well as machine-based analysis in digital transformation [19]. It is based on general-purpose or domain-specific modeling methods that define how abstractions of a system under study are created by instantiating elements of a modeling language and how the resulting models can be processed by algorithms [19]. Due to the size of the models, these modeling methods are today offered in the form of modeling tools, which typically provide graphical editors for creating and modifying models [20]. Besides traditional applications in the field of enterprise modeling, where conceptual models serve to analyze all aspects of IS [21], most recently conceptual models were proposed for supporting the design and analysis of sustainable systems. In particular, models can be used to understand the multidimensional nature of sustainability and the trade-offs between different dimensions, to improve and control sustainability attributes, or to formalize ethical, legal, and equity principles [22].

Our GLSS approach will contribute to these aspects by integrating environmental sustainability aspects into process-oriented QM, more specifically model-based GLSS, from a holistic perspective. As such, to the best of our knowledge, it represents a first artifact for integrating environmental sustainability attributes into a modeling prototype for GLSS. For that purpose, we develop conceptual model types for selected quality techniques that are widely used in GLSS projects. We analyze the functioning and application of these quality techniques to achieve environmental goals and consider modeling constructs related to environmental sustainability. This research addresses a common challenge in practice, namely the lack of structured GLSS methods and guidelines for their construction [7, 18]. Following the ideas of ME, the proposed model types and metamodels represent GLSS method knowledge, which is consolidated into a knowledge artifact (GLSS approach) and instantiated in the form of a prototype [9].

3 Research Procedure

This study follows a DSR approach [23, 24] to prototypically develop a modeling tool, which supports the execution of GLSS projects with the help of conceptual model types. An overview of the procedure is given in Fig. 1, which adapts the steps as introduced by *Peffers et al.* [25]. The process is iterative as the findings from the evaluation are used to further develop the artifact (prototype) in future. The research is currently in the first iteration cycle of the process.

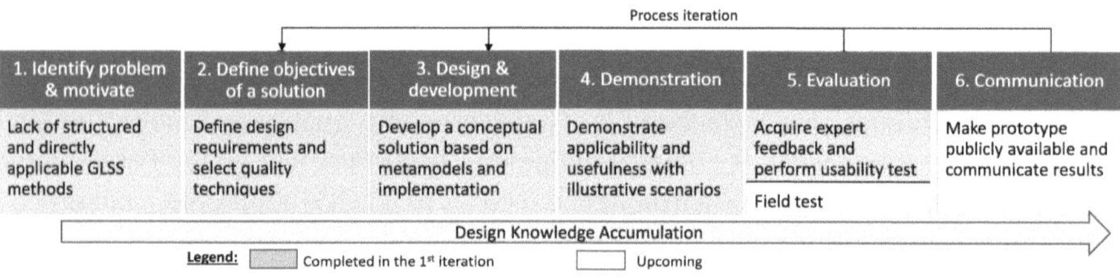

Fig. 1. Research procedure – adapted from *Peffers et al.* [25].

In the introduction, the problem is outlined and the research is motivated (step 1 – Fig. 1). In a second step, initial design requirements (DRs) for the prototype were derived by scrutinizing GLSS case studies from literature (step 2). Simultaneously, the DRs were reflected against quality techniques described in GLSS literature, and a set of techniques was selected to be incorporated into our GLSS approach. For the 'design & development' stage (step 3), it was analyzed how the quality techniques were used in GLSS projects to meet quality objectives related to environmental sustainability and whether the quality techniques were modified for this purpose in any way. Afterwards, these findings were used to transform the quality techniques into model types and corresponding metamodels. A prototype was then realized with the help of the freely available metamodeling platform ADOxx (adoxx.org). The general applicability and usefulness of the prototype were demonstrated by using two illustrative scenarios (cf. [26]) (step 4). This allowed us to check whether the modeling tool-based GLSS approach met the DRs, could address typical GLSS problem scenarios and to uncover any design drawbacks. Then, a first evaluation was performed in form of three written expert interviews and a System Usability Scale (SUS) [40] usability study (step 5). Further evaluations (e.g., field studies) will be conducted before releasing the artifact (step 6).

4 Objectives of a Solution

4.1 Literature Review

To come up with DRs for the modeling tool-based GLSS approach, a literature review was undertaken [27, 28]. For this purpose, the following databases were searched: *Emerald Insight, EBSCO Business Source Premier, Springerlink, AIS Electronic Library, IEEE Xplore* and *Science Direct*. These databases comprise the leading journals and conference proceedings in the field of entrepreneurial QM and were thus chosen for this study. We used the search terms 'Green Six Sigma', 'Green Lean Six Sigma' and combinations of the terms 'green' with 'quality technique' and 'quality tool' (e.g., 'green' AND 'quality technique'). The last three search terms were used to also cover the 'toolbox' perspective on Six Sigma that can be found in the literature [17]. In order to filter the 2197 publications found that way for relevance, titles and abstracts were scanned to find articles that clearly focused on the GLSS method, rather than casually mentioning GLSS without applying or analyzing the method in more detail. Also, we expected the publications to describe the application of at least one quality technique used in GLSS initiatives, as quality techniques form the basis of our modeling tool-based GLSS approach. For the remaining 45 publications, a forward and backward search [27] was performed, 11 additional articles were added that way, and finally a basic sample set of 56 publications was considered for a first iteration of the DSR cycle.

4.2 Definition of Design Requirements

To arrive at the DRs, case studies detailing the implementation of a GLSS initiative and outlining all the relevant steps of the GLSS project were filtered from the set of publications. This resulted in 24 case studies, which were scrutinized with the help of qualitative content analysis [29] to identify the milestones of a GLSS project. For each milestone a corresponding DR was defined, and categorized according to the phases of the DMAIC cycle. We refer to these DRs as 'project phase-related DRs' in the following. Table 1 gives an example. It presents three statements that highlight the specification of goals (related to customers, stakeholders and the environment) as a key milestone in a GLSS project. As shown, a corresponding DR was derived from this. Following this procedure, all statements across the included studies were coded and abstracted into the set of DRs as summarized in Table 2.

Table 1. Example for deriving project phase-related DRs

Author statements	GLSS milestone	Derived DR
"(…) The requirements, standards, needs and preferences of the customers and users are defined as "Voice of Customers" (VOC). (…)" ([30], p. 2173)	Goals with regards to customers, stakeholders and environment	**D1:** The specification of goals from the perspective of environmental sustainability, customer needs and stakeholder expectations must be enabled
"(…) For the Define phase, three key aspects are taken into account when defining the Six Sigma objectives of the particular case study. These are Voice of Customer (VOC), Critical to Quality (CTQ), (…) analysis (…)." ([4], p. 338)	*Same milestone*	*Contributes to same DR (D1)*
(…) The Define step is vital in embedding green goals into the improvement activities (…)." ([31], p. 773)	*Same milestone*	*Contributes to same DR (D1)*
…	…	…

In addition, DRs affecting the sound construction of the modeling tool-based GLSS approach were formulated using the established framework for method design requirements proposed by *Greiffenberg* [32]. We refer to these as 'general DRs' hereafter. Hence, general DRs regarding completeness (e.g., coverage of all DMAIC phases), intended purpose (e.g., adequacy for designing eco-friendly processes) and consistency (e.g., quality techniques are logically arranged) with regard to the modeling tool-based GLSS approach were specified. Table 2 provides an overview distinguishing between 'general' and 'project phase-related' DRs.[1]

---

[1] Additional information (supplementary material) can be provided by the authors on request.

Table 2. List of DRs (general & project phase-related)

General Design Requirements	Project phase-related Design Requirements *(derived from GLSS milestones)*	
Completeness (C)	**Define-Phase (D)**	**Improve-Phase (I)**
C1: Input/Output	**D1:** Specification of goals from the perspective of customers, stakeholders and the environment	**I1:** Classification of improvement suggestions
C2: Process	**D2:** Visualization of the process with environmental issues	**I2:** Prioritize suggestions
C3: Method elements	**D3:** Assignment of CTQ, CTB and CTE factors to corresponding quality dimensions	**I3:** Use of an action plan to organize the implementation of improvement suggestions
Purpose (P)	**Measure-Phase (M)**	**Control-Phase (Con)**
P1: Simplicity	**M1:** Definition of KPIs	**Con1:** Assignment of countermeasures to specific KPIs
P2: Structuredness	**M2:** Alignment of performance metrics and environmental goals	**Con2:** Define responsibilities to countermeasures
P3: Construction and language adequacy	**M3:** Precise operationalization of each KPI	**Examples for DR specifications:**
P4: Applicability and Comparability	**M4:** Analysis of performance data	**C2:** The modeling tool-based GLSS approach must cover all steps (DMAIC-phases) of a GLSS project.
Consistency (Co)	**Analyze-Phase (A)**	
Co1: Consistency in the procedure model	**A1:** Identification of problem causes	
Co2: Consistency of the result documents to be produced	**A2:** Prioritization of problem causes	**D1:** The specification of goals from the perspective of environmental sustainability, customer needs and stakeholder expectations must be enabled.
Co3: Support **Co4:** Concurrency	**A3:** Automated analysis of performance data	

4.3 Selection of Quality Techniques

A set of 107 quality techniques was then compiled from our basis sample set of 56 publications (see Sect. 4.1). All techniques were clustered in terms of their ability to support project phase-related DRs. For instance, the 'CTQ/CTB-Matrix' is a technique to support the fulfillment of D1 (Table 1), as it enables the analysis of requirements and the explicit specification of project goals [11]. Consequently, each project phase-related DR was assigned potential quality techniques for its fulfillment. Then, we used the following three filters to reduce the number of techniques to a manageable number for the prototype:

(I) First, we focused on those techniques with the highest number of mentions across all publications considered in our sample, as this was judged to be an important indicator of their acceptance in GLSS projects.

(II) Second, evaluations of quality techniques described in the literature were used to filter out those with the highest practicability ratings [33, 34].

(III) As a last filter, we considered a ranking of popular quality techniques that we had derived in a previous long-term Six Sigma collaboration with an automotive bank over a period of almost three years (cf. [35]). Using these three filters, the following set of quality techniques emerged: *SIPOC Diagram, CTQ/CTB-Matrix (Critical-to-Quality/Critical-to-Business) Matrix, Performance Indicators, Measurement Matrix, Data Collection Plan, Box Plots/Control Charts/Scatterplots, Ishikawa (Cause-and-Effect) Diagram, Failure-Mode-and-Effects Analysis (FMEA), Value Stream Map (VSM), Affinity Diagram* and *Reaction Plan.*

5 Design and Development

It was then analyzed how the above quality techniques were applied in GLSS projects and whether any modifications were made to the techniques for their application in the GLSS context in comparison to Six Sigma projects without a focus on environmental sustainability. For this purpose, all papers in the basic sample set (N = 56) were analyzed with respect to examples for the use of the mentioned quality techniques in GLSS (e.g., use cases). Further, any theoretical descriptions of modifications made to these techniques were of interest. Of the basic sample set, 27 publications provided corresponding examples or descriptions. To enhance this sample, the literature databases (see Sect. 4.1) were examined once more. Now, the names of the quality techniques above mentioned (e.g., 'SIPOC', 'FMEA', etc.) and the terms 'Green Six Sigma', 'Green Lean Six Sigma' and 'environmental sustainability' were used as search terms (e.g., 'SIPOC' AND 'Green Lean Six Sigma' AND 'environmental sustainability'). Six additional publications that were not yet considered were found. Hence, 33 publications were examined to analyze the use of the above mentioned (Sect. 4.3) quality techniques in GLSS projects or potential modifications made to them. Table 3 provides an example for a modification of the 'CTQ/CTB-Matrix' [11] in GLSS.

These findings were then used to create model types and metamodels for each quality technique that was selected for our modeling tool-based GLSS approach. For metamodel creation, the steps proposed by *Johannsen and Fill* [35] were followed. This included the identification of core concepts for each quality technique, an analysis of the interplay between the concepts to produce results, and finally the translation of these concepts into classes of a metamodel along with relationships and cardinalities.

Table 3. Example of the CTQ/CTB-Matrix in GLSS

Quality technique: 'CTQ/CTB-Matrix'
Description
The CTQ/CTB-Matrix summarizes the requirements of customers (VOC – Voice of the Customer) and stakeholders (VOB – Voice of the Business) and derives measurable targets from them, namely CTQ factors ('Critical-to-Quality') and CTB factors ('Critical-to-Business').
Identified modification for a GLSS project
It is proposed that the 'Voice of the Environment (VOE)' (e.g., reduced material usage, etc.) [36] be considered in addition to the 'VOC' or 'VOB' statements (customer and stakeholder needs). This results in the derivation of 'Critical-to-Environment (CTE)' factors, which capture environmental sustainability goals and complement the 'CTQ' and 'CTB' factors that determine the project goals from the perspective of customers and stakeholders.

Figure 2 exemplarily shows the derivation of the metamodel for the 'Green CTQ/CTB Model' for our approach, which is based on the 'CTQ/CTB-Matrix' (Table 3). Hence, the 'Green CTQ/CTB Model' condenses requirements from the perspective of customers, stakeholders and environmental sustainability (VOCs, VOBs and VOEs) to core statements, from which project goals are derived (CTQs, CTBs and CTEs). In the metamodel the concepts 'VOC', 'VOB' and 'VOE' were translated into corresponding classes. Similarly, this was done for the concepts 'core statement', 'CTQ', 'CTB' and 'CTE' factor and relationships and cardinalities were defined (markings 1–3). By that, the model type includes all required constructs to specify goals for a GLSS project from various perspectives as demanded by DR D1 (Table 1). In total 11 model types for GLSS were created that way to address our DRs. Additionally, synergies were identified between these model types at the metamodel level. Synergy was treated when the results produced and codified with the help of a model type were directly referenced and further processed by another model type. Hence, data transfer between different model types could be enabled in the prototype.

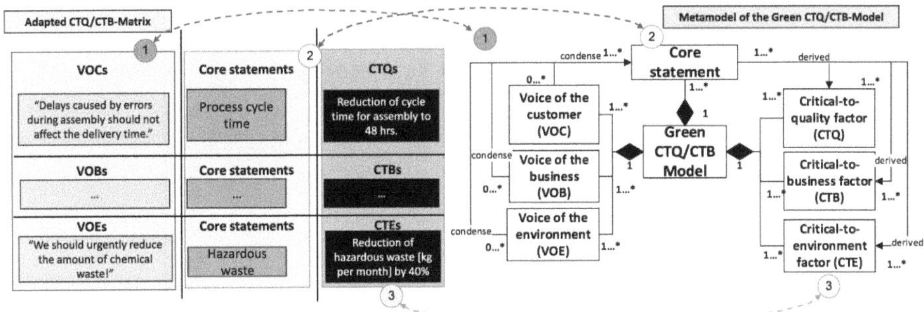

Fig. 2. Example of the Green CTQ/CTB Model (metamodel)

On the base of the integrated metamodel, which is shown in the Appendix, a first version of the prototype was developed by using the low code metamodeling platform ADOxx, allowing the easy realization of modeling tools [37]. Thereby, the metamodel concepts were transferred into corresponding ADOxx Library Language (ALL) classes, attributes and relations (cf. [38]). In the prototype, the user is guided through all DMAIC phases of a GLSS project, while the model types support in eliciting user knowledge to arrive at improvement suggestions, codifying knowledge and documenting results.

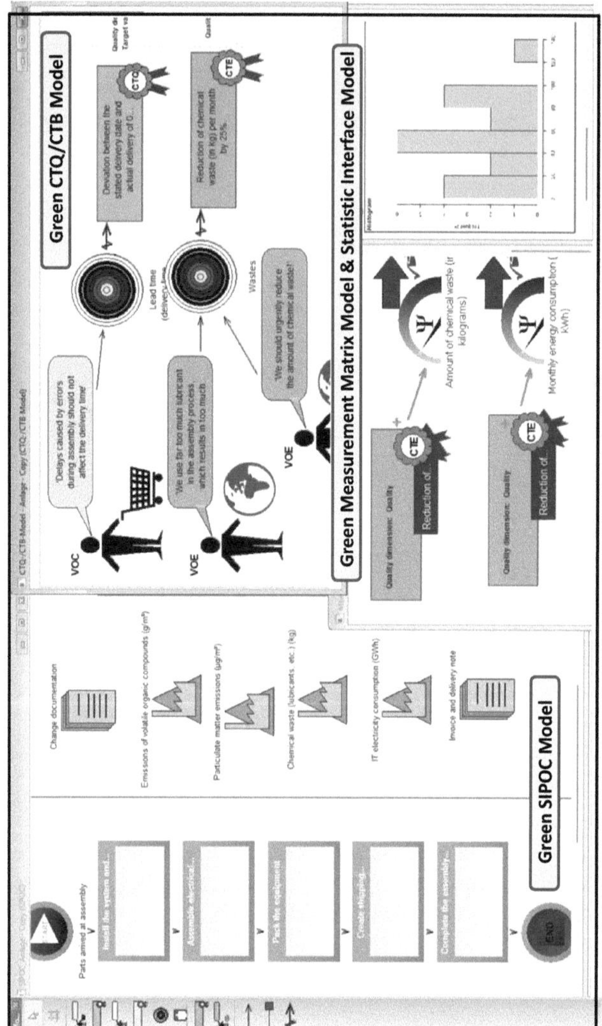

Fig. 3. Screenshot from the prototype

Figure 3 shows a screenshot of the implemented prototype and exemplarily illustrates instances of four model types. The excerpt from the 'Green SIPOC Model' provides an overview of the central process steps and their outputs including. Environmental emissions (e.g., particulate emissions). The 'Green CTQ/CTB Model' instance links VOCs and VOEs (e.g., 'we should urgently reduce the amount of chemical waste') to project goals (e.g., CTE: 'reduction of chemical waste (in kg) per month by 25%'). Further, the 'Green Measurement Matrix Model' enables the linking of quality goals to performance indicators (e.g., 'amount of chemical waste [kg/month]'). Once the relevant data has been collected, it can be imported into the prototype via a CSV interface for direct analysis or visualization using the 'Statistic Interface Model', which is enabled by coupling to the R environment (r-project.org).

6 Demonstration and Evaluation

6.1 Illustrative Scenarios

For demonstration purposes, two synthetic illustrative scenarios (cf. [26]) were created on base of process descriptions for industrial manufacturing as presented in *Staud* [39]. The first scenario was the 'parts production' process, and the second was the 'machine assembly' process. In line with *Peffers et al.* [26], syntactic illustrative scenarios are a well-established way of demonstrating the utility of an artifact by showing, how it works in a problem setting to solve an organizational issue.

Scenario 1 (Parts Production): The first scenario described a fictive company that has recently introduced an environmental management system (EMS) in response to market pressures and requirements from business partners. Additionally, high energy prices and rising waste disposal costs are driving the company to enhance its environmental performance. The parts production process also results in hazardous chemical substances, which must be stored, handled, and disposed according to the Hazardous Substances Ordinance. The goal was to significantly reduce the waste and lower costs.

Scenario 2 (Machine Assembly): The second scenario was an extension of the first, but focused on a different process. Following the introduction of the EMS, it became apparent that the environmental requirements imposed (e.g., the Energy Saving Ordinance) were not being met adequately. Furthermore, there had been repeated delivery delays in the past. The machine assembly process was identified as one of the core processes responsible for both the delays and the environmental emissions. The purpose of the scenario was to improve the process in order to reduce delay times and emissions.

Based on the scenarios, the logical arrangement of model types to solve organizational issues, as well as complete coverage of all DMAIC phases, could be acknowledged. However, weaknesses were identified during the scenario walkthroughs by the authors. For example, it was felt that different symbols should be offered to indicate the segregation of waste from other types of process input/output (e.g., physical components). Furthermore, it was suggested that highlighting environmentally-related KPIs would help distinguish them from other KPIs, such as cycle times. These revisions were made to the prototype before proceeding.

6.2 Expert Feedback

Following these revisions, the prototype was evaluated further with the help of three experts to ascertain its general usefulness and applicability. To this end, the prototype was presented at face-to-face meetings with a former process manager from the university administration department (that has anchored sustainability in its mission statement), who is now pursuing her PhD, a current process manager of the university administration, and a Data & BI specialist at an energy and automation technology group who has extensive experience in environmental sustainability projects. We consider these participants to be suitable experts for an initial evaluation, as they have gained a great deal of experience in modelling, optimizing and monitoring business processes in their work. The prototype was presented to the experts in individual meetings, its application was demonstrated using the illustrative scenario 'machine assembly' as an example, and a link was provided for independent testing of the prototype. Spontaneous questions could be answered immediately in the face-to-face meetings, and any uncertainties could be resolved. However, to obtain more precise and well-founded answers, the experts were asked to provide written feedback within a two-week period. This enabled them to engage with the prototype in more detail.

In summary, the experts considered the selection of the implemented quality techniques to be helpful for a GLSS project, since the available model types support every key activity in the DMAIC cycle. The integration of environmental aspects into quality techniques (Sect. 5) was considered effective in helping practitioners to better understand environmental-related inputs and outputs. Avenues for further development suggested the integration of prepared templates for typical GLSS use cases, along with information on statutory emission limits for certain industries during KPI definition. This would provide users with further guidance when working with the tool. Furthermore, the idea of a green KPI dashboard was proposed. Challenges for application in companies or institutions include insufficient conceptual modelling skills among the workforce, as well as the lack of availability of environmental-related measurement data. Furthermore, suggestions for change management on how to implement the derived process improvements could be provided. Furthermore, the tool should include mechanisms for data security. This feedback provided valuable insights into the artifact's applicability and usefulness, as well as opportunities for further development.

6.3 Usability Study

To supplement the feedback received so far, a usability study of the prototype, based on the SUS scale [40], was performed. The SUS scale was chosen as it has established as a well-recognized usability scale that can be applied rather quickly and provides results of high reliability [41]. The SUS questionnaire consists of ten items (alternately phrased positively and negatively), which are rated on a 5-point Likert scale (1: "strongly disagree" – 5: "strongly agree") [40, 41]. In this study, all SUS questions were formulated positively, as this has been shown to improve understanding for participants, resulting in findings that are easier to interpret [42]. The participants were ten Master's degree students of Management Information Systems (MIS) at a German university. Each student attended a course on 'Quality Management', which covered the fundamentals of GLSS and process improvement. As they have received dedicated training in the application of quality techniques from the Six Sigma toolset, the students can be regarded as proxies for practitioners in business process improvement. Previous studies have found students of this type to be adequate proxies for novice practitioners, meaning no prior knowledge needs to be considered [43, 44].

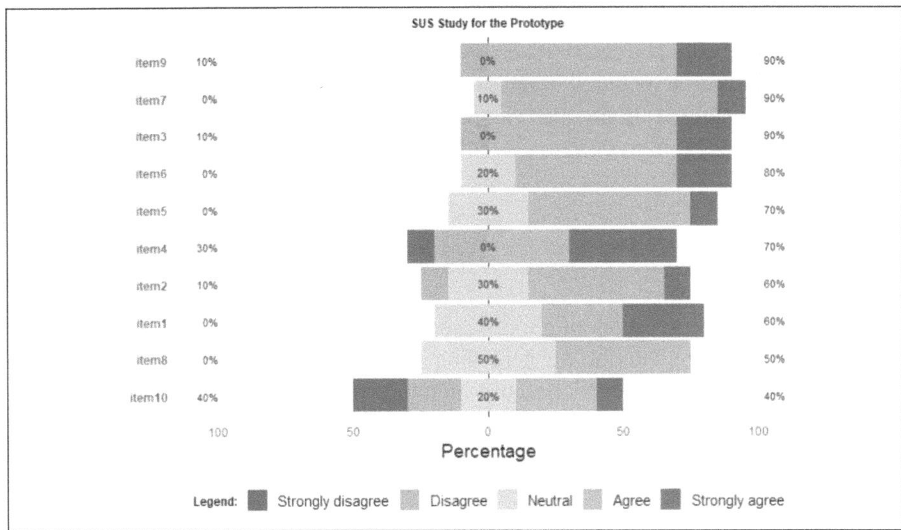

Positively formulated SUS items: *(https://www.handwerkwirddigital.de/wp-content/uploads/2022/02/System-Usability-Scale_Fragebogen.pdf)*
item 1: *"I think that I would like to use this system frequently"*; **item 2:** *"I found the software simple"*, **item 3:** *"I thought the system was easy to use"*, **item 4:** *"I think I could use the software without the help of a technically skilled person"*; **item 5:** *"I found the various functions in this system were well integrated"*; **item 6:** *"I think the software was very consistently designed"*; **item 7:** *"I would imagine that most people would learn to use this system very quickly"*; **item 8:** *"I found the software very intuitive to use"*; **item 9:** *"I felt very confident using the system"*; **item 10:** *"I was able to use the software without having to learn anything new"*.

Fig. 4. Results of the usability study

The material for testing usability was a case study based on the illustrative scenario 'machine assembly' as described above. Therefore, the students received a description of the process along with the problem situation. From an environmental perspective, the problems with this process were defined as excessive fine dust emissions, the production of too much chemical waste (lubricants, etc.) and the generation of a large amount of packaging waste. Furthermore, a reduction of defects during the assembly process as well as a reduction of process costs were required. Based on this information, students were supposed to develop suggestions for improving the process by following our GLSS approach. This included a precise definition of measurable project goals, the specification of KPIs, the identification of process weaknesses and the analysis of provided sample data amongst others. As an incentive to take the study seriously, students could earn a certificate of participation. Therefore, the students submitted their case study solutions after completion, which were reviewed by two lecturers to assess completeness and quality. In addition, students were asked to fill out the SUS questionnaire.

The results from the analysis is shown in Fig. 4. Overall, 90% of participants found the prototype easy to use and learn, and felt confident using it (items 3, 7 and 9). The prototype's design and offered functionalities were appreciated as well (items 5 and 6). However, in view of the disagreement expressed by some participants on items 4 and 10, hints to improve the usability of the software became apparent. For instance, the Statistic Interface Model type (see Fig. 3) works on base of a coupling to the software

R, whereby the path to it has to be set once. Based on the feedback received, this configuration step could be automatized. Further, students would have appreciated more supporting information included in the prototype to create model instances.

Overall the results from the interviews and the SUS study confirm the applicability and usefulness of the prototype in its current version. Though, suggestions for optimizing usability got evident, which we will realize in upcoming steps.

7 Discussion

This research proposes a modeling tool-based GLSS approach based on selected quality techniques that are suitable for achieving environmental objectives and have been designed as model types. This is because literature lacks general standards and recommendations for the operational conduct of GLSS projects. While there are a number of case studies in the literature that describe the conduction of company-specific GLSS projects, these do not address the construction of a GLSS method itself or do not show transferability of practices to other companies. Moreover, the appropriate codification and documentation of results in GLSS projects with the help of software is an under-researched topic. Hence, we see this study's contribution as follows:

First, given the mostly theoretical discussion on GLSS and the general lack of theories for 'green quality' we see our approach as an important step towards better understanding which quality techniques are promising for successfully achieving environmental-related process objectives and how these should be applied in this context. This can enable companies to develop their own customized GLSS approaches that are tailored to their business environment by carefully selecting and arranging promising quality techniques. This work thus adopts a ME perspective and applies it to GLSS, as it demonstrates how individual metamodels can be composed into a coherent GLSS method. In doing so, the metamodels represent GLSS method knowledge that researchers and practitioners can utilize to construct their own GLSS methods tailored to their organizational context.

Second, the research contributes to the discussion in the context of Industry 5.0 (cf. [45]), on how to make production processes environmentally sustainable, by proposing a modeling-tool based GLSS approach. This solution can help companies improve their resource efficiency and reduce their carbon footprint by analyzing business processes at the model level on base of the DMAIC cycle and with respect to environmental sustainability. Our modeling-tool based GLSS approach is novel for several reasons. As outlined in the introduction, it addresses the lack of generally accepted, operationalized GLSS methods. Further, it was designed against DRs that were derived from a comprising literature search to cope with the most current challenges and tasks in GLSS. Furthermore, the artifact leverages the advantages of conceptual modelling for systematically supporting business process improvement (cf. [46]). Prior research has shown that modelling-based tools can be beneficial in terms of usability and effectiveness compared to spreadsheet-based solutions (e.g., office applications enhanced with scripts such as VBA) that are freely available and widely used in practice [46]. This is highly relevant for GLSS, because with our solution users explicitly relate and visualize environmentally relevant concepts (e.g., VOE, CTE, CTQ, CTB, KPIs) to one another. Such an explicit representation positively influences cognitive processing and supports tasks that require the integration of multiple perspectives (environmental, customer, stakeholder), which are central to a GLSS initiative (cf. [46]). This structuring and relating of sustainability-specific concepts is what makes our solution particularly innovative, as knowledge about these explicit relations is essential for developing standardized GLSS approaches.

Third, metamodels have proven as helpful means to analyze and visualize the integration of environmental issues into established quality techniques (e.g., 'Voice of the Environment' into the CTQ/CTB-Matrix). This suggests depicting further quality techniques that have not yet been considered but are potentially relevant for GLSS as metamodels. It may then be possible to identify general patterns on this basis of how environmental aspects can be incorporated into quality techniques for environmental-oriented QM.

Accordingly, the feedback received will be used to further develop the modeling tool-based GLSS approach in upcoming steps. This will include providing information on how to use particular model types, along with templates for typical GLSS project scenarios in the prototype. Subsequently, the GLSS approach will be expanded to include additional quality techniques (model types) and filters to select quality techniques on demand based on parameters such as 'employee skill level', 'ease of learning' and 'process data availability'. This will enable companies to develop their own GLSS approaches with the help of the prototype, which they can then use straight away. After that, the prototype will undergo further evaluations in practical projects.

This research has limitations. As we are in the first iteration of the research cycle (Fig. 1), the DRs, together with the findings on the use and possible modifications of techniques in GLSS, were derived from literature. In addition, the prototype contains only a limited number of quality techniques. This number will increase as more quality techniques are going to be added in the future. Nevertheless, we think that a limited number of quality techniques is appropriate for a first version of the prototype, as this allows us to examine how the techniques work for environmental sustainability and interact in GLSS projects more closely.

8 Conclusion

In this work, a modeling tool-based GLSS approach was created and realized as a prototype to support practitioners in redesigning business processes to be more eco-friendly with the help of conceptual modeling. The next step of the research will entail the evaluation of the prototype in real-life projects at companies of varying sizes and from disparate industry sectors, with a view to ascertaining its applicability and usefulness. Moreover, the consistency of the prototype with its specification (integrated metamodel) is investigated at this juncture (cf. [47]). Based on the feedback obtained, modifications or enhancements of the metamodels will be conducted. This could subsume introducing a new concept 'Voice of the Government (VOG)' for industries highly regulated in view of environmental sustainability. The use of AI in model creation will also be a topic of discussion.

Acknowledgments. The authors would like to express their gratitude to the OMiLAB Nodes in Schmalkalden and Fribourg. Financial support for this research is gratefully acknowledged by the SmartLiving Lab (https://www.smartlivinglab.ch/en/) funded by the University of Fribourg, EPFL, and HEIA-FR.

Disclosure of Interests. The authors have no competing interests to declare that are relevant to the content of this article.

Appendix

The integrated metamodel shows all the metamodels created for the corresponding model types and the synergies between them enabling data transfer (references) (Fig. 5).

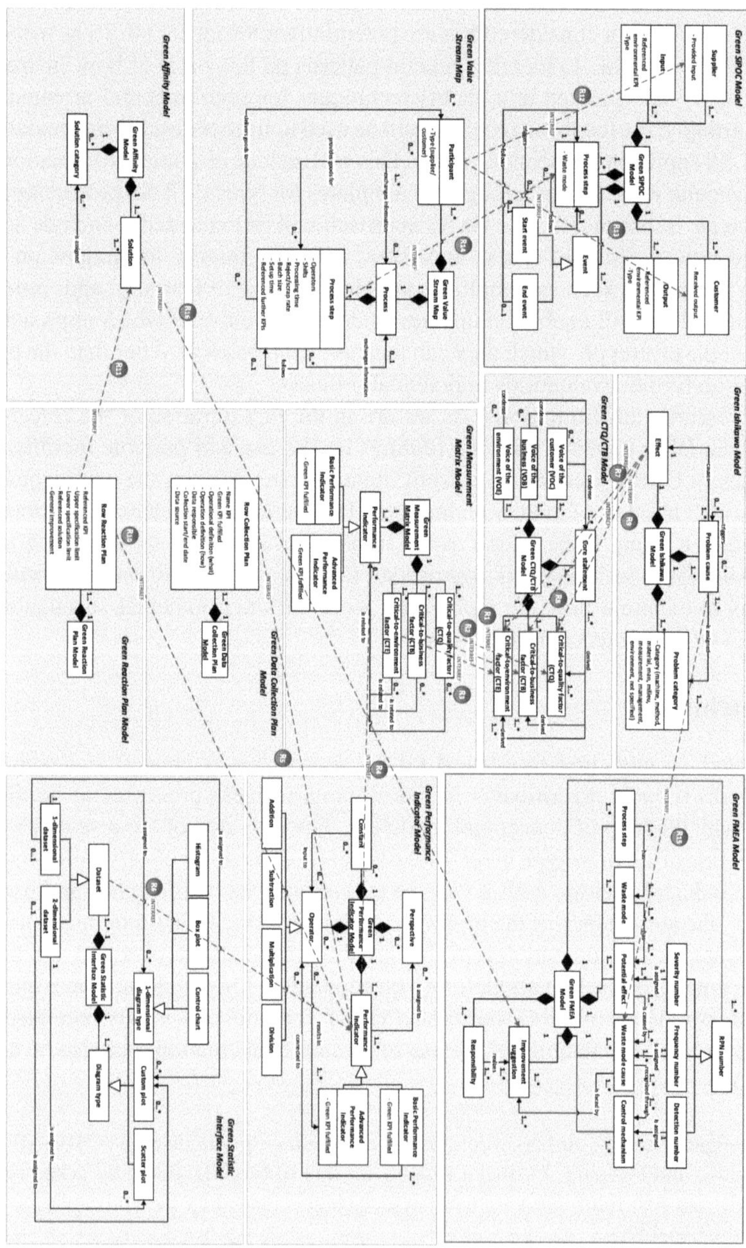

Fig. 5. Integrated metamodel of the modeling tool-based GLSS approach along with references

References

1. United Nations. https://www.undp.org/sustainable-development-goals. Accessed 28 Mar 2026
2. Albloushi, B., Alharmoodi, A., Jabeen, F., Mehmood, K., Farouk, S.: Total quality management practices and corporate sustainable development in manufacturing companies: the mediating role of green innovation. Manag. Res. Rev. **46**(1), 20–45 (2023)
3. Naeemah, A.J., Wong, K.Y.: Positive impacts of lean manufacturing tools on sustainability aspects: a systematic review. J. Ind. Prod. Eng. **39**(7), 552–571 (2022)
4. Delgadillo, R., Medini, K., Wuest, T.: A DMAIC framework to improve quality and sustainability in additive manufacturing—a case study. Sustainability **14**(1), 581 (2022)
5. Rajak, S., Kumar, P., Modi, A., Swarnakar, V., Antony, J., Sony, M.: An assessment of barriers to integrate lean six sigma and industry 4.0 in manufacturing environment: case based approach. Int. J. Comput. Integr. Manuf. **28**(3), 386–407 (2025)
6. Johannsen, F.: Green (lean) six sigma: an analysis and agenda for research from the perspective of method engineers. In: European Conference on Information Systems (ECIS 2024), Cyprus (2024)
7. Gaikwad, L.M., Sunnapwar, V.K.: Integrated lean-green-six sigma practices to improve the performance of the manufacturing industry. In: Concepts, Applications and Emerging Opportunities in Industrial Engineering. IntechOpen (2021)
8. Brinkkemper, S.: Method engineering: engineering of information systems development methods and tools. Inf. Softw. Technol. **38**(4), 275–280 (1996)
9. Goldkuhl, G., Karlsson, F.: Method engineering as design science. J. Assoc. Inf. Syst. **21**(5), 1237–1278 (2020)
10. Johannsen, F., Fill, H.-G.: Supporting knowledge elicitation and analysis for business process improvement through a modeling tool. In: 12. Internationale Tagung Wirtschaftsinformatik, Osnabrück (2015)
11. Lunau, S. (ed.): Six Sigma+Lean Toolset. Springer, Berlin (2013)
12. Yadav, V., et al.: Green lean six sigma for sustainability improvement: a systematic review and future research agenda. Int. J. LSS **14**(4), 759–790 (2023)
13. Deif, A.M.: A system model for green manufacturing. J. Clean. Prod. **19**(14), 1553–1559 (2011)
14. Gholami, R., Watson, R.T., Hasan, H., Molla, A., Bjorn-Andersen, N.: Information systems solutions for environmental sustainability: how can we do more? J. Assoc. Inf. Syst. **17**(8), 521–536 (2016)
15. Gouda, S.K., Awasthy, P., Krishnan, T., Sreedevi, R.: What does "green quality" really mean? TQM J. **31**(1), 52–69 (2018)
16. Johannsen, F.: Prozessorientiertes Qualitätsmanagement zur Gestaltung ökologisch nachhaltiger Geschäftsprozesse in Zeiten der sozialökologischen transformation. In: Gerth, S., Heim, L. (eds.) Entrepreneurship der Zukunft - Nachhaltigkeit durch digitale Innovation und Transformation. Springer/Gabler (2025)
17. Magnusson, K., Kroslid, D., Bergman, B.: Six Sigma the Pragmatic Approach. Professional Pub Serv. (2004)
18. Cherrafi, A., Elfezazi, S., Govindan, K., Garza-Reyes, J.A., Benhida, K., Mokhlis, A.: A framework for the integration of Green and Lean Six Sigma for superior sustainability performance. Int. J. Prod. Res. **55**(15), 4481–4515 (2017)
19. Fill, H.-G., Muff, F.: Bridging the mental and the physical world: conceptual modeling and augmented reality. In: Strecker, S., Jung, J. (eds.) Informing Possible Future Worlds - Essays in Honour of Ulrich Frank, pp. 197–212. Logos (2024)

20. Karagiannis, D., Lee, M., Hinkelmann, K., Utz, W.: Domain-Specific Conceptual Modeling: Concepts, Methods and ADOxx Tools. Springer, Cham (2022). https://doi.org/10.1007/978-3-030-93547-4
21. Sandkuhl, K., et al.: From expert discipline to common practice: a vision and research agenda for extending the reach of enterprise modeling. Bus. Inf. Syst. Eng. **60**(1), 69–80 (2018)
22. Bork, D., David, I., España, S., Guizzardi, G., Proper, H.A., Reinhartz-Berger, I.: The role of modeling in the analysis and design of sustainable systems: a panel report. Commun. Assoc. Inf. Syst. **54**(1), 911–936 (2024)
23. Tuunanen, T., Winter, R., vom Brocke, J.: Dealing with complexity in design science research: a methodology using design echelons. MIS Q. **48**(2), 427–458 (2024)
24. Gregor, S., Hevner, A.R.: Positioning and presenting design science research for maximum impact. MIS Q. **37**(2), 337–355 (2013)
25. Peffers, K., Tuunanen, T., Rothenberger, M.A., Chatterjee, S.: A design science research methodology for information systems research. J. Manag. Inf. Syst. **24**(3), 45–77 (2007)
26. Peffers, K., Rothenberger, M., Tuunanen, T., Vaezi, R.: Design science research evaluation. In: Peffers, K., Rothenberger, M., Kuechler, B. (eds.) DESRIST 2012. LNCS, vol. 7286, pp. 398–410. Springer, Heidelberg (2012). https://doi.org/10.1007/978-3-642-29863-9_29
27. Webster, J., Watson, R.: Analyzing the past to prepare for the future: writing a literature review. MIS Q. **26**(2), xiii–xxiii (2002)
28. Snyder, H.: Literature review as a research methodology: an overview and guidelines. J. Bus. Res. **104**, 333–339 (2019)
29. Mayring, P.: Qualitative content analysis. Forum Qual. Soc. Res. **1**(2), 1–10 (2000)
30. Talapatra, S., Gaine, A.: Putting green lean six sigma framework into practice in a jute industry of Bangladesh: a case study. Am. J. Ind. Bus. Manag. **9**(12), 2168–2189 (2019)
31. Belhadi, A., Kamble, S.S., Gunasekaran, A., Zkik, K., Touriki, F.E.: A big data analytics-driven Lean Six Sigma framework for enhanced green performance: a case study of chemical company. Prod. Plan. Control **34**(9), 767–790 (2023)
32. Greiffenberg, S.: Methodenbewertung mittels quality function deployment. In: Modellierung betrieblicher Informationssyteme (MobIS 2003), Bamberg, pp. 131–153 (2003)
33. Johannsen, F., Leist, S.: Evaluation ausgewählter qualitätstechniken in six-sigma-projekten. In: Moormann, J., Heckl, D., Lamberti, H. (eds.) Six Sigma in der Finanzbranche, pp. 361–379. Frankfurt School Verlag, Frankfurt a. M. (2009)
34. Hagemeyer, C., Gershenson, J.K., Johnson, D.M.: Classification and application of problem solving quality tools: a manufacturing case study. TQM Mag. **18**(5), 455–483 (2006)
35. Johannsen, F., Fill, H.-G.: Codification of knowledge in business process improvement projects. In: European Conference on Information Systems (ECIS 2014). Tel Aviv (2014)
36. Trappey, A.J., Ou, J.J., Lin, G.Y., Chen, M.-Y.: An eco-and inno-product design system applying integrated and intelligent QFDE and TRIZ methodology. J. Syst. Sci. Syst. Eng. **20**(4), 443–459 (2011)
37. Völz, A., Amlashi, D.M., Burzynski, P., Utz, W.: ADOxx: Eine Low-Code-Plattform für die Entwicklung von Modellierungswerkzeugen. HMD Praxis der Wirtschaftsinformatik **61**(5), 1295–1316 (2024)
38. Johannsen, F., Fill, H.-G.: Supporting business process improvement through a modeling tool. In: Karagiannis, D., Mayr, C.H., Mylopoulos, J. (eds.) Domain-Specific Conceptual Modeling, pp. 217–237. Springer, Heidelberg (2016). https://doi.org/10.1007/978-3-319-39417-6_10
39. Staud, J.: Geschäftsprozessanalyse mit Ereignisgesteuerten Prozessketten. Springer, Heidelberg (1999)
40. Brooke, J.: SUS-a quick and dirty usability scale. Usability Eval. Ind. **189**(194), 4–7 (1996)
41. Assila, A., Ezzedine, H.: Standardized usability questionnaires: features and quality focus. Electron. J. Comput. Sci. Inf. Technol. **6**(1), 15–31 (2016)

42. Perrig, S.A., von Felten, N., Vollenwyder, B., Opwis, K.: Development and psychometric validation of a positively worded german version of the system usability scale (SUS). Int. J. Hum. Comput. Interact. **41**(16), 10399–10419 (2025)
43. Parsons, J., Cole, L.: What do the pictures mean? Guidelines for experimental evaluation of representation fidelity in diagrammatical conceptual modeling techniques. Data Knowl. Eng. **55**(3), 327–342 (2005)
44. Gemino, A., Wand, Y.: A framework for empirical evaluation of conceptual modeling techniques. Requir. Eng. **9**(4), 248–260 (2004)
45. Maddikunta, P.K.R., et al.: Industry 5.0: a survey on enabling technologies and potential applications. J. Ind. Inf. Integr., 100257 (2021)
46. Johannsen, F., Mang, F., Fill, H.-G., Hofmann, S.: Tool-based codification in business process improvement and the impact on problem-solving. Enterp. Model. Inf. Syst. Archit. **18**(1), 1–30 (2023)
47. Sonnenberg, C., vom Brocke, J.: Evaluations in the science of the artificial – reconsidering the build-evaluate pattern in design science research. In: Peffers, K., Rothenberger, M., Kuechler, B. (eds.) DESRIST 2012. LNCS, vol. 7286, pp. 381–397. Springer, Heidelberg (2012). https://doi.org/10.1007/978-3-642-29863-9_28

Designing Mobile Applications for Spontaneous Volunteers: Insights from a Design Science Research Approach

Enrico Milutzki[1]([⊠]) [iD], Lucas Memmert[2] [iD], Marten Borchers[1]([⊠]) [iD], Ramazan Zeybek[1], Valeria Magdych[1], Martin Semmann[1] [iD], and Eva Bittner[2] [iD]

[1] University of Hamburg, Hamburg, Germany
{enrico.milutzki,marten.borchers,martin.semmann}@uni-hamburg.de,
{ramazan.zeybek,valeria.magdych}@studium.uni-hamburg.de
[2] University of Zurich, Zurich, Switzerland
lucas.memmert@uzh.ch, bittner@ifi.uzh.ch

Abstract. Spontaneous volunteers provide essential assistance during crises yet integrating them into official response structures remains challenging. This paper examines how a mobile application can support spontaneous volunteers' recruitment and coordination in storm surge scenarios. Following the design science research paradigm, we conducted a systematic literature review and six semi-structured interviews with citizens and emergency stakeholders to identify key issues. From this analysis, we derived design principles, which were instantiated in a high-fidelity Figma prototype. The prototype was evaluated with twelve participants using scenario-based walkthroughs with concurrent think-aloud and qualitative interviews. Findings confirm the value of centralized information, flexible registration, and accessible safety preparation, while also highlighting needs for moderated communication, configurable recognition mechanisms, and features for visual salience and social engagement. We articulate seven design principles that balance autonomy and oversight, reduce cognitive load, and foster trust. These contribute actionable guidance for designing digital systems that empower citizens and enhance disaster resilience.

Keywords: Crisis Response · Spontaneous Volunteers · Mobile Application

1 Introduction

Climate change represents one of the most pressing global challenges of our time, with profound implications for human societies and ecosystems alike. Global surface temperatures have already risen by about 1.1 °C since pre-industrial times and continue to increase [1]. Rising ocean temperatures accelerate evaporation and increase atmospheric moisture capacity, thereby intensifying rainfall [2]. At the same time, sea level rise is progressing, and more than 100 million people already live in areas below present-day sea level, a number projected to exceed 450 million by 2050 [3]. These developments pose growing risks to urban populations and critical infrastructures [4] and are closely

J. vom Brocke et al. (Eds.): DESRIST 2026, LNCS 16606, pp. 114–130, 2026.
https://doi.org/10.1007/978-3-032-28313-9_7

linked to the United Nations Sustainable Development Goals 11 on resilient cities and 13 on climate action [5].

Recent flood disasters since 2024 across the United States and Western Europe, including Germany, Spain, Poland, and the Czech Republic, with more than 466 fatalities and damages exceeding 4.2 billion euros, underscore the urgency of these challenges [4, 6–8]. While emergency management agencies provide warnings, evacuations, and relief, their capacities are often strained in the early phases of large-scale events. In such situations, spontaneous volunteers (SVs) emerge as an important resource, providing rapid assistance in search, rescue, and logistics [9, 10]. However, their integration remains difficult, as ambiguous responsibilities, missing communication channels, and safety concerns frequently limit their effective deployment [11, 12].

Digital crisis applications have the potential to support communication and coordination between institutions and citizens. Yet existing systems are still largely designed for one-way warning and information dissemination [13], while interaction, incident reporting, and volunteer coordination remain poorly supported [14, 15]. Prominent examples such as the mobile crisis apps NINA and KATWARN illustrate this gap: they are effective at broadcasting alerts but do not enable the structured recruitment and coordination of SVs. While prior research has established abstract design principles and theories for coordinating SVs [16], less is known about how such design knowledge can be operationalized in mobile crisis apps. To address this gap, we investigate the following research question (**RQ**):

RQ: How should a mobile application for citizens be designed to support their recruitment and coordination as spontaneous volunteers in storm surge scenarios?

To answer the **RQ**, we adopted the *design science research* (DSR) approach [17, 18]. Based on a literature review and interviews with citizens and emergency professionals, we identified key issues and derived design principles. These were instantiated in a functional prototype and evaluated using a mixed-methods study. Our findings show that mobile crisis applications can lower entry barriers, enhance safety, and support trustful coordination of SVs, while also revealing tensions between flexibility, oversight, and recognition. With this study, we contribute a situated instantiation as well as specific design principles for integrating SVs into emergency response scenarios.

The remainder of this paper is structured as follows. We first review related work on emergency management, spontaneous volunteering, and crisis applications. We then describe the research method and present the derived design principles and prototype. After reporting on the evaluation, we discuss the results in relation to existing research, outline limitations and future work, and conclude the paper.

2   Related Work

2.1   Spontaneous Volunteers in Disaster Management

SVs are individuals who engage in disaster response in a self-initiated and unpaid manner without formal affiliation to emergency organizations [10, 19, 20]. They often emerge directly at the disaster site, either as local residents or as unaffiliated helpers from outside the affected area [10]. While their motivation and local knowledge can be highly valuable, their lack of coordination with official structures creates risks such as overcrowding, misinformation, or unsafe behavior, a tension described as the involvement-exclusion paradox [12, 21]. To address this challenge, recent research has explored how digital platforms and crisis apps can support the structured integration of SVs by matching their skills and availability with operational needs and by enabling bidirectional communication and situational awareness [22–24]. Betke et al. [16] further formalized this design space by proposing a design theory for SVs' coordination systems. We extend this line of work by contributing situated design knowledge at the artifact level, showing how coordination principles can be instantiated and evaluated in a mobile crisis app used by citizens under time pressure and stress.

2.2 Emergency Management Phases

The existing literature on crisis and emergency management outlines various approaches and frameworks that can assist stakeholders and entire organizations in structuring their activities, thereby safeguarding human lives and minimizing damage to property and ecosystems. For this work, we follow the *emergency management phase*, as described by Rodrigues et al. [25], in which SVs can be integrated, as the framework relies on a set of capabilities and competencies organized into three phases: risk mitigation, response, and recovery (cf. Fig. 1).

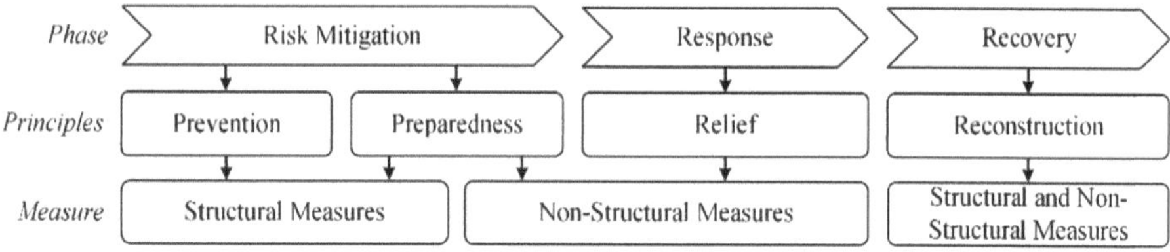

Fig. 1. Overview of the Emergency Management Phases, Principles, and Measures according to Rodrigues et al. [25].

The first phase of emergency management, *risk mitigation*, involves preventive and preparedness measures to address floods [25]. This includes structural interventions, such as dikes and flood protection gates, and non-structural approaches, such as contingency planning, training, and awareness campaigns. These tasks are typically managed by ministries of the interior and local authorities [26] and include activities to inform and raise awareness among citizens about existing risks and behavioral guidelines in case of emergencies. Moreover, this can also include training citizens as volunteer helpers, similar to SVs, but with the added feature of being registered in databases, allowing authorities to contact them if needed [27].

In the second phase, *response*, coordination is characterized by the rapid convergence of heterogeneous actors, emergent collaboration, and high levels of uncertainty, which often challenge formal command-and-control structures [28]. Coordinated efforts among agencies such as police and fire departments are essential for addressing immediate needs like search and rescue, food, medical care, and evacuations [29]. Communication and collaboration are critical during chaotic flooding events [4, 30], while emergency operation centers manage resources, logistics, and public communication [31]. At this stage, SVs become particularly visible by assisting affected individuals, disseminating information, organizing relief goods, or providing basic psychosocial support [10], sometimes spanning approximately 100,000 SVs within several weeks [11].

The final phase, *recovery*, focuses on restoring normal operations and strengthening resilience post-disaster [25]. It involves debris removal, utility restoration, and long-term rebuilding [32]. SVs also play an important role here, contributing to clean-up, reconstruction, and community support. In some cases, such efforts have even evolved into permanent organizations [10].

2.3 Existing Mobile Emergency Applications and Guidelines

Many mobile emergency applications exist, yet adoption remains limited and key operational requirements are often unmet [33]. In Germany, Katwarn and NINA have been widely deployed and evaluated [45]. While both systems cover a wide range of emergencies, they primarily provide generic information and offer little contextual adaptation or interaction. Users cannot easily contribute situational reports, which restricts the development of comprehensive situational awareness from within affected areas [34]. The FEMA app in the United States allows users to request assistance or access hotline support, but sustained bidirectional communication between citizens and emergency responders remains limited. At the same time, large volumes of user-generated data can create information overload, especially during high-stress events [35].

These shortcomings have motivated the development of design guidelines for disaster applications. Because such systems are used infrequently but under extreme stress, they must be immediately usable without prior training and remain functional under constrained conditions [36]. Prior work therefore emphasizes reducing cognitive load through simple, consistent interfaces with minimal input requirements [36], supporting situational awareness through context-sensitive and location-based information [37], and ensuring that critical alerts are salient through prioritization and visual or auditory highlighting [36]. However, existing mobile emergency applications and related design guidelines primarily address citizens in general, providing limited guidance on how mobile apps can operationalize the recruitment and coordination of SV in crisis conditions.

3 Methodology

Our research approach follows the DSR paradigm, a problem-solving approach that generates new knowledge by creating an innovative artifact. The outcomes of DSR consist of the artifact itself and the underlying design knowledge [18]. In this work, we apply DSR according to Kuechler and Vaishnavi [17], which involves the five phases illustrated in Fig. 2. One DSR cycle was conducted for this paper. In the first phase, *problem awareness*, we combined a systematic literature review with semi-structured interviews involving citizens and emergency experts, allowing us to draw both from a rich body of knowledge and the practical experience of potential users. This process identified issues in the recruitment and coordination of spontaneous volunteers, which in the *suggestion* phase were translated into meta-requirements and design principles guiding the design activities.

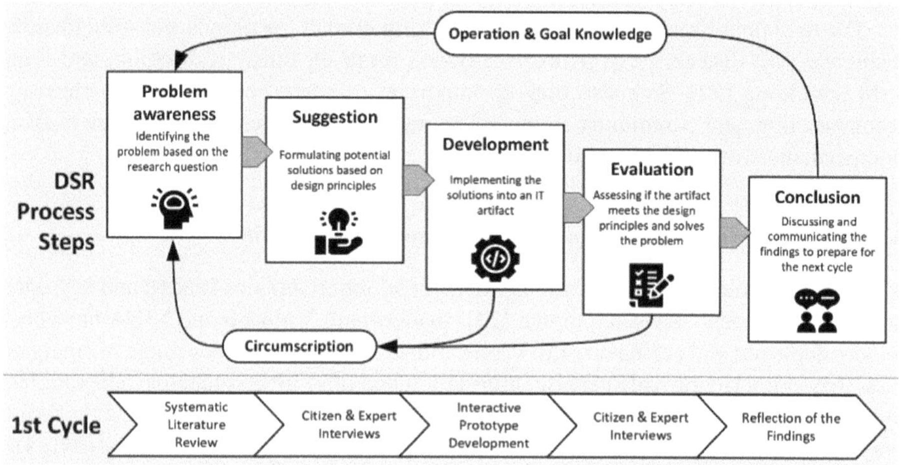

Fig. 2. Overview of Design Science Research and the conducted Steps [17].

The *development* phase translated these requirements and design principles into an interactive IT prototype using user-centered design practices. The evaluation phase employed a qualitative approach, with citizens and experts participating in semi-structured interviews combined with scenario-based walkthroughs using a think-aloud technique. The interviews examined how the prototype supported the intended design principles and provided in-depth insights into participants' perceptions and experiences. All interviews were recorded, if allowed, and analyzed following Mayring's qualitative content analysis, using paraphrasing as a core analytic technique [38]. Finally, in the conclusion phase, we elaborate and conclude on our findings in the context of the existing literature and knowledge base. In line with DSR, the following sections present the iterative progression from problem awareness to design knowledge and evaluation, rather than strictly separating method and results.

4   Awareness of the Problem and Suggestions

To explore the problem space of recruiting and coordinating SVs in disaster contexts, we combined a systematic literature review with a set of semi-structured interviews involving citizens and emergency stakeholders. The systematic review followed the established guidelines by Kitchenham and Charters [39]. We searched in three commonly used bibliographic databases: ACM Digital Library, ScienceDirect, and AIS Library. The search string was developed to align with the **RQ** and combine core concepts of spontaneous volunteering and crisis management: *("spontaneous volunteer" OR "ad-hoc volunteer")*

AND ("recruitment" OR "mobilization" OR "coordination" OR "organization" OR "management") AND ("storm surge" OR "disaster"). To ensure topical relevance, we restricted the search to publications from 2015 onwards, yielding an initial set of 202 records. We then applied successive filtering steps, including title and abstract screening, to ensure that the papers focused on crisis management, storm surges, and similar topics, thereby addressing the **RQ**. After this process, nine publications remained, which form the main body of insights synthesizing academic work and official reports on the challenges of engaging SVs.

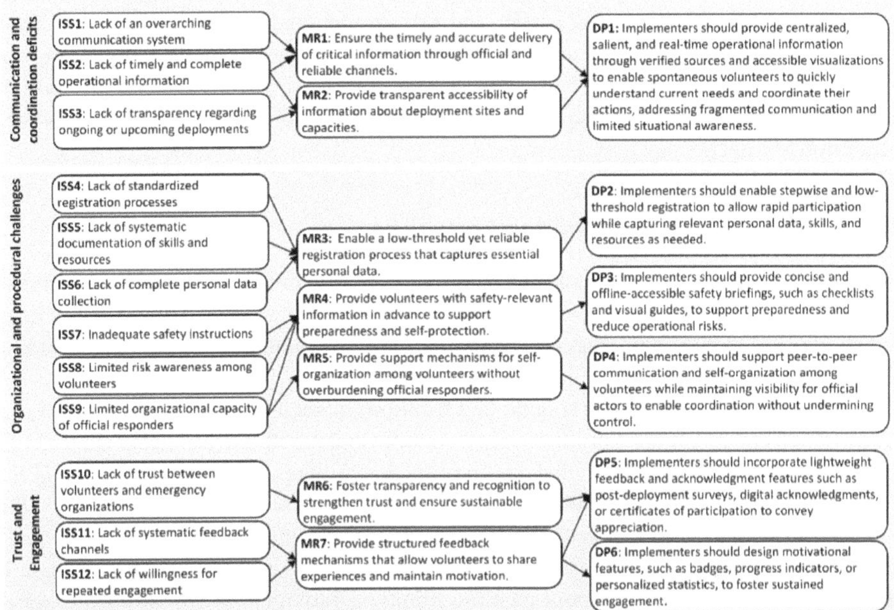

Fig. 3. Overview of the identified Issues (ISS), the formulated Meta-Requirements (MR), and the derived Design Principles (DP).

To extend the literature perspective and theoretical insights, we conducted six individual semi-structured interviews, including three citizens and three emergency stakeholders. Both groups comprised two men and one woman. The citizen participants were aged between 26 and 30, while the experts were aged between 29 and 41, representing emergency management, fire services, and governmental crisis response. The citizens' interviews captured perceptions and expectations of potential end users of a mobile application. In contrast, stakeholder interviews provided expert perspectives on floods, storm surges, and organizational practices in emergency response. The interviews allowed us to validate and contextualize the categories derived from the literature. For both the literature corpus and the interview transcripts, we applied structured qualitative content analysis [38], which integrates deductive and inductive coding. First, the literature was analyzed deductively to identify explicit issues reported in prior research. Second, the interview material was analyzed inductively to validate and, where appropriate, extend these categories with practice-oriented insights. Relevant passages were openly coded, consolidated across sources, and merged into subcategories, which were then grouped into overarching categories. This combined analysis produced three overarching categories, each comprising a set of issues (**ISS**). These issues informed the derivation of meta requirements (**MR**), which specify essential system capabilities, and design principles (**DP**), as summarized in Fig. 3. The design principles are formulated to reflect their intended aim, underlying mechanisms, and rationale in line with established DSR guidelines [40]. The categories should be understood as analytical lenses rather than mutually exclusive domains, as several **ISS**, **MR**, and **DP** cut across them, reflecting the socio-technical interdependencies of spontaneous volunteer coordination.The categories and their respective **ISS**, **MR**, and **DP** are detailed in Sects. 4.1 to 4.3. Data saturation, defined as the point at which no new subcategories or insights emerged, was reached early in the analysis. This was confirmed through iterative coder discussions and is consistent with prior research showing that saturation in qualitative studies may occur quickly [41].

4.1 Communication and Coordination Deficits

In the literature, a major issue identified is the lack of structured and coordinated communication across organizations involved in crisis management (**ISS1**). This issue has been widely discussed in prior research [12] and leads to insufficient official communication and coordination channels.

Many organizations rely on fragmented solutions or social media and messenger services, which can result in contradictory information and parallel streams that are difficult to monitor and control. As one incident commander explained: *"The organization in the <specific crisis name> was largely done via social media and messenger services. That can be useful, but it needs a central instrument, a platform that everyone can connect to"* (E2). A second recurring issue is the insufficient provision of operational details (**ISS2**). Critical information about meeting points, deployment times, or hazard zones often reaches SVs too late, incompletely, or not at all [10]. Related to this is a third difficulty, the lack of transparency regarding ongoing or upcoming deployments (**ISS3**). Without visibility into actual needs, SVs frequently make autonomous decisions about where to help, resulting in overcrowding at some sites while others remain underserved [10, 42]. From these issues, we derived two meta requirements. First, we call for a system that ensures the timely and accurate delivery of critical information through official and reliable channels (**MR1**), addressing the lack of an overarching communication system (**ISS1**) and the need for operational details (**ISS2**). **MR2** responds to **ISS2** and **ISS3** by emphasizing the need for transparent access to information on deployment sites and capacities. Building on these requirements, we formulated **DP1**, which integrates **MR1** and **MR2**. **DP1** highlights the need for salient and structured operational information, provided in real time and via verified sources, to counteract fragmented communication flows, strengthen situational awareness, and enable more coordinated SVs' participation.

4.2 Organizational and Procedural Challenges

A recurring issue concerns the lack of standardized registration processes for SVs (**ISS4**). Registration is often improvised and differs widely depending on local capacity, which creates legal uncertainty and complicates supra-regional coordination [11, 12]. Closely related is the insufficient documentation of skills and resources (**ISS5**). Specific competencies or equipment are rarely captured systematically, resulting in both underutilized potential and increased safety risks if SVs are assigned tasks without the necessary expertise and caution [10]. Even basic personal data is often collected only partially (**ISS6**), despite its importance for communication, insurance coverage, and accountability. As one incident commander emphasized: *"In flood zones, anything can happen, and it is essential to trace where people have been in case of insurance or health claims"* (E2). From these issues, we derived **MR3**, which calls for a low threshold yet reliable registration process that captures both essential personal data and, where possible, additional skills and resources. Building on **MR3**, we articulated **DP2**, which emphasizes the importance of stepwise registration: a minimal entry barrier for urgent deployment combined with the option to provide more detailed information later. This balances speed with reliability and enables better coordination. A further set of issues concerns the insufficient preparation and protection of SVs. Many engage without receiving adequate safety instructions (**ISS7**) or without sufficient awareness of risks and organizational procedures (**ISS8**), thereby exposing themselves and others to unnecessary hazards [12, 20]. To address this, we derived **MR4**, which emphasizes the need to provide SVs with safety-relevant information in advance, supporting both preparedness and self-protection. From **MR4** follows **DP3**, which highlights the value of concise digital safety briefings, such as checklists or visual guides. While it is not replacing in-person training, these resources can mitigate risks and enable safer participation. Finally, the limited capacity of official responders (**ISS9**) represents a significant organizational barrier. Emergency professionals are heavily burdened during large-scale events [11] and, as one expert noted, *"[...]cannot simultaneously handle our tasks and organize spontaneous volunteers. We need them (SV) to come as a ready-to-use package"* (E1). This issue informed **MR5**, which calls for mechanisms that enable SVs to organize themselves without overburdening official responders. Addressing **MR5**, we formulated **DP4**, which emphasizes horizontal communication and coordination tools among SVs, complemented by mechanisms that preserve visibility for official agencies. Group chats or broadcast functions can support self-organization, while prominently highlighted official messages ensure situational awareness and maintain authority.

4.3 Trust and Engagement

Another persistent issue described in the literature concerns the fragile relationship of trust between SVs and official emergency organizations (**ISS10**). A lack of communication and transparency can leave SVs with the impression that their support is unwelcome. At the same time, emergency professionals perceive uncoordinated assistance as disruptive, even though its necessity and potential are widely acknowledged [11, 12]. As one expert noted, *"We work within our structures. Our personnel are well-trained for these situations and speak the same language. Suddenly, many others arrive wanting to help,* *and synchronizing all of this has been, and still is, the greatest challenge"* (E2). This trust gap is amplified by the absence of systematic feedback channels (**ISS11**). Current communication remains largely top-down, without opportunities for SVs to provide feedback or engage in dialogue. As a result, experiences and lessons learned are not systematically captured, limiting the potential for improvement and recognition [12, 20]. Over time, such frustrations can reduce SVs' willingness to volunteer and engage again (**ISS12**). Prior research shows that a lack of appreciation and negative experiences undermine repeat engagement. This problem is particularly problematic as spontaneous, project-based SVs increasingly replace long-term organizational commitment [42].

From these issues, we derived two meta requirements. **MR6** emphasizes the need for transparency and recognition to strengthen trust and ensure sustainable engagement. **MR7** highlights the importance of structured mechanisms that allow SVs to share their experiences and maintain motivation over time. Building on these requirements, we formulated two DPs. **DP5** follows from **MR6** and **MR7** and therefore underscores the value of lightweight feedback and acknowledgment features, such as post-deployment surveys, digital acknowledgments, or certificates of participation. These not only contribute to system improvement but also convey appreciation. **DP6** builds on **MR7** and suggests the integration of motivational features, for instance, through gamification elements such as badges, progress indicators, or personalized statistics. While optional, such features can foster sustained engagement by making contributions visible and strengthening SV's sense of achievement. Together, these directions address the trust deficit and support the conditions necessary for recurring SV participation in future disaster scenarios.

5   Design and Development

To implement the proposed design principles as described in Sect. 4, we developed a mobile prototype as shown in Fig. 4. The prototype is designed as a citizen-facing mobile application for spontaneous volunteers and conceptually depends on backend integration with official emergency management systems to provide verified information and deploy tasks.

Guided by a user journey mapping approach [43], we structured the design into five stages that reflect the typical activities of SVs. Each stage was informed by user stories that captured volunteers' needs and goals, and iteratively refined through sketches, wireframes, and ultimately a high-fidelity click model in Figma. Figma enables the creation of a (mobile) web app that participants can explore interactively and, therefore, receive an authentic impression of the solution [44]. The visual style follows design recommendations for crisis apps [36], emphasizing clarity, robustness, and minimal cognitive load under stressful conditions. Across stages, the design strikes a balance between providing sufficient structure and leaving space for volunteer initiative.

The coordination map instantiates **DP1** (Information & Coordination) and **DP4** (Self-Organization & Communication), addressing issues of fragmented communication and unbalanced task distribution. It displays real-time information on available deployments, associated requirements, and current volunteer capacities, as partly shown in (Fig. 4a). A combination of filter and sorting functions enables users to identify suitable opportunities quickly. Volunteers can self-organize through group communication features, while official broadcasts are highlighted to maintain. The registration flow (Fig. 4b) implements **DP2** (Registration) by offering a stepwise process that requires only minimal personal data for immediate access while enabling optional input of skills and resources. This design acknowledges the urgency of storm surge scenarios, where time pressure should not prevent participation, and at the same time prepares the ground for competence-based task allocation.

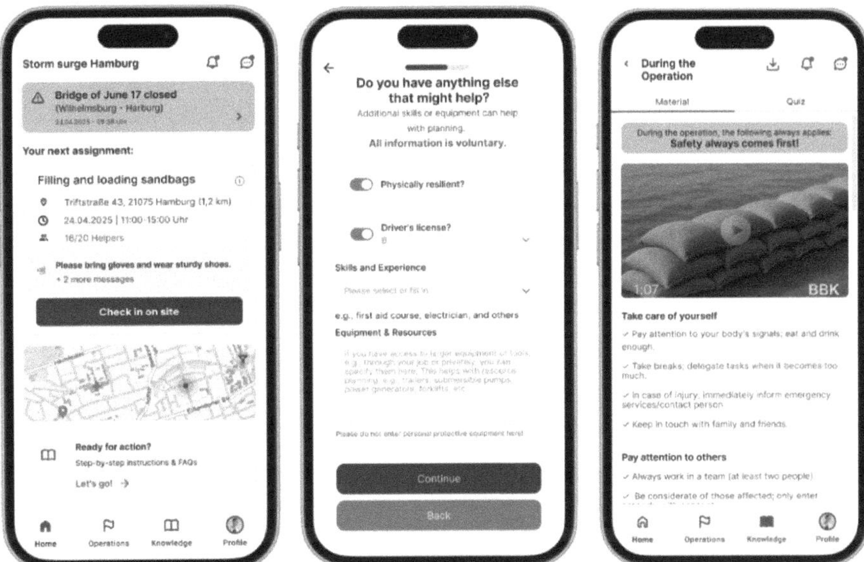

Fig. 4. Overview of the Prototype showing: (a) Home-Dashboard with volunteer activities (DP1, DP4), (b) Registration Process (DP2), and a (c) Safety Briefing (DP3).

The transparent presentation of required app permissions, such as location sharing and notifications, further supports trust in the system and its handling of personal data. To address gaps in safety awareness, the prototype includes a dedicated knowledge and briefing module (Fig. 4c). This feature embodies **DP3** (Safety Preparation) by providing concise checklists and visual guides covering core safety practices and common tasks such as filling sandbags. Content is designed for both pre-event preparation and in-situ consultation, with offline availability ensuring robustness in case of unstable networks. A progress tracker and badges make the learning process visible and reinforce motivation, directly supporting sustained engagement (**DP6**).

The reflection stage supports feedback and recognition. After deployment, SVs are encouraged to provide a lightweight evaluation through ratings and short comments. This feature responds to **DP5** (Feedback & Recognition) by establishing a feedback channel between SV and organizations and simultaneously signaling appreciation. In addition, the profile area documents past deployments, hours contributed, and training modules completed. Automatically generated certificates offer formal recognition, while gamification elements such as badges visualize progress and reinforce long-term motivation (**DP5, DP6**).

6 Evaluation and Findings

The evaluation examined how the prototype enacted the proposed design principles in use and served to validate, refine, and extend the design principles based on empirical feedback. To evaluate the prototype, we conducted a qualitative study based on in-depth interviews with twelve participants, comprising spontaneous volunteers and emergency experts (cf. Table 1).

Table 1. Overview of evaluation interviews conducted with citizens (C) and experts (E).

No	Age	Gender	SV Experience	Crisis App Experience
C1	30	M	No	NINA
C2	29	F	No	NINA
C3	26	M	No	NINA
C4	24	F	No	None
C5	22	M	No	None
C6	30	M	No	None
C7	27	M	No	None
C8	29	F	No	Katwarn

No	Age	Gender	Expert Background	Responsibility
E1	41	M	Fire Department	Crisis Response & Rescue Operations
E2	29	M	Technical Relief Agency	Emergency Management
E3	40	M	Fire Department	Crisis Response & Rescue Operations
E4	31	F	Government	Crisis Management Expert

The sample consisted of eight potential spontaneous volunteers without prior response experience and four experts from German emergency organizations at national and local levels. Two experts (E1, E2) participated in both the problem awareness and evaluation phases, while all other participants were distinct. Each participant explored the prototype in an individual remote session lasting 45–60 min. Participants were given direct access to the interactive Figma prototype via a web link and independently navigated through the interface during a scenario-based walkthrough with concurrent think-aloud. This ensured active interaction with the artifact rather than passive observation. All sessions were recorded, transcribed, and pseudonymized. Following the walkthrough, semi-structured interviews were conducted to capture participants' perceptions, experiences, and improvement suggestions [18]. All collected data were analyzed, and related statements were aggregated [38]. The evaluation examined how different aspects of the identified issues, meta-requirements, and design principles manifested in use. Regarding **DP1** (Information & Coordination), both citizens and experts praised the clarity of the information display. One SV appreciated that *"important information was quickly recognizable"* (S1), while experts stressed the value of structured overviews to avoid redundant deployments. However, experts also highlighted a missing requirement: tasks and information should be filterable by qualifications and skills to avoid mismatches between volunteers' capabilities and operational needs (E1, E2). This indicated that centralization alone was not sufficient; information needed to be targeted and adaptive to support effective coordination. In addition, several participants reported that, despite the structured presentation, it was not always immediately obvious which information was most critical in stressful situations. They called for stronger visual highlighting and clearer structuring of key elements to support rapid orientation and reduce cognitive load. This revealed a further limitation of **DP1**, namely that information availability and structuring alone do not guarantee perceptual salience under pressure. Based on this gap, we derive **DP7** (Visual Salience), which warrants further investigation due to its unclear implementation.

DP7: Implementers should visually highlight and clearly structure critical information to facilitate rapid orientation and decision-making under stress, reducing cognitive load in high-pressure situations.

DP2 (Registration) was widely perceived as practical and trustworthy. One expert described it as *"low threshold enough to be practical"* (E8). SVs valued the idea that only minimal information was required initially (C1, C3, C5, C6, C7), while experts appreciated the option of adding further details, such as skills or available resources, when needed (E1, E2, E3). Transparent consent dialogs were repeatedly mentioned as essential for building trust and willingness to share personal data in emergency situations (E1, E2, E3, E4). **DP3** (Safety Preparation) introduced digital safety briefings and offline materials. All participants in both groups considered these features highly valuable. SVs found them helpful for saving time and for orientation, and offline availability was seen as particularly important under unstable connectivity. Experts, however, stressed that digital briefings could only complement, but not replace, physical instructions and supervision on site (E2, E4). With respect to **DP4** (Self-Organization & Communication), which focused on peer-to-peer communication and self-organization through layered chat structures, six SVs welcomed the possibility to coordinate with others and to organize themselves, even if this required limited data sharing. Experts, by contrast, expressed concerns about misinformation and emphasized the need for temporary moderation mechanisms to ensure that communication remains reliable and does not undermine operational control. This indicated that while **DP4** enabled coordination, it did not fully address issues of trust, reliability, and sustained engagement. In particular, experts pointed out that volunteers would be more motivated and dependable if they could act together with people they already know, such as friends or family. Existing social ties were seen as increasing both commitment and confidence during spontaneous engagement. This revealed a gap in **DP4**, which supported interaction but not the formation of trusted social units. Based on this limitation, we introduce an additional design principle.

DP8: Implementers should enable volunteers to connect with trusted individuals or form ad hoc groups to strengthen motivation, reliability, and confidence, leveraging existing social ties to support engagement.

DP5 (Feedback & Recognition) and **DP6** (Motivation), which addressed feedback, recognition, and gamification, produced the most divergent reactions. Lightweight feedback mechanisms and digital certificates were generally perceived as meaningful and appropriate forms of acknowledgment (C1–C7). Experts cautioned, however, that feedback is only valuable if it leads to concrete action or learning (E1, E2, E4). Gamified elements such as badges and statistics divided opinion: while five SVs found them motivating, three considered them "out of place in a disaster context" (C1, C6, C7). These mixed reactions highlight the need for further specifications and refinement. In addition, feedback or, more generally speaking, information can also lead to an overflow and slow down reaction and action. Therefore, this mechanism should also be carefully provided in the context of the current emergency management phases (cf. Sect. 2.2), as the phase risk mitigation does not require fast action, while this is crucial in the response phase and in recovery also still of high value. Based on these insights and divergence, we refine both **DP5** and **DP6** as follows, to support transparency and engagement, with a phase-based approach.

Adjusted DP5: Implementers should incorporate lightweight, semi-automated feedback and acknowledgment mechanisms during *response* phases to ensure that spontaneous volunteers feel valued and recognized, strengthening trust and supporting continued engagement.

Adjusted DP6: Implementers should provide optional motivational features, such as badges, progress indicators, or personalized statistics, particularly in *risk mitigation* and *recovery* phases, to foster sustained engagement.

Across all design principles, participants consistently praised the prototype's reduced complexity and clear structure, often referring to its *"easy handling"* (C1, C2, C5, C6). Suggestions for improvement mainly focused on faster access to critical information and stronger visual salience in stressful situations (C3, C7, C8). Experts further suggested extending the application to better connect spontaneous engagement with longer-term volunteering opportunities. Overall, the findings indicate that the prototype was perceived as useful and usable, while also revealing several concrete directions for refinement.

7   Discussion and Conclusion

This paper addressed the **RQ,** "How should a mobile application for citizens be designed to support their recruitment and coordination as spontaneous volunteers in storm surge scenarios?" Following DSR, we developed design principles, instantiated them in a functional prototype, and qualitatively evaluated them. The positive reception by both volunteers and emergency professionals aligns with prior work in crisis informatics, showing that digital tools can lower participation barriers and support preparedness and coordination when they are embedded in institutional response structures [16]. Similar to earlier studies on mobile crisis applications [45], our findings indicate that citizen-facing systems can meaningfully contribute to emergency management beyond one-way warning infrastructures.

Beyond validating the general feasibility of this approach, the study revealed several fundamental tensions that are characteristic of crisis volunteering. Participants valued low-threshold access, autonomy, and self-organization, echoing observations on spontaneous volunteering in disasters [25]. At the same time, experts emphasized the need for filtering, moderation, and governance, which resonates with prior work on institutional control and accountability in digital volunteer coordination [22]. Motivational and recognition mechanisms were perceived as meaningful by some but inappropriate by others, reflecting the ambivalent role of gamification and incentives in crisis contexts discussed in earlier studies [11, 19]. Together, these tensions underscore that SVs' coordination is not merely a technical problem, but a socio-technical challenge that involves trust, responsibility, and situational stress.

Importantly, the resulting design implications span all phases of emergency management (cf. Sect. 2.2). Design principles related to onboarding and safety briefings (**DP2** and **DP3**) primarily strengthen preparedness and risk mitigation, as emphasized in prior work on disaster readiness and citizen education [25]. Design principles related to information consolidation, task coordination, and rapid orientation under pressure (**DP1**, **DP4**, **DP7**) mainly support the response phase, which aligns with established models of operational crisis management [45]. Finally, design principles related to feedback, recognition, and social connection (**DP5, DP6, DP8**) extend into recovery and longer-term engagement by fostering reflection, acknowledgment, community and continuity. This dimension has been highlighted as critical for sustaining volunteer involvement after disasters [19]. By covering the *preparedness*, *response*, and *recovery* phases in an integrated manner, the design responds to a long-standing ambition in crisis informatics to move beyond fragmented, phase-specific tools toward comprehensive digital support across the full emergency management cycle [45].

From a theoretical perspective, this study contributes a situated instantiation of design knowledge for mobile digital spontaneous volunteer recruitment and coordination by synthesizing insights from prior literature with empirical findings from a prototype evaluation. In doing so, the study contributes towards a nascent design theory in this domain, extending recent formalizations of design knowledge [46]. Rather than aiming for a system-level design theory, the contribution emphasizes context-sensitive, artifact-centered insights for citizen-facing mobile crisis applications [16]. From a practical perspective, the high-fidelity prototype illustrates how these insights can be instantiated in mobile crisis applications. For emergency management organizations and public authorities, the findings underline the importance of embedding mobile volunteer coordination tools into governance frameworks that define activation, oversight, and data protection, as argued in earlier work on institutional integration of crisis technologies [17, 22].

While the findings provide meaningful insights, the newly derived design principles (**DP7** and **DP8**) have not yet been fully instantiated or rigorously evaluated. In addition, the first design cycle resulted in a prototype rather than a fully operational application. This work reports on a first design cycle with a small and digitally literate sample, including a limited number of evaluation participants, which constrains generalizability, as is common in early-stage design research [47]. Moreover, the evaluation focused on qualitative insights derived from interviews and think-aloud sessions, which capture early perceptions but do not fully reflect long-term use or large-scale deployment in real crisis situations. Future research should therefore include larger and more diverse participant groups and incorporate richer adoption models such as UTAUT [48], as well as evaluate the system under more realistic conditions, such as disaster exercises or field simulations, as recommended in prior crisis informatics research [45].

In conclusion, this study provides actionable design implications for mobile applications that support the recruitment and coordination of spontaneous volunteers in storm surge scenarios. These insights offer practitioners valuable guidance for designing communication and coordination mechanisms for spontaneous volunteers and extend the existing knowledge base on mobile crisis applications. However, the limitations described should be acknowledged, and future research should focus on addressing these limitations and evaluating such applications in realistic emergency environments.

References

1. Intergovernmental Panel On Climate Change (IPCC): Climate Change 2021 – The Physical Science Basis: Working Group I Contribution to the Sixth Assessment Report of the Intergovernmental Panel on Climate Change. Cambridge University Press (2023). https://doi.org/10.1017/9781009157896
2. Wang, J., et al.: Atmospheric water vapor transport between ocean and land under climate warming. J. Clim. **36**, 5861–5880 (2023). https://doi.org/10.1175/JCLI-D-22-0106.1
3. Kulp, S.A., Strauss, B.H.: New elevation data triple estimates of global vulnerability to sea-level rise and coastal flooding. Nat. Commun. **10**, 4844 (2019). https://doi.org/10.1038/s41467-019-12808-z
4. Lourenço Neves, J.: Urban planning for flood resilience under technical and financial constraints: the role of planners and competence development in building a flood-resilient city in Matola, Mozambique. City Environ. Interact. **22**, 100147 (2024). https://doi.org/10.1016/j.cacint.2024.100147
5. Henriksen, H.Z., Thapa, D., Elbanna, A.: sustainable development goals in IS research. Scand. J. Inf. Syst. **33** (2021)
6. Center for Disaster Philanthropy: 2024 US Floods. https://disasterphilanthropy.org/disasters/2024-us-floods/. Accessed 01 Feb 2025
7. Hartmann, F.: So teuer könnten die Überschwemmungen in Mittel- und Osteuropa werden. https://www.fr.de/wirtschaft/so-teuer-koennten-die-ueberschwemmungen-in-mittel-und-osteuropa-werden-zr-93309508.html. Accessed 28 Oct 2024
8. Welz, F.: Nach der Flutkatastrophe protestieren Zehntausende in Valencia. https://www.tagesschau.de/ausland/europa/valencia-flut-protest-100.html. Accessed 11 Nov 2024
9. Twigg, J., Mosel, I.: Emergent groups and spontaneous volunteers in urban disaster response. Environ. Urban. **29**, 443–458 (2017). https://doi.org/10.1177/0956247817721413
10. Whittaker, J., McLennan, B., Handmer, J.: A review of informal volunteerism in emergencies and disasters: definition, opportunities and challenges. Int. J. Disaster Risk Reduct. **13**, 358–368 (2015). https://doi.org/10.1016/j.ijdrr.2015.07.010
11. Merkes, S.T., Zimmermann, T., Voss, M.: Whose disaster? Disaster response as a conflicted field between cooperation and competition. Int. J. Disaster Risk Reduct. **106**, 104459 (2024). https://doi.org/10.1016/j.ijdrr.2024.104459
12. Nahkur, O., et al.: The engagement of informal volunteers in disaster management in Europe. Int. J. Disaster Risk Reduct. **83**, 103413 (2022). https://doi.org/10.1016/j.ijdrr.2022.103413
13. Haunschild, J., Kaufhold, M.-A., Reuter, C.: Perceptions and use of warning apps – did recent crises lead to changes in Germany? In: Mensch und Computer 2022, Darmstadt Germany, pp. 25–40. ACM (2022). https://doi.org/10.1145/3543758.3543770

14. Kaufhold, M.-A., Reuter, C., Amelunxen, C., Cristaldi, M.: 112. Social: design and evaluation of a mobile crisis app for bidirectional communication between emergency services and citizens (2018). https://doi.org/10.26083/tuprints-00020741
15. Kotthaus, C., Ludwig, T., Pipek, V.: Persuasive system design analysis of mobile warning apps for citizens (2016)
16. Betke, H., Sperling, M., Schryen, G., Sackmann, S.: A design theory for spontaneous volunteer coordination systems in disaster response. Presented at the Hawaii International Conference on System Sciences (2024). https://doi.org/10.24251/HICSS.2024.258
17. Kuechler, B., Vaishnavi, V.: On theory development in design science research: anatomy of a research project. Eur. J. Inf. Syst. 17, 489–504 (2008). https://doi.org/10.1057/ejis.2008.40
18. Vom Brocke, J., Winter, R., Hevner, A., Maedche, A.: special issue editorial –accumulation and evolution of design knowledge in design science research: a journey through time and space. JAIS 21, 520–544 (2020). https://doi.org/10.17705/1jais.00611
19. Cottrell, A.: Research report - A survey of spontaneous volunteers. Australian Red Cross, Australia (2021)
20. Elkady, S., Hernantes, J., Muñoz, M., Labaka, L.: What do emergency services and authorities need from society to better handle disasters? Int. J. Disaster Risk Reduct. 72, 102864 (2022). https://doi.org/10.1016/j.ijdrr.2022.102864
21. Harris, M., Shaw, D., Scully, J., Smith, C.M., Hieke, G.: The involvement/exclusion paradox of spontaneous volunteering: new lessons and theory from winter flood episodes in England. Nonprofit Volunt. Sect. Q. 46, 352–371 (2017). https://doi.org/10.1177/0899764016654222
22. Kaufhold, M.-A., Reuter, C.: The self-organization of digital volunteers across social media: the case of the 2013 European floods in Germany. J. Homel. Secur. Emerg. Manag. 13, 137–166 (2016). https://doi.org/10.1515/jhsem-2015-0063
23. Lorenz, D.F., Schulze, K., Voss, M.: Emerging citizen responses to disasters in Germany. Disaster myths as an impediment for a collaboration of unaffiliated responders and professional rescue forces. Contingencies Crisis Manag. 26, 358–367 (2018). https://doi.org/10.1111/1468-5973.12202
24. Reuter, C., Kaufhold, M.-A., Leopold, I., Knipp, H.: Katwarn, Nina, or Fema? Multi-method study on distribution, use, and public views on crisis apps. Presented at the European Conference on Information Systems (ECIS) (2017)
25. Rodrigues, A.S., Santos, M.A., Santos, A.D., Rocha, F.: Dam-break flood emergency management system. Water Resour. Manag 16, 489–503 (2002). https://doi.org/10.1023/A:1022225108547
26. Federal Ministry of the Interior: The Crisis Management System in Germany. https://www.bmi.bund.de/EN/topics/civil-protection/crisis-management/crisis-management.html. Accessed 15 Nov 2024
27. Eriksson, K., Danielsson, E.: Framing volunteers identifying and integrating volunteers in crises response operations. Int. J. Disaster Risk Reduct. 74, 102912 (2022). https://doi.org/10.1016/j.ijdrr.2022.102912
28. Boin, A., Bynander, F.: Explaining success and failure in crisis coordination. Geogr. Ann. Ser. B 97, 123–135 (2015). https://doi.org/10.1111/geoa.12072
29. Bera, M.K.: Flood emergency management in a municipality in the Czech Republic: a study of local strategies and leadership. Nat. Hazards Res. 3, 385–394 (2023). https://doi.org/10.1016/j.nhres.2023.06.004
30. Bräker, J., Fischer, M., Semmann, M.: RescueMate – rethinking innovation in natural disasters: building an AI & data platform to better deal with storm surges. In: ICIS 2022 TREOs, Denmark (2022)
31. Feagan, M., et al.: Co-producing new knowledge systems for resilient and just coastal cities: a social-ecological-technological systems framework for data visualization. Cities 156, 105513 (2025). https://doi.org/10.1016/j.cities.2024.105513

32. Salvo, G., Karakikes, I., Papaioannou, G., Polydoropoulou, A., Sanfilippo, L., Brignone, A.: Enhancing urban resilience: managing flood-induced disruptions in road networks. Transp. Res. Interdiscip. Perspect. **31**, 101383 (2025). https://doi.org/10.1016/j.trip.2025.101383

33. Kangana, N., Kankanamge, N., De Silva, C., Mahamood, R., Ranasinghe, D., Goonetilleke, A.: Harnessing mobile technology for flood disaster readiness and response: a comprehensive review of mobile applications on the Google play store. Urban Sci. **9**, 106 (2025). https://doi.org/10.3390/urbansci9040106

34. Klafft, M.: Risk and crisis communication for disaster prevention and management (2017)

35. Navarro de Corcuera, L., del Mar Barbero-Barrera, M., Campos Hidalgo, A., Recio Martínez, J.: Assessment of the adequacy of mobile applications for disaster reduction. Environ Dev Sustain. **24**, 6197–6223 (2022). https://doi.org/10.1007/s10668-021-01697-2

36. Tan, M.L., Prasanna, R., Stock, K., Doyle, E.E.H., Leonard, G., Johnston, D.: Modified usability framework for disaster apps: a qualitative thematic analysis of user reviews. Int. J. Disaster Risk Sci. **11**, 615–629 (2020). https://doi.org/10.1007/s13753-020-00282-x

37. Bonaretti, D., Fischer-Pressler, D.: Timeliness, trustworthiness, and situational awareness: three design goals for warning with emergency apps. In: ICIS (2021)

38. Mayring, P., Fenzl, T.: Qualitative inhaltsanalyse. In: Baur, N., Blasius, J. (eds.) Handbuch Methoden der empirischen Sozialforschung. Springer VS, Wiesbaden, pp. 633–648 (2019). https://doi.org/10.1007/978-3-658-21308-4_42

39. Kitchenham, B., et al.: Systematic literature reviews in software engineering – a tertiary study. Inf. Softw. Technol. **52**, 792–805 (2010). https://doi.org/10.1016/j.infsof.2010.03.006

40. Gregor, S., Kruse, L., Seidel, S.: Research perspectives: the anatomy of a design principle. JAIS **21**, 1622–1652 (2020). https://doi.org/10.17705/1jais.00649

41. Guest, G., Bunce, A., Johnson, L.: How many interviews are enough?: an experiment with data saturation and variability. Field Methods **18**, 59–82 (2006). https://doi.org/10.1177/1525822X05279903

42. Lindner, S., Kuehnel, S.: Design and instantiation of IS2SAVE: an information system to predict the influx of spontaneous volunteers at operating sites. Presented at the Hawaii International Conference on System Sciences (2023). https://doi.org/10.24251/HICSS.2023.221

43. Samson, S., Granath, K., Alger, A.: Journey mapping the user experience. CRL **78**, 459 (2017). https://doi.org/10.5860/crl.78.4.459

44. Borchers, M., Tavanapour, N., Bittner, E.: Designing mobile applications for citizen participation in urban planning. Presented at the Hawaii International Conference on System Sciences (2023). https://doi.org/10.24251/HICSS.2023.054

45. Milutzki, E., Borchers, M.: Facing climate change: a literature review on crisis apps for warning and engaging citizens during storm surges. Presented at the PACIS (2025)

46. Gregor, S., Hevner, A.R.: Positioning and presenting design science research for maximum impact. MIS Q. **37**, 337–355 (2013). https://doi.org/10.25300/MISQ/2013/37.2.01

47. Legris, P., Ingham, J., Collerette, P.: Why do people use information technology? A critical review of the technology acceptance model. Inf. Manag. **40**, 191–204 (2003). https://doi.org/10.1016/S0378-7206(01)00143-4

48. Venkatesh, V., Thong, J., Xu, X.: The Hong Kong polytechnic university: unified theory of acceptance and use of technology: a synthesis and the road ahead. JAIS **17**, 328–376 (2016). https://doi.org/10.17705/1jais.00428

Design Principles for Trauma-Informed Information Systems for Refugees

Olena Ocheredko[1(✉)] [iD], Dominik Siemon[1] [iD], and Jamile Teles Hamideh[1,2] [iD]

[1] Lappeenranta–Lahti University of Technology LUT, Mukkulankatu 19, 15210 Lahti, Finland
{olena.ocheredko,dominik.siemon}@lut.fi,
jamile.teleshamideh@hanken.fi
[2] Hanken School of Economics, Arkadiankatu 22, 00100 Helsinki, Finland

Abstract. Information systems (IS) increasingly mediate refugee reception and integration, shaping access to legal status, healthcare, education, and employment. While IS research has examined digital divides, e-government, and sociotechnical inclusion, trauma remains largely absent from design-oriented theorizing, despite extensive evidence that forced displacement profoundly affects cognition, emotion, and trust. This study adopts a trauma-informed design perspective to investigate how integration-related IS are experienced by refugees. Following an echelons design science research (eDSR) approach, we ground prescriptive design knowledge in lived experience. Empirical data were collected through 35 interviews with Ukrainian adults residing in 22 Finnish cities and analyzed using qualitative content analysis informed by digital divide theory and trauma-informed design. The findings show that language barriers, fragmented information ecosystems, opaque system logic, repeated data requests, and rigid interaction flows transform routine administrative encounters into emotionally charged and high-risk experiences. Trauma-related vulnerability amplifies cognitive overload, fear of error, and avoidance, while informal human mediation emerges as a critical compensatory mechanism. Based on these insights, we derive seven empirically grounded design principles for trauma-informed IS, emphasizing emotional and cognitive safety, transparency and predictability, graduated engagement, integrated human mediation, linguistic and institutional legibility, data dignity and user agency, and ecosystem coherence. The study contributes intermediate design knowledge by articulating empirically grounded trauma-informed actionable design principles for IS.

Keywords: Information Systems · Design Principles · Trauma-Informed Information Systems · Refugees

1 Introduction

The increasing number of conflicts and natural disasters is currently leading to unprecedented levels of forced displacement. At the end of 2024, over 123 million people were forcibly displaced worldwide [1]. By the end of November 2025, the European

J. vom Brocke et al. (Eds.): DESRIST 2026, LNCS 16606, pp. 131–151, 2026.
https://doi.org/10.1007/978-3-032-28313-9_8

Union member states hosting the largest populations of people benefiting from temporary protection (TP) due to the war in Ukraine were Germany with approximately 1,241,000 people, Poland with around 968,750, Czechia with about 392,670, and Finland with 77,805 beneficiaries under TP [2]. These events are not only disruptive in socio-economic and political terms, but they are also profoundly traumatic experiences for people. Forcibly displaced populations are frequently exposed to multiple, cumulative forms of trauma, including violence, loss of family members, homes, prolonged uncertainty, and forced adaptation to unfamiliar institutional and cultural environments [3, 4]. Trauma can manifest in heightened stress, anxiety, post-traumatic stress disorder (PTSD), cognitive overload, emotional dysregulation, and diminished trust in institutions [5]. These effects shape how individuals process information, make decisions, and engage with information systems (IS) [6].

While IS have become critical infrastructures in the governance and facilitation of refugee integration across Europe and globally, IS mediate critical encounters between individuals and the state, from registering personal data and navigating legal entitlements to booking online appointments and accessing integration programs [7, 8]. However, while IS research has extensively examined digital inequality, e-government, and sociotechnical systems design in refugee contexts [7–9], the concept of trauma remains largely under-theorized in IS scholarship [10, 11]. This gap is particularly striking given that forced displacement profoundly affects cognition, emotion, and trust dimensions that fundamentally shape how individuals interact with IS. Prior research has shown that access to digital services does not automatically translate into meaningful use or inclusion [12–14]. Yet, the psychological mechanisms underlying these patterns of exclusion remain underexplored. For refugees who have experienced trauma, routine administrative interactions can become sources of distress, cognitive overload, and avoidance when systems are not designed with sensitivity to their needs [15, 16]. We therefore pose the following research question: **How can trauma-informed design principles manage and inform the development of IS that support refugee integration without retraumatization?**

Drawing on an in-depth qualitative study of Ukrainian refugees' encounters with IS in Finland, we examine how refugees experience IS, what forms of distress and disengagement emerge, and how design principles could foster emotional safety, trust, and agency. Finland, widely recognized as one of the most digitally advanced countries in the world, has invested heavily in e-government platforms, enterprise architectures, and interoperable public-sector systems. Refugee integration is managed through a hybrid ecosystem involving national authorities, municipal actors, NGOs, and volunteer initiatives, each relying on different IS to support functions such as application processing, housing, employment, and healthcare [17]. By grounding this investigation in Finland's highly digitalized public sector, this study contributes to IS research by: conceptualizing trauma as a critical, yet overlooked, dimension of IS use, developing empirically grounded design principles for trauma-informed IS, and demonstrating how digital divide theory and trauma-informed design can be integrated to analyze and improve IS in humanitarian contexts. Our findings reveal that language barriers, fragmented information ecosystems, repeated disclosure demands, and opaque system logic transform routine administrative encounters into emotionally distressing experiences for refugees. Trauma-related vulnerability amplifies cognitive overload and avoidance, while informal human mediation emerges as a critical compensatory mechanism. Based on these insights, we derive seven design principles emphasizing relational trust.

2 Theoretical Background and Research Gap

2.1 IS for Refugee Integration: Progress and Limitations

IS have become central to how refugee integration is managed and experienced. Across Europe and globally, digital platforms mediate access to housing, healthcare, education, employment, and legal status [7, 9, 18]. The IS literature has extensively examined both the potential and the limitations of digital technologies in refugee contexts, with particular attention to digital inequality, e-government, and sociotechnical systems design. A foundational lens in this domain is digital divide theory, which has evolved from an initial focus on disparities in physical access to technology (first-level divide) to encompass differences in digital skills and forms of use (second-level divide), and further to inequalities in the social, institutional, and life outcomes enabled through technology (third-level divide) [13, 19, 20].

Research in refugee contexts has shown that even when refugees are technically connected, they may remain excluded from meaningful engagement with digital IS [9]. Andrade and Doolin [9] demonstrated that while ICTs can support social inclusion, they simultaneously create new forms of exclusion when systems presume linguistic proficiency, institutional familiarity, and stable living conditions. Similarly, Pethig and Kroenung [8] showed that specialized systems designed for "disadvantaged users" may unintentionally stigmatize their users, reinforcing social markedness and avoidance behavior. Despite these advances, the digital divide literature has primarily focused on structural and skills-based barriers. While we know that access alone is insufficient for inclusion, we know less about why refugees disengage from systems even when they have the necessary skills and infrastructure. This gap points to the need for a complementary lens that foregrounds users' emotional and psychological experiences. Trauma-informed design offers precisely this complementary lens, as discussed in the following section.

2.2 Trauma-Informed Design: A Missing Lens in IS

Trauma-informed approaches have gained traction in healthcare, education, and social services as frameworks for designing services that do not inadvertently retraumatize vulnerable populations [20, 21]. In computing, trauma-informed design has recently emerged as a critical perspective. Chen et al. [15] introduced the concept of trauma-informed computing (TIC), arguing that digital systems can inadvertently retraumatize users when emotional safety and predictability are not addressed. They propose that TIC principles can guide system design to avoid retraumatization, enhance emotional safety, and promote user empowerment. Similarly, Randazzo et al. [16] demonstrated how trauma-informed design can be applied to online spaces, emphasizing that digital environments are not neutral but can either mitigate or exacerbate trauma depending on how they are designed. Despite its promise, trauma-informed design has limitations. Tseng et al. [22] argue that TIC principles are often too diffuse for prospective system design, being better suited for retrospective analysis than guiding real-time development. There is no standardized metric to assess the impact of TIC-informed systems on user well-being, and trade-offs may exist between principles such as safety and enablement. Nevertheless, TIC provides a promising foundation for embedding trauma-awareness into IS, especially when paired with participatory approaches that involve users in co-design and iterative evaluation [15, 22].

2.3   Synthesis and Research Gap

Taken together, Sects. 2.1 and 2.2 reveal two parallel bodies of knowledge that have not yet been integrated: digital divide research, which documents structural and skills-based barriers but leaves the psychological dimensions of exclusion underexplored, and trauma-informed design, which addresses emotional safety but has not been applied to institutional IS for refugee integration. Our study addresses this gap by asking the main research question and by integrating digital divide theory and trauma-informed design as dual analytical lenses, we examine how refugees experience integration-related IS, and we develop empirically grounded design principles that respond to the psychological dimensions of digital exclusion. Figure 1 illustrates how first-, second-, and third-level digital divides intersect with trauma-informed principles.

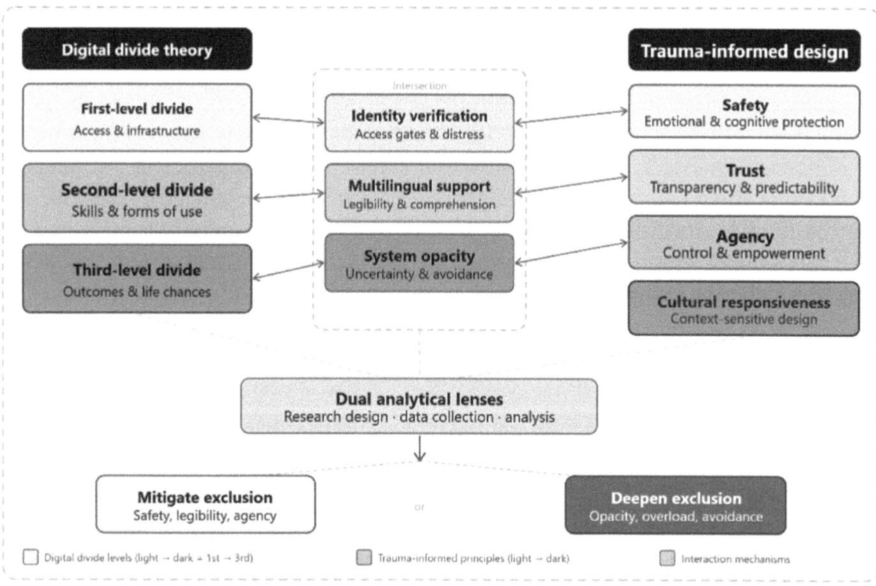

Fig. 1. Theoretical framework – digital divide theory and trauma-informed design.

The framework guided our research design, data collection, and analysis. In particular, it enabled the examination of how identity verification processes, multilingual support, and system opacity interact with trauma-related vulnerabilities to either mitigate or deepen digital exclusion.

3 Methodology

3.1 Research Approach and eDSR Framework

Our study adopts an eDSR approach to develop prescriptive design knowledge in the form of design principles for trauma-informed IS supporting refugee integration [23]. The eDSR framework is particularly suited for complex sociotechnical contexts characterized by heterogeneous users, evolving institutional arrangements, and emotionally charged interactions. Following Tuunanen et al. [24], this paper focuses on the problem analysis and the derivation of initial design principles key outputs of early echelons in the DSR process. This foundational work sets the stage for future instantiation, evaluation, and refinement of the design principles in subsequent research cycles.

3.2 Data Collection

To examine how IS shape refugee integration through a trauma-informed lens, we adopted a qualitative research design. We conducted 35 semi-structured interviews with Ukrainian refugees residing in 22 cities across Finland between February 1 and April 8, 2025. Interviews lasted between 25 and 60 min and were conducted in Ukrainian and Russian, with participants given full choice over interview language to ensure accessibility and emotional comfort. Interviews were conducted using a combination of online (Google Meet, Microsoft Teams) and in-person formats, depending on participant preference and location.

Participants were recruited through multiple channels to ensure inclusivity, such as social media groups for Ukrainians in Finland (Telegram, WhatsApp), snowball sampling through initial participants. Ages ranged from 20 to 63 years. To protect anonymity, interviewees are referenced throughout the paper using participant identifiers (e.g., U1…U35). Participants included both individuals who had arrived in Finland after February 2022 and who had TP status under temporary protection directive, representing diverse lengths of stay, family compositions, and geographic locations across Finland. Participants were asked to reflect on their interactions with all IS used for integration purposes. This included: public e-government portals, municipal and healthcare systems, employment platforms, educational platforms, etc. This broad operationalization allowed participants to describe their full range of digital experiences rather than being limited to a predefined set of systems.

3.3 Ethical Considerations

Given the sensitive nature of trauma-related discussions and the vulnerability of the participant group, ethical safeguards were central to our research design. The study was conducted in accordance with ethical research principles of LUT University. Key ethical measures included that participants received study information and consent forms in

Ukrainian, detailing voluntary participation, data protection procedures, right to pause or withdraw anytime and anonymity assurances. Written consent was obtained before each interview. The research team created a safe interview atmosphere by building rapport before sensitive discussions, allowing participants to guide the conversation, avoiding unsolicited probing on traumatic events, and monitoring for distress. All interview recordings and transcripts were stored securely on university servers with restricted access. Identifying information was removed during transcription, and participants are identified only by anonymized codes in all outputs.

3.4 Data Analysis

Data were analyzed using qualitative content analysis following Mayring's [25] methodological framework, supported by the software Atlas.ti. This approach was selected because it enables a systematic integration of deductive and inductive coding, aligning well with the study's dual theoretical objectives. The analysis followed a structured process. First, interviews were transcribed using Transkriptor, with transcripts initially produced in the original interview language. Transcripts were subsequently translated into English using DeepL, followed by manual review for accuracy and contextual meaning by the research team, which includes native Ukrainian speakers.

Second, a deductive-inductive coding scheme was developed. Deductive codes were derived from digital divide theory (e.g., "access barriers," "skill limitations," "outcome inequalities") and trauma-informed design principles (e.g., "safety concerns," "trust issues," "agency"). Inductive codes emerged from the data to capture unanticipated themes. Codes capturing institutional barriers to access or skills were assigned to the digital divide dimension, while codes capturing emotional and psychological responses to those barriers were assigned to the trauma-informed dimension. Where both dimensions were simultaneously present, for instance, when a skill barrier triggered avoidance rather than a workaround, the data point was flagged as an intersection node, signaling high relevance for design principle derivation.

3.5 From Data to Design Principles: The Analytic Pipeline

To ensure transparency in how empirical insights were translated into design principles, we followed a systematic analytic pipeline. This pipeline consisted of five steps:

Step 1: Open coding. In the first step, we conducted open coding of interview transcripts. Step 2: Theme development. Through iterative discussion and grouping, we consolidated open codes into higher-level themes. This process involved clustering related codes and identifying patterns across participants. Key themes included: linguistic barriers, fragmented information ecosystem, opaque system logic, repeated data requests, administrative transitions, uncertainty about future, informal mediation.

Step 3: Problem specification. For each theme, we specified the core problem in terms of its manifestation and impact. For example, under linguistic barriers, we identified the problem: "Administrative content available primarily in Finnish or Swedish, with machine translation insufficient for complex concepts, leads to fear of non-compliance and error." Step 4: Design objective/requirement derivation. We translated each problem specification into a design objective or requirement. Continuing the example, we derived:

"IS must provide linguistic and institutional legibility, not just translation, enabling users to understand administrative concepts, legal implications, and practical consequences." Step 5: Design principles abstraction. Finally, we abstracted related requirements into design principles using the anatomy proposed by Gregor et al. [26]. This involved articulating each principle's aim, context, mechanisms, enactors, and rationale. Requirements that addressed similar mechanisms were grouped into a single design principle (e.g., requirements for transparency and predictability were integrated into DP2).

4 Results

4.1 Linguistic and Institutional Barriers

Across interviews, language emerged as the most pervasive barrier shaping refugees' interactions with IS. Participants consistently reported that official websites, applications, and platforms were available primarily in Finnish or Swedish, with limited or unreliable translation options. Machine translation tools were frequently described as insufficient for understanding complex administrative content: *"When you download the app or page, it's only in Finnish... Google can't translate correctly." (U14)*

Language inaccessibility transformed routine administrative tasks such as filling out forms, booking appointments, or understanding eligibility criteria into sources of anxiety and fear of error: *"Every day there is stress because you don't know if you understood correctly." (U21)*. Importantly, participants emphasized that literal translation was insufficient. Administrative concepts, legal categories, and institutional responsibilities were often unfamiliar, and machine translation tools failed to convey their practical implications: *"It translates the words, but I still don't understand what they want from me. What is 'municipality of residence'? Why does it matter? Nobody explains." (U18)*

Administrative content presented primarily in Finnish/Swedish, with machine translation insufficient for complex institutional concepts, leads to fear of non-compliance, loss of benefits, and emotional distress. Misunderstanding legal and administrative terms has potentially severe consequences, transforming routine interactions into high-stakes encounters. IS must provide linguistic and institutional legibility not just translation. This requires simplifying administrative language, contextualizing legal and institutional terms, explaining institutional roles and decision authority, and supplementing or replacing machine translation with interpretive support. This requirement is the foundation for DP5: Design for Linguistic and Institutional Legibility, Not Mere Translation. These language-related challenges were further compounded by the fragmented nature of the information landscape refugees had to navigate, as described in the following section.

4.2 Fragmented Information Ecosystems

Information was scattered across multiple platforms, requiring repeated searches, logins, and authentication steps. Participants described confusion and exhaustion when navigating what they perceived as an opaque digital landscape: *"You google in Finnish and get redirected to a million sites." (U3)*. As a result, refugees frequently relied on informal

IS, such as Telegram and Facebook groups, as primary sources of information. While these networks offered accessibility and peer support, participants also expressed concerns about misinformation and lack of trust: *"Sometimes I find a lot of information on Facebook... but I can't trust it a lot." (U31)*

Information required for integration is distributed across multiple uncoordinated platforms, causing confusion, exhaustion, and over-reliance on informal sources of uncertain reliability. The resulting requirement is not simply centralization, but greater *coherence, cross-referencing, and transparency across IS*, such that refugees can reliably assess the credibility of information and understand how different services and platforms relate to each other. This requirement is the foundation for DP7: Design for Ecosystem Coherence Rather Than Platform Completeness. The cognitive and emotional burden of this fragmentation became especially acute when refugees were required to repeatedly re-disclose personal information as they moved between systems, an issue examined in the next section.

4.3   The Burden of Administrative Transitions and Repeated Disclosure

Administrative fragmentation is particularly pronounced during the first year of arrival, as individuals are often required to move between multiple service systems, reception centers, municipal services, education providers, health and employment-related institutions, and, in many cases, across municipalities. These transitions frequently necessitate repeated re-disclosure of personal histories and circumstances: *"First we live in help center in Helsinki, then we moved to another municipality and then we transferred to another city for Finnish courses, because it was so far from our town and then my husband find a job and get a permanent contract and we moved to another city." (U7).* This burden is particularly evident in healthcare interactions, where continuity of care is disrupted by relocation: *"I have three children, we moved three times, it's so difficult for me to explain their health situation to nurse and to doctor and then again and again." (U34)*

This dynamic is especially significant in the context of war-related trauma. Many participants reported ongoing symptoms such as nightmares months after arrival, and some explicitly expressed a preference to avoid verbal recounting of their experiences, favoring minimal communication or digital form-based interactions. Repeated data requests and requirements to re-disclose personal histories across uncoordinated systems cause distress, particularly for trauma-affected individuals for whom recounting experiences may be harmful. IS must support data dignity and user agency by minimizing redundant data collection, clearly explaining data usage, and providing users with control over how their information is shared across systems. This requirement is the foundation for DP6: Enable trust through data dignity and user agency. Beyond the burden of disclosure itself, the opacity of administrative processes, unclear timelines, unexplained delays, and unpredictable decisions, constituted a further and distinct source of psychological distress, as described next.

4.4 Opaque System Logic and Institutional Uncertainty

Psychological distress extended beyond initial displacement and was closely tied to ongoing uncertainty surrounding TP status. Participants described a prolonged inability to plan for the future, resulting in chronic anxiety: *"You cannot plan your life." (U6).* The annual renewal of TP reinforced a sense of instability, with participants expressing fear about what would happen next: *"Every year they extend it, but what happens after? This is our everyday problem and fear for future... because we wanted to stay here, he has a job, our children learning at school, they speak Finnish even better than I." (U12)*

Participants consistently reported distress caused by unclear decision processes, unexplained delays, and lack of transparency about application statuses and timelines. Unclear system logic, unexplained delays, and lack of transparency about administrative processes heighten anxiety and contribute to avoidance behavior, particularly for trauma-affected populations who are sensitive to unpredictability. IS must be transparent and predictable, explicitly communicating procedural steps, process stages, application statuses, and consequences of user actions. This requirement is the foundation for DP2: Make system logic transparent and predictable. The uncertainty produced by opaque system logic not only caused emotional distress but also directly exacerbated the cognitive overload that refugees experienced when attempting to complete administrative tasks, which is the focus of the next section.

4.5 Cognitive Overload and Rigid Interaction Demand

Many refugees experienced exhaustion, concentration difficulties, and avoidance when systems required sustained attention or immediate completion of complex tasks. Trauma-related cognitive load reduced tolerance for prolonged or high-stakes interaction: *"When I see a long form with many questions, I just close it. I come back later, but sometimes I forget." (U20).* Participants described difficulty concentrating on administrative tasks when emotionally distressed, and the inability to pause and resume processes without penalty created additional stress. Systems that require sustained attention, impose time pressure, or penalize incomplete interactions cause cognitive overload and disengagement among trauma-affected users. IS must support graduated engagement and user-controlled pace, allowing users to decompose complex tasks into manageable steps, pause and resume processes without penalty, and avoid strict time constraints. This requirement is the foundation for DP3: Support graduated engagement and user-controlled pace. Faced with these cognitive and emotional barriers in formal IS, many refugees turned to informal human networks as a primary coping mechanism, a pattern that reveals an important and underappreciated dimension of the refugee integration ecosystem, explored in Sect. 4.6.

4.6 The Critical Role of Informal Human Mediation

Despite their challenges, participants demonstrated significant resilience and adaptive capacity. Volunteers, churches, and local communities played a crucial role in facilitating integration, providing emotional, informational, and practical support where formal systems fell short: *"Volunteers helped more than our center, originally Finns helped a lot." (U5).* Participants repeatedly expressed gratitude toward Finnish society and emphasized the importance of human contact alongside digital services: *"It'll be good if we can have some platform or website where we can find answers and Finnish friends."* *(U26).* Refugees consistently rely on informal human mediation to interpret digital information, verify decisions, and cope with emotional stress. Formal IS often treat these practices as "workarounds" rather than as legitimate components of the sociotechnical system. IS must integrate human mediation as a legitimate design element, explicitly providing pathways to human support (volunteers, caseworkers, interpreters) rather than treating human mediation as a system failure. This requirement is the foundation for DP4: Integrate Human Mediation as a Legitimate Design Element.

4.7 Summary: Problem Specification and Design Objectives

Table 1 summarizes the problem specifications and derived design objectives that form the basis for the design principles presented in the next section.

Table 1. Problem specifications and design objectives

Theme	Problem Specification	Design Objective
Linguistic and institutional barriers	Translation insufficient for complex administrative concepts; fear of error	Linguistic and institutional legibility
Fragmented information ecosystems	Information scattered across uncoordinated platforms; over-reliance on informal sources	Ecosystem coherence
Repeated disclosure	Repeated data requests across uncoordinated systems cause distress	Data dignity and user agency
Opaque system logic	Unclear processes, delays, and lack of transparency heighten anxiety	Transparency and predictability
Cognitive overload	Sustained attention demands and time pressure cause disengagement	Graduated engagement and user-controlled pace
Informal mediation	Reliance on informal support networks as workarounds	Integrated human mediation

5 Design Principles for Trauma-Informed IS

Building on the problem specifications and design objectives summarized in Table 1, this section presents seven design principles for trauma-informed IS supporting refugee integration. Following the eDSR logic [24], each principle synthesizes empirically grounded insights into actionable means-end guidance that can inform the design, evaluation, and refinement of refugee-facing IS across contexts. Each principle is presented using the anatomy proposed by Gregor et al. [26], specifying its aim, implementer and user, context, mechanisms, enactors, and rationale.

DP1: Prioritize Emotional and Cognitive Safety Before Administrative Efficiency. IS supporting refugee integration should prioritize emotional and cognitive safety over administrative efficiency, ensuring that system interactions do not induce fear, overload, or retraumatization. Empirical findings demonstrate that refugees' interactions with IS are frequently accompanied by anxiety, fear of making irreversible mistakes, and cognitive overload. Participants described routine digital tasks, such as completing forms, booking appointments, or interpreting eligibility rules as emotionally distressing experiences, particularly when systems were linguistically inaccessible or procedurally opaque. Trauma-related vulnerability amplifies the cost of errors and uncertainty, transforming ostensibly neutral administrative interactions into sources of psychological strain. The following table presents DP1, presented according to the anatomy of a design principles by Gregor [26] (Table 2).

Table 2. DP1: Prioritize Emotional and Cognitive Safety.

Component	Specification
DP Title	DP1: Prioritize Emotional and Cognitive Safety
Aim, Implementer, and User	For implementers of refugee-facing IS to allow emotional and cognitive safety during system interaction for refugee users, particularly those affected by trauma and displacement
Context	In highly digitalized public-sector refugee integration contexts, where IS mediate access to legal status, healthcare, education, and employment, and where users may experience trauma-related stress, cognitive overload, linguistic barriers, and institutional uncertainty
Mechanisms	Design IS interactions that (1) minimize cognitive load during high-stakes administrative tasks, (2) avoid time pressure and irreversible actions, (3) reduce fear of errors through clear feedback and recoverability, and (4) limit exposure to emotionally distressing content during routine system use. These mechanisms may involve interface structure, process flow design, task decomposition, and interaction pacing
Enactors	Digital systems and interfaces that structure interaction flows; public-sector organizations configuring and governing IS processes; human support actors

(continued)

Table 2. (*continued*)

Component	Specification
Rationale	Empirical findings show that refugees frequently experience anxiety, fear of mistakes, and cognitive overload when interacting with IS, transforming routine administrative tasks into emotionally distressing encounters. Realizing this principle requires not only interaction design choices but also organizational policy decisions, including configuring administrative workflows that allow for recoverability, avoid penalizing incomplete submissions, and empower caseworkers to override rigid system rules when user distress is evident

DP2: Make System Logic Transparent and Predictable. IS should communicate system logic, procedural steps, and consequences of user actions in a transparent and predictable manner, enabling users to anticipate outcomes and maintain a sense of control (Table 3).

Table 3. DP2: System Logic Transparent and Predictable.

Component	Specification
DP Title	DP2: Make System Logic Transparent and Predictable
Aim, Implementer, and User	For implementers of refugee-facing IS to enable predictability and sensemaking in system interaction for refugee users, allowing them to anticipate outcomes and maintain a sense of control over administrative processes
Context	In public-sector refugee integration settings characterized by complex bureaucratic procedures, multiple interconnected IS, legal uncertainty, and trauma-affected users who are particularly sensitive to unpredictability, delays, and opaque decision-making
Mechanisms	Design IS to (1) explicitly communicate procedural steps and process stages, (2) provide clear and continuous feedback on application status and timelines, (3) explain the consequences of user actions before submission, and (4) signal delays, system changes, or decision points in advance. These mechanisms may involve process visualization, status indicators, explanatory messages, and structured information architecture across platforms
Enactors	Digital IS that present procedural information and feedback; public authorities configuring workflows and decision processes; organizational actors responsible for maintaining consistency and alignment across interconnected platforms

(*continued*)

Table 3. (*continued*)

Component	Specification
Rationale	Empirical findings show that unclear decision processes, unexplained delays, and fragmented information flows cause significant distress among refugees. Transparency and predictability therefore serve as core design conditions that support sensemaking and mitigate uncertainty in complex institutional environments

DP3: Support Graduated Engagement and User-Controlled Pace. IS should allow refugees to engage at their own pace by supporting graduated interaction, optional pauses, and the ability to resume tasks without penalty (Table 4).

Table 4. DP3: Support Graduated Engagement and User-Controlled Pace.

Component	Specification
DP Title	DP3: Support Graduated Engagement and User-Controlled Pace
Aim, Implementer, and User	For implementers of refugee-facing IS to allow graduated and self-paced engagement with system tasks for refugee users, enabling interaction that adapts to fluctuating emotional and cognitive capacity
Context	In refugee integration contexts where users interact with complex administrative IS under conditions of trauma, fatigue, uncertainty, and unfamiliar institutional procedures
Mechanisms	Design IS to (1) decompose complex tasks into smaller, manageable steps, (2) allow users to pause and resume processes without penalty or data loss, (3) avoid strict time constraints for task completion, and (4) visibly indicate progress and remaining effort. These mechanisms may be realized through modular workflows, save-and-resume functionality, flexible deadlines, and progressive disclosure of information
Enactors	Digital IS that structure task flows and persistence mechanisms; organizational actors responsible for configuring deadlines, process rules, and exception handling within administrative systems
Rationale	Empirical findings show that refugees frequently experience exhaustion, concentration difficulties, and avoidance when IS require sustained attention or immediate completion of high-stakes tasks. Trauma-related cognitive load reduces tolerance for prolonged or rigid interaction, particularly in unfamiliar institutional environments

DP4: Integrate Human Mediation as a Legitimate Design Element. IS should explicitly integrate pathways to human support, such as volunteers, caseworkers, or interpreters, rather than treating human mediation as a system failure (Table 5).

Table 5. **DP4:** Integrate Human Mediation as a Legitimate Design Element.

Component	Specification
DP Title	DP4: Integrate Human Mediation as a Legitimate Design Element
Aim, Implementer, and User	For implementers of refugee-facing IS to enable access to human mediation and support during system interaction for refugee users, particularly when digital processes are complex, emotionally distressing, or difficult to interpret
Context	In refugee integration contexts characterized by trauma, institutional complexity, linguistic barriers, and reliance on heterogeneous support actors, where digital IS coexist with volunteers, caseworkers, interpreters, NGOs, and community organizations
Mechanisms	Design IS to (1) explicitly provide pathways to human support such as volunteers, caseworkers, or interpreters, (2) signal when human mediation is appropriate or recommended, (3) enable escalation from digital interaction to human assistance, and (4) integrate human support channels within system workflows rather than treating them as external exceptions. These mechanisms may involve contact features, referral logic, hybrid workflows, and coordination interfaces
Enactors	Digital IS that expose and route mediation pathways; human actors including volunteers, caseworkers, interpreters, and community organizations; public-sector organizations coordinating sociotechnical workflows across digital and human support structures
Rationale	Empirical findings show that refugees consistently rely on informal human mediation to interpret digital information, verify decisions, and cope with emotional stress. Recognizing human mediation as a designed affordance aligns with eDSR by accounting for the embeddedness of IS within broader social systems and enables trust, interpretability, and emotional support without undermining digital efficiency

DP5: Design for Linguistic and Institutional Legibility, Not Mere Translation. IS should be designed for linguistic and institutional legibility, ensuring that administrative content is not merely translated but made interpretable in context (Table 6).

Table 6. Design for Linguistic and Institutional Legibility, Not Mere Translation.

Component	Specification
DP Title	DP5: Design for Linguistic and Institutional Legibility, Not Mere Translation
Aim, Implementer, and User	For implementers of refugee-facing IS to enable linguistic and institutional legibility during system interaction for refugee users, allowing them to understand administrative content, institutional roles, and legal implications rather than merely translated text
Context	In refugee integration settings where users encounter unfamiliar legal categories, administrative procedures, and institutional responsibilities through digital IS, often under conditions of limited host-country language proficiency and trauma-related cognitive strain
Mechanisms	Design IS to (1) simplify administrative language and avoid unnecessary bureaucratic terminology, (2) contextualize legal and institutional terms with explanations and examples, (3) explain institutional roles, responsibilities, and decision authority, and (4) supplement or replace machine translation with interpretive support. It could also include the use of pictures, audio, or video [27, 28] These mechanisms may be implemented through plain-language content, contextual help, glossaries, guided explanations, and layered information structures
Enactors	Digital IS presenting administrative content; public-sector organizations responsible for content governance and legal communication; translators, content designers, and institutional actors defining terminology and explanatory structures
Rationale	Empirical findings show that while language barriers are pervasive, literal translation is insufficient for meaningful interaction. Refugees frequently misunderstand administrative concepts, legal categories, and institutional responsibilities, as machine translation fails to convey practical implications. These misunderstandings generate fear of non-compliance and loss of benefits. Designing for linguistic and institutional legibility extends digital inclusion beyond access toward meaning-making under institutional complexity, supporting interpretive accessibility rather than surface-level translation

DP6: Enable Trust Through Data Dignity and User Agency. IS should enable trust by providing users with meaningful agency over their data, including clear explanations of why data are collected, how they are used, and what consequences follow (Table 7).

Table 7. DP6: Enable Trust Through Data Dignity and User Agency.

Component	Specification
DP Title	DP6: Enable Trust Through Data Dignity and User Agency
Aim, Implementer, and User	For implementers of refugee-facing IS to enable trustful interaction through data dignity and user agency for refugee users, allowing them to understand, control, and make informed decisions about their personal data
Context	In refugee integration contexts where IS require extensive personal data collection, identity verification, and cross-system data sharing, and where users may have prior exposure to coercive, opaque, or hostile institutional data practices
Mechanisms	Design IS to (1) clearly explain why specific data are collected, (2) communicate how data are processed, stored, and shared, (3) specify the consequences of providing or withholding data, and (4) provide users with meaningful choices and control over data submission where legally possible. These mechanisms may include transparent consent flows, contextual explanations, user-accessible data views, and reversible or staged data submission processes
Enactors	Digital IS that manage data collection and authentication; public-sector organizations defining data governance and compliance requirements; institutional actors responsible for communicating data practices and enforcing user rights
Rationale	Conceptualizing trust as a design outcome rather than a contextual given highlights the role of data dignity, transparency, and agency in shaping user–system relationships and supporting trauma-informed values of empowerment and control

DP7: Design for Ecosystem Coherence Rather Than Platform Completeness. IS should be designed to function coherently within an ecosystem of formal and informal information sources, acknowledging platform multiplicity rather than striving for a single comprehensive solution (Table 8).

Table 8. DP7: Design for Ecosystem Coherence Rather Than Platform Completeness.

Component	Specification
DP Title	DP7: Design for Ecosystem Coherence Rather Than Platform Completeness
Aim, Implementer, and User	For implementers of refugee-facing IS to enable coherent navigation and sensemaking across multiple systems for refugee users, rather than requiring engagement with a single, comprehensive platform

(continued)

Table 8. (*continued*)

Component	Specification
Context	In refugee integration environments characterized by a heterogeneous ecosystem of formal public-sector IS, informal digital platforms (e.g., messaging apps and social media), and interpersonal support networks, where users differ in age, digital skills, and support needs
Mechanisms	Design IS to (1) support interoperability and data alignment across platforms, (2) provide cross-references to complementary formal and informal information sources, (3) ensure consistency of core information and terminology across systems, and (4) acknowledge and accommodate platform multiplicity rather than enforcing centralized interaction. These mechanisms may involve shared standards, reference links, coordinated content governance, and boundary-spanning interfaces
Enactors	Digital IS operating within the refugee integration ecosystem; public-sector organizations coordinating platforms and information governance; community actors and informal platforms that complement formal systems
Rationale	Treating refugee integration as a complex adaptive system rather than a bounded platform problem shifts design focus from exhaustive "one-stop-shop" solutions toward interoperability, cross-referencing, and consistency. Accommodating emergence and plurality aligns with eDSR logic and supports more resilient and inclusive system design

Together, these seven design principles articulate a trauma-informed approach to IS design that reframes efficiency, transparency, and integration through the lens of emotional safety, trust, and agency. In accordance with eDSR, they represent accumulated and validated intermediate design knowledge, grounded in empirical evidence yet open to refinement through future instantiation and evaluation. Our principles are situated within the context of a highly digitalized welfare state and may require adaptation in settings with different institutional infrastructures or cultural norms. They also offer a theoretically grounded foundation for advancing trauma-informed IS design and for organizing future DSR efforts in humanitarian contexts.

6 Discussion

Our study contributes to IS research by developing empirically grounded design principles for trauma-informed IS for refugee integration. Consistent with prior IS research, our findings confirm that access to digital infrastructure does not ensure meaningful use or equitable outcomes [9, 12, 13]. While in Finland, where e-government services and digital identification systems are highly developed, refugees encounter second- and third-level digital divides driven by language barriers, fragmented information landscapes, institutional opacity, and trust deficits. These findings align with earlier studies showing that refugee integration IS often reproduce exclusion when systems presume linguistic proficiency, institutional familiarity, and stable cognitive capacity [8, 18]. Our study extends this stream of research by showing how trauma-related vulnerability amplifies these divides. In line with trauma research documenting heightened anxiety, cognitive overload, and impaired sensemaking among forcibly displaced populations [29–32], refugees in our study experienced routine IS interactions as emotionally charged and high-risk. Language barriers, unclear system logic, repeated data requests, and unpredictable timelines were not merely usability issues but sources of psychological distress and avoidance. This finding complements emerging IS and HCI research arguing that digital systems can inadvertently retraumatize users when emotional safety and predictability are not addressed [15, 16]. From a DSR perspective, our findings underscore the limitations of efficiency-oriented and rational-user assumptions that still dominate many public-sector IS. Prior IS research has already questioned the applicability of generic adoption and acceptance models in marginalized contexts [9, 30]. Our results reinforce this critique by empirically demonstrating that trauma disrupts core assumptions about sustained attention, error tolerance, and institutional trust. As a result, emotional safety, sensemaking, and user agency emerge as foundational design objectives rather than secondary design considerations.

Situating these contributions within existing design knowledge, the seven design principles both draw on and extend the foundational SAMHSA trauma-informed care framework, which emphasizes safety, trustworthiness, collaboration, empowerment, and cultural responsiveness [31]: where SAMHSA's principles were developed for interpersonal service delivery, our principles operationalize these values at the level of institutional IS, specifying concrete mechanisms such as process visualization, save-and-resume functionality, and integrated referral pathways that make trauma-awareness actionable for system designers rather than service practitioners. Compared to Chen et al.'s [15] TIC framework, which focuses primarily on avoiding retraumatization in digital interactions, our principles extend the scope to encompass ecosystem-level concerns: DP7 on ecosystem coherence and DP6 on data dignity address challenges, cross-platform fragmentation and repeated disclosure, that are largely absent from prior TIC frameworks oriented toward single-system or single-session interactions. No equivalent design knowledge currently addresses these ecosystem-level dimensions in refugee IS contexts, confirming that the principles presented here constitute a substantive extension of the existing body of trauma-informed design guidance rather than a restatement of it.

Importantly, our findings resonate with sociotechnical perspectives that view IS as embedded within broader organizational and social systems [30]. Rather than treating informal human mediation as workarounds, our design principles acknowledge them as integral components of the refugee integration ecosystem. This perspective aligns with prior IS research showing that meaningful inclusion often depends on hybrid arrangements that combine digital systems with human mediation and social support [7, 32]. While grounded in refugee experiences, our design principles align with Chen et al.'s [15] observation that trauma-informed design principles benefit everyone, not just trauma-affected refugees, thereby offering insights applicable to IS design more broadly.

6.1 Limitations and Future Research

Several limitations of this study should be acknowledged. First, our empirical findings are based on interviews with adults under TPD, which may not represent refugees with other legal statuses or undocumented individuals, and that participants self-selected through different IS channels, which likely over-represents those who are already digitally engaged, potentially underrepresenting the most digitally excluded. Second, the principles have not yet been instantiated or evaluated in real-world design contexts future research will translate them into concrete sociotechnical interventions through participatory design with refugees, service providers, and trauma experts, followed by iterative field evaluation [15, 16, 26]. Third, the study captures only refugee perspectives, future work will incorporate service providers, system designers, and policymakers to understand implementation constraints and boundary conditions across service domains [15, 16, 26].

7 Conclusion

In this paper, we set out to develop trauma-informed design principles for IS that support refugee integration. Building on digital divide research and trauma-informed design, we examined how Ukrainian refugees experience integration-related IS in a highly digitalized welfare-state context [9, 12, 13, 15, 18, 33]. Our results align with evidence that trauma and prolonged uncertainty shape stress, cognition, and institutional engagement among displaced populations [9, 33–35]. Following a DSR approach, we used these empirical insights to ground problem analysis and requirements elicitation and to derive initial, projectable design principles [25, 36, 37]. The design principles emphasize emotional and cognitive safety, transparency and predictability, user-controlled pacing, integrated human mediation, linguistic and institutional legibility beyond literal translation, and trust through data dignity and user agency [15, 16]. Our intent is that these principles guide subsequent design and evaluation efforts in refugee-facing IS, contributing to more humane, inclusive, and trauma-sensitive digital infrastructures for some of the most vulnerable members of our societies.

Acknowledgments. This research was funded by the Research Council of Finland, decision number 365952.

References

1. United Nations High Commissioner for Refugees: Global Trends: Forced displacement in 2024 (Global Trends Report) (2025). https://www.unhcr.org/global-trends-report-2024.html
2. Eurostat: Temporary protection for persons fleeing Ukraine – monthly statistics: Data extracted on 6 January 2026. European Commission, 12 January 2026

3. Sukiasyan, S.G.: The mental health of refugees and forcibly displaced people: a narrative review. Consort. Psychiatr. **5**(4), 78–92 (2024)
4. Mak, C., Wieling, E.: A systematic review of evidence-based family interventions for trauma-affected refugees. Int. J. Environ. Res. Public Health **19**(15), 9361 (2022)
5. Bryant, R.A.: Post-traumatic stress disorder: a state-of-the-art review of evidence and challenges. World Psychiatry **18**(3), 259–269 (2019)
6. Diaz, M., Lundell, I.W.: Hidden scars: the impact of torture, traumatic brain injury, and PTSD on executive functions-a narrative review. Torture J. **35**(1) (2025)
7. AbuJarour, S., Ajjan, H., Fedorowicz, J., Köster, A.: ICT support for refugees and undocumented immigrants. Commun. Assoc. Inf. Syst. **48**(1) (2021)
8. Pethig, F., Kroenung, J.: Specialized information systems for the digitally disadvantaged. J. Assoc. Inf.Syst. **20**(10) (2019)
9. Andrade, A.D., Doolin, B.: Information and communication technology and the social inclusion of refugees. MIS Q. **40**(2), 405–416 (2016)
10. Reeves, E.: A synthesis of the literature on trauma-informed care. Issues Ment. Health Nurs. **36**(9), 698–709 (2015)
11. Levy-Carrick, N.C., Lewis-O'Connor, A., Rittenberg, E., Manosalvas, K., Stoklosa, H.M., Silbersweig, D.A.: Promoting health equity through trauma-informed care: critical role for physicians in policy and program development. Fam. Community Health **42**(2), 104–108 (2019)
12. DiMaggio, P., Hargittai, E.: From the "digital divide" to "digital inequality": studying internet use as penetration increases (Working Paper). Princeton University, Center for Arts and Cultural Policy Studies (2001)
13. Warschauer, M.: Technology and Social Inclusion: Rethinking the Digital Divide. The MIT Press (2003)
14. Ocheredko, O., Siemon, D.: Toward trauma-informed information systems: challenges and opportunities in supporting refugee integration in Finland. In: ICIS 2025 Proceedings (2025). https://aisel.aisnet.org/icis2025/is_good/is_good/5
15. Chen, J.X., et al.: Trauma-informed computing: towards safer technology experiences for all. In: Proceedings of the 2022 CHI Conference on Human Factors in Computing Systems, pp. 1–20 (2022)
16. Randazzo, C., et al.: Trauma-informed design: a collaborative approach to building safer online spaces. In: Proceedings of the ACM Conference on Computer-Supported Cooperative Work (CSCW) (2023)
17. Finnish Immigration Service: Immigration statistics 2023: The effects of international conflicts and of the economic downturn on immigration to Finland (2024)
18. Schreieck, M., Wiesche, M., Usachova, O., Krcmar, H.: Digital platforms for social inclusion: the case of an information platform for refugees. MIS Q. **48**(4), 1835 (2024)
19. van Dijk, J.A.G.M.: A Theory of the Digital Divide. In The Digital Divide. Routledge (2013)
20. Goldstein, E., Chokshi, B., Melendez-Torres, G.J., Rios, A., Jelley, M., Lewis-O'Connor, A.: Effectiveness of trauma-informed care implementation in health care settings: systematic review of reviews and realist synthesis. Permanente J. **28**(1), 135–150 (2024)
21. Maynard, B.R., Farina, A., Dell, N.A., Kelly, M.S.: Effects of trauma-informed approaches in schools: a systematic review. Campbell Syst. Rev. **15**(1–2), e1018 (2019)
22. Tseng, E., Ristenpart, T., Dell, N.: Mitigating trauma in qualitative research infrastructure: roles for machine assistance and trauma-informed design. In: Proceedings of the ACM on Human-Computer Interaction, 9(CSCW2), Article no. 137, pp. 1–31 (2025)
23. Bichler, M.: Design science in information systems research. Wirtschaftsinformatik **48**(2), 133–135 (2006). https://doi.org/10.1007/s11576-006-0028-8
24. Tuunanen, T., Winter, R., vom Brocke, J.: Dealing with complexity in design science research: a methodology using design echelons. MIS Q. **48**(2), 427–458 (2024)

25. Mayring, P.: Qualitative content analysis: theoretical foundation, basic procedures and software solution. Social Science Open Access Repository (2014). https://nbn-resolving.org/urn: nbn:de:0168-ssoar-395173
26. Gregor, S., Chandra Kruse, L., Seidel, S.: Research perspectives: the anatomy of a design principle. J. Assoc. Inf. Syst. **21**(6), 1622–1652 (2020)
27. Romeo, R.R., et al.: Neuroplasticity associated with conversational turn-taking following a family-based intervention. Dev. Cogn. Neurosci. **49**, 100967 (2021)
28. Georgiou, A., Katkov, M., Tsodyks, M.: Forgetting dynamics for items of different categories. Learn. Mem. **30**(2), 34–41 (2023)
29. Lushchak, O., Velykodna, M., Bolman, S., Strilbytska, O., Berezovskyi, V., Storey, K.B.: Prevalence of stress, anxiety, and symptoms of post-traumatic stress disorder among Ukrainians after the first year of Russian invasion: a nationwide cross-sectional study. Lancet Reg. Health Europe **36**, 100773 (2024)
30. Kvasny, L.: Cultural (Re)production of digital inequality in a US community technology initiative. Inf. Commun. Soc. **9**(2), 160–181 (2006)
31. Huang, L.N., et al.: SAMHSA's concept of trauma and guidance for a trauma-informed approach. Substance Abuse and Mental Health Services Administration (2014)
32. Bostrom, R., Heinen, J.: MIS problems and failures: a socio-technical perspective PART 1: the causes. Manag. Inf. Syst. Q. **1**(1) (1977). https://aisel.aisnet.org/misq/vol1/iss1/9
33. Venkatesh, V., Sykes, T.A.: Digital divide initiative success in developing countries: a longitudinal field study in a village in India. Inf. Syst. Res. **24**(2), 239–260 (2013)
34. Neria, Y., Nandi, A., Galea, S.: Post-traumatic stress disorder following disasters: a systematic review. Psychol. Med. **38**(4), 467–480 (2008)
35. Fazel, M., Wheeler, J., Danesh, J.: The burden of trauma in the lives of refugees. World Psychiatry **23**(2), 239–251 (2024)
36. Ocheredko, O., Siemon, D.: Beyond access: rethinking refugee integration through information systems. In: ICIS 2025 Proceedings, 8 (2025). https://aisel.aisnet.org/icis2025/public_is/public_is/8
37. Gregor, S., Jones, D.: The anatomy of a design theory. J. Assoc. Inf. Syst. **8**(5), 312–335 (2007)

Future of Design Science Education

Generative AI in Knowledge Management: Designing a GenAI Chatbot for Tacit Knowledge Externalization

Oliver Dinand[(✉)] [iD], Vincent Heimburg [iD], and Manuel Wiesche [iD]

TU Dortmund University, Dortmund, Germany
`{oliver.dinand,vincent.heimburg,manuel.wiesche}@tu-dortmund.de`

Abstract. Knowledge is a critical organizational resource. Yet organizational restructuring, project-based work, employee mobility, and demographic change threaten the loss of vital tacit knowledge. To retain this knowledge within organizations, it must be externalized into explicit forms that can be shared and reused. While Generative AI (GenAI) offers promising opportunities through its natural-language-based, situationally adaptive interactions, the Information Systems (IS) field lacks prescriptive guidance on designing artifacts for this purpose. Adopting the echeloned Design Science Research (^{e}DSR) methodology, we design and evaluate the GenAI chatbot artifact externalAIze as an instrument for knowledge externalization. We derived four design principles: phased reflective questioning, curated input options with free-text fallback, adaptive motivational feedback, and human-in-the-loop knowledge validation. We evaluated the artifact via a quantitative study with 53 participants, comparing three interaction modalities. The evaluation demonstrates that curated input options with free-text fallback optimally balance users' cognitive effort and efficiency with expressive freedom. Furthermore, phased reflective questioning effectively elicits deep expertise, adaptive motivational feedback supports user engagement and willingness to articulate knowledge, and human-in-the-loop knowledge validation successfully improves the overall quality of externalized knowledge and mitigates GenAI hallucination risks. Our results contribute to the literature by moving beyond the descriptive potential of GenAI in knowledge externalization to provide prescriptive design knowledge.

Keywords: Knowledge Management · Knowledge Externalization · Organizational Learning · Artificial Intelligence · Generative AI · Design Science

1 Introduction

Multiple organizational and workforce-related dynamics, such as organizational restructuring, project-based work, workforce mobility, and demographic change, cause organizations to lose deep, experiential knowledge [1, 2]. This tacit knowledge represents the unarticulated know-how, insights, and context-dependent expertise deeply embedded within individuals [3]. The failure to externalize this knowledge—that is, to transform

© The Author(s), under exclusive license to Springer Nature Switzerland AG 2026
J. vom Brocke et al. (Eds.): DESRIST 2026, LNCS 16606, pp. 155–172, 2026.
https://doi.org/10.1007/978-3-032-28313-9_9

personal, experience-based know-how into explicit, communicable, and organizationally accessible forms—before it leaves the organization poses a risk to organizational continuity and competitive advantage [4].

Systems that utilize Generative Artificial Intelligence (GenAI) technologies offer a potential solution to this impasse. Unlike systems constrained by pre-defined logic trees, foundational GenAI models appear to possess an unprecedented breadth of topical understanding and the capability to generate context-aware, coherent content [5]. This highly generative nature of GenAI promises to transform how users interact with knowledge management systems [6, 7]. Specifically, the capability of GenAI models to process natural language inputs allows for chatbots that are situationally adaptive—capable of generating highly personalized, high-fidelity responses that are proactive in shaping the dialogue [5].

While emerging research suggests that GenAI chatbots are fundamentally capable of externalizing tacit knowledge [e.g., 8], the Information Systems (IS) field lacks prescriptive guidance on how to design such systems effectively. Existing research primarily focuses on demonstrating the potential of such systems rather than the mechanisms of their application [9–11]. Consequently, design choices remain implicit. It remains unclear which specific design choices effectively support the process of knowledge externalization.

This gap is particularly evident in the design of conversational interfaces for knowledge externalization systems. Most conversational interfaces rely on open-ended text input. While flexible, this imposes a high cognitive load on users. Users must recall, structure, and articulate complex knowledge without guidance [5]. Conversely, non-conversational interfaces with predefined closed-ended input options reduce user effort but lack the nuance required to capture complex, tacit domains. Here lies a key potential of GenAI: it can facilitate a "dynamic closed-endedness" rather than relying on predefined closed-ended input options. The GenAI model can generate situationally relevant selection options and follow-up proposals based on the user's initial input. To address these challenges, we pose the following research question:

RQ: *How can a GenAI chatbot be designed to externalize tacit knowledge?*

To answer this question, we adopt a Design Science Research (DSR) approach, following the echeloned DSR (ᵉDSR) methodology [12, 13]. We design a sociotechnical artifact centered on a GenAI chatbot, *externalAIze*, that helps users to externalize their knowledge interactively: the user provides initial input, and the artifact dynamically generates inquisitive follow-up questions to expand and refine that knowledge.

We contribute to research in three primary ways. First, we extend the discourse on externalization of tacit knowledge within organizational contexts [14]. Second, while prior research has focused on explaining GenAI's capabilities for knowledge externalization, we shift toward a prescriptive understanding of how to design specific artifacts that leverage these capabilities [8]. Third, we contribute prescriptive design knowledge on how specific design choices—particularly differing reflective questioning techniques and interaction modalities—influence the knowledge externalization process. Finally, we offer a practical contribution by providing organizations with an adaptive, scalable approach to facilitating knowledge externalization.

2   Theoretical Background

Knowledge is a central organizational resource, making it a key challenge for organizations to develop, preserve, and transfer it [15]. When organizations fail to actively manage their organizational knowledge, they face risks of inefficiencies, reduced innovation capabilities, and declining customer satisfaction [16]. Particularly tacit knowledge is vulnerable to loss due to multiple organizational and workforce-related dynamics, including organizational restructuring, project-based work, workforce mobility, and demographic change such as the retirement of the baby boomer generation in western economies [1, 2, 4]. Consequently, knowledge management has gained strategic importance as it enables the systematic retention and distribution of critical expertise, thereby supporting informed decision-making and organizational learning [17].

2.1   Knowledge Externalization

Knowledge externalization plays a pivotal role in knowledge management. Knowledge externalization transforms tacit knowledge into explicit forms that can be shared and understood, thereby providing the foundation for subsequent knowledge creation [3, 18]. This process varies in complexity depending on the degree of tacitness of the knowledge involved [19, 20]: experience-based insights, practical intelligence, and rules of thumb are more amenable to articulation, whereas intuition and gut-feelings can typically only be transferred through observation, apprenticeship, and learning-by-doing. To externalize these forms of tacit knowledge that are more amenable to articulation, organizations commonly rely on analyst-mediated elicitation methods such as interviews [14]. These methods, however, are time- and resource-intensive, often restricted by the analyst's own lack of domain-specific nuance, and difficult to scale in dynamic organizational environments [8, 14].

2.2   Potential of GenAI in Knowledge Externalization

Advances in generative AI offer a viable solution to address these challenges. Especially Large Language Models (LLMs) can be steered via system prompts—meta-instructions that define the knowledge externalization system's persona and objectives—to simulate the investigative behavior of a human analyst [21]. This allows organizations to guide the GenAI model in analyzing user inputs and dynamically generating context-aware, coherent responses [22].

Thus, GenAI opens new opportunities for knowledge management by enabling natural-language-based, situationally adaptive, personalized, and proactive interactions that can facilitate the externalization of tacit knowledge [5, 23]. At the same time, GenAI can reduce time and resource requirements compared to manual approaches, enabling the rapid extraction and synthesis of relevant knowledge.

Building on this potential, GenAI chatbot approaches for knowledge externalization have been proposed in research. Prior work demonstrates that combining generative AI with reflective questioning may support the elicitation of tacit knowledge across different domains, including production, education, and professional learning [8, 9, 24]. Other studies show how tacit knowledge can be contextualized for GenAI systems and transformed into explicit knowledge, documented in learning materials, documents, or knowledge graphs [11, 25]. However, existing research remains fragmented and focuses on demonstrating potential rather than providing prescriptive guidance on how to design GenAI systems that systematically support the externalization of tacit knowledge.

3 Research Design

Design Science Research (DSR) fundamentally aims to generate prescriptive knowledge through the design and evaluation of innovative artifacts. Traditional DSR approaches, such as the method presented by Peffers et al. [26], suggest a sequential process from problem formulation to final evaluation. However, this structure faces two main challenges related to complexity. First, both the problem and solution space often emerge and become refined in the course of the process, which requires nonlinear DSR iterations. Second, the research process must remain responsive to situational conditions, which evolve as a project progresses [13].

To address these challenges, Tuunanen et al. [13] introduced the echeloned DSR (^{e}DSR) methodology, which decomposes the DSR process into logically coherent self-contained parts referred to as "echelons". This structure enables the research problem to be divided into a hierarchy of several logical subproblems whose solutions can be developed, validated, and communicated independently. As a result, an iterative development process emerges in which potential problems can be identified at an early stage and intermediate results can be quickly validated and adjusted. The five types of echelons encompassed by ^{e}DSR are (1) problem analysis, (2) objectives and requirements definition, (3) design and development, (4) demonstration, and (5) evaluation. Due to the high complexity and dynamics of GenAI systems, our study follows the ^{e}DSR methodology [13] for the development and evaluation of a GenAI chatbot for the externalization of tacit knowledge.

4 Designing and Evaluating a GenAI Chatbot for Externalization

Figure 1 provides an overview of the design echelons at the macro and micro levels. The design process comprises seven echelons, which are described in the following sections.

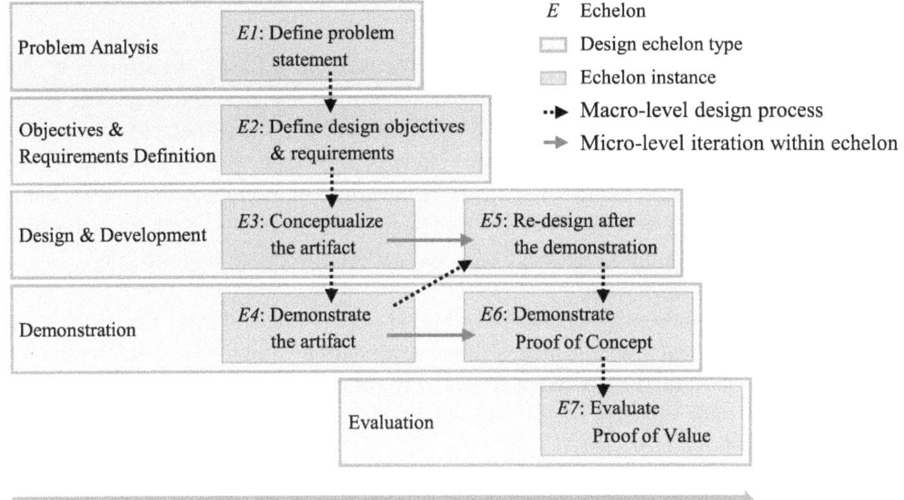

Fig. 1. Overview of the design echelons at the macro and micro levels.

4.1 Problem Analysis

[e]DSR starts by identifying and validating a real-world problem. In *Echelon 1*, we set the following validation criteria [13]: the degree to which the problem has been solved and the extent to which the problem is solvable. To address this, we conducted a literature review to examine the current state of research related to the externalization of tacit knowledge in organizations. We found that tacit knowledge constitutes a substantial share of organizational knowledge bases, while organizations struggle to systematically consider it in their knowledge management and organizational learning processes [27]. This becomes increasingly critical due to multiple organizational and workforce-related dynamics, including organizational restructuring, project-based work, workforce mobility, and demographic change, which heighten the risk of losing vital tacit knowledge [1, 2, 4]. As a consequence, organizations face growing pressure to establish effective mechanisms for capturing, preserving, and transferring tacit knowledge in order to remain competitive [15].

Addressing this critical challenge, and considering the unique capabilities of GenAI, we posit that GenAI chatbots can significantly enhance the externalization of tacit knowledge. Specifically, GenAI enables situationally adaptive interfaces that proactively shape the dialogue. By leveraging an unprecedented breadth of topical knowledge, these systems synthesize analogies and cross-domain connections that human interviewers often lack the background to suggest [5, 28]. However, existing literature lacks prescriptive guidance on how to design such systems effectively. Existing research remains fragmented across disparate domains, interaction modalities, and objectives, primarily focusing on demonstrating the potential of GenAI rather than the mechanisms of its application [9–11]. Consequently, it remains unclear which specific design choices effectively support the process of knowledge externalization.

4.2 Objectives and Requirements Definition

Based on the problem statement, *Echelon 2* focuses on defining the objectives and requirements that contribute to addressing the identified research problem. We set the following validation criteria [13]: fit to the validated problem statement and design operationality. The overarching objective of this study is to generate prescriptive knowledge on how to design a GenAI chatbot for the externalization of tacit knowledge effectively. Based on a literature review, we identify five design requirements, each representing a necessary condition for the knowledge externalization process or its outcome.

DR1: Elicit tacit knowledge
Tacit knowledge is inherently experiential, context-dependent, and often not consciously accessible to individuals, which makes direct articulation difficult [3, 29]. In practice, the externalization of tacit knowledge typically relies on reflective methods that engage individuals with concrete experiences, decisions, and outcomes before such knowledge can be articulated explicitly [8].

DR2: Minimize cognitive load in knowledge articulation
Most conversational interfaces rely on open-ended text input. While flexible, this imposes a high cognitive load on users. Users must recall, structure, and articulate complex knowledge without guidance [5]. As a result, users may experience fatigue or disengagement, which can limit the depth and completeness of the articulated knowledge.

DR3: Facilitate efficient interactions
In addition to cognitive effort, the process of knowledge externalization is constrained by employees' limited time resources in organizational contexts [30]. Especially in dynamic environments such as the shop floor, work is characterized by frequent adjustments, time pressure, and continuous problem solving, leaving little room for time-intensive knowledge externalization [8].

DR4: Foster motivation for knowledge sharing
The knowledge externalization process is frequently constrained by motivational barriers, including employees' reluctance to share their own knowledge [30, 31]. Prior research further indicates that insufficient motivation and a low perceived ability to articulate tacit knowledge are among the primary reasons why established knowledge externalization approaches often fail in practice [14, 31].

DR5: Assure quality of externalized knowledge
The use of GenAI in knowledge externalization introduces the risk of erroneous or hallucinated content, which can undermine trust in the system and compromise the reuse of externalized knowledge in organizational knowledge management systems [7, 32].

4.3 Design and Development

We conducted two design and development echelons. In *Echelon 3*, we set the following validation criteria [13]: applicability to instantiate the artifact, internal consistency, and justification of the design choice rationale. Building on the design requirements defined in Sect. 4.2, we derived four design principles (DP), which are summarized in Table 1 following the schema proposed by Gregor et al. [33].

DP1: Phased reflective questioning addresses the complexity of tacit knowledge externalization by employing a reflective questioning approach, which has been shown to effectively support users in becoming aware of and articulating their tacit knowledge [8, 9, 24]. The chatbot poses reflective questions in sequential, increasingly abstract phases, guiding users step by step from concrete experiences toward higher-level insights.

DP2: Curated input options aims to reduce users' cognitive load while promoting efficient interaction and content consistency during knowledge externalization [21, 34]. For each reflective question, the chatbot provides a predefined set of context-specific answer options, including fallback options such as *"None of these answers"* and *"I don't know/can't express"*.

DP3: Adaptive motivational feedback addresses the role of motivational factors in knowledge sharing. Prior research indicates that insufficient motivation and low perceived ability to articulate knowledge are among the primary reasons why established knowledge externalization approaches fail in practice [14, 31]. Accordingly, positive and empathetic feedback—particularly in conversational agents—has been shown to enhance user engagement [35]. Building on this insight, the chatbot provides empathic and affirmative responses to users' inputs in order to strengthen their willingness and confidence to externalize and share tacit knowledge.

DP4: Human-in-the-loop knowledge validation aims to ensure the overall quality of externalized knowledge generated by GenAI systems, including the mitigation of hallucinated or erroneous content. To achieve this, a feedback loop is introduced at the end of the interaction in which users review and cross-check a structured summary of the externalized knowledge. Users assess the summary with regard to completeness, correctness, quality, and accuracy and can revise or correct the content where necessary. This validation step ensures that only verified knowledge is retained for further use and integration into knowledge management systems [7, 36].

Table 1. Design requirements and design principles.

Design Requirements	Design Principles	Expected Outcomes
DR1: Elicit tacit knowledge	DP1: Phased reflective questioning	Users progressively become aware of and articulate their tacit knowledge
DR2: Minimize cognitive load in knowledge articulation	DP2: Curated input options *(adapted to "curated input options with free-text fallback" in Echelon 5)*	Users externalize their tacit knowledge with reduced cognitive and temporal effort
DR3: Facilitate efficient interactions		
DR4: Foster motivation for knowledge sharing	DP3: Adaptive motivational feedback	Users are willing and confident in their ability to share their tacit knowledge
DR5: Assure quality of externalized knowledge	DP4: Human-in-the-loop knowledge validation	Users assure the completeness, correctness, quality and accuracy of their externalized knowledge summary

To instantiate our DPs into a functional software artifact, we developed *externalAIze* designed to guide users through a structured knowledge externalization process. Drawing on a framework for effective knowledge conversion [37], we adopted a tripartite interaction workflow. This workflow guides the user through three distinct phases of engagement: Extraction, Formalization, and Documentation.

In the initial phase, the **extraction phase**, tacit knowledge elements are identified and elicited from the dialogue with users. To establish a shared context and enhance the coherence of subsequent questions, users are first prompted to provide an initial open-ended description of their knowledge on a specific topic. The artifact is designed to ingest this initial input and dynamically adapt the subsequent dialogue to progressively deepen the level of reflection.

In line with DP1, we employ the Systematic Reflection Method [38], dynamically adapted to the conversational flow. This method supports learning from both failures and successes by posing reflective questions that encourage users to critically examine their own actions and support the articulation of tacit knowledge [8, 38]. The questioning strategy comprises three sub-steps: self-explanation, data verification, and feedback. Self-explanation refers to the process by which users analyze their behavior and develop explanations for success or failure. Data verification confronts users with alternative perspectives on the same situation, thereby challenging and refining their mental models. Feedback facilitates reflection on prior decisions.

Following DP2, user input is constrained to reduce cognitive load; interaction occurs exclusively through a predefined but generative set of answer options. To account for the elusive nature of tacit knowledge, users may select *"None of these answers"* or *"I don't know/can't express"*, which triggers the artifact to reframe the question or offer alternative perspectives. To prevent the option *"I don't know/can't express"* from being used as an avoidance strategy due to the tacit nature of the knowledge, its use is limited to every second question.

In accordance with DP3, the artifact generates empathetic and affirmative responses prior to each reflective question to strengthen users' willingness and confidence to externalize and share tacit knowledge.

In the **formalization phase**, once the dialogue concludes, *externalAIze* synthesizes the unstructured conversational data, organizing the elicited insights into dynamically codified representations. This process transforms the fragmented dialogue into a cohesive, structured summary.

In the **documentation phase**, in accordance with DP4, a human-in-the-loop knowledge validation mechanism is triggered. The user is presented with a structured summary of the externalized knowledge. This feedback loop empowers the user to confirm, revise, or correct the content, thereby ensuring high data quality and mitigating the risk of GenAI hallucinations.

To operationalize this, we used prompt engineering to iteratively develop, test, and optimize the system prompt [21]. An excerpt of the system prompt[1] illustrating the instantiation of the DPs is shown in Fig. 2. User inputs were processed and responses generated by Gemini-2.5-Flash model, a large language model provided by Google. The model was accessed via an application programming interface (API).

---

[1] To support transparency and replicability, we kindly provide the full system prompt on request.

```
DP1

2. **Data Verification:** Question the described procedure
      to solidify the knowledge and explore
      alternatives. Make your questions here
      especially varied. Avoid constantly starting
      with "What would have happened if...". Instead,
      actively use phrases like "How would that have
      affected things if...", "Could you have also
      imagined...?" or other examples from the pool.
   * **Counterfactual Alternatives:** What would have
      happened if something had been done differently?
   * **Context Variations:** How would the procedure
      change if the context changed? …

DP2

   case ChatbotMode.C:
     modeDescription = 'Mode C (Answer Options): You ask a
        question and create THREE plausible, distinct
        answer options. The user can select MULTIPLE
        options. A fourth option "D: None of these
        answers" and a fifth option "E: I don't know/
        can't express" are always automatically added by
        the user interface. Therefore, you must NEVER
        generate these options yourself as one of your
        three options. Return your response in JSON
        format: {"question": "your question", "options":
        ["Option 1", "Option 2", "Option 3"],"phase":
        "CURRENT_PHASE"}';
     break; …
```

```
DP3

   **Conversation Style: Empathetic, Motivating, and
        Efficient**
   - **Regular Feedback:** Before the reflective questions,
        provide regular short feedback to show empathy,
        motivation, and appreciation without disrupting
        the conversation flow. …
   - **Empathetic Feedback (approx. 20% of messages):** Use
        this after emotional or personal assessments to
        show understanding and compassion, but only if
        the content is suitable. Examples: "I can
        imagine that was a special moment.", "I'm glad
        that worked out so well.", …

DP4

   `You are an AI tasked with revising the previous summary
        based on the user's last feedback.
   **Your Task:** Please create a new, improved version of
        the summary. Carefully analyze the last feedback
        message and integrate the desired corrections or
        additions. Maintain the original structure and
        formatting rules.
   **Formatting and Structure Requirements:** Strictly
        structure the summary according to the following
        three aspects. Use the exact headings and emojis
        as shown below. …
```

Fig. 2. Excerpt from the system prompt with the instantiated DPs .

Echelon 5 represents the second design and development echelon conducted in this study. We set the following validation criteria [13]: internal consistency and justification of the design choice rationale. Building on the insights gained from the initial demonstration of the artifact, this echelon focused on refining DP2 in response to observed limitations and user feedback, while DP1, DP3, and DP4 were confirmed as appropriate and effective in supporting the externalization of tacit knowledge.

In line with participants' feedback, we adapted DP2 to **curated input options with free-text fallback** to include a free-text input field to mitigate misunderstandings during interaction and to allow for the externalization of additional, individual knowledge. At the same time, the provision of predefined answer options was retained, as it continues to support efficient interaction and promotes content consistency. The final instantiation of the DPs from the users' perspective is illustrated in Fig. 3.

While the hybrid input modality (DP2) emerged as the most promising design direction, we implemented three different chatbot interaction modalities to systematically validate this design choice and to examine trade-offs between open-endedness and closed-endedness.

Chatbot C (Closed-ended) was designed as a closed-ended GenAI chatbot relying exclusively on a predefined set of answer options to guide users through the interaction. Users articulated their knowledge solely by selecting one or more of the provided answer options.

Chatbot H (Hybrid) combined predefined answer options with free-text input. In this interaction modality, users could either select from a curated set of answer options or complement and refine their responses using open-ended text input. This modality is illustrated in Fig. 3.

Chatbot O (Open-ended) was designed as an open-ended GenAI chatbot relying exclusively on free-text input, allowing users to articulate their knowledge through unconstrained textual responses.

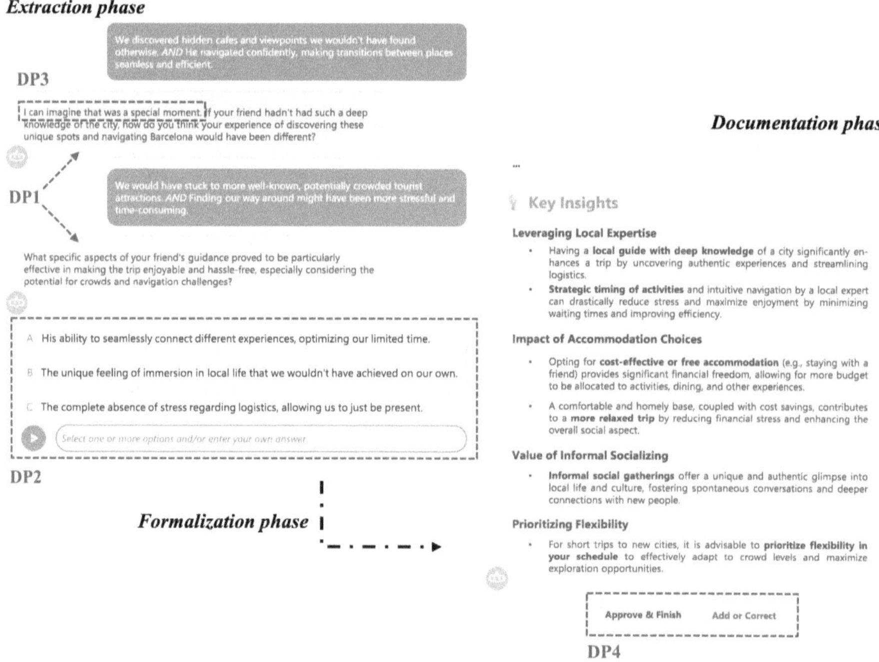

Fig. 3. Screenshots of GenAI chatbot *externalAIze* (Chatbot H) with the final instantiated DPs.

4.4 Demonstration

We conducted two demonstration echelons. *Echelon 4* constitutes the first practical demonstration of *externalAIze*. In this echelon, we set the following validation criteria [13]: fit to the validated design of the artifact, ease of use, and robustness. The objective of this demonstration is to provide an initial proof of concept to demonstrate the functional feasibility and whether its design meets the intended objectives and requirements. The demonstration is conducted as an experiment with the artifact in an artificial context. As a demonstration scenario, participants are asked to reflect on a past weekend trip taken with friends, family, or alone. This scenario involves numerous context-specific decisions related to planning and execution and is therefore characterized by a high proportion of tacit knowledge. At the same time, it is accessible to participants across heterogeneous professional backgrounds, thereby enabling a controlled validation of the design principles. Due to its retrospective nature and the opportunity to reflect on both successes and failures, the scenario is well suited for applying the Systematic Reflection Method proposed by Ellis et al. [38].

The demonstration follows a within-subject design and is conducted with three participants recruited from the researchers' networks. During the interaction with *externalAIze*, participants are observed and encouraged to verbalize their thoughts, enabling the collection of initial insights into the artifact's comprehensibility, usability, and functionality. Following the interaction, we conducted semi-structured interviews to examine user impressions and qualitative feedback.

The results indicate that *externalAIze* is fundamentally functional and that the proposed DPs largely operate as intended. In particular, *phased reflective questioning*, *adaptive motivational feedback*, and *human-in-the-loop knowledge validation* mechanisms received positive feedback. However, participants' feedback indicates that curated input options were perceived as restrictive and should be complemented by free-text fallback to allow for more precise articulation of situational knowledge.

"In most cases, the suggestions were helpful. However, when misunderstandings occurred, I felt that the proposed options did not fully fit the situation. In those cases, I would have preferred to point out the issue myself and correct it directly. For example, the chatbot misunderstood that there were not multiple groups but only a single carpool, which would have led the dialogue in a different direction." (Interview #B02)

Echelon 6 constitutes the second demonstration echelon conducted in this study. In this echelon, we set the following validation criteria [13]: fit to the validated design of the artifact, ease of use, and robustness. Using the same experimental setting and scenario as in Echelon 4, we carried out a demonstration with three participants recruited from the researchers' networks, providing a proof of concept for a fully anonymized procedure intended for the main test. Based on the results, it can be concluded that *externalAIze* exhibits the required stability and that the implemented technical adjustments function as intended.

4.5 Evaluation

To systematically validate *externalAIze's* proof of value from users' perspectives, in *Echelon 7*, we derive a summative approach. We set the following validation criteria [13]: fit to the validated instance of the artifact, efficacy and utility of the artifact.

We developed a post-interaction questionnaire to capture subjective perceptions of *externalAIze*. The instrument consists of six multi-item constructs, adapted from prior research on chatbot evaluation and knowledge management systems.

To enhance construct validity, item-sorting exercises were conducted following Moore and Benbasat [39]. Two iterative rounds with three participants each were performed, resulting in six final constructs: *Satisfaction with Interaction Process (SI)*, *Perceived Quality (PQ)*, *Reflection Facilitation (RF)*, *Hindrances to Knowledge Articulation (HK)*, *Articulation Effort (AE)*, and *Future Use Intention (FU)*.

The construct *SI* captures the extent to which *externalAIze's* questioning strategy is perceived as goal-oriented and supportive for knowledge externalization. *PQ* assesses users' perceptions of the comprehensibility, correctness, completeness, and usefulness of the knowledge summary generated by *externalAIze*, as well as overall satisfaction with the outcome. To examine whether the questioning strategy stimulates reflective processes and supports deeper understanding, the construct *RF* is employed. The construct *HK* focuses on challenges arising from the tacit nature of knowledge. The construct *AE* captures the perceived temporal and cognitive effort required to externalize the knowledge. Finally, *FU* assesses users' willingness and perceived suitability for regularly using *externalAIze* for knowledge externalization.

All constructs were measured using multi-item seven-point Likert scales with *1 strongly disagree – 7 strongly agree* or *1 extremely inaccurate – 7 extremely accurate* anchors. All measures are reflective and demonstrated acceptable internal consistency (Cronbach's $\alpha = 0.759$–0.868 [40]). The study protocol was reviewed and approved by the Ethics Committee of TU Dortmund University prior to data collection.

We deliberately composed a sample to include users with varying levels of professional experience and familiarity with generative AI. This approach enabled the evaluation of *externalAIze* and its DPs across both more experienced user groups—such as members of older generations for whom the risk of tacit knowledge loss due to retirement is particularly salient—and younger generations who may be more accustomed to interacting with generative AI systems.

The final sample consisted of 53 participants and is described in Table 2.

Table 2. Sample characteristics

Variable	Category (n)
Gender	male (30), female (23), non-binary (0)
Age group (years)	18–29 (23), 30–39 (4), 40–49 (5), 50–59 (13), 60–69 (8)
Professional experience	no professional experience - e.g., still in school, apprenticeship, or university (17), <5 years (6), 5–14 years (4), 15–24 years (5), 25–34 years (11), >35 years (10)
Use of GenAI systems	never (13), 1–2 times per week (11), 3–6 times per week (11), daily (14), multiple times per day (4)

Participants were randomly assigned to one of three chatbot interaction modalities, with 19 participants interacting with Chatbot H and 17 participants each assigned to Chatbot C and Chatbot O.

Log data indicate substantial differences in interaction time across chatbot interaction modalities. Chatbot O required the longest average interaction time (26:18 min), Chatbot C the shortest (9:55 min), with Chatbot H falling in between (16:59 min). For Chatbot H, predefined answer options accounted for 85% of all entries, while free-text inputs comprised 15%.

DP1 aims to facilitate the externalization of tacit knowledge through *phased reflective questioning* based on the Systematic Reflection Method [38]. Overall, this DP was evaluated very positively. Participants perceived the *phased reflective questioning* as meaningful and supportive for externalizing their knowledge, which is reflected in the consistently high ratings of the *satisfaction with interaction process*. These results indicate that the phased progression—from self-explanation to data verification and feedback—helped users to gradually surface and structure their experience-based knowledge.

However, evaluations varied depending on users' prior familiarity with GenAI systems. Participants with no prior exposure reported lower levels of *reflection facilitation* and weaker *future use intention*, suggesting that unfamiliarity with GenAI constrained their willingness to engage deeply with the reflective dialogue. In contrast, users with moderate to frequent GenAI experience reported substantially stronger reflection support, indicating that DP1 is particularly effective once a basic level of system familiarity is established.

DP2 builds on the assumed trade-off between open-ended and closed-ended input options, which motivated the comparison of three distinct chatbot interaction modalities. Users of the closed-ended chatbot (Chatbot C) reported increased hindrances in articulating their knowledge, particularly when predefined options did not adequately capture their individual experiences. This limitation was repeatedly highlighted in participants' feedback, who expressed a desire for greater expressive flexibility.

"The purely answer-based interaction was very restrictive. Being able to combine predefined options with a field to write one's own answer would be more suitable, especially when dealing with specific expert knowledge." (Main test #B625483)

In contrast, participants interacting with the Chatbot H, *curated input options with free-text fallback*, emphasized the added flexibility and expressive freedom afforded by the hybrid interaction modality:

"I found the chatbot very good—being able to either select predefined options or formulate my own response gave me much flexibility." (Main test #C860221)

Log data showed that users of Chatbot H primarily relied on predefined options while selectively complementing them with free-text input when necessary. This combination enabled both efficiency and expressive freedom, allowing users to specify nuances beyond the predefined answer options. Importantly, the hybrid design was perceived as significantly less demanding in terms of *articulation effort* compared to the fully open-ended Chatbot O, while still maintaining flexibility. However, the results suggest a potential trade-off: users may underutilize open-ended input even when predefined options do not fully capture their knowledge.

DP3 targets motivational challenges that frequently limit the effectiveness of traditional approaches to tacit knowledge externalization. Overall, the integration of empathetic and affirmative responses contributed positively to users' engagement and willingness to reflect, as several participants highlighted its supportive character during the interaction. At the same time, the results reveal clear boundary conditions for its effectiveness. Participants in later career stages and higher age groups reported greater *hindrances to knowledge articulation* and expressed lower *future use intention*. This suggests that *adaptive motivational feedback* alone is insufficient to address reservations toward GenAI systems and that additional design and organizational measures are required.

DP4 aims to ensure the overall quality of externalized knowledge generated by GenAI systems, including the mitigation of hallucinated or erroneous content by integrating a feedback loop at the end of the interaction, where users cross-check their externalized knowledge. This mechanism enables users to review, correct, and confirm a structured summary of their externalized knowledge before it is retained. Overall, DP4 received the most positive evaluations across all DPs, reflecting high *perceived quality* of the resulting knowledge representations.

Evidence from the interaction logs further demonstrates the importance of this validation mechanism. In some cases, users actively corrected misinterpretations in the generated summary, thereby preventing inaccurate content from being retained. For example, one user clarified that an event interpreted by the chatbot as the outcome of the trip—"the return journey ended with a speeding violation"—was in fact only a salient incident rather than the conclusion of the trip. The user explicitly corrected the summary, noting that "the trip did not end with the speeding violation; this was just an event that remained particularly memorable, the rest of the summary is accurate" (Log #A297413). Such corrections illustrate how *human-in-the-loop knowledge validation* effectively supports error detection and refinement of the externalized knowledge.

5 Discussion

In an iterative research process, following the ^{e}DSR methodology [13], we developed the GenAI chatbot artifact *externalAIze* as an instrument for knowledge externalization. In the first demonstration echelon, we demonstrated a closed-ended interface where the artifact guided users solely through a predefined but generative set of answer options. Our demonstration revealed a critical tension: while users valued the reduction in typing effort, they deemed the lack of free expression restrictive—suggesting that closed-ended user inputs alone are insufficient for the complex process of knowledge externalization. Consequently, while the remaining DPs proved robust, DP2 was refined from *curated input options* to *curated input options with free-text fallback* to better balance users' cognitive effort and efficiency with expressive freedom. The resulting set of four DPs was subsequently instantiated and confirmed in a final quantitative evaluation echelon.

5.1 Contributions to Literature

This study contributes to research on GenAI chatbots and knowledge management in three ways. First, we extend the discourse on tacit knowledge externalization within organizational contexts by proposing and evaluating a new solution to a known problem [14, 41]. The evaluated artifact *externalAIze* demonstrates how situationally adaptive and individualized questions and answer options can be generated proactively without the involvement of human analysts. By leveraging an unprecedented breadth of topical knowledge, GenAI systems synthesize analogies and cross-domain connections that human interviewers may lack the background to suggest [5, 28]. This allows organizations to externalize tacit knowledge with comparatively low time requirements, making this approach efficient and particularly suitable for organizational contexts characterized by dynamic knowledge [8].

Second, we shift the focus from explaining the capabilities of GenAI toward prescriptive knowledge of how real-world artifacts can be designed to leverage these capabilities for knowledge externalization [8]. To this end, the study derives and empirically evaluates four DPs: *phased reflective questioning, curated input options with free-text fallback, adaptive motivational feedback*, and *human-in-the-loop knowledge validation*.

Third, the study contributes empirical design knowledge by evaluating how design choices influence the knowledge externalization process. In particular, a systematic comparison of three interaction modalities shows that combining closed-ended and open-ended inputs improves usability and reduces articulation effort [21, 34]. However, the results also indicate a potential trade-off: users may underutilize open-ended inputs out of convenience even when predefined options do not fully capture their knowledge.

5.2 Practical Contributions

Finally, this study offers a practical contribution by providing organizations with design knowledge to facilitate the externalization of tacit knowledge. The proposed artifact, *externalAIze,* enables continuous knowledge externalization in everyday work contexts, requires comparatively few time and resource investments, and reduces reliance on human analysts.

5.3 Limitations and Future Research

This study is subject to several limitations that provide directions for future research. First, it focuses on forms of tacit knowledge that are more amenable to articulation, such as experience-based insights, practical intelligence, and rules of thumb. More deeply embedded forms, including intuition and gut-feelings, can typically only be transferred through observation, apprenticeship, and learning-by-doing. Future research should explore how GenAI chatbots can be combined with complementary elicitation approaches to extend the boundaries of tacit knowledge externalization.

Second, although the selected scenario enabled a controlled validation of the design principles, it does not fully reflect the complexity of actual organizational tasks. Future research should therefore conduct experiments in domain-specific organizational environments to assess real-world applicability.

Third, the closed-ended and hybrid interaction modalities rely on curated input options, whose non-deterministically generated composition may have influenced user behavior and perceptions. Future research should experimentally examine whether users underutilize open-ended input out of convenience and how interface nudges or usage prompts can encourage richer self-formulated knowledge.

Fourth, the evaluation primarily relies on subjective perception measures. Future research should complement these with independent expert ratings and NeuroIS methods such as eye tracking or Electroencephalography (EEG) to more objectively assess knowledge quality and users' cognitive states during the externalization process.

6   Conclusions

This study presented a design-oriented approach to a GenAI chatbot for the externalization of tacit knowledge. Applying the ^{e}DSR methodology [13], we derived, instantiated, and evaluated a set of DPs that guide the development of such systems. Specifically, the study proposes four DPs to researchers and practitioners: (DP1) the use of *phased reflective questioning* to progressively elicit and structure tacit knowledge, (DP2) the provision of *curated input options with free-text fallback* to balance users' cognitive effort and efficiency with expressive freedom, (DP3) the integration of *adaptive motivational feedback* to foster engagement and reflection, and (DP4) the implementation of *human-in-the-loop knowledge validation* mechanisms to ensure user control and accuracy over the externalized knowledge.

Disclosure of Interests. The authors have no competing interests to declare that are relevant to the content of this article.

References

1. Adesina, A.O., Ocholla, D.N.: Tacit knowledge management strategies of small- and medium-sized enterprises: an overview. South Afr. J. Inf. Manag. **26**(1), a1711 (2024). https://doi.org/10.4102/sajim.v26i1.1711
2. Bakker, R.M., Cambré, B., Korlaar, L., Raab, J.: Managing the project learning paradox: a set-theoretic approach toward project knowledge transfer. Int. J. Proj. Manag. **29**(5), 494–503 (2011). https://doi.org/10.1016/j.ijproman.2010.06.002
3. Nonaka, I., Takeuchi, H.: The Knowledge-Creating Company: How Japanese Companies Create the Dynamics of Innovation. Oxford University Press, Oxford (1995)
4. Massingham, P.R.: Measuring the impact of knowledge loss: a longitudinal study. J. Knowl. Manag. **22**(4), 721–758 (2018). https://doi.org/10.1108/JKM-08-2016-0338
5. Subramonyam, H., Pea, R., Pondoc, C., Seifert, C.: Bridging the gulf of envisioning: cognitive challenges in prompt based interactions with LLMs. In: Proceedings of the 2024 CHI Conference on Human Factors in Computing Systems, Honolulu, pp. 1–19. Association for Computing Machinery (2024)
6. Niehaus, F., Wiesche, M.: A Socio-technical perspective on organizational interaction with AI: a literature review. In: Proceedings of the 29th European Conference on Information Systems, Marrakech. AIS Electronic Library (2021)
7. Alavi, M., Leidner, D.E., Mousavi, R.: Knowledge management perspective of generative artificial intelligence (GenAI). J. Assoc. Inf. Syst. **25**(1), 1–12 (2024). https://doi.org/10.17705/1jais.00859
8. Kernan Freire, S., Wang, C., Ruiz-Arenas, S., Niforatos, E.: Tacit knowledge elicitation for shop-floor workers with an intelligent assistant. In: Extended Abstracts of the 2023 CHI Conference on Human Factors in Computing Systems, Hamburg, pp. 1–7. Association for Computing Machinery (2023)
9. Favero, L., Pérez-Ortiz, J.A., Käser, T., Oliver, N.: Enhancing critical thinking in education by means of a socratic chatbot. In: Bellas, F., Fontenla-Romero, O. (eds.) AIEER 2024. CCIS, vol. 2519, pp. 17–32. Springer, Cham (2025). https://doi.org/10.1007/978-3-031-93409-4_2
10. Matsumoto, T., Nishikawa, R., Morimoto, C.: Reflection through interaction with digital twin AI in the human-AI-collaboration SECI model. In: 28th International Conference on Knowledge-Based and Intelligent Information & Engineering Systems, Sevilla, pp. 3743–3752. Elsevier (2024). https://doi.org/10.1016/j.procs.2024.09.182
11. Singh, H., Shi, Y., Van Toorn, C.: Generative AI-powered knowledge management in education: a dual perspective of design and use. In: Proceedings of the 35th Australasian Conference on Information Systems, Canberra. AIS Electronic Library (2024)
12. Hevner, A.R., March, S.T., Park, J., Ram, S.: Design science in information systems research. MIS Q. **28**(1), 75–105 (2004). https://doi.org/10.2307/25148625

13. Tuunanen, T., Winter, R., Vom Brocke, J.: Dealing with complexity in design science research: A methodology using design echelons. MIS Q. **48**(2), 427–458 (2024). https://doi.org/10.25300/MISQ/2023/16700
14. Gavrilova, T., Andreeva, T.: Knowledge elicitation techniques in a knowledge management context. J. Knowl. Manag. **16**(4), 523–537 (2012). https://doi.org/10.1108/13673271211246112
15. Donate, M.J., Sánchez de Pablo, J.D.: The role of knowledge-oriented leadership in knowledge management practices and innovation. J. Bus. Res. **68**(2), 360–370 (2015). https://doi.org/10.1016/j.jbusres.2014.06.022
16. Omotayo, F.O.: Knowledge management as an important tool in organisational management: a review of literature. Libr. Philos. Pract. **1**, 1–23 (2015)
17. Du Plessis, M.: Drivers of knowledge management in the corporate environment. Int. J. Inf. Manag. **25**(3), 193–202 (2005). https://doi.org/10.1016/j.ijinfomgt.2004.12.001
18. Seghroucheni, O.Z., Al Achhab, M., Lazaar, M.: Systematic review on the conversion of tacit knowledge. In: 2023 7th IEEE Congress on Information Science and Technology, Agadir, pp. 123–128. IEEE (2023)
19. Chennamaneni, A., Teng, J.T.C.: An integrated framework for effective tacit knowledge transfer. In: Proceedings of the Seventeenth Americas Conference on Information Systems, Detroit. AIS Electronic Library (2011)
20. Weldemariam, G.S., Garfield, M.J.: Framework for externalization of tacit knowledge in participatory agricultural research in Ethiopia: the case of farmers research group (FRG). In: Proceedings of the 52nd Hawaii International Conference on System Sciences, Maui, pp. 5339–5347. AIS Electronic Library (2019)
21. Heimburg, V., Schreieck, M., Wiesche, M.: Complementor value co-creation in generative AI platform ecosystems. J. Manag. Inf. Syst. **42**(2), 491–528 (2025). https://doi.org/10.1080/07421222.2025.2487310
22. Banh, L., Strobel, G.: Generative artificial intelligence. Electron. Mark. **33**, 63 (2023). https://doi.org/10.1007/s12525-023-00680-1
23. Vadari, S., Desik, P.H.A.: The role of AI/ML in Enhancing knowledge management systems. IUP J. Knowl. Manag. **19**(2), 7–31 (2021)
24. Kocielnik, R., Avrahami, D., Marlow, J., Lu, D., Hsieh, G.: Designing for workplace reflection: a chat and voice-based conversational agent. In: Proceedings of the 2018 Designing Interactive Systems Conference, New York, pp. 881–894. Association for Computing Machinery (2018)
25. Shen, W.-C., Lin, F.-R.: The design of AI-enabled experience-based knowledge management system to facilitate knowing and doing in communities of practice. In: Uden, L., Ting, I.-H. (eds.) KMO 2024. CCIS, vol. 2152, pp. 292–303. Springer, Cham (2024). https://doi.org/10.1007/978-3-031-63269-3_22
26. Peffers, K., Tuunanen, T., Rothenberger, M.A., Chatterjee, S.: A design science research methodology for information systems research. J. Manag. Inf. Syst. **24**(3), 45–77 (2007). https://doi.org/10.2753/MIS0742-1222240302
27. Fenoglio, E., Kazim, E., Latapie, H., Koshiyama, A.: Tacit knowledge elicitation process for industry 4.0. Discov. Artif. Intell. **2**(1), 6 (2022). https://doi.org/10.1007/s44163-022-00020-w
28. Ding, Z., Srinivasan, A., Macneil, S., Chan, J.: Fluid transformers and creative analogies: exploring large language models' capacity for augmenting cross-domain analogical creativity. In: Proceedings of the 15th Conference on Creativity and Cognition, pp. 489–505. Association for Computing Machinery (2023)
29. Polanyi, M.: The Tacit Dimension. University of Chicago Press, Chicago (1966)
30. Gan, J., Sundaram, D.: Why knowledge management system needs to be "intelligent" in professional service providing organisations. In: 2023 IEEE Asia-Pacific Conference on Computer Science and Data Engineering, Nadi, pp. 1–6. IEEE (2023)

31. Kankanhalli, A., Tan, B.C.Y., Wei, K.-K.: Contributing knowledge to electronic knowledge repositories: an empirical investigation. MIS Q. **29**(1), 113–143 (2005). https://doi.org/10.2307/25148670
32. Hanelt, A., Wiesche, M., Benlian, A., Hinz, O.: Opening the network of trust: how domain experts in triadic relationships build trust in AI-based counterparts. MIS Q. **50**(1), 299–326 (2026). https://doi.org/10.25300/MISQ/2025/18041
33. Gregor, S., Kruse, L.C., Seidel, S.: Research perspectives: the anatomy of a design principle. J. Assoc. Inf. Syst. **21**(6), 1622–1652 (2020). https://doi.org/10.17705/1jais.00649
34. Nguyen, Q.N., Sidorova, A., Torres, R.: User interactions with chatbot interfaces vs. menu-based interfaces: an empirical study. Comput. Hum. Behav. **128**, 107093 (2022). https://doi.org/10.1016/j.chb.2021.107093
35. Bickmore, T.W., Picard, R.W.: Establishing and maintaining long-term human-computer relationships. ACM Trans. Comput. Hum. Interact. **12**(2), 293–327 (2005). https://doi.org/10.1145/1067860.1067867
36. Wu, X., Xiao, L., Sun, Y., Zhang, J., Ma, T., He, L.: A survey of human-in-the-loop for machine learning. Future Gener. Comput. Syst. **135**, 364–381 (2022). https://doi.org/10.1016/j.future.2022.05.014
37. Seghroucheni, O.Z., Lazaar, M., Al Achhab, M.: Bridging tacit knowledge and explicit knowledge: an ontological model for effective knowledge conversion. Int. J. Eng. Pedagogy **15**(2), 93–105 (2025). https://doi.org/10.3991/ijep.v15i2.53389
38. Ellis, S., Carette, B., Anseel, F., Lievens, F.: Systematic reflection: implications for learning from failures and successes. Curr. Dir. Psychol. Sci. **23**(1), 67–72 (2014). https://doi.org/10.1177/0963721413504106
39. Moore, G.C., Benbasat, I.: Development of an instrument to measure the perceptions of adopting an information technology innovation. Inf. Syst. Res. **2**(3), 192–222 (1991). https://doi.org/10.1287/isre.2.3.192
40. Cronbach, L.J.: Coefficient alpha and the internal structure of tests. Psychometrika **16**(3), 297–334 (1951). https://doi.org/10.1007/BF02310555
41. Gregor, S., Hevner, A.R.: Positioning and presenting design science research for maximum impact. MIS Q. **37**(2), 337–355 (2013). https://doi.org/10.25300/MISQ/2013/37.2.01

From Passive Consumption to Creative Engagement: Designing and Evaluating Scaffolded Augmented Reality Authoring

Dana Hofmann[(✉)] [iD], Kay Hönemann [iD], and Manuel Wiesche [iD]

TU Dortmund University, Dortmund, Germany
`{dana.hofmann,kay.hoenemann,manuel.wiesche}@tu-dortmund.de`

Abstract. Augmented Reality (AR) offers novel opportunities for creative engagement in education, cultural heritage, and participatory design, yet many applications remain limited to passive content consumption. This study investigates how scaffolded support can enhance creativity in novice-oriented AR authoring environments. Following an Action Design Research (ADR) approach, we iteratively designed and evaluated a voxel-based AR authoring tool in two configurations: an unstructured baseline and a semi-structured, example-based scaffold. The design leverages principles from Scaffolding Theory and the Paradox of Choice to balance structural guidance with creative freedom, enabling users to create, manipulate, and reflect on digital content in situ. Evaluation results demonstrate that the scaffolded environment achieved higher creativity ratings from external experts, while participants' subjective perceptions of creativity were similar across conditions. Cognitive load analyses indicate that scaffolds may simultaneously increase germane load, supporting meaningful engagement, and introduce extraneous load, highlighting the nuanced effects of structural guidance. These findings provide empirically grounded design principles for AR authoring tools, showing how partial, example-based scaffolds can actively shape creative processes, support novice users, and promote higher-quality creative outcomes without constraining perceived autonomy.

Keywords: Augmented Reality · Creativity Support · Action Design Research · Example-based Scaffolds

1 Introduction

Augmented reality (AR) has reached mass adoption through mobile and web-based platforms such as Snapchat [1], Pokémon Go [2], and many more AR-enabled consumer and enterprise applications. AR refers to technologies that overlay digital content onto the physical world in real time, allowing users to perceive and interact with virtual elements within their immediate environment. Millions of users now routinely consume AR experiences in everyday contexts. Beyond entertainment, AR has enormous potential in creative domains such as education, cultural heritage, museum design, and participatory design, where creativity drives engagement and the construction of meaningful, contextually situated experiences [3–5]. In these domains, engagement is not only a matter of information access but also of active meaning-making, where users interpret, contextualize, and contribute to digital content.

Despite these opportunities, current AR implementations in these application domains are predominantly characterized by passive consumption. In museum settings, for instance, AR applications typically present supplementary information through digital overlays [6], while in educational contexts, learning materials are augmented with digital content to enhance instruction [7]. Such approaches primarily support information delivery rather than active knowledge construction or creative expression. However, this passive reception of AR content represents only the superficial level of engagement [8]. While passive AR can be effective for guidance and information presentation, it often limits opportunities for users to explore, reinterpret, or extend content in personally meaningful ways [9]. To achieve this deeper level of engagement, users would need to transition from consumers to creators of AR content. Enabling users to create their own AR experiences allows them to actively engage with content, externalize ideas, and construct situated meaning, which is particularly valuable in learning and participatory contexts [9].

Creating AR applications and creative content, however, is complex. Existing AR authoring tools often demand extensive technical expertise and familiarity with 3D modeling or programming, posing high entry barriers for novice users [9, 10]. This complexity constrains engagement, limits creative exploration, and restricts who can contribute to the AR ecosystem [11, 12].

AR authoring tools can help mitigate this complexity [4, 5, 7]. Authoring tools are software programs that allow users to create and publish AR experiences on different platforms on different types of hardware [10]. Prior research has demonstrated the feasibility of block-based and in-situ authoring paradigms for supporting novice users in content creation [13]. In particular, scaffolded support structures—such as templates, parameterized examples, and structured workflows—can guide novice users through the authoring process, reducing cognitive load and lowering entry barriers [14, 15].

However, structuring the authoring process introduces a fundamental tension: providing guidance can reduce complexity but may also constrain creativity, while leaving too much freedom risks overwhelming novice users [16]. The "Paradox of Choice" from psychological research suggests that an abundance of options can lead to decision paralysis, cognitive overload, and reduced satisfaction, particularly for novice users who lack clear prior knowledge or preferences [16]. Translating this insight to AR authoring implies that scaffolds must balance structural guidance with opportunities for creative exploration.

One promising approach to address this tension is the use of example-based scaffolds—pre-structured, context-sensitive starting points within the authoring environment that can guide novices while leaving room for creative exploration [14, 17], by offering partially completed artifacts that illustrate possible solutions while remaining modifiable. Although prior work has explored AR authoring tools with example-based scaffolds, it remains unclear how those example-based scaffolds can be designed to simultaneously reduce complexity and foster creative engagement for novice users.

To address this gap, we pose the following research question: *How can AR authoring tools be designed to effectively support novice users' creativity while reducing
complexity?*

To answer this challenge, we adopt a Design Science Research (DSR) approach
[18]. Evaluating the effectiveness of creativity-supporting scaffolds in AR authoring
tools requires human-in-the-loop studies with real users. Therefore, we follow an Action
Design Research–based approach (eADR) [19] to iteratively design and evaluate a voxel-
based AR authoring artifact, where virtual content is constructed from discrete, cube-
shaped building blocks (voxels) that simplify 3D design through modular composition,
aiming to develop empirically grounded design knowledge for novice-oriented creative
AR authoring. Building on theories of scaffolding [15] and the Paradox of Choice [16],
our study investigates how structured guidance can navigate novice users through the
authoring process while preserving creative freedom and opportunities for meaningful
experimentation.

Through this work, we contribute prescriptive design knowledge for future AR
authoring tools, providing insights into how example scaffolds can foster user-driven,
creative content creation and unlock the full educational and societal potential of AR.

2 Theoretical Background and Related Work

2.1 Creativity in AR Authoring as a Practical Design Problem

AR authoring tools such as Blender [20] and Unreal Engine [21] are established platforms
for developing AR applications, but they require substantial programming expertise
and are typically detached from the physical context of use. Authors often design AR
experiences in abstract environments rather than in the spatial setting in which content
will be deployed, which undermines spatio-temporal coherence, particularly in domains
such as education, cultural heritage, and participatory design [4].

To address these limitations, a range of novice-oriented AR authoring approaches
based on direct manipulation, WYSIWYG principles, visual block programming, trigger–action rules, and programming by demonstration has been proposed [22–25]. Existing AR authoring tools are software environments that enable users to design, configure,
and deploy augmented reality experiences without necessarily developing underlying
system functionality from scratch. Empirical studies indicate that AR authoring tools
can support inexperienced users when tools are appropriately designed [11]. For example,
Funk et al. [26] and Hönemann et al. [12] demonstrate that users without programming
experience can create situational AR content through accessible, in-situ authoring tools.

Despite these advances, novice-oriented AR authoring remains cognitively demanding. Open-ended creative tasks require users to simultaneously generate ideas, structure
content, and understand the tool's interaction and representational logic. From a cognitive perspective, this combination places substantial demands on working memory and
can lead to cognitive overload, particularly for novices [27].

This highlights the need for design interventions that explicitly address cognitive
load by reducing unnecessary complexity while preserving opportunities for creative
experimentation.

2.2 Creative Orientation and Anchoring in Example-Based AR Authoring

Beyond cognitive demands, novice-oriented AR authoring tools must also contend with how users orient themselves in open design spaces. Example-based guidance and pre-configured starting points have emerged as promising design interventions to support orientation in these early stages [17, 28]. By providing concrete reference structures, examples can reduce initial uncertainty and help users understand what is possible within an authoring environment. However, theoretical perspectives such as Anchoring Theory suggest that examples may function as cognitive reference points that shape how users interpret both the task and the available solution space, even when no explicit constraints are imposed [29].

Insights from creativity research in adjacent design domains further indicate that example-based guidance can have conditional effects on creative performance [30]. While examples can support orientation and reduce initial uncertainty, overly complete, semantically rich, or highly task-proximal examples have been associated with fixation effects and reduced originality, particularly when designers closely align their solutions with the presented reference [31–33]. These findings suggest that the creative impact of examples depends less on their mere presence than on their level of completeness, specificity, and similarity to the target task.

This creates a central tension in AR authoring: examples provide orientation but can also constrain creativity. However, this trade-off is rarely examined, as research still focuses on usability and technical feasibility [34, 35].

Together, these perspectives highlight that novice-oriented AR authoring tools must carefully balance cognitive accessibility and creative orientation. Rather than rejecting examples altogether, these considerations emphasize the need for scaffold designs that provide orientation without inducing fixation. This tension motivates the selection of Scaffolding Theory and the Paradox of Choice as the primary kernel theories in the following section, as they jointly frame the central design problem of balancing guidance and freedom in creativity-supporting AR authoring environments.

2.3 Scaffolding in AR Authoring (Kernel Theory 1)

The concept of scaffolding originates from Wood et al. [15] and describes support structures that enable learners to perform complex tasks by providing a framework for problem solving and exploration. In the context of AR authoring, scaffolds can be defined as in-tool, context-coupled support structures that simplify the design process and guide users' creative activity. These include parameterized examples, worked-example-like templates, and structured workflows that reduce the initial search space and lower entry barriers [14].

Prior research has implemented heterogeneous scaffolding mechanisms in AR authoring, including predefined components, restricted interaction palettes, guided workflows, and example-based starting points. Example-based scaffolds provide small executable AR applications with placeholder objects, default parameters, and predefined anchors that users can run and adapt [5, 25] These scaffolds reduce initial search processes, provide concrete points of entry into the design space, and lower technical hurdles for novice users [5, 25].

Similarly, Rajaram and Nebeling's [36] Paper Trail system demonstrates the potential of example-driven and capture-based workflows for low-threshold AR authoring, while also revealing users' need for structured guidance to translate goals into meaningful AR interactions and concerns about reliability and task structuring [36].

While these approaches provide empirical support for the feasibility and usability of example-based scaffolds, they primarily evaluate perceived usefulness and adoption rather than how scaffold structure shapes creative exploration or originality. Prior work leaves open how scaffolds should be designed to provide orientation without fixing users' solution spaces or constraining creative outcomes.

2.4 Choice Overload and Creative Freedom (Kernel Theory 2: Paradox of Choice)

The Paradox of Choice [16] posits that excessive options can lead to cognitive overload, decision paralysis, and reduced satisfaction. In creative tools, large and unstructured design spaces may therefore undermine engagement, particularly for novices with limited domain knowledge.

Applied to AR authoring, this perspective suggests that empty workspaces impose substantial cognitive demands, as users must simultaneously decide what to create, how to structure it, and how to operate the tool [7].

While creative freedom is a core value, the Paradox of Choice justifies introducing structural guidance that constrains early choice spaces in a way that supports engagement rather than suppressing creativity.

Together with Scaffolding Theory, this perspective frames the balance between freedom and guidance as a central design problem and provides justificatory knowledge for introducing example-based scaffolds that reduce initial complexity while preserving opportunities for creative divergence.

3 Research Method and Design Process

3.1 Action Design Research-Based Approach

Design Science Research (DSR) focuses on designing and evaluating innovative IT artifacts to address practically relevant problems while generating prescriptive design knowledge [37, 38]. Action Design Research (ADR), as a specific DSR approach, emphasizes sustained engagement with stakeholders throughout the artifact development process [39]. Unlike traditional design cycles, ADR integrates researcher-stakeholder interaction (in this study: novice users) into iterative artifact refinement, with evaluation occurring continuously throughout each design iteration [19].

However, the original ADR framework offers considerable latitude in its operationalization. Therefore, IS scholars have noted that artifact development typically progresses through multiple intermediate instantiations, each offering opportunities to extract design knowledge [19]. To systematically capture insights at all stages of artifact design, we adopted an elaborated ADR (eADR) approach that executes all core ADR activities, *problem formulation and planning, artifact creation, evaluation, reflection, and learning,* within each intervention [19].

In the problem formulation and planning phase, limitations of existing novice-oriented AR authoring tools were identified, and meta-requirements were derived a priori from kernel theories, including Scaffolding Theory and the Paradox of Choice.

These meta-requirements directly informed an initial reflection and learning step, in which they were abstracted into prescriptive design principles that structured the subsequent artifact design.

During artifact creation, the design principles were operationalized in a voxel-based AR authoring tool instantiated in two configurations: an unstructured baseline and a semi-structured example scaffold as a targeted design intervention.

The evaluation phase comprised a controlled laboratory experiment with novice users, combining self-report measures, cognitive load assessments, and an external creativity evaluation of the resulting artifacts.

The empirical findings were then reflected upon to assess how well the instantiated artifacts realized the design principles, thereby refining and validating the proposed prescriptive design knowledge. Based on these meta-requirements, prescriptive design principles were subsequently abstracted to translate theoretical insights into actionable design guidance. These design principles informed the development of two artifact instantiations: a semi-structured scaffold artifact implementing both structural guidance and universal constructability, and an unstructured baseline artifact implementing universal constructability without scaffolded guidance.

Both artifacts were evaluated in a controlled laboratory experiment with novice users, complemented by an external creativity assessment. Based on the evaluation results, the proposed design principles were empirically examined, contributing reusable prescriptive design knowledge for creativity-supporting AR authoring environments.

3.2 Synthesizing Literature for a Theory-Informed Artifact Design

In this diagnosis stage, we identified and conceptualized the research object of this study: creativity-supporting scaffolds for novice-oriented AR authoring environments. Following the elaborated Action Design Research process [40], meta-requirements (MRs) were derived from the literature a priori to artifact instantiation. To this end, we conducted a focused analysis of prior work on AR authoring tools, novice interaction, and creativity support to examine (a) typical challenges faced by novice AR authors during early ideation, (b) limitations of existing authoring environments with respect to creative guidance, (c) previously proposed forms of scaffolding and example-based support, and (d) design characteristics that may balance guidance, freedom, and cognitive accessibility.

The preceding discussion establishes a fundamental design tension in novice-oriented AR authoring: creative freedom must be preserved while providing sufficient structural guidance to reduce overwhelm and cognitive disorientation. This work derives prescriptive meta-requirements for creativity-supporting AR authoring tools, grounded in prior research on novice-oriented design [10, 13, 14, 28], cognitive accessibility [3, 16, 27], and in-situ spatial interaction [26, 41]. These meta-requirements consolidate the core design objectives and guide the development of the voxel-based AR authoring artifact.

MR1 (Structural Guidance without Over-Constraint).
Drawing on, Scaffolding Theory [15] and the Paradox of Choice [16], AR authoring tools should provide sufficient structural guidance to reduce initial search processes and support task engagement, while preserving enough degrees of freedom to enable original and exploratory design [7]. Prior research on example-based AR authoring demonstrates that guided examples can effectively reduce entry barriers and support task engagement by providing concrete points of orientation [5, 25, 26]. Such guidance should help users navigate the design space efficiently without restricting the range of creative possibilities they can explore.

MR2 (Universal Constructability without Creative Restriction).
To support creative exploration and originality, AR authoring tools should afford universal constructability—that is, the ability to realize any structure or idea in principle using the provided building elements [3, 14, 31]. Building blocks should remain semantically neutral and broadly composable, avoiding domain-specific or meaning-laden forms that privilege particular interpretations.

This requirement directly addresses the risk of creative restriction identified in Anchoring Theory [29], which cautions that semantically rich elements may implicitly define "appropriate" outcomes and narrow the explored solution space [33]. By prioritizing expressive completeness over semantic specificity, universal constructability ensures that structural guidance (MR1) does not undermine creative freedom, aligning with the objective of balancing guidance and freedom [11].

MR3 (Cognitive Accessibility through Simple and Familiar Forms for Novice Users).
To minimize extraneous cognitive load and lower the entry barrier for novice users, AR authoring tools should employ simple, perceptually and conceptually familiar forms that can be readily understood and manipulated without prior expertise [10, 13, 14, 28, 34]. According to Cognitive Load Theory, unnecessary representational complexity increases extraneous load and detracts from germane processes such as ideation and creative elaboration [27, 34].

In open-ended authoring environments, this effect is amplified by the Paradox of Choice, where complex or unfamiliar elements increase decision difficulty and cognitive overwhelm [16]. Simple and familiar forms reduce interpretive overhead, enabling rapid experimentation and helping users focus on what they want to create rather than how to understand the representational system. This requirement ensures that the expressive power enabled by universal constructability (MR2) remains cognitively accessible to novice users.

MR4 (Orientation without Anchoring Bias).
To support in-situ spatial authoring while avoiding creative fixation, AR authoring tools should provide orientation through modifiable and incomplete example structures rather than finalized solutions [31, 33]. Example-based scaffolds can lower entry barriers and support task engagement by offering concrete spatial reference points [14, 17, 36], particularly in immersive environments.

However, consistent with Anchoring Theory [29] and creativity research, such examples must be designed to avoid anchoring bias [31–33]. Parameterizable, transformable, and partially underspecified examples invite users to adapt, reinterpret, and extend the initial structure, balancing guidance and freedom while preserving originality.

3.3 Design and Development

In accordance with Mullarkey and Hevner's [19] conception of design science research as the production of reusable, prescriptive design knowledge, the contribution of this study not only lies in the voxel-based AR authoring artifact itself, but in the abstraction of empirically grounded insights into design principles derived from the formulated meta-requirements (MR1–MR4). We formulate our DPs following the framework proposed by Gregor et al. [42].

Design Principle 1 (DP1: Semi-Structured Example Scaffolds) To support early ideation without over-constraining users, AR authoring tools should provide semi-structured example scaffolds with deliberate gaps, rather than fully specified templates or empty workspaces. This operationalizes MR1 by offering orientation and reducing initial search effort [14, 15, 17], while MR4 is addressed by keeping scaffolds underspecified to avoid fixation on predefined solution paths [32, 33].

Design Principle 2 (DP2: Simple, Universally Composable Building Elements) To preserve creative freedom and maintain cognitive accessibility, scaffolds should be composed of a small set of simple, semantically neutral, and universally composable building elements. This fulfills MR2 by preventing implicit bias from rich or domain-specific forms [29, 33], and MR3 by keeping extraneous cognitive load and decision difficulty manageable [16, 27]. Simple, familiar forms enable expressive completeness, allowing any structure or idea to be realized while keeping the design space navigable [13].

Together, these design principles capture the core design insight of this study: creativity-supporting AR authoring tools for novice users should deliberately calibrate the degree of structure and choice.

3.4 Design of a Voxel-Based AR Authoring Tool

This section describes the design instantiation that operationalizes the meta-requirements derived in Sect. 3.2 and the design principles presented in 3.3. Following Mullarkey and Hevner's elaborated ADSR [19], we developed two voxel-based AR authoring artifacts in which the proposed design principles are instantiated and made empirically testable.

To operationalize these objectives, we developed two custom AR authoring applications inspired by the Blocks system proposed by Guo et al. [13] (see table 1). Both applications follow a voxel-based interaction paradigm emphasizing modularity, direct manipulation, and low-threshold entry for novice users. Voxels afford universal constructability, enabling users to create any structure through their combination while maintaining cognitive accessibility due to their geometric simplicity.

Within the application, the ground surface functions as a spatial grid onto which users can place individual voxels. From an affordance perspective, voxels provide clear and

Table 1. Implementation of Design Principles Across Artifacts

Artifact	Name of Artifact	Implemented Design Principles
Artifact 1	Semi-Structured Scaffold	DP1, DP2
Artifact 2	Unstructured Baseline	DP2

immediately perceivable action possibilities: they can be placed, combined, removed, and reconfigured through direct manipulation, enabling users to explore the design space through interaction rather than abstract planning. Voxels are placed by tapping on the grid; users may preselect colors to differentiate structural elements. Existing voxels can be deleted or repositioned through direct interaction. When voxels are placed in close proximity, they automatically connect, supporting the incremental construction of larger structures. This interaction design preserves expressive completeness while remaining accessible to novice users.

To ensure consistent evaluation of creative outcomes, the tool includes a camera function that exports the authored artifact as a standardized 3D image from a fixed perspective without background. This enables outcome-based comparison across participants while remaining decoupled from subjective self-reports.

All authoring takes place in situ using an image-based anchor placed in the physical environment. This preserves a tight coupling between physical context and virtual authoring space and reflects realistic AR creation scenarios outside abstract development environments.

Both artifacts constitute solution design entities in the sense of design science research, operationalizing the derived meta-requirements (MR1–MR4) through concrete interaction and representation choices. They are designed to support creative AR authoring by balancing structural guidance and creative freedom while reducing cognitive barriers.

The first artifact operationalizes both DP1 and DP2 through a semi-structured example scaffold (see Fig. 1). This scaffold takes the form of a partially specified, tree-like voxel structure containing deliberate gaps and underspecified elements, providing orientation without fixing the solution space or constraining creative exploration. Users can freely modify, extend, reinterpret, or partially discard the scaffold, ensuring that structural guidance supports early ideation without biasing outcomes. The second artifact implements only DP2 (see Fig. 1), without any scaffold, representing an unstructured baseline condition. Participants start from an empty design space containing only a single initial voxel; no structural guidance (DP1) is provided.

Both artifacts share the same interaction paradigm and differ only in the presence of the scaffold, enabling a controlled comparison of creative outcomes, user experience, and cognitive effects.

Fig. 1. Left and middle: Scaffolds in the and Semi-structured example scaffold condition. Right: Scaffolds in the unstructured authoring baseline without scaffolds.

3.5 Demonstration Context

To demonstrate the applicability of the proposed artifacts in a realistic setting, the voxel-based AR authoring tool was embedded in an open-ended creative design task. The task required no technical or programming knowledge and could be approached intuitively through direct voxel manipulation in physical space, while still allowing for meaningful design decisions and creative variation.

Two separate artifacts were used: an unstructured baseline artifact, starting from a single voxel, and a semi-structured scaffold artifact, providing a partially specified tree-like starting structure that participants could freely modify, extend, or reinterpret. All content was authored in situ using an image-based anchor, enabling participants to move around their creations and refine designs from multiple perspectives.

Together, the task, artifacts, and physical setup form a socio-technical context in which creative outcomes emerge from the interaction between novice users and the AR authoring tool, supporting the evaluation of artifact utility and the validity of the derived design principles.

4 Evaluation

The artifact was evaluated to assess its utility and to validate the proposed design principles derived from the meta-requirements. To this end, a controlled laboratory study with novice users and an external assessment of the generated creative artifacts were conducted. The evaluation focused on the performance of the Solution Design Entity within its usage context.

4.1 Evaluation Design and Participants

We recruited 38 participants from a pool of students enrolled in an undergraduate economics course. In total, 330 students were enrolled in the course, from which 38 students volunteered to participate in the study. Recruitment was conducted via an in-class announcement distributed to all students in the course. Participants received bonus points toward a passing grade for their participation.

As part of this survey, participants reported their prior experience with AR authoring tools through self-assessment items. The results indicated that the majority of participants had very limited prior exposure to AR authoring. This sample was deliberately chosen because it represents novice users with limited prior experience, which aligns with the relevance problem addressed in this study.

After excluding outliers and straightliners to ensure data quality, the final sample comprised 36 participants. We employed a between-subjects design contrasting two authoring conditions:

(1) an unstructured baseline condition without scaffolding, and
(2) a semi-structured example scaffold condition.

Both conditions were implemented within the same voxel-based AR authoring artifact but differed with respect to the instantiation of the derived design knowledge. In the unstructured baseline condition, the artifact did not implement the proposed meta-requirements and design principles; participants were provided with an empty authoring environment without structural guidance or example-based orientation. In contrast, the semi-structured example scaffold condition instantiated the proposed design principles derived from the meta-requirements by providing a partially structured, example-based starting point intended to support ideation while preserving creative freedom.

The participants were distributed between the experimental conditions (Group 1: n = 17; Group 2: n = 19). Participants were between 18 and 28 years old (M = 20.67), with comparable mean ages across all experimental groups, indicating a balanced age distribution. The sample consisted of 23 male and 13 female participants. With respect to educational background, most participants reported having obtained a high school diploma (n = 33). Two participants reported holding a bachelor's degree, one a master's degree. At the time of the study, all participants were enrolled as students.

Crucially for the research objective, participants reported very limited prior experience with AR authoring tools. This confirms that the sample represents the intended target group of novice AR authors and supports the ecological validity of the evaluation. From a design science perspective, this sampling strategy is appropriate because the derived design principles are intended to support inexperienced users in early-stage creative AR authoring, rather than expert developers. Consequently, the sample provides a suitable empirical basis for evaluating whether the proposed scaffold designs address the identified relevance problem and fulfill the formulated meta-requirements.

4.2 Task and Procedure

Participants received an iPad Pro with the voxel-based AR authoring application installed. After a short instruction session, participants were asked to complete the task "Build a tree of the future that can withstand changing climatic conditions." The task was intentionally designed to provide a clear thematic frame while preserving a high degree of creative openness. It required participants to translate an abstract problem into a concrete, spatial AR artifact, while leaving freedom with respect to form, structure, and interpretation. Rather than following predefined instructions, participants had to conceptualize and externalize their own design ideas. In this way, the task reflects a realistic creative authoring scenario in which novelty, interpretation, and exploratory construction are central. After the task, participants completed a questionnaire assessing user experience, perceived creativity support, and cognitive load, followed by open-ended feedback.

Since the investigation of example scaffolds in AR authoring environments and the tool itself have not yet been extensively studied, this study also included an analysis of

184   D. Hofmann et al.

open questions, which addressed participants' sense of freedom during creation and the helpful or disruptive aspects of specific features.

To obtain external creativity ratings, 112 raters were recruited via Prolific; after data cleaning, the final sample comprised 111 raters (M = 35.6 years, SD = 11.9). Each rater evaluated randomly selected artifacts (see Fig. 2 & 3). To ensure data quality and task engagement, we included manipulation checks and excluded responses that failed these checks.

In contrast, for the student sample in the experimental study, data quality was ensured through straightlining checks and response pattern analysis. Given that participants completed the study in a controlled educational context with direct task involvement and supervision, the risk of inattentive responding was substantially lower than in anonymous online settings such as Prolific.

4.3 Measures

User experience was measured using the User Engagement Scale – Short Form (UES-SF) [43] (α = .89), excluding aesthetic appeal.

Cognitive load was measured using the Cognitive Load Scale [44], distinguishing intrinsic, extraneous, and germane load (α = .66).

Perceived creativity support was measured using the Creativity Support Index (CSI) [45] (α = .89).

Creative outcomes were assessed using the Creative Product Semantic Scale (CPSS) [46] based on external ratings. Internal consistency was α = .94.

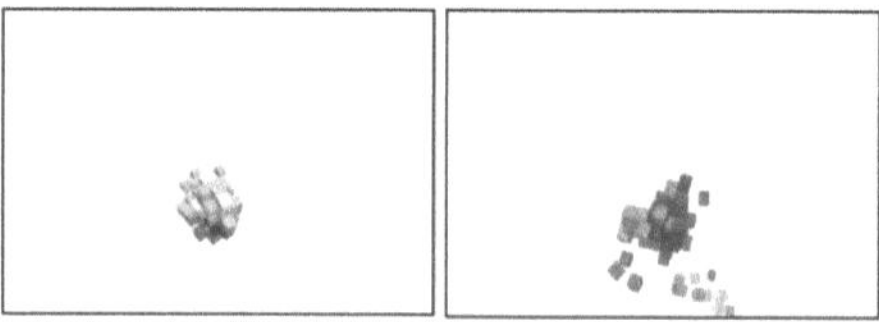

Fig. 2. Example Outputs of the Group with unstructured authoring baseline without scaffolds.

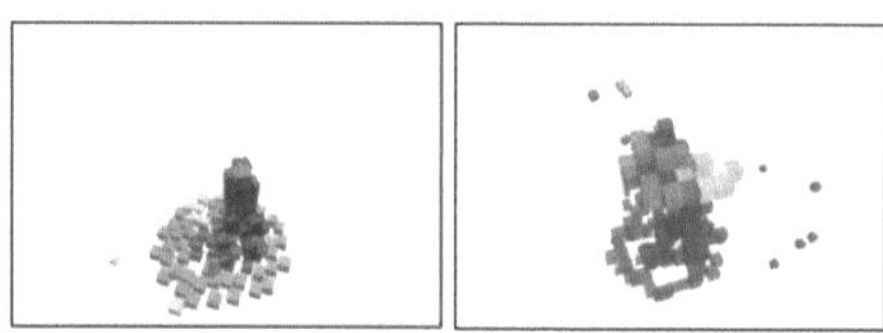

Fig. 3. Example Outputs of the Group with Semi-structured example scaffold condition.

4.4 Evaluation Results

Participants' experiences with the voxel-based AR authoring artifacts generally support the operationalization of the four meta-requirements. Regarding MR1 (structural guidance without over-constraint), participants using the semi-structured scaffold artifact reported satisfaction levels nearly identical to those in the unstructured baseline artifact

(M = 2.96 vs. M = 2.95), indicating that the scaffold provided effective orientation without limiting autonomy. Perceived creativity support was slightly lower in the scaffold artifact (M = 4.72) than in the baseline (M = 4.91), and this difference was not statistically significant (t(27) = 0.30, p = .765, d = 0.11) suggesting that while the scaffold offered guidance, it did not impose a preferred solution path. Open-ended responses confirm this: scaffold users valued the structured starting point as a point of orientation but emphasized that they were able to freely extend, modify, or reinterpret the initial design. For example, participants reported "very free, I could design it however I wanted" and "I felt very free", indicating that the scaffold provided guidance without restricting creative autonomy. Baseline users similarly appreciated the unconstrained nature of the artifact, though some noted challenges with precise 3D placement and camera maneuvering that occasionally restricted their sense of freedom. In terms of MR2 and MR3—universal constructability without creative restriction and cognitive accessibility through simple and familiar forms—the voxel-based AR artifacts supported both creative freedom and usability for novice users. External creativity ratings showed that artifacts created with the semi-structured scaffold were evaluated as more creative than those produced without scaffolds (M = 4.21, SD = 0.12 vs. M = 4.09, SD = 0.16), and this difference was statistically significant (t(27) = − 2.54, p = .017, d = − 0.95) indicating that the scaffold did not limit expressive completeness but rather supported the production of more creative outcomes. Cognitive load measures revealed a nuanced pattern: overall load was higher in the scaffold artifact (M = 3.62 vs. M = 3.21), but this difference was not statistically significant (t(27) = − 1.15, p = .260, d = − 0.43). Germane load was descriptively higher in the scaffold artifact (M = 3.59 vs. M = 3.12), yet again without a significant difference (t(27) = − 0.79, p = .439, d = − 0.29). Extraneous load was also higher in the scaffold artifact (M = 3.91 vs. M = 3.27), but remained non-significant (t(27) = − 1.30, p = .204, d = − 0.49). In contrast, intrinsic load was slightly lower in the scaffold artifact (M = 3.50 vs. M = 3.58), with no significant group difference (t(27) = 0.18, p = .861, d = 0.07). Together, these findings suggest that the scaffold encouraged meaningful engagement and exploration while introducing no statistically reliable increase in cognitive burden.

Both artifacts used simple, perceptually familiar voxel forms, enabling participants to manipulate and combine them without prior domain knowledge. Participants highlighted the utility of direct manipulation, stacking, deletion, and color selection. These insights confirm that cognitive accessibility was maintained and that both scaffolded and baseline designs supported creative expression.

Finally, MR4 (orientation without anchoring bias) was clearly supported by the semi-structured scaffold design. Participants reported high perceived autonomy, noting that the scaffold acted as an invitation rather than a prescriptive template. Illustrative comments include "I could freely express my creativity and design my work as I liked without interference", and "Quite free, one can definitely let their creativity flow". While some operational limitations were encountered, such as "Blocks were difficult to move upward in space, and it was hard to judge their exact position", these did not diminish participants' sense of creative freedom. The scaffold allowed users to interpret, adapt, and extend the initial design in multiple ways, demonstrating that orientation can coexist with exploration and novelty.

Overall, the results indicate that the semi-structured scaffold artifact successfully balances guidance and freedom, supporting engagement, cognitive accessibility, and expressive completeness. Participants' qualitative feedback complements the quantitative findings, highlighting both the supportive aspects of the scaffold and areas where minor operational improvements could further enhance the authoring experience.

5 Discussion

This study investigated how creativity-supporting scaffolds can be designed for novice-oriented AR authoring environments and how varying degrees of structural guidance influence creative experience, cognitive load, and creative outcomes. Rather than treating scaffolds as neutral usability aids, the findings position them as consequential design interventions that actively shape ideation processes, creative exploration, and resulting artifacts in immersive AR authoring.

5.1 Theoretical Implications

These findings extend Scaffolding Theory by demonstrating that partial, example-based support can meaningfully influence creative performance without constraining perceived autonomy, consistent with its conceptualization as temporary support for complex tasks [15]. This perspective is consistent with research on tool-mediated creativity, which highlights how system design actively shapes creative processes and outcomes [47]. The results also reinforce the Paradox of Choice in creative tools: completely open design spaces may overwhelm novice users, while partial structure can reduce early decision friction without biasing outcomes toward a single solution path [13]. This aligns with prior work on creativity support tools, which emphasizes the importance of balancing guidance and freedom to foster creative exploration [48]. Cognitive Load Theory further elucidates that interaction design factors—such as interface stability—mediate whether scaffolds reduce or add to cognitive burden [27].

Anchoring Theory helps explain why participants remained sensitive to structural cues; even underspecified structures can shape attention and interpretation in ways that call for careful scaffold design [29].

Taken together, these theoretical linkages show how scaffold structures interact with cognitive processes and creative behavior in immersive authoring settings. They also illustrate that structure, freedom, and cognitive demands are co-constitutive design dimensions rather than independent variables.

5.2 Design and Evaluation Implications

We found that external creativity ratings provided meaningful additional insight into participants' creative outcomes, complementing self-reported perceptions. This is consistent with Amabile's work on the *Consensual Assessment Technique (CAT)*, which has repeatedly demonstrated in other domains that creativity is best evaluated by domain-relevant judges rather than relying solely on creators' own assessments [49]. By applying such an externally grounded evaluation approach, the study captured aspects of creativity that might not be reflected in participants' subjective experience, supporting a more comprehensive understanding of the effects of scaffolds on creative performance.

5.3 Limitations

The validity of these design principles is bounded by several contextual conditions. That also inform directions for future research. First, the evaluation focused exclusively on novice AR authors; leaving open whether the findings generalize to more experienced users. This also suggests that the effectiveness of scaffolds may depend on user characteristics, such as prior design experience or domain familiarity, pointing to potential person–structure fit effects that were not examined in this study. Future studies should therefore examine how scaffold effectiveness varies across user types and explore potential person–structure fit effects, such as differences in prior design experience or domain familiarity. Second, the creative task was an open-ended, exploratory and the semi-structured scaffold was conceptually aligned with the task, which may have introduced anchoring effects. Future research should investigate the applicability of the principles in more constrained or domain-specific tasks and assess how different types of scaffolds influence creative outcomes under varying task conditions. Third, the artifact was based on a voxel-based interaction paradigm, leaving the generalizability of the principles to other AR authoring paradigms uncertain. Furthermore, the study employed a between-subjects design, which may have introduced additional variance due to individual differences in creativity and prior experience, potentially reducing statistical sensitivity. Future design cycles should therefore explore alternative paradigms and scaffold designs, including adaptive scaffolds, process-oriented guidance, or rule-based constraints, to better understand their effects on creative engagement and cognitive load. Given that creativity often occurs collaboratively, future studies should investigate scaffolds in group-based AR authoring to inform socially aware design mechanisms.

References

1. Snapchat (2019). https://whatis.snapchat.com/
2. Pokémon Go (2016)
3. Liaqat, A., Liu, F., Berengard, B., Cao, J., Monroy-Hernández, A.: Understanding young people's creative goals with augmented reality. Proc. ACM Hum.-Comput. Interact. **9**, 1–21 (2025). https://doi.org/10.1145/3711097
4. Shi, J., Jain, R., Chi, S., Doh, H., Chi, H., Quinn, A.J., Ramani, K.: CARING-AI: towards authoring context-aware augmented reality instruction through generative artificial intelligence. In: Proceedings of the 2025 CHI Conference on Human Factors in Computing Systems, pp. 1–23. ACM, Yokohama Japan (2025). https://doi.org/10.1145/3706598.3713348
5. Numan, N., Brostow, G., Park, S., Julier, S., Steed, A., Van Brummelen, J.: CoCreatAR: enhancing authoring of outdoor augmented reality experiences through asymmetric collaboration. In: Proceedings of the 2025 CHI Conference on Human Factors in Computing Systems, pp. 1–22. ACM, Yokohama Japan (2025). https://doi.org/10.1145/3706598.3714274
6. Arnaboldi, M., Diaz Lema, M.L.: The participatory turn in museums: the online facet. Poetics **89**, 101536 (2021). https://doi.org/10.1016/j.poetic.2021.101536
7. Dengel, A., Iqbal, M.Z., Grafe, S., Mangina, E.: A review on augmented reality authoring toolkits for education. Front. Virtual Real. **3**, 798032 (2022). https://doi.org/10.3389/frvir.2022.798032
8. Spitzer, B.O., Ma, J.H., Erdogmus, E., Kreimer, B., Ryherd, E., Diefes-Dux, H.: Framework for the use of extended reality modalities in AEC education. Buildings **12**, 2169 (2022). https://doi.org/10.3390/buildings12122169

9. Hönemann, K., Konopka, B., Wiesche, M.: The Importance of Separation in the Creation and Usage Phases of Augmented Reality Content Using Social Cognitive Theory. Presented at the Hawaii International Conference on System Sciences (2024). https://doi.org/10.24251/HICSS.2024.070

10. Nebeling, M., Speicher, M.: The trouble with augmented reality/virtual reality authoring tools. In: 2018 IEEE International Symposium on Mixed and Augmented Reality Adjunct (ISMAR-Adjunct), pp. 333–337. IEEE, Munich, Germany (2018). https://doi.org/10.1109/ISMAR-Adjunct.2018.00098

11. Konopka, B., Hönemann, K., Brandt, P., Wiesche, M.: WizARd: A No-Code Tool for Business Process Guidance through the Use of Augmented Reality

12. Hönemann, K., Konopka, B., Wiesche, M.: Designing an effective augmented reality interaction technique to develop AR instructions. In: Local Solutions for Global Challenges: 20th International Conference on Design Science Research in Information Systems and Technology, DESRIST 2025, Montego Bay, Jamaica, June 2–4, 2025, Proceedings, Part II, pp. 130–145. Springer-Verlag, Berlin, Heidelberg (2025). https://doi.org/10.1007/978-3-031-93979-2_10

13. Guo, A., Canberk, I., Murphy, H., Monroy-Hernández, A., Vaish, R.: Blocks: collaborative and persistent augmented reality experiences. Proc. ACM Interact. Mob. Wearable Ubiquitous Technol. **3**, 1–24 (2019). https://doi.org/10.1145/3351241

14. Rau, L., Horst, R., Liu, Y., Dorner, R.: A Nugget-based concept for creating augmented reality. In: 2021 IEEE International Symposium on Mixed and Augmented Reality Adjunct (ISMAR-Adjunct), pp. 212–217. IEEE, Bari, Italy (2021). https://doi.org/10.1109/ISMAR-Adjunct54149.2021.00051

15. Wood, D., Bruner, J.S., Ross, G.: The role of tutoring in problem solving*. J. Child Psychol. Psychiatry **17**, 89–100 (1976). https://doi.org/10.1111/j.1469-7610.1976.tb00381.x

16. Schwartz, B.: The Paradox of Choice: Why More Is Less. Ecco, New York, NY, USA (2004)

17. Rau, L., Döring, D.C., Horst, R., Dörner, R.: Pattern-based augmented reality authoring using different degrees of immersion: a learning nugget approach. Front. Virtual Real. **3**, 841066 (2022). https://doi.org/10.3389/frvir.2022.841066

18. Hevner, A.R., March, S.T., Park, J., Ram, S.: Design science in information systems research. MIS Q. Manag. Inf. Syst. **28**, 75–105 (2004). https://doi.org/10.2307/25148625

19. Mullarkey, M.T., Hevner, A.R.: An elaborated action design research process model. Eur. J. Inf. Syst. **28**, 6–20 (2019). https://doi.org/10.1080/0960085X.2018.1451811

20. Blender Foundation: Blender - Open Source 3D Creation Software (2023). https://www.blender.org/

21. Epic Games: Unreal Engine (2023). https://www.unrealengine.com/

22. Ha, T., Woo, W., Lee, Y., Lee, J., Ryu, J., Choi, H., Lee, K.: ARtalet: tangible user interface based immersive augmented reality authoring tool for digilog book. In: 2010 International Symposium on Ubiquitous Virtual Reality, pp. 40–43. IEEE, Gwangju, Korea (South) (2010). https://doi.org/10.1109/ISUVR.2010.20

23. Lee, J., et al.: ImaginateAR: AI-Assisted In-Situ Authoring in Augmented Reality (2025). http://arxiv.org/abs/2504.21360. https://doi.org/10.48550/arXiv.2504.21360

24. Lee, G.A., Nelles, C., Billinghurst, M., Kim, G.J.: Immersive authoring of tangible augmented reality applications. In: Third IEEE and ACM International Symposium on Mixed and Augmented Reality, pp. 172–181. IEEE, Arlington, VA, USA (2004). https://doi.org/10.1109/ISMAR.2004.34

25. Lee, G.A., Kim, G.J., Billinghurst, M.: Immersive authoring: what you experience is what you get (WYXIWYG). Commun. ACM **48**, 76–81 (2005). https://doi.org/10.1145/1070838.1070840

26. Funk, M., Bächler, A., Bächler, L., Kosch, T., Heidenreich, T., schmidt, a.: working with augmented reality?: a long-term analysis of in-situ instructions at the assembly workplace. In: Proceedings of the 10th International Conference on Pervasive Technologies Related to Assistive Environments, pp. 222–229. ACM, Island of Rhodes Greece (2017). https://doi.org/10.1145/3056540.3056548
27. Sweller, J.: Cognitive load during problem solving: effects on learning. Cogn. Sci. **12**, 257–285 (1988). https://doi.org/10.1207/s15516709cog1202_4
28. Brij, Y., Belhadaoui, H.: Virtual and augmented reality in school context: a literature review. In: 2021 Third International Conference on Transportation and Smart Technologies (TST), pp. 16–23 (2021). https://doi.org/10.1109/TST52996.2021.00010
29. Tversky, A., Kahneman, D.: Judgment under Uncertainty: Heuristics and Biases. 185 (1974)
30. Bako, H.K., Liu, X., Battle, L., Liu, Z.: Understanding how designers find and use data visualization examples. IEEE Trans. Vis. Comput. Graph. 1–11 (2022). https://doi.org/10.1109/TVCG.2022.3209490
31. Bako, H.K., Liu, X., Ko, G., Song, H., Battle, L., Liu, Z.: Unveiling how examples shape visualization design outcomes. IEEE Trans. Vis. Comput. Graph. **31**, 1137–1147 (2025). https://doi.org/10.1109/TVCG.2024.3456407
32. Wadinambiarachchi, S., Kelly, R.M., Pareek, S., Zhou, Q., Velloso, E.: The effects of generative AI on design fixation and divergent thinking. In: Proceedings of the CHI Conference on Human Factors in Computing Systems, pp. 1–18. ACM, Honolulu HI USA (2024). https://doi.org/10.1145/3613904.3642919
33. Agogué, M., et al.: The impact of type of examples on originality: explaining fixation and stimulation effects. J. Creat. Behav. **48**, 1–12 (2014). https://doi.org/10.1002/jocb.37
34. Xia, Z., Monteiro, K., Van, K., Suzuki, R.: RealityCanvas: augmented reality sketching for embedded and responsive scribble animation effects. In: Proceedings of the 36th Annual ACM Symposium on User Interface Software and Technology, pp. 1–14. ACM, San Francisco CA USA (2023). https://doi.org/10.1145/3586183.3606716
35. Monteiro, K., Vatsal, R., Chulpongsatorn, N., Parnami, A., Suzuki, R.: Teachable reality: prototyping tangible augmented reality with everyday objects by leveraging interactive machine teaching. In: Proceedings of the 2023 CHI Conference on Human Factors in Computing Systems, pp. 1–15. ACM, Hamburg Germany (2023). https://doi.org/10.1145/3544548.3581449
36. Rajaram, S., Nebeling, M.: Paper trail: an immersive authoring system for augmented reality instructional experiences. In: Proceedings of the 2022 CHI Conference on Human Factors in Computing Systems. Association for Computing Machinery, New York, NY, USA (2022). https://doi.org/10.1145/3491102.3517486
37. vom Brocke, J., Winter, R., Hevner, A., Maedche, A.: Special issue editorial – accumulation and evolution of design knowledge in design science research: a journey through time and space. J. Assoc. Inf. Syst. **21**, 520–544 (2020). https://doi.org/10.17705/1jais.00611
38. Peffers, K., Tuunanen, T., Niehaves, B.: Design science research genres: introduction to the special issue on exemplars and criteria for applicable design science research. Eur. J. Inf. Syst. **27**, 129–139 (2018). https://doi.org/10.1080/0960085X.2018.1458066
39. Sein, M.K., Henfridsson, O., Purao, S., Rossi, M., Lindgren, R.: Action design research. MIS Q. **35**, 37–56 (2011)
40. Chandra, L., Seidel, S., Gregor, S.: Prescriptive knowledge in IS research: conceptualizing design principles in terms of materiality, action, and boundary conditions. In: 2015 48th Hawaii International Conference on System Sciences, pp. 4039–4048. IEEE, HI, USA (2015). https://doi.org/10.1109/HICSS.2015.485
41. Arora, R., Habib Kazi, R., Grossman, T., Fitzmaurice, G., Singh, K.: SymbiosisSketch: Combining 2D & 3D sketching for designing detailed 3D objects in situ. In: Proceedings of the

2018 CHI Conference on Human Factors in Computing Systems, pp. 1–15. ACM, Montreal QC Canada (2018). https://doi.org/10.1145/3173574.3173759

42. Gregor, S., Kruse, L.C., Seidel, S.: Research perspectives: the anatomy of a design principle. J. Assoc. Inf. Syst. 21, (2020). https://doi.org/10.17705/1jais.00649

43. O'Brien, H.L., Cairns, P., Hall, M.: A practical approach to measuring user engagement with the refined user engagement scale (UES) and new UES short form. Int. J. Hum.-Comput. Stud. **112**, 28–39 (2018). https://doi.org/10.1016/j.ijhcs.2018.01.004

44. Klepsch, M., Schmitz, F., Seufert, T.: Development and validation of two instruments measuring intrinsic, extraneous, and germane cognitive load. Front. Psychol. **8**, 1997 (2017). https://doi.org/10.3389/fpsyg.2017.01997

45. Cherry, E., Latulipe, C.: Quantifying the creativity support of digital tools through the creativity support index. ACM Trans. Comput.-Hum. Interact. **21**, 1–25 (2014). https://doi.org/10.1145/2617588

46. Han, J., Hua, M., Shi, F., Childs, P.R.N.: A further exploration of the three driven approaches to combinational creativity. Proc. Des. Soc. Int. Conf. Eng. Des. **1**, 2735–2744 (2019). https://doi.org/10.1017/dsi.2019.280

47. Shneiderman, B.: Creating creativity: user interfaces for supporting innovation. ACM Trans. Comput.-Hum. Interact. **7**, 114–138 (2000). https://doi.org/10.1145/344949.345077

48. Resnick, M., Myers, B.A., Nakakoji, K., Shneiderman, B., Pausch, R., Selker, T., Eisenberg, M.: Design Principles for Tools to Support Creative Thinking

49. Amabile, M.: Social psychology of creativity: a consensual assessment technique. J. Pers. Soc. Psychol. **5**, (1982)

Orchestrating Scaffolding AI Agents: Design Principles for Mechanism-Specific Learner Support

Diana Kozachek$^{(\boxtimes)}$ [ID] and Andreas Janson [ID]

Institute of Information Systems, University of St. Gallen, St. Gallen, Switzerland
`{diana.kozachek,andreas.janson}@unisg.ch`

Abstract. AI agents are increasingly adopted in higher education, yet current systems handle requests uniformly, promoting cognitive offloading over sustained skill development. With the rise of orchestrated multi-agent systems, learning goals can be targeted by specialized AI agents that each address a distinct scaffolding mechanism: conceptual, procedural, strategic, or metacognitive. This study follows a Design Science Research approach to derive design requirements from 32 student interviews, iteratively refine a prototype with 22 IS experts, 6 educators, and 34 students, and computationally analyze scaffold effectiveness. We contribute three design principles: (1) multi-agent coordination through a lead orchestrator that delegates to mechanism-specific sub-agents, (2) adaptive learner profiling that enables cross-session scaffolding fading, and (3) continuous institutional knowledge integration grounding scaffolds in verified course materials. Our effectiveness analysis reveals that delivery order predicted learning behavior, positioning orchestration as a key design concern for AI-assisted educational systems.

Keywords: AI Agents · Orchestration · Design Science Research

1   Introduction

Consider a novice analyzing a business case: they start understanding frameworks, navigate multiple resources, develop a solution and a strategy towards it, and ideally, they reflect on their approach. Each of these steps requires distinct support, rather than generic answers [25].

Nowadays, learners often consult Generative AI agents, autonomous, goal-directed systems that can adapt to user needs and coordinate tools across tasks, to identify key information and generate results [9,14]. AI agent-assisted learning has emerged as the fourth most prevalent use case globally [58], with recent implementations in higher education supporting foreign language acquisition [60], innovation management [12], and software development [40]. And while many tools already hold the potential to personalize learning experiences, especially when tutors are scarce [32,43], generic AI tools are not built with human

J. vom Brocke et al. (Eds.): DESRIST 2026, LNCS 16606, pp. 191–208, 2026.
https://doi.org/10.1007/978-3-032-28313-9_11

learning as their core functionality [46]. Recent studies suggest that this lack of pedagogic grounding may harm the learning process by motivating cognitive offloading and over-reliance [26,59], indicating that mechanism-specific support has yet to transcend knowledge-transfer to foster sustained skill-development [46].

AI agents that adapt to human learning are designed to follow pedagogic frameworks, such as the Zone of Proximal Development (ZPD) [50], defined as the space between a learners' independent skills and what they can achieve with targeted support from a more knowledgeable other [56]. Within a learners' individual ZDP, scaffolding is a method that structures temporary and progressively adjusted support by educators [41]. Aiming to gradually reduce a learners' dependence to facilitate skill development, conceptual, procedural, strategic, and metacognitive scaffolding mechanisms each activate a distinct cognitive process [3,23]. While a human teacher can easily adapt support mechanisms throughout a learning session [41], scaffolding AI agents need to leverage architectural possibilities to move beyond isolated conversational interventions, into dynamic, mechanism-specific tutoring encounters [8,9]. One of these architectural approaches consider orchestration as framework to streamline multiple AI agents' internal planning logic into a unified workflow [1], capable of supporting humans in a targeted manner [15]. As multiple specialized AI agents are needed [57] to scaffold the right cognitive process at the right time [5], orchestration poses a useful mechanism to prioritize and sequence tasks tied to learning [15,21]. This leads to the following research question **(RQ): How can AI agents be designed to orchestrate scaffolding mechanisms for sustained learning support?**

To address this, we follow a Design Science Research (DSR) approach by Peffers et al. [39], emphasizing iterative artifact development, grounded in real-world problems and user needs [28]. Scaffolding poses as a kernel theory that informs implementation, the design rationale is derived from orchestrating distinct scaffolding AI agents, targeting cognitive processes [24]. Orchestration becomes the novel technical lens to improve the issue with AI-agent assisted scaffolding towards mechanism-specific tutoring [16]. This study elaborates on the first design cycle: the introduction covers problem identification and objective definition. The design and development is discussed in the method section, informed by management student interviews (N = 32), a demonstration with experts from IS research (N = 22), and a system evaluation by educators (N=6) and a focus group of students (N = 34), as well as a computational analysis of the effectiveness of AI agent scaffolds. This study contributes three design principles that specify how orchestration coordinates scaffolding AI agents: (1) multi-agent coordination through a lead orchestrator that delegates to mechanism-specific sub-agents, (2) adaptive learner profiling that enables cross-session fading of support, and (3) continuous institutional knowledge integration that grounds scaffolds in verified course materials. These principles, operationalized through five design features, offer reusable design knowledge for AI-agent assisted educational systems that need to coordinate multiple support mechanisms.

2   Conceptual Background

2.1   AI Agents

Artificial intelligence refers to artifacts that demonstrate reasoning, learning, or decision-making [4]. With the introduction of agentic capabilities into Generative AI, AI agents are regarded as the next step in the evolution of the frontier technology [62]. We define AI agents through four capabilities that distinguish them from static prompt-response systems [42,57]: **(1)** operating across domains and time horizons (environmental complexity), **(2)** prioritizing understanding over task completion (goal complexity), **(3)** responding to shifting user needs (adaptability), and **(4)** coordinating tools and planning to sequence tasks effectively (independent task execution). While generic AI agents display an absence of coordination toward overarching goals [57], this architectural shortcoming has prevented differentiated scaffolding aligned with educational theory [9]; novel orchestration mechanisms for multi-agent communication, organization, and task coordination, including tool usage and sustained memory [57], indicate that this deficit is solvable and may present a solution to a known challenge [16].

Orchestration frameworks manage AI agents' planning logic within a workflow [1], addressing delegation of tasks and roles in Multi-Agent-Systems [20,33]. Systems containing multiple AI agents pose design challenges regarding task and role delegation [1,7,29]. Since scaffolding requires the coordinated delivery of distinct support mechanisms, the delegation provided by orchestration frameworks offers a way to assign mechanisms to specialized agents and coordinate their deployment based on learner state [6,21]. We refer to this as *mechanism-specific* support: the targeted activation of a particular scaffold type, combined with orchestration logic that determines delivery order and coordinates across agents.

2.2   Scaffolding AI Agents

Tutoring encounters, whether human- or AI-mediated, deliver scaffolding interventions [23,41], catalyzing external support mechanisms into self-regulatory competencies [2]. AI agents have demonstrated effectiveness in delivering instruction that adapt support frequency support based on domain knowledge [9,10,23], but have failed to implement multiple support mechanism at once [3]. Facilitating mechanism-specific learner-AI interaction necessitates a scaffolding framework that is attuned to orchestrated AI agents, since advanced systems introduce novel possibilities such as sustained learner-adaption [8,32]. Literature identifies four scaffold types to structure scaffolds [3,24]:

1. Conceptual scaffolds highlight key knowledge and relationships between frameworks and information [5,43].
2. Procedural scaffolds guide navigation of learning environments, including tools, resources and functionality [22].
3. Strategic scaffolds help learners to select and sequence the learning process in terms of planning and problem-solving [5,36].

4. Metacognitive scaffolds prompt learners to plan, monitor, and regulate thinking along the process [2], mediating not only knowledge transmission [54], but also motivational support [10].

While each scaffold mechanism addresses a distinct cognitive need, effective AI agent-assisted educational systems requires a coordinated deployment: a learner struggling with a concept may first need metacognitive prompting to recognize their gap, then conceptual explanation to address it, and finally strategic guidance to integrate their ideas. The rise of AI agent orchestration enables novel directions to develop design knowledge for such mechanism-specific support. The following section presents our methodological approach to deriving design requirements, principles, and features for orchestrated scaffolding AI agents.

3   Method and Design

3.1   Setting, Participants and Procedure

We aim to develop an artifact that supports management students during the two-semester qualification phase of a leading European business school. This phase challenges novices to unify and conceptualize information across subjects and contexts. To ensure a user-centered design, we recruited 32 students (13 female, 19 male; ages 19–25; M = 23.2) who had successfully completed this phase, and were enrolled in the third semester or beyond of their bachelor's program. Prior to the study, participants completed a beginnerâĂŹs course on AI agent fundamentals to ensure a shared conceptual baseline. Each unpaid, semi-structured interview lasted approximately 30 min. The approach follows the informative and consultative user involvement steps proposed by [28], emphasizing relevance and user-centricity as guiding principles in DSR.

The interview protocol consisted of three parts: (1) five questions on AI usage and observed limitations when working on business cases, (2) nine theory-informed use cases derived from AI agent theory, and (3) five open-ended prompts to elicit additional needs. Interviews were transcribed and analyzed using focused coding, based on thematic analysis of orchestrated AI agents and scaffolding theory [3,23], and refined based on emergent themes. The coding was conducted by the first author and reviewed by another researcher to ensure consistency. Themes were mapped to design requirements through iterative comparison with theory, ensuring that they reflected conceptual grounding and user relevance [13].

3.2   Deriving Scaffolding AI Agent Design Requirements

Building on the scope of AI agents, each orchestration functionality has been mapped to a corresponding scaffold mechanism, divided into strategic, conceptual, procedural, and metacognitive scaffolds. Table 1 summarizes the mapping rationale, linking AI agent requirements to learner-facing use cases and scaffold types. To complement the theoretical mapping with empirical exploration, we conducted user interviews (N = 32) on predefined technical functionalities to validate relevance [19]. By combining theory-driven mapping with user-centered validation, we aim to ensure that the resulting scaffolding structures align with the experiences and expectations of learners navigating continuous, personalized learning journeys. The interviews result in two core observations:

Observation 1: Interaction with non-educational AI agents invite cognitive offloading [46,47]. Generic AI agents (e.g., ChatGPT) cannot infer which cognitive mechanisms support effective learning from prompts alone, especially novice students default to simple copy-pasting usage without reflection on their broader learning journey. This user behavior promotes cognitive offloading and undermines problem-solving and critical thinking [3,26,59].

Observation 2: AI agent implementation forces continuous re-prompting. Even if students intend to engage with resources more deeply, current AI agents operate as standalone session without domain specialization, contextual memory, or coordination across support mechanisms [46,61], resulting in generic task-completion [42].

Table 1. Learner-facing design requirements mapped to scaffold types.

Scaffold Type	Learner Needs (Interviews)	Design Requirement	Testability Criteria
Conceptual: Clarifying domain knowledge and concept relationships	"Explains better than professors; adapts to my speed" (I1, I4)	**DR1:** The AI agent shall provide domain-specific explanations that adapt in complexity to the learner's demonstrated understanding level.	Explanation accuracy; adaptation frequency
Strategic: Supporting planning and task decomposition	"Don't know where to start; helps me structure" (I4, I5, I8)	**DR2:** The AI agent shall support learners in decomposing complex tasks into manageable steps and sequencing activities.	Plan quality ratings; task completion rates
Procedural: Guiding resource and tool usage	"Knows what was covered in lecture; connected to old exams" (I4, I5)	**DR3:** Learners shall receive scaffolds grounded in verified institutional materials relevant to their current task.	Retrieval accuracy; guidance uptake
Metacognitive: Sustaining self-monitoring and reflection	"Tracks where I'm stuck; recognizes my mistake patterns" (I5, I8)	**DR4:** Learners shall receive reflection prompts adapted to their demonstrated learning patterns and progress over time.	Profile-accuracy; scaffolding fading rate

We derive four learner-facing design requirements (DR1-DR4) from the interview findings, following de Weck's criteria for clarity, testability, and feasibility [52]. DR1 and DR2 address the absence of context-specific cognitive support identified in Observation 1: scaffolding theory requires that support be contingent on the learner's current understanding [41], which generic AI agents cannot assess from prompts alone [3]. DR3 and DR4 address the system-level deficits identified in Observation 2: effective scaffolding depends on continuity across learning sessions [56] and alignment with institutional curricula [24], neither of which standalone AI agents provide [42]. The orchestration of the scaffolding mechanisms, describing how and when they are delivered, is addressed below.

3.3 Developing Design Principles and Features

The four learner-facing design requirements inform three system-level design principles (DP1-DP3) (Table 2), formulated according to Gregor et al.'s anatomy of design principles [17]. Each principle specifies its mechanism, aim, context, and theoretical rationale. We then derive five design features (DF1-DF5) that translate these principles into an orchestrated AI agent architecture (Fig. 1).

DP1: Orchestrated Multi-agent Coordination. *Derived from DR1 and DR2.* For scaffolding AI agents to achieve coherent support across diverse cognitive tasks in higher education contexts, implement a lead orchestrator agent that delegates to specialized sub-agents based on scaffold type, as learners require seamless transitions between conceptual, strategic, procedural, and metacognitive support without context loss [57]. This principle enacts the scaffold functions of *contingency* (responding to learner state) and *intersubjectivity* (maintaining shared understanding across agents). DP1 is implemented through DF1 (Lead Orchestrator Agent) and DF2 (Specialized Sub-Agents).

DP2: Adaptive Learner Profiling. *Derived from DR1 and DR4.* For scaffolding AI agents to achieve appropriate support intensity in sustained learning activities, implement persistent learner profiles that track demonstrated understanding and learning patterns, because scaffolding effectiveness depends on accurate assessment of the learner's zone of proximal development [50]. This principle enacts the scaffold functions of *fading* (reducing support as competence grows) and *transfer* (applying insights across domains) [56]. DP2 is implemented through DF3 (Learner Memory Store).

DP3: Continuous Institutional Knowledge Integration. *Derived from DR3 and DR4.* For scaffolding AI agents to achieve curriculum-aligned support in institutional learning environments, implement verified connections to course materials and educator oversight mechanisms [9,55], because learners require scaffolds grounded in approved content, while instructors require visibility into AI-mediated learning [24]. This principle enacts the scaffold functions of *procedural guidance* (directing resource use) and *recruitment* (maintaining orientation toward institutional goals) [41]. DP3 is implemented through DF4 (Institutional Resource Connector) and DF5 (Educator Oversight Dashboard).

Scaffolding theory anticipates gradual *fade-out* as learners develop competence within their ZDP [56]. DF3 enables this by tracking skill progression

Table 2. Mapping of design requirements to principles and features.

Design Requirement	Design Principle	Design Feature	Scaffold Function
DR1: Adaptive domain explanation	DP1: Multi-Agent Coordination	DF1: Lead Orchestrator	Contingency
DR2: Task decomposition support		DF2: Specialized Sub-Agents	Intersubjectivity
DR1: Adaptive domain explanation	DP2: Adaptive Learner Profiling	DF3: Learner Memory Store	Fading
DR4: Pattern-based reflection			Transfer
DR3: Curriculum-grounded scaffolds	DP3: Institutional Knowledge Integration	DF4: Resource Connector	Procedural guidance
DR4: Pattern-based reflection		DF5: Educator Dashboard	Recruitment

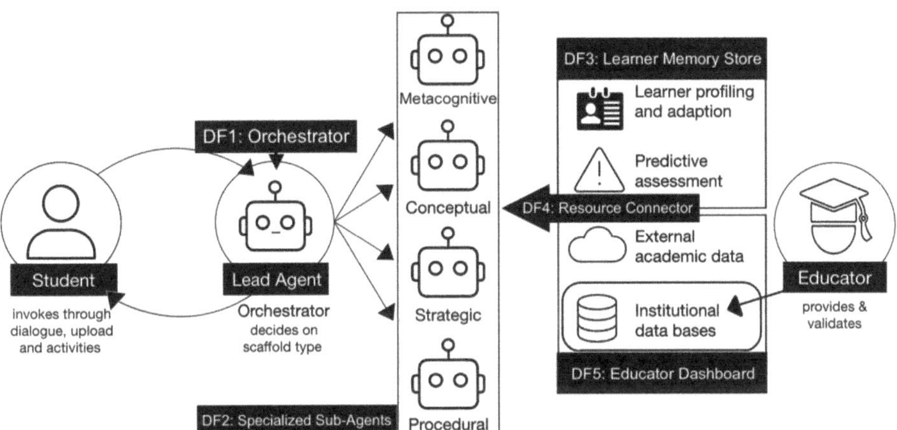

Fig. 1. Design features of the scaffolding AI agent architecture.

across sessions, allowing the orchestrator (DF1) to reduce intervention intensity for mastered topics. Interview participants emphasized the importance of human oversight during this transition, as they value the expertise of an educator over the generic explanations they would receive otherwise: DF5 ensures educators can monitor fade-out timing and intervene when the AI misjudges learner readiness.

3.4   Demonstrating the Scaffolding AI Agent Prototype

System Description and Orchestration Logic. The system [27] implements a hierarchical multi-agent architecture (Fig. 1). A **lead agent (DF1)** serves as the orchestrator, managing the workflow, sub-agent activation, and learner state. Upon each concept map submission, the orchestrator follows a fixed delegation sequence: it first dispatches input to the content ingestion agent, which parses and tracks concept map changes across rounds; then to the example map agent, which compares the learner's map against an expert reference without revealing it; and finally to the scaffolding agent assigned to the current round. The active **scaffolding agent (DF2)** is determined by the experimental condition, which assigns one of four specialized agents per round. Each scaffolding agent adjusts its support intensity (high, medium, low) based on the **learner's memory store (DF3)**, which the profiling component updates by analyzing concept map complexity relative to previous submissions. This enables scaffolding fading: as the learner's assessed competence increases, support intensity decreases. Agent activation and deactivation are controlled through the **educators' configuration (DF5)**, allowing design features to be enabled or disabled for experimental conditions, which is directly tied to the **resource connector (DF4)** on a task content-level.

The environment is built on Python 3.12 [48] with a Streamlit interface [45], and integrates LLM-based natural language generation for agent responses, MongoDB [34] for data persistence, and Cytoscape [38] for real-time concept map interaction. A progress tracking dashboard provides visual feedback on learner development across rounds.

Task Description. The concept mapping exercise focused on a fictional market entry challenge for a foreign software startup to prevent external knowledge contamination and ensure experimental control (Fig. 2). *"Adaptive Market Gatekeeping (AMG)"* could neither be found online, nor did generic AI agents provide suitable information on it. The task required participants to construct concept maps illustrating the interconnections between four core domains: Market analysis, resources and capital, entry strategies, and the fictional AMG mechanisms: dynamic adaptation, rule-changing, network control, and resource blocking by incumbent firms. Concept mapping externalizes learners' knowledge structures and misconceptions in a machine-parseable graph [37] and has strong evidence for learning benefits and assessment validity [22,53]. Scaffolding in concept mapping tasks demonstrates feasibility to provide structured support [31].

Demonstration Procedure. We recruited 22 experts from IS research (9 female, 13 male) with experience in design and implementation of GenAI-based systems from a leading European Business School. Experts tested the prototype individually by working through the case task, providing think-aloud commentary on system interaction (Figure 3). Sessions lasted one hour and were screen-recorded. During this phase, experts identified more than 20 usability barriers at the interface level, which were resolved prior to proceeding to the evaluation.

Stage 1: IS Expert Evaluation of Design Principles. The same 22 experts participated in a structured evaluation session assessing principle validity and feature utility. Our evaluation follows FEDS [49], adopting a Human Risk & Effectiveness strategy appropriate for educational AI deployment. Experts received descriptions of each design principle (DP1-DP3) and their corresponding features (DF1-DF5), then rated: (1) whether features adequately operationalized their parent principles (*principle-feature traceability*); (2) whether the orchestration logic produced appropriate scaffold sequencing (*DP1 validity*); (3) whether

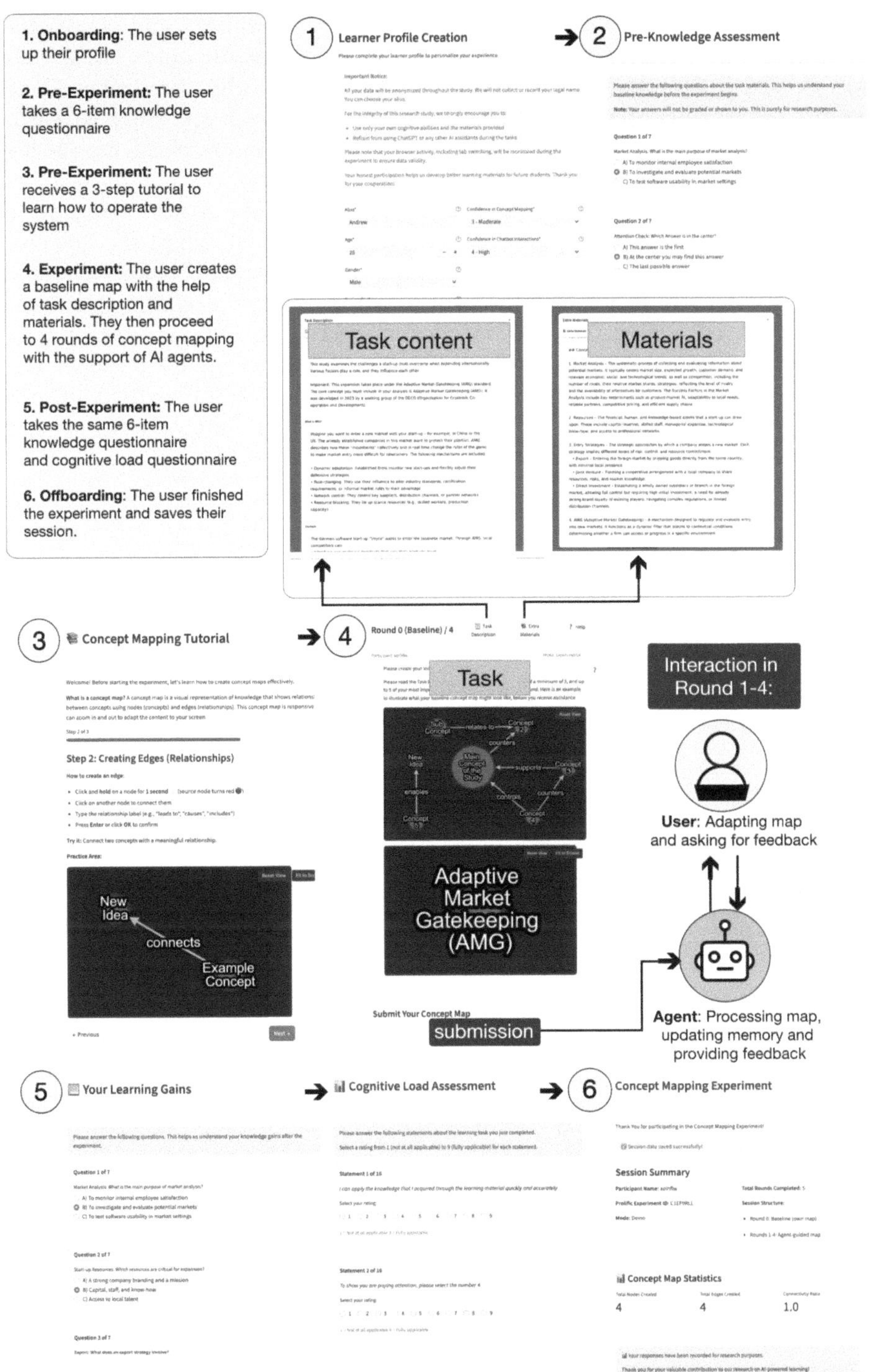

Fig. 2. Implemented design features within a workflow.

learner profiles enabled meaningful adaptation (*DP2 validity*); and (4) whether institutional resource integration maintained curriculum alignment (*DP3 validity*). Feedback was collected in a follow-up discussion. This assessment identified two refinement categories: *system persistence* to improve memory, so learner profiles persisted across sessions, and *scaffolding effectiveness*, clarifying the lead agents' orchestration logic was transparent to evaluators.

Stage 2: Educators Evaluation of Scaffolding AI Agent Output. To ensure that the AI agents delivered the intended scaffold types, six educators (all female), each experienced in scaffolding novice learners, blindly classified agent outputs by mechanism (conceptual, procedural, metacognitive, strategic) through focused coding. Ratings were conducted in rotating groups of three; only prompts with consistent classifications were implemented. Educators then provided coded edits to the prompt-templates [47] to increase contextualization for the problem-solving task (Table 3). Their adaptions aim to cater towards more contextualized learner feedback during the problem-solving task.

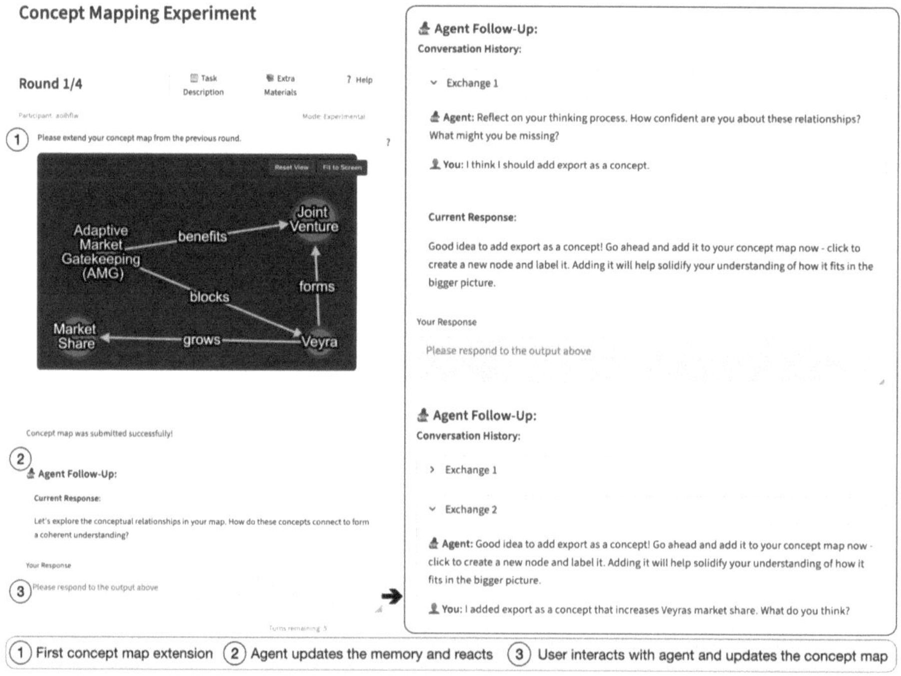

Fig. 3. Prototype displaying the design features within in an interaction.

Stage 3: Student Focus Group Evaluation (N = 34). A focus group with 34 first-semester management students (20 male, 14 female), none with prior experience in business case analysis, revealed findings along two dimensions. Regarding *usability*, simultaneous novelty of the interface and multi-agent

Table 3. Prompt templates of the scaffold types iteratively refined by educators (N=6).

Prompt before edits	Prompt after edits
Conceptual: Can you explain the difference between {concept A} and {concept B}?	The concept of {concept A} relates to {concept B} in international markets. How does this theoretical understanding change how you see these relationships?
Procedural: Have you considered alternative ways to organize these concepts? What might work better?	I notice {observation}. Let me walk you through a method for adding complex relationships: (1) identify the placement of {concept A}, (2) determine the relationship with {node A}, (3) create the linking phrase.
Strategic: What's your strategy for identifying the most critical relationships first? How do you prioritize connection-building?	Looking at your challenge with {observation}, what strategy would be most effective here? Have you considered breaking {observation} down into smaller concepts as with {concept A}?
Metacognitive: What was challenging about creating this concept map?	How has your understanding of {concept A} changed since you started working on this map? What specific insights have you gained?

interaction caused information overload, and unfamiliarity with the task domain confounded task difficulty with system complexity. Regarding *scaffolding reception*, expectations shaped by ChatGPT usage limited some students' engagement with reflective scaffolding, while others noted that the metacognitive agent prompted deeper engagement with their own learning process, particularly in priming self-reflection early in the task. These findings indicate that summative evaluation requires incremental feature introduction and task familiarization before assessing scaffolding effectiveness in the full orchestrated system.

Stage 4: Scaffold Effectiveness Analysis (N = 153). To assess whether the AI agents delivered scaffolding as designed and whether these scaffolds translated into observable learning behavior, we conducted a computational analysis of 153 agent-learner interactions from the metacognition-first condition using two complementary methods.

LLM-as-a-Judge Classification. Following recent advances in automated content analysis [62], we employed a custom LLM-based classifier to evaluate each agent response along two dimensions: (1) *scaffolding act* (elaboration, prompting, or feedback), reflecting whether the agent provided explanatory content, posed reflective questions, or offered corrective input; and (2) *scaffold mechanism* (conceptual, strategic, procedural, or metacognitive), indicating which cognitive process the response targeted. Additionally, elaborations were rated for *quality* (helpful, neutral, or unhelpful) based on whether they provided actionable guidance aligned with the learner's current task state. The classifier achieved mean confidence of 0.93 across these classifications.

Effectiveness Measure. We operationalized scaffold effectiveness through concept map growth: for each agent interaction, we computed Δconcepts as the difference in node count between consecutive rounds. An elaboration was coded as *behaviorally effective* if the learner added at least one concept following the interaction (Δconcepts > 0). This measure captures whether scaffolds translated into externalized knowledge construction, the creation of new nodes and edges.

Analysis Procedure. We fitted mixed-effects regression models with random intercepts by session to account for repeated measures within learners. The dependent variable was Δconcepts per round; predictors included agent type (delivery position), helpful elaboration count, total interactions, and baseline concept map size, which represents the first round, where students did nor receive AI agent support. A Bootstrap resampling (1,000 iterations) at the session level provided robust confidence intervals [18].

Results. Table 4 presents scaffold effectiveness by agent type in the early metacognitive group. Delivery position strongly predicted concept addition: the metacognitive agent delivered first and produced the highest growth ($M = 2.66$, $SD = 3.50$), while the conceptual agent, who delivered last, showed minimal effect ($M = 0.43$, $SD = 1.15$). Bootstrap analysis confirmed that only the metacognitive agent effect was robust (95% CI $[1.24, 1.91]$, excluding zero). The effect size between best- and worst-performing agents was large (Cohen's $d = 0.96$), indicating that position accounted for the variance in learning behavior.

Table 4. Scaffold effectiveness by agent type (N=153).

Agent Type	Pos.	M	SD	n	95% CI	Sig.
Metacognitive	1st	2.66	3.50	31	[1.24, 1.91]	*
Strategic	2nd	1.40	2.81	23	[–0.02, 1.20]	—
Procedural	3rd	0.84	2.79	48	[-0.45, 1.53]	—
Conceptual	4th	0.43	1.15	51	ref.	—

*CI excludes zero. Reference: conceptual. Δconcepts = concepts added per round.

These findings reveal a primacy effect: metacognitive scaffolds delivered early produced greatest immediate behavioral change. This supports DP1 by demonstrating that orchestration—specifically, delivery coordination is a consequential design parameter. The pattern suggests that early scaffolds capture learner attention and cognitive resources, while later scaffolds may encounter diminishing reception. Practitioners designing multi-agent systems should therefore consider not only *which* scaffold to deploy but *when* in the sequence to deploy it.

4   Discussion

4.1   Findings and Contributions

This study contributes design knowledge for orchestrated scaffolding AI agents in higher education, as well as an accessible prototype [27]. The contribution is threefold: (1) design principles that specify how a lead orchestrator coordinates mechanism-specific sub-agents, with evidence that orchestration affects scaffold effectiveness (DP1); (2) a persistent learner profiling approach that enables cross-session scaffolding fading based on assessed ZPD (DP2); and (3) an institutional knowledge integration architecture that grounds AI-generated scaffolds in course materials (DP3). These principles, grounded in scaffolding theory and validated through learner interviews (N=32), IS expert evaluation (N = 22), educator refinement (N = 6), and a student focus group (N=34), are formulated following Gregor et al. [17] and reusable design knowledge for multi-agent systems in education. Our scaffold effectiveness analysis revealed that delivery position predicted learning behavior: early metacognitive scaffolds produced the largest concept map growth (Cohen's $d = 0.96$), suggesting a primacy effect that orchestration policies must account for.

A Framework Linking Scaffolding and AI Agent Orchestration. Prior educational AI has treated scaffolding as monolithic: Systems either scaffold or they do not, utilizing a single support mechanism [3,23,47]. Through novel possibilities introduced by orchestrated AI agents, our framework decomposes this known issue into coordinated, distinct mechanisms and maps each to specialized agents, enabling researchers to study *which* scaffold affects *which* outcome [16]. Our empirical analysis demonstrates that mechanism-specific support alone is insufficient: the same scaffold type (metacognitive) produced high effectiveness when delivered first. This finding elevates orchestration from implementation detail to first-order design concern. While prior work explores AI-assisted education [32,35,43], these single-agent systems cannot address position-dependent effectiveness. DP1 responds by establishing coordination logic, how agents sequence interventions, as consequential as the scaffolds themselves, addressing the reusability gap [11].

Validated Design Knowledge for Mechanism-Specific Support. The design requirements (DR1-DR4) translate scaffold types [3,24] into testable AI agent orchestration following de Weck [52]. The design principles (DP1-DP3) follow Gregor et al.'s anatomy [17], supporting cumulative knowledge building.

DP1: Orchestrated Multi-agent Coordination. While Lange and Schlimbach [30] differentiate cognitive levels, they do not address cross-level coordination. Our primacy finding concerning early scaffolds as capturing learner receptivity regardless of type, demonstrates why orchestration matters: practitioners must sequence scaffolds strategically, not just select appropriate types. This extends Belland et al.'s [3] observation that scaffolding requires mechanism-specific adaptation by showing that *timing* of adaptation is equally critical. Designers should: (1) implement scaffold-type classifiers; (2) design position-aware sequencing policies; (3) log orchestration decisions for pattern analysis.

DP2: Adaptive Learner Profiling. Wambsganss and Schmitt [51] enhance learning through post-hoc trace analysis. Our contribution enables real-time profiling: persistent learner profiles allow orchestrated AI agents to calibrate intensity and delivery order based on assessed understanding. While Neis et al. [35] adapt their system within sessions, it resets across conversations. DP2 maintains cross-session continuity, enabling the fading function central to scaffolding [56].

Designers could: (1) implement lightweight diagnostics; (2) store profiles with privacy safeguards; (3) design fading policies informed by position effects.

DP3: Continuous Institutional Knowledge Integration. Steinherr et al. [44] address infrastructure for human-designed materials, not AI agents, other AI agents operated independently of institutional content [35,43]; orchestration now enables dedicated resource-retrieval agents that validate curriculum alignment before scaffolds reach learners. The orchestrated AI agents coordinate when and what to retrieve, and how to integrate it into ongoing scaffolding sequences, leading to the following suggestions for Designers: (1) implementation of retrieval agents within the orchestrated architecture; (2) designing validation protocols for curriculum alignment; (3) providing educator dashboards for oversight.

4.2   Limitations and Future Work

Our evaluation remains formative-artificial [49]: experts and students assessed validity and utility, while LLM-as-a-judge analysis validated scaffold delivery, but summative outcome measurement is pending. The focus group revealed that simultaneous novelty (interface, task, agents) obscured effects, requiring feature-by-feature evaluation. The primacy effect we observed warrants replication across sequences, as our analysis examined early metacognitive scaffolds. The interview sample (N = 32) from one European institution limits generalizability. Institutional integration (DP3) was demonstrated in controlled conditions; production embedding remains unaddressed. The next cycle will compare feature-ablated versions (planned N = 200) and test adaptive scaffolding orchestration policies to isolate position from mechanism effects.

Subsequent work addresses cross-domain generalization and longitudinal deployment to assess scaffolding persistence. By establishing AI agent orchestration as the architectural foundation for mechanism-specific scaffolding (DP1 and DP2), this study demonstrates how advances in multi-agent coordination can now address a long-standing challenge in AI-assisted educational systems: delivering the right support, at the right time, adapted to the learner's evolving needs.

Disclosure of Interests. The authors have no competing interests to declare.

References

1. Allmendinger, S., Bonenberger, L., Endres, K., et al.: Multi-agent ai. Electr. Markets **36** (2026). https://doi.org/10.1007/s12525-025-00862-z
2. Azevedo, R., Hadwin, A.F.: Scaffolding self-regulated learning and metacognition: implications for the design of computer-based scaffolds. Instr. Sci. **33**, 367–379 (2005). https://doi.org/10.1007/s11251-005-1272-9
3. Belland, B.R., Lee, E., Zhang, A.Y., Kim, C.: Characterizing the most effective scaffolding approaches in engineering and technology education: a clustering approach. Comput. Appl. Eng. Educ. **30**(6), 1795–1812 (2022)

4. Berente, N., Gu, B., Recker, J., Santhanam, R.: Managing artificial intelligence. MIS Q. **45**(3) (2021)

5. Borchers, C., Fleischer, H., Schanze, S., Scheiter, K., Aleven, V.: High scaffolding of an unfamiliar strategy improves conceptual learning but reduces enjoyment compared to low scaffolding and strategy freedom. Comput. Educ. **236** (2025). https://doi.org/10.1016/j.compedu.2025.105364

6. Charisi, V., Malinverni, L., Rubegni, E., Schaper, M.M.: Empowering children's critical reflections on ai, robotics and other intelligent technologies. In: NordiCHI 2020, Association for Computing Machinery, New York(2020). https://doi.org/10.1145/3419249.3420090

7. Constantinescu, M., Kaptein, M.: Responsibility gaps, llms & organisations: many agents, many levels, and many interactions. Sci. Eng. Ethics **31** (2025). https://doi.org/10.1007/s11948-025-00560-1

8. Dai, L., Jiang, Y.H., Chen, Y., Guo, Z., Liu, T.Y., Shao, X.: Agent4edu: advancing AI for education with agentic workflows. In: Proceedings of the 3rd International Conference on Artificial Intelligence and Education (ICAIE 2024), p. 6. ACM, Xiamen, China (Nov 2024) https://doi.org/10.1145/3722237.3722268

9. D'Mello, S.K., Graesser, A.: Intelligent tutoring systems: how computers achieve learning gains that rival human tutors. In: Schutz, P.A., Muis, K.R. (eds.) Handbook of Educational Psychology, pp. 603–629. Routledge, 4 edn. (2024)

10. Duffy, M.C., Azevedo, R.: Motivation matters: interactions between achievement goals and agent scaffolding for self-regulated learning within an intelligent tutoring system. Comput. Hum. Behav. **52**, 338–348 (2015)

11. Elshan, E., Engel, C., Ebel, P., Siemon, D:. Assessing the reusability of design principles in the realm of conversational agents. In: Drechsler, A., Gerber, A., Hevner, A. (eds.) DESRIST 2022. LNCS, vol. 13229. Springer, Cham (2022). https://doi.org/10.1007/978-3-031-06516-3_10

12. Füller, J., Tekic, Z., Hutter, K.: Rethinking innovation management-how ai is changing the way we innovate. J. Appl. Behav. Sci. **60**(4), 603–612 (2024). https://doi.org/10.1177/00218863241287323, Accessed 30 April 2025

13. Gioia, D.: A systematic methodology for doing qualitative research. J. Appl. Behav. Sci. **57**(1), 20–29 (2021). https://doi.org/10.1177/0021886320982715

14. Goddard, Q., Moton, N., Hudson, J., He, H.A.: A chatbot won't judge me: an exploratory study of self-disclosing chatbots in introductory computer science classes. In: Proceedings of the 26th Western Canadian Conference on Computing Education (WCCCE 2024), vol. 9, pp. 1–7. Association for Computing Machinery (2024). https://doi.org/10.1145/3660650.3660662

15. Gonzalez, C., et al.: .: Toward a science of human-ai teaming for decision making: a complementarity framework. PNAS Nexus **5**(3), pgag030 (2026). https://doi.org/10.1093/pnasnexus/pgag030

16. Gregor, S., Hevner, A.R.: Positioning and presenting design science research for maximum impact. Manag. Inf. Syst. Q. **37**(2), 337–355 (2013). https://doi.org/10.25300/MISQ/2013/37.2.01

17. Gregor, S., Kruse, L., Seidel, S.: The anatomy of a design principle. J. Associat. Inform. Syst. **21**(6), 1622–1652 (2020). https://doi.org/10.17705/1jais.00649, https://aisel.aisnet.org/jais/vol21/iss6/2/

18. Henderson, A.R.: The bootstrap: A technique for data-driven statistics. using computer-intensive analyses to explore experimental data. Clinica Chimica Acta **359**(1), 1–26 (2005). https://www.sciencedirect.com/science/article/pii/S0009898105002433https://doi.org/10.1016/j.cccn.2005.04.002

19. Hevner, A.R.: A three cycle view of design science research. Scandinavian J. Inform. Syst. **19**(2), 87–92 (2007). http://aisel.aisnet.org/sjis/vol19/iss2/4
20. Holldack, F., Banh, L., Strobel, G.: Agentic information systems. Electron. Mark. **36** (2026). https://doi.org/10.1007/s12525-025-00861-0
21. Hunke, F., Seebacher, S., Thomsen, H.: Please tell me what to do – towards a guided orchestration of key activities in data-rich service systems. In: Hofmann, S., Müller, O., Rossi, M. (eds.) DESRIST 2020. LNCS, vol. 12388, pp. 426–437. Springer, Cham (2020). https://doi.org/10.1007/978-3-030-64823-7_41
22. Janson, A., Söllner, M., Leimeister, J.M.: Ladders for learning: is scaffolding the key to teaching problem-solving in technology-mediated learning contexts? Acad. Manag. Learn. Educ. **19**(4), 439–468 (2020). https://doi.org/10.5465/amle.2018.0078
23. Kim, M.C., Hannafin, M.J.: Scaffolding problem solving in technology-enhanced learning environments (teles): bridging research and theory with practice. Comput. Educ. **56**(2) (2011). https://doi.org/10.1016/j.compedu.2010.08.024
24. Kim, N.J., Belland, B.R., Walker, E.A.: Effectiveness of computer-based scaffolding in the context of problem-based learning for stem education: bayesian meta-analysis. Educ. Psychol. Rev. **30**(3) (2018). https://doi.org/10.1007/s10648-017-9419-1
25. Koedinger, K.R., Aleven, V.: Exploring the assistance dilemma in experiments with cognitive tutors. Educ. Psychol. Rev. **19**, 239–264 (2007). https://doi.org/10.1007/s10648-007-9049-0
26. Kosmyna, N., et al.: Your brain on chatgpt: accumulation of cognitive debt when using an ai assistant for essay writing task (2025)
27. Kozachek, D., Göldi, A., Schwarz, K., Kiafard, A.: Multi-Agent Scaffolding System for Higher Education Research (Aug 2026). https://github.com/koizachek/scaffolding_multiagentsystem
28. Kujala, S.: Effective user involvement in product development by improving the analysis of user needs. Behav. Inform. Technol. **27**(6), 457–473 (2008). https://doi.org/10.1080/01449290601111051
29. Kumar, N., Wei, X., Zhang, H.: Agentic artificial intelligence as a new frontier in information systems: promise, peril, and research opportunities. Inform. Manag. **63**(3), 104317 (2026)
30. Lange, T.C., Schlimbach, R.: Designing knowledge for conversational AI applications: a bloom's taxonomy perspective. In: Chatterjee, S., vom Brocke, J., Anderson, R. (eds.) DESRIST 2025. LNCS, vol. 15703. Springer, Cham (2025). https://doi.org/10.1007/978-3-031-93976-1_14
31. Luchini, K., et al.: Scaffolding in the small: designing educational supports for concept mapping on handheld computers. In: CHI 2002 Extended Abstracts on Human Factors in Computing Systems, CHI EA 2002, pp. 792–793. Association for Computing Machinery, New York (2002). https://doi.org/10.1145/506443.506600
32. Maedche, A., et al.: Ai-based digital assistants. Bus. Inform. Syst. Eng. **61**, 535–544 (2019). https://doi.org/10.1007/s12599-019-00600-8
33. Masters, C., et al.: Orchestrating human-ai teams: the manager agent as aunifying research challenge. In: Proceedings of the 2025 7th International Conference on Distributed Artificial Intelligence, DAI 2025, pp. 91–107. Association for Computing Machinery, New York (2025). https://doi.org/10.1145/3772429.3772439
34. MongoDB Inc: Mongodb community server (version 8.0) (2025). https://www.mongodb.com/docs/

35. Neis, N., Spleth, P., Kudlek, C., Zarnekow, R., Winkelmann, A.: Designing a large language model based conversational agent for language acquisition. In: Local Solutions for Global Challenges. Proceedings of the 20th International Conference on Design Science Research in Information Systems and Technology (DESRIST 2025). LNCS, vol. 15703. Springer, Cham (2025). https://doi.org/10.1007/978-3-031-93976-1_15
36. NGoon, T.J.: Inventive scaffolds catalyze creative learning. In: Extended Abstracts of the 2019 CHI Conference on Human Factors in Computing Systems (CHI EA 2019), pp. 1–5. Association for Computing Machinery (2019). https://doi.org/10.1145/3290607.3299073
37. Novak, J.D., Cañas, A.J.: The theory underlying concept maps and how to construct and use them. Tech. Rep. IHMC CmapTools 2006–01 Rev 01–2008, Florida Institute for Human and Machine Cognition, Pensacola, FL (2008)
38. Otasek, D., Morris, J.H., Bouças, J., Pico, A.R., Demchak, B.: Cytoscape automation: empowering workflow-based network analysis. Genome Biol. **20**(1), 185 (2019)
39. Peffers, K., Tuunanen, T., Rothenberger, M., Chatterjee, S.: A design science research methodology for information systems research, vol. 24(3) (2007). https://doi.org/10.2753/MIS0742-1222240302
40. Petrovska, O., Clift, L., Moller, F., Pearsall, R.: Incorporating generative ai into software development education. In: Waite, J., Crosby, R. (eds.) CEP 2024: Proceedings of the 8th Conference on Computing Education Practice, pp. 37–40. Association for Computing Machinery, Durham, United Kingdom (2024). https://doi.org/10.1145/3633053.3633057
41. van de Pol, J., Volman, M., Beishuizen, J.: Scaffolding in teacher-student interaction: a decade of research. Educ. Psychol. Rev. **22**, 271–296 (2010). https://doi.org/10.1007/s10648-010-9127-6
42. Shavit, Y., et al.: Practices for governing agentic ai systems. Technical report, OpenAI (2023). https://cdn.openai.com/papers/practices-for-governing-agentic-ai-systems.pdf
43. Sjöström, J., Dahlin, M.: Tutorbot: a chatbot for higher education practice. In: Hofmann, S., Müller, O., Rossi, M. (eds.) DESRIST 2020. LNCS, vol. 12388, pp. 93–98. Springer, Cham (2020). https://doi.org/10.1007/978-3-030-64823-7_10
44. Steinherr, V.M., Brehmer, M., Stöckl, R., Reinelt, R.: Design science research as a guide for innovative higher education teaching: towards an application-oriented extension of the proficiency model. In: Mandviwalla, M., Sollner, M., Tuunanen, T. (eds.) DESRIST 2024. LNCS, vol. 14621. Springer, Cham (2024). https://doi.org/10.1007/978-3-031-61175-9_15
45. Streamlit Inc: Streamlit (2025). https://github.com/streamlit/streamlit, gitHub-Repository; Commit COMMIT; 2025–09-11
46. Tankelevitch, L., et al.: Tools for thought: research and design for understanding, protecting, and augmenting human cognition with generative ai. In: Proceedings of the Extended Abstracts of the CHI Conference on Human Factors in Computing Systems, CHI EA 2025, Association for Computing Machinery, New York (2025). https://doi.org/10.1145/3706599.3706745
47. Thomann, H., Deutscher, V.: Scaffolding through prompts in digital learning: a systematic review and meta-analysis of effectiveness on learning achievement. Educ. Res. Rev. **47**, 100686 (2025). https://doi.org/10.1016/j.edurev.2025.100686
48. Van Rossum, G., Drake, F.L., Jr.: Python tutorial. Centrum voor Wiskunde en Informatica Amsterdam, The Netherlands (1995)
49. Venable, J., Pries-Heje, J., Baskerville, R.: Feds: a framework for evaluation in design science research. Eur. J. Inf. Syst. **25**(1), 77–89 (2016)

50. Vygotsky, L.S.: Mind in Society: Development of Higher Psychological Processes. Harvard University Press (1978). http://www.jstor.org/stable/j.ctvjf9vz4
51. Wambsganss, T., Schmitt, A.: Enhancing personalized learning through process mining. Bus. Inform. Syst. Eng. (2024). https://doi.org/10.1007/s12599-024-00901-7
52. de Weck, O.L.: Requirements definition. https://ocw.mit.edu/courses/16-842-fundamentals-of-systems-engineering-fall-2015 (2015), lecture notes, Session 2, 16.842 Fundamentals of Systems Engineering, MIT OpenCourseWare
53. Whitelock-Wainwright, A., Laan, N., Wen, D., Gašević, D.: Exploring student information problem solving behaviour using fine-grained concept map and search tool data. Comput. Educ. **145**, 103731 (2020). https://doi.org/10.1016/j.compedu.2019.103731
54. Winkler, R., Hobert, S., Fischer, T., Salovaara, A., Soellner, M., Leimeister, J.M.: Engaging learners in online video lectures with dynamically scaffolding conversational agents. In: Proceedings of the 28th European Conference on Information Systems (ECIS), 15–17 June. Association for Information Systems, Virtual Conference (2020), https://aisel.aisnet.org/ecis2020_rp/97
55. Winkler, R., Roos, J.: Bringing ai into the classroom: designing smart personal assistants as learning tutors. In: ICIS 2019 Proceedings (2019). https://aisel.aisnet.org/icis2019/learning_environ/learning_environ/10/
56. Wood, D., Bruner, J.S., Ross, G.: The role of tutoring in problem solving. J. Child Psychol. Psychiatry **17**(2), 89–100 (1976). https://doi.org/10.1111/j.1469-7610.1976.tb00381.x
57. Yao, S., Zhao, J., Yu, D., Du, N., Shafran, I., Narasimhan, K.R., Cao, Y.: React: synergizing reasoning and acting in language models. In: Proceedings of the Eleventh International Conference on Learning Representations. (2023) ICLR 2023
58. Zao-Sanders, M.: How people are really using gen ai in 2025. Harvard Business Review (April 2025). https://hbr.org/2025/04/how-people-are-really-using-gen-ai-in-2025
59. Zhai, C., Wibowo, S., Li, L.D.: The effects of over-reliance on ai dialogue systems on students' cognitive abilities: a systematic review. Smart Learn. Environ. **11**(28), (2024). https://doi.org/10.1186/s40561-024-00316-7
60. Zhai, C., Wibowo, S.: A systematic review on artificial intelligence dialogue systems for enhancing english as foreign language students' interactional competence in the university. Comput. Educ. Artifi. Intell. **4**, 100134 (2023)
61. Zhang, Y., et al.: Position: trustworthy AI agents require the integration of large language models and formal methods. In: Proceedings of the 42nd International Conference on Machine Learning, pp. 1–19, Vancouver, Canada (2025)
62. Zhiheng, X., Wenxiang, C., et al.: The rise and potential of large language model based agents: A survey (2023)

Designing Immersive Game-Based Pretraining for Business Simulations: An Action Design Research Study

Anna Wenzel[1]($\boxtimes$) (iD), Jan-Martin Geiger[2] (iD), and Andreas Liening[1]

[1] TU Dortmund University, Friedrich-Wöhler-Weg 6, 44227 Dortmund, Germany
{anna.wenzel,andreas.liening}@tu-dortmund.de
[2] University of Münster, Bispinghof 3, 48143 Münster, Germany
jan-martin.geiger@uni-muenster.de

Abstract. Highly complex learning environments in experiential entrepreneurship education, e.g., business simulation games, place substantial cognitive demands on learners, which may lead to cognitive overload, reduced motivation, and ineffective early gameplay experiences. Although pretraining has been established as an effective instructional support strategy in multimedia learning, existing implementations in game-based contexts are often limited to passive information delivery. At the same time, advances in immersive virtual world technologies enable embodied and interactive forms of learning that may support both cognitive and motivational readiness prior to gameplay but can simultaneously introduce additional cognitive demands for learners. Adopting an Action Design Research approach, theory-informed and context-specific challenges emerging in early gameplay were analyzed to derive meta-requirements and design principles for immersive game-based pretraining. These principles were instantiated and iteratively refined within an immersive virtual pretraining environment. The artifact was evaluated with student teachers in an exploratory setting and subsequently deployed in a large-scale field study with actual users of a business simulation game. As a result, the study contributes a set of theoretically grounded and actionable design principles for immersive pretraining in complex simulation-based learning environments and presents a contextually instantiated artifact. The findings also provide descriptive insights into learners' perception of cognitive and motivational readiness and highlight both the promises and the potential pitfalls of immersive pretraining for subsequent business simulation gameplay.

Keywords: Action Design Research · Pretraining · Immersive Environment · Business Simulation Game

1 Introduction

Within entrepreneurship education, students are expected to develop an understanding of entrepreneurship as a dynamic process of vision, change, and innovation that requires initiative, persistence, and a willingness to take calculated risks. Successful entrepreneurial

J. vom Brocke et al. (Eds.): DESRIST 2026, LNCS 16606, pp. 209–226, 2026.
https://doi.org/10.1007/978-3-032-28313-9_12

activity further depends on the ability to form effective teams, mobilize resources, and develop viable business concepts while identifying and exploiting opportunities under conditions of uncertainty [1]. Accordingly, entrepreneurship education aims to foster an entrepreneurial mindset that enables learners to cope with ambiguity and to engage in opportunity-driven decision-making [2]. To support these goals, experiential learning approaches are increasingly applied in entrepreneurship education as they enable student-centered and active engagement with realistic entrepreneurial activities. Specifically, game-based interventions have gained prominence, as they enable learners to engage in entrepreneurial decision-making without exposure to real-world financial or organizational risks. Through simulated market dynamics, competition, and feedback, such environments enable learners to experience complex entrepreneurial processes in a safe setting [3, 4]. However, they may also overwhelm students, particularly novices [5]. The simultaneous presentation of numerous interdependent variables, interfaces, and decision options can increase cognitive demands, distract learners from core learning objectives, and hinder deep cognitive processing [6, 7]. Thus, experiential entrepreneurship education requires adequate guidance to help students to develop and achieve their goals [8]. To address these challenges, pretraining has been identified as a central instructional support strategy for learning in complex multimedia and game-based environments [9]. Especially for novice learners, pretraining can facilitate learning by introducing key concepts and system components prior to the main instructional activity [10]. By enabling learners to build initial component models in advance, pretraining can reduce perceived task complexity and free cognitive resources for meaningful interaction and cognitive processing during subsequent learning activities [11]. Although meta-analytic results generally support the effectiveness of pretraining in multimedia learning [9], concrete design choices of pretraining does not always yield the expected results [12]. While initial studies implement technological advanced methods such as virtual reality games [12], most studies frequently operationalize pretraining in rather passive formats, such as narrated information [13] or an information sheet [14]. Yet, research on cognitive engagement emphasizes that effective instruction should foster more active, ideally constructive or interactive, learning processes to enable deep generative processing [15]. Accordingly, it remains unclear how pretraining for complex business simulation games can be designed to move beyond passive information delivery and actively prepare learners for experiential entrepreneurial learning. Beyond cognitive considerations, supporting learners' sense of autonomy, fostering positive achievement-related emotions, and reducing anxiety are central to effective learning experiences [16, 17]. In line with the inherent tension between learner autonomy and instructional guidance in experiential learning settings [16], these perspectives suggest that pretraining environments should be designed to support perceived control, enable meaningful interaction, and provide opportunities for competence development, while avoiding overly restrictive guidance that may undermine autonomy. Consequently, pretraining should not only address cognitive readiness but also foster motivational and emotional preparedness prior to engagement in complex learning environments. At the same time, recent technological developments enable the creation of immersive three-dimensional virtual environments that allow learners to explore realistic scenarios and interact with digital artifacts and social agents. Immersive virtual environments may extend traditional instruction by enabling learners to actively explore spatially organized information, interact with task-relevant objects, and engage with embodied social agents. Rather than passively receiving information, learners can construct understanding through heightened agency, social presence, and increased environmental realism [15, 17], thereby offering particular potential for experiential learning [18]. Prior research suggests that such embodied and interactive learning experiences can foster deeper cognitive engagement and support the integration of conceptual and procedural knowledge [10]. However, how these affordances can be systematically leveraged for pretraining purposes, particularly in preparation for complex business simulation games, remains insufficiently understood. This raises the question of *how immersive virtual environments can be designed to introduce learners to relevant concepts, mechanics, and decision logics in preparation for subsequent business simulation gameplay.* To address this design challenge, this study adopts an iterative Action Design Research (ADR) approach [19]. While the overall ADR project aims to contribute prescriptive design knowledge by (1) deriving design principles grounded in theory and informed by a practice-oriented needs analysis, (2) developing a functioning artifact to inform subsequent research on immersive pretraining effects, and (3) providing utility for students by fostering cognitive and motivational readiness for the business simulation, this paper focuses primarily on the derivation of design principles and the development of the artifact (1–2).

2 Theoretical Background

For theoretically grounding our ADR approach, we first draw on the Cognitive Affective Theory of Learning with Media (CATLM) [20] as an established framework at the intersection of educational psychology and educational technology. CATLM posits that learning with media is shaped by the dynamic interplay of cognitive and affective processes. Building on Cognitive Load Theory [21], the model assumes that learners possess limited working-memory resources and that meaningful learning depends on managing intrinsic and extraneous cognitive load while fostering germane processing. At the same time, CATLM [20] further emphasizes that motivational and emotional factors, such as interest, perceived relevance, and affective states, influence how learners allocate cognitive resources during learning. Accordingly, effective instructional design should not only minimize unnecessary extraneous cognitive load and support the management of intrinsic load but also create motivational and emotional conditions that encourage learners to invest cognitive effort in learning activities. In line with Self-Determination Theory (SDT) [22], intrinsic motivation is shaped by the fulfilment of the psychological needs for autonomy, competence, and relatedness. Similarly, Control-Value Theory of Achievement Emotions (CVT) [23] posits that learners' emotions are influenced by their perceived control over tasks and the value they assign to them. Beyond individual learning facets, digital game-based learning is further shaped by social forms of engagement. Learners frequently interact with tutors, peers, or artificial agents, and meaningful learning experiences emerge through social interaction. Grounded in research on computer-supported collaborative learning [24], meaningful social interactions are influenced by the sociability of the learning environment, resulting from concrete design choices, the perceived social presence of interaction partners, and the underlying pedagogical design of the system [24]. To further specify how productive cognitive engagement can be supported within such environments, we additionally draw on the ICAP framework [15]. ICAP differentiates levels of cognitive engagement ranging from passive to active, constructive, and interactive engagement, with constructive and interactive activities providing the greatest potential for deep generative processing. From this perspective, instructional designs should enable learners to actively construct knowledge, engage in dialogic interaction with peers or instructional agents, and support autonomy, competence, and meaningful social interaction, thereby promoting deep generative learning.

3   Research Method: Action Design Research

This study is situated in a university-level business simulation game in which students participate in five consecutive rounds of entrepreneurial decision-making within the textile manufacturing industry. In each round, teams make up to 15 interdependent decisions, including pricing, investments, personnel planning, and research and development. The simulation incorporates dynamic macroeconomic conditions, including a simulated crisis in the third round, exposing students to complex decision-making under changing market conditions, which may lead to cognitive overload, particularly for novice learners. Although the simulation includes a pretraining intervention that introduces the narrative and provides essential information, it remains largely passive, relying on an introductory video and potentially limiting deeper cognitive engagement [15]. Moreover, as students are oftentimes unfamiliar with the textile industry, the underlying value creation process is often abstract, which may hinder self-efficacy, intrinsic motivation, and task value. To address these challenges, this study develops a problem-solving artifact for immersive pretraining while deriving prescriptive design knowledge. Accordingly, we adopt ADR as a design science research approach suited for investigating complex socio-technical problems through theory-informed artifact design and iterative evaluation [25]. Following ADR, the study comprises four stages: (1) problem formulation, (2) build–intervention–evaluation cycles, (3) reflection and learning, and (4) formalization of learning [19]. Given the technology-driven nature of the artifact, we follow the IT-dominant BIE schema. The study includes an initial pre-study to identify learning challenges in the baseline simulation, followed by two ADR design cycles in which the artifact was developed, implemented, and evaluated. The overall research process is illustrated in Fig. 1.

After conducting a needs analysis based on qualitative responses from students interacting with the business simulation game (n = 21 responses from 100 invited participants), we derived theory-informed and practice-validated meta-requirements, corresponding design principles, and concrete design features, which guided the instantiation of an initial prototype. This prototype was subsequently evaluated in a small-scale formative study (n = 12), collecting preliminary quantitative measures and qualitative feedback to identify design strengths and potential breakdown with student teachers as future practitioners. Based on insights from this first iteration, the prototype was refined and evaluated in a second iteration through a large-scale field deployment with participants of the business simulation game (n = 82 active participants from 119 invited students).

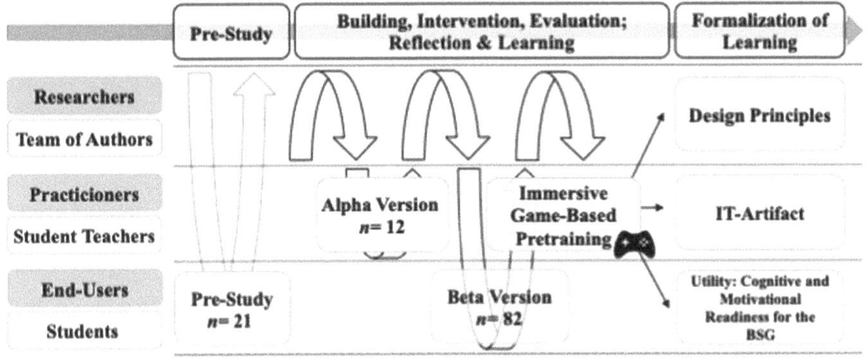

Fig. 1. Action Design Research Approach.

This evaluation combined quantitative data and qualitative feedback to assess whether the implemented design features adequately instantiated the intended design principles. Based on the results, the design principles were verified or refined, and the resulting design knowledge was formalized to inform future immersive game-based pretraining initiatives.

4   Needs Analysis Results of the Pre-Study

For the needs analysis as part of the pre-study, qualitative data were collected from students who participated in the business simulation game within an undergraduate entrepreneurship course during the winter term 2023/2024 as part of a prior field-study. Participants were on average 23.1 years old (SD = 2.41) and primarily majored in economics and business administration or complemented their studies with entrepreneurship courses. Data were collected through a pre-structured questionnaire administered after completion of the first simulation round, when students had gained initial exposure to the complexity of the simulation. Participants were invited to reflect on experienced learning-related hurdles by responding to the open-ended question: "Did you encounter personal hurdles during the learning process? If yes, in which areas?" Responding to this question was voluntary. Of the 100 invited participants, 21 students provided explicit qualitative responses describing perceived challenges. **Cognitive Overload and Novice Status:** Learners described the simulation as cognitively demanding due to the large amount of information and interdependent variables that had to be processed simultaneously (e.g., *"it was difficult to keep track of all costs and figures,"* S5). These challenges were amplified by learners' lack of prior experience: *"I had difficulties because I had no previous experience with the simulation game,"* (S12), indicating high intrinsic cognitive load during early interaction. Such complexity places substantial demands on working memory and may hinder the construction of initial mental models and germane cognitive processing. **Game-Related Uncertainty:** Participants also expressed uncertainty regarding the overall objective of the business simulation and consequences of their decisions, as one student noted that *"it was not clear what exactly the goal of the simulation game was"* (S4). One student reported that *"it was unclear what consequences* *our decisions would have"* (S9), while another questioned, *"How do our decisions affect sales? How is the pricing of the other enterprises?"* (S13). Such uncertainty is characteristic of entrepreneurship and experiential entrepreneurial learning environments [26, 27], where outcomes are often probabilistic and interdependent. However, uncertainty can elicit negative emotions that potentially deactivate students' engagement [23]. **Stress and Overwhelm:** Indeed, students also reported signs of stress and feelings of being overwhelmed. One participant highlighted the time pressure associated with the simulation (*"time pressure during the simulation,"* S21), while another noted, *"I felt extremely overwhelmed during the simulation with everything"* (S17). **Early Low Ease of Use:** Additionally, one student described the simulation software as *"somewhat tricky and confusing at the beginning"* (S15), although they later reported improved handling of the system. Such usability constraints are particularly salient during initial interactions with complex digital systems. While perceived ease of use may increase as learners gain experience, negative early interactions can undermine users' behavioral intention and reduce subsequent engagement with the system [28]. In the context of business simulation games, early usability barriers may therefore divert cognitive resources away from learning-related activities and hinder productive engagement during initial learning phases. Taken together, the reported challenges, including high information density, lack of prior experience, uncertainty regarding goals and decision consequences, feelings of stress and being overwhelmed and navigation issues with the game's interface, indicate that learners experienced negative affective states and substantial cognitive overload during the early stages of the simulation. These challenges informed the derivation of the meta-requirements guiding the subsequent design of the immersive game-based pretraining artifact.

5   Deriving Meta-Requirements

Based on our theoretical rationale and the identified challenges, we derived outcome-oriented and process-oriented meta-requirements (MRO) that specify what the immersive game-based pretraining should achieve in preparation for subsequent participation in the business simulation. On the **outcome level**, while pretraining primarily aims to ease learners' initial interaction with complex learning environments [11], we argue that effective pretraining must also intentionally support learners' cognitive and motivational readiness for digital game-based learning. **Cognitive Readiness:** Findings from the needs analysis revealed substantial cognitive overload during early simulation phases, particularly among novice learners. In line with cognitive load theory [6, 7, 21], limited prior knowledge likely increased intrinsic cognitive load, while complex interfaces and information density contributed to extraneous load. To enable deep cognitive processing early in the simulation, pretraining for game-based learning should therefore reduce early extraneous cognitive load (**MRO1**), support the management of moderate levels of intrinsic load (**MRO2**) and enable cognitive resources to be allocated to generative processing (**MRO3**). **Motivational Readiness:** In addition to cognitive challenges, students reported experiencing substantial uncertainty during the initial simulation rounds. Although uncertainty represents a core characteristic of entrepreneurial contexts and is intentionally emphasized within experiential entrepreneurship education [26, 27], it may also elicit negative achievement-related emotions such as anxiety or hopelessness, which can exert deactivating effects on learning [23]. Consequently, learners should be prepared to engage with uncertainty productively rather than experiencing it as overwhelming. Drawing on SDT [22], intrinsic motivation is associated with greater persistence, curiosity, and sustained engagement in challenging and ambiguous learning situations. Accordingly, pretraining should strengthen learners' motivational readiness for participation in the subsequent business simulation game **(MRO4)**, thereby supporting engagement and persistence when learners encounter uncertainty during entrepreneurial decision-making. On the **process level,** we derive a set of meta-requirements that specify how the pretraining environment should be designed to foster learners' engagement during interaction with the pretraining environment. In digital game-based learning, design elements shape not only cognitive processes but also learners' emotional, motivational, and social engagement [29]. Accordingly, effective pretraining design must intentionally support these experiential dimensions. First, drawing on the ICAP framework [15], the pretraining environment should enable active, constructive, and ideally interactive learning processes **(MRP1)** in order to promote deep generative cognitive engagement. Specifically, emphasizing collaboration in cognitive processing, the pretraining should provide a positive social space **(MRP2)** that facilitates meaningful social interaction with peers or instructional agents, thereby supporting collaborative sensemaking [24]. Furthermore, the environment should foster positive emotional experiences **(MRP3)**, as emotions play a central role in learners' willingness to engage and persist during learning activities [23]. Third, pretraining should support motivational engagement **(MRP4)**, encouraging learners to invest effort and explore the learning environment voluntarily [22].

6 Deriving Design Principles

Based on the derived meta-requirements, which define the problem space of our study, we formulate reusable design principles that guide the subsequent artifact instantiation. Following a supportive approach [30], these principles translate the identified requirements into actionable solution concepts [19] that guide the subsequent instantiation of the artifact. Figure 2 depicts the derived meta-requirements and proposed design principles, following [30]. On the outcome level, addressing **MRO1–MRO3**, pretraining should reduce early cognitive overload in complex simulation environments [11]. Novice learners are often confronted with numerous interdependent variables, resulting in excessive intrinsic and extraneous cognitive load [3, 5, 7]. Structured introduction of core concepts can support initial mental model construction and free cognitive resources for generative processing. As a result, we introduce **DP1: Progressive Structuring of Domain Complexity**. *Objective*: Reduce cognitive load and support mental model construction. *Mechanism*: Decompose complex systems into smaller, conceptually coherent units to limit initial element interactivity, and gradually increase complexity by integrating these elements over time, thereby enabling schema construction and supporting germane processing. *Context:* Novice learners in complex simulation environments. Addressing **MRO4**, pretraining should support learners' motivational readiness for engaging with the simulation. In entrepreneurship education, uncertainty and ambiguous outcomes can challenge sustained engagement, particularly for novice learners [26]. To remain engaged, learners require baseline motivational beliefs such as task value, goal orientation, and self-efficacy [31]. Accordingly, pretraining should foster positive beliefs about the relevance, purpose, and attainability of simulation tasks, enabling learners to approach uncertainty as a meaningful learning opportunity. Thus, we propose: **DP2: Framing Tasks to Foster Perceived Value and Attainability.** *Objective*: Strengthen motivational readiness and persistence under uncertainty. *Mechanism*: Frame tasks in ways that enhance perceived value and expectancy of success by clarifying relevance, providing meaningful goals, and offering achievable entry points aligned with learners' prior knowledge and capabilities. *Context*: Unstructured, uncertainty-rich learning environments, particularly for novice learners encountering complex problem spaces.

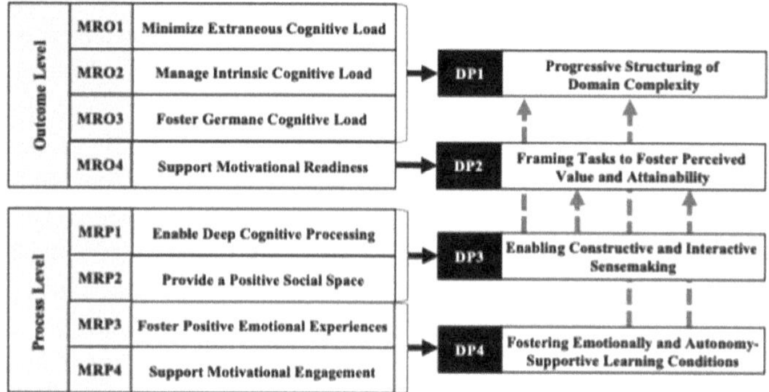

Fig. 2. Overview of Meta-Requirements and Design Principles.

Addressing **MRP1-MRP2**, pretraining should support deep cognitive engagement through constructive and interactive learning processes. In line with ICAP, constructive and interactive activities, such as dialogue with peers or digital agents, enable generative processing and collaborative sensemaking in complex environments [15]. Moreover, a supportive social space facilitates collaboration and shared understanding, allowing learners to jointly interpret complex system dynamics. [24, 29]. Accordingly, pretraining should provide opportunities for dialogue, explanation, and collaborative reflection to support cognitive and social engagement. Therefore, we introduce **DP3: Enabling Constructive and Interactive Sensemaking.** *Objective*: Foster generative cognitive processing and shared understanding during pretraining. *Mechanism:* Engage learners in constructive (e.g., self-explanation) and interactive (e.g., dialogue, collaboration) activities that require articulation, negotiation, and integration of knowledge. Where applicable, align interaction with task-relevant actions so that learners can externalize and manipulate system elements, thereby supporting meaning-making through both cognitive and embodied engagement while avoiding unnecessary interaction complexity. Context (cursive): Virtual environments offering high degrees of learner freedom (not cursive). Addressing **MRP3 and MRP4,** pretraining should foster positive emotional and motivational conditions that support engagement [29]. In complex and uncertain environments, negative emotions such as anxiety can reduce learning and participation [23]. Drawing on SDT, learning environments should enable autonomous exploration and experiences of competence [22]. Provide low-stakes, autonomous exploration and competence-supportive feedback to enhance perceived control and reduce anxiety. Thereby, we propose **DP4: Fostering Emotionally Supportive and Autonomy-Supportive Learning Conditions.** *Objective:* Support positive affect, perceived control, and sustained engagement during pretraining. *Mechanism:* Provide low-stakes, autonomous exploration and competence-supportive feedback. *Context:* Complex and uncertain learning environments with potential for cognitive and emotional overload.

7 First Design Cycle

Based on the proposed design principles (DP1–DP4), the immersive game-based pretraining intervention was instantiated accordingly. For the implementation of the pretraining environment, we selected the gaming platform Roblox, which provides an open-access development environment (Roblox Studio) for the creation of user-generated 3D virtual worlds. The platform was chosen for several reasons. First, it enables the development of immersive environments that support interactive exploration and social interaction, thereby aligning with the process-oriented design principles. Second, Roblox allows free deployment and hosting of custom-built environments, making it a particularly suitable solution for iterative design and large-scale field testing in higher education contexts. Finally, its accessibility across devices and its low technical entry barriers for users supported the practical feasibility of the second iteration field study. The content of the immersive 3D pretraining environment builds upon an informational pretraining video developed by one of the authors, which served as the initial pretraining solution for the business simulation game. It includes an introduction to the narrative of the business simulation game: the previous CEOs have left the startup, and the players must now take over its operations. Students are guided through the company's departments and the entire value creation process as well as the profit and loss statement based on the decisions made by the previous CEOs.

7.1 Building: Introducing Design Features

To realize **DP1: Progressive Structuring of Domain Complexity**, the design focuses on the primary objective of the business simulation game: making managerial decisions under conditions of uncertainty. This requires students to analyze the financial statements of the previous week as the basis for subsequent decision-making. In line with the initial pretraining video of our use case and the pretraining principle in multimedia learning, students are guided to systematically derive decisions for a baseline scenario in relation to the corresponding organizational departments (**DF1**). Through this process, they become familiar not only with the most relevant financial statements and their implications for decision parameters, but also with the various departments and their core functions within the business simulation game. Furthermore, in accordance with the coherence principle [10], only information essential for the initial rounds of the business simulation is included, while advanced topics (e.g., coping with macroeconomic changes) are deliberately omitted (**DF2**). In contrast to the video-based pretraining, which follows a guided tutorial format, the immersive 3D pretraining environment requires students to actively search for relevant information, e.g., by interacting with non-player characters (NPCs) or exploring objects placed within the virtual world, and to perform required calculations themselves. In line with the segmenting principle [10], the pretraining allows user-paced exploration of the virtual environment (**DF3**). This active exploration is intended to help manage intrinsic cognitive load and foster deeper cognitive engagement compared to passive video consumption. Furthermore, enhancing the bodily engagement in pretraining, users can actively interact with most important objects [32], e.g., zooming and or rotating on cross-wound yarn package on the weaving machine (**DF4**). To further support learning while managing cognitive load, established instructional support principles from multimedia learning theory are incorporated. To reduce extraneous cognitive load, and following the spatial contiguity principle [10], corresponding narration and graphical information are presented simultaneously rather than sequentially (**DF5**). In addition, essential information is visually highlighted in accordance with the signaling principle, for example by emphasizing fields that need to be completed and corresponding sections in the financial statement sheet (**DF6**). Together, these design features translate the previously passive pretraining approach into an interactive, self-directed learning experience while preserving the underlying instructional structure of the business simulation game. To realize **DP2**: **Framing Tasks to Foster Perceived Value and Attainability,** the immersive pretraining environment is designed to strengthen learners' motivational beliefs, including task value, goal orientation, and self-efficacy. As the business simulation confronts students with high levels of uncertainty that may evoke anxiety and deactivation [23], the design aims to foster motivational readiness prior to entering actual gameplay. To support perceived competence, the system provides achievement badges for successfully completed tasks (**DF7**) and an overview of previously mastered calculations and decision parameters (**DF8**). To support autonomy, learners are granted high agency through unrestricted exploration of the virtual environment (**DF9**) but receive guidance through a quest field at the top of the screen (**DF10**). To support relatedness, friendly NPCs provide guidance, content-related explanations, and information on how to proceed to subsequent steps within the pretraining environment (**DF11**). To realize **DP3: Enabling Constructive and Interactive Sensemaking,** NPCs initiate interaction by signaling availability through gestural cues (e.g., waving) during first encounters (**DF12**), aligning with the embodiment principle [10]. Furthermore, students can take notes in a notebook, e.g., when interacting with an object that included specific information that was necessary for calculations afterwards (**DF13**). In addition, text-based chat and voice communication features enable peer interaction and collaborative sensemaking, as provided by the default functionality of Roblox Studio (**DF14**). To realize **DP4: Fostering Emotionally Supportive and Autonomy-Supportive Learning Conditions**, a structured tutorial is included to support initial orientation within the immersive environment (**DF15**). Furthermore, NPC language is designed to be friendly and supportive, and NPC characters vary in names and appearance to represent multiple genders and ethnic backgrounds (**DF16**). To ensure a respectful learning climate, peer communication is protected against inappropriate wording through moderation features provided by Roblox Studio (**DF17**). Together, the proposed design principles and corresponding design features operationalize an immersive pretraining approach that prepares learners for subsequent engagement in the business simulation game.

7.2 Intervention: Small-Scale Testing

In the first design cycle, student teachers enrolled in an economics education program were invited to evaluate an alpha version of the immersive game-based pretraining environment. Participation was voluntary and incentivized by the opportunity to earn three bonus points toward their final exam (equivalent to 3% of the exam score). In total, 12 students participated in the evaluation (50% female). Students were on average 22.1 years old (SD = 4.11). Participants were introduced to the alpha version of the pretraining environment and were given 15 min to freely explore the virtual world and attempt to solve the embedded objectives; completion of all objectives was not required. When possible, two students were placed within the same virtual world while being physically located in separate rooms, enabling the collection of initial insights into social and peer-related aspects of the design. As future teachers, they were also asked to reflect from the perspective of the player but also from a pedagogical lens. Following the exploration phase, participants completed an online questionnaire administered via LimeSurvey. The questionnaire focused on students' perceptions of the learning and interaction processes supported by the immersive pretraining environment. As the participating student teachers did not subsequently engage in the business simulation game itself, the primary purpose of this design cycle was not to evaluate learning outcomes, but rather to gather formative feedback on the perceived learning process, with particular emphasis on the proposed process-oriented design principles. In alignment with **DP3,** quantitative data were collected on students' perceived extraneous, intrinsic, and germane cognitive load using the scale by [33] as well as on the perceived sociability of the environment based on [24]. Furthermore, in alignment with **DP4,** data were gathered on perceived enjoyment and anxiety [34], as well as on autonomy, competence, and relatedness [35]. Each dimension was gathered on a 7-point Likert-scale (0 = don't agree – 6 = fully agree). Qualitative data was collected through open-ended questions, asking students to describe encountered hurdles and potential improvement areas to inform subsequent refinements of the artifact.

7.3 Evaluation: Process-Level Outcomes

To support interpretation of the descriptive statistics, values are considered relative to the theoretical scale midpoint (3): values below 2 are interpreted as low, values between 2 and below 3 as relatively low, values between 3 and below 4 as moderate, and values of 4 and above as high. Descriptive results indicate generally favorable perceptions of the immersive pretraining environment. Participants reported moderate levels of germane cognitive load (M = 3.06, SD = 1.10), while perceived intrinsic (M = 2.02, SD = 0.90) and extraneous cognitive load (M = 1.78, SD = 1.30) remained low. These findings suggest that the environment was perceived as cognitively manageable during the short exploration phase. Perceived sociability of the environment was rated moderately (M = 3.32, SD = 0.56), indicating initial support for interactive and socially oriented sensemaking processes. Regarding emotional and motivational perceptions, participants reported moderate to high enjoyment (M = 3.92, SD = 1.31) and rather low anxiety (M = 2.10, SD = 1.55). Concerning basic psychological needs, perceived autonomy was rated moderately (M = 3.30, SD = 1.83), while perceived relatedness received the highest ratings (M = 5.00, SD = 1.13). In contrast, perceived competence was relatively low (M = 2.42, SD = 1.57). The relatively high standard deviations across emotional and motivational constructs indicate heterogeneous perceptions, suggesting that participants experienced the pretraining environment in different ways. These quantitative findings are reflected in the qualitative feedback. While some participants reported that "everything was included" (S3) or indicated "nothing" that should be changed (S2, S5), others explicitly pointed to areas for improvement. Several students emphasized the need for clearer onboarding and navigation support. One participant requested "a more detailed explanation before the start of the game regarding how the controls work" (S4), while another stated that "it should be explained how the 360-degree rotation works" (S7). One student further specified that "360-degree movement [should be possible] without requiring the mouse button to be held down continuously" (S12). In addition, one participant reported difficulties with spatial orientation and suggested a "display showing where the avatar is currently located on the map" (S1). Another student expressed the need for improvements to the note-taking functionality, requesting "the possibility to edit my notes afterwards" as well as "a better visualization of the note-taking block, more freely like a note sheet rather than fixed lines" (S11). Regarding task structure and guidance, one participant perceived the overall objectives as unclear and requested clearer feedback (S10). Similarly, another one noted that "tasks should be formulated more briefly, as I had difficulties understanding them the first time" (S9). In this context, one student suggested "a hint field when users cannot proceed with a task, so that they can decide themselves whether to use a hint" (S8).

8 Second Design Cycle

8.1 Building: Refining the Design Features

Based on the findings of the first design cycle, several targeted refinements were implemented prior to the second design cycle, as outlined in Fig. 3. These refinements addressed the previously identified improvement areas related to onboarding and navigation support, interface usability, as well as guidance and task clarification.

Regarding **onboarding and navigation support**, to improve initial orientation, a control GUI was added at the beginning of the game to introduce relevant navigation and interaction controls (**DF18**). In addition, camera settings were adjusted from a fixed perspective to a follow-camera mode, thereby reducing students' effort when navigating the 360-degree environment. Furthermore, while the initial version provided visual cues in the form of light points indicating where to proceed next based on the quest field displayed at the top of the screen, an optional "?" GUI-button was added in the 3D environment. When activated, this button displays the direct pathway to the next objective within the game (**DF19**). In terms of **interface usability**, to improve usability of the note-taking functionality, the notebook was refined to allow notes to be deleted and revised. Regarding **guidance and task clarification,** to support clearer task understanding, an introductory window was extended at the beginning of the game to introduce the narrative context of the pretraining intervention more explicitly prior to gameplay

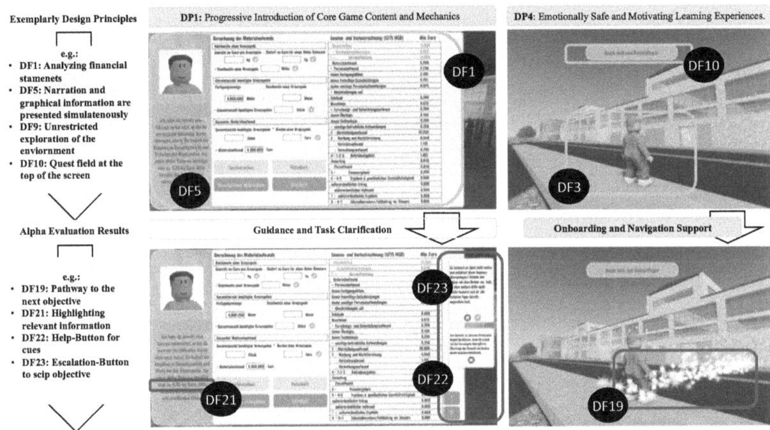

Fig. 3. Example of artifact refinement across design cycles.

(**DF20**). In addition, signaling of relevant information was strengthened by not only highlighting the fields in which information must be entered, but also emphasizing relevant keywords within conversations with NPCs (**DF21**). Furthermore, additional guidance mechanisms were integrated into the NPC conversation interfaces. A help ("?") button was introduced to provide optional instructional support on how to complete the current objective (**DF22**), while an escalation ("!") button allows learners to skip an objective and proceed to the next step (**DF23**). This design decision was intended to ensure that students can complete the pretraining environment even when individual objectives cannot be solved. Together, these refinements aimed to improve orientation, reduce frustration, and strengthen motivational readiness prior to the second evaluation cycle.

8.2 Intervention: Field-Study Deployment

In the second design cycle, the immersive game-based pretraining environment was implemented in a field-study setting with 238 students participating in a business simulation course during the winter term 2025/2026 at a German university. Of these, 119 students were randomly assigned to the experimental group, while the remaining 119 served as a control group and were instructed to watch a pretraining video. Log data showed that 107 students of the control group accessed the video and were included in the analysis. Students in the intervention group were enrolled in a separate *Moodle* course and asked to create a Roblox account to access the pretraining environment. They were informed that no personal data was required and that the account could be deleted afterward. Following a joint introductory session, all students were given four days to complete the pretraining. Afterward, participants were invited to complete an online questionnaire. Those who opted out of the Roblox-based pretraining were provided with a written handbook covering the same content. Participation and gameplay duration were tracked within the system, and the study received ethical approval from the university's ethics committee. Of the 119 students in the experimental group, 82 actively engaged with the Roblox environment and completed the questionnaire, forming the final sample for descriptive analysis. Evaluation included both process level (see measures of first design cycle) and outcome level, emphasizing on extraneous, intrinsic and germane cognitive load during the first round of the business simulation [33] with regard to DP1 and task value, self-efficacy and intrinsic goal orientation [31] after completion of the pretraining intervention with regard to DP2. During the first evening of deployment, a technical bug occurred that limited progression within the environment for a subset of participants. The issue was identified and resolved by the following morning. Based on log data, participants could be categorized into three groups: students who only interacted with the initial buggy version (n = 32), students who exclusively experienced the fixed version (n = 27), and students who completed the environment after the bug had been fixed, thus interacting with both versions (n = 23). Therefore, not all participants encountered identical system conditions, which may have influenced individual experiences.

8.3 Evaluation: Process- and Outcome-Level Results

Due to the temporary technical issue during deployment, participants experienced different system states. These are treated as contextual exposure groups rather than experimental conditions. Table 1 presents descriptive results of the second design cycle evaluation, separated by exposure group due to the temporary technical issue during deployment. These findings provide exploratory insights into participants' perceptions of the pretraining experience and their initial engagement with the simulation. Thus, the results serve to evaluate the artifact and the associated design principles within the ADR process, while offering preliminary insights into how different system configurations may shape user experience. Across all groups, participants reported relatively low to low levels of extraneous cognitive load and moderate to high levels of germane cognitive load during the pretraining phase. Enjoyment was consistently high, while anxiety remained low across groups. Moreover, autonomy differed from low to moderate while competence and relatedness showed stable moderate to high values.

On the outcome level, descriptive results indicate low to relatively low levels of intrinsic and extraneous cognitive load and comparatively high levels of germane cognitive load following the first game round. In addition, intrinsic goal orientation was rated moderate, while task value and self-efficacy were rated high across exposure groups. While the control group (video-based pretraining) showed overall comparable patterns, with peak average values in sociability and autonomy, the Buggy + Fixed group tended to report the most favorable average values across several outcomes, such as germane cognitive load, task value, intrinsic goal orientation, and self-efficacy.

9 Discussion

This ADR study aimed to derive theory-informed and practice-driven meta-requirements and design principles that guided the instantiation and iterative refinement of an immersive game-based pretraining environment across two build–intervention–evaluation cycles. **First design cycle:** Quantitative results indicated that the initial instantiation was

Table 1. Descriptive Results of Second Iteration Cycle Evaluation

Dimension	Buggy (n = 32)		Fixed (n = 27)		Buggy + Fixed (n = 23)		Control (n = 117)	
Process Level	*M*	*SD*	*M*	*SD*	*M*	*SD*	*M*	*SD*
Extraneous Load	2.61	1.11	1.98	1.51	**1.91**	**1.66**	2.06	1.31
Intrinsic Load	1.76	1.17	1.74	0.98	1.92	1.36	2.41	1.24
Germane Load	3.79	1.08	3.86	1.05	**4.06**	**0.97**	3.86	0.87
Sociability	3.50	1.32	3.32	1.31	3.76	1.24	**3.95**	**1.11**
Enjoyment	3.87	1.08	4.21	1.33	**4.28**	**1.23**	3.98	1.10
Anxiety	1.14	1.22	1.06	1.18	**0.97**	**1.12**	1.08	1.19
Autonomy	2.28	1.54	3.06	1.33	2.67	1.52	**3.31**	**1.01**
Competence	3.46	1.08	**3.77**	**0.92**	3.59	1.04	3.37	0.83
Relatedness	3.67	1.38	3.78	1.11	**3.97**	**1.26**	3.79	1.14
Outcome Level								
Extraneous Load (1. Round)	2.24^1	0.96	**2.02^2**	**1.03**	2.09^1	1.29	2.27^2	1.22
Intrinsic Load (1. Round)	2.39^1	0.92	2.16^2	1.12	2.45^1	1.36	2.66^2	1.20
Germane Load (1. Round)	4.07^1	0.84	4.15^2	0.70	**4.42^1**	**0.67**	4.00^2	0.79
Task Value	3.76	1.11	4.44	1.11	**4.67**	**0.84**	4.38	0.93
Intrinsic Goal Orientation	3.05	1.12	3.50	0.95	**3.84**	**0.95**	3.59	0.98
Self-Efficacy	4.07	0.84	4.13	0.88	**4.42**	**0.67**	4.12	1.05

[1] one missing value, [2] two missing values

overall perceived as aligned with the four proposed design principles. However, qualitative feedback revealed notable challenges related to navigation and spatial orientation within the virtual environment. These findings underline that ease of use in immersive learning environments should not be taken for granted, even for learners often characterized as "digital natives." From a theoretical perspective, this observation aligns with the Technology Acceptance Model, which posits that perceived ease of use plays a central role in shaping users' engagement with digital systems [28]. In addition, consistent with cognitive load theory [21], students explicitly requested additional cues, suggesting that inefficient navigational support may have imposed extraneous cognitive load. These insights informed targeted refinements implemented in the second design cycle.

Second design cycle: A noteworthy finding of the second evaluation concerned comparatively low perceived autonomy, potentially having implications for intrinsic motivation [22]. This outcome can be attributed to the deliberately linear structure of the pretraining intervention, which was inherited from the original video-based pretraining format. The linear storyline was intentionally designed to introduce organizational departments sequentially and to allow learners to conceptually trace the production process from production through sales. While this structure supported progressive introduction of core content, it may have constrained learners' sense of agency. This highlights a design tension between instructional guidance and autonomy support, which is explicitly salient in experiential entrepreneurship education [26]. Future refinements should therefore explore alternative designs that allow greater freedom in task selection, enabling investigation of how increased autonomy influences perceived competence and cognitive load. **Breakdowns and recovery mechanisms:** The technical breakdown encountered during field deployment provided additional design insights. Log data indicated that fewer than half of the students who initially experienced the buggy version returned once the issue had been resolved. From a design perspective, this underscores the importance of optional guidance and recovery mechanisms that allow learners to re-enter the learning process after interruptions or moments of disorientation, e.g., by implementing automated save points. Such mechanisms appear particularly relevant in immersive learning environments, where technical breakdowns or cognitive overload may otherwise quickly lead to frustration and disengagement.

9.1 Limitations and Future Research Directions

This study is subject to several limitations that also provide directions for future research. First, while the study derives design knowledge for immersive pretraining environments, pretraining represents only one component of business simulation gaming. Consequently, the proposed meta-requirements and design principles cannot be directly generalized to the design of complete immersive digital game-based learning environments. Future studies should build on the presented design knowledge to investigate how immersive business simulation games can be holistically designed and integrated across multiple gameplay phases. Second, although the study combines quantitative and qualitative evaluation approaches, the findings are primarily interpretive in nature and do not allow causal conclusions between learning process and outcome variables. Future research could complement this work by examining how immersive pretraining influences learning effectiveness, decision quality, or performance trajectories during subsequent game rounds. Third, while additional guidance cues and escalation mechanisms were implemented in the second design cycle, these supports followed predefined rule-based logic. Future research could explore adaptive feedback mechanisms, for example through AI-assisted NPCs, to provide individualized guidance based on learners' progress, behavior, or prior knowledge. Such adaptive designs may further enhance both cognitive and motivational readiness in immersive pretraining environments.

10 Contributions

Theoretical contribution: From a theoretical perspective, this ADR study contributes to design knowledge across three levels. First, it addresses a specific problem space i.e., how to prepare novice learners for complex business simulation environments characterized by high cognitive and motivational demands. Second, it abstracts this problem into a broader class of solutions by conceptualizing immersive pretraining to support cognitive and motivational readiness as well as active sensemaking in complex learning environments. Third, it formalizes this understanding into meta-requirements and reusable design principles that specify how immersive environments can be designed to achieve these outcomes. By linking multimedia learning theory with practical design challenges and the distinctive affordances of immersive environments, the study extends existing design knowledge on the purposeful use of immersive technologies beyond engagement-oriented applications. **Practical contribution:** From a practical perspective, the study provides a validated design blueprint for implementing immersive pretraining in game-based education. The developed artifact demonstrates how abstract design principles can be operationalized through concrete design features, including interactive onboarding, embodied object interaction, optional guidance mechanisms, and socially supportive NPC design. Despite initial technical breakdowns during deployment, the artifact was successfully implemented in a large-scale field setting. The resulting design features and refinement logic offer actionable guidance for educators and designers seeking to prepare learners for complex simulation-based courses.

References

1. Kuratko, D.F., Hodgetts, R.M.: Entrepreneurship: Theory, process, practice. TN: Nashville South-Western (2004)
2. Fayolle, A., Gailly, B., Lassas-Clerc, N.: Assessing the impact of entrepreneurship education programmes: a new methodology. J. Eur. Ind. Train. **30**(9), 701–720 (2006)
3. Goi, C.-L.: The use of business simulation games in teaching and learning. J. Educ. Bus. **94**(5), 342–349 (2019)
4. Neck, H.M., Greene, P.G.: Entrepreneurship education: known worlds and new frontiers. J. Small Bus. Manage. **49**(1), 55–70 (2011)
5. Wouters, P., Van Oostendorp, H.: A meta-analytic review of the role of instructional support in game-based learning. Comput. Educ. **60**(1), 412–425 (2013)
6. Sweller, J.: Element interactivity and intrinsic, extraneous, and germane cognitive load. Educ. Psychol. Rev. **22**, 123–138 (2010)
7. Paas, F., Renkl, A., Sweller, J.: Cognitive load theory and instructional design: recent developments. Educ. Psychol. **38**(1), 1–4 (2003)
8. Van Gelderen, M.: Autonomy as the guiding aim of entrepreneurship education. Educ.+ Training, **52**(8–9), 710–721 (2010)
9. Mayer, R.E.: Computer games in education. Annu. Rev. Psychol. **70**, 531–549 (2019)
10. Mayer, R.E.: Using multimedia for e-learning. J. Comput. Assist. Learn. **33**(5), 403–423 (2017)
11. Mayer, R.E.: Multimedia Learning (2nd ed.). Cambridge University Press (2009)
12. Lawson, A.P., Mayer, R.E.: Effect of pre-training and role of working memory characteristics in learning with immersive virtual reality. Int. J. Hum.–Comput. Interact. 1–18 (2024)
13. Petersen, G.B., et al.: The virtual field trip: Investigating how to optimize immersive virtual learning in climate change education. Br. J. Edu. Technol. **51**(6), 2099–2115 (2020)
14. Meyer, O.A., Omdahl, M.K., Makransky, G.: Investigating the effect of pre-training when learning through immersive virtual reality and video: a media and methods experiment. Comput. Educ. **140**, 103603 (2019)
15. Chi, M.T., Wylie, R.: The ICAP framework: linking cognitive engagement to active learning outcomes. Educ. Psychol. **49**(4), 219–243 (2014)
16. Kirschner, P., Sweller, J., Clark, R.E.: Why unguided learning does not work: an analysis of the failure of discovery learning, problem-based learning, experiential learning and inquiry-based learning. Educ. Psychol. **41**(2), 75–86 (2006)

17. Makransky, G., Petersen, G.B.: The cognitive affective model of immersive learning (CAMIL): a theoretical research-based model of learning in immersive virtual reality. Educ. Psychol. Rev. **33**(3), 937–958 (2021)
18. Kolb, D.A.: The process of experiential learning. Experiential learning: Experience as the source of learning and development, 20–38 (1984)
19. Sein, M.K., et al.: Action design research. MIS Q. 37–56 (2011)
20. Moreno, R., Mayer, R.: Interactive multimodal learning environments: special issue on interactive learning environments: contemporary issues and trends. Educ. Psychol. Rev. **19**, 309–326 (2007)
21. Chandler, P., Sweller, J.: Cognitive load theory and the format of instruction. Cogn. Instr. **8**(4), 293–332 (1991)
22. Ryan, R.M., Deci, E.L.: Self-determination theory and the facilitation of intrinsic motivation, social development, and well-being. Am. Psychol. **55**(1), 68 (2000)
23. Pekrun, R.: The control-value theory of achievement emotions: assumptions, corollaries, and implications for educational research and practice. Educ. Psychol. Rev. **18**(4), 315–341 (2006)
24. Kreijns, K., et al.: Measuring perceived sociability of computer-supported collaborative learning environments. Comput. Educ. **49**(2), 176–192 (2007)
25. Peffers, K., Tuunanen, T., Niehaves, B.: Design science research genres: introduction to the special issue on exemplars and criteria for applicable design science research, pp. 129–139. Taylor & Francis. (2018)
26. Crosina, E., et al.: From negative emotions to entrepreneurial mindset: a model of learning through experiential entrepreneurship education. Acad. Manage. Learn. Educ. **23**(1), 88–127 (2024)
27. Fayolle, A.: Personal views on the future of entrepreneurship education. In: A Research Agenda for Entrepreneurship Education, pp. 127–138. Edward Elgar Publishing (2018)
28. Venkatesh, V., Davis, F.D.: A theoretical extension of the technology acceptance model: four longitudinal field studies. Manage. Sci. **46**(2), 186–204 (2000)
29. Plass, J.L., Homer, B.D., Kinzer, C.K.: Foundations of game-based learning. Educ. Psychol. **50**(4), 258–283 (2015)
30. Möller, F., Guggenberger, T.M., Otto, B.: Towards a method for design principle development in information systems. In: International conference on design science research in information systems and technology. Springer (2020)
31. Pintrich, P.R., et al.: Reliability and predictive validity of the motivated strategies for learning questionnaire (MSLQ). Educ. Psychol. Measur. **53**(3), 801–813 (1993)
32. Skulmowski, A., Rey, G.D.: Embodied learning: introducing a taxonomy based on bodily engagement and task integration. Cogn. Res. Principles Implications **3**(1), 6 (2018)
33. Krieglstein, F., et al.: Development and validation of a theory-based questionnaire to measure different types of cognitive load. Educ. Psychol. Rev. **35**(1), 9 (2023)
34. Pekrun, R., Goetz, T., Perry, R.P.: Achievement emotions questionnaire (AEQ). User's manual. Unpublished Manuscript, University of Munich, Munich (2005)
35. Sheldon, K.M., Filak, V.: Manipulating autonomy, competence, and relatedness support in a game-learning context: new evidence that all three needs matter. Br. J. Soc. Psychol. **47**(2), 267–283 (2008)

Authentic Learning by Design: Meta-Requirements for AI Support for Students and Educators

Anna Wolters[1]([⊠]) [iD], Gregor Kipping[2] [iD], Sofie Wass[3] [iD], Michael Gau[2] [iD], Dennis M. Riehle[1] [iD], and Leona Chandra Kruse[3] [iD]

[1] University of Koblenz, Koblenz, Germany
awolters@uni-koblenz.de
[2] University of Liechtenstein, Vaduz, Liechtenstein
[3] University of Agder, Kristiansand, Norway

Abstract. Large language models (LLMs) have transformed learning and educational practices, yet concerns persist about whether authentic learning occurs when cognitive tasks are outsourced to artificial intelligence (AI) systems. We examined how AI systems can support educators in facilitating student's authentic learning. This paper reports on the first two echelons of our echeloned design science research (eDSR). We evaluated 200 AI systems deployed across European educational institutions and interviewed 11 experienced educators in three countries. Based on the findings, we formulated and validated meta-requirements for AI systems that support authentic learning from the perspectives of students, educators, and educational institutions.

Keywords: Authentic Learning · Design Science Research · Meta-Requirements · AI Learning Support · Pedagogical Design

1 Introduction

Students no longer search for information in books or databases; they prompt large language models (LLMs) to explain concepts, generate examples, and assemble arguments in seconds. This shift has sparked growing concern about whether—and what—students actually learn when substantial cognitive work is delegated to LLMs. In the UK, reports show that students themselves fear that such delegation is eroding their ability to study and research, even as LLM use becomes widespread in educational institutions [1]. Across educational institutions more broadly, observers warn that LLM support does not automatically lead to deeper understanding [2] and may even dull core capacities for critical thinking [3]. These accounts point to a central dilemma for contemporary education: now that there is no going back, how can we ensure that authentic learning is supported when learning activities are increasingly mediated by LLMs?

To address this dilemma, we turn to the notion of authentic learning. Authentic learning emphasizes learners' active construction of knowledge through disciplined inquiry and learning activities that have value beyond the academic setting [4]. In contrast to

© The Author(s), under exclusive license to Springer Nature Switzerland AG 2026
J. vom Brocke et al. (Eds.): DESRIST 2026, LNCS 16606, pp. 227–245, 2026.
https://doi.org/10.1007/978-3-032-28313-9_13

traditional approaches focused on the reproduction of information, authentic learning encourages learners to ground understanding in experience [5]. It is commonly supported through pedagogical design such as group discussions, case-based projects, and cooperative tasks, which aim to foster intellectual quality and student engagement [5]. To operationalize authentic learning, we draw on the framework by Newmann & Wehlage [6], which specifies five dimensions for authentic instruction: higher-order thinking, depth of knowledge, connectedness to the world beyond the classroom, substantive conversation, and social support for student achievement. Existing concerns among educational institutions suggest that current LLM integration has not yet facilitated the core dimensions of authentic learning.

This perspective shifts attention from whether LLMs should be used in education to how they should be designed and integrated to meaningfully facilitate authentic learning. Our echeloned design science research (eDSR) addresses these challenges, and this paper reports on the first two echelons. The aim of this paper is the identification of meta-requirements for the design of LLM-based solutions for facilitating authentic learning. We analyzed 200 artificial intelligence (AI) systems used at educational institutions across Europe and interviewed 11 educators in three countries. Following Maedche et al. [7] we constructed the problem space, derived meta-requirements for the (a) contents, (b) user experience, and (c) governance of AI systems for authentic learning, and validated them. This paper contributes to design knowledge for AI systems in facilitating authentic learning.

2 Background

2.1 AI-Supported Learning Platform in Higher Education

The integration of AI systems in educational institutions has accelerated dramatically in recent years, with educators increasingly adopting diverse AI-powered applications to enhance teaching and learning experiences. Among various AI-based technologies, pedagogical conversational agents (PCAs) have received particular attention, illustrating their effectiveness for teaching but also the complexity in their adoption [8]. Weber et al. [9] illustrate the variety of PCAs, which, among others, are characterized by varying interaction modalities, intended roles to imitate in the learning process, or the addressed target group. Such conversational technologies enable learning support, which can be used for improving argumentative writing [10], or for solving legal cases [11], among other use cases.

The increasing presence of AI systems in professional contexts also puts pressure on educational institutions to integrate AI literacy development in their curriculum [12]. Thereby, AI literacy is now perceived as a fundamental skill of knowledge workers across industries, instead of being a professional skill exclusive to knowledge workers in IT-related disciplines. Hönigsberg et al. [12] argue that AI literacy needs to be established through structured learning and practical experiences with AI.

Research demonstrates that AI-enhanced education benefits from active learning, where students build knowledge through practical use cases supported by AI [13]. However, educators also need to ensure that AI systems are incorporated to enhance the students' learning process instead of allowing them to use AI systems as a shortcut to success [13]. The design of learning platforms and digital learning environments has therefore emerged as a complementary area of inquiry, offering insights into how technological systems can be structured to support pedagogical goals. However, the intersection of authentic learning principles and AI system implementation in educational institutions contexts remains under-explored, creating an urgent need for empirically grounded design requirements.

2.2 Authentic Learning

Authentic learning is a core element of current pedagogy, emphasizing how learners' active construction of knowledge, disciplined inquiry, and value beyond the academic setting improve learning outcomes [4]. Compared to more traditional approaches, authentic learning encourages learners to ground their understanding in experience rather than absorbing and reproducing knowledge [5]. This is often achieved through techniques such as group discussions, case-based projects, arts and crafts materials, and cooperative tasks. These techniques seek to foster not only in-depth understanding, but also intellectual quality and engagement [5].

Newmann & Wehlage [6] provide a framework for authentic instruction that presents a set of standards for how educators can move towards a more authentic learning instruction. While all standards might be far reached in some settings, the framework can serve as a guide for prioritizing and reflecting on forms of instruction. This framework consists of higher-order thinking, depth of knowledge, connectedness to the world beyond the classroom, substantive conversation, and social support for student achievement. Table 1 gives a brief overview of the standards.

Table 1. Standards for Authentic Learning for Educators [6]

Standard	Description
Higher-order thinking (H)	Transforming the meaning and implications of information to discover new understandings (i.e., synthesis, generalize, explain etc.)
Depth of knowledge (D)	Demonstrating understanding of the central idea of the topic by making arguments, solving problems, making distinctions
Connectedness to the world beyond the classroom (C)	Connecting learning to the larger social context by engaging with real-world public problems and personal experiences
Substantive conversation (SC)	Engaging in considerable interaction through sharing of ideas and questions, that improves the collective understanding of the topic
Social support for student achievement (S)	Fostering high expectations of all students and mutual respect among all members of the learning environment

With the rapid spread of generative artificial intelligence systems, particularly in education, new opportunities have emerged in how to access, apply, interpret, and reproduce knowledge [14, 15]. As AI reshapes how knowledge is acquired and processed, the roles of both educators and students are changing, making authentic learning more relevant than ever.

3   Research Method

Effective information systems (IS) design requires comprehensive problem understanding to achieve lasting impact [16]. The recently introduced eDSR methodology [17] addresses this need by providing a structured approach to managing complex socio-technical challenges in DSR projects. eDSR's core innovation lies in decomposing projects into discrete, self-contained echelons, thereby enhancing project structure, manageability, and stakeholder communication. Unlike linear DSR approaches, eDSR embraces iterative, non-linear cycles that reflect how complex problems naturally evolve. Knowledge flows dynamically across echelons rather than following rigid sequential paths, enabling the agility and adaptability essential for addressing intricate design challenges. As such, adopting an eDSR approach helps to ensure flexibility in structuring this DSR project.

The proposed eDSR methodology comprises five interconnected stages (1) problem analysis, (2) objectives and requirements definition, (3) design and development, (4) demonstration, and (5) evaluation. Each stage systematically contributes to design knowledge through rigorous validation. The given research focuses on the first two stages. Figure 1 illustrates the different phases of the eDSR process and the activities conducted (grey) as well as the planned activities (white) for future research. The contribution of this study is the generated design knowledge for phase one and two.

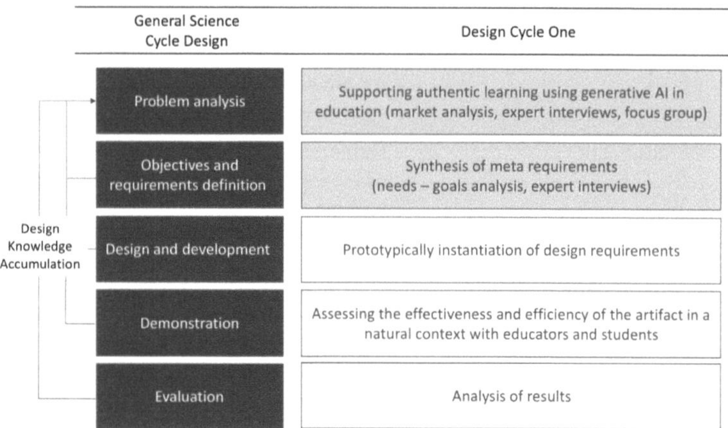

Fig. 1. Overview of the eDSR Process and the Conducted and Planned Activities

The problem analysis stage requires a clear articulation of problem characteristics, boundaries, and stakeholder perspectives to form the foundation for subsequent design decisions. In particular, we conducted a market review of AI systems used by educational institutions in higher education (HE) and conducted interviews with experts. The objectives and requirements definition focuses on deriving design objectives and requirements, and on supporting designers in formulating the needs and goals of relevant stakeholders based on the problem analysis. Based on the results of the previous phase, we derived an initial set of meta-requirements. In future activities, we plan to instantiate the derived requirements in the design and development phase. Furthermore, we will demonstrate the prototype to educators in a natural setting to assess the efficiency and effectiveness of the artifact. Finally, we plan to analyze the results of the artifact used by educators and students.

4 Problem Analysis and Requirements Definition

4.1 Analysis of AI Systems Deployed in European Educational Institutions

The market review focuses on identifying AI systems currently used at European educational institutions. First, a comprehensive collection of European educational institutions was compiled using the Microdata Access of the European Higher Education Sector Observatory (EHESO)[1], which encompasses approximately 3,500 educational institutions across the European Union, the United Kingdom, and the European Free Trade Association (EFTA) countries. The latest version of the microdata was used.

Second, the collection was refined to include only larger institutions within each country, which resulted in a subset of approximately 1,400 organizations for the market review. Third, the market review was conducted through systematic online searches to identify information publicly shared by the educational institutions regarding their use or adoption of AI systems. All available online information was documented for analysis. The search resulted in a collection of approximately 230 AI systems. For each AI system the following data were collected: name, purpose and key functionality, target user group, and additional information on the technology used or its service provider.

For the analysis of data, AI systems were grouped into categories based on their provided functionality. System categories were further structured based on learning and teaching activities for which the underlying key functionality is applicable for. The final grouping is used for an analysis of authentic learning standards.

4.2 Interviews and Requirements Definition with Educators

In addition to the market analysis, semi-structured interviews were conducted with eleven experienced educators (experts E1–E11) from HE institutions to gain insights into current work and practice in the field of AI-supported teaching and learning. By experts from educational institutions, we mean "knowledgeable agents" [18] who have considerable teaching experience and initial experience with the use of AI in their daily work. We considered experts from institutions of different sizes and with varying degrees of maturity in terms of the implementation and use of AI technologies. These insights help to understand the needs of educators and the requirements for AI systems in HE. As

---

[1] https://national-policies.eacea.ec.europa.eu/eheso/micro-data-access.

part of the problem analysis, the focus was on deriving the needs and goals of relevant stakeholders in order to ultimately formulate meta-requirements. According to Maedche et al. [7], these three concepts—needs, goals, and requirements—in conjunction with the stakeholders, serve to describe and explore the problem space. Our analysis revealed a number of recurring needs that influence the way AI is adopted and used in educational institutions for teaching and learning. Stakeholders may have different and potentially conflicting requirements for a solution, with needs forming the core of the problem. The goals should reflect the interests of the stakeholders and solve the problems underlying the needs, and are fulfilled by requirements such as, in our case, requirements for AI-supported authentic learning in HE [7].

All interviews were conducted between November 2025 and December 2025 by three co-authors. They took place via digital video communication tools (e.g., Microsoft Teams) and lasted an average of about 30 min. The interview guide was developed using a combination of theoretical and methodological frameworks. As a conceptual foundation, recent IS and educational technology literature was used to identify key dimensions relevant for understanding the adoption of AI for authentic learning [14, 19–22]. The interview guide consisted mainly of open-ended questions and provided detailed insights into specific aspects. Accordingly, the interviewers were able to react flexibly throughout the interview process. These neutral, open-ended questions and systematic follow-up questions also helped to avoid interviewer bias. All interviews were transcribed and coded using *ATLAS.ti* software.

We used purposive sampling [23] to select experts with different roles from different educational institutions to consider a variety of perspectives and practical experiences and ultimately gain a comprehensive understanding of AI-supported teaching and learning in HE. The experts include senior lecturers, managing directors, AI officer, professors, and program managers, each of whom contributes different but complementary perspectives on AI-supported teaching and learning in educational institutions. Table 2 provides an overview of all the experts interviewed, their respective roles, the size of their respective educational institution, and relevant experience.

The analysis was based on the inductive approach proposed by Gioia et al. [18]. Since similar issues were repeated after eleven interviews and no new conceptual categories emerged, theoretical saturation was assumed and no further interviews were conducted [24, 25]. The coding was carried out independently by two co-authors, ensuring that no interviewer coded a transcript of an interview they had conducted themselves. The interview transcripts were coded into 591 emerging quotes and 278 1st-order concepts. Based on this, similarities and relationships between the individual codes were analyzed and condensed into eleven 2nd-order themes. From this, we developed three aggregate dimensions articulated as three problem statements.

Further data analysis followed an abductive approach [26], moving between empirical data and existing theory. While coding was conducted inductively [18], authentic learning theory [6] informed the abstraction of identified needs into goals. Specifically, drawing on the eleven second-order themes and their underlying concepts, 14 needs were identified. The subsequent derivation of 13 goals from these needs was theory-informed, drawing on authentic learning theory by Newmann & Wehlage [6] to strengthen our theoretical grounding. In the next step, ten meta-requirements were derived from these

Table 2. Interview Partners

Expert	Role	Institution size (Employees)	Relevant Experience (Years)
E1	Lecturer & AI Officer	~1'200	10
E2	Lecturer & Institute Managing Director	~8'000	10
E3	Senior Lecturer	~1'200	7,5
E4	Professor	~1'200	20
E5	Senior Lecturer & Managing Director	~8'000	26
E6	Senior Lecturer & Academic Director	~200	16
E7	Program Manager	~200	5
E8	Senior Lecturer	~200	15
E9	Senior Lecturer & Program Manager	~1'600	17
E10	Senior Lecturer & Program Manager	~1'600	11
E11	Associate Professor	~1'600	8

goals. A 45-min in-person focus group at a European HE institution with twelve educators was conducted to additionally inform this derivation of meta-requirements. The focus group participants consisted of doctoral candidates and postdoctoral scholars from the disciplines of finance, entrepreneurship, and IS, with one participant representing additional professional practice in management consulting. This focus group also served as an additional validation of the identified problem statements. Throughout the coding process, the team of authors met regularly to discuss preliminary results, references to recent literature, and potential theoretical perspectives to iteratively improve the problem analysis process [24, 27].

5 Findings

5.1 AI Systems Analysis

The consolidated findings of the market review are based on publicly available information on approximately 230 AI systems used by educational institutions in Europe. AI systems were categorized by functionality into 28 categories, structured into seven sets, and further clustered according to the main areas of HE institution: administration, research, and teaching. An additional cluster for systems that could not be mapped was created. An overview of the categorization is given in Table 3.

Grouping was performed independent of the target user group. Two main user groups were identified: educators and students, with a few cases mentioning other target user groups such as administrative staff or addressing employees in general. Only AI systems specifically targeting either educators or students were identified. The further analysis is therefore limited to the two main target groups.

The first set (S1) encompasses AI systems dedicated for overall support of educators and students working or studying in an educational institution. AI systems within the set provided general support for (prospective) students, providing administrative information. Among others, these AI systems covered information regarding student life, enrollment, study programs or specific courses. This category only addresses students and represents the category that was identified the most in the dataset. Further, supporting systems for IT- or HR-related questions were identified. The final set within this category provides support for mental health concerns, such as exam anxiety.

Set 2, *Office Work*, covers AI systems supporting educators and students with general desk work. The group includes AI systems for text generation and editing, image generation, transcription of audio files, translations, and text summarization. All of the AI systems covered in the categories were provided for educators and students. The last category of AI systems deals with the issue of detecting AI-generated content. None of the AI systems were targeted at educators only.

Table 3. Set and Categorization of AI Systems

	Group	List of Categories	Cluster
S1	Support	General Support for (Prospective) Students, IT Support, HR Support, Mental Health Support	Administration
S2	Office Work	Text Generation and Editing, Image Generation, Transcription of Audio Files, Translation, Text Summarization, AI-generated Content Detection	
S3	Organization	Self-Management, Teaching Preparation incl. Content Generation, Study Preparation, Curriculum Planning	
S4	Learning	Personalized Learning, Content-specific Learning, Immersive Learning, Access to Learning Resources, Search Support, Idea Development	Teaching
S5	Feedback	Task-oriented Feedback, Grading Assistant, Teaching Support	
S6	Research	Academic Writing Support, Research Support, Library Services	Research
S7	Exploration	LLM Access Provider, Chatbot Builder, Experimentation with AI Content and Tools	General-Purpose

For organization of teaching and studying multiple AI systems were classified, which are covered in set 3. AI systems for supporting self-management such as time management were identified. Particularly targeted at educators, AI systems for the preparation of teaching including generation of the teaching content itself or curriculum planning are presently used at European educational institutions. Similarly, AI systems for study preparation are provided for students to support them in organizing their work.

Set 4 covers system categories focusing on the learning process itself and providing learning environments for educators and students. A share of the AI systems focused on creating personalized learning experiences or focused on creating an immersive learning system using additional technology such as Virtual Reality (VR). Other AI systems were specifically designed to target content-specific learning. This group also encompasses AI systems enabling students to access learning resources and support searching for suitable material or resources. Other AI systems support educators or students in the in-depth development of an idea, supporting critical and creative thinking.

In set 5, AI systems dedicated towards providing feedback are covered. This group includes AI systems that provide feedback on different academic tasks or grading assistance. The latter category is primarily targeted at educators. Teaching support in the form of feedback on teaching quality, for instance, is covered in the grouping.

AI systems supporting research activities were identified in the dataset as well (set 6). This group consists of AI systems for academic writing or research support. Other AI systems provide additional benefits such as information on library services.

The final set, *Exploration*, covers system categories that deal with the experimentation with different AI systems. The largest share of AI systems within this category covers AI systems, which provide interfaces to commercial or self-hosted LLMs, enabling educators or students to use LLMs for their individual purposes. Other AI systems provided further exploration possibilities such as a chatbot builder or general AI learning experiences targeted at exploring AI functionalities and different related content.

Table 4. Mapping of AI Systems Categories to Authentic Learning Standards

Authentic Learning Standards	AI Systems Categories
Higher-Order Thinking	Idea Development
Depth of Knowledge	Personalized Learning, Content-specific Learning, Immersive Learning, Access to Learning Resources
Connectedness to the World	Search Support
Substantive Conversation	-
Social Support for Student Achievement	Task-oriented Feedback, Grading Assistant, Teaching Support

This categorization and grouping provide the foundation for a further analysis of the results regarding the application of AI systems in HE for authentic learning. Table 4 depicts a mapping of the identified system categories to the standards of authentic learning proposed by Newmann & Wehlage [6]. The analysis is only performed on AI systems that represent teaching-oriented AI systems, i.e., only sets 4 and 5 are considered.

The standard on higher-order thinking [6] indicates the degree to which students are able to combine factual information for a more in-depth analysis of content. At the lower end of the standard's spectrum lower-order thinking is placed which represents mere recitation of facts. We identified AI systems directed at supporting in-depth idea development as suitable AI systems for supporting higher-order thinking. Supported idea development may lead to more creative and critical thinking among students.

The second standard, *Depth of Knowledge*, represents the extent to which students have understood the classroom material. Our analysis shows that this standard of authentic learning is most strongly supported within the identified group of existing AI systems. Multiple system categories support the learning process of students, which could lead to an improvement of their understanding of the content. These system categories thereby support personalized learning, content-specific learning to target specific subjects, or immersive learning. Presumably these AI systems follow a didactic concept and therefore enable a suitable learning experience. AI systems that provide access to learning material support students in improving their understanding of a topic.

As for the improvement of providing value beyond the instructional context, which is captured in the standard of *Connectedness to the World*, we were able to identify AI systems supporting search functionality to enable students to access further material that may link theoretical concepts learned in a classroom setting to real-world cases.

AI systems that could provide social support for student achievement are task-based feedback AI systems, grading assistant AI systems, and teaching support AI systems to improve teaching quality. AI systems supporting feedback and grading functionality could provide positive encouragements for students to improve their participation and willingness to express their opinions on topics. No AI systems that support substantive conversations among students were identified. As such, authentic learning is given very little consideration in the design of AI systems for HE institutions.

5.2 Results from Interviews & Requirements Development

Based on eleven interviews with experienced educators we derived needs [7] for the development of meta-requirements [28]. The identified needs relate to the educators' challenges in adopting AI for teaching and learning activities in HE. The meta-requirement development is depicted in Fig. 2 and the requirement descriptions are given in Table 5. This development was additionally informed by a 45-min focus group with twelve educators, providing further practice-oriented input that complement the interview findings. In Fig. 2, goals are ordered by stakeholders and authentic learning standards are assigned using abbreviation from Table 1. Requirements are color-coded to indicate three clusters: light-gray for content-related, gray for user experience-related, and dark-gray for governance-related requirements.

Most interviewees reported positive attitudes towards AI in educational contexts. E8 explains "I'm not afraid or panicking about it. It's a tool. It will take two or three years, or whatever, to master the tool", pointing towards a temporary disruption in the field that will mature over time. Educators actively encourage students to use AI effectively. E8 claims that "it's not about being critical or reflective or avoiding it altogether but simply learning how to use the tool".

Despite the positive attitudes, the interviewees reported on challenges they face and concerns they have regarding the use of AI in education. Three key problems were identified: educators' lack of competency and resources to integrate AI effectively (P1), students' uncritical AI use negatively impacting their learning outcome (P2), and insufficient support for AI adoption provided by educational institutions (P3). These issues manifest in barriers for AI adoption and point towards different needs for improvement.

For more effective AI integration, participants highlighted the value of best-practice examples (N1). E11 requests "a platform to see how other teachers use it" for inspiration for their own teaching. E3 complained that existing training formats are too generic: "all the training courses and experts who tell you things tend to be very general, and in the end, you have to find a program that's specifically tailored to your situation". This led to the goal of providing established or best-practice learning material (G1) to address the depth of knowledge authentic learning standard. This goal is fulfilled by R1, specifying that verified training resources should be provided by the system.

Learning alongside other duties presents challenges for educators individual AI competency building (N2). E4 noticed that "even if there were courses or programs available, people don't have the time", which E8 agrees since they said "I don't really have the time to play around and experiment", which partially contradicts N1. E10 wishes that educational institutions "give them that time" if there are interested in learning. Educators, therefore, require access to learning material (G2) and microlearning tutorials (G3) to fit learning into their schedule. Both goals again support the depth of knowledge standard of authentic learning and are addressed by R2 (Open and Free Access to Learning) and R3 (Generation of Relevant Learning Resources).

Educators' motivation to participate in training opportunities is driven by their own self-assessed low AI literacy and a desire for improvement (N3). E9 reported "I don't know anything about AI", or E1 said "I would never call myself an expert". E10 response to the key barrier is "it's expertise". Similarly, E3 claims they "don't know [their] way around particularly well", or E11 expresses a lack of technical expertise but they "would probably like some more knowledge". Educators are aware of their need for AI literacy, particularly in teaching settings, as E10 reports on the need that "to demonstrate something to the students, I really need more expertise". Low levels of AI literacy correspond with legal uncertainties, for instance, present in discussing AI use for grading, where E6 reports that they "don't even know if that would be allowed". We derived the goal of cultivating AI literacy (G7) which addresses the depth of knowledge standard. To fulfil the goal, R5 (Interactive Learning Modules) has been established, focusing on providing features for interactive learning.

Another adoption barrier are limited AI system capabilities for domain-specific contexts (N4). E4 highlights that "demands and requirements in the different disciplines are very different", which complicates organizational decisions on AI system and training offerings. E4 gave an example of failures of AI use in their teaching. They expressed concerns regarding the generated content since it "didn't turn out well" and "wasn't differentiated enough". Domain-specific customization possibilities should be enabled (G4), which targets the standards of depth of knowledge and connectedness and requires the generation of relevant learning resources (R3).

Educators are concerned about negative impacts AI use has on students' skill development, particularly deskilling (N5). E7 emphasizes "anyone who just uses it and switches off their brain will definitely become more stupid over time", pointing to the issue of deskilling. E1 even fears that students "don't reach that expert level" during their studies due to over-reliance on AI systems. As a possible reason for this observed behavior, interviewees point to efficiency improvements in solving tasks. E10 claims that students "can take shortcuts and get through their studies" and continues by saying that "if you use it to take shortcuts, to avoid thinking for yourself, then you won't get any smarter". This presents a misalignment of the use of AI and desired pedagogical outcomes. To prevent deskilling, students need to improve their AI literacy (G7).

Participants report a lack of insight into students' AI use but suspect that "all the students are already using it anyway" (E7) or that "they probably write all their emails and even their homework assignments using ChatGPT" (E4). Thus, educators feel forced to redesign their didactic concepts and assignment formats (N6). Due to the uncertainty on students' AI use, E10 claims that "we can't control it in the current format of the assignments" and that "we are probably a little behind in terms of adjusting our educational programs so that we can use AI". Educators express the need to rely more on assessment format where students cannot use AI easily, such as oral exams or presentations. This concern was not shared by all participants, as E9 reports that they "haven't changed school exams and assessment methods much". While the majority supported the need for changes in assessment formats, we derived the goal of supporting the design of AI-aware assessment formats (G6), addressing depth of knowledge, higher-order thinking, and substantive conversation. This goal is covered by R4, *Templates for Assessment Formats*, supporting features to assess topic understanding.

The interviewed educators observe different levels of student AI literacy as an additional challenge for designing AI-supported teaching. E1 explains that differences in AI knowledge led to disparities in how effectively students apply AI systems. More experienced students may use AI to surpass their pervious performances. Others remain "just completely uncritical, copying and pasting" (E1) without reflection. E3 describes this as a spectrum of student behaviors towards AI use. At the one end are high-performing students who use AI "in a very sensible, efficient, and reflective way" (E3), while at the other end are students who use AI for unfair advantages. This diversity may be characterized as a polarizing effect, where for high-performing students AI provides additional advantages, while for less motivated students AI might reduce their learning performance. These observations underscore the need for uniform AI literacies among students (N7), with the goal to cultivate AI literacy (G7) and establish learning communities (G9). G9 addresses the social support for student achievement standard of authentic learning. To facilitate learning communities, we defined requirement R7 (*Peer-Learning*), which focuses on features for collaborative learning.

Educators report that they perceive high value from AI systems for the creation of real-word teaching cases to enrich learning content and support authentic learning. E9 notes that AI systems are "surprisingly good at case generation", while E5 explains, "I try to encourage students to generate real-world cases in order to demonstrate the applicability of the concepts". E1 highlights the potential of AI systems to "create a better practical reference" and "more realistic learning environments". However, educators approach case generation with caution. E7 acknowledges uncertainties inherent in AI-generated content, saying that "you can really create exercises like this in the hope [...] that they're correct". E3 expresses quality concerns, describing generated content as "too poor, too general, too broad [...] it's too superficial". This reflects the need to use

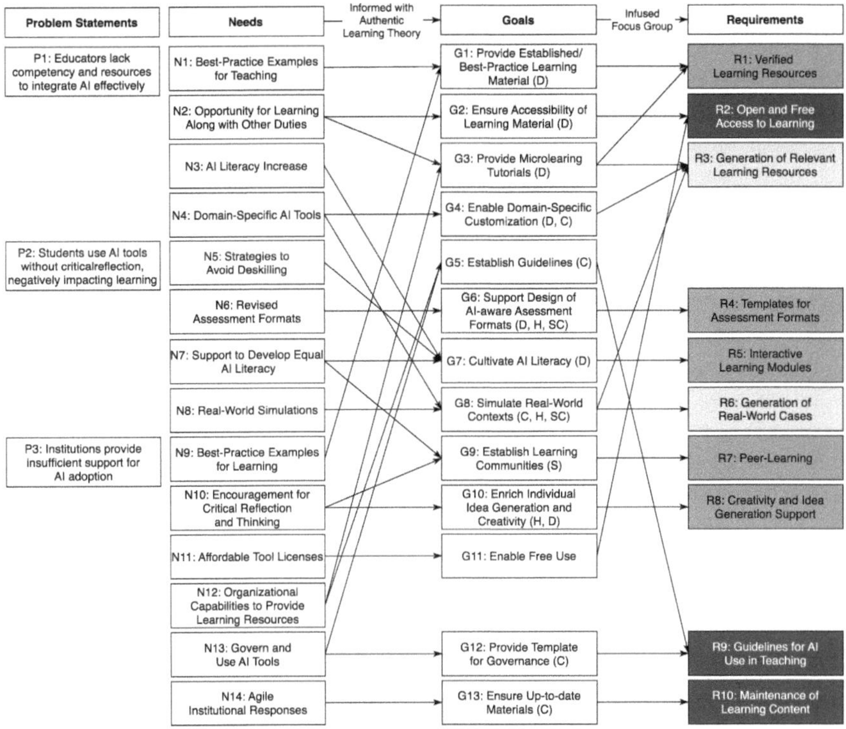

Fig. 2. Requirements Development

AI systems for simulating real-world cases for practical learning (N8) with the goal to simulate real-world cases (G8), which addresses the authentic learning standards of higher-order thinking, connectedness, and substantive conversation. This goal leads to requirement R6, which covers features supporting case generation.

Educators identify several areas where students require guidance and best-practice examples for effective AI use (N9). E9 and E11 report students' uncertainty on the use of AI systems due to possible academic misconduct, with E11 noting, "the students are very afraid of using AI, they are afraid of being caught for cheating". For effective AI use, E7 claims that students need to learn prompt engineering. They state "the results will naturally be better and better […] it would be a good idea to really show students how to do this". Participants report on students being unaware of AI offerings from their educational institution. E10 presents a situation, where "one of the teachers mentioned which AI systems they had access to through the institution and the students didn't know that". These observations similarly reflect G1, and therefore fit to R1.

Educators recognize AI systems' value for supporting critical reflection and expanding students' opinion on the topic (N10). E4 describes personal experiences with the use of AI for idea generation: "I've used it myself and noticed that it mentions points that I hadn't thought of, so that additional ideas suddenly become interesting". AI systems can help to expand the solution space, but educators emphasize that professional expertise is essential to judge the applicability of AI-generated suggestions. E11 emphasizes the need for reflection: "I don't have to use the suggestions, but I can at least get some perspectives or examples or something similar, then I can bring what I want". AI systems are understood as sparring partners to encourage critical thinking, improving higher-order thinking. We derived the goal to support individual idea generation and enrich individual creativity (G10), which addresses the authentic learning standard of higher-order thinking and depth of knowledge. To address this goal, we have defined requirement R8 (Creativity and Idea Generation Support).

The lack of funding for AI system licenses provided by educational institutions is a barrier to educators' exploration and adoption of AI systems. E3 expresses frustration when using free versions, stating, "I tried different ones until I reached the point where I would have had to buy them". E3 perceives the lack of funding as limitations in exploration possibilities: "it would really be helpful to have more money available so you could [...] try things out". E7 highlighted the absence of institutions support for paid AI systems as they "don't know anyone who has a paid model from the institution". The lack of funding expresses the need for affordable system licenses (N11). Free use of these AI systems should be enabled (G11). This goal is covered in requirement R2.

When discussing institutional support for AI adoption, educators report a lack of training resources but express interest in participating, provided they are tailored to disciplinary contexts. E8 claims that training opportunities "have to be tailored, so it would probably be difficult to find a topic that is equally relevant to everyone across the whole institution". Instead of structured training opportunities organized by their institution, E3 rather prefers individual exploration of AI systems, as they "don't need further instructions because I find it exciting to figure things out for myself", expressing different learning styles and preferences among educators. These findings indicate a need for organizational capabilities to provide suitable learning resources (N12), which can be addressed through learning tutorials (G3) and the development of AI usage guidelines (G5). This leads to requirement R9 (Guidelines for AI Use in Teaching), stating that the system should provide features to support the definition of guidelines.

Educators feel the need to have more guidelines to support their use of AI systems in teaching, so there is the need for governance (N13). E6 responds with a wish for "guidelines on dos and don'ts, i.e., on possibilities and areas in which AI may be used for whatever reason". E10 asks for official approvals from the institution on system usage. Most of the participants reported that they are not aware about any guidelines, while some reported about guidelines being in development. Although the interviewees wish for clear guidelines, they also express concerns regarding the applicability of guidelines. E1 points to the differences between departments and concludes that "the needs regarding guidelines differ greatly". E7 claims that established guidelines might be neglected, which would cause that forbidden AI systems might still be used. They express a clear opinion on official restrictions regarding the use, which they frame as "if I give you guidelines, saying you're not allowed to use something, it doesn't make sense". These findings imply the goal to provide templates for governance (G12), which was taken into consideration for the development of requirement R9. Goal G12 supports the authentic learning standard of connectedness.

Further concerns expressed by the interviewees are related to the speed of development of AI technologies and the speed in response on an organizational level (N14). E10 reports a fear of falling behind, which put additional pressure on educators to regularly improve their knowledge on AI systems. While educators are fully aware of the speed in development, they equally report about slow AI adoptions at their educational institutions. E9 noticed slow progress in AI integration due to slow decision-makings at the institution. As such, it should be ensured that materials are up-to-date (G13), supporting the standard of connectedness to the world beyond the classroom. To deal with this goal we propose requirement R10, *Maintenance of Learning Content*, which defines that a system should support features to update content and technologies.

A focus group with twelve educators revealed that many of the identified needs were familiar to the participants from their own teaching practice. Participants addressed several issues that overlapped with the problem statements, while also expressing uncertainty about how some of these aspects might unfold in practice. Participants reported particularly students' uncritical reliance on AI outputs (cf. N9), increasing effort in assessment (cf. N6), and the growing difficulty of evaluating individual learning contributions. The discussion emphasized the potential of AI as a sparring partner (cf. N10) when used to stimulate reflection rather than to replace students' own reasoning, which is also reflected in our findings from the interviews. Several participants highlighted the need for clearer guidance (cf. N13) and alternative assessment formats that focus on learning processes instead of final results. These insights informed and refined the derivation of the meta-requirements, ensuring that they address teaching and learning experiences, and pedagogical goals.

Table 5. Requirements Definitions

	Title	Requirement Description
R1	Verified Learning Resources	The system should provide features to make well-established and evaluated teaching resources available for educators to support authentic learning
R2	Open and Free Access to Learning	The system should support open and free access to the learning material
R3	Generation of Relevant Learning Resources	The system should provide and support creating additional, individual learning resources for a given topic to create knowledge spaces
R4	Templates for Assessment Formats	The system should support conversational features to assess the understanding of topics
R5	Interactive Learning Modules	The system should support features for interactive learning modules for engaging students in AI interactions

(continued)

Table 5. (*continued*)

	Title	Requirement Description
R6	Generation of Real-World Cases	The system should support features to generate real-world cases for a given topic
R7	Peer-Learning	The system should support features for collaborative learning to enhance mutual respect among learners
R8	Creativity and Idea Generation Support	The system should support conversational features to enhance creativity and reflection on topics
R9	Guidelines for AI Use in Teaching	The system should support features for building guidelines for AI use in higher education institutions
R10	Maintenance of Learning Content	The system should support features for updating content and features provided regularly to keep up with technology advancements

6 Validation and Discussion

For the validation of our derived needs, goals, and requirements, we conducted three additional interviews with educators (E5, E6, E11) from the problem analysis stage of around 25 min each. Participants were shown Fig. 2 and asked a set of focused questions addressing the structure, completeness of needs, completeness and relevancy of requirements, and further improvement suggestions. Overall, the experts found the structure coherent, but E6 recommended offering pre-defined courses as guidelines might be too weak. They confirmed the importance of fostering students' AI literacy (cf. P2), addressing potential deskilling (N5), revising assessment formats (N6), case generation possibilities (N8), and supporting critical thinking (N10). They highlighted the need for ethical reflection, which however can be covered in AI literacy development (G7). E5 questioned the value of templates for assessment formats (R4) since organizational regulations might restrict educators' freedom in changing established formats. They additionally highlight differences in peer-learning (R7) in between student groups and AI-enabled peer-learning. For the latter they suggest to take critical engagement (G10) into consideration. Documentation support for students on their AI usage for assignments was suggested by E11, which will be explored in future research.

Beyond the evaluation insights, this study deals with the shift in HE from discussing whether LLMs should be used to how they should be designed and integrated to meaningfully facilitate authentic learning, we applied an eDSR approach [17]. In particular, in this study, we focus on the problem space exploration, contributing (1) an elaborated and evaluated understanding of the problem domain and context, and (2) an initial set of design goals and meta-requirements. We provide design knowledge for the class of

AI-based learning systems in HE supporting authentic learning. In our problem analysis echelon, we conducted a market analysis to explore AI systems currently used in HE and identified relevant stakeholders. Additionally, we conducted interviews with the identified stakeholder to understand their needs. As an intermediate artifact, we propose an initial set of problem statements regarding the use of AI in HE. The problem analysis reveals three key problems addressing the needs of educators, students, and institutions. We evaluated the problem statements in a focus group with educators in HE regarding their validity, whereby the derivation of meta-requirements was also informed. In the Objectives and Requirements definition echelon, we derived a preliminary set of meta-requirements. Following the conceptual model of the problem space proposed by Maedche et al. [7], we first derived design goals based on the needs of the identified stakeholders. Second, we informed our goals by the concepts of authentic learning [6]. Finally, we derived meta-requirements from the design goals and evaluated them through interviews. Based on the findings, we envision future artifacts that serve as teaching support systems that integrate conversational agents, teaching materials, and opportunities for interaction.

This study has several limitations. The market analysis is limited to educational institutions located in Europe only. Another limitation of this study is the small number of participants in the evaluation of the problem statements and the preliminary meta-requirements. The validation of the findings is limited to short interviews with participants from the original sample. Large-scale evaluations of the intermediate artifacts at both echelons are needed to strengthen validation and deepen our understanding of the problem. We will continue the eDSR and conduct the next echelon, named Design and Development. We aim to develop an information system that addresses the meta-requirements we derived. Moreover, we plan to evaluate the intermediate artifact following a naturalistic and summative evaluation strategy [29].

7   Conclusion

This study contributes design knowledge on how AI systems can be integrated into HE to support authentic learning. Using an evidence-based design science research approach, we constructed an empirically grounded problem space based on an analysis of 230 AI systems across European educational institutions and interviews with 11 experienced educators from three countries. The findings highlight three interrelated challenges: limited educator competencies and resources for AI integration, students' uncritical use of AI support, and insufficient institutional structures.

We formulated and validated meta-requirements for AI systems that support authentic learning, organized across content, user experience, and governance dimensions. Together, they provide prescriptive guidance for the design and integration of AI systems that move beyond administrative efficiency toward meaningful support for authentic learning from the perspectives of students, educators, and educational institutions. Future research will deal with the development and evaluation of an information systems artifact addressing the meta-requirements.

Acknowledgments. This work was funded by the European Union [EU Funding Erasmus+ 2025-1-LI01-KA220-HED-000361836: "Higher Education AI Resources & Teaching"].

Disclosure of Interests.   The authors have no competing interests to declare that are relevant to the content of this article.

References

1. Adams, R.: Pupils fear AI is eroding their ability to study, research finds (2025). https://www.theguardian.com/technology/2025/oct/15/pupils-fear-ai-eroding-study-ability-research
2. United Nations: The AI Generation: Youth in the Artificial Intelligence Era (2025). https://unric.org/en/the-ai-generation-youth-in-the-artificial-intelligence-era/
3. Mineo, L.: Is AI dulling our minds? (2025). https://news.harvard.edu/gazette/story/2025/11/is-ai-dulling-our-minds/
4. Lynch, M., Sage, T., Hitchcock, L.I., Sage, M.: A heutagogical approach for the assessment of Internet communication technology (ICT) assignments in higher education. Int. J. Educ. Technol. High. Educ. **18**, 55 (2021)
5. Newmann, F.M., Marks, H.M., Gamoran, A.: Authentic pedagogy and student performance. Am. J. Educ. **104**, 280–312 (1996)
6. Newmann, F.M., Wehlage, G.G.: Five standards of authentic instruction. Educ. Leadersh. **50**, 8–12 (1993)
7. Maedche, A., Gregor, S., Morana, S., Feine, J.: Conceptualization of the problem space in design science research. In: Tulu, B., Djamasbi, S., Leroy, G. (eds.) Extending the Boundaries of Design Science Theory and Practice, pp. 18–31. Springer, Cham (2019)
8. Winkler, R., Soellner, M.: Unleashing the Potential of Chatbots in Education: A State-Of-The-Art Analysis. AOM Proceedings. (2018)
9. Weber, F., Wambsganss, T., Rüttimann, D., Söllner, M.: Pedagogical Agents for Interactive Learning: A Taxonomy of Conversational Agents in Education. ICIS Proceedings. (2021)
10. Wambsganss, T., Benke, I., Maedche, A., Koedinger, K., Käser, T.: Evaluating the impact of learner control and interactivity in conversational tutoring systems for persuasive writing. Int. J. Artif. Intell. Educ. **35**, 791–822 (2025)
11. Weber, F., Neshaei, S.P., Wambsganss, T., Soellner, M.: Intelligent Tutoring for Law Courses: Design and Evaluation of an LLM-based System. ICIS Proceedings. (2025)
12. Hönigsberg, S., Mallek, S., Watkowski, L., Weritz, P.: Measuring AI literacy of future knowledge workers: a mediated model of AI experience and AI knowledge. In: Wirtschaftsinformatik Proceedings (2025)
13. Richter, S., Giroux, M., Piven, I., Sima, H., Dodd, P.: A constructivist approach to integrating AI in marketing education: bridging theory and practice. J. Mark. Educ. **47**, 94–111 (2025)
14. Van Slyke, C., Johnson, R., Sarabadani, J.: Generative artificial intelligence in information systems education: challenges, consequences, and responses. CAIS **53**, 1–21 (2023)
15. Sooriamurthi, R., Tu, X.: Fostering and Assessing Authentic Learning: Preliminary Report on Building a Generative AI Tool to Teach SQL. SaudiCIS Proceedings. (2024)
16. vom Brocke, J., Winter, R., Hevner, A., Maedche, A.: Special issue editorial –accumulation and evolution of design knowledge in design science research: a journey through time and space. JAIS. **21**, 520–544 (2020)
17. Tuunanen, T., Winter, R., Brocke, J.V.: Dealing with complexity in design science research: a methodology using design echelons. MIS Q. **48**, 427–458 (2024)
18. Gioia, D.A., Corley, K.G., Hamilton, A.L.: Seeking qualitative rigor in inductive research: notes on the Gioia methodology. Organ. Res. Methods **16**, 15–31 (2013)
19. Hönigsberg, S., Watkowski, L., Drechsler, A.: Generative artificial intelligence in higher education: mediating learning for literacy development. CAIS. **56**, 1044–1076 (2025)
20. Gimpel, H., et al.: Using generative AI in higher education: a guide for instructors. JISE. **36**, 237–256 (2025)

21. Hughes, L., Malik, T., Dettmer, S., Al-Busaidi, A.S., Dwivedi, Y.K.: Reimagining higher education: navigating the challenges of generative AI adoption. Inf. Syst. Front. (2025)
22. Sun, R., Deng, X.: Using generative AI to enhance experiential learning: an exploratory study of ChatGPT use by university students. JISE. **36**, 53–64 (2025)
23. Etikan, I.: Comparison of convenience sampling and purposive sampling. AJTAS. **5**, 1 (2016)
24. Glaser, B.G., Strauss, A.L.: The Discovery of Grounded Theory: Strategies for Qualitative Research. Routledge (2017)
25. Saunders, B., et al.: Saturation in qualitative research: exploring its conceptualization and operationalization. Qual. Quant. **52**, 1893–1907 (2018)
26. Tavory, I., Timmermans, S.: Abductive Analysis. The Univ. of Chicago Press, Chicago, IL (2014)
27. Wiener, C.: Making teams work in conducting grounded theory. In: The SAGE Handbook of Grounded Theory, pp. 292–310. SAGE Publications (2007)
28. Walls, J.G., Widmeyer, G.R., El Sawy, O.A.: Building an information system design theory for vigilant EIS. Inf. Sys. Res. **3**, 36–59 (1992)
29. Venable, J., Pries-Heje, J., Baskerville, R.: FEDS: a framework for evaluation in design science research. EJIS **25**, 77–89 (2016)

Future of Design Science Methodology

Critical Incident Technique for Semi-Naturalistic DSR Evaluation: A Methodology and an Illustration

Charon Abbott[1]($\boxtimes$) (iD), Mary Tate[2] (iD), Wasana Bandara[1] (iD), and Lisa Tam[1] (iD)

[1] Queensland University of Technology, Brisbane, QLD, Australia
charon.abbott@hdr.qut.edu.au, w.bandara@qut.edu.au,
l.tam@qut.edu.eu
[2] Victoria University of Wellington, Wellington, New Zealand
mary.tate@vuw.ac.nz

Abstract. Evaluation is a key part of Design Science Research (DSR). Evaluations can take place in artificial or naturalistic environments, which may be chosen, depending on the type of artifact being developed, and each with their own advantages and disadvantages. With the advent of Industry 5.0, naturalistic evaluations will be more in demand, however these can be difficult, time-consuming and expensive. This study outlines the use of the Critical Incident Technique (CIT) as a useful way to obtain many of the benefits of naturalistic evaluation, such as verisimilitude, and other benefits such as the ability to evaluate in a broader range of settings and improved engagement of participants in the evaluation process. An illustration of the use of this technique is provided, demonstrating how CIT can be a valuable addition to the DSR researcher's toolbox.

Keywords: Design Science Research (DSR) · Critical Incident Technique · Evaluation · Case study

1 Introduction

Design Science Research (DSR) is well established, aiming to create and evaluate innovative or unique solutions to important, unsolved problems [6]. DSR artifacts are intended to offer useful solutions to classes of real-world design problems [6]. "Useful solutions" should be novel, make a positive difference to practice, and be superior to what was previously used [13]. To establish if this has occurred, naturalistic evaluation (evaluation in a 'real-world' context) is considered in many cases to have more face validity and be a more reliable measure of impact [19].

As the world progresses towards Industry 5.0, described as the next industrial evolution, where digital data-driven tools will combine with humans [17] there is increasing pressure on DSR evaluation. There is likely to be a requirement for more naturalistic evaluations (both ex-ante and ex-post) to ensure the digital tools deliver as designed and

J. vom Brocke et al. (Eds.): DESRIST 2026, LNCS 16606, pp. 249–266, 2026.
https://doi.org/10.1007/978-3-032-28313-9_14

are fit for purpose. Furthermore, the speed with which industry is changing is increasing and therefore the expected timeframe for delivering useful artifacts is increasingly shorter.

However, it is surprisingly difficult to evaluate DSR artifacts in real-world settings. This can be uncertain, costly, time-consuming [19] and lack generalizability [10]. This is especially the case for artifacts intended for use in dynamic, evolving settings where it is unclear at the outset how a phenomenon will evolve. For example, while stakeholder engagement tools are commonly employed in projects, the practice of stakeholder engagement remains inherently challenging; its specific issues are seldom visible at the outset and remain difficult to anticipate even as they begin to unfold.

There is, therefore, an important gap in current DSR evaluation options for a method that captures the advantages of naturalistic evaluation, while mitigating the disadvantages. In this study, we present a novel "semi-naturalistic" evaluation approach using Critical Incident Technique (CIT).

The remainder of this paper situates our work within DSR evaluation literature, focusing on artificial and naturalistic evaluation. We then introduce the Critical Incident Technique (CIT) and present our semi-naturalistic evaluation approach, illustrated through a recent project. This is followed by an evaluation of the approach from two perspectives: (a) participant experiences and (b) its effectiveness in capturing useful artifact-related feedback. We conclude with guidelines for CIT use, discussion, and concluding remarks.

2 Background: Evaluation in Design Science Research

In this section, we briefly situate our work within the broader landscape of DSR evaluation and clarify the distinction between artificial and naturalistic evaluation. Given the diversity of DSR projects, evaluation design is a non-trivial task, and a substantial body of work has proposed classifications, strategies, and guidance for researchers [e.g. 1, 10, 12, 15, 18, 19]. We do not attempt a full review here but focus on the aspects most relevant to positioning our study.

DSR evaluation methods can be distinguished along several dimensions, including whether they occur before or after artifact instantiation (ex-ante or ex-post), the stage of artifact maturity, to improve the characteristics or performance (formative), to derive a shared meaning (summative) and the type of setting in which evaluation takes place [10, 12, 19]. Ex-ante evaluation typically supports the clarification of needs and design requirements, whereas ex-post evaluation assesses the artifact itself at varying levels of maturity [13] - including assessing the overall value of implementing the designed artefact [19]. Multiple evaluation cycles are often undertaken as the artifact is refined [6, 15]. For example, an early ex-post evaluation may focus on usability or conformance to requirements in an artificial setting, while later cycles may focus on effectiveness in real-world use contexts [10, 12].

A foundational distinction in DSR evaluation is between artificial and naturalistic evaluation. These types of evaluation can be seen through the "three realities" perspective [16], which characterizes naturalistic evaluation as involving real users interacting with real systems to address real problems in real contexts. Artificial evaluation occurs when one or more of these elements is substituted, abstracted, or simulated [19]. Artificial evaluations can include laboratory experiments, logical arguments, mathematical proofs, and simulations, among other methods [10, 19]. These approaches are often useful in the earlier stages of DSR, or for all stages with purely technical artifacts, because they enable control, repeatability, and relatively efficient feedback [19]. By contrast, naturalistic evaluation is conducted with artifact users and systems in real organizational contexts [18]. It offers stronger contextual grounding, but is typically more difficult, time-consuming, and costly to conduct [19]. These evaluations can be conducted through methods such as case studies, action research, and field experiments [19]. Table 1 provides a comparison of the key criteria for artificial and naturalistic evaluation types and provides the basis for later positioning CIT as a semi-naturalistic evaluation technique.

Table 1. Comparison of key criteria for artificial and naturalistic evaluation types [12, 18]

Key Criteria	Artificial Evaluation	Naturalistic evaluation
Methodology	Empirical or non-empirical	Empirical
Perspective	Positivist and reductionist	Interpretive, Positivist, and/or Critical
Setting	Fabricated or simulation	Industry
Focus	Hypothesis testing, theoretical arguments	How an artifact operates in complex environments
Time	Generally quicker	Generally, more time-consuming
Cost	Generally lower	Generally higher
Variables	Controlled	Can be subject to confounding variables
Outcomes	Clear but narrow. May not work in the 'real-world'	Demonstrates application in the 'real world'. Often difficult to generalize

While conceptually useful, this binary distinction is often too coarse for contemporary DSR settings, particularly in complex socio-technical environments where fully naturalistic evaluation may be impractical, but purely artificial evaluation may be insufficient. We therefore introduce the notion of *semi-naturalistic* evaluation to refer to evaluation arrangements that preserve some, but not all, of the three realities - namely, real users, real tasks, and real contexts. Such approaches typically retain real users and real problem contexts, while introducing some degree of mediation, abstraction, or reconstruction in order to improve feasibility, analytical structure, and scalability. In this sense, semi-naturalistic evaluation should be understood not as eliminating the trade-offs between artificial and naturalistic evaluation, but as reconfiguring them in a different balance. This positioning is consistent with calls in the DSR literature to balance rigor, relevance, and efficiency across evaluation cycles [1, 19].

Naturalistic evaluation remains highly valuable because it reflects how an artifact performs in the complexity of real use settings. However, it also presents well-known challenges. Because it is conducted in context, findings may be harder to generalize, confounding variables may be difficult to isolate, and studies may be vulnerable to organizational change or disruption [10, 12, 19]. Naturalistic studies are also often resource-intensive and difficult to sustain over time, especially in time-bounded research such as Masters, PhD or industry funded projects [12–14, 19]. Further complications can arise when the phenomena of interest are dynamic, emergent, or politically sensitive, including situations in which organizations may be reluctant to expose problematic or failed initiatives. These constraints help explain why naturalistic evaluation, while desirable, remains difficult to execute in many DSR contexts.

3 Critical Incident Technique (CIT)

The Critical Incident Technique (CIT) was developed in the mid-20th century by Flanagan [3], who defined a 'critical incident' as an event that significantly impacts (positively or negatively) a task or activity in which the respondent is engaged. The basic unit of analysis is the critical incident, which is a participant's recollection of an event that made a significant contribution to the outcome of an activity [3]. Such incidents typically have a clear sequence of events, identifiable actors, and a defined outcome. CIT has been widely applied across domains, including psychology, communication, education, nursing, and job evaluation [2].

In this study, we position CIT as an evaluation technique that enables semi-naturalistic evaluation - an intermediate mode in which real users engage with real, experience-based problem contexts, while artifact interaction is mediated through structured reflection rather than direct real-time deployment. In this configuration, some of the "three realities" [16] - real users, real tasks, and real contexts - are preserved (i.e., users and tasks), while others are partially abstracted (i.e., context), enabling a balance between contextual realism and evaluation feasibility. CIT operationalizes this configuration by eliciting structured accounts of critical incidents, capturing how artifacts are experienced and interpreted in context without requiring in-situ observation [3]. From the perspective of the three realities framework [16], this involves (i) real users drawing on lived experience, (ii) real problems captured through authentic incidents, and (iii) mediated system interaction based on reflection rather than direct use. As such, CIT occupies a position between artificial and naturalistic evaluation, preserving contextual grounding and experiential richness while maintaining feasibility and analytical structure, thereby rebalancing, rather than eliminating, the trade-offs between these evaluation modes [1, 19].

To further position CIT within the broader DSR evaluation landscape, we draw on the taxonomy proposed by Prat et al. [11], which distinguishes evaluation along dimensions such as technique, form, level, and participants. Within this framework, CIT can be understood as a qualitative, participant-driven evaluation technique operating at the level of artifact use and experience. Unlike simulation or laboratory-based techniques, which assess artifacts under controlled or abstracted conditions, CIT captures context-sensitive, experience-based insights into how artifacts perform in realistic situations. Compared to full case study or field study approaches, CIT provides a more structured and scalable mechanism for eliciting evaluative data across multiple contexts without requiring continuous field immersion. In this sense, CIT complements existing evaluation techniques by enabling the systematic capture of rich, contextually grounded evidence of artifact utility, particularly where direct observation is infeasible.

From a strategy perspective, CIT does not replace evaluation frameworks such as FEDS [19] or MEDS [1], but complements them at the level of evaluation technique selection. These frameworks provide procedural guidance for determining why, when, and under what conditions to evaluate, including the choice between artificial and naturalistic settings and the sequencing of evaluation cycles. In contrast, CIT contributes to the "how" dimension of evaluation by providing a data-generative, theory-sensitive mechanism for capturing evaluative evidence through critical incidents. It enables the systematic elicitation of contextually grounded, actor-centered accounts, revealing insights into the research topic [2, 3]. Accordingly, CIT should be understood not as an alternative evaluation strategy, but as a complementary technique that enriches the evidential depth of evaluation within a given strategy.

While CIT may be operationalized in ways that resemble "quick-and-simple" or "human risk and effectiveness" evaluation strategies [19] in terms of feasibility and resource efficiency, its contribution lies in the nature of the evidence it produces rather than in the evaluation strategy it represents. By enabling researchers to capture rich, experience-based insights without requiring full organizational deployment, CIT supports semi-naturalistic evaluation while navigating the trade-offs between realism, control, and feasibility that characterize DSR evaluation [1, 10, 19].

Further motivations for selecting CIT include its ability to overcome temporal and geographical constraints [8, 9], capture dynamic and evolving behaviors [5], and generate detailed, experience-based narratives that support behavioral analysis [5]. It has been shown to capture largely accurate recollections of real events and can serve as an efficient alternative to more resource-intensive approaches such as action research. While still relatively underutilized in Information Systems (IS) research, there is a growing body of work demonstrating its applicability in IS contexts [5].

Classic accounts of the CIT describe five core steps, originally articulated by Flanagan [3] and consistently reaffirmed in later syntheses [e.g. 2, 7]. They are outlined below:

Step 1: Establishing the General Aim of the Activity. The first step involves clearly defining the purpose and boundaries of the activity under study, including what constitutes effective and ineffective performance relative to that aim [2, 3]. This shared orientation provides the reference frame against which incidents are judged as "critical." From a DSR evaluation perspective, this step aligns with clarifying the intended purpose of the artifact, the design goals it seeks to achieve, and the evaluation focus (e.g., utility, appropriateness, or impact), ensuring that incident collection is explicitly tied to artifact objectives rather than diffused user impressions.

Step 2: Planning and Setting Specifications. This step specifies what types of incidents are relevant, who should report them, and under what conditions incidents should be considered significant [3]. Decisions are made regarding sampling, prompts, data collection modes, and consistency across participants. For DSR evaluation, this step enables researchers to strategically delimit which artifact interactions, stakeholder roles, or usage contexts are of interest, allowing evaluation to focus on meaningful moments of artifact use without requiring continuous observation or full-scale naturalistic immersion.

Step 3: Collecting Critical Incidents. Data is collected as detailed accounts of concrete events, typically through interviews, questionnaires, or written narratives, capturing sequences of actions, actors involved, and perceived outcomes [2, 3]. While originally emphasizing direct observation, Flanagan [3] explicitly acknowledged the validity of carefully elicited recalled incidents. In DSR contexts, this step supports semi-naturalistic evaluation by capturing rich, situated experiences of where the artifact can be used. Well-elicited incidents allow evaluators to access tacit judgments and experiential consequences that are otherwise difficult to observe directly.

Step 4: Analyze To identify patterns, categories, or dimensions that meaningfully summarize recurring behaviors, outcomes, or conditions [2, 3]. This step is widely regarded as the most analytically demanding, requiring careful judgment to preserve specificity while enabling abstraction. For DSR evaluation, this step enables researchers to systematically trace how particular artifact features, design decisions, or configurations contribute to observed successes, breakdowns, or unintended consequences, thereby supporting design learning across iterations.

Step 5: Interpreting and Reporting Results. The final step involves interpreting findings in light of the original aims, making analytic judgments explicit, and transparently discussing limitations, credibility, and implications [3]. Emphasis is placed on articulating the practical and theoretical value of the results. In DSR evaluation, this step supports reflective learning by linking incident-based insights back to design principles, artifact refinement, and theoretical contribution, strengthening the traceability between evaluation evidence and design knowledge claims.

4   An Illustrative Example of Using CIT for Evaluation

The context of the study was an evaluation of a stakeholder engagement tool designed for use in Business Process Management (BPM) projects. The tool is aimed to assist practitioners with identifying and characterizing their stakeholders and then evaluate the risk to their engagement with the BPM initiative. CIT was applied in the second cycle of tool-evaluation - the first of which having been conducted in a purely artificial setting (and the third planned in a fully naturalistic setting), as part of an overall "human risk and effectiveness" evaluation strategy [19]. While gathering the evaluation information from the participants, the researchers also took the opportunity to ask three questions in relation to using CIT for artifact evaluation, outlined in Sect. 4.3. Sections 4.1 to 4.5 describe how the CIT steps outlined in Sect. 3 were applied in the example study. Section 4.6 describes the evaluation insights while Sect. 4.7 provides a summary synthesis of CIT as a semi-naturalistic evaluation technique.

4.1   Step 1 - Establish General Aims

The aim of this evaluation was an ex-post evaluation of an artifact in the second evaluation round, to determine its efficacy in supporting experienced BPM practitioners in real-life contexts to analyze their stakeholders and their degree of engagement on various dimensions. The evaluation cycle was aimed to have multiple initiatives of different sizes, types, and industries so the usefulness, satisfaction, and ease of use of the tool could be established, in addition to refining who the target audience for the tool was. It was also important that the evaluation effort was not onerous for the time-poor professionals who were to be the participants.

4.2 Step 2 - Establish Plans and Specifications

This step included setting requirements for recruitment and the screening and selection of incidents and participants. It was decided that the focus for the evaluation should be on stakeholders with whom the responding-practitioners had experienced engagement issues, so it could be ascertained if the tool could have assisted them in the situation (or not), had it been available to them at the time. It was therefore important that the phenomenon of stakeholder engagement challenges was present in the initiatives studied. Recruitment materials and interview protocols were planned and had ethical clearance. These included questions relating to both the tool evaluation and using CIT as an evaluation method. We then recruited ten experienced BPM practitioners with 5–20 years' experience in BPM (hereafter referred to as Participant #1–10). All participants were actively involved in managing stakeholder engagement.

4.3 Step 3 - Collect the Data

In this step, the participants were interviewed twice. An initial discussion was held with prospective participants to determine a suitable incident from their experience. The research team screened the incidents to ensure they had the characteristics required to evaluate the tool (i.e. challenges with stakeholder engagement that resulted in initiative issues), an example of which is displayed in Fig. 1.

> *"The initiative was to merge 46 volunteer units of an organization with a government service. The BPM manager was required to develop common HR and governance processes. Many of the 46 stakeholder groups had issues with trust, communication, slow and hierarchical decision-making, the pace of change, unrealistic goals and resourcing due to staff turn-over increasing workload"* (Participant #2).

Fig. 1. A summarized example of a selected incident.

For artifact evaluation, once the incident had been selected, the participant was then given time to use the artifact to analyze the stakeholders involved and the profile of the engagement risk associated with the stakeholder groups in detail, with a particular focus upon the stakeholders they had challenges with. The participants then attended a second interview, usually one week later, in which they provided: a) additional feedback about the artifact and its effectiveness for the selected incident, and b) their opinions about using critical incident technique for artifact evaluation. This second part of the interview supports the methodological aspect of the study, which is reported in this paper. Specifically, the participants were asked whether they believed the method was appropriate for evaluating the artifact, in addition to what they saw as the advantages and disadvantages are with this technique compared with use of an artificial scenario or a fully naturalistic evaluation, the results of which are presented in Sect. 4.6.1.

In this step, ten cases were collected from practitioners which covered multiple industries and organization types, including four private companies, one public company, three government organizations and two educational settings.

4.4   Step 4 - Analyze the Data

The interview data, from both interview sets, was coded using NVivo 15. Initial codes were set up for both the tool evaluation, based upon the criteria of usefulness, satisfaction, and ease of use, and for the CIT comments. This also included initial child codes, e.g. advantages and disadvantages with CIT. A grounded approach was taken to the analysis of the data as new themes emerged [4].

4.5   Step 5 - Interpret and Report Findings

The tool evaluation by the participants provided insight into how the tool was perceived by the practitioners. The information enabled the researchers to refine for whom the tool would be most useful, when it would be used, and for which types of initiatives it would be most useful. For example, in the case outlined in Fig. 1, Participant #2 stated that they believed the artifact would be useful during Agile retrospectives, adding the requirement that the tool allow - repeated use of the risk assessment as part of the tool - to be able to be created and compared over time within the initiative. The data revealed unexpected results to the research team, such as the way in which the exercise had transformed the participants thinking about the situation. The findings also provided improvements for the tool, which will be incorporated into the tool before the next phase of evaluation, which will be in a fully naturalistic setting.

4.6   CIT Evaluation

The rest of this section will outline the feedback received regarding the use of CIT for evaluation. First, the participant's feedback and experience is presented, followed by the experience of the research team.

4.6.1   CIT Evaluation – Participants Perspective

The participants of the study had some key observations using CIT for the purposes of evaluation, with three key themes clearly supported by the data: verisimilitude, engagement, and deep reflection. When asked - they also mentioned that they did not encounter any disadvantages of using this approach – but acknowledged the importance of selecting 'the right' scenario to reflect on.

Verisimilitude: In order to be an effective substitute for naturalistic evaluation, it is essential that the critical incidents as recalled by the participants have high verisimilitude to real incidents. Participants found that the approach was authentic and reported a high degree of verisimilitude compared to a made-up scenario. Participant #6 stated

"...recalling a real project that I was personally involved in, is more authentic - to give us better ideas and analysis... they have the deep understanding so they can dive into great detail, and everything is real. No assumption will be, absorbed into your tool". And Participant #7 stated *"It was way more meaningful using a real situation."* The impact of this is that the research results could be more trusted. Participant #3 noted *"if you're using a simulation you don't build up the same level of trust because it feels contrived or it's like - here a jigsaw piece and here is the thing that it goes in. So, tell me if it works and .... of course it works because you designed both pieces".* These quotes demonstrate the participants believe in depth of authenticity this approach provides.

Engagement: The participants in this study indicated that the use of a real incident that they had experienced and had a deep understanding of led to a greater level of engagement with the artifact they were assessing. Participant #7 stated; *"definitely a lot more meaningful......it was a lot more interesting...when it was something that you could relate to".* This is in contrast to completing the evaluation with an artificial scenario, which Participant # 10 said *"often when it's a simulated one, I would question the simulation more rather than engaging with the tool more".*

Deep Reflection: An emergent theme from participants using the CIT method was that - like fully naturalistic evaluations, it encouraged deep reflection that allowed fresh and unexpected insights about the incident to be uncovered. Participant #5 stated *"I had a bit of an a - ha moment...".* The majority of the participants noted that using a real scenario enabled the complexity of real-life scenarios and facilitated a deeper, more authentic and comprehensive evaluation of the artifact.

4.6.2 CIT Evaluation – Researchers' Perspective

From the perspective of the research team carrying out the evaluation, there were a number of advantages to critical-incident-based evaluation. The resources required were very much lower than for a naturalistic evaluation. In terms of time and cost - ten detailed evaluations were able to be carried out by the research team over 20 h of participant interactions (which occurred within a few weeks). Each evaluation took approximately two hours - arranged as two one-hour sessions. The time and cost required to observe and capture insights about ten BPM initiatives being conducted in real-time would almost certainly be largely more expensive and time-consuming. The approach provided the research team with a high degree of control over the appropriateness of the evaluation context and the resources expended, as opposed to a more open-ended naturalistic study, with a risk of uncertain or unusable findings (if no relevant incident(s) occurred). Furthermore, the structure of the interviews enabled the research approach to be repeatable, even though the situations were very different. This additional control for the research team made comparisons between the cases to be easier, enabling the emergence of similarities and differences to be more evident. The breadth of cases also enabled the research team to have a greater understanding of what types of BPM initiatives the tool should be used in and by whom (i.e. what the tool target user should be). This would have been unlikely to have been achieved had a fully naturalistic evaluation been carried out at this point in the DSR cycle due to the time this would have required and the number of resources available.

The critical incident approach was a good fit for the requirements of the tool evaluation. In a dynamic and evolving situation involving stakeholder relationships, it is impossible to tell at the outset of a project if and how these challenges develop. Relatedly, in naturalistic evaluations, the detailed characteristics of the incident forming the basis of the evaluation will not be evident until after it has occurred, while using a critical incident allowed the researchers to ensure that the incident had the required characteristics. This may not have been found in a fully naturalistic setting, as the tool is designed to provide insight regarding stakeholders in order to avoid engagement issues. In a naturalistic setting, it is therefore difficult to determine whether the *absence* of stakeholder engagement issues is due to the tool having worked as intended, or simply because no such issues would have occurred in that context regardless of the tool. By contrast, selecting a critical incident ensured that situations in which the tool was intended to add value were already present, rather than evaluating the tool in contexts where its need may not yet have materialized.

4.7 Comparison of Artificial, CIT and Naturalistic Methods

Based on the data and analysis above and mapping to the DSR evaluation discussions, we present a summary synthesis here on how the CIT approach fits neatly between artificial and naturalistic approaches. It captures the advantages of naturalistic evaluation and mitigates the disadvantages in terms of resource requirements, fit to DSR evaluation, and scope and completeness. For example, there was a lower requirement for time and cost than naturalistic evaluation, while offering a high degree of control, verisimilitude, and depth. There was a high degree of breadth in industry and scenario types. Further, the deep reflection that the critical incidents encouraged resulted in unexpected insights, such as the way in which the artifact caused the participant to have a change of perspective on the incident they were using for the evaluation. Table 2 positions CIT as a semi-naturalistic evaluation technique by comparing its key characteristics with those of artificial and naturalistic evaluation approaches.

Table 2. Positioning CIT as a Semi-Naturalistic Evaluation Technique: Comparison with Artificial and Naturalistic Evaluation

Characteristic	Artificial	CIT (semi-naturalistic)	Naturalistic
Resource requirements and control			
Cost/Resources	Low requirement for resources compared with naturalistic evaluations [12, 18]	Low requirement for resources and medium requirement for participants	Can have a high requirement for resources, both from researcher and organizational perspective [12, 18, 19]

(continued)

Table 2. (*continued*)

Characteristic	Artificial	CIT (semi-naturalistic)	Naturalistic
Length of study	Tends to be shorter than naturalistic [19]	Short- medium additional step for recruitment and interview	Tends to be longer than artificial [10, 18, 19] – requires partner organization, recruitment, study can take a long time, e.g. through the time of a project
Level of control	Control is high in an artificial setting as the study is narrowly focused on testing the certain aspects of the artifact [12, 19]	Control is medium. While some control is exercised (e.g. through screening the scenario) and the evaluation questions, there is limited control beyond this	As the setting is in the real-world there is low control. Control is sacrificed for understanding how the artifact operates in the real world [18, 19]

Suitability of a Critical Incident for Evaluation Context

Characteristic	Artificial	CIT (semi-naturalistic)	Naturalistic
Phenomena	Stated prior to commencement	Can be validated to be in the study prior to commencement	May or may not exist as the study unfolds
Scenario	Artificially created and aims to provide required evidence to test the study's hypotheses [12]	Validated early in the process	In a real life setting the scenario will develop as the study progresses [12, 16]
Verisimilitude	As these are set in artificial environment verisimilitude is low [12, 18]	As real-life examples are used, however in retrospect verisimilitude is medium /high	A naturalistic evaluation has high verisimilitude as it is in a real-life setting [12, 18]
Depth of analysis	The evaluations are narrow and reductionist and so the depth of analysis required is also low [12, 19]	There is a medium-high depth of analysis required, while confounding factors are less than fully naturalistic, careful interpretation of participant's evaluation is required	Deep analysis is required due to the complexity of the real environment, and the need to understand potential confounding variables [12, 19]

Scope and completeness of the evaluation

(*continued*)

Table 2. (continued)

Characteristic	Artificial	CIT (semi-naturalistic)	Naturalistic
Breadth of testing	The testing is usually narrowly focused on efficacy [12, 18]	The use of CIT allows for a much higher number of scenarios across different settings, and is broader than artificial, but less broad than fully naturalistic	The evaluation encompasses broad aspects of the context in which it takes place, however often in limited scenarios due to the resources required to test broadly [12, 19]
Measures	Primarily measures efficacy in a narrow sense, not including how the artifact functions in a broader setting [18, 19]	Semi-focused – can start with measures, but also open so that additional observations can be added	Primarily measures effectiveness, which includes how the artifact functions in its real-world setting. [12, 19]
Unexpected insights	This is low as it is hypothesis testing and the study is positivist and reductionist [12, 19]	This is high as real-world situations across a wide range of scenarios are used	This is high, however the effect of confounding factors need to be considered [18, 19]

5   CIT Application Guidelines

Further to the comparison of artificial, semi-naturalistic (using CIT) and naturalistic evaluations this section provides practical guidelines for researchers to follow in selecting and using CIT as a DSR evaluation technique:

1. **Determine the suitability of CIT for evaluation.** We propose the following technical rules to provide guidance to researchers as to when CIT is appropriate to be used in a DSR evaluation
a. *IF a fully naturalistic evaluation is infeasible but desired (e.g. if the artifact is socio-technical):* Due to cost, time, safety, access, regulatory constraints, or the inability to repeat real-world scenarios with and without the artifact, *THEN* use CIT to overcome the restraints and use stakeholders' time effectively *and/or.*
b. *IF the environments are contextually diverse or heterogeneous*: When the artifact must operate across a wide range of settings, roles, or organizational conditions, making single-site naturalistic trials may be insufficient, *THEN* use CIT to improve the understanding of how the artifact will operate in a *broad* range of settings *and/or;*
c. *IF* processes unfold over time and are hard to predict upfront, *THEN* use CIT to screen scenarios in advance to ensure it will be suitable to use for evaluation *and/or;*

d. *IF* there is a high reliance on practitioner experience and judgement: When meaningful evaluation requires participants to draw on deep domain knowledge and prior lived experiences, *THEN* CIT achieves greater engagement of practitioners in the evaluation and thus facilitates richer insights *and/or;*
e. *IF* there is a need for repeatable evaluations across DSR cycles and there are resource constraints, *THEN* CIT offers a both rigorous and practically sustainable alternative to fully naturalistic evaluations *and/or;*
f. *IF* reflective insight is important, not just performance outcomes, *THEN* CIT is preferable to a tightly controlled artificial evaluation *and/or;*
g. *IF* the evaluation must surface diverse experiential viewpoints, *THEN* CIT facilitates the capturing of multiple perspectives in a cost and time effective way *and/or;*
h. *IF* evaluation across a breadth of scenarios is more valuable than depth in one or two settings, *THEN* CIT provides a consistent, focused approach to the evaluations.

2. **Consider the Overall Evaluation Strategy and Position CIT Appropriately in the Evaluation and Iteration Cycles**. Our illustrative example was conducted ex-post, but we believe the technique has relevance for ex-ante evaluation as well. As per guidelines provided in [13], ex-ante evaluation supports the *process* of design and provides an approach for theoretically evaluating a design without actually implementing the material system or technology. The artifact is evaluated (and improvements identified) on the basis of its design specifications alone. Use of CIT ex-ante can provide rich feedback on the specifications anchored in real-world practice. For ex-post evaluation, CIT is valuable for late-stage or final evaluation cycles with experienced professionals.

3. **Determine the characteristics required for the critical incidents**. These should be specified *a priori* in direct relation to the evaluation objectives and the intended role of the artifact. Rather than treating any memorable event as suitable, researchers should define what constitutes a "critical" incident for the purposes of evaluation. In general, critical incidents should:

a. *Exercise the core design intentions of the artifact:* The incident should require the types of decisions, judgements, or sensemaking activities the artifact is designed to support (e.g., in our case, interpreting complex situations and exploring alternative courses of action using the artifact).

b. *Involve meaningful consequences or trade-offs:* The situation should matter to the participant or organization so that the artifact's potential value can be assessed (e.g., incidents associated with operational, compliance, or coordination challenges).

c. *Reflect realistic complexity and contextual constraints*: Incidents should contain sufficient organizational, social, or technical nuance to test the artifact under practical conditions (e.g., multiple actors, rules, or interdependencies similar to those described in the case).

d. *Be specific, bounded, and recallable:* Participants should be able to clearly describe what happened, who was involved, and why the incident was critical (e.g., a concrete episode personally experienced by the participant).

e. *Enable comparison with and without the artifact:* The incident must allow participants to plausibly reflect on how the situation might have unfolded differently if the artifact had been available *(as demonstrated in the illustrative evaluation).*

4. **Select and screen incidents.** The research team must engage with prospective participants to screen their proposed critical incidents and ensure they have the properties required for the evaluation.
5. **Participants conduct artifact evaluation based on their critical incident recall.** It is recommended for most contexts that the evaluation can be conducted on an unassisted basis by the participants, otherwise the verisimilitude with real contexts is compromised. This may mean that information or training material is required to support artifact comprehension and use. This material is considered part of the artifact package and also receives rigorous evaluation. This can be augmented with additional techniques such as observation, think-aloud, or diary method, if appropriate.
6. **Debrief the evaluator and capture insights.** Researchers should conduct a structured debrief to surface participants' reflections on both the artifact and the evaluation experience itself. This can include:
a. *Prompted reflection on the evaluation experience*: Invite participants to comment on what the artifact enabled or constrained, how it shaped their thinking or actions, and what surprised them *(e.g., reflections that led to "aha" moments)*.
b. *Elicitation of perceived value and limitations*: Ask participants to identify what they found useful, confusing, or missing, and under what conditions the artifact would or would not add value *(as captured in post-evaluation reflections in the illustrative case)*.
7. **Analysis and coding.** Researchers should analyze the collected material using both *pre-defined evaluation criteria* and *open, inductive coding* to surface emergent insights. While the *a priori* criteria provide structure and comparability across evaluations, researchers should remain attentive to unanticipated themes, including new advantages, limitations, and patterns of artifact use.
8. **Record evaluation insights.** Evaluation insights should be systematically documented to support both immediate artifact refinement and cross-iteration learning. This involves:
a. *Aligning insights with the artifact's design logic and use guidance*: Link each insight to the specific artifact elements, design requirements, or underlying assumptions it relates to, and note implications for refining features, extending functionality, or clarifying user guidance (including differences across contexts, roles, or use situations).
b. *Capturing rationale and context:* Record not only what was observed, but why it mattered, under what conditions it emerged, and how it was experienced by participants.
c. *Preparing insights for iteration and synthesis:* Structure notes and records so they can directly inform the next design cycle and contribute to later cross-case or cross-iteration synthesis.
9. **Plan next iteration of the DSR cycle (if relevant):** Use the recorded evaluation insights to prioritize design changes, refine requirements, and determine which aspects of the artifact should be retained, modified, or extended in the next cycle. This step closes the evaluation–design loop by explicitly translating empirical findings into design decisions, ensuring that each iteration builds cumulatively on the learning generated through CIT-based evaluation.

6 Discussion

The findings presented in Sect. 4 demonstrate that the use of the CIT evaluation technique **offers several advantages** for both researchers and participants in DSR evaluation. In particular, it provides a practical means of addressing a key limitation of fully naturalistic evaluation - namely, the significant time, cost, and organizational constraints associated with conducting in-situ studies [12–14, 19]. By enabling evaluation through real, experience-based incidents, CIT allows researchers to incorporate contextually grounded insights while maintaining a manageable level of effort and control. This is particularly valuable in contemporary contexts, such as Industry 5.0, where rapid development cycles and close human–technology interaction increase the demand for timely yet realistic evaluation approaches [17].

A further strength of CIT lies in its ability to support evaluation across a broader range of scenarios and contexts than would typically be feasible in fully naturalistic studies. While it does not fully overcome the well-documented limitations of naturalistic evaluation in terms of generalizability [10], it enables the inclusion of diverse, experience-based scenarios across industries and organizational settings. This breadth enhances the relevance of evaluation insights while maintaining feasibility within constrained research settings.

The results also indicate that CIT is particularly well suited to experienced practitioners, who can draw on rich prior experiences to evaluate artifacts in meaningful ways. Compared to artificial scenarios, which may be perceived as contrived or overly simplified, the use of real incidents enhances both engagement and verisimilitude. Participants reported that evaluating the artifact in relation to their own experiences allowed for deeper reflection and more nuanced assessment. This, in turn, led to the emergence of unexpected insights, including shifts in how participants understood and interpreted the situations they were analyzing. Such insights are less likely to emerge in artificial settings, where scenarios may lack depth, or in naturalistic settings, where controlled comparison is often difficult to achieve.

An additional benefit of the CIT evaluation technique is the ability to compare participants' retrospective understanding of an incident with their interpretation of the same situation when supported by the artifact. Although such comparisons are based on reflective accounts rather than direct observation, the presence of strong engagement and "a-ha" moments suggests that the artifact can meaningfully influence how practitioners analyze and interpret complex situations. The experienced practitioners who participated in the evaluation's testimony added to the case for the tool to have real-world impact and applicability.

While these findings provide strong support for the experiential and practical value of the CIT-based semi-naturalistic evaluation approach, **several limitations should be acknowledged**. First, the empirical evidence presented is primarily illustrative and focuses on participants' perceptions, including engagement, verisimilitude, and depth of reflection. Although these are important indicators of evaluation quality, they do not directly demonstrate improvements in artifact effectiveness, design quality, or evaluative validity when compared to alternative evaluation approaches.

This limitation reflects the methodological focus of the study. The primary contribution is to introduce and position CIT as an evaluation technique that enables semi-naturalistic evaluation within the DSR evaluation landscape, rather than to empirically establish its superiority in terms of outcome performance. Accordingly, the evaluation reported here should be interpreted as an initial demonstration of feasibility and value, rather than a definitive assessment of impact.

In addition, the use of retrospective critical incidents introduces potential sources of bias. Participants' accounts may be influenced by hindsight bias, selective recall, and retrospective reconstruction of events, as well as social desirability effects. While these risks are inherent to experience-based evaluation approaches, steps were taken to mitigate them through structured incident selection, clearly defined criteria, and systematic data collection procedures. Nevertheless, these biases may influence the nature and interpretation of the insights generated and should be considered when applying and interpreting CIT-based evaluation findings.

More broadly, while semi-naturalistic evaluation using CIT offers a pragmatic balance [19] between artificial and naturalistic approaches, it does not eliminate the trade-offs between these modes. Rather, it reconfigures them. Although CIT benefits from contextual grounding through real users and real incidents, it relies on retrospective accounts rather than real-time observation, which may limit temporal accuracy and the ability to capture dynamic interactions as they unfold. Similarly, while it improves feasibility and scalability compared to naturalistic evaluation, it does not achieve the same level of ecological validity as in-situ deployment, nor does it provide the same level of experimental control as artificial evaluation. Semi-naturalistic evaluation should therefore be understood as offering a distinct balance of strengths and limitations, rather than a complete integration of the advantages of both approaches [15, 19].

Future research should extend this work by examining how CIT-based evaluation influences artifact design outcomes over time. Comparative studies could investigate differences between artifacts evaluated using CIT, artificial methods, and fully naturalistic approaches, assessing outcomes such as usability, effectiveness, and stakeholder acceptance. Longitudinal and multi-cycle DSR studies may also provide insight into how CIT contributes to iterative design refinement and whether it supports the development of more robust and context-sensitive artifacts. In addition, quantitative and mixed-method approaches could be used to assess the reliability, consistency, and predictive validity of insights generated through critical incidents.

7 Conclusion

The CIT method allows for rich exploration of experiences across multiple scenarios without the high cost and time-consuming disadvantages of a fully naturalistic evaluation. This is particularly helpful during ex-ante evaluations, when developing artifacts for optional use. It enables users' feedback to be incorporated into the development of systems prior to roll out, reducing costly mistakes. It sits neatly between artificial and naturalistic evaluation and is a valuable addition to the DSR evaluation toolkit and allows the participants to evaluate the artifact *as they would use it* in a real-life situation.

References

1. Baskerville, R., Pries-Heje, J., Venable, J.R.: MEDS: methodology for evaluation in design science. Eur. J. Inf. Syst. 1–18 (2026). https://doi.org/10.1080/0960085X.2026.2627280
2. Butterfield, L.D., Borgen, W.A., Amundson, N.E., Maglio, A.-S.T.: Fifty years of the critical incident technique: 1954–2004 and beyond. Qual. Res. QR **5**, 475–497 (2005). https://doi.org/10.1177/1468794105056924
3. Flanagan, J.C.: The critical incident technique. Psychol. Bull. **51**, 327–358 (1954). https://doi.org/10.1037/h0061470
4. Glaser, B., Strauss, A.: Discovery of grounded theory: strategies for qualitative research. Routledge (2017). https://doi.org/10.4324/9780203793206
5. Gogan, J.L., McLaughlin, M.-D., Thomas, D.: Critical incident technique in the basket. In: 35th International Conference on Information Systems (ICIS) (2014)
6. Hevner, A.R., March, S.T., Park, J., Ram, S.: Design science in information systems research. MIS Q. **28**, 75–105 (2004). https://doi.org/10.2307/25148625
7. Jacobs, R.L.: Critical incident technique. Work Analysis in the Knowledge Economy, pp. 129–143 (2019). https://doi.org/10.1007/978-3-319-94448-7_9
8. Nili, A.: Digital service problems: Prevention and user persistence in solving them. Open Access Te Herenga Waka-Victoria University of Wellington (2016)
9. Nili, A., Tate, M., Johnstone, D., Gable, G.: Consumer's persistence in solving their own problem with self-service technology. In: Proceedings of the 25th Australasian Conference on Information Systems, pp. 1–10. ACIS/Auckland University of Technology (2014)
10. Peffers, K., Rothenberger, M., Tuunanen, T., Vaezi, R.: Design science research evaluation. In: DESRIST: International Conference on Design Science Research in Information Systems and Technology, pp. 398–410. Springer, Berlin, Heidelberg (2012). https://doi.org/10.1007/978-3-642-29863-9_29
11. Prat, N., Comyn-Wattiau, I., Akoka, J.: A taxonomy of evaluation methods for information systems artifacts. J. Manag. Inf. Syst. **32**, 229–267 (2015). https://doi.org/10.1080/07421222.2015.1099390
12. Pries-Heje, J., Baskerville, R., Venable, J.R.: Strategies for design science research evaluation. In: 16th European Conference on Information Systems (2008)
13. Recker, J.: Scientific Research in Information Systems : A Beginner's Guide. Springer, Cham, Switzerland (2021). https://doi.org/10.1007/978-3-030-85436-2_5
14. Reiners, S., Kipping, G., Tingelhoff, F., Gau, M.: Past lessons, future directions: an author-informed review of design science research in information systems. In: International Conference on Design Science Research in Information Systems and Technology, pp. 99–115. Springer (2025). https://doi.org/10.1007/978-3-031-93976-1_7
15. Sonnenberg, C., vom Brocke, J.: Evaluations in the science of the artificial – reconsidering the build-evaluate pattern in design science research. In: Design Science Research in Information Systems. Advances in Theory and Practice, pp. 381–397. Springer Berlin Heidelberg (2012). https://doi.org/10.1007/978-3-642-29863-9_28
16. Sun, Y., Kantor, P.B.: Cross-evaluation: a new model for information system evaluation. J. Am. Soc. Inform. Sci. Technol. **57**, 614–628 (2006). https://doi.org/10.1002/asi.20324
17. Szelągowski, M., Berniak-Woźny, J.: BPM challenges, limitations and future development directions – a systematic literature review. Bus. Process. Manag. J. **30**, 505–557 (2024). https://doi.org/10.1108/BPMJ-06-2023-0419
18. Venable, J., Pries-Heje, J., Baskerville, R.: A comprehensive framework for evaluation in design science research. In: DESRIST: International Conference on Design Science Research in Information Systems and Technology, pp. 423–438. Springer, Berlin, Hiedelberg (2012). https://doi.org/10.1007/978-3-642-29863-9_31

19. Venable, J., Pries-Heje, J., Baskerville, R.: FEDS: a framework for evaluation in design science research. Eur. J. Inf. Syst. **25**, 77–89 (2016). https://doi.org/10.1057/ejis.2014.36

Generating Design Knowledge Without Doing Design: The Design Researcher as Curator

Pedro Antunes[1]([⊠]) [iD] and Andreas Drechsler[2] [iD]

[1] Faculty of Sciences of the University of Lisbon, Lisbon, Portugal
padantunes@fc.ul.pt
[2] Victoria University of Wellington, Wellington, New Zealand
andreas.drechsler@vuw.ac.nz

Abstract. In this study, we explore different types of engagement in research within the Design Science Research paradigm. We also identify and elaborate on a new form of engagement where the researcher, acting as a curator, accomplishes design science research projects that rely on accounts of design by practitioners. We define a set of requirements that curators should follow when conducting their research. To illustrate the approach, we present an illustrative project in which changes in the design function in systems engineering are investigated, using accounts of practice shared on a blogging platform. The unique form of engagement discussed in this paper enables researchers to rapidly generalize design knowledge emerging from practice.

Keywords: Design Science Research · Research Engagement · Curator

1 Introduction

Researchers tend to gravitate toward research communities, which in turn tend to converge around research paradigms, defining specific ways of thinking about research problems, practices, and achievements [39]. As researchers immerse themselves in a community, they become aware of what makes their role in that community distinctive.

One recognized characteristic of the Design Science Research (DSR) community is that its members engage with research objects as *players*, whereas researchers in more traditional communities engage as *observers* [19]. While observers independently and objectively analyze, describe, and explain reality, players subjectively change reality through design. In the early days of DSR, this raised the debate of whether DSR researchers were operating "within the compass of science" or not [58]. Given the current legitimacy of DSR, we consider this debate as already set [47].

The player metaphor highlights changing reality as an essential characteristic of DSR. However, it also reveals some limitations: there is no single game or playfield; both are highly diverse and contextualized [48]. A widely recognized problem in DSR is how to accumulate design knowledge, given that it spans so many unique areas, interests, viewpoints, and types of design artifacts [9, 54]. No less important, design science also concerns practitioners. A significant amount of knowledge and experience

J. vom Brocke et al. (Eds.): DESRIST 2026, LNCS 16606, pp. 267–280, 2026.
https://doi.org/10.1007/978-3-032-28313-9_15

exists in the minds of practitioners, containing valuable lessons, but remains inaccessible to DSR due to its tacit nature. And yet, there are outlets where designers document some knowledge, albeit in an unstructured, narrative way (e.g., professional blogging sites), making that knowledge explicit, yet also making it difficult to process from a DSR standpoint. We propose a curating approach to structure, systematise, and summarise this design knowledge. Curating thus makes this formerly tacit knowledge more easily accessible for other designers, including design researchers.

The paper is structured as follows. First, we review the literature and identify different modes of engagement in DSR, including some variations of the player metaphor. Then, we discuss the proposed new metaphor and elaborate on its main characteristics. We also provide an illustrative project of engaging in DSR as a curator. Finally, we compare modes of engagement and provide some points for discussion about this new type of engagement.

2 The Player and Other Forms of Engagement

In this section, we further extend our metaphorical or analogical examination of the different roles a DSR researcher can take, which we began with the player-versus-observer distinction in the Introduction. Such metaphors allow analysis and reflection on the range of distinct roles a DSR researcher can take on over the course of a DSR project, the characteristic tasks each role entails, and the corresponding contributions each role can make to human knowledge and to achieving practical impacts.

One characteristic that clearly separates the player from the observer is the utilization of abductive thinking [30]. Abduction is a key ingredient in design. It relies neither on extensive analysis nor systematic application of rules to make an informed design argument [19]. Instead, it entangles trial and error, intuitive insights, and the emergence of creative ideas [13]. This is what makes the player an agent of change. However, abduction can appear as a "methodological hodgepodge" [12]. It needs to be integrated into the research in a way that preserves rigor. This is often accomplished through the adoption of methodologies that control the boundaries within which players use abductive thinking [13]. As such, players have been observed to exhibit ritualistic behaviors [3].

Players operate in a two-dimensional field, which combines the "science of design" with "designing with science" [12]. This duality led to the emergence of two camps [11]: the artifact camp, which emphasizes designing with science, and the design theory camp, which emphasizes the science of design. The artifact camp takes a pragmatic approach, highlighting that the essential contribution of DSR is the design of innovative artifacts. The design theory camp stresses that the essential contribution of DSR has a theoretical nature, advancing science in a normative sense, with clear progress pathways [2]. Thus, the designed artifacts are merely vehicles for exhibiting progress in design theory [32]. Despite the considerable differences, it is acknowledged that the two camps are complementary [31]: the player should simultaneously deliver concrete and abstract contributions. Likewise, in football, attackers play defense and vice versa.

Some literature suggests that DSR researchers should change their role metaphors throughout the design process, acting as players when building artifacts, but becoming observers when evaluating them [25]. This articulation seems empowering, especially when considering the design theory camp: as a player, the researcher can deviate from the status quo and argue for novel, radical, and inspired outcomes; and as an observer, the researcher can reinforce the conjectural aspect of the contributions. However, such empowerment can be illusory, as this "heroic" researcher [59] will be entangled in paradigmatic debates, conflicting discourses, and different norms and assumptions about the research. Additionally, from the pragmatic camp, the researcher may become entangled in two very different research projects rather than just one, where the second project focuses on naturalistic evaluation. Not acting as an observer allows the researcher to engage with other forms of evaluation, such as artificial and formative evaluations [60].

Researchers can also engage in DSR as *collaborators* [55]. This type of engagement is found in research strategies that place the researcher in solving specific problems encountered by clients, such as Action Design Research (ADR) [56]. In this type of engagement, the researcher faces a conflict of interest between pursuing local outcomes, which may satisfy the client but not the research community, and pursuing broader contributions, which could satisfy the research community but may encounter friction from the client [36, 55]. This type of engagement may shift the research from well-defined to more casuistic projects, with constant opportunistic decisions and micro evaluations made by the client [55]. This reduces intellectual control over the research [46] and increases the risk of not delivering sound research contributions [29].

Noting the challenges with collaboration, Mullarkey and Hevner [46], citing McKay and Marshall [43], suggested a future type of engagement that would divide the design into two parallel processes, one that encapsulates practice and another that caters to research. The authors characterized this type of engagement as *consulting*.

3 A New Type of Engagement: The Researcher as a Curator

Vom Brocke et al. [61] pointed out that DSR projects can be accomplished by building on "design processes that are not conducted as part of the DSR project itself but at another place and time." In this study, we focus on **DSR projects that rely on accounts of design by practitioners**. Considering this context, we propose a new form of engagement that we designate as *curator*. The Cambridge Dictionary defines curator as "a person who organizes [...] and arranges a showing [...] of objects of interest"[1]. Applying this definition to our context, the "showing" is an artifact designed by the researcher to characterize design products, processes, as well as options and decisions documented by practitioners. In our context, the "organizing and arranging" aspect of curation also reflects the researcher's capacity to explore the boundaries of such characterizations, asking and answering new questions, and adding new perspectives [53]. These relationships can be more accurately expressed using Nonaka's [50] theory of knowledge creation: the curator *externalizes* design artifacts by reflecting on tacit design knowledge and artifacts *socialized* by practitioners.

Externalization must be conducted within the scope of the DSR paradigm. However, socialization does not. In this study, we focus on **DSR projects that utilize blogging platforms for socialization**.

---

[1] https://dictionary.cambridge.org/dictionary/english/curator.

In relation to the knowledge creation cycle, the curator assumes several responsibilities: 1) distinguish between their design generalization and the targeted design practices, leaving the latter to others; 2) exert boundary control over generalization, which requires aligning it with the knowledge base and the problem environment, assuring both rigor and relevance; and 3) apply abductive logic to the generalization, integrating ideas arising from both practice and research. In Fig. 1, we link these responsibilities to the DSR framework by Hevner et al. [34].

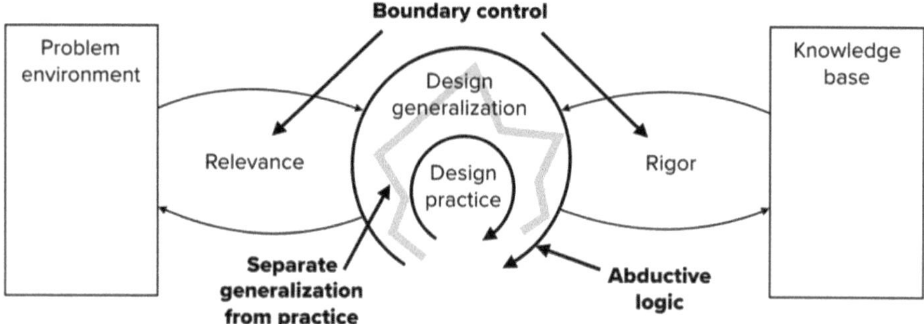

Fig. 1. The curator's responsibilities.

Before detailing this type of engagement, we first outline and address a few preliminary questions about its nature and purpose.

Is curation the same as observation? Curation is a particular form of playing, not of observing. The curator investigates targeted design practices; however, with some distance, considering time and place, and self-determination in relating the generalization to the targeted practices.

Is curation the same as design archaeology? Design archaeology uses artifacts and material signs from the past to reconstruct prescriptive knowledge [17]. Curation also involves a shift in time, but with a more contemporary focus, seeking to identify and characterize new and emerging trends from practice. As curation becomes more closely tied to practice, it tends to take on a more ethnographic nature. Finally, curation adds a layer of abductive thinking on top of these approaches, making it significantly different.

Is curation the same as a literature review? There are some similarities, but also some differences. We find similarities with grey literature reviews, as data is acquired from diverse and heterogeneous materials that exist beyond research literature [1]. This includes, in particular, professional outlets where practitioners discuss design and related topics. Guidelines developed to control the quality of grey literature reviews can and should be applied by the curator. However, a key distinction is that the curator employs a type of reasoning that aligns with DSR, focusing on artifact design, abductive thinking, and prescriptive knowledge [12].

Is curation the same as a meta-analysis or meta-design? Meta-studies build on the scientific studies of others. Curation builds on the thoughts of practitioners; they lie in a grey area, available outside the traditional academic processes [1]. Curation also lies in a grey area not yet covered by DSR.

What kind of problems can be addressed? Curation does not apply to solving concrete problems faced by specific organizations—that is the domain of ADR. It can also be challenging to design utterly unique artifacts—that is the domain of the designing—and not curating— player. Curation applies to widespread classes of design problems and artifacts, about which emergent design practices proliferate, but generalizations remain elusive. This includes, for example, new information systems architectures (e.g., microservices, event-based architectures, choreography) and development approaches (e.g., DevOps, BizDevOps, BizOps, DevSecOps, and MLOps) [8, 10].

What is the potential value brought by curation? The literature highlights that the DSR domain is characterized by a wide range of problems researched in various environments and contexts, resulting in concrete artifact instantiations rather than abstract contributions [15]. This makes it challenging to accumulate knowledge through refinement [54]. Curation may transform less abstract and more specific knowledge into more abstract and more general knowledge [31]. This can be accomplished at an accelerated pace by relying on communities of practice, a strategy that has similarities with crowdsourcing. Finally, considering that IS is characterized by constantly evolving technologies, processes, and tools, tapping into grey literature allows researchers to focus on new, emergent technology-driven problems.

4 Detailed Curation Approach

We now elaborate on the curation concept, outlining a set of steps and associated requirements for conducting curation. This characterization provides logical reasoning; it is not intended to prescribe a procedure.

4.1 Data Sourcing

The curator needs to identify relevant data sources. Research on grey literature assigns different levels of credibility to various sources, with more credibility attributed to controlled outlets, such as books, moderate credibility assigned to blog posts, and less credibility assigned to uncontrolled outlets like social media [27]. Our primary focus is on professional blogging platforms with moderate credibility, where practitioners independently communicate to an unknown audience that primarily consists of other practitioners. Sources focused on marketing and consulting services should be avoided, as their content is not as independent. We also suggest focusing on long-form posts, rather than short exchanges (such as Reddit). Long-form posts provide space for structuration and rationalization, making it easier to extract knowledge and assess credibility. A good example is the Medium.com platform, which embraces the following motto: "write about what they're working on, what's keeping them up at night, what they've lived through, and what they've learned that the rest of us might want to know too."[2]

Posts differ structurally from scientific content. They can be structured around episodes, intents, problems, and how-to assertions, enriched with "war stories," anecdotal

---

[2] https://medium.com/about.

evidence, metaphors, and practical examples. Therefore, data selection requires flexibility from the curator. Only a fraction of data may end up having assigned symbolic meaning by the curator.

One issue to consider is that authors can retract posts. The collected data is volatile and must be downloaded and stored by the curator.

4.2 Analysis

The targeted type of data consists of reflections on artifacts, design decisions, and contextual elements, including, for example, success and failure in organizational contexts, as well as emerging trends. The selection should focus on soundness, novelty, insightfulness, and interestingness. In a context of moderate credibility, the curator must carefully assess the soundness of arguments, considering contextual elements, such as the quality of writing and the value of examples and stories [37]. Curation is not concerned with confirmation. A novel concept is therefore more relevant than familiar ones. Insightfulness is essential for determining the "actability" of a concept in the practice community [35]. Interestingness is key to the curator's role, as the researcher does not aim to build a comprehensive representation of all concepts in the selected data, but instead to choose specific concepts that raise interesting "so what" questions [7]. This criterion is particularly relevant when the purpose is to challenge current assumptions [5]. Specifically, in DSR, this criterion provides a heuristic for realizing design novelty [22].

The data analysis has a qualitative focus, a standard procedure in which coding plays a significant role [44]. However, there is a stronger emphasis on finding emerging and unexpected concepts and patterns.

4.3 Generalization

Curation aims to elevate concepts from the practical level to the more abstract and generalized level. This can be achieved by design, producing conceptual artifacts such as typologies, concept maps, and conceptual frameworks [6]. Following the DSR paradigm, multiple design cycles can be involved in generalization [53]: from an embryonic cycle, where novel concepts are distinguished, to a growth cycle that explores emerging features, and culminating in a maturity cycle where the conceptual artifact is consolidated and refined, organizes thinking, and conveys purposefulness [6].

Evaluation is an integral component of the design cycle, and several evaluation actions can be integrated into the cycles mentioned above. Given the conceptual progression, a hierarchy of goals can be considered for the evaluations, ranging from more utilitarian at the embryonic cycle to more subjective and perceptual at the mature cycle [33]. Criteria such as innovation and evolution can be considered for evaluations at the maturity cycle. Innovation is particularly well-suited for curation, as it enables a comparison between the knowledge emerging from practice, the knowledge incorporated into the finalized conceptual artifact, and the existing knowledge base.

4.4 Abductive Logic

Abductive logic is essential to design, bringing intuition, creativity, and thinking outside the box into the cycles of elevating concepts from the practical to the abstract [13]. The concept helps distinguish curation from the grey literature reviews on which it builds. It blends well with curatorial processes developed in research methodology [52], extending beyond selection and structuration to ask new questions and promote new answers. This way, the curator builds an open conceptual artifact, which invites users to make their own interpretations. Concepts brought from the grey literature provide examples and suggest images, rather than justifications. The artifact helps allocate attention in a controlled way [21].

4.5 Boundary Control

Curation involves ample freedom in selecting and organizing design concepts, but also constant care in crafting a narrative that simultaneously builds on rigor and relevance to deliver generalization. The tacit design knowledge extracted from the grey literature is broken down, reassembled, and recreated as it goes through the cycles of elevating concepts from the practical to the abstract. The adoption of existing (kernel) theories to support this process helps clarify the path toward generalization and legitimize the curator's choices and the artifact design [30].

5 Illustrative Project

Design is an essential component of systems engineering, supporting the analysis of the as-is situation and the design of an improved to-be system [4]. Traditional systems engineering models incorporate design tasks into several stages of the Software Development Life Cycle (SDLC), e.g., preliminary design and detailed design [20]. However, the Agile movement [26] significantly changed the situation, advocating for more flexible, dynamic, adaptable, and lightweight approaches with a stronger connection to users and emerging needs [57]. This evolution led to what is commonly referred to as Agile Design [18]. Another significant evolution involved DevOps, which introduced a set of operational practices supported by technology, significantly reducing development time and altering the relationship between developers and users [57]. Various practices stemming from DevOps are changing the design function (as opposed to a task), leading to new approaches such as Emergent Design and DesignOps [38, 62]. However, the pace of change is accelerating because generative AI is transforming both the DevOps landscape [14, 45] and the design landscape [41, 42].

Given that these changes emerge from practice, as researchers, we are still trying to understand what is going on with the design function [8, 49, 51]. This illustrative case focuses on characterizing the design transformation path based on the practitioner's viewpoint. As noted by Siau et al. [57], different eras require different abstractions, so we aim to create an abstraction that characterizes design in the evolving systems engineering landscape.

Data Sourcing: The selected data source was Medium.com. It was chosen because it is a prominent platform with approximately 100 million users[3]. The platform has extensive coverage of technology (the third most popular category) and features longer

---

[3] https://thesmallbusinessblog.com/medium-statistics.

articles,[4] which helps to appraise credibility. A variety of initial searches on Medium were conducted to identify the most effective keywords for data collection, resulting in the categories and keywords listed in Table 1. These searches and associated categories ultimately shaped the artifact design. Considering data volatility, the selected writings were downloaded in PDF to ensure they would not be lost.

Table 1. Selection of keywords.

Categories		Keywords	Comments
1	Agile	agile/scrum/lean design, agile design thinking	Provided a plethora of results, although with views not as recent as the keywords below
2	DevOps and xOps	DevOps design, xOps design	No relevant results, as design discussions were focused on systems architecture instead of product design
3	Ops	DevOps product design, DevOps 2.0 design, DesignOps, ProductOps, DevOps design thinking, DevOps product thinking	More recent views on the topic. The keyword "xOps design" returned results related to systems and architecture design, which were not used in this study
4	Product design	Product design, product thinking, platform engineering, platform engineering design	Significant number of results with high recency
5	Evolving role	Product design future/evolving role/new realities/evolution/relevance/trends	Only writings published in 2025 were considered. Most writings about the future provide diagnostics of the current situation of product design

The selected type of data considered writings by individuals self-characterized as designers, product owners, digital consultants, and engineers (IT, software architects, developers, DevOps, etc.). The sourced data for this project consisted of about 92.766 words.

Analysis: The results from the keyword searches listed in Table 1 were screened based on two criteria: consideration of the design function, even if not the primary concern of the writing, and interestingness. Data chunks were extracted from the writings, and key concepts were identified, following the same approach as in qualitative data analysis [44]. The selected concepts focused on specific design practices (e.g., adaptive feature delivery and stream-aligned teams), as well as reflections on what works, what does not work, and what could work.

Although no frequency analysis was conducted, multiple occurrences of the same concepts were considered indicative of current trends.

Generalization: The primary goal of the project was to achieve a generalizable understanding of the transformation path of the design function. The process was organized into two cycles. The first cycle involved structuring the identified concepts around the categories in Table 1. The second step applied process theory [16] to explain and characterize changes in the design function from an organizational perspective.

---

[4] https://mediumcourse.com/what-is-medium.

Figure 2 illustrates the adopted conceptual structure based on process theory. A defining event signifies a change, which is further elucidated by a set of drivers and patterns. Drivers identify the leading causes of change. The nature of change is characterized by social and sociotechnical patterns, which examine how people and technology interact within the context of the defining event.

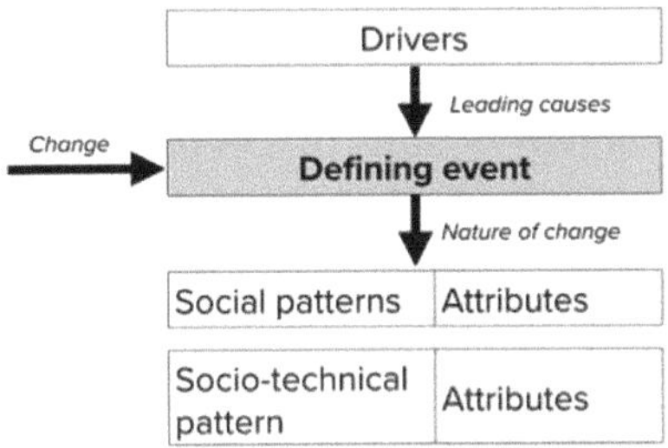

Fig. 2. Adopted characterization of the process of change

The artifact that resulted from applying this conceptual structure is presented in Fig. 3. It characterizes changes in the design function that result from four defining events: Agile adaptation, DevOps adaptation, platform alignment, and coexistence with AI.

Abductive Logic: This artifact helps understand the design function from a historical perspective. However, it also affords more interesting narratives, e.g., concerning levels of maturity and organizational enactment, where Agile adaptation is seen as a prerequisite for DevOps adaptation, which is a prerequisite for platform alignment, and a prerequisite for coexisting with AI (in a way that resolves the identity crisis, i.e., the realization of how designers can coexist with AI). For instance, sharing requires tight communication, and infrastructure standardization requires automation and high-performance workflows.

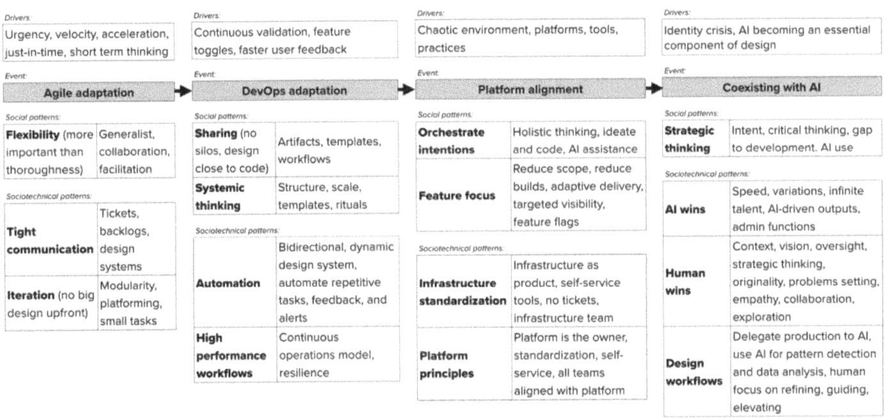

Fig. 3. Conceptual artifact characterizing changes in the design function, based on process theory.

The separation between social and sociotechnical patterns highlights how designers and organizations, on the one hand, and designers and technology, on the other hand, operate within the context of each event. The Agile adaptation involves flexibility, tight communication, and iteration; the DevOps adaptation involves sharing, systemic thinking, automation, and high-performance workflows; and so forth. For each one of these concepts, sub-concepts are identified that further explain the involved behaviors. Due to a lack of space, these sub-concepts are not detailed.

Boundary Control: The selected topic has an extensive knowledge base related to Agile software development [23, 28, 40]. To accomplish relevance, the novelty of the chosen concepts was continuously checked against that baseline.

In parallel, the artifact also integrates concepts from process theory that provide a coherent narrative about the generalization. This helped accomplish rigor.

In summary, this artifact demonstrates how curation can provide value to both research and practice. From a research perspective, the artifact offers a holistic understanding of how the design function is evolving through the lens of process theory. The first two events, Agile and DevOps adaptations, do not deliver significant novelty, considering that they occurred many years ago. The start of the Agile movement is dated to around 2001 [26], and DevOps to around 2009 [24]. Therefore, there are already ample accounts of these phenomena in the research literature. However, the more recent events, considering platform alignment and coexistence with AI, still lack conceptualization. This illustrative project demonstrates how conceptualizations of emergent phenomena can be presented in dialogue with, as well as in conflict with, prior accounts.

6 Discussion and Conclusion

In Table 2, we compare the different types of engagement discussed in this paper. For the comparison, we use three criteria: type of knowledge, knowledge buildup, and validation.

Regarding the type of knowledge, curation stands out from the other forms of engagement by focusing on abstract, general knowledge that covers a range of viewpoints emerging from practice. This contrasts, in particular, with the player, where knowledge is subjective and in-depth. On the other hand, the player can direct the generation of knowledge, controlling essential factors such as problematization, requirements, constraints, and contextualization, while the curator can only filter it.

Considering the knowledge buildup, crowdsourcing enables the curator to generate knowledge more quickly than other types of engagement, while covering an extended range of issues. Also distinctive is that curation can cover recent practices and technologies coming from the front line. This presents a dilemma: on the one hand, there is the risk of spending research effort trying to conceptualize phenomena that may fade rapidly; on the other hand, a slow buildup risks irrelevance in changing times.

Regarding validation, curation emphasizes abstract justifications. Such understanding aligns with the hierarchy of goals defined by Hevner et al. [33], which suggests adapting validation to the level of abstraction in knowledge generation. Example goals include innovation and interestingness. In contrast, if we consider that the knowledge

Table 2. Comparison between modes of engagement.

Engagement	Type of knowledge	Knowledge buildup	Validation
Observer	Conjectural, regulated	Slow, exclusive	Robust
Player	Subjective, in-depth, directed	Slow, clustered	Flexible
Collaborator	Subjective, uncontrolled	Slow, volatile	Contextual
Consultant	Subjective, filtered	Slow, diffused	Contextual
Curator	Abstract, general, filtered	Fast, recent, extended	Abstract

generated by collaboration and consulting is less abstract and more contextual, the validation needs to move down the hierarchy of goals, for example, by considering utilitarian goals such as efficacy and effectiveness.

Beyond the novel curator role, we also contribute a blueprint for the curation process, along with a demonstration to curate design knowledge about recent evolutions of design(ing) through analysis of articles on a professional blogging platform. As this is merely an example, the curating process can encompass other design-relevant topics, various types of data sources (which may have different advantages and disadvantages compared to Medium.com, as outlined above), and alternative analysis and design methods. Future research can further explore the range of feasible curation processes. Exploring the creative nature of curation is also a relevant topic that warrants further investigation.

In conclusion, we make two remarks. The first remark is that a discussion of modes of engagement, using metaphors such as player and curator, contributes to a discussion of the range, possibilities, and configurations afforded by the DSR paradigm. This is accomplished in a manner that is not rigid and proceduralized, but instead indicative of what the community is like [39].

The second remark is that the curation metaphor raises new imaginative ways for design knowledge development while keeping close (albeit somewhat unidirectional) ties between research and practice. Still, there are risks involved. One risk is that curation may not be viewed as a sophisticated endeavor, resulting in uninteresting artifacts that fail to gain traction in both the research and practice communities. A related risk is that curation may be undertaken opportunistically, in pursuit of immediate gains, but lacking long-term theoretical resonance. We also consider the risk of normalizing curation as a form of theory-building, rather than embracing pragmatism, which introduces many preconceptions, constraints, and rules.

Acknowledgements. This work is funded by national funds through FCT – Fundação para a Ciência e a Tecnologia, I.P., under the LASIGE Research Unit, ref. UID/00408/2025, DOI: https://doi.org/https://doi.org/10.54499/UID/00408/2025.

References

1. Adams, R., et al.: Shades of grey: guidelines for working with the grey literature in systematic reviews for management and organizational studies. Int. J. Manag. Rev. **19**(4), 432–454 (2017)

2. Aier, S., Fischer, C.: Criteria of progress for information systems design theories. IseB **9**(1), 133–172 (2011)

3. Alter, S.: long live design science research!.... and remind me again about whether it is a new research paradigm or a rationale of last resort for worthwhile research that doesn't fit under any other umbrella. In: Thirty Third International Conference on Information Systems. Orlando (2012)

4. Alter, S.: Work system theory: overview of core concepts, extensions, and challenges for the future. J. Assoc. Inf. Syst. **72** (2013)

5. Alvesson, M., Sandberg, J.: Generating research questions through problematization. Acad. Manag. Rev. **36**(2), 247–271 (2011)

6. Antunes, P., et al.: Construction of conceptual frameworks in research: an information systems design perspective. Commun. Assoc. Inf. Syst. **57** (2025)

7. Antunes, P., Tate, M.: Examining the canvas as a domain-independent artifact. IseB **20**, 495–514 (2022). https://doi.org/10.1007/s10257-022-00556-5

8. Antunes, P., Tate, M.: "What's going on" with BizDevOps: a qualitative review of BizDevOps practice. Comput. Ind. **157–158**(104081), 1–14 (2024). https://doi.org/10.1016/j.compind.2024.104081

9. Barquet, A., et al.: Knowledge accumulation in design-oriented research. In: International Conference on Design Science Research in Information System and Technology, pp. 398–413 Springer (2017)

10. Baškarada, S., et al.: Architecting microservices: practical opportunities and challenges. J. Comput. Inf. Syst. **60**(5), 428–436 (2020). https://doi.org/10.1080/08874417.2018.1520056

11. Baskerville, R., et al.: Design science research contributions: finding a balance between artifact and theory. J. Assoc. Inf. Syst. **19**(5), 358–376 (2018)

12. Baskerville, R., et al.: Genres of inquiry in design-science research: justification and evaluation of knowledge production. MIS Q. **39**(3), 541–564 (2015)

13. Baskerville, R., et al.: Inducing creativity in design science research. In: International Conference on Design Science Research in Information Systems and Technology, pp. 3–17 Springer (2019)

14. Berardinelli, L., et al.: Model driven engineering, artificial intelligence, and devops for software and systems engineering: a systematic mapping study of synergies and challenges. ACM Trans. Softw. Eng. Methodol. (2025)

15. Brendel, A., et al.: Towards an integrative view on design science research genres, strategies, and pivotal concepts in information systems research. ACM SIGMIS Datab. Database Adv. Inf. Syst. **53**(4), 9–23 (2022)

16. Burton-Jones, A., et al.: Theoretical perspectives in IS research: from variance and process to conceptual latitude and conceptual fit. Eur. J. Inf. Syst. **24**(6), 664–679 (2015)

17. Chandra Kruse, L., et al.: Design archaeology: generating design knowledge from real-world artifact design. In: Tulu, B. et al. (eds.) Extending the Boundaries of Design Science Theory and Practice, pp. 32–45. Springer International Publishing, Cham (2019). https://doi.org/10.1007/978-3-030-19504-5_3

18. Crowder, J., Friess, S.: Systems Engineering Agile Design Methodologies. Springer, New York, NY (2013). https://doi.org/10.1007/978-1-4614-6663-5

19. Daase, C., et al.: Classifying design science research in terms of types of reasoning from an epistemological perspective. In: International Conference on Design Science Research in Information Systems and Technology, pp. 155–167 Springer (2024)

20. Darrin, M., Devereux, W.: The Agile Manifesto, design thinking and systems engineering. In: 2017 Annual IEEE International Systems Conference, pp. 1–5 IEEE (2017)

21. Davis, J.: Theorizing curation. In: The Oxford handbook of digital media sociology. Oxfords University Press (2022). https://doi.org/10.1093/oxfordhb/9780197510636.013.5

22. Deng, Q., Ji, S.: A review of design science research in information systems: concept, process, outcome, and evaluation. Pacific Asia J. Assoc. Inf. Syst. **10**(1), 2 (2018)
23. Dingsøyr, T., et al.: A decade of agile methodologies: towards explaining agile software development. J. Syst. Softw. **85**, 1213–1221 (2012). https://doi.org/10.1016/j.jss.2012.02.033
24. Dörnenburg, E.: The path to devops. IEEE Softw. **35**(5), 71–75 (2018)
25. Drechsler, A.: A postmodern perspective on socio-technical design science research in information systems. In: International Conference on Design Science Research in Information Systems, pp. 152–167 Springer (2015)
26. Fowler, M., Highsmith, J.: The agile manifesto. Softw. Dev. **9**(8), 28–35 (2001)
27. Garousi, V., et al.: Introduction to the special issue on: grey literature and multivocal literature reviews (MLRs) in software engineering. Inf. Softw. Technol. **141** (2022)
28. Gill, A., et al.: Scaling for agility: a reference model for hybrid traditional-agile software development methodologies. Inf. Syst. Front. **20**(2), 315–341 (2018). https://doi.org/10.1007/s10796-016-9672-8
29. Gill, A., Chew, E.: Configuration information system architecture: insights from applied action design research. Inf. Manage. **56**(4), 507–525 (2019)
30. Gregor, S.: Reflections on the practice of design science in information systems. In: Engineering the Transformation of the Enterprise: A Design Science Research Perspective, pp. 101–113 Springer (2022)
31. Gregor, S., Hevner, A.: Introduction to the special issue on design science. IseB **9**(1), 1–9 (2011)
32. Gregor, S., Jones, D.: The anatomy of a design theory. J. Assoc. Inf. Syst. **8**(5), 312–335 (2007)
33. Hevner, A., et al.: A pragmatic approach for identifying and managing design science research goals and evaluation criteria. In: AIS SIGPrag Pre-ICIS workshop on Practice-based Design and Innovation of Digital Artifacts (2018)
34. Hevner, A., et al.: Design science in information systems research. MIS Q. **28**(1), 75–105 (2004)
35. Iivari, J., et al.: A proposal for minimum reusability evaluation of design principles. Eur. J. Inf. Syst. **30**(3), 286–303 (2021)
36. Iivari, J.: Distinguishing and contrasting two strategies for design science research. Eur. J. Inf. Syst. **24**(1), 107–115 (2015). https://doi.org/10.1057/ejis.2013.35
37. Kamei, F., et al.: Grey literature in software engineering: a critical review. Inf. Softw. Technol. **138**, 106609 (2021)
38. Kosicki, M., et al.: Towards designops design development, delivery and operations for the AECO industry. In: Design Modelling Symposium Berlin, pp. 61–70. Springer (2022)
39. Kuhn, T.: The Structure of Scientific Revolutions. University of Chicago Press (2012)
40. Kuhrmann, M., et al.: What makes agile software development agile? IEEE Trans. Softw. Eng. **48**(9), 3523–3539 (2022). https://doi.org/10.1109/TSE.2021.3099532
41. Lee, S., et al.: When and how to use AI in the design process? implications for human-AI design collaboration. Int. J. Hum. Comput. Interact. **41**(2), 1569–1584 (2025)
42. Luo, Y.: Designing With AI: A systematic literature review on the use, development, and perception of AI-enabled UX design tools. Adv. Hum. Comput. Interact. **1**, 3869207 (2025)
43. McKay, J., Marshall, P.: The dual imperatives of action research. Inf. Technol. People **14**(1), 46–59 (2001)
44. Miles, M., et al.: Qualitative Data Analysis: A Methods Sourcebook. Sage Publications, Thousand Oaks, CA (2014)
45. Moreschini, S., et al.: The evolution of technical debt from devops to generative AI: a multivocal literature review. J. Syst. Softw. **231**, 112599 (2026)
46. Mullarkey, M., Hevner, A.: An elaborated action design research process model. Eur. J. Inf. Syst. **28**(1), 6–20 (2019)

47. Nagle, T. et al.: The research method we need or deserve? a literature review of the design science research landscape. Commun. Assoc. Inf. Syst. **50**, 1, 358–395 (2022). https://doi.org/10.17705/1CAIS.05015
48. Niehaves, B.: On episemological diversity in design science: new vistas for a design-oriented IS research? In: ICIS 2007 Proceedings (2007)
49. Niu, X., et al.: Research on the transformation path of devops in the digital era. In: 2024 26th International Conference on Advanced Communications Technology, pp. 248–251 IEEE (2024)
50. Nonaka, I.: A dynamic theory of organizational knowledge creation. Organ. Sci. **5**(1), 14–37 (1994). https://doi.org/10.1287/orsc.5.1.14
51. Parizi, R., et al.: How has design thinking being used and integrated into software development activities? a systematic mapping. J. Syst. Softw. **187**, 111217 (2022). https://doi.org/10.1016/j.jss.2022.111217
52. Persohn, L.: Curation as methodology. Qual. Res. **21**(1), 20–41 (2021). https://doi.org/10.1177/1468794120922144
53. Raabe, J.-P., et al.: Towards Phenomenon-driven Design Science Research (2021)
54. Reining, S., et al.: Knowledge accumulation in design science research: ways to foster scientific progress. ACM SIGMIS Datab. Database Adv. Inf. Syst. **53**(1), 10–24 (2022)
55. Schmid, S.: Bridging the gap: analyzing collaboration between practitioners and researchers across different stages of the design science research process. In: Technologies for Organizations and Society: Balancing Sustainable Innovations and Social Implications, pp. 439–455 Springer (2025)
56. Sein, M., et al.: Action design research. MIS Q. **35**(1), 37–56 (2011)
57. Siau, K., et al.: Information systems analysis and design: past revolutions, present challenges, and future research directions. Commun. Assoc. Inf. Syst. **50**(1), 33 (2022)
58. Simon, H.: The Sciences of the Artificial. The MIT Press, Cambridge, USA (1996)
59. Stahl, B.: The ideology of design: a critical appreciation of the design science discourse in information systems and Wirtschaftsinformatik. In: Wissenschaftstheorie und gestaltungsorientierte Wirtschaftsinformatik, pp. 111–132 Springer (2009)
60. Venable, J., et al.: FEDS: a framework for evaluation in design science research. Eur. J. Inf. Syst. **25**(1), 77–89 (2016)
61. Vom Brocke, J., Maedche, A.: The DSR grid: six core dimensions for effectively planning and communicating design science research projects. Electron. Mark. **29**(3), 379–385 (2019)
62. Wiesche, M., et al.: Digital desire paths: exploring the role of computer workarounds in emergent information systems design. Eur. J. Inf. Syst. **33**(2), 145–160 (2024)

Design Science Research in the Age of Generative AI: A Systematic Literature Review and Research Agenda

Ransome Bawack[1]($\boxtimes$) (iD) and Kevin Carillo[2] (iD)

[1] 8 Rte de La Jonelière, 44300 Nantes, France
`rbawack@audencia.com`
[2] TBS Education, 20 Bd Lascrosses, 31000 Toulouse, France

Abstract. Generative artificial intelligence (GenAI) challenges several assumptions that have long underpinned design science research (DSR), including that artifacts can be clearly bounded, evaluation results can be treated as evidence about stable contributions, and prescriptive knowledge can travel across contexts with limited boundary specification. This paper critically reviews how empirical DSR studies engage with these tensions when designing GenAI artifacts. Using a PRISMA-guided systematic literature review, we analyze the emerging corpus through a configuration-centric lens that examines how studies define the artifact, stabilize evidence, formulate reusable knowledge, and address governance in use. The review shows that most GenAI artifacts are not bounded tools but socio-technical configurations that combine models, prompts, retrieval mechanisms, orchestration logic, and human oversight. It also identifies recurring weaknesses, including under-specified artifact boundaries, limited configuration disclosure, unstable evaluation evidence, incomplete portability conditions, and governance concerns that are acknowledged but rarely operationalized as design features. Based on these findings, we argue that GenAI should be treated as a boundary condition that intensifies key DSR challenges and requires adaptations in artifact conceptualization, evaluation, reporting, and the formulation of reusable design knowledge.

Keywords: Generative artificial intelligence · Design Science · Systematic Literature Review

1 Introduction

Generative artificial intelligence (GenAI) refers to a family of models, such as large language models (LLMs), capable of producing novel content such as text, code, and images, typically through large-scale pretraining and subsequent adaptation via prompting, retrieval, or fine-tuning [1]. This paper analyzes design science research (DSR) on GenAI artifacts, which are IT artifacts whose core functionality depends on generative capacity. Before GenAI, the DSR body of knowledge assumed that the IT artifact can be meaningfully bounded, that evaluation can generate evidence about a sufficiently stable

J. vom Brocke et al. (Eds.): DESRIST 2026, LNCS 16606, pp. 281–296, 2026.
https://doi.org/10.1007/978-3-032-28313-9_16

designed object, and that prescriptive knowledge can be expressed in forms that remain useful beyond the original instantiation when relevant boundary conditions are specified [2–6].

GenAI challenges these assumptions because its outputs are probabilistic, sensitive to prompting and context, and often dependent on external components that are partly outside the researcher's control, such as vendor-managed models, evolving application programming interfaces (APIs), safety layers, and changing retrieval corpora. Under such conditions, the artifact is often no longer well represented as a bounded IT instance. Instead, it increasingly appears as a socio-technical configuration whose behavior is jointly produced by model/version, prompt regime, retrieval, and data provenance, orchestration logic, and governance controls. This shift reactivates longstanding questions in information systems research (IS) in general and DSR in particular about what the IT artifact is, how it should be bounded analytically, and how artifact claims relate to theoretical claims [7–9].

Despite the rapid growth of DSR for GenAI artifacts, how empirical DSR studies are addressing these GenAI-driven challenges, and what adjustments are required if DSR is to remain rigorous, relevant, and cumulative for GenAI artifacts, remain unclear. Without a critical exploration of this issue, results from DSR studies on GenAI artifacts risk remaining anecdotal and conceptually limited to instantiations. This paper examines how GenAI exposes tensions in DSR's justification of claims about that artifact through evaluation, abstraction, and theorization. Systematic literature reviews (SLRs) are well-suited to this objective because they enable the integration of dispersed evidence, the identification of recurrent patterns, and the articulation of mechanisms and boundary conditions that support cumulative theorizing [10, 11]. Thus, we systematically synthesize empirical DSR on GenAI artifacts to theorize GenAI as a boundary condition for DSR and to derive a research agenda for extending DSR's treatment of artifact conceptualization, evaluation, cumulative knowledge formats, and reporting norms. Guided by this objective, we address the following research questions:

RQ1 (Foundations): What methodological and epistemic commitments in the DSR knowledge base are most relevant to GenAI artifacts?

RQ2 (Boundary condition): How does the emerging DSR literature on GenAI artifacts align with, extend, or expose gaps in those commitments?

RQ3 (Agenda): How can future research contribute to addressing the gaps identified?

We make three main contributions. First, we clarify the DSR commitments most consequential for GenAI artifact research and propose a configuration-centric framework for analyzing artifact boundary, evidence, portability, and governance. Second, we synthesize how DSR studies on GenAI artifacts are currently designed and evaluate the artifacts, highlighting recurring practices and systematic weaknesses. Third, we derive a research agenda specifying where DSR requires explicit methodological and reporting extensions to produce rigorous and reusable design knowledge under GenAI conditions.

2   Analyzing DSR Foundations in the GenAI Era

This section introduces a configuration-centric framework for analyzing how GenAI acts as a boundary condition for DSR. The framework is primarily an analytic lens, but it also has normative implications because it highlights where DSR may require revision or extension to clarify how GenAI sharpens longstanding DSR questions about artifact definition, evaluation, cumulative knowledge, and practical validity. The framework has four main dimensions.

The first dimension is artifact composition and boundary. Traditional DSR often treats the artifact as a sufficiently bounded IT instantiation that can be evaluated as a coherent object [4, 5]. GenAI complicates this assumption because the behavior of a GenAI artifact depends not only on the model itself but also on prompts, retrieval sources, orchestration logic, safety constraints, and human oversight. For this reason, the artifact is often better understood not as a standalone tool but as a configuration in use. It means that some elements previously treated as implementation details may now fall within the artifact boundary because they materially shape its behavior. By contrast, context refers to the organizational setting, domain, stakeholder environment, and institutional conditions in which the artifact is used and evaluated. Distinguishing boundaries from context is therefore essential.

The second dimension is evidentiary stability. DSR assumes that evaluation can provide interpretable evidence about whether an artifact meets its objectives under sufficiently stable conditions [12, 13]. GenAI makes this more difficult because outputs are probabilistic, sensitive to prompt variations, and vulnerable to drift due to vendor updates, API changes, and evolving retrieval corpora. Under such conditions, evaluation results are only credible if the configuration that produced them is sufficiently stabilized and disclosed. Transparency and replication, therefore, become constitutive requirements for inference rather than optional reporting improvements [14, 15].

The third dimension is cumulative portability, which refers to whether GenAI-DSR studies produce prescriptive knowledge that remains reusable across settings once the relevant mechanisms and boundary conditions are made explicit. A core ambition of DSR is to produce prescriptive knowledge that remains useful beyond a single instantiation, for example, in the form of design principles or design theories [2, 3, 16]. GenAI raises the threshold for such portability because reusable knowledge must specify which configuration elements must remain stable, which may vary, and which governance or drift-management assumptions travel with the design. Without such specification, prescriptive knowledge risks becoming brittle rather than cumulative.

The fourth dimension is governance-conditioned pragmatic validity. DSR has long emphasized utility and relevance in context [17, 18]. GenAI does not displace this concern, but it makes utility inseparable from accountability. A system may appear useful in a pilot while still being unsafe, biased, opaque, or unacceptable at scale. Practical validity must therefore be assessed not only in terms of whether the artifact works, but also for whom, under what oversight, and under what risk and accountability conditions.

These four dimensions are analytically distinct but conceptually interdependent. A single artifact may be socio-technical, under-specified, difficult to evaluate, and weakly portable at the same time. Figure 1 summarizes the components of the configuration-centric framework, which should therefore be read as a framework for analyzing how GenAI exposes tensions in DSR and where more explicit methodological and reporting guidance is needed. The contextual foundations derived from seminal DSR literature capture the elements typically used to describe and justify a study: problem framing and design goal, justificatory knowledge, contribution type and novelty locus, application

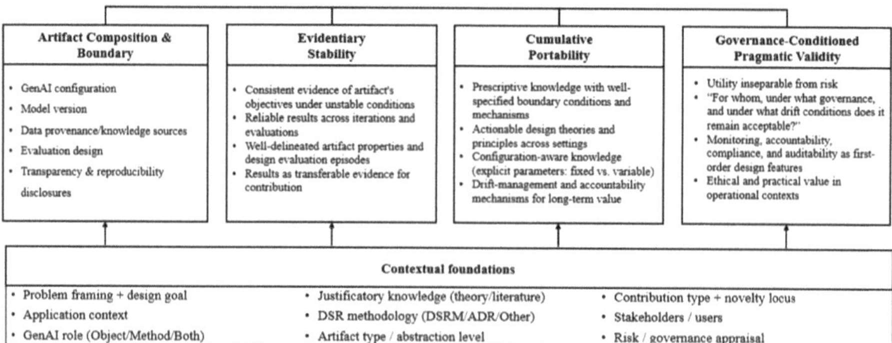

Fig. 1. Analytic framework linking artifact boundary, evidence, portability, and pragmatic validity in DSR research on GenAI artifacts.

context, DSR methodology, stakeholders/users, GenAI role, artifact type/abstraction level, and risk/governance appraisal. The arrows pointing to the four dimensions from the contextual foundations indicate that the four central dimensions are grounded in and interpreted through these established DSR descriptors. The four boxes represent the framework's focal analytical dimensions: artifact composition and boundary, evidentiary stability, cumulative portability, and governance-conditioned pragmatic validity. The lines connecting them indicate their mutual dependence, showing that choices about artifact boundary shape evaluation, portability, and governance claims. In coding and synthesis of the extant literature, the contextual foundations structured data extraction, while the four dimensions guided cross-study comparison and interpretation (details in the next section).

3   Method

3.1   Review Design

We conducted an SLR to synthesize how DSR is being enacted in relation to GenAI and to assess whether and how GenAI functions as a boundary condition that reshapes DSR assumptions about artifacts, evidence, cumulation, and pragmatic validity. Consistent with established IS guidance on review rigor and transparency, we report the review process in accordance with the Preferred Reporting Items for Systematic reviews and Meta-Analyses (PRISMA) 2020 guidelines [19].

To analyze and compare GenAI-DSR studies, we used the configuration-centric DSR framework as an interpretive lens. The framework guided both coding and synthesis by structuring interpretation around artifact composition & boundary, evidentiary stability, cumulative portability, and governance-conditioned pragmatic validity. For transparency and comparability, the core synthesis table was organized using the following conceptual foundation elements (columns), extracted for each included study: problem framing + design goal, application context, GenAI role (Object/Method/Both), justificatory knowledge (theory/literature), DSR methodology (DSRM/ADR/Other), artifact type/abstraction level, contribution type + novelty locus, stakeholders/users, risk/governance appraisal.

3.2 Information Sources and Search Strategy

To identify relevant GenAI-DSR studies, we searched seven bibliographic sources: Web of Science, Business Source Complete, ScienceDirect, SAGE Journals, Taylor & Francis Online, Wiley Online Library, and the AIS eLibrary. In addition, we conducted a backward reference list screening of all retained articles to assess the full text. Searches were last consulted on January 27, 2026.

We implemented a high-recall strategy that queried "anywhere" (Topic/Anywhere/All fields/All text, depending on platform) using a core string and syntax-adapted variants: ("design science") AND ("generative ai" OR "generative artificial intelligence" OR ChatGPT), with minor expansions where supported (e.g., "design science research"/DSR and equivalent GenAI terms). We applied no date restrictions, and we avoided restrictive document-type filters at the query stage to reduce the risk of inadvertently excluding relevant work.

We included studies that were published in English and met at least one of two relevance conditions: (a) the study uses DSR to design and evaluate a GenAI-enabled artifact (GenAI as the object of design), or (b) the study uses a GenAI artifact to support the DSR methodology/process (GenAI as a methodological instrument to understand when GenAI enters the design/evaluation process itself and thereby modifies DSR practice). We excluded conceptual-only publications (e.g., commentaries, position pieces, speculative frameworks without an enacted DSR instantiation and corresponding artifact/method instantiation) and publications that mentioned GenAI or DSR only tangentially.

All retrieved records were screened in two stages: title/abstract screening followed by full-text assessment against the predefined inclusion and exclusion criteria. Two reviewers independently screened each record at each stage and documented inclusion decisions. Disagreements were resolved through discussion until consensus was reached; a third reviewer was available to adjudicate if needed. Screening and eligibility decisions were conducted manually, without automated tools (e.g., machine learning-based prioritization).

3.3 Data Extraction and Coding

Data were extracted from each included full text by two reviewers working independently, using a structured coding form, with discrepancies reconciled through discussion. No automation tools were used for extraction or verification. The extraction scheme was designed to enable a configuration-centric interpretation while remaining anchored in DSR-relevant descriptors. The primary outputs of extraction were (1) the synthesistable columns listed above and (2) supporting evidence notes (short paraphrases or brief excerpts) used to justify coding and later interpretations. When information was missing or ambiguous, we coded it conservatively as "not reported/unclear" rather than imputing. Given the heterogeneity of design artifacts and evaluation approaches in GenAI-DSR work, we assessed study quality using an explicit appraisal rubric applied independently by two reviewers. The rubric focused on threats most salient to configuration-dependent artifacts: clarity of artifact description, evaluation rigor, transparency of GenAI configuration, and alignment between evidence and contribution claims. Disagreements were resolved by consensus. Figure 2 summarizes the extraction results.

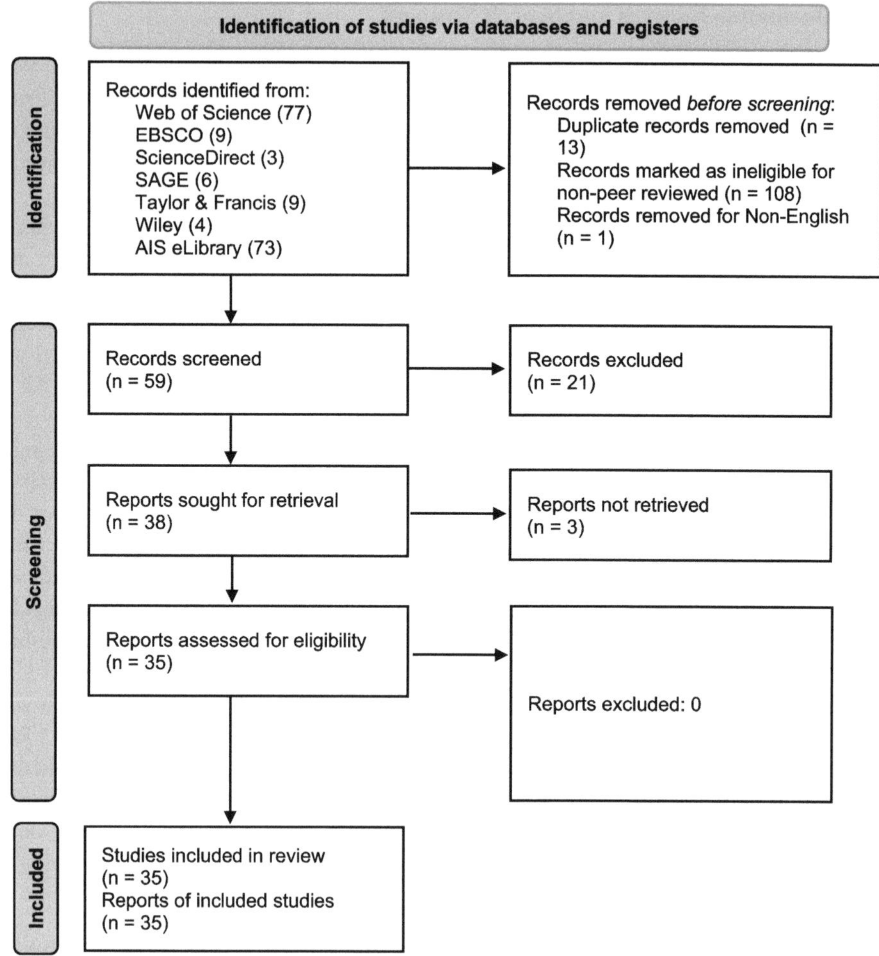

Fig. 2. Data extraction process.

3.4 Synthesis and Analysis

We conducted a structured qualitative synthesis oriented to explanation rather than aggregation of effect sizes. Studies were first organized by GenAI role (object of design (17 studies), methodological instrument (3 studies), or "both" (15 studies)) and then compared using the synthesis-table columns to identify recurring design patterns, evaluation logics, and contribution types. Eligibility for each synthesis strand was determined by tabulating study characteristics against the planned groupings and assigning each study to the appropriate group.

To support interpretive consistency, we standardized terminology across papers (e.g., harmonizing labels for DSR approaches and artifact abstraction levels). We treated missing information as "not reported" without statistical imputation, given the qualitative nature of the synthesis. We examined heterogeneity qualitatively through subgroup comparisons (e.g., by GenAI role, application context, and contribution locus) and traced divergences to differences in methodological choices and disclosure practices. Robustness was assessed through sensitivity checks on coding (e.g., re-coding a subset and verifying that central themes and gap claims persisted) and by comparing conclusions when focusing on higher-rigor studies per the appraisal rubric.

To assess the risk of bias due to missing results (reporting bias), we examined selective reporting signals that are consequential for configuration-dependent artifacts (e.g., absent configuration details or under-specified evaluation protocols) and reflected these limitations in the synthesis. Finally, we assessed confidence in each synthesized claim using a narrative certainty judgment (high/moderate/low) based on convergence across studies, methodological rigor, transparency, and contextual consistency.

4   Results

4.1   Artifact Composition and Boundary

A central regularity in the corpus is that the artifact is rarely a bounded IT instance whose behavior can be attributed solely to researcher-authored logic. Instead, most artifacts are better described as compositional ensembles in which an LLM is embedded within retrieval infrastructures, orchestration workflows, and interaction scaffolds that discipline generative behavior. In our coding, pipeline-style architectures appear in most studies (25/35), and retrieval augmentation is a common boundary-defining element (20/35), sharpening a longstanding DSR concern regarding what belongs to the artifact and what belongs to the context.

A first and dominant pattern positions GenAI as one component within a system-level artifact whose identity is defined by how generation is grounded, constrained, and integrated. Studies that design retrieval-augmented assistants make the artifact boundary explicit as a multi-stage pipeline that includes document ingestion, chunking, embedding, retrieval, and response generation, rather than treating it as a chatbot in isolation [20, 21]. In manufacturing, the boundary is thickened further through vector stores, knowledge graphs, and citation-grounded answering, making provenance logic part of the artifact's mechanism [22]. Likewise, real-time text-to-graph query systems locate novelty in intermediate representations and query-execution boundaries rather than in the LLM alone [23].

A second pattern treats GenAI as part of an agentic or orchestration architecture. Here, intelligence emerges from the coordination of specialized agents, tools, and inter-action protocols, so the artifact cannot be bounded at the level of a single model or interface without misrepresenting the mechanism [24, 25]. The strongest contributions in this stream, therefore, situate novelty in orchestration choices such as task decomposition, tool constraints, and coordination logic.

A third pattern incorporates human oversight and validation into the artifact boundary. In these studies, the working artifact is the socio-technical configuration that makes generative behavior acceptable in use, not the generative component alone [26–29]. However, human oversight may be constitutive of the artifact in some cases and contextual in others, depending on the contribution claim. This distinction also helps separate a socio-technical artifact from an underspecified boundary: the former deliberately includes human and governance elements as part of the design, whereas the latter leaves decisive configuration elements unclear [27, 30].

Overall, the corpus suggests that GenAI sharpens rather than replaces existing DSR boundary concerns. Where studies explicitly define the artifact as a configuration-in-use, they make evaluation and contribution claims more interpretable. Where they do not, novelty attribution and reusability become harder to justify.

4.2 Evidentiary Stability

A central epistemic problem is that with GenAI artifacts, DSR evidence becomes hard to interpret when the evaluated configuration is unstable or incompletely disclosed. Across the corpus, many studies reaffirm a core DSR commitment that evaluation is the warrant for contribution claims [5, 13]. Yet with GenAI, evidence is credible only when it can be tied to a sufficiently specified configuration, including model version, prompt set, retriever settings, corpus version, and tool constraints. In this sense, evidentiary stability is where the paper's broader epistemic concern becomes empirical: what researchers evaluate determines what they can legitimately claim.

The strongest studies pursue stability through four recurring strategies: controlled comparison, robustness testing, iterative evaluation, and configuration disclosure. First, some studies use explicit baselines and controlled comparisons to position GenAI-enabled artifacts against non-GenAI or weaker-configured alternatives, thereby linking outcomes to design choices rather than vendor capability alone [20, 22]. Others compare families of retrieval-augmented generation (RAG) configurations under standardized tasks, turning the LLM from a black box into a parameterized design space [31]. Related work on natural-language-to-graph queries uses measurable evaluation harnesses to stabilize what counts as success and reduce ambiguity about what the artifact actually accomplishes [23].

Second, some studies address stochasticity through robustness-oriented testing. Repeated runs, structured judging, and simulation-heavy trials help reduce dependence on single outputs and make claims less brittle under output variance, especially in multi-agent and workflow-oriented artifacts [32]. Technical systems for extraction or learning similarly rely on repeatable benchmarks and systematic measurement to strengthen claims beyond illustrative demonstrations [33, 34].

Third, several studies pursue stability through iterative and multi-cycle evaluation. Action design research and repeated prototyping cycles use stakeholder feedback, successive revisions, and triangulation across qualitative and quantitative indicators to surface brittle prompts, grounding failures, and unanticipated misuse that one-shot evaluations may miss [26, 28, 35]. It extends DSR's relevance tradition, but under GenAI, it also becomes a practical strategy for making evidence more reliable over time [25, 28].

However, the corpus also reveals a recurring weakness: evidence often outpaces disclosure. Many studies report evaluation activity but under-specify the configuration that produced the results. Missing details about system instructions, prompt libraries, retriever settings, corpus composition, or tool constraints weaken the inferential chain from design decisions to artifact properties, evaluation results, and contribution claims. This problem is especially visible when studies refer only to broad classes such as "ChatGPT" or "GPT-4", despite likely sensitivity to model updates [25, 28]. Only a few report stable model identifiers or snapshots that would support faithful replication [23, 31, 32]. Prompt transparency is also uneven, as some document prompt logic without sharing reusable prompt artifacts, logs, or traces [27].

Overall, evidentiary stability emerges as a hinge condition for credible GenAI-DSR. Where studies stabilize and disclose the evaluated configuration, GenAI extends DSR toward configuration-aware testing. Where they do not, evidence risks collapsing into a transient runtime demonstration rather than a durable scientific contribution.

4.3 Cumulative Portability

DSR has always faced the challenge of making design knowledge travel beyond the original setting. GenAI makes this concern even more configuration-dependent and, therefore, more fragile. In the corpus, this ambition is evident in 23/35 studies that artic-ulate contributions in portable forms such as design principles, design requirements, guidelines, toolkits, frameworks, or architectural blueprints [24, 35–37]. The distinc-tive pressure introduced by GenAI artifact studies is the need to encode configuration dependencies into prescriptive knowledge.

A first portability pattern consists of codified prescriptive artifacts that package GenAI-specific design knowledge for reuse. Several studies translate experiential learn-ing into reusable guidance. For example, a card-based toolkit codifies UX guidelines and recommendations for GenAI assistants for multidisciplinary design settings [37]. Design principles for text-to-image systems similarly aim to travel beyond a single domain or prompt set by specifying how model behavior and interaction design should be con-trolled [38]. In process contexts, design requirements for LLM-supported knowledge acquisition are linked to theory and demonstrated through a multi-agent instantiation [24]. These studies validate a classic DSR aspiration (codifying mid-range prescriptions) while shifting the unit of prescription from static features toward configuration elements such as prompting structures, grounding strategies, and human validation points.

A second pattern expresses portability through architectures and implementa-tion blueprints. Multi-agent conversational systems combining retrieval and structured querying are presented as reusable designs for transparency-oriented answering [39]. Compliance-checking architectures similarly seek portability by specifying how LLMs, structured prompting, and tool-calling should be assembled to improve auditability [40]. Knowledge-grounding pipelines and hybrid advisory architectures follow the same logic by offering generalized design blueprints rather than one-off prototypes [21, 41].

A third, and especially instructive, pattern binds prescriptions explicitly to bound-ary conditions. Strategic foresight research, for example, specifies where automation is appropriate, where SMEs must remain in the loop, and how prompt decomposition and version control support portability under variability and drift [28]. Work on heteroge-neous LLM agents similarly shows that generalization is not about the artifact itself, but about the conditions under which particular agent designs outperform naïve prompt-ing or narrow the gap to fine-tuning [32]. This is where GenAI most clearly intensifies traditional DSR concerns, because portable knowledge must describe not only what to design but also the configuration assumptions that must accompany the design.

At the same time, the corpus reveals a recurring weakness. Many contributions are not configuration-complete, which limits their reuse as cumulative design knowledge.

Frameworks and methods sometimes remain silent about which parameters must stay stable for the guidance to hold [42, 43]. Boundary conditions are also often underspecified around provenance, retrieval corpus composition, and model/version dependence [20, 30]. Where these dependencies remain implicit, design knowledge risks becoming brittle rather than portable.

4.4 Governance-Conditioned Pragmatic Validity

In DSR studies on GenAI artifacts, pragmatic validity becomes inseparable from ethical acceptability and governance. Ethics provides the normative rationale - fairness, harm prevention, accountability, contestability, privacy, and legitimacy - while governance operationalizes these commitments in artifact design and evaluation. Across the corpus, "works in practice" is therefore increasingly re-specified as "works acceptably under accountability constraints". It extends DSR's relevance doctrine by showing that utility alone is insufficient when generative outputs may be biased, misleading, harmful, or difficult to challenge [44].

This shift is most visible in domains where outputs have institutional consequences. In public-management foresight, trustworthiness concerns include hallucinations, bias, interpretability limits, compliance and accountability requirements, and the risk that generative systems distort human reasoning; the proposed response is not full automation, but expert review as a condition of valid use [42]. Similarly, public-sector foresight work treats opacity, source-selection bias, and legitimacy risks as central design concerns and responds through SME validation, traceability structures, and stakeholder engagement [28]. In such studies, pragmatic validity is not simply whether the artifact fits the task, but whether it remains ethically and institutionally acceptable for particular users and decisions.

A second pattern is governance-by-design, in which traceability, verifiability, and contestability are built into the artifact itself. In civic transparency, a multi-agent RAG plus Text-to-SQL pipeline is justified not only by efficiency gains, but also by its ability to ground answers, reduce hallucinations, and support auditability [39]. In compliance checking, structured representations, clause decomposition, and RAG grounding are similarly used to contain errors and make outputs more defensible in high-stakes settings [40]. In financial-report question answering, evaluation focuses on relevance, faithfulness, and verifiability rather than on answer quality alone, making accountability part of the performance logic [20, 31].

Human oversight is the most common governance mechanism, but it takes different forms. In accounting automation, governance comprises human validation, privacy-conscious processing, and alignment with GDPR [25]. In public-sector foresight, SMEs act not merely as error correctors but as epistemic gatekeepers and legitimacy providers [28]. In startup support tools, by contrast, governance remains largely implicit, appearing more as cautionary guidance than as a designed accountability regime [27]. This variation suggests that human-in-the-loop is a family of governance arrangements whose validity depends on whether humans are positioned as validators, editors, auditors, or accountable decision owners.

The corpus also shows that ethics is often acknowledged without being fully operationalized. Studies frequently note risks such as bias, privacy breaches, misinformation, and hallucinations, yet stop short of specifying bias audits, monitoring routines, escalation procedures, or formal compliance mechanisms [27, 35, 39]. Even so, sensitive-domain studies make clear that privacy, safety, and fairness are not peripheral concerns: they are part of what makes the artifact practically valid in the first place [29, 30, 45]. Overall, GenAI strengthens DSR's relevance imperative, but only by making usefulness conditional on explicit, testable, and ethically grounded governance arrangements.

5 Discussion

Taken together, our findings show a cumulative logic regarding how DSR researchers define the GenAI artifact boundary conditions and what can count as evidence. The quality and specificity of that evidence condition whether design knowledge can travel as a portable prescription. Portability, in turn, is credible only when practical validity is specified under explicit governance conditions. Some of these are longstanding DSR concerns (boundary specification, evaluation rigor, contextual contingency, and generalization). Still, GenAI makes them materially sharper through vendor mediation, stochasticity, drift, prompt sensitivity, retrieval dependence, and governance requirements that now shape utility itself. The implication for DSR theory and method is that researchers must specify the configuration they designed, report the parameters that stabilize results, evaluate robustness and accountability alongside utility, and avoid claiming portability when boundary conditions, provenance assumptions, and oversight arrangements remain implicit.

5.1 Future Research Agenda

Table 1 presents our proposed future research agenda based on our findings. It is organized around the four analytic dimensions of the configuration-centric framework to show where GenAI most clearly pressures extant DSR assumptions and potential future research directions.

Table 1. Future research agenda for GenAI-DSR research.

Dimension	Key gap	Research direction	Example questions
Artifact composition and boundary	The distinction between artifact boundary and context is often unclear in GenAI ensembles	Develop a boundary doctrine for configuration-based artifacts	When is a system a bounded artifact vs. a socio-technical configuration? How should DSR handle vendor-managed components?

(continued)

Table 1. (*continued*)

Dimension	Key gap	Research direction	Example questions
Evidentiary stability	Under-specified configurations weaken evaluation claims	Design drift-aware, configuration-aware evaluation approaches	Which evaluation designs support claims under stochasticity and drift? What disclosure is minimally necessary?
Cumulative portability	Design knowledge is often not configuration-complete	Encode dependencies and boundary conditions into prescriptive knowledge	How can principles capture configuration dependencies without becoming brittle? Which conditions must travel across contexts?
Governance-conditioned pragmatic validity	Governance is noted but rarely tested as a design feature	Treat governance as part of the artifact's functional core	How can auditability, contestability, and accountability be designed and evaluated? Under what governance conditions is a GenAI artifact practically valid?

5.2 Theoretical Contributions

This study makes three related contributions to DSR scholarship. First, conceptually, it offers a configuration-centric framework for analyzing GenAI-related tensions in DSR. Rather than claiming that GenAI creates an entirely new ontology of artifacts, the framework refines and extends how artifact boundaries should be specified in GenAI-DSR by treating many artifacts as governed configurations-in-use rather than as static system instances. This conceptualization is grounded in the corpus's dominant design reality, where artifacts frequently combine retrieval, orchestration, and structured representations with an LLM core [22, 23, 39].

Second, the paper synthesizes extant empirical DSR on GenAI artifacts to provide systematic evidence showing where GenAI validates extant DSR commitments and where it exposes recurring misalignments. The review shows that DSR's core design-and-evaluate logic remains useful when studies treat evaluation as configuration-aware testing, for example, through benchmarking RAG variants, grounding strategies, or architectural alternatives [22, 31]. At the same time, it identifies recurring fragilities in boundary specification, configuration disclosure, and the attribution of outcomes to designed mechanisms rather than vendor capabilities [25, 27, 30].

Third, methodologically and programmatically, the paper translates these findings into a research agenda that specifies where DSR methods, evaluation approaches, and reporting norms must be extended so that contributions remain rigorous, relevant, and cumulative under GenAI conditions.

5.3 Limitations

The GenAI-DSR literature remains emergent and heterogeneous. Many studies are recent and exploratory, and reporting is uneven, particularly regarding configuration disclosure (e.g., model versioning, prompt regimes, provenance assumptions), which constrains replication and cumulative comparison. The evidence also appears clustered in particular application archetypes (assistants, RAG systems, compliance/transparency pipelines), potentially underrepresenting other organizational settings and long-horizon post-deployment dynamics. Also, our review relied on seven major bibliographic sources and English-language publications, which may exclude relevant work in other languages or in practitioner/grey literature. While we used dual screening and dual extraction to reduce subjectivity, interpretive coding inevitably involves judgment, especially when assessing boundary definitions and governance implications from heterogeneous reporting formats. Therefore, our analysis and conclusions drawn from the SLR should be considered with these limitations in mind.

6 Conclusion

This study argues that GenAI pressures DSR to rethink how artifact boundaries are specified, how evaluation evidence is interpreted, and how design knowledge is made portable and accountable. Empirically, the reviewed studies show a clear shift toward ensemble- and configuration-based artifacts in which models, prompts, retrieval mechanisms, orchestration logic, and governance controls jointly shape outcomes. Conceptually, it suggests that configuration specification should become central to how DSR defines the designed object and justifies contribution claims. Methodologically, it implies that DSR must strengthen its reporting and evaluation doctrines so that claims remain interpretable under stochasticity, drift, and vendor mediation. We therefore contribute a configuration-centric analytical framework, a critical synthesis of current GenAI-DSR practice, and a research agenda for extending DSR in ways that preserve rigor, relevance, and cumulative knowledge under GenAI conditions.

Disclosure of Interests.   The authors have no competing interests to declare that are relevant to the content of this article.

References

1. Banh, L., Strobel, G.: Generative artificial intelligence. Electron. Mark. **33**, 63 (2023). https://doi.org/10.1007/s12525-023-00680-1
2. Gregor, S., Kruse, L., Seidel, S.: Research perspectives: the anatomy of a design principle. J. Assoc. Inf. Syst. **21**, 1622–1652 (2020). https://doi.org/10.17705/1jais.00649
3. vom Brocke, J., Winter, R., Hevner, A., Maedche, A.: Special issue editorial –accumulation and evolution of design knowledge in design science research: a journey through time and space. J. Assoc. Inf. Syst. **21**, 520–544 (2020). https://doi.org/10.17705/1jais.00611
4. Hevner, M.: Park, ram: design science in information systems research. MIS Q. **28**, 75 (2004). https://doi.org/10.2307/25148625
5. March, S.T., Smith, G.F.: Design and natural science research on information technology. Decis. Support. Syst. **15**, 251–266 (1995). https://doi.org/10.1016/0167-9236(94)00041-2
6. Gregor, S., Hevner, A.R.: Positioning and presenting design science research for maximum impact. MIS Q. Manag. Inf. Syst. **37**, 337–355 (2013). https://doi.org/10.25300/MISQ/2013/37.2.01
7. Orlikowski, W.J., Iacono, C.S.: Research commentary: desperately seeking the "IT" in IT research - a call to theorizing the IT artifact. Inf. Syst. Res. **12**, 121–134 (2001). https://doi.org/10.1287/isre.12.2.121.9700
8. Iivari, J.: Distinguishing and contrasting two strategies for design science research. Eur. J. Inf. Syst. **24**, 107–115 (2015). https://doi.org/10.1057/ejis.2013.35
9. Lee, A.S., Thomas, M., Baskerville, R.L.: Going back to basics in design science: from the information technology artifact to the information systems artifact. Inf. Syst. J. **25**, 5–21 (2015). https://doi.org/10.1111/isj.12054
10. Paré, G., Trudel, M.C., Jaana, M., Kitsiou, S.: Synthesizing information systems knowledge: a typology of literature reviews. Inf. Manag. **52**, 183–199 (2015). https://doi.org/10.1016/j.im.2014.08.008
11. Templier, M., Paré, G.: A framework for guiding and evaluating literature reviews. Commun. Assoc. Inf. Syst. **37**, 112–137 (2015). https://doi.org/10.17705/1cais.03706
12. Peffers, K., Tuunanen, T., Rothenberger, M.A., Chatterjee, S.: A design science research methodology for information systems research. J. Manag. Inf. Syst. **24**, 45–77 (2007). https://doi.org/10.2753/MIS0742-1222240302
13. Venable, J., Pries-Heje, J., Baskerville, R.: FEDS: a framework for evaluation in design science research. Eur. J. Inf. Syst. **25**, 77–89 (2016). https://doi.org/10.1057/ejis.2014.36
14. Brendel, A.B., Lembcke, T.-B., Muntermann, J., Kolbe, L.M.: Toward replication study types for design science research. J. Inf. Technol. **36**, 198–215 (2021). https://doi.org/10.1177/02683962211006429
15. Hevner, A.R., et al.: Transparency in design science research. Decis. Support. Syst. **182**, 114236 (2024). https://doi.org/10.1016/j.dss.2024.114236
16. Jones, D., Gregor, S.: The anatomy of a design theory. J. Assoc. Inf. Syst. **8**, 312–335 (2007). https://doi.org/10.17705/1jais.00129
17. Holmström, J., Ketokivi, M., Hameri, A.-P.: Bridging practice and theory: a design science approach. Decis. Sci. **40**, 65–87 (2009). https://doi.org/10.1111/j.1540-5915.2008.00221.x
18. van Aken, J., Chandrasekaran, A., Halman, J.: Conducting and publishing design science research. J. Oper. Manag. **47–48**, 1–8 (2016). https://doi.org/10.1016/j.jom.2016.06.004
19. Page, M.J., et al.: The PRISMA 2020 statement: an updated guideline for reporting systematic reviews. Syst. Rev. **10**, 89 (2021). https://doi.org/10.1186/s13643-021-01626-4
20. Mokashi, A., Puthuparambil, B., Daniel, C., Hanne, T.: Analysis of large language models for company annual reports based on retrieval-augmented generation. Information **16**, 786 (2025). https://doi.org/10.3390/info16090786

21. Tran, S.V.-T., et al.: Leveraging large language models for enhanced construction safety regulation extraction. J. Inf. Technol. Constr. **29**, 1026–1038 (2024). https://doi.org/10.36680/j.itcon.2024.045

22. Knollmeyer, S., Caymazer, O., Grossmann, D.: Document GraphRAG: knowledge graph enhanced retrieval augmented generation for document question answering within the manufacturing domain. Electronics **14**, 2102 (2025). https://doi.org/10.3390/electronics14112102

23. Hornsteiner, M., Kreussel, M., Steindl, C., Ebner, F., Empl, P., Schönig, S.: Real-time text-to-cypher query generation with large language models for graph databases. Futur. Internet. **16**, 438 (2024). https://doi.org/10.3390/fi16120438

24. Schinckus, M., Simonofski, A., Bono Rosselló, N.: Large language models for process knowledge acquisition. Bus. Inf. Syst. Eng. (2025). https://doi.org/10.1007/s12599-025-00976-w

25. Resende, M.: AI agents and no-code tools in accounting: a case study. FinTech. **4**, 65 (2025). https://doi.org/10.3390/fintech4040065

26. Schlimbach, R., Lange, T.C., Wagner, F., Robra-Bissantz, S., Schoormann, T.: An educational business model ideation tool – insights from a design science project. Commun. Assoc. Inf. Syst. **54**, 642–661 (2024). https://doi.org/10.17705/1CAIS.05423

27. Ahlgren, T.L., Sunde, H.F., Kemell, K.-K., Nguyen-Duc, A.: Assisting early-stage software startups with LLMs: effective prompt engineering and system instruction design. Inf. Softw. Technol. **187**, 107832 (2025). https://doi.org/10.1016/j.infsof.2025.107832

28. Picavet, M.E.B., Maroni, P., Sandhu, A., Desouza, K.C.: Human-machine collaboration for strategy foresight: the case of generative AI. Public Adm. Rev. (2025). https://doi.org/10.1111/puar.70048

29. Giunti, G., Doherty, C.P.: Cocreating an automated mHealth apps systematic review process with generative AI: design science research approach. JMIR Med. Educ. **10**, e48949 (2024). https://doi.org/10.2196/48949

30. Walter, D., Pengel, J., Steuck, P.-F., Di Maria, M., Knackstedt, R., Meissner, A.: Designing an AI companion to support informal caregivers in role transition: insights from a design science approach. BMC Nurs. **24**, 1165 (2025). https://doi.org/10.1186/s12912-025-03868-2

31. Iaroshev, I., Pillai, R., Vaglietti, L., Hanne, T.: Evaluating retrieval-augmented generation models for financial report question and answering. Appl. Sci. **14**, 9318 (2024). https://doi.org/10.3390/app14209318

32. Xing, F.: Designing heterogeneous LLM agents for financial sentiment analysis. ACM Trans. Manag. Inf. Syst. **16**, 1–24 (2025). https://doi.org/10.1145/3688399

33. Li, H., Gao, H., Wu, C., Vasarhelyi, M.A.: Extracting financial data from unstructured sources: leveraging large language models. J. Inf. Syst. **39**, 135–156 (2025). https://doi.org/10.2308/ISYS-2023-047

34. Xia, L., Shen, W., Fan, W., Wang, G.A.: Knowledge-aware learning framework based on schema theory to complement large learning models. J. Manag. Inf. Syst. **41**, 453–486 (2024). https://doi.org/10.1080/07421222.2024.2340827

35. Gimpel, H., Laubacher, R., Meindl, O., Wöhl, M., Dombetzki, L.: Advancing content synthesis in macro-task crowdsourcing facilitation leveraging natural language processing. Gr. Decis. Negot. **33**, 1301–1322 (2024). https://doi.org/10.1007/s10726-024-09894-w

36. Karst, F.S., Li, M.M., Leimeister, J.M.: SynDEc: a synthetic data ecosystem. Electron. Mark. **35**, 7 (2025). https://doi.org/10.1007/s12525-024-00746-8

37. Peláez, C.A., et al.: Toolkit for inclusion of user experience design guidelines in the development of assistants based on generative artificial intelligence. Informatics **12**, 10 (2025). https://doi.org/10.3390/informatics12010010

38. Herath, S., Bashardoust, A., Bole, Y., Shrestha, Y.R.: Design principles for text-to-image generative artificial intelligence creativity support tools for visual design. Eur. J. Inf. Syst. 1–26 (2026). https://doi.org/10.1080/0960085X.2026.2616042
39. Flores, N., Ramirez, C., Mauricio, D.: Expert Multi-agent conversational system using retrieval-augmented generation and dynamic text-to-SQL for government transparency. IEEE Access. **13**, 198178–198200 (2025). https://doi.org/10.1109/ACCESS.2025.3635530
40. Iversen, O., Huang, L.: Leveraging large language models for BIM-based automated compliance checking. Autom. Constr. **182**, 106707 (2026). https://doi.org/10.1016/j.autcon.2025.106707
41. Asemi, A., Sebrek, S.S., Pérez Garrido, B.: Transforming financial decision-making with hybrid artificial intelligence (AI). Manag. Decis. 1–34 (2025). https://doi.org/10.1108/MD-05-2025-1403
42. Panizzon, M., Janissek-Muniz, R., Borges, N.M., Cainelli, A.: Assessment method for generative AI technology in foresight and policy design in public management: expanding AI trustability for anticipatory governance. BAR - Brazilian Adm. Rev. **22** (2025). https://doi.org/10.1590/1807-7692bar2025240196
43. Bonnet, S., Teuteberg, F.: Unfolding the potential of generative artificial intelligence. Int. J. Knowl. Manag. **21**, 1–25 (2025). https://doi.org/10.4018/IJKM.368223
44. Myers, M.D., Venable, J.R.: A set of ethical principles for design science research in information systems. Inf. Manag. **51**, 801–809 (2014). https://doi.org/10.1016/j.im.2014.01.002
45. Falegnami, A., Tomassi, A., Corbelli, G., Nucci, F.S., Romano, E.: A generative artificial-intelligence-based workbench to test new methodologies in organisational health and safety. Appl. Sci. **14**, 11586 (2024). https://doi.org/10.3390/app142411586

Toward a Science of the Unexpected: Serendipity as an Epistemic Mechanism in Design Science Research

Hanna Buyssens[✉] [iD]

ESCP Business School, Berlin, Germany
hbuyssens@escp.eu

Abstract. Design science research (DSR) is increasingly conducted in contexts in which neither the problem space nor the effects of artifacts can be fully specified in advance. Wicked socio-technical challenges, participatory settings with heterogeneous stakeholders, and technologies with emergent capabilities (e.g., generative AI) often yield outcomes that are unexpected yet epistemically significant. Nevertheless, prevailing DSR method guidance tends to treat such outcomes as anomalies to be reduced through iterative refinement rather than as resources for knowledge production. This paper advances Toward a Science of the Unexpected by conceptualizing serendipity as an epistemic mechanism that can be systematically incorporated into DSR. Building on research on serendipity, pragmatist epistemology, abductive reasoning, and the concept of epistemic objects, we develop a four-phase iterative model comprising (i) an unexpected encounter, (ii) recognize and reflect, (iii) abductive leap, (iv) materialization. We further derive three guiding principles (treating artifacts as epistemic objects, cultivating a prepared mind, and conducting reflexive evaluation) to complement refinement-oriented iteration with discovery-oriented inquiry. The paper contributes a conceptual foundation and methodological guidance for DSR scholars seeking to engage systematically with unexpected outcomes under conditions of emergence and uncertainty.

Keywords: Serendipity · Design Science Research · Abduction · Epistemic Objects · Iteration

1 Introduction

The history of scientific progress is often told as a story of meticulous planning and linear advancement. However, breakthrough innovation often emerges from episodes of disruption and fortuitous encounters with the unexpected. Serendipity, the phenomenon of making surprises and valuable discoveries by accident, has long served as a silent partner in scientific inquiry [1]. From the accidental molding of bacterial cultures that led to penicillin to the melting chocolate bar that inspired the invention of the microwave, significant insights emerged when observant minds encountered the unexpected [1, 2].

This paper presents an initial step toward a conceptual, theory-building account of serendipity in Design Science Research (DSR) [3]. Although serendipity has received

J. vom Brocke et al. (Eds.): DESRIST 2026, LNCS 16606, pp. 297–314, 2026.
https://doi.org/10.1007/978-3-032-28313-9_17

scholarly attention across fields, ranging from laboratory-based science to entrepreneurship, it remains comparatively undertheorized within the field of information systems (IS) research, and particularly within DSR. This, by itself, is surprising, because DSR increasingly engages with contexts that call for explicit attention to serendipity: wicked problems with evolving framings, emerging technologies with unpredictable capabilities and participatory design settings where artifacts are often appropriated in unexpected ways [4, 5].

DSR is commonly presented as a systematic approach to developing and evaluating artifacts that address organizational problems [6, 7]. Rooted in Simon's Sciences of the Artificial [8], many established approaches emphasize purposeful intervention, iterative build-evaluate cycles, and learning through progressively improving artifact utility and performance against predefined criteria [6, 7, 9, 10]. This orientation has enabled decades of rigorous DSR. At the same time, contemporary DSR increasingly operates in settings where evaluation does not merely confirm performance against stable criteria, but also reveals shifts in stakeholder values, emergent uses, and behaviors that reconfigure what the problem is and what constitutes a suitable solution [4, 5].

A prominent example is the rise of generative AI (GenAI) and Large Language Models (LLMs). These systems have fundamentally different epistemic properties than traditional technological artifacts because they carry emergent properties that often appear at scale and cannot be reliably inferred from earlier versions or design intentions [11, 12]. Designing these systems means that unexpected outcomes are not exceptions but almost expected. They can surface gaps between expectation and observation that invite further inquiry. However, treating all surprises as mere feedback for refinement risks missing moments where an anomaly signals that the underlying problem–solution space warrants reconsideration.

We therefore propose a complementary lens on DSR: a Science of the Unexpected, in which serendipity is not treated as luck, but as a potential epistemic mechanism through which surprise can become transferable design knowledge. Importantly, we do not claim that DSR ignores surprise, emergence or learning. Canonical frameworks acknowledge these things through iterative cycles [6, 9], guided emergence [10] and abductive reasoning [13]. However, an important distinction exists: surprise is an unexpected observation, such as an anomaly or unexpected outcome. Serendipity is what happens when researchers recognize that surprise as meaningful, investigate it carefully and turn it into design knowledge. In much of DSR, unexpected outcomes are typically treated as feedback within iteration cycles, oriented toward refinement, rather than being explicitly theorized as a mechanism for discovery and reframing. However, as the problems and solutions that DSR aims to tackle are becoming inherently more fluid [11, 12] and discovery is becoming more prominent within DSR practice [14, 15], this vocabulary of refinement alone may be too restrictive: it offers limited conceptual resources for explaining when an anomaly should count as an epistemic signal that legitimizes redirection and how such redirection can be converted into design knowledge. Against this background, we ask: *How can serendipity be conceptualized as an epistemic mechanism in DSR?*

To address this question, we synthesize concepts from the serendipity literature [1, 2, 16], abductive reasoning [13, 17–19] and Rheinberger's theory of epistemic things (here used as a basis for conceptualizing design artifacts as epistemic objects) [20, 21]. We develop an initial conceptual account of serendipitous discovery in DSR and specify its internal structure as a four-phase iteration cycle, through which unexpected outcomes can be turned into design knowledge and publishable knowledge claims.

Following Gregor's [3] taxonomy, we position this work primarily as a theory for analyzing, supplemented with explanatory elements that clarify how serendipitous discovery operates within design inquiry. The paper contributes to DSR in three ways. First, we conceptualize serendipity as an epistemic mechanism in DSR: while surprise denotes an unexpected observation (e.g., anomaly, breakdown, unanticipated use), serendipity denotes the disciplined process of recognizing that surprise as meaningful and converting it into legitimate design knowledge. Second, we articulate a four-phase iteration cycle (trigger, recognition, abductive leap and materialization) that makes explicit when and how anomalies can warrant reframing of the problem–solution space, and how such reframing can be translated into publishable knowledge claims. Third, we propose three guiding principles for structuring serendipity in practice, clarifying how researchers can remain open to discovery while sustaining rigor and traceability in contexts characterized by epistemic instability.

2   The Simonian Heritage and the Search Paradigm

DSR finds its ontological and epistemological roots in Herbert Simon's seminal work, the Sciences of the Artificial [8]. Within his opus, Simon established design as a rigorous endeavor by framing it as a purposeful, goal-oriented activity aimed at changing existing situations into preferred ones. Within this paradigm, design is articulated as a form of bounded, rational problem-solving. Designers do not seek optimal solutions but rather "satisficing" outcomes that are acceptable given the constraints [8]. Simon's search logic assumes that while problems may be ill-structured at the outset, they can ultimately be clarified and stabilized through systematic search and refinement [8, 22].

This technical rationality has provided the foundation for most DSR methodologies that dominate the field today. Canonical approaches, such as the DSR guidelines by Hevner [6], the DSR methodology (DSRM) by Peffers et al., [9], the action design research (ADR) method [10] and the more recent echelons-based DSR (eDSR) [7] stress the importance of purposeful intervention and evaluation against predefined objectives. Artifacts are broadly understood as constructs, models or instantiations designed as causal interventions intended to produce desirable outcomes [6]. Iteration serves as a primary mechanism for analytical refinement in which designers test a hypothesis, measure performance against predefined criteria, and then tweak parameters to better meet objectives.

Most of the methodologies that acknowledge emergence explicitly retain this Simonian assumption. ADR foregrounds organizational intervention and mutual shaping; however the emphasis on guided emergence still points toward intended outcomes. FEDS, the framework for evaluating design science [23], distinguishes between formative and summative evaluation, enabling learning during design; but formative evaluation primarily refines artifacts against evolving criteria. The question remains: when search itself presupposes a space to search within, how does DSR account for constituting entirely new spaces through encounter with the unexpected?

These limitations of predictability become visible in contexts marked by emergence, uncertainty, and interdisciplinary ambiguity [4]. In these "wicked" environments, the parameters of the "search" do not merely wait to be discovered, but they may shift as designers interact with the problem and context, inviting greater attention to processes of learning, discovery and serendipity instead of the more traditional logic of search and control. The designer is no longer searching for an existing point in a stable space, but is instead participating in the co-constitution of the problem and solution simultaneously [4, 24].

In this context, the artifact becomes a generative instrument for exploration rather than a finalized solution [4]. Iteration then serves not merely as a way to refine the outcome, but to actively explore and discover what could be possible. This shift is particularly pronounced in participatory socio-technical contexts, where multiple stakeholders interact and bring conflicting values [10, 25]. In such settings, design artifacts are often appropriated in unforeseen ways, revealing hidden affordances that the designer did not intend [4]. Here, the designer is not a sovereign problem-solver, but rather a facilitator navigating contested terrain, where surprise and deviations are constituent features of the design process itself [26].

These challenges suggest that while the traditional, rationalist paradigm of design remains valuable for well-structured problems, it may be insufficient for contemporary and future DSR practices that operate in interdisciplinary contexts marked by uncertainty. Nevertheless, the idea that design knowledge emerges through reflective engagement with surprising outcomes is not entirely new. Schön's [27] notion of the reflective practitioner already challenged this technical rationality by showing how designers learn through "reflection-in-action": when the context "talks back" unexpectedly, skilled practitioners reframe the situation rather than forcing it into a predefined solution. Similarly, Dorst and Cross [28] argue that in creative design, unexpected connections drive the process forward. These insights provide important micro-foundations for the present argument. However, they were developed primarily for individual design practice rather than for the methodological structuring of DSR inquiry. What remains less explicit is how such reflective encounters with surprise can be systematically incorporated into DSR as an epistemic mechanism for producing transferable design knowledge. This motivates a complementary epistemology that treats the unexpected and surprise not just as noise, but as a legitimate and productive source of knowledge production.

3   Serendipity as a Mechanism of Discovery in DSR

In this section we briefly touch upon the concept of serendipity. We describe the concept, how it positions within DSR and demonstrate how it can be used as a logic for iteration.

3.1   The Concept of Serendipity

To integrate serendipity into DSR, it is necessary to move beyond its colloquial use as a synonym for "luck." The term is often referred to as *the faculty of making happy and unexpected discoveries by accident* [29]. However, contemporary scholarship across fields, ranging from information science [30] to human-computer interaction [31] and biomedicine [32] has reconceptualized serendipity as a structured process that combines unexpected events with an active, prepared, and reflective mind.

Building on an extensive review of the literature, Busch [1] identifies serendipity as requiring the alignment of three necessary conditions: surprise, agency, and value. Chance may introduce the unexpected event, but it is human agency and interpretive effort that transform surprise into insight and value. Hence, serendipity is situated, effortful, and deeply embedded in ongoing inquiry. According to Busch, these three elements are necessary conditions that must align for serendipity to occur. Table 1 summarizes these conditions and illustrates how they manifest in DSR practice. Since these are interdependent aspects of a single epistemic event, they are not tied to specific stages of the DSR process. All three aspects need to be present in order for true serendipity to occur, making it distinctly different from randomness and blind luck.

Table 1. Conditions for Serendipity

Condition	Definition	Application in DSR
Surprise	An unexpected, unplanned, or unusual event that captures attention	Encounters with unanticipated user behavior or technical anomalies during prototyping
Agency	Human-driven actions involving recognition, interpretation, and purposeful effort	The designer's choice to investigate an anomaly rather than dismiss it as an error
Value	The subjective assessment of a discovery as meaningful or beneficial	The transformation of an unexpected observation into a new design principle or artifact feature

This understanding of serendipity aligns closely with pragmatist philosophy, which emphasizes action, experience, and reflection as the foundations of knowledge creation. Within the pragmatist tradition, inquiry unfolds through engagement with real-world situations that are inherently open-ended and evolving [33]. Actions are situated within a specific context, and because contexts change continuously, so do their outcomes. Pragmatism suggests treating these surprises not as noise or errors, but as signals that suggest that the current hypotheses or framing may be incomplete or erroneous [34], which can prompt abductive reasoning [17]. When researchers encounter surprises during (design) inquiry, they can either attempt to suppress them in pursuit of predefined objectives or engage with them reflectively as potential sources of learning. We argue that serendipity emerges in the latter case when surprise is recognized and interpreted as epistemically relevant.

Importantly, this interpretation positions serendipity not as a deviation from disciplined inquiry, but as a mode of discovery that operates within the design process. By foregrounding agency, reflection, and contextual engagement, serendipity also aligns with a pragmatist view of knowledge as provisional, practice-based, and oriented toward possible futures rather than fixed endpoints. In this sense, we argue that serendipity can be understood as a mechanism through which design inquiry advances in processes that allow or demand exploration.

The connection between serendipity and the pragmatist mode of abductive reasoning deserves closer attention, as these concepts are closely related. Abduction, as characterized by Peirce, refers to the process of generating plausible hypotheses from surprising or uncertain observations [35]. Unlike deduction (which derives consequences from theory) or induction (which generalizes from repeated observations), abduction is oriented toward discovery and exploration: it creates tentative explanations that guide further inquiry and action. When designers therefore encounter unexpected outcomes, deductive reasoning cannot explain them (since the rules do not predict the observation), and inductive reasoning is insufficient (because the pattern has not been seen before). Abduction, however, can provide an explanation by inferring a plausible explanation.

In DSR, abduction has already been presented and recognized as a central component of design theorizing [36], but, to the best of our knowledge, its connection to serendipity and serendipitous discovery has not yet been explored. We argue that serendipity, in fact, operationalizes abduction through material engagement: the artifact and its context serve as sources of surprise that actually trigger the abductive inference. Consequently, the iterative cycles of design become opportunities for encountering the unexpected and engaging in abductive sensemaking [37]. It differs from "plain abduction" because it encompasses more than an inferential leap; while abduction generates a hypothesis, serendipity includes a conversion process in which the researcher recognizes the anomaly and materializes it into transferable (and publishable) design knowledge (value).

3.2 Positioning of Serendipity in DSR

To position serendipity as a rigorous epistemic mechanism in DSR, we differentiate it from (and relate it to) the epistemic logics from the prevailing methodologies that define the field. This positioning requires care: established DSR approaches already acknowledge (to varying degrees) emergence, reframing, and formative evaluation. Our argument is not that existing frameworks reject surprise, but that they carry a difference in default orientation toward it. Most of the DSR methods treat anomalies as input for refinement within a broader goal-directed inquiry, whereas a Science of the Unexpected foregrounds it as a potential portal to reframe discovery. We refer to Table 2 for a structured analysis of the epistemic logics in the DSR frameworks.

To illustrate concretely: Hevner's [6] Three-Cycle Model frames DSR as a "search process" (guideline 6) to find effective solutions within a predefined problem space. DSRM [9] allows for "backward iterations", but those are typically treated as corrective measures to align the artifact with the initial project objectives. ADR [10] goes further by acknowledging "guided emergence," and "concurrent evaluation" acknowledging that artifacts are shaped by the unpredictability of organizational contexts. However, its orientation remains toward stabilization of the artifact and does not theorize how researchers might cultivate surprise as a discovery source, nor provide criteria for evaluating emergence-driven pivots. Similarly, eDSR [7] permits echeloned pathways that skip or reorder phases, managing complexity through structural adaptation. However, the focus remains on planning and structuring of DSR projects. Serendipity could act as the catalyst for "echelon jumping": an unexpected discovery at a lower echelon (e.g., a Demonstration echelon) may suddenly invalidate the current theoretical foundation, forcing an unplanned leap to a higher or entirely different echelon of design theory that was not part of the original research design.

Table 2. Comparative analysis of epistemic logics in DSR

Dimension	Search Paradigm (Hevner, 2004)	Process Model (Peffers et al., 2007)	Guided Emergence (ADR) (Sein et al., 2011)	Echelon DSR (eDSR) (Tuunanen et al. 2024)	Science of the Unexpected (Proposed)
Foundational Logic	Search & Optimization: Finding a solution in a defined space	Procedural Rigor: Sequential execution of research stages	Intervention: Mutual shaping of artifact and social context	Hierarchical Decomposition: Organizing DSR into self-contained echelons	Abductive Discovery: Converting surprises into new knowledge
Nature of the Artifact	Instrumental: Evaluated for performance/outputs	Final Output: The culmination of a planned process	Ensemble: A fusion of technology and organization	Intermediate Knowledge: Self-contained units of design/validation	Epistemic Object: A "probe" designed to reveal the unknown
Primary Mechanism	Iteration: To close the gap to a desired state	Nominal Sequence: To ensure methodological alignment	BIE Cycles: To stabilize the artifact socially	Echeloned Pathways: Concurrent execution of decision units	Serendipity Cycle: To capture and materialize sagacity
Researcher Stance	The Expert: Navigating a problem space	The Planner: Following a methodological map	The Participant: Co-creating with stakeholders	The Coordinator: Managing complexity via hierarchical logic	The Prepared Mind: Detecting and capturing "triggers
Accommodation of Surprise	Implicit in relevance cycle iteration	Acknowledged through backward iteration	Explicit via guided emergence and organizational shaping	Explicit via emergent echelon pathways	Central: Theorized as epistemic mechanism with internal structure

Note: This comparison highlights dominant orientations rather than absolute positions. Most frameworks accommodate multiple epistemic modes; the distinction concerns which mode is explicitly theorized and methodologically supported.

Based on this, we identify three elements that a Science of the Unexpected can contribute. (1) An explicit account of serendipity's internal structure. Existing frameworks acknowledge that reframing occurs, but the process through which anomalies transition from noise to signal remains implicit. (2) Methodological vocabulary for legitimate fundamental reframing. When researchers pivot or iterate due to unexpected findings, current frameworks offer criteria for evaluating artifacts against objectives, but not for evaluating the (epistemic) quality of the pivot itself. (3) A generative orientation toward surprise. Existing frameworks instrumentalise emergence toward expected outcomes. The unexpected is therefore accommodated but not theorized as an independent source of design knowledge.

3.3 Two Logics of Iteration: Refinement and Discovery

If serendipity is to serve as a rigorous epistemic mechanism, it must be grounded in the practices that structure DSR inquiry. The most fundamental of these, we argue, is iteration. Iteration is the repeated cycles of building and evaluating through which design knowledge emerges [6]. Yet iteration itself can operate according to different logics.

In many projects, iteration usually denotes refinement of the overall artifact between building and evaluating [6]. Evaluation produces feedback about performance, relative to predefined objectives, and subsequent iteration cycles aim to close the gap between current and desired performance [23]. Iterations are considered successful insofar as they converge the solution closer to the predefined criteria. We refer to this as refinement-oriented iteration.

Alongside refinement-oriented iteration, we propose a second mode of iteration, more explicitly grounded in serendipity: discovery-oriented iteration. Here, iteration between building and evaluating not only tests whether artifacts meet predefined criteria, but it is sparked by a surprising moment that reveals incompleteness in the current problem–solution space. In this mode, iteration is not only a convergence mechanism, but a mechanism for reframing, abductive theorizing and thus, divergence. Table 3 shows the distinct differences between the two iteration modes.

The difference between the two modes of iteration lies in epistemic purpose and is not unlike single and double loop learning where the former corrects action within an existing frame, while the latter questions and revises the governing assumptions and frames themselves: they produce different outcome kinds, demand different evaluation practices, and justify different knowledge claims [38]. Refinement-oriented iteration ensures convergence toward criteria, where success is primarily measured as improvements [39]. Discovery-oriented iteration focuses on reframing through surprise. During build and evaluation, outcomes may occur that do not simply indicate underperformance but actually signal underlying framing of incompleteness. These moments are not noise but act as epistemic triggers for new pathways for knowledge creation. Importantly, discovery-oriented iteration tends to precede refinement-oriented iteration: discovery-oriented cycles help open and stabilize the problem–solution space, after which refinement-oriented iteration can converge toward robust artifacts and well-defined evaluative criteria [4, 5]. In the next section, we describe a four-phase iteration cycle that operationalizes this discovery logic explicitly.

Table 3. Refinement-oriented iteration vs discovery-oriented iteration

Dimension	Refinement-oriented iteration	Discovery-oriented iteration
Primary goal	Converge on a better solution	Expand/reframe the problem–solution space
Problem status	Largely known / stabilizing	Uncertain, evolving, contested
Role of evaluation	Verify performance against criteria	Surface surprises and generate new inquiry
Unexpected outcomes	Deviations/bugs to eliminate	Epistemic triggers to investigate
Dominant reasoning	Deduction + induction (tuning, optimization)	Abduction (plausible explanations + pivots)
Iteration output	Improved artifact version	Reframed goals + new mechanism/theory + new problem space
Typical success metric	Criteria met; utility improved	Insight materialized into transferable knowledge
Risk if overused	Premature convergence; blind to emergence	Drift / opportunism if not disciplined

4   The Structure of Serendipitous Discovery

To understand how serendipity functions as an epistemic mechanism, we unpack its internal structure by synthesizing Busch's framework for conceptualizing serendipity [1] with insights from Sætre and Van de Ven's [17] four-step process for theory generation through abduction. We adapt this integrated framework to the DSR context to capture the distinctive temporal and material dynamics of iterative design work and the material role of artifacts in producing unexpected design knowledge. Figure 1 visualizes this process as an iterative cycle embedded within DSR build evaluate cycle [6, 10].

(1) **Encountering an unexpected outcome – the trigger**: During iterative design work, designers can encounter an outcome, behavior or pattern that deviates from expectations. In other words, they "observe an anomaly": a phenomenon that cannot be explained using existing knowledge [17]. In DSR, triggers can manifest as technical anomalies (the artifact behaves unexpectedly), unanticipated user responses (stakeholders appropriate the artifact in novel ways), or emergent affordances (the artifact reveals undesigned capabilities). This trigger is not random noise but contains latent information about the problem–solution space, which was not previously recognized. As Sætre and Van de Ven [17] note, anomalies do not exist objectively "out there"; they are perceived by attentive individuals as a deviation from their expectations (p. 688).

(2) **Recognize and reflect – prepared mind:** The prepared and trained mind (or prepared researcher) recognizes this trigger as potentially significant. Following Pasteur's dictum that "fortune favors the prepared mind", this phase requires what Glaser [40] termed "theoretical sensitivity", a combination of domain expertise, familiarity with relevant theories and a cultivated openness to deviation. For Sætre and Van de Ven [17] recognizing these anomalies requires grounding them both "up close" (in particular instances) and "from afar" (understanding their pervasiveness and context).

In DSR, the prepared mind encompasses domain knowledge, theoretical fluency across design theories and adjacent literatures, and crucially, a reflexive disposition toward inquiry rather than mere execution [41]. The prepared mind asks not, "how do we fix this deviation?" but "what might this deviation reveal?" This may require temporarily suspending commitment to initial problem framings to genuinely explore what the artifact's unexpected behavior might indicate.

At this point, DSR inquiry involves a methodological choice: not every unexpected outcome warrants immediate abductive theorizing. As shown in Fig. 1, researchers may choose to pursue the anomaly as a source of insight or deliberately either abort it, or park and document it for later. As an example of how such judgments might be guided, we suggest that researchers assess whether the anomaly has potential to generate one of the three knowledge claim types identified in recent validity research [42]: Does it suggest unexpected artifact utility compared to existing solutions or the state of the art (criterion claim)? Does it reveal how specific design features produce outcomes (causal claim)? Does it indicate boundary conditions—where the artifact does or does not work (context claim)? Anomalies with potential to generate at least one such claim warrant pursuit; those without may be documented and parked for later reconsideration. Additionally, pursuit should be consistent with affordable loss [43], meaning that exploratory probes should not jeopardize core project commitments, and the anomaly should be rendered reflexively evaluable through documentation practices (see Principle 3).

(3) **Generating plausible explanation – Abductive leap:** Upon recognizing the significance of the unexpected trigger, the designer engages in abductive reasoning to construct a plausible explanation of this unexpected observation [37]. As Peirce [35] formulated it: "The surprising fact C is observed. But if A were true, C would be a matter of course. Hence, there is reason to suspect that A is true." Following this logic, a new hypothesis ought to be generated that could render the surprising phenomenon understandable.

In DSR, the abductive leap might propose a revised problem framing, identify hidden stakeholder needs or suggest alternative theoretical lenses [4]. Importantly, the abductive leap should not be understood as an instantaneous flash of insight but as a disciplined, iterative practice of interpretation. Goldkuhl's [44] multi-grounding framework positions design knowledge development as iterative movement between empirical evidence, theoretical insights, and internal coherence, a process that Cronholm et al. [13] operationalize as structured alternation between inductive and deductive moves within DSR iterations. Through this process, designers reframe the problem space itself, constructing plausible explanations not in a single cognitive flash but progressively, through materially supported inquiry. The process might benefit from what Weick [45] called disciplined imagination, i.e., deliberate creative thought to avoid premature convergence. However, the criterion for evaluating surprise's potential is not validity or truth, but plausibility: which explanation, if true, would make the observed anomaly comprehensible [17].

(4) **Materialization – From insight to knowledge:** Finally, the researcher must materialize the selected hunch by enacting it within the ongoing design inquiry. The serendipitous event, in short, needs to be put into effect by going from "evaluating hunches" to emphasizing enactment [17]. This means embodying the discovery into artifacts, problem framings or design knowledge that can further guide the research community.

In DSR, materialization is not automatic, because the generation of plausible explanations does not guarantee design outcomes. The insight, in short, must be "put into effect" through deliberate design effort. This might involve a redesign of the artifact, articulation of design principles or the development of a mid-range theory. Essentially, materialization means moving from an indeterminate to a determinate situation, not closure, but sufficient clarity to enable productive next steps [46].

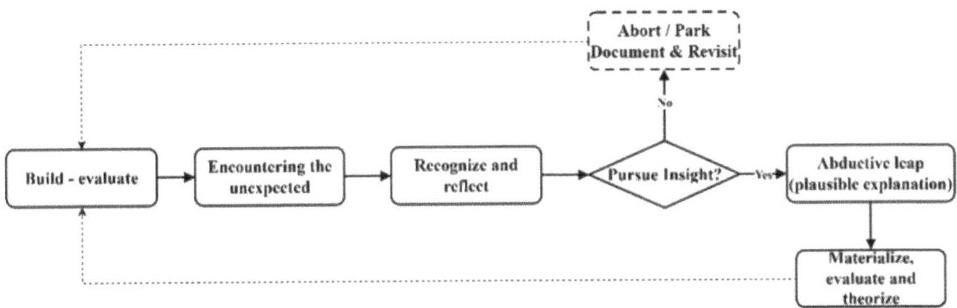

Fig. 1. Four-phase iteration cycle in DSR (Serendipity cycle)

Importantly, although these steps are discussed and presented as conceptually distinct and logically sequential, these four phases "may overlap, iterate, and unfold in stochastic ways over time" [17] (p.693). This recursive quality is particularly pronounced in DSR, where artifacts mediate between researchers, users, and contexts. Each iteration may create an opportunity for new triggers as the evolving artifact changes over time. Serendipitous discovery, therefore, can be seen as a recursive cycle embedded within iterative design practice, not as a linear problem–solution process. While grounded in abductive inquiry, serendipitous discovery in DSR goes a step further as it requires some aspect of materialization, where insight must be enacted through artifact, principles, or mid-range theorizing.

Illustrative Vignette: We illustrate the four phases through a documented DSR project by Buyssens and Viaene [4, 47], in which two industry partners and one research partner set out to design a blockchain-based exchange platform for the transparent trading and donation of potable water, explicitly emphasizing sustainability aligned with United Nations Sustainable Development Goal 6 (SDG 6: Clean Water and Sanitation). In the initial framing, the central goal was trustworthy, sustainable exchange, operationalized through traceability/provenance requirements for all transactions.

Encountering the Unexpected: As stakeholders interacted with early versions of the platform, the team encountered an unanticipated possibility: blockchain was not only useful for provenance, but it could also turn water into digital assets that could be traded and used for offsetting. This was not part of the original intent and emerged through iterative experimentation and stakeholder engagement.

Recognize and Reflect: Rather than treating this as scope creep, the team treated it as an epistemic signal: the artifact was acting as a probe that revealed hidden degrees of freedom in the problem–solution space. This interpretation was made conceptually legible by shifting the project's theoretical lens toward affordance theory, focusing on action potentials, not just intended features [47].

Abductive Leap: They hypothesized: if water can be digitized into tokens/credits, then sustainability could be advanced not only by transparent trade, but by creating incentive mechanisms that reshape behavior, making "offsetting water waste" feasible in the same way carbon credits operationalize emission offsets.

Materialization: The team reoriented the artifact toward tokenization and a secondary offset marketplace, which generated new requirements and culminated in generalizable design principles (prescriptive/provisional knowledge) for blockchain-based platforms. The team explicitly theorized through affordances (non-deterministic action potential) rather than linear causality.

5 Principles for Serendipity in DSR

The preceding sections conceptualize serendipity as a structured epistemic mechanism in DSR and unpack its internal logic as a four-phased cycle. We now synthesize these insights into an initial set of guiding principles that enable serendipity in the DSR process. The selection of these principles follows from Busch's three necessary conditions for serendipity (see Sect. 3.1 and Table 1).

For serendipity to occur there must be a source of *surprise*, which can be generated through the artifact design (see Principle 1). There must be the *agency* to recognize significance in those triggers (hence Principle 2 for cultivating a prepared mind). Finally, there must be practices that realize *value* by capturing and legitimizing unexpected discoveries rather than filter them out (hence Principle 3 for developing evaluation approaches that enable materialization). The abductive leap, while central to the mechanism, is a cognitive act that is enabled when these three conditions are in place.

We do not claim these principles are exhaustive. Serendipitous discovery is also shaped by contextual factors such as organizational conditions and resource constraints. The three principles focus on dimensions over which researchers have direct agency and are intended as reflective guidance for discovery-oriented iteration rather than prescriptive steps [39]. These principles apply most directly to DSR contexts characterized by epistemic uncertainty, co-evolving problem and solution space, or projects with emerging technologies; projects with highly stable contexts may find refinement-oriented iteration more than sufficient [4, 39].

5.1   Guiding Principle 1: Design Artifacts as Epistemic Objects

The first principle states that in contexts of uncertainty, artifacts should be constructed with a degree of "deliberate incompleteness" to allow them to function as epistemic objects [20, 21]. It draws on the philosophy of experimental science, particularly Rheinberger's distinction between "epistemic objects" and "technical objects" [20]. In pharmaceutical science and laboratory research, epistemic objects are relatively common. They specifically refer to entities whose unknown characteristics are the target of inquiry. They embody what we do not yet know and are characterized by "irreducible vagueness" and openness to ongoing investigation [48]. Technical objects, by contrast, are well-defined instruments with stable background conditions that enable experimentation but are not themselves under investigation. Epistemic objects, that eventually are well understood can transform into technical objects, but also vice versa.

A classic illustration is Alexander Fleming's discovery of penicillin. Fleming was growing Staphylococcus bacteria on petri dishes as part of routine lab work. These dishes were just tools for him (technical objects). However, when he returned to the lab after some time away, he noticed that some parts of his dishes had been contaminated by mold. Normally, this would have meant throwing them away as failed experiments. But Fleming noticed something unusual: the bacteria were not growing near the mold. There was a clear ring around it. Instead of discarding it completely, the mold and the surprise became the focus of his inquiry. In Rheinberger's terms, the dishes shifted from a technical object (a stable setup for routine culturing) into an epistemic object, a material configuration whose latent properties generated new questions [2].

Within the DSR context, this suggests that artifacts should not be conceptualized exclusively as solutions that need to be optimized, but they can also function as epistemic objects that generate questions, as much as they answer them. The artifacts are then seen as incomplete, with a capacity that continuously unfolds while revealing new aspects as researchers and users deal with them [21]. Whenever the artifacts are treated as complete solutions too early in the research process, they risk becoming purely technical objects, losing their capacity to generate surprises.

Practically, this principle involves resisting the pressure to "lock down" artifacts specification prematurely. A researcher might even deliberately maintain ambiguity in certain features (e.g., the emergent capabilities of GenAI applications [12]) allowing them to afford different things depending on the use and context, thereby opening new pathways within both the problem and the solution space [4, 49].

5.2   Guiding Principle 2: Cultivate a Prepared Mind

The second principle addresses the cognitive and dispositional capacities that enable researchers to recognize and act upon the serendipitous triggers. As discussed, serendipity does not just involve a happy accident, but also the "sagacity" or prepared mind that can perceive significance in surprise. This sagacity, as argued by Busch [1] and Dew [2], entails the combination of domain expertise, theoretical sensitivity and a disposition towards inquiry rather than mere execution. Akin to theoretical sensitivity in grounded theory methodology, researchers must cultivate this mindset in order to develop the capacity to recognize what could be significant in the data, and to give meaning to it

[40]. In the serendipity context, this translates to the ability to perceive unexpected observations not as noise to be filtered out but as potential signals worthy of investigation. The sensitivity is not innate but requires deep engagement with a domain, familiarity with relevant theories and frameworks, and a reflexive awareness of one's own assumptions and expectations, thereby providing researchers with the correct insight into pursuing or aborting the serendipitous trigger.

Returning to the example of Fleming, the prepared mind is exactly what transformed the contaminated mold from a potential error into an epistemic opportunity: without the expertise of Fleming in bacteriology and medicine as well as his interpretive sensitivity, the anomaly would likely have been discarded as a failed experiment [29].

For DSR researchers, cultivating a prepared mind involves several practices. First, a deep engagement with both the problem domain and the design theory provides the conceptual vocabulary needed to interpret the surprises meaningfully. Second, maintaining conversational openings and conceptual flexibility that invite unexpected connections, creates conditions for triggers to be registered [1]. Third, reflexive documentation practices of peripheral observations, anomalies, and perhaps even "interesting failures" may create a record from which serendipitous patterns can emerge later. Finally, researchers might deliberately expose themselves to perspectives outside their primary domain, as interdisciplinary cross-fertilization often enables [17].

5.3 Guiding Principle 3: Legitimize and Materialize the Unexpected Through Reflexive Evaluation

The third principle addresses how surprises can be captured and converted into legitimate design knowledge. Even when artifacts are configured to render surprises (Principle 1) and researchers are able to recognize their potential relevance (Principle 2), serendipitous insights can still fail to enter the knowledge base if the research logic treats them as an irrelevant deviation. In other words, serendipity cannot become epistemically productive by recognition alone, but it must become productive when it is methodically accommodated and evaluatively legitimized. This requires evaluation practices that do more than just verify whether an artifact meets predefined objectives as they must also be able to capture and translate unexpected outcomes into defensible contributions.

Continuing the Fleming example illustrates this. Fleming recognized the anomaly and documented that the mold inhibited bacterial growth, but he struggled to isolate and stabilize the active substance in a form that could be reliably reproduced and developed further. Historical accounts suggest that he eventually lost momentum and produced limited follow-up work after the early 1930s. Years later, two Oxford scientists, having their own serendipitous moment, stumbled on Fleming's article, and advanced penicillin through systematic purification and clinical development. In this sense, without proper evaluation the same serendipitous trigger can either remain an intriguing observation or become legitimate and transferable knowledge, depending on whether the inquiry is structured to stabilize, test, and materialize the unexpected [29]. Within DSR, evaluation thus functions as an epistemic gatekeeper: it determines which observations count as evidence and which are discarded. Conventional evaluation approaches (e.g. FEDS [23]) mostly emphasize assessment against predefined criteria, which is appropriate in stable problem contexts. However, they can prematurely foreclose learning in exploratory phases by treating deviations from expected behavior as errors rather than signals.

Practically, this implies the following in DSR evaluation practice: first, evaluation should be concurrent rather than sequential. This is something that has long been argued by ADR [10], in which building, intervention, and evaluation are interwoven to sustain learning while design commitments remain revisable. Second, evaluation should be collective and critical rather than purely confirmatory. Collective evaluation facilitates creative abduction by challenging assumptions and exposing emerging ideas to multiple perspectives [17]. Constructive criticism, in this context, can be highly productive [50]. Third, researchers should adopt reflexive evaluation practices that explicitly document and interpret unexpected outcomes and reflect upon the process itself [5, 51]. For example, expectation–outcome contrasts and reflective annotation during evaluation can create a record of where experience diverged from expectations, enabling abductive hypothesis generation and opening new research directions.

6   Limitations and Future Research

This paper develops an initial conceptual framework for serendipity in DSR. As a theoretical contribution, it remains provisional and invites future research. First, while we have articulated how serendipity operates (four-phase iteration cycle) and what conditions can enable it (three principles), we have not clearly demonstrated when serendipity-oriented approaches are appropriate versus when more Simonian search remains superior. As such, we recognize that there are some boundary conditions which make serendipity and discovery-oriented iteration more warranted. Namely when problem–solutions are uncertain and when the artifact exhibits emergent abilities (i.e. contexts with low problem and solution space maturity) [39]. Conversely, when objectives or project boundaries are fixed or highly constrained by budget and resources, researchers may find less opportunity for serendipity-oriented inquiry. Relatedly, "the decision gate" in Fig. 1 is mentioned but not fully operationalized. What criteria should govern whether to pursue an anomaly or to park it? When exactly should researchers just focus on refinement-oriented iteration versus discovery-oriented iteration? Future research could investigate how serendipity operates under varying conditions and develop more refined guidance for balancing openness with various constraints.

Second, the framework presents the four phases of serendipity as analytically distinct, even though in practice they are likely to overlap. In particular, the boundary between trigger and recognition may be difficult to specify, and the distinction between abduction and materialization may be less sequential than the model suggests [13, 17]. Future research could investigate whether researchers experience serendipity as discrete phases or as continuous processes.

Third, our principles emphasize researcher agency and design choices, but serendipitous discovery may be constrained by structural and institutional factors beyond individual control [1]. Funding and review regimes often favor predictable plans and linear narratives, making reframing hard to legitimize. Future work should examine how evaluation criteria, funding models, publishing norms, and doctoral training could better accommodate discovery-oriented DSR without sacrificing rigor.

Finally, we have emphasized serendipity's productive potential, but surprises can also be misleading or harmful. Future research should specify safeguards and evaluation practices for distinguishing fruitful anomalies from dangerous or spurious ones.

7 Conclusion

This paper proposes serendipity as an epistemic mechanism in DSR. Grounded in pragmatist epistemology, abductive reasoning, and Rheinberger's notion [20] of epistemic objects, we conceptualize how unexpected outcomes can be treated as legitimate epistemic signals and converted into defensible design knowledge rather than being dismissed as noise. The four-phase iteration cycle (unexpected encounter, recognize and reflect, abductive leap, materialization) offers an initial methodological vocabulary for legitimizing pivots when anomalies indicate an incomplete problem–solution space. The three guiding principles translate this cycle into actionable guidance for structuring discovery-oriented iteration alongside refinement-oriented iteration: designing artifacts as epistemic objects that generate surprise, cultivating the prepared mind that can recognize significance in anomalies, and adopting reflexive evaluation practices that capture and legitimize unexpected discoveries. For researchers navigating uncertain contexts, this provides conceptual legitimacy for pivots that might otherwise appear as methodological drift [4]. For the community, it addresses a gap between what researchers often do: adapt, pivot, learn from surprise, and what established methodologies explicitly describe. By naming serendipity as a legitimate mechanism with specifiable structure, we offer vocabulary that allows discovery-driven inquiry to be reported and accumulated as rigorous design knowledge, rather than retrospectively rationalized or quietly omitted from publication narratives.

References

1. Busch, C.: Towards a theory of serendipity: a systematic review and conceptualization. J. Manag. Stud. **61**, 1110–1151 (2024)
2. Dew, N.: Serendipity in entrepreneurship. Organ. Stud. **30**, 735–753 (2009)
3. Gregor, S.: The nature of theory in information systems. MIS Q. **30**, 611–642 (2006)
4. Buyssens, H., Viaene, S.: Reframing the problem space: a layered model for coevolving problems and solutions. In: DESRIST 2025 Proceedings, Montego Bay (2025)
5. Strong, D.M., Tulu, B., Agu, E., Pedersen, P.C.: Search and evaluation of coevolving problem and solution spaces in a complex healthcare design science research project. IEEE Trans. Eng. Manag. **70**, 912–926 (2020)
6. Bichler, M.: Design science in information systems research. Wirtschaftsinformatik **48**(2), 133–135 (2006). https://doi.org/10.1007/s11576-006-0028-8
7. Tuunanen, T., Winter, R., vom Brocke, J.: Dealing with complexity in design science research: a methodology using design echelons. MIS Q. **48**, 427–458 (2024)
8. Simon, H.A.: The Sciences of the Artificial, 3rd edn. MIT Press, Cambridge (2019)
9. Peffers, K., Tuunanen, T., Rothenberger, M.A., Chatterjee, S.: A design science research methodology for information systems research. J. Manag. Inf. Syst. **24**, 45–77 (2007)
10. Sein, M.K., Henfridsson, O., Purao, S., Rossi, M., Lindgren, R.: Action design research. MIS Q. **35**, 37–56 (2011)

11. Wei, J., et al.: Emergent abilities of large language models. arXiv preprint arXiv:2206.07682 (2022)
12. Woodside, T.: Emergent abilities in large language models: an explainer. CSET Center for Security and Emerging Technology (2024)
13. Cronholm, S., Göbel, H., Cao, L.: Abductive design science research: the interplay between deduction and induction. In: ACIS 2023 Proceedings (2023)
14. Seckler, C., et al.: Design science across disciplines: building bridges for advancing impactful business research. Schmalenbach J. Bus. Res., 1–43 (2025)
15. Hevner, A., Gregor, S.: Envisioning entrepreneurship and digital innovation through a design science research lens: a matrix approach. Inf. Manag. **59**, 103350 (2022)
16. Garud, R., Gehman, J., Giuliani, A.P.: Serendipity arrangements for exapting science-based innovations. Acad. Manag. Perspect. **32**, 125–140 (2018)
17. Sætre, A.S., Van de Ven, A.: Generating theory by abduction. Acad. Manag. Rev. **46**, 684–701 (2021)
18. Goldkuhl, G.: Design research in search for a paradigm: pragmatism is the answer. In: European Design Science Symposium (EDSS), Leixlip, pp. 84–95. Springer (2011)
19. Goldkuhl, G.: Meanings of pragmatism: ways to conduct information systems research. In: Action in Language, Organisations and Information Systems, pp. 13–26 (2004)
20. Rheinberger, H.-J.: Experimental systems and epistemic things. In: Toward a History of Epistemic Things: Synthesizing Proteins in the Test Tube, pp. 24–37. Stanford University Press, Stanford (1997)
21. Knorr Cetina, K.: Objectual practice. In: Knorr Cetina, K., von Savigny, E. (eds.) Knowledge as Social Order, pp. 83–97. Routledge (2016)
22. Buchanan, R.: Wicked problems in design thinking. Des. Issues **8**, 5–21 (1992)
23. Venable, J., Pries-Heje, J., Baskerville, R.: FEDS: a framework for evaluation in design science research. Eur. J. Inf. Syst. **25**, 77–89 (2016)
24. Jones, P.H.: Systemic design principles for complex social systems. In: Social Systems and Design, pp. 91–128. Springer (2014)
25. Haj-Bolouri, A., Bernhardsson, L., Rossi, M.: PADRE: a method for participatory action design research. In: DESRIST 2016 Proceedings, St. John's, pp. 19–36. Springer (2016)
26. Orlikowski, W.J.: Using technology and constituting structures: a practice lens for studying technology in organizations. Organ. Sci. **11**, 404–428 (2000)
27. Schön, D.A.: The Reflective Practitioner: How Professionals Think in Action. Routledge (2017)
28. Dorst, K., Cross, N.: Creativity in the design process: co-evolution of problem–solution. Des. Stud. **22**, 425–437 (2001)
29. De Rond, M.: The structure of serendipity. Cult. Organ. **20**, 342–358 (2014)
30. Agarwal, N.K.: Towards a definition of serendipity in information behaviour. Inf. Res. **20**, n3 (2015)
31. de Gemmis, M., Lops, P., Semeraro, G., Musto, C.: An investigation on the serendipity problem in recommender systems. Inf. Process. Manag. **51**, 695–717 (2015)
32. Ban, T.A.: The role of serendipity in drug discovery. Dialogues Clin. Neurosci. **8**, 335–344 (2006)
33. Goldkuhl, G.: Pragmatism vs interpretivism in qualitative information systems research. Eur. J. Inf. Syst. **21**, 135–146 (2012)
34. Simpson, B., den Hond, F.: The contemporary resonances of classical pragmatism for studying organization and organizing. Organ. Stud. **43**, 127–146 (2022)
35. Peirce, C.S.: Collected Papers. Harvard University Press, Cambridge (1931)
36. Lee, J.S., Pries-Heje, J., Baskerville, R.: Theorizing in design science research. In: DESRIST 2011 Proceedings, Milwaukee, pp. 1–16. Springer (2011)

37. Douven, I.: Abduction. In: Zalta, E.N., Nodelman, U. (eds.) The Stanford Encyclopedia of Philosophy, Summer 2025 edn. (2025)
38. Argyris, C.: Double loop learning in organizations. Harv. Bus. Rev. **55**, 115–125 (1977)
39. Gregor, S., Hevner, A.R.: Positioning and presenting design science research for maximum impact. MIS Q. **37**, 337–355 (2013)
40. Glaser, B.: Theoretical Sensitivity: Advances in the Methodology of Grounded Theory. Sociology Press, Mill Valley (1978)
41. Reich, Y.: The principle of reflexive practice. Des. Sci. **3**, e4 (2017)
42. Larsen, K.R., et al.: Validity in design science. MIS Q. **49**, 1267–1294 (2025)
43. Sarasvathy, S.D.: Causation and effectuation: toward a theoretical shift from economic inevitability to entrepreneurial contingency. Acad. Manag. Rev. **26**, 243–263 (2001)
44. Goldkuhl, G.: Design theories in information systems—a need for multi-grounding. J. Inf. Technol. Theory Appl. **6**, 59–72 (2004)
45. Weick, K.E.: Theory construction as disciplined imagination. Acad. Manag. Rev. **14**, 516–531 (1989)
46. Dewey, J.: How We Think, 2nd edn. D.C. Heath & Co. (1933)
47. Buyssens, H., Viaene, S.: Design principles for a blockchain-based multi-sided platform for the sustainable trade of water: an affordance approach. J. Clean. Prod. **471** (2024)
48. Bloor, D.: Toward a sociology of epistemic things. Perspect. Sci. **13**, 285–312 (2005)
49. Markus, M.L., Majchrzak, A., Gasser, L.: A design theory for systems that support emergent knowledge processes. MIS Q. **26**, 179–212 (2002)
50. Verganti, R.: Overcrowded: Designing Meaningful Products in a World Awash with Ideas. MIT Press (2017)
51. vom Brocke, J., Gau, M., Maedche, A.: Journaling the design science research process: transparency about the making of design knowledge. In: DESRIST 2021 Proceedings, Kristiansand, pp. 131–136. Springer (2021)

Fundamental Patterns – A Taxonomy for Archetype Development in Information Systems

Christian Koldewey[1,2]([⊠]) [iD], Celina Maleen Avermeyer[1], Hendrik van der Valk[3,4] [iD], Julian Zerbin[1] [iD], and Roman Dumitrescu[1,2] [iD]

[1] Heinz Nixdorf Institute, Paderborn University, Paderborn, Germany
{Christian.koldewey,celina.maleen.avermeyer,julian.zerbin,
roman.dumitrescu}@hni.uni-paderborn.de
[2] Fraunhofer Institute for Mechatronic Systems Design, Paderborn, Germany
[3] TU Dortmund University, Dortmund, Germany
hendrik.van-der-valk@tu-dortmund.de
[4] Fraunhofer Institute for Software and Systems Engineering, Dortmund, Germany

Abstract. Archetypes are widely used in information systems (IS) research to structure and interpret complex socio-technical phenomena. Despite their widespread use, however, archetype development often lacks methodological rigor. Many studies rely on ad hoc and situational configurations of methods, which limit comparability and transparency. To address this gap, we developed a taxonomy of 114 archetype development approaches identified through a systematic literature review in the IS domain. The taxonomy captures common contexts of use, objects of analysis, and procedures employed in archetype construction. The analysis reveals dominant and less common archetype development practices clarifying how archetypes are understood and constructed in IS and giving guidance for future studies. Beyond its theoretical contribution, the taxonomy also supports practical applications, such as constructing archetypes of IT services as a structured solution space. Overall, our taxonomy strengthens the methodological foundations of archetype development and provides reusable design knowledge for future studies in IS and related fields.

Keywords: Archetype Development · Design Knowledge · Taxonomy Development · Conceptual Artifact · Theory Building

1 Introduction

Many papers in the Information Systems (IS) domain develop "archetypes" as design artifacts to describe abstract categories of real-world phenomena. Yet they often research archetypes without sufficient definitions, theoretical foundations, or methodological rigor. However, archetypes are not unique to IS and have a long intellectual history. One of the most prominent examples is Jung's "archetypes of the unconscious," whereby Jung refers back to Plato in his argumentation [1].

© The Author(s), under exclusive license to Springer Nature Switzerland AG 2026
J. vom Brocke et al. (Eds.): DESRIST 2026, LNCS 16606, pp. 315–329, 2026.
https://doi.org/10.1007/978-3-032-28313-9_18

Archetypes are commonly understood as recurring, fundamental patterns across cases. Identifying archetypes within a set of objects is essential as it offers both theoretical implications and practical benefits. The classification into archetypes often provides a structured starting point for further research, guiding future studies in the field [2]. Archetypes provide an overview of existing research and help researchers and practitioners identify gaps in the literature while also contributing new insights and enhancing the theoretical development of the discipline [3–6]. Additionally, they can help bridge theoretical and empirical findings into practical guidelines [7]. With archetypes, decision-making can be significantly improved, as archetypes allow for deeper insights, which are valuable in comparing with competitors and understanding industry dynamics [8, 9]. Archetypes serve as reference points, allowing organizations to tailor their approaches better or to navigate the market more effectively, for example, by using archetypes to align management direction to better meet organizational goals [10, 11]. Depending on the research field, they can enable the identification and comparison of substitutable technologies, which aids in decision-making processes [12].

As archetypes are generally understood as abstractions, researchers often combine various analytical tools, such as taxonomies, theoretical frameworks, and clustering techniques, to characterize and identify archetypes. This motivates the assumption that the development of archetypes lacks a formalized methodology, as no clear or standardized methodological approach currently exists. For instance, Wissuchek and Zschech utilize a concept matrix and taxonomy as foundational tools, yet their approach appears to be tailored or adapted for their specific objectives rather than following an established, widely accepted methodological framework [13]. Similarly, Lauf et al. describe their process of identifying archetypes as "exploring patterns," suggesting an exploratory and relatively unstructured approach, which underscores the absence of clear guidelines for the archetype identification process [14]. They analyzed their sample's characteristics and devised their own methods to identify archetypes. Holler et al. explicitly note the lack of universal terminology and methodology concerning archetypes, further highlighting the need for a standardized framework in this area [15]. As a preliminary step to developing a research methodology, one needs to know the central features of the design process in question. This follows the principles of inductive modeling [16]. The actual design process for an overarching method builds upon distinctive elements of individual instantiations [17]. These considerations have led us to our **research question**:

What are the key dimensions and characteristics of archetype development in information systems?

Answering the research question this paper makes two **contributions** to design-oriented research in IS. First, we develop a taxonomy of archetype development projects in IS, unveiling contexts of use, objects of analysis, and procedural options. Second, we provide descriptive insight into dominant and exotic practices in archetype development. The results codify reusable design knowledge that supports systematically designing, documenting, and reflecting on archetype studies. By structuring the fragmented methodological practices into a coherent framework, the taxonomy provides a foundation for a nascent design methodology and future prescriptive guidance on archetype development.

After the hitherto introduction, the paper is structured as follows: Sect. 2 will introduce the concept of archetype in detail. In Sect. 3, the research design is described, and a systematic literature review is composed as the foundation for a taxonomic analysis of archetype development. Section 4 presents the taxonomy. Then, the results are discussed before the paper closes with a short conclusion.

2 Archetypes in Information Systems

The **concept** of "archetypes" lacks a universally accepted definition across literature [15], with most studies approaching it as a type with specific properties rather than providing a precise meaning. In several reviewed papers, researchers approach archetypes through classifications or categorizations grounded in empirical evidence. Dolata et al., Holler et al., and Walsh et al. all reference Greenwood and Hinings' 1993 work in the *Academy of Management Journal*, which conceptualizes organizational archetypes as coherent arrangements of structures and systems that reflect underlying interpretive schemes [15, 18, 19]. Van der Valk describes archetypes as "foundational and distinguishable types," while Soh and Markus, Nkwe and Cohen, and Cullen et al. conceptualize archetypes in ways that align more closely with their specific research aims. Nkwe and Cohen and Cullen et al. emphasize archetypes as behavioral patterns, while Soh and Markus define strategic archetypes as sets of firms sharing similar attributes [7, 11, 20, 21].

Archetypes are sometimes described as conceptual categories or types characterized by distinct, identifiable features [20]. They are theoretical constructs or models that describe typical patterns of systems, actors, or organizational structures. In some cases, archetypes may build on ideal types as described by Weber, which emphasize essential characteristics for analytical comparison [22]. However, archetypes are broader than ideal types: they can also be empirically grounded, serving both descriptive functions – explaining dominant patterns observed in practice – and prescriptive functions – offering design guidance and possible future directions [23, 24]. Importantly, archetypes may be empirically grounded, derived from observed data through methods such as classification, taxonomy-building, or cluster analysis [2, 12], yet they need not always reflect existing reality. As shown by Göldi and Rietsche, archetypes can also represent logically possible or future configurations that may never exist in practice [25]. This positions archetypes as tools for both understanding what is and speculating about what could be. Archetypes aid in understanding complex phenomena by reducing diverse data sets to a manageable number of abstract patterns, highlighting salient characteristics. They serve as tools to explain specific properties, behaviors, or structures of IS-related phenomena, such as technologies, user behavior, or business strategies [11, 12, 26]. The number of archetypes within a field is not constrained, allowing for the identification of multiple archetypes as needed.

In IS, the **scope and nature** of research can vary significantly, leading to diverse application scenarios for archetype identification, with distinct objects being categorized depending on the context. Eickhoff et al., for example, identify archetypes specifically for fintech companies, while Geiger et al. classify crowdsourcing platforms [27, 28]. Gerlach et al. develop a decision-tree analysis of archetypes for AI-driven cybersecurity applications [29]. Mueller et al. focus on classifying apps related to depression, whereas Knote et al. categorize smart personal assistants [2, 30]. Berger et al. provide a broader classification of digital technologies, while Weking et al. focus on archetypes related to business model innovation [12, 26]. Katsma and Spil and Hodapp et al. also address business model archetypes, with Katsma and Spil's focus on digital music services and Hodapp's on IoT [31, 32].

Archetypes may be understood as **design science** artifacts, i.e., models, following March and Smith [24], in a sense that they structure knowledge about socio-technical phenomena. Referring to Gregor and Hevner [23], archetypes may also contribute to nascent design theory codifying knowledge in the form of generalized architectures or constellations of objects. Accordingly, when researching archetypes for design-oriented purposes, the paradigms and goals of design science should be considered. Basic assumptions are that design artifacts are artificial and result from conscious design activities; they have intended purposes and functionalities to solve meaningful problems [24, 33–35]. Design science goals are, as summarized by Moeller et al., to accumulate design knowledge, to make it available for reuse, and to generalize knowledge gained from singular instances [36]. In terms of contributions to the knowledge base, according to Gregor and Hevner [23], archetypes can deliver both descriptive knowledge and prescriptive knowledge.

Several concepts are closely related to or frequently discussed in the context of archetypes, offering alternative or complementary ways of organizing, understanding, and analyzing phenomena in IS research. Among these, classification, typology, taxonomy, and configuration serve as key frameworks for structuring and interpreting complex data and organizational patterns. Classification refers to the process of grouping entities into classes based on similarity, either conceptually or empirically, and in one or multiple dimensions [37, 38]. Its purpose is to reduce complexity and minimize within-group variance while maximizing between-group variance [37]. By highlighting similarities and differences across cases, classification provides a descriptive tool that summarizes data and supports pattern recognition [37]. Typology represents a conceptual classification system organized around ideal types, which are abstract and often extreme theoretical constructs [37, 39]. Typically, multidimensional and conceptually derived rather than empirically based, typologies function as abstract models that emphasize specific characteristics, guide hypothesis construction, and allow deviations to be interpreted meaningfully [39, 40]. Taxonomy is another form of classification and is often used interchangeably with typology [37]. Like classification, it can refer to both the process of organizing entities and the resulting structure [37]. In contrast to typologies, however, taxonomies classify empirical rather than conceptual entities [37, 38]. Although the term originates from biological sciences, taxonomies have been widely applied to analyze design principles of observed artifacts and are historically important in research [41, 42]. Configuration, in turn, refers to the alignment or constellation of multiple organizational elements around a unifying theme [43].

Hence, for this paper, we understand archetypes as recurring, coherent configurations of salient characteristics across instances of a focal phenomenon. In contrast to classifications, typologies, and taxonomies, which primarily serve as schemes for ordering entities, archetypes reveal meaningful, recurring configurations. They may be derived empirically or conceptually and can be used for analytical and design-oriented purposes. Often, classifications, typologies, and taxonomies are used as foundations and contribute to archetype development. Yet, they are applied inconsistently and do not constitute a formalized methodology for archetype development.

3   Research Design

Taxonomies are a suitable artifact to structure dimensions and characteristics of objects. For this paper, we applied the taxonomy development method according to Nickerson et al. [38]. First, we determined the meta-characteristic; we aim for a taxonomy that describes the fundamental elements of the development process for the archetype derivation. Then we chose the ending conditions and decided to use the classic thirteen subjective and objective ending conditions [38]. To identify our objectives to be investigated, we applied the proven method for a Structured Literature Review (SLR) from vom Brocke et al. partially [44]. Thus, we employed three of the five steps of an SLR: 1) Definition of Review Scope, 2) Conceptualization of Topic, and 3) Literature Search; the remaining two steps were substituted by the investigation approaches from the taxonomy development method. The review scope is scientific papers from IS scholars in which archetypes are developed. For the conceptualization of the topic, we use the definition and explanation of archetypes provided in Sect. 2. Although concepts such as typology, taxonomy, classification, and configuration are frequently discussed in the literature, and archetypes are sometimes referred to simply as "types," we deliberately constrained the scope of our review to studies explicitly addressing archetypes. Expanding the search to encompass all related concepts would have yielded an unmanageable volume of literature. Additionally, our review was confined to research within the domain of IS. Extending the scope to include other disciplines would likewise have produced an excessive number of studies and diverted attention from IS-specific phenomena. Hence, we selected AISeL as the sole database as it covers the core IS conferences and journals and allowed us to maintain a clear boundary. By narrowing the focus in this manner, we ensured that our analysis remained both tractable and conceptually coherent, while retaining relevance to IS research.

The search for the literature corpus was conducted within the database AISeL using the search term "archetyp*". The search was filtered for title and abstract. The initial search yielded 207 papers. All abstracts of the papers were read to check whether the paper was relevant to our research. Ambiguous cases were resolved through discussions among the authors. All papers that developed archetypes were included, others were excluded. This reduced the number of hits to 114. To build our taxonomy, we then chose to use an empirical-to-conceptual (E2C) approach first, followed by two conceptual-to-empirical (C2E) iterations. For the first E2C iteration we analyzed 37 papers regarding archetype development to inductively derive characteristics related to our meta-characteristics (Context, Objects' Aspects, and Process). For the next iteration, we utilized the C2E approach by reflecting on the existing taxonomy and, informed by our experience in taxonomy and archetype development as well as seminal literature, e.g., Bailey [37], Nickerson et al. [38], Doty and Glick [39], derived new characteristics and reorganized dimensions. We then analyzed 31 additional papers and classified them using the newly conceptualized characteristics. In the third iteration, we revised the taxonomy and determined new characteristics, followed by an analysis of the remaining

46 papers to test the usefulness of these new characteristics. We used a concept matrix (https://bit.ly/3NwFWXk) with studies as rows and taxonomy characteristics as columns to ensure traceability across iterations. The taxonomy was finalized once all papers in the corpus could be coded consistently without introducing additional dimensions or characteristics, and once the predefined ending conditions were judged to be met. The conceptual saturation suggests that the taxonomy sufficiently captures the design space of archetype development processes within IS research.

Following Kundisch et al., we also evaluated the taxonomy and applied specific cases of our own archetype development experience [45]. The taxonomy was able to characterize these studies without requiring a revision of dimensions or characteristics. This indicates that the taxonomy is sufficiently expressive and usable to characterize real archetype development projects.

4   A Taxonomy for Archetype Development

The final taxonomy includes 43 characteristics across eleven dimensions grouped into three meta-dimensions: **Context**, **Objects' Aspects**, and **Process** (cf. Table 1). The final meta-dimensions were created by clustering the identified dimensions into meaningful, higher-level categories. In the table, the most common categories within each dimension are highlighted in grey. The dimensions and their corresponding characteristics are described in the next subsections. Some dimensions are mutually exclusive, meaning that each item belongs to only one category. In these dimensions, there is no overlap between classes, so a single case cannot be a member of two different groups. Mutually exclusive dimensions are marked as "ME" in Table 1.

4.1   Context of Archetype Development

This meta-dimension includes the three dimensions: **Timing**, **Perspective**, and **Purpose**. The dimensions describe the conceptual environment in which the archetypes are to be developed.

Timing: This dimension contains two characteristics, *ex ante* and *ex post*. The characteristics refer to the point in time at which the archetypes are derived, i.e., before or after the instantiation of the objects. Most of the literature describes an archetype development process that is ex post (97%), whereas only 3% of the literature shows the opposite. The dimension is mutually exclusive.

Perspective: The perspective of the archetypes is closely related to the timing. They can either be *prescriptive* or *descriptive*. Here, the focus lies on the individual point of view the archetypes' developers possess. While a descriptive archetype is self-explanatory, i.e. it is an archetype representing a cluster of objects, a prescriptive archetype is vaguer and describes the space to aim for during the design of a certain number of objects so that they belong to one cluster, i.e., the archetype. Nevertheless, the potential purpose of a descriptive archetype serving as a knowledge base for further prescriptive developments remains. Again, 98% of the papers contain archetypes of a descriptive nature, and just the remaining 2% present prescriptive archetypes. This dimension is also mutually exclusive.

Table 1. Taxonomy of Archetype Development.

Meta-Dimension	Dimension	Characteristics							Exclusivity
Context	Timing	Ex ante			Ex post ●●				ME
	Perspective	Prescriptive			Descriptive ●●				ME
	Purpose	Conceptual Map	Theory Builder		Assessment Instrument ●○		Design Guide ●○		NE
Objects' Aspects	State	Theoretical ●			Empirical ●○				NE
	Source	White Literature ●○	News / Articles ○	Practitioner Insights ●○	Practice Reports ○	Websites ○	Practitioner Database	Case Material ○	NE
Procedure	Object Identification	(S)LR ●○	Case Study ○	Interviews ●		Survey	Grey Literature Search ○		NE
	Object Description	Taxonomy ●●		Typology		Text			NE
	Archetype Identification	Clustering ○		Coding & Analysis		Derivation from Classification ●			ME
	Iterations	Single ●●			Multiple				ME
	Documentation	Free Text ●●		Template		Visual			NE
	Analysis	None ●		Same Level of Abstraction		Super/ Sub level of Abstraction ○			ME
	Evaluation	Interviews	Exemplary Cases	Statistical methods		Focus Group	None ●●		NE

Showcases – ●: Lauf et al. [14] / ○ : Weking et al. [26].

While ex-post archetypes are often descriptive and ex-ante archetypes are often prescriptive, Dehling et al. show that an ex-ante approach can still yield descriptive archetypes, illustrating that timing and perspective are related but independent dimensions [46].

Purpose: The analysis showed four purposes for which archetypes are developed. *Conceptual Map* (42%) represents the use of archetypes as analytical structures for theoretical insights and development. In this context, the archetypes sort the knowledge base or create a common ground for the emerging literature. *Theory Builder*, which appears in 30% of the studies, captures the use of archetypes as building blocks for theoretical construction. For example, archetype structure objects that are analyzed and decomposed for the derivation of design principles. Often, a group of specific design principles is defined for the objects belonging to a certain archetype, and the difference between the archetypes varies, while some design principles are common for all archetypes. In our analysis, archetypes have been used to derive privacy-by-design rules for service systems [47], to define design parameters for ICOs [48], or to establish chatbot design principles that address reskilling and feedback exchange [49]. Furthermore, the archetypes can be integrated into existing IS theories (e.g., platform theories, governance, data economy). *Assessment Instrument* (37%) emphasizes the diagnostic use of archetypes in real-world contexts. Using archetypes is especially beneficial for the development of inductive reference models. These models are a derivative of existing objects. The general core of the reference model is the similarities between the archetypes, while the differences provide for either the individual instantiations of the reference model or allow for modularization of the model with alternating system elements according to the corresponding archetype. *Design Guide* constitutes the most prevalent purpose, with 65% of archetypes supporting concrete design activities. Here, archetypes are developed as a tool to support decision-making processes, helping practitioners make informed choices based on established patterns. These archetypes can offer ideal-typical configurations that have proven beneficial and, therefore, aid practitioners in design-related decisions. For example, archetypes can inform strategic choices such as selecting cooperation partners [9], tailoring agile practices to avoid pitfalls [50], or guiding e-health providers in commercialization strategies [51]. The archetypes can also serve as templates for recurring solution options that can be adapted to specific contexts. By systematizing design alternatives, they support practitioners in developing concrete instantiations, for example, when identifying business model configurations for IoT platforms [31] or when creating new data trustee models [14]. A study can be coded with multiple purposes simultaneously; the dimension is non-exclusive.

4.2 Objects' Aspects

The meta-dimension Objects' Aspects describe the nature of the objects that belong to the respective archetypes. Its dimensions are **State** and **Source**.

State: This dimension is split into two main categories: *empirical* and *theoretical*. The majority of objects were measurable, observable characteristics gathered through data or experimentation, i.e., *empirical* (88%), while *theoretical* objects were used less (19%). The dimension is not mutually exclusive, as some researchers used both theoretical and empirical objects to enhance their archetypes. Geiger et al. provide an example of integrating both object states by enriching crowdsourcing information system archetypes with empirical objects and theoretical concepts from systems theory [28].

Source: The sources the researchers use for the acquisition of the objects that build up the archetypes are manifold. In total, seven characteristics are noticeable: *White Literature* (40%), *News/ Articles* (12%), *Practitioner Insights* (37%), *Practice Reports* (13%), *Websites or Blogs* (37%), *Practitioner Databases* (27%) and *Case Material* (22%). The dimension is not mutually exclusive. Diederich et al., e.g., utilize both white literature from a literature review and data from the startup database CrunchBase as sources on conversational agent platforms [52].

4.3 Archetype Development Procedure

This meta-dimension consists of seven dimensions that describe the procedure of developing the archetypes. They are **Object Identification, Object Description, Archetype Identification, Iterations, Documentation, Analysis,** and **Evaluation**.

Object Identification: This dimension captures the approaches applied to determine the objects used for the archetype derivation. The most frequently applied methods are *Case Studies* (42%). *(Systematic) Literature Reviews* are used in 36% of the papers. *Interviews or Focus Group*s are applied in 30% of the papers, while *Surveys* are only used in 7%. Additionally, 27% of the papers draw on *Grey Literature Searches*, which include database searches or the use of internet search engines. The category is non-exclusive, meaning that several methods can be combined within one study.

Object Description: This dimension reports on the type of different descriptions in which the objects for the archetype derivation are represented. The majority of the papers present their objects in a *taxonomy* (53%). This is most often a morphological box, yet other visualizations can also be noted. Only a few papers show their objects in a *typology* (10%). A distinctive assignment to one of these categories is often complex, as the differentiation between taxonomies and typologies is not obvious because both terms can be used interchangeably [37]. Thus, we follow the designation the respective authors chose. The third characteristic is the *textual description* of the objects (38%). These papers describe the archetypes' objects in plain text. The dimension is non-exclusive.

Archetype Identification: The dimension involves the identification of archetypes from objects (i.e., the method that produced the archetype partition), primarily using two methods: *Clustering*, which accounted for 45%, and *Coding/Analysis* of objects, which accounted for 34%. Within clustering, researchers employed hierarchical methods (Ward's agglomerative clustering, 40%, k-means/partitioning (26%), and two-stage hybrids combining hierarchical and k-means (8%), while a few used qualitative or unspecified clustering techniques (26%). This variety shows that both statistical and iterative approaches are used to identify meaningful archetypes depending on the dataset and research goal. Coding and analysis were predominantly applied to data derived from interviews and surveys. *Derivation from Classification* constitutes a third approach, emphasizing the use of previously established object descriptions such as typologies and taxonomies. As both terms refer not only to documentation formats but also the process, many researchers build upon such classifications to derive archetypes. The development of a typology or taxonomy inherently facilitates the emergence of archetypes, as the existence of structural categories enables the identification of combinations, clusters, or stable patterns within them. This approach accounted for 21%. This dimension is mutually exclusive.

Iterations: The dimension depicts whether the researchers analyze their database *Once* or *Multiple* times to derive the archetypes. 64% used a single pass, whereas 36% used multiple iterations. The dimension is mutually exclusive.

Documentation: The documentation style of archetypes is characterized by three non-mutually exclusive categories. The majority of archetypes (97%) were documented in *free-text* format, which encompasses descriptions ranging from brief, two-word phrases to more detailed explanations. Alternative documentation styles included *template-based* formats (10%) and *visual or graphical* representations of the archetypes (14%). This dimension is non-exclusive.

Analysis: The dimension categorizes dependencies into three distinct types: *No Dependency* (72%), *Same-level Dependency* (16%), and *Hierarchical Dependency* (12%). The last one encompasses the classification into super- and sub-archetypes. These dependency types are mutually exclusive.

Evaluation: The dimension classifies the evaluation methods applied to the developed archetypes. A significant proportion of studies (80%) did not include any form of evaluation of their archetypes (*No Evaluation*). In cases where evaluation was conducted, the most frequently used methods were *Focus Groups* and reviews by independent researchers (4%), followed by testing the archetypes against *Exemplary Field Cases* (4%). Other evaluation techniques included *Interviews* (4%), and *Statistical Analyses* such as Cohen's Kappa and ANOVA (9%). The dimension is non-exclusive.

## 5	Discussion

Our study contributes to the development of archetypes within the IS community, with our taxonomy offering an overview of how IS researchers approach the topic, which methods they use, and which perspectives they employ. We highlight the applicability of the taxonomy by providing examples. Thus, we showcase the archetype development of Lauf et al. [14] and Weking et al. [26] in Table 1. While they align with the majority of studies in many dimensions, they also address characteristics besides the majority, e.g., [14] derives the archetypes from a classification, while [26] aligns with the majority and derives the archetypes through a cluster analysis. Nevertheless, also [26] diverts and uses grey literature or incorporates hierarchical dependencies for their archetypes. The applications show the suitability of the taxonomy to describe archetype development processes.

While most of the approaches are of an ex-post and more descriptive nature, it becomes visible that archetypes are often used as a tool for further research on a certain topic. They sort existing objects, of which then other artifacts are designed inductively. Yet the taxonomy also sheds light on pitfalls and limited standardization of procedures. For instance, most researchers do not apply a template for the description of their archetypes. Thus, it becomes difficult to compare different archetypes with one another. Further advantages of using templates for the archetypes, analogous to the formulation of design principles [53], are neglected. Furthermore, most researchers rarely evaluate their archetypes, limiting the significance of their findings. The choice of identification method has only a minor influence on evaluation practices. Across the three archetype identification approaches, the absence of evaluation is comparably prevalent (Clustering: 73%, Coding & Analysis: 89%, Derivation: 79%). Still, patterns emerge: Coding & Analysis studies rarely report evaluation beyond focus groups; Derivation studies rely on exemplary cases but remain largely unevaluated; Clustering increases the likelihood of interviews and statistical validation. These findings suggest that methodological choices may subtly shape the kinds of evaluation that are perceived as appropriate. However, evaluation is widely neglected, suggesting a structural issue in archetype research and highlighting the need for dedicated methodological guidance rather than ad hoc adaptations of generic research methods. More work is needed to establish robust, field-wide practices that encourage evaluation independent of the chosen identification approach.

The analysis shows that researchers do not follow a shared methodology to develop archetypes. Instead, generic research methods are adapted to fit to the respective purpose, with some applying a Design Science Research approach for example. From a DS perspective, archetypes can be represented by a set of features and characteristics, presenting as multidimensional configurations that underscore their non-trivial nature. Thus, they may be considered as complex artifacts within a design science research lens, which necessitates a more rigorous development process. Our analysis demonstrates that while concepts such as classification, typologies, taxonomies, and configurations provide useful reference points, they alone are not sufficient to guide archetype development. Researchers frequently draw on these concepts, but inconsistently and without a shared methodological foundation. Classification, for example, serves primarily as a descriptive grouping tool, while typologies and taxonomies are invoked as conceptual or empirical structures without a standard procedure for translating them into archetypes. Reflecting on the research approaches of the papers investigated, our findings support the assumption that archetype development currently lacks a shared, formalized methodological foundation. Consequently, archetypes continue to be developed in fragmented and heterogeneous ways, making comparisons across studies difficult and limiting the accumulation of reusable design knowledge.

Following the analysis of the taxonomy, a dominant approach to archetype development emerges (cf. Grey boxes in Table 1). The taxonomy thus serves as a foundation for subsequently developing a more structured and cumulative research method for archetype development. Moreover, it enables comparability through a shared set of dimensions and characteristics, allowing archetype studies to be systematically compared rather than remaining fragmented. Furthermore, by providing a morphological box, the taxonomy can already guide researchers in systematically positioning their study.

We propose using the morphological box as a reporting instrument for future archetype studies. Researchers should provide information on their design choices for the three meta-dimensions context, objects, and procedure. For context they should argue for their choice of timing, perspective, and primary purpose. For objects they should report on the object state and origin. For procedure they should explain the method for object identification, the object description technique, the archetype identification approach, the number of iterations run, the choice of documentation format, the dependency structure, and the evaluation method or justification for omission. By making those decisions transparent, researchers may increase the rigor and transparency of their methodological choices.

Additionally, we discovered that the majority of papers appear in a limited set of core IS venues, most notably ICIS, HICSS, and ECIS. Journal publications account for approximately 11% of the total output. We also observe a clear overall increase in publications on archetype development over the past two decades, with particularly notable growth from the mid-2010s onward. This trend reflects a steadily rising scholarly interest in the topic.

The development of the taxonomy is also subject to limitations. First, as with every literature-based analysis, the taxonomy development was subject to interpretive judgement. We mitigated this risk by iterative discussions among four researchers while refining dimensions and characteristics. We achieved a theoretical saturation with our database. Nevertheless, we are aware that we only covered archetype development projects from the IS domain. In particular, we observe an imbalance between empirical objects (88%) and theoretical archetypes (19%), reflecting the IS-focused orientation of the literature and introducing potential biases. Broadening the search to other disciplines could be a promising direction for future research, both to mitigate these biases and to investigate whether the proposed taxonomy of archetype development in IS is applicable or transferable to other fields. Investigating other domains like engineering or management might uncover further practices. Finally, the current form of instantiation-based evaluation does not replace an independent empirical evaluation.

6   Conclusion

Our taxonomy aggregates the diverse approaches researchers adopt in developing archetypes, structured through key dimensions and characteristics. It provides insights into the primary concerns of archetype development, i.e., context, objects' aspects, and process. The taxonomy serves a dual purpose: to characterize past archetype development processes and as a guide for future archetype development processes. It hereby supports researchers and practitioners in crafting meaningful archetypes. Future work should include a thorough evaluation of the taxonomy and the development of an archetype development method grounded in the identified best practices.

References

1. Jung, C.G.: The Archetypes and the Collective Unconscious. Routledge, London (2014)
2. Mueller, N.S., Werth, O., Koenig, C.M., Breitner, M.H.: How is your mood today? - A taxonomy-based analysis of apps for depression. In: AMCIS 2022 Proceedings (2022)
3. Fruhwirth, M., Rachinger, M., Prlja, E.: Discovering business models of data marketplaces. In: Proceedings of the 53rd Hawaii International Conference on System Sciences, pp. 5738–5747 (2020)
4. Fadler, M., Legner, C.: Understanding the impact of machine learning on enterprise data management: a taxonomic approach. In: Proceedings of the 2019 Pre-ICIS SIGDSA Symposium (2019)
5. Weber, F., Wambsganss, T., Soellner, M.: Supporting human cognitive writing processes: towards a taxonomy of writing support systems. In: ICIS 2023 Proceedings (2023)
6. Guillemette, M., Pare, G.: understanding the role and transformation of the information technology function in organizations. In: ICIS 2005 Proceedings (2005)
7. Soh, C., Markus, M.L.: Business-to-business e-marketplaces: a strategic archetypes approach. In: ICIS 2002 Proceedings, pp. 835–845 (2002)
8. Schulze, L., Trenz, M., Nickerson, R.C.: Fingers in the pie: characterizing decision rights partitioning on digital labor platforms. In: ICIS 2021 Proceedings (2021)

9. Dremel, C., Stöckli, E., Wulf, J., Herrmann, A.: Archetypes of data analytics providers in the big data era. In: AMCIS 2018 Proceedings (2018)
10. Xue, Y., Liang, H., Boulton, W.R.: Information technology governance in information technology investment decision processes: the impact of investment characteristics, external environment, and internal context. MIS Q. **32**(1) (2008)
11. Cullen, S., Shanks, G., Davern, M., Willcocks, L.: A framework for relationships in outsourcing: contract management archetypes. In: Proceedings of the 50th Hawaii International Conference on System Sciences, pp. 5380–5389 (2017)
12. Berger, S., Denner, M.-S., Roeglinger, M.: The nature of digital technologies - development of a multi-layer taxonomy. In: ECIS 2018 Proceedings (2018)
13. Wissuchek, C., Zschech, P.: Survey and systematization of prescriptive analytics systems: towards archetypes from a human-machine-collaboration perspective. In: ECIS 2023 Proceedings (2023)
14. Lauf, F., Scheider, S., Friese, J., Kilz, S., Radic, M., Burmann, A.: Exploring design characteristics of data trustees in healthcare - taxonomy and archetypes. In: ECIS 2023 Proceedings (2023)
15. Holler, M., Uebernickel, F., Brenner, W.: Defining archetypes of E-collaboration for product development in the automotive industry. In: ECIS 2017 Proceedings, pp. 114–130 (2017)
16. Fettke, P.: Eine Methode zur induktiven Entwicklung von Referenzmodellen. In: Tagungsband Multikonferenz Wirtschaftsinformatik, pp. 1034–1047 (2014)
17. Brinkkemper, S., Saeki, M., Harmsen, F.: Assembly techniques for method engineering. In: Goos, G., Hartmanis, J., van Leeuwen, J., Pernici, B., Thanos, C. (eds.) Advanced Information Systems Engineering. Lecture Notes in Computer Science, vol. 1413, pp. 381–400. Springer, Heidelberg (1998)
18. Dolata, M., Crowston, K., Schwabe, G.: Project archetypes: a blessing and a curse for AI development. In: ICIS 2022 Proceedings (2022)
19. Walsh, C., OReilly, P., Gleasure, R., Feller, J., Li, S., Cristoforo, J.: New kid on the block: a strategic archetypes approach to understanding the Blockchain. In: ICIS 2016 Proceedings (2016)
20. van der Valk, H., Haße, H., Möller, F., Otto, B.: Archetypes of digital twins. Bus. Inf. Syst. Eng. **64**, 375–391 (2022)
21. Nkwe, N., Cohen, J.F.: Social network site user archetypes: an exploratory study of implications for workplace outcomes. In: PACIS 2020 Proceedings (2020)
22. Weber, M.: "Objectivity" in social science and social policy. Methodol. Soc. Sci., 49–112 (1949)
23. Gregor, S., Hevner, A.R.: Positioning and presenting design science research for maximum impact. MIS Q. **37**(2), 337–355 (2013)
24. March, S.T., Smith, G.F.: Design and natural science research on information technology. Decis. Support. Syst. **15**(4), 251–266 (1995)
25. Göldi, A., Rietsche, R.: Making sense of large language model-based AI agents. In: ICIS 2024 Proceedings (2024)
26. Weking, J., Stocker, M., Kowalkiewicz, M., Bohm, M., Krcmar, H.: Archetypes for industry 4.0 business model innovations. In: AMCIS 2018 Proceedings (2018)
27. Eickhoff, M., Muntermann, J., Weinrich, T.: What do FinTechs actually do? A taxonomy of FinTech business models. In: ICIS 2017 Proceedings (2017)
28. Geiger, D., Rosemann, M., Fielt, E., Schader, M.: Crowdsourcing information systems - definition, typology, and design. In: ICIS 2012 Proceedings (2012)
29. Gerlach, J., Werth, O., Breitner, M.H.: Artificial intelligence for cybersecurity: towards taxonomy-based archetypes and decision support. In: ICIS 2022 Proceedings (2022)

30. Knote, R., Janson, A., Söllner, M., Leimeister, J.M.: Classifying smart personal assistants: an empirical cluster analysis. In: Proceedings of the 52nd Hawaii International Conference on System Sciences, pp. 2024–2033 (2019)
31. Hodapp, D., Remane, G., Hanelt, A., Kolbe, L.M.: Business models for internet of things platforms: empirical development of a taxonomy and archetypes. In: Proceedings of the 14th International Conference on Wirtschaftsinformatik, pp. 1769–1783 (2019)
32. Katsma, C., Spil, T.: A taxonomy of digital music services. In: AMCIS 2010 Proceedings (2010)
33. Hilpinen, R.: Belief systems as artifacts. Monist **78**(2), 136–155 (1995)
34. Baker, L.R.: The shrinking difference between artifacts and natural objects. Newslett. Philosophy Comput. **07**(2) (2008)
35. Simon, H.A.: The Sciences of the Artificial. MIT Press, Cambridge, Mass (1996)
36. Möller, F., Guggenberger, T.M., Otto, B.: Towards a method for design principle development in information systems. In: Hofmann, S., Müller, O., Rossi, M. (eds.) Designing for Digital Transformation. Co-Creating Services with Citizens and Industry. Lecture Notes in Computer Science, vol. 12388, pp. 208–220. Springer, Cham (2020)
37. Bailey, K.D.: Typologies and Taxonomies: An Introduction to Classification Techniques. Sage (1994)
38. Nickerson, R.C., Varshney, U., Muntermann, J.: A method for taxonomy development and its application in information systems. Eur. J. Inf. Syst. **22**, 336–359 (2013)
39. Doty, D.H., Glick, W.H.: Typologies as a unique form of theory building: toward improved understanding and modeling. Acad. Manag. Rev. **19**(2), 230–251 (1994)
40. Smith, K.B.: Typologies, taxonomies, and the benefits of policy classification. Policy Stud. J. **30**(2), 379–395 (2002)
41. Williams, K., Chatterjee, S., Rossi, M.: Design of emerging digital services: a taxonomy. Eur. J. Inf. Syst. **17**, 505–517 (2008)
42. Fiedler, K.D., Grover, V., Teng, J.T.: An empirically derived taxonomy of information technology structure and its relationship to organizational structure. J. Manag. Inf. Syst. **13**(1), 9–34 (1996)
43. Miller, D.: Configurations revisited. Strateg. Manag. J. **17**(7), 505–512 (1996)
44. vom Brocke, J., Simons, A., Niehaves, B., Reimer, K., Plattfaut, R., Cleven, A.: Reconstructing the Giant: on the importance of Rigour in documenting the literature search process. In: ECIS Proceedings (2009)
45. Kundisch, D., et al.: An update for taxonomy designers. Bus. Inf. Syst. Eng. **64**, 421–439 (2021)
46. Dehling, T., Schmidt-Kraepelin, M., Demircan, M., Szefer, J., Sunyaev, A.: User archetypes for effective information privacy communication. In: Proceedings of the Pre-ICIS Workshop on Information Security and Privacy (2016)
47. Kurtz, C., Vogel, P., Semmann, M.: Exploring archetypes of value co-destructive privacy practices. In: Proceedings of the 52nd Hawaii International Conference on System Sciences, pp. 1396–1405 (2022)
48. Bachmann, N., Drasch, B., Miksch, M., Schweizer, A.: Dividing the ICO jungle: extracting and evaluating design archetypes. In: Proceedings of the 14th International Conference on Wirtschaftsinformatik, pp. 1709–1723 (2019)
49. Lechler, R., Stoeckli, E., Rietsche, R., Uebernickel, F.: Looking beneath the tip of the iceberg: the two-sided nature of Chatbots and their roles for digital feedback exchange. In: ECIS 2019 Proceedings (2019)
50. Zaitsev, A., Tan, B., Gal, U.: Collaboration amidst volatility: the evolving nature of boundary objects in agile software development. In: ECIS 2016 Proceedings (2016)
51. Mettler, T., Eurich, M.: What is the business model behind E-Health? A pattern-based approach to sustainable profit. In: ECIS 2012 Proceedings (2012)

52. Diederich, S., Brendel, A.B., Kolbe, L.M.: Towards a taxonomy of platforms for conversational agent design. In: Proceedings of the 14th International Conference on Wirtschaftsinformatik, pp. 1100–1114 (2019)
53. Chandra, L., Seidel, S., Gregor, S.: Prescriptive knowledge in IS research: conceptualizing design principles in terms of materiality, action, and boundary conditions. In: Proceedings of the 48th Hawaii International Conference on System Sciences, pp. 4039–4048 (2015)

Fruitfulness in Design Science: Evaluating Contributions by What They Make Possible

Roland M. Mueller[(✉)] [iD]

Berlin School of Economics and Law, Badensche Straße 52, 10825 Berlin, Germany
roland.mueller@hwr-berlin.de

Abstract. Design Science Research (DSR) has traditionally evaluated contributions by their effectiveness in solving specified problems within given contexts. While this problem-solving orientation and its focus on "fitness" have proven valuable, they provide limited guidance for assessing contributions whose primary impact lies in expanding the space of future design options. This paper introduces the concept of "fruitfulness" as a complementary evaluative dimension for DSR, defined as the capacity of design knowledge to expand or restructure the set of reachable future design states within a structured possibility space. Building on philosophical accounts of fruitfulness, insights from non-objective search in computer science, and possibility-centered views of science, this paper develops a conceptual model that distinguishes problem-specific fitness landscapes from a possibility lattice governed by prerequisite relations. It further differentiates artifact types by how they support problem-solving or option-making and illustrates fruitfulness through real-world and speculative examples. By reframing evaluation around what contributions make possible, the paper provides an epistemic foundation for anticipatory, speculative, and future-oriented design research.

Keywords: Design Science Research · Fruitfulness · Design Evaluation · Adjacent Possible · Anticipatory Design · Future-Oriented Design

1 Introduction

Design Science Research (DSR) has traditionally evaluated design contributions primarily in terms of their effectiveness in addressing articulated problems. While this orientation has been instrumental in producing immediately useful artifacts, it offers limited guidance for assessing design contributions whose primary impact lies in anticipating and expanding the space of design options. This makes it difficult to justify, compare, and systematically accumulate contributions in the field of anticipatory, speculative [20], or future-oriented design [48] that focus on opening new design trajectories or restructuring and discussing what becomes possible over time. The current dominant epistemic commitment in Information Systems (IS) is that only phenomena that are actual, observable, or instantiated can be legitimately studied, while merely possible phenomena remain outside the scope of rigorous inquiry [13]. This paper addresses this gap by developing a framework of fruitfulness: the capacity of design knowledge to unlock possible design trajectories.

© The Author(s), under exclusive license to Springer Nature Switzerland AG 2026
J. vom Brocke et al. (Eds.): DESRIST 2026, LNCS 16606, pp. 330–347, 2026.
https://doi.org/10.1007/978-3-032-28313-9_19

Evaluating design contributions solely in terms of immediate performance is insufficient for capturing how design knowledge advances over time. Many influential contributions do not primarily improve the utility for a specific problem in a given context, but instead function as stepping stones that unlock new regions of the design space. They are reconfiguring assumptions, introducing new conceptual building blocks, or establishing prerequisites that make previously unattainable solutions reachable.

Information Systems is inherently a future- and world-making discipline, as it studies and designs socio-technical artifacts that actively shape how work and social life will be configured going forward. Recent work in IS has argued that the field must take futures seriously as a legitimate site of inquiry rather than treating them as mere extrapolations of the present. Frank [13] argues that IS theory should not be restricted to describing the factual world, but may also contribute to articulating and constructing possible future worlds. Chiasson et al. [4] call for a stronger philosophical foundation for informing future(s) in IS, highlighting how conceptual frameworks, metaphors, and assumptions actively shape which futures can be envisioned, debated, and enacted. Hovorka and Peter [20] argue that IS research has a responsibility to engage speculatively with alternative possible futures as a core part of scholarly inquiry, calling for approaches that meaningfully explore uncertainty, imagination, and the emergence of unprecedented digital phenomena. Schlagwein et al. [41] emphasize the plurality of futures, the limits of prediction-centered epistemologies, and the need for imaginative, speculative, and design-oriented approaches that explore what might become possible rather than what is most probable.

Why is establishing the fruitfulness concept in DSR important? Research guidelines and validation frameworks influence what scientific knowledge is shared and built upon [43]. According to Foucault [12], labels and taxonomies are not neutral containers, but ordering devices that reflect value assumptions about the world. Streven [46] conceptualizes science as an "epistemic machinery" in which scientific knowledge production is governed by institutionalized selection rules that determine which claims are admitted, retained, and accumulated as legitimate knowledge. Introducing fruitfulness should be understood in this sense: not just as an addition of another evaluative label, but as a reordering of what counts as a meaningful design contribution. It could be seen as a suggestion of alternative selection rules governing the sharing and accumulation of design knowledge.

This raises the following research question: How can DSR conceptualize and evaluate contributions whose primary value lies in what they make possible for future design rather than in their immediate utility?

This paper frames design science as a science of the possible rather than solely a science of the artificial. It goes beyond problem-solving artifacts toward option-making artifacts and a systematic model of how new design knowledge shapes the space of possible futures. Our model of fruitfulness, as the capacity of design knowledge to enable future possibilities, can therefore serve as an epistemic foundation for anticipatory and future-oriented design.

The paper is structured as follows. In Sect. 2, fruitfulness and related concepts from different fields are discussed. Section 3 introduces a model of fruitfulness in design science. Section 4 distinguishes fruitfulness from other concepts. Section 5 discusses implications for communicating and evaluating fruitfulness.

2 Theoretical Foundations

2.1 Philosophical Origins of the Fruitfulness Concept

Peirce [35, pp. 186–199] distinguishes three fundamental modes of reasoning: deduction, induction, and abduction. He uses the term "security" to denote the degree to which a mode of reasoning guarantees correctness [36, pp. 463–474]. He also coined the new term "uberty", denoting the fruitfulness or productiveness of a reasoning [36, p. 465]. Uberty is derived from the Latin "ubertas", meaning abundance or fertility. Deduction derives necessary conclusions from given premises and has therefore high security but low uberty. Induction generalizes from observations to probable rules and offers moderate security and moderate uberty. Abduction reasons from an outcome to a possible explanation or (design) intervention. It has low security but high uberty. While uberty concerns the generative power of reasoning processes, we define fruitfulness as a property of design knowledge situated within a possibility space, capturing how a contribution expands or restructures the space of reachable future design states.

Kuhn [26, p. 322] identifies fruitfulness as one of five criteria by which scientific theories are judged, alongside accuracy, consistency, scope, and simplicity. By fruitfulness, Kuhn refers to a theory's capacity to generate new research problems, novel applications, and further empirical inquiry over time. Importantly, this criterion captures a forward-looking dimension of scientific progress that is not reducible to accuracy or simplicity alone. Ivani [21] develops this insight further by explicating fruitfulness as the capacity of a research program to develop through the questions and heuristics it enables, emphasizing that fruitfulness concerns the structured expansion of inquiry. Building on this insight, the present paper extends the notion of fruitfulness from a theory-evaluation criterion to a structural property of design science contributions, conceptualizing it not merely as the generation of new findings, but as the expansion of reachable future design states within a possibility space.

2.2 Non-objective Search in Computer Science

In computer science, a growing body of work argues that objective-based optimization can be fundamentally brittle when progress depends on discovering stepping stones whose value is not visible from the objective [44]. Ethayarajh and Jurafsky [10] critique leaderboard-based evaluation in machine learning, showing that optimizing against narrow performance objectives often misrepresents real-world utility and suppresses alternative design directions. Their analysis highlights how institutionalized objectives can distort search behavior, reinforcing the need for evaluative concepts that capture generativity and future potential beyond immediate performance. These concerns are further reinforced by the "No Free Lunch" theorems [51], which show that no single optimizer is uniformly best across all possible problems. Performance gains on some classes of problems are necessarily offset by losses on others, undermining the idea of a general-purpose objective-driven search strategy. In response, non-objective search processes were suggested, such as novelty search [30], which reward behavioral novelty, thereby maintaining exploration pressure and avoiding deceptive gradients that trap objective-based search in local optima. Other work discusses robustness under "Knightian uncertainty" [29]. Knightian uncertainty describes situations in which the space of possible outcomes and their associated probabilities is unknown, in contrast to risk, where the possible outcomes are known and meaningful probabilities can be assigned to them [33]. In such settings, many machine-learning methods struggle because they optimize against a predefined objective under an assumed distribution, whereas evolution-like processes that reward exploration and novelty can produce robustness without requiring an explicit objective or a fully specified model of future conditions [29]. The open-ended evolution literature [34] frames the deepest challenge as sustaining continual innovation rather than converging to a fixed target, emphasizing dynamics that keep producing novelty and new niches over time.

Taken together, these lines of research in computer science motivate the concept of fruitfulness in design science. When futures are open-ended, and objectives are incomplete or potentially misleading, the most valuable contributions are often those that expand the reachable search space. Such contributions create stepping stones, capabilities, and prerequisites that enable new design trajectories, rather than merely optimizing performance with respect to today's objective.

2.3 Possibility in Science

The prediction-centered view of science [e.g., 14] views the role of science as developing increasingly accurate theories to predict what will happen. Then, given the system's initial state and the natural laws governing it, we can predict its state at any future time. For example, if we know the mass of an object, its distance from the surface, and the gravitational force, we can calculate when the object will hit the surface. This powerful view has existed since the time of Galileo and Newton. In this view, the best way to understand the behavior of more complex systems is to reduce them to their subsystems, apply the applicable theoretical laws on this sublevel, and then infer the global behavior of the more complex system. Uncertain knowledge about the initial state leads to probabilistic predictions of the future state, while the prevailing predictive logic remains unchanged.

Because the future state is, in this view, fully determined by the initial state and the governing natural laws, the future is treated as epistemically fixed, differing from the past only in terms of uncertainty. Alternative futures and counterfactuals, therefore, do not play an explanatory role within this framework. Consequently, these prediction-centered theories are not intended to be generative. They aim to describe and predict what will happen, rather than to account for what futures might be produced.

This prediction-centered view of science has problems capturing some emergent phenomena of reality. Even if, in principle, these emergent phenomena could be predicted by underlying basic natural laws, such reductions would not provide any meaningful explanation.

Deutsch [7, p. 22, emphasis added] gives an example of why this reductionism is often inappropriate: "Consider one particular copper atom at the tip of the nose of the statue of Sir Winston Churchill that stands in Parliament Square in London. Let me try to explain why that copper atom is there. It is because Churchill served as prime minister in the House of Commons nearby; and because his ideas and leadership contributed to the Allied victory in the Second World War; and because it is customary to honour such people by putting up statues of them; and because bronze, a traditional material for such statues, contains copper, and so on. Thus *we explain a low-level physical observation* – the presence of a copper atom at a particular location *through extremely high-level theories about emergent phenomena* such as ideas, leadership, war and tradition. There is no reason why there should exist, even in principle, any lower-level explanation of the presence of that copper atom than the one I have just given. Presumably a reductive 'theory of everything' would in principle make a low-level prediction of the probability that such a statue will exist, given the condition of (say) the solar system at some earlier date. It would also in principle describe how the statue probably got there. But such descriptions and predictions (wildly infeasible, of course) *would explain nothing*. They would merely describe the trajectory that each copper atom followed [...]. But even if you had the superhuman capacity to follow such lengthy predictions of the copper atom's being there, you would still not be able to say 'Ah yes, now I understand why they are there'." Therefore, higher-level phenomena are not simply derivable from lower-level theories, but rather require higher-level theories that refer directly to those phenomena [7, p. 30].

The non-generative property of prediction-centered theories is further illustrated with the following thought experiment: imagine a hypothetical mousetrap oracle that could perfectly predict which mousetrap would catch how many mice [7, p. 7]. This mousetrap oracle would still not help us build a better mousetrap. Prediction alone presupposes that we already know which designs to test, but it does not indicate how to generate those candidates. Without explanations of how and why a design works or fails, the oracle offers no guidance for modifying, improving, or inventing new designs. Prediction alone cannot generate new possibilities. It can only assess those options that have already been conceived.

Addressing this gap requires a shift from a prediction-centered view of science to a possibility-centered view [16]. There are various approaches from different scientific fields that aim to capture how complex systems (including human individuals, teams, companies, societies, but also ecosystems, or technical systems) navigate and explore new possibilities. These interdisciplinary endeavors are sometimes referred to under the umbrella term of possibility studies [16] and span both social and natural sciences.

In theoretical physics, e.g., Deutsch [6] proposed the constructor theory. Central to the constructor theory is the concept of counterfactuals: statements about what is possible and what is impossible. The constructor theory treats counterfactuals as fundamental because they specify the space of transformations a system can and cannot support, independent of whether those transformations are ever realized. In the same counterfactual manner, this paper conceptualizes fruitfulness by evaluating design knowledge according to the extent to which a contribution changes what designers can, in principle, build next.

Possibility studies seek to understand how individuals and collectives become aware of, imagine, and explore new possibilities across psychological, material, technological, social, and cultural domains, focusing on human engagement with what is possible and impossible in shaping future action [16, p. x]. New possibilities are a pervasive feature of everyday life, as individuals continually encounter, explore, and adopt new ideas, technologies, relationships, and situations [31]. However, what can be discovered or acted upon in any given situation is constrained by the adjacent possible, such that only a limited set of nearby possibilities is available to specific agents within particular environments, depending on their affordances and capacities [3, p. 17].

The adjacent possible refers to the set of possibilities that are reachable from the current state of a system, given existing elements, capabilities, and constraints [3, p. 18]. Originating in evolutionary biology [25], it characterizes how complex systems – from biospheres to technologies and ideas – evolve by incrementally exploring nearby possibilities that become available as new combinations of existing components are formed. It is "a kind of shadow future, hovering on the edges of the present state of things, a map of all the ways in which the present can reinvent itself" [22, p. 31]. As adjacent possibilities are actualized, they expand the space of what can be explored next, creating cascades of new opportunities that unfold through successive steps of discovery and recombination (see Fig. 1).

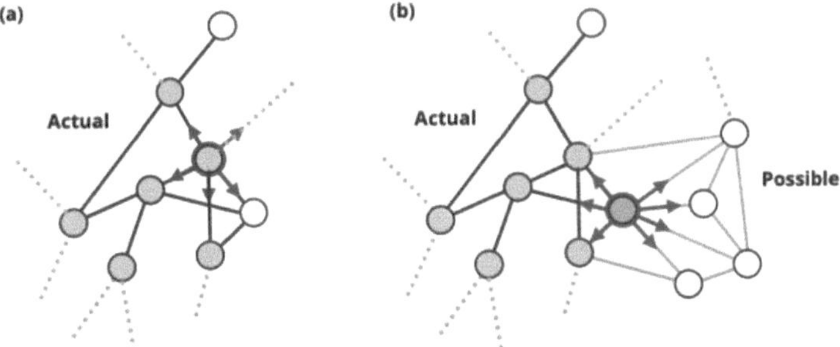

Fig. 1. Illustration of the *adjacent possible* as a graph that expands conditionally from state (a) to state (b) when a previously unvisited node becomes actualized, thereby making new neighboring possibilities reachable (adapted from [31]).

Fruitfulness captures this generative dimension by evaluating design knowledge according to the new possibilities it unlocks within a structured space of reachability. From a possibility-centered perspective, fruitfulness concerns whether a design contribution increases the range of possible transformations, rather than trying to predict what transformation will occur.

3   A Model of Fruitfulness in Design Science

This section develops a conceptual model of fruitfulness in design science by treating design as search in a structured space of possibilities rather than only optimization on a problem-specific fitness landscape. We define fruitfulness as the evaluative property of a design science contribution that expands the set of reachable future design states within a structured possibility space. This section explains how search logics in DSR relate to both fitness and reachability, introduces the coupled model of fitness landscape and possibility lattice, and shows how different artifact types engage the possibility lattice to make new regions of the design space accessible, activatable, or critically examinable.

3.1 Design as a Search Process in the Possibility Space

Simon [42, p. 127] describes design as fundamentally a search process in a solution space, in which designers explore alternatives under constraints. Similarly, Perkins [37, p. 496] mentions that "the work of any creative system can be viewed as a process of search through a space of possibilities or a 'possibility space'". This view is picked up in DSR, where Hevner et al. [19, p. 88] state that "design is essentially a search process to discover an effective solution to a problem", emphasizing the navigation of a fitness landscape through heuristics aimed at optimizing utility.

Yet Simon himself already questioned whether this purely optimization-centered view is always appropriate [42, p. 162]. He argued that designing with fixed final goals can be inconsistent with our limited ability to foresee the future [42, p. 163]. Instead, he characterizes design as an evolving activity in which the real outcome of action is to set initial conditions for what comes next, guided at times by general notions of interestingness and novelty, and oriented toward "keep[ing] open the options for the future or perhaps even to broaden them a bit by creating new variety and new niches" [42, p. 167]. Fruitfulness operationalizes Simon's intuition about designing for future flexibility by providing a conceptual model for assessing how design knowledge shapes what can be designed next.

3.2 Conceptual Model Overview

Before introducing the conceptual model, consider the following illustrative case of fruitfulness: the invention of the iPod, which emerged from Apple's "digital hub" strategy [23, p. 62]. As personal computing increasingly became the center for managing digital photos, videos, and music, Apple's software teams recognized that existing MP3 players were unsatisfactory, prompting an exploration of whether a better device could be designed. The effort initially stalled because available components implied unacceptable trade-offs between size, battery life, and storage capacity [24]. The decisive stepping stone came not from Apple's own roadmap, but from a chance encounter with a prototype 1.8-inch hard drive developed by Toshiba, for which its creators had no clear application [23, p. 57]. The Toshiba hard drive represents a stepping stone from outside Apple's own design trajectory, while the iPod instantiated this externally originating knowledge and opened a new region in the space of what could be designed for portable music devices. The drive itself had little standalone value, but its significance lay in enabling design configurations that were previously unreachable, thereby expanding the space of possible designs that could subsequently be realized. The conceptual model introduced below provides the formal vocabulary to analyze cases like this systematically.

We conceptualize design science as a process of distributed cognition in which multiple designers collectively explore a structured design space. This space comprises two distinct but coupled topographies: a fitness landscape, representing the functional utility of material artifact instantiations, and what we call a "possibility lattice", representing the path-dependent dependencies and prerequisite structures that govern which design knowledge states become reachable.

Figure 2 provides an overview of the conceptual model, clarifying how fitness and fruitfulness operate at different levels. It distinguishes material entities (left side of the figure) from abstract entities (right side) and follows the distinction between material and abstract artifacts of Gregor & Hevner [18, p. 341].

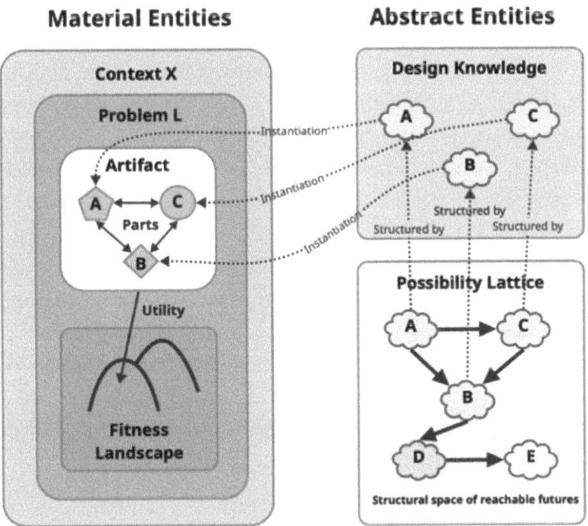

Fig. 2. Overview of the conceptual model linking artifacts, fitness, design knowledge, and the possibility lattice.

On the left side, instantiated artifacts are situated within a concrete context, solving a concrete problem. Artifacts consist of multiple interrelated parts or components [28, p. 1273]. Each part instantiates different abstract design knowledge elements [32]. The artifact's performance is evaluated through utility or performance and represented on a fitness landscape [15], which captures how well a given instantiation performs with respect to a particular problem framing in a context.

A context (or setting) refers to the situational conditions under which an artifact is designed, instantiated, and evaluated, including the task, organizational or industry environment, and whether the setting is experimental (e.g., laboratory) or real-world (in vivo) [28, p. 1273]. A problem denotes a specific design challenge or goal arising within a context. Multiple distinct problems may exist within a single context, while similar or identical problems can arise across different contexts. Each problem defines its own fitness landscape with its own goodness criteria. The left side of the figure emphasizes that fitness is inherently context- and problem-dependent and tied to the material instantiation of design knowledge.

On the right side, the figure depicts abstract entities, consisting of abstract design knowledge elements (A, B, C). Design knowledge can be instantiated into materialized artifacts. Design knowledge is structured by the possibility lattice, which encodes prerequisite and dependency relations that determine which future design states can be reached. Importantly, the lattice contains not only currently instantiated knowledge elements but also latent possible elements (D, E) that are not yet realized in any artifact. This structural space of reachable futures represents the domain in which fruitfulness operates: design contributions differ not by their immediate fitness, but by how they expand, delay, or foreclose access to future design possibilities across contexts.

3.3 Possibility Lattice

We conceptualize sets of design knowledge elements as nodes in a possibility lattice. In mathematics, a lattice is a partially ordered structure that represents how elements are related through dependency and combination. A prerequisite relation specifies that a knowledge element becomes reachable only once one or more other elements are already in place, thereby inducing a partial ordering over the possibility lattice. As a result, some possibilities are latent rather than adjacent: they exist within the space of the possible but remain inaccessible until their prerequisites are satisfied.

Prerequisite relations thus explain why different sequences of design activity are not equivalent and why certain contributions function as stepping stones or gateway nodes by unlocking entire regions of future possibilities. Nodes in the possibility lattice differ in their generative capacity: some contributions unlock only narrow extensions, while highly fruitful ones open up an entire surrounding region of new, thematically related possibilities that can be activated thereafter.

A possibility lattice is characterized by a topology that is inherently path dependent, such that the sequence in which possibilities are explored shapes which future possibilities become reachable [50, p. 6]. New possibilities emerge through combinatorial emergence, arising from novel recombinations of existing elements. This process is marked by the irreversibility of expansion: once a possibility is actualized and its adjacent possibilities are revealed, the space of the possible is permanently reconfigured. The structure of this space is unprestatable [3, p. 4], meaning it cannot be fully specified or predicted in advance, as each newly realized possibility reshapes the topology itself. Together, these properties render the adjacent possible fundamentally open-ended, with its structure and extent revealed only through ongoing exploration and enactment.

Fruitfulness denotes a capacity rather than a deterministic prediction. Whether a given possibility is ultimately realized depends on human agency, contextual conditions, and contingent events.

3.4 Artifact Types by Their Relation to the Possibility Lattice

Different artifact types contribute to fruitfulness in distinct ways by expanding the adjacent possible along different dimensions of the possibility lattice. Artifacts in design science can be distinguished by how they relate to the structure of the possibility lattice and by the kinds of design knowledge they instantiate or engage. Only actual design knowledge can be instantiated directly in an artifact. Latent and impossible design knowledge, by definition, cannot be realized as part of an artifact directly. However, we can engage indirectly by probing, speculating, or imagining artifacts that are not yet possible or that will never be (see Fig. 3).

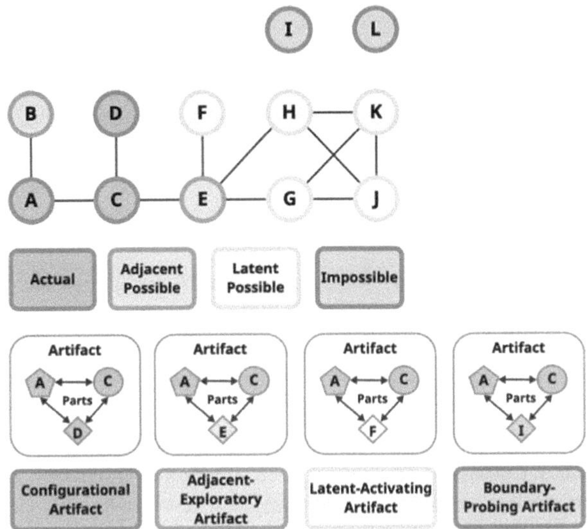

Fig. 3. Artifact Types by the Relation to the Possibility Lattice.

Configurational artifacts are composed entirely of design knowledge elements that are already actual, yet whose specific configuration, integration, or contextual instantiation has not previously existed. Even when all underlying knowledge elements are established, bringing them together into a concrete artifact for a particular problem and context constitutes a novel design act. Such artifacts are primarily evaluated in terms of fitness, rigor, and validity, while contributing incremental fruitfulness by demonstrating new viable configurations within the existing design space.

Adjacent-exploratory artifacts instantiate at least one design element drawn from the adjacent possible, where the underlying knowledge has become reachable but is not yet widely adopted. These artifacts explore emerging regions of the possibility lattice. Their evaluation combines considerations of immediate utility with consideration to their fruitfulness in extending new design trajectories.

Latent-activating artifacts do not instantiate latent design knowledge directly, as such knowledge is not yet realizable but possible in principle. They are designed to approximate the prerequisites required for latent possibilities to become adjacent in subsequent design cycles. These prerequisites could be technical, organizational, conceptual, or institutional. These artifacts include speculative and anticipatory designs that explore whether emerging possibilities should be pursued and under what conditions they might be realized responsibly. Their primary contribution lies not in near-term utility, but in restructuring the design space by expanding, redirecting, or critically reframing which possibilities are considered reachable or acceptable. Accordingly, such artifacts are evaluated predominantly for their fruitfulness rather than their immediate fitness.

Boundary-probing artifacts, by contrast, engage with design states that are impossible even in principle given current or foreseeable constraints, including physical laws, logical contradictions, or fundamental ethical prohibitions. These artifacts do not aim to activate future realizations, but to probe, expose, or interrogate the boundaries of the possible itself. They may do so through exaggeration or speculative enactment, including critical design practices that question whether certain futures should exist, even if hypothetically achievable. Their epistemic value lies in clarifying impossibility conditions, revealing hidden assumptions, and critically examining the values and worldviews that structure the design space.

3.5 Examples of Artifact Types

Pillet et al. [39] present *RATER*, an AI-based system for assessing the content validity of psychometric scales. Although content validation is a core step in rigorous measurement, practical barriers such as cost, cognitive load on human judges, and limited replicability have constrained its widespread adoption. The decisive stepping stone came from outside psychometric research: transformer-based large language models, originally developed for general natural language processing, constituted adjacent possible design knowledge that made automated, domain-independent content validation feasible. *RATER* functions as an adjacent-exploratory artifact that instantiates newly available design knowledge into a new class of solution that had been theoretically desirable but practically difficult to reach before.

Thoring et al. [49] introduce the *Speculens* system, an AI-augmented mixed-reality environment designed to support imaginative knowledge creation and critical engagement with possible socio-technical futures. *Speculens* enables participants to external-ize conjectural futures, encounter them as embodied "artifacts-from-the-future," [38] and reflect on the values, assumptions, and trajectories embedded in those imaginaries. The system exemplifies a latent-activating artifact because it establishes the concep-tual, epistemic, and institutional prerequisites that enable currently latent possibilities to become meaningfully explorable and potentially realizable in subsequent design cycles. Its fruitfulness lies in expanding what designers can meaningfully inquire into, debate, and prepare for, thereby activating regions of the possibility lattice that would otherwise remain inaccessible under utility- or performance-centered evaluation regimes.

El Sawy and Rydén [9] describe *Phygitar*, a non-digital planet in the year 2050, using futures studies, science-fiction prototyping, and speculative theorizing. The paper envisions an extreme, holistic future to surface new concepts such as rhythmic fabric, phygital pulsing, and hybrid intelligence. *Phygitar* functions as a boundary-probing arti-fact: it engages with design states that are currently impossible or radically indeterminate to interrogate the limits, assumptions, and values that structure contemporary thinking. Its fruitfulness lies in this boundary work. By clarifying what may be impossible, unde-sirable, or ethically problematic, the paper reshapes the possibility lattice for design science, redirecting attention toward alternative futures and reframing what kinds of design knowledge are worth pursuing next.

4 What Fruitfulness is Not

Sometimes it is a good practice not just to describe what a concept is, but also what it is not, as Sutton & Staw [47] did for theories.

4.1 Fruitfulness is not Generalization or Exaptation.

Figure 4 illustrates two established pathways through which design science artifacts extend beyond their original problem and context: generalization and exaptation. An artifact is initially developed to address a specific problem (Problem L) within a given context (Context X).

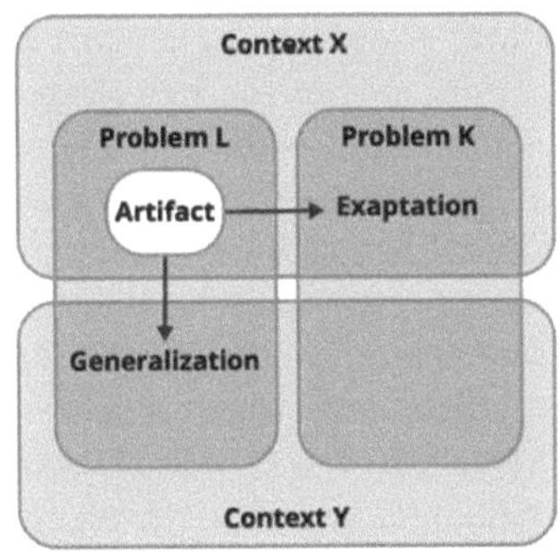

Fig. 4. Generalization and exaptation as two pathways by which a design artifact extends beyond its original problem and context.

One form of extension generalizes the usefulness or utility claim to other contexts or settings [5]. In this figure, this would be the claim that the fitness of the artifact is similar in a new context Y as it was in the original context X. This is related to context claims, which "explicate the situations or conditions in which the proposed outcomes of the artifact are expected to hold" [28, p. 1274].

In evolutionary biology, exaptation refers to a trait that originally evolved for one function (or with no adaptive function at all) but was later co-opted for a different use, thereby becoming evolutionarily significant without having been selected for that role in the first place [17]. One example is feathers, which likely evolved in dinosaurs for insulation or display, and were only later co-opted for flight in birds [17, p. 7]. In DSR, exaptation extends existing design knowledge by adapting known artifacts or principles to address a new problem domain [18, p. 347].

While both generalization and exaptation describe how an artifact can be transferred or reused beyond its original problem context, they do not capture the generative expansion of future design possibilities. Fruitfulness differs in that it concerns how a design contribution restructures the space of what can be designed next, rather than how well an existing artifact performs or can be repurposed across contexts or problems.

4.2 Fruitfulness is not Artifact Generativity

Drechsler [8] argues that design science should look beyond immediate utility and introduces artifact generativity as a lens for sustained utility and transformation. He distinguishes between technical generativity [52], social generativity [27], and informational generativity [1]. However, he focuses on how artefacts should be designed to remain adaptable and transformative over time. By contrast, fruitfulness evaluates the design science contributions themselves, conceptualizing them as a structural property of design knowledge that determines which future design states become reachable.

4.3 Fruitfulness is Not Just Basic Research

The static view of research [45, p. 8] treats basic and applied research as opposing categories along a single spectrum, implying an inherent trade-off between the pursuit of understanding and practical use. In the dynamic form [45, p. 9], there is a linear model of innovation, in which knowledge flows sequentially from basic research to applied research, development, and ultimately production.

Stokes's quadrant model [45, p. 73] challenges the static and dynamic views by rejecting the assumption that understanding and use must trade off against one another. Stokes [45, p. 73] conceptualizes research by distinguishing two independent dimensions: the quest for fundamental understanding and considerations of practical use. Crossing these dimensions yields four quadrants. "Bohr's Quadrant" represents pure basic research, driven by fundamental understanding without immediate concern for use. "Edison's Quadrant" represents pure applied research, focused on practical problem-solving without seeking general theory. "Pasteur's Quadrant" captures use-inspired basic research, which simultaneously advances fundamental knowledge while addressing real-world problems. The fourth quadrant, low on both dimensions, represents work that contributes neither to theory nor to application.

Fruitfulness cannot be equated with basic research, because it is not defined by the pursuit of fundamental understanding alone. A contribution may be highly fruitful by opening new design trajectories, enabling novel combinations, or establishing critical prerequisites for future innovation, even when it does not advance general theory in the sense associated with Bohr's Quadrant. Conversely, much basic research may deepen understanding without materially expanding what can be designed or enacted next. Fruitfulness instead concerns how a contribution restructures the space of possible future actions across theory, design, and practice.

4.4 Fruitfulness is Not Citation Count

To determine whether a contribution is fruitful, counting its past citations is insufficient. Bhattacharya and Packalen [2] show that citation-based evaluation systematically biases scientific activity toward incremental, low-risk work in crowded areas, while discouraging exploratory contributions that are unlikely to be cited early but are essential as stepping stones for later breakthroughs. Their analysis demonstrates that many highly fruitful ideas emerge during an exploratory phase in which immediate impact and citations are low, yet these contributions restructure the knowledge space by enabling subsequent advances. From a fruitfulness perspective, the epistemic value of a design contribution lies not in how often it is cited, but in how it expands the adjacent possible by creating new capabilities, concepts, or prerequisites that future designers and researchers can build upon; even if recognition arrives late or indirectly.

4.5 Fruitfulness It not "Anything Goes"

Paul Feyerabend's famous slogan "anything goes" is often misunderstood as an endorsement of arbitrariness or the abandonment of any standards. Feyerabend [11] argues instead that rigid methodological rules can inhibit scientific progress by prematurely excluding unconventional approaches that later prove productive. His claim is historical and critical rather than just anarchic.

In contrast, epistemologies such as critical rationalism [40] focus primarily on the convergent side of scientific progress: conjectures are subjected to criticism, testing, and refutation, and knowledge advances by eliminating what does not survive this process. As Popper [40, p. 7] explicitly notes, the question of how genuinely new conjectures arise "may be of great interest to empirical psychology," but is "irrelevant to the logical analysis of scientific knowledge".

Fruitfulness addresses precisely this neglected divergent aspect of inquiry: not how conjectures are selected or falsified, but how new conjectures, design directions, and possibilities come into being. While fruitfulness shares Feyerabend's concern that excessive rigidity can stifle creativity, it does not collapse into an "anything goes" position. Instead, it remains a structured evaluative criterion: design contributions are assessed by how they expand, reorganize, or delimit a shared space of reachable possibilities. In this sense, fruitfulness complements rather than rejects critical rationalism by making the generative side of design knowledge explicit and assessable without abandoning epistemic discipline.

5 Implications for Evaluating Design Science Contributions

Evaluating design science contributions can be expanded beyond assessing how well an artifact performs for a specified problem and context. While fitness remains essential for judging the quality of an instantiation, it does not capture how design knowledge advances over time. Fruitfulness highlights a complementary dimension of evaluation that focuses on how a contribution reshapes the space of future design possibilities, including the prerequisites, assumptions, and capabilities that condition what can be designed next across contexts.

Fruitfulness draws attention to design contributions whose primary value lies in enabling future work rather than delivering immediate utility. Stepping-stone contributions, speculative and anticipatory designs, and artifacts with delayed or indirect impact can be recognized as meaningful scientific outputs when they expand, redirect, or clarify the design space. Distinguishing among different relations to the possibility lattice, such as configurational, adjacent-exploratory, latent-activating, and boundary-probing artifacts, suggests that evaluative expectations should vary based on how a contribution engages with and reshapes the space of future design possibilities, thereby contributing to fruitfulness through the expansion of the adjacent possible.

Fruitfulness supports a view of design science as a cumulative enterprise in which knowledge grows by opening new trajectories rather than by converging solely on optimal solutions. It reframes rigor to include careful articulation of counterfactual possibilities, dependencies, and constraints, and it aligns evaluation practices with future-oriented, speculative, and anticipatory forms of design inquiry. In doing so, fruitfulness helps bridge the gap between the expanding ambitions of design science and the criteria used to assess its contributions.

Taken together, these implications suggest the need for evaluation practices that explicitly attend to fruitfulness alongside fitness. Reviewers, editors, and authors are therefore encouraged to articulate and assess not only what a design contribution accomplishes in its immediate context, but also how it opens, redirects, or constrains future design trajectories. Making such expectations explicit can support more pluralistic, forward-looking assessments of design science contributions.

To support such assessments, we suggest the following guiding questions when evaluating a contribution for fruitfulness: Does the contribution reconfigure existing design knowledge into a novel arrangement that enables solutions not achievable before? Does it introduce new conceptual primitives, components, or configurations that others can recombine in future design efforts? Does it relax constraints or remove dependencies that previously blocked a class of solutions? Does it make visible or explorable a region of the design space that was previously inaccessible or unarticulated? And does it establish technical, conceptual, or institutional prerequisites that condition what can be designed next, beyond the immediate problem context? These questions are not intended as a checklist, but as an orienting frame that can help authors communicate, and reviewers recognize, the forward-looking dimension of a design contribution.

6 Conclusion

In conclusion, this paper introduces the concept of fruitfulness as a complementary evaluative dimension for design science contributions – one that captures how design knowledge expands or restructures what can be designed next, rather than only how well a particular artifact performs in a given problem–context configuration. By modeling design knowledge in a possibility lattice coupled to problem-specific fitness landscapes, the paper makes visible why stepping stones, prerequisite-setting contributions, and speculative or critical artifacts can be methodologically valuable even when their immediate utility is modest. This shift supports a more future-facing and cumulative design science: one that can justify and accumulate contributions by the trajectories they enable, the dependencies they clarify, and the counterfactual design futures they make intelligible and discussable.

This paper opens several fruitful avenues for future research. First, the conceptual model of fruitfulness could be extended through agent-based simulations of idealized design science communities operating under different epistemic regimes. By varying institutional selection rules, such as fitness-based evaluation, fruitfulness-based evaluation, or hybrid regimes, it would be possible to explore how different knowledge institutions shape long-term innovation dynamics, path dependencies, and the emergence of gateway contributions. This kind of "computational thought experiment" or "epistemic simulation" would give validity [28] to a potential claim that fruitfulness should be part of the design science evaluation. Second, future work could explore semi-automated extraction of fruitfulness-related claims from the literature using information extraction techniques. Such methods could identify statements about enabling conditions, prerequisites, future trajectories, and unlocked possibilities, helping to build longitudinal datasets that support cumulative analysis of fruitfulness across design science research. Finally, future work could develop computational proxies for fruitfulness by measuring how a design contribution expands or diverges from the existing design knowledge corpus at a given point in time, thereby capturing structural novelty and potential reach.

Together, these avenues suggest that taking fruitfulness seriously as an evaluative concern would allow design science to better recognize, cultivate, and accumulate contributions that shape the long-term evolution of its knowledge space.

Disclosure of Interests. The authors have no competing interests to declare.

References

1. Avital, M., Te'eni, D.: From generative fit to generative capacity: exploring an emerging dimension of information systems design and task performance. Inf. Syst. J. **19**(4), 345–367 (2009). https://doi.org/10.1111/j.1365-2575.2007.00291.x
2. Bhattacharya, J., Packalen, M.: Stagnation and scientific incentives. Nat. Bureau Econ. Res. (2020). https://doi.org/10.3386/w26752
3. Björneborn, L.: Adjacent possible. In: Glăveanu, V.P. (ed.) The Palgrave Encyclopedia of the Possible, pp. 16–28. Palgrave Macmillan, Cham (2022)
4. Chiasson, M., et al.: Philosophical foundations for informing the future(S) through IS research. Eur. J. Inf. Syst. **27**(3), 367–379 (2018). https://doi.org/10.1080/0960085X.2018.1435232
5. Cronholm, S., et al.: Generalisation of design science research. In: ECIS 2024 Proceedings (2024)
6. Deutsch, D.: Constructor theory. Synthese **190**(18), 4331–4359 (2013). https://doi.org/10.1007/s11229-013-0279-z
7. Deutsch, D.: The Fabric of Reality. Penguin, London (1998)
8. Drechsler, A.: Designing for change and transformation: exploring the role of IS artefact generativity. In: Australasian Conference on Information Systems (2017)
9. El Sawy, O., Rydén, P.: Phygitar: envisioning the rhythmic Phygital ecosystem in 2050. Commun. Assoc. Inf. Syst. **56**, 1 (2025)
10. Ethayarajh, K., Jurafsky, D.: Utility is in the eye of the user: a critique of NLP Leaderboards. In: Webber, B., et al. (eds.) Proceedings of the 2020 Conference on Empirical Methods in Natural Language Processing (EMNLP), pp. 4846–4853 Association for Computational Linguistics, Online (2020). https://doi.org/10.18653/v1/2020.emnlp-main.393
11. Feyerabend, P.: Against Method: Outline of an Anarchistic Theory of Knowledge. Verso, London (2010)
12. Foucault, M.: The Order of Things: Archaeology of the Human Sciences: An Archaeology of the Human Sciences. Routledge, London (2006)
13. Frank, U.: Theories in the light of contingency and change: possible future worlds and well-grounded hope as a supplement to truth. In: Proceedings of the 50th Hawaii International Conference on System Sciences (HICSS) (2017)
14. Friedman, M.: The methodology of positive economics. In: Hausman, D.M. (ed.) The Philosophy of Economics: An Anthology, pp. 145–178 Cambridge University Press, Cambridge (2007). https://doi.org/10.1017/CBO9780511819025.010
15. Gill, T.G., Hevner, A.R.: A fitness-utility model for design science research. ACM Trans. Manag. Inf. Syst. **4**(2), 1–24 (2013). https://doi.org/10.1145/2499962.2499963
16. Glăveanu, V.P. (ed.): The Palgrave Encyclopedia of the Possible. Palgrave Macmillan, Cham (2022)

17. Gould, S.J., Vrba, E.S.: Exaptation-a missing term in the science of form. Paleobiology **8**(1), 4–15 (1982)
18. Gregor, S., Hevner, A.R.: Positioning and presenting design science research for maximum impact. MIS Q. **37**(2), 337–355 (2013)
19. Bichler, M.: Design science in information systems research. Wirtschaftsinformatik **48**(2), 133–135 (2006). https://doi.org/10.1007/s11576-006-0028-8
20. Hovorka, D.S., Peter, S.: Speculatively engaging future(s): four theses. MIS Q. **45**(1), 461–466 (2021). https://doi.org/10.25300/MISQ/2021/15434.1.2
21. Ivani, S.: What we (should) talk about when we talk about fruitfulness. Eur. J. Philosophy Sci. **9**(1), 4 (2019). https://doi.org/10.1007/s13194-018-0231-7
22. Johnson, S.: Where Good Ideas Come From: The Natural History of Innovation. Penguin Publishing Group, New York (2011)
23. Jones, D.: IPod, Therefore I am. Orion Publishing, London (2005)
24. Kahney, L.: An illustrated history of the iPod and its massive impact [Updated]. https://www.cultofmac.com/news/an-illustrated-history-of-the-ipod-and-its-massive-impact-ipod-10th-anniversary. Accessed 30 Jan 2026
25. Kauffman, S.A.: Prolegomenon to patterns in evolution. Biosystems **123**, 3–8 (2014). https://doi.org/10.1016/j.biosystems.2014.03.004
26. Kuhn, T.S.: The Essential Tension: Selected Studies in Scientific Tradition and Change. University of Chicago Press, Chicago, Ill (1977)
27. Lane, D.A.: Complexity and innovation dynamics. In: Handbook on the Economic Complexity of Technological Change. Edward Elgar Publishing (2011)
28. Larsen, K.R., et al.: Validity in design science. MIS Q. **49**(4), 1267–1294 (2025). https://doi.org/10.25300/MISQ/2024/18064
29. Lehman, J., et al.: Evolution and the Knightian Blindspot of machine learning. http://arxiv.org/abs/2501.13075 (2025). https://doi.org/10.48550/arXiv.2501.13075
30. Lehman, J., Stanley, K.O.: Abandoning objectives: evolution through the search for novelty alone. Evol. Comput. **19**(2), 189–223 (2011). https://doi.org/10.1162/EVCO_a_00025
31. Loreto, V., et al.: Dynamics on expanding spaces: modeling the emergence of novelties. In: Degli Esposti, M. et al., (eds.) Creativity and universality in language, pp. 59–83. Springer, Cham (2016). https://doi.org/10.1007/978-3-319-24403-7_5
32. Lukyanenko, R., et al.: Instantiation validity in IS design research. In: Tremblay, M.C., et al. (eds.) Advancing the Impact of Design Science: Moving from Theory to Practice, pp. 321–328. Springer, Cham (2014). https://doi.org/10.1007/978-3-319-06701-8_22
33. Nishimura, K.G., Ozaki, H.: Search and Knightian uncertainty. J. Econ. Theory **119**(2), 299–333 (2004)
34. Packard, N., et al.: An overview of open-ended evolution: editorial introduction to the open-ended evolution II special issue. Artif. Life **25**(2), 93–103 (2019)
35. Peirce, C.S.: The Essential Peirce, Volume 1: Selected Philosophical Writings (1867–1893). Indiana University Press, Bloomington (1992)
36. Peirce, C.S.: The Essential Pierce, Volume 2: Selected Philosophical Writings (1893–1913). Indiana University Press, Bloomington (1998)
37. Perkins, D.N.: Insight in minds and genes. In: The Nature of Insight, pp. 495–533. The MIT Press, Cambridge, MA (1995)
38. Peter, S., et al.: Artefacts from the future: engaging audiences in possible futures with emerging technologies for better outcomes. In: ECIS Proceedings (2020)
39. Pillet, J.-C., et al.: AI-augmented content validation in behavioral research: development and evaluation of the RATER system. MIS Q. **50**(1), 59–86 (2026)
40. Popper, K.R.: The Logic of Scientific Discovery. Routledge, London (2010)
41. Schlagwein, D., et al.: Digital futures: definition (what), importance (why) and methods (how). J. Inf. Technol. **40**(1), 2–8 (2025). https://doi.org/10.1177/02683962241301544

42. Simon, H.A.: The Sciences of the Artificial. The MIT Press, Cambridge, MA (2019). https://doi.org/10.7551/mitpress/12107.001.0001
43. Siponen, M., et al.: Research perspectives: reconsidering the role of research method guidelines for interpretive, mixed methods, and design science research. J. Assoc. Inf. Syst. **22**, 4 (2021). https://doi.org/10.17705/1jais.00692
44. Stanley, K.O., Lehman, J.: Why Greatness Cannot Be Planned: The Myth of the Objective. Springer, Cham (2015). https://doi.org/10.1007/978-3-319-15524-1
45. Stokes, D.E.: Pasteur's Quadrant: Basic Science and Technological Innovation. Bloomsbury Publishing, New York (2011)
46. Strevens, M.: The Knowledge Machine: How Irrationality Created Modern Science. Liveright Pub Corp, New York (2020)
47. Sutton, R.I., Staw, B.M.: What theory is not. Adm. Sci. Q. **40**(3), 371–384 (1995). https://doi.org/10.2307/2393788
48. Thoring, K., et al.: Mind the future gap: introducing the FOD framework for future-oriented design. In: Proceedings of the 56th Hawaii International Conference on System Sciences (HICSS) (2023)
49. Thoring, K., et al.: Speculens: AI-augmented mixed reality for imaginative knowledge creation and critical futures discourse. In: Proceedings of the 59. Hawaii International Conference on Information Systems (HICSS) (2026)
50. Tria, F., et al.: The dynamics of correlated novelties. Sci. Rep. **4**, 5890 (2014). https://doi.org/10.1038/srep05890
51. Wolpert, D.H., Macready, W.G.: No free lunch theorems for optimization. IEEE Trans. Evol. Comput. **1**(1), 67–82 (2002)
52. Zittrain, J.: The Future of the Internet: and How to Stop It. Penguin UK, London (2009)

Design Science at Scale: Applying Consortium Research Methodology in Open Source Ecosystems

Markus Spiekermann[1(✉)] ⬤, Boris Otto[1,2] ⬤, and Julia Pampus[2] ⬤

[1] TU Dortmund University, Dortmund, Germany
{markus.spiekermann,boris.otto}@tu-dortmund.de
[2] Fraunhofer ISST, Dortmund, Germany
julia.pampus@isst.fraunhofer.de

Abstract. The pursuit of relevance and rigor in Design Science Research (DSR) has spurred collaborative methods that tightly integrate researchers and practitioners. Consortium Research (CR) has emerged as a structured approach operationalizing DSR in multi-organization settings, enabling the co-creation of artifacts that are both scientifically sound and immediately applicable. This paper examines how CR can be applied at scale in an enterprise-grade open source project, using the Eclipse Dataspace Components (EDC) project as a case study. We adopt the established CR and map it onto the open source context. The EDC case involves a multi-partner open source initiative for building dataspaces and inter-organizational data sharing, illustrating how CR facilitates knowledge exchange between academia and industry. Beyond relevance, the study emphasizes how open source initiatives can strengthen scientific rigor under conditions of increasing technological and organizational dynamism of research activities. The findings highlight that open source projects can serve as DSR engines that produce broadly applicable solutions and insights at scale. The paper delivers methodological guidance for researchers and contributes to the Design Science Research knowledge base by integrating practical insights from a real-world consortium setting.

Keywords: Design Science Research · Consortium Research · Open Source Ecosystems · Eclipse Dataspace Components · Multi-Stakeholder Collaboration · Knowledge Transfer · Dataspaces

1 Introduction

1.1 Motivation and Problem Statement

In the information systems (IS) community, a long-standing debate concerns the relevance of research outcomes to practice [1, 2]. DSR proposes a response to this challenge by emphasizing the purposeful design of IT artifacts that are both rigorously grounded and practically useful [3, 4]. Methodological frameworks such as the Design Science Research Methodology (DSRM) structure this process across phases from problem identification to artifact design, evaluation, and communication [5]. Nevertheless, ensuring

© The Author(s), under exclusive license to Springer Nature Switzerland AG 2026
J. vom Brocke et al. (Eds.): DESRIST 2026, LNCS 16606, pp. 348–364, 2026.
https://doi.org/10.1007/978-3-032-28313-9_20

that research addresses relevant problems and systematically incorporates knowledge remains challenging, particularly in dynamic and technology-intensive domains [1, 6]. These challenges are amplified by innovation increasingly being distributed across organizational contexts and no longer confined to academia [7]. Large technology organizations maintain substantial in-house research and development capacities exceeding those of universities [2]. This raises concerns that pressures for speed and applicability may undermine methodological rigor [8]. As a result, new forms of collaboration between academic and industry communities are required to sustain both relevance and rigor in DSR [2].

One established response to this challenge is CR, a collaborative and design-oriented research approach involving multiple industry partners and academic researchers [9]. Related collaborative approaches in the DSR domain include engaged scholarship [10], action and action design research [11, 12], participatory design [13], living labs [14], and open innovation [15]. While these approaches effectively support relevance through practitioner engagement, they are typically grounded in localized contexts and offer limited methodological guidance for scalable, multi-organizational settings.

This paper argues that CR, particularly when combined with open source ecosystems, is well suited to address these limitations, as it offers structured governance arrangements, supports shared and reusable artifact development, and enables cumulative and scalable knowledge production across heterogeneous industrial environments. Prior studies characterize CR projects by close collaboration across all DSR phases, systematic evaluation in real-life contexts, strong emphasis on practical utility, and sustained industry participation and funding [2, 6, 16]. Through its structured phases, defined roles, and explicit knowledge exchange mechanisms, CR offers methodological guidance for conducting DSR in contexts of problem complexity. Evidence from prior implementations, such as the Competence Center Corporate Data Quality (CC CDQ), demonstrates that CR can facilitate knowledge transfer and enable access to tacit practitioner knowledge that would otherwise remain difficult to capture [2, 9, 17].

Despite these advantages, CR has been applied only selectively in emerging research contexts, most notably in enterprise-grade open source ecosystems [18]. Such ecosystems are increasingly relevant for IS research, as they constitute large-scale, multistakeholder environments in which digital artifacts are collaboratively designed, implemented, and evolved [19, 20]. Industry-driven open source projects represent settings in which DSR is effectively conducted "at scale", involving heterogeneous stakeholders, rapid iterations, and continuous interaction between design and use. Foundations such as the Eclipse Foundation (EF) exemplify this development by hosting hundreds of projects and engaging thousands of contributors from industry and research [21]. However, it remains unclear how DSR can be methodologically structured in such environments and whether established approaches such as CR can be adapted to support systematic accumulation of design knowledge.

Addressing this gap is timely, as IS innovation increasingly unfolds in open, distributed, and stakeholder-rich settings that challenge traditional research designs [7, 19]. This paper therefore argues that combining CR with enterprise-grade open source practices constitutes a promising methodological paradigm for DSR at scale. In doing so, the paper contributes to ongoing discussions on methodological innovation in Design Science (DS) and proposes new ways of building futures with DS in complex, contexts.

1.2 Research Question and Approach

To investigate the above, we formulate the following research question: *How to apply CR methodology within enterprise-grade open source ecosystems to produce rigorous and relevant artifacts according DSR principles?* In particular, we examine how CR enables knowledge transfer between researchers and practitioners in a multi-organizational open source project, and how it ensures both the practical utility and scientific rigor of the designed artifact. We approach this question through a participatory design activity [10, 22] in the Eclipse Dataspace Components (EDC) project. The project serves as a core technology in data ecosystems and complex data sharing endeavors [23], such as Catena-X for the automotive industry [24] and EONA-X for mobility and aviation industries [25].

This case provides a rich setting to observe CR "in action" within an open source project. It represents a new way of bridging theory and practice, increasingly important due to the raise of open source activities in IS research [26, 27]. The research design is qualitative and interpretive as we draw on documentation and observations from the EDC project over its lifecycle, adopting an "inside" viewpoint, and aligning observations with the CR methodology's constructs. By mapping EDC project activities to the CR framework, we explicitly identify the DSR relevance cycle, the rigor cycle, and the iterative design-evaluate cycles within the project. By mirroring the structure of prior CR studies, we ensure that our analysis is comparable and rooted in established CR literature [2, 16]. The goal is to derive insights into how CR can be scaled and adapted to an open source context, and to distill contributions to the DSR knowledge base and methodology from this experience.

The remainder of the paper is organized as follows. First, we review the CR methodology as a vehicle for collaborative DSR, describing its key components and underlying model (Sect. 2). We then introduce the EDC case (Sect. 3) documenting details on the research domain, consortium setup, project phases, results, and a discussion of encountered challenges. Finally, we conclude with implications for DSR and guidelines for researchers and consortia aiming to leverage the CR approach in open source ecosystems (Sect. 4).

2 Background

2.1 Organization of Design-Oriented Research

DSR often entails collaboration among diverse stakeholders such as academic researchers, industry practitioners, technology providers, etc., each bringing unique expertise [6, 17]. Organizing such collaboration is essential for success, yet remains non-trivial. Traditional research models typically revolved around single organizations or bilateral partnerships. In DSR projects, however, bilateral setups can limit the generalizability of results of artifacts [2, 22]. As digital transformation challenges grew more complex and inter-organizational, this limitation became more pronounced [28].

CR is one model, explicitly designed to involve multiple stakeholders in a coordinated research program [9]. In broad terms, a corresponding IS research consortium is an partnership where several companies work jointly with academic teams on a shared research agenda and governance [2, 6]. Each partner contributes resources and knowledge, participates in steering activities, and gains early access to results. Unlike contract research, no single company has exclusive rights to the outcomes. Results are ultimately made public for wider benefit [29]. This aligns well with scenarios where stakeholders face common problems or share a common interest, so that no proprietary advantage is sought from the solutions [6, 17, 28]. Open source ecosystems are a prime example, as companies collaborate on a shared technology platform without exclusive ownership, aiming to co-create infrastructure that all can use [30, 31]. CR thus offers methodological guidance that mirrors the open knowledge creation ideal, similar to what [29] termed collaborative R&D without exclusive exploitation rights. What distinguishes CR from other approaches is the scale and structure of participation as engaged, partnership-based model [2]. Rather than a single company's context, CR operates across a network of organizations, often mediated by a neutral entity such as a university institute, industry association, or foundation [2, 9]. From an organizational design perspective, CR embodies the "triple helix" model where academia, industry, and sometimes government collaborate to create and apply knowledge [32]. Universities may act as knowledge mediators, facilitating innovation that no single firm or purely academic research could achieve alone.

2.2 Consortium Research Method

CR is a research methodology for conducting collaborative, design-oriented research. As defined by [9], CR is a DSR approach that enables multilateral knowledge transfer between research and practice. This is achieved through knowledge socialization, externalization, combination, and internalization [33], yielding relevant and rigorously designed artifacts. In a consortium setting, practitioners grant researchers access to their knowledge base, participate in specifying solutions, test artifacts in their business environment, and finance the research activities. This cooperative arrangement is underpinned by a clear methodical structure, derived from the Competence Center (CC) model [34], evident from existing CR case studies [2, 6, 17]. Further, it is built on principles of Method Engineering, i.e., domain (meta-model), phases, results, techniques, and roles [35, 36]. Figure 1 visualizes the below introduced CR phases and activities, highlighting the covered/applied activities within the EDC project setup and elucidating the phases iterative character.

A CR project begins in the *Analysis phase* by identifying the problem and consolidating requirements [9]. Unlike an individual research project where a scholar might derive a research gap from literature alone, CR's analysis heavily involves practitioners to sharpen the artifact and requirements [6]. Existing practical solutions are surveyed, and the consortium discusses which research gaps are truly relevant to address. The outcome of the analysis phase is typically a formal consortium agreement and research agenda and project plan that all partners commit to [9]. Notably, CR projects often exhibit an expanding character, as new partners may join over time, requiring renewed analysis and refinement of problem understanding and design objectives [2].

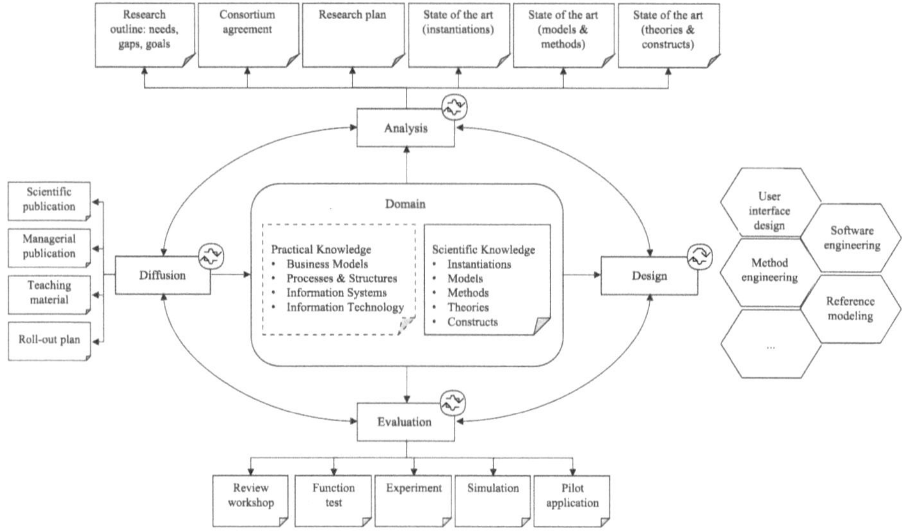

Fig. 1. Mapping EDC setup with CR overview (adapted from [9])

During the *Design phase*, the consortium focuses on creating the artifact(s). This is usually done through collaborative activities, where alternatives are discussed, based on both academic and practitioner input, and specialized working groups may tackling different facets of the artifact [2, 6, 17]. The design artifacts are developed iteratively and then implemented in controlled settings [2]. Knowledge exchange in this phase is intensive due practitioners share tacit knowledge and context specifics (facilitating socialization), while researchers introduce relevant theories or design principles (knowledge combination).

The *Evaluation phase* is closely intertwined, often running in parallel and also as an iterative cycle [9]. Pilots may be framed as action research interventions [12], where partner companies running a pilot project to implement the new solution, with researchers observing. Multiple evaluation activities such as focus group [37] evaluations at industry events can occur. Practically, the design-evaluation loop in CR continues until the consortium agrees that the artifact meets the defined objectives and performs adequately in real use cases [2].

Finally, the *Diffusion phase* ensures broadly dissemination and institutionalization [9]. Since consortium projects lack exclusive ownership, there is strong incentive to publish the results for the wider IS community and to share them among all partners' organizations [29]. Diffusion activities often include joint presentations by researchers and practitioners at industry conferences or trade events, demonstrating the artifact and its benefits [9]. Internally, partner firms may carry out roll-outs or training [2]. In academic terms, diffusion also means producing scholarly publications to contribute to the formal knowledge base. By the end of the diffusion phase, the artifact ideally transitions into sustained use by the industry partners, while the researchers extract generalized findings and prescriptive knowledge that add to theory [9].

Prior studies confirm that CR serves as a vehicle to merge the relevance and rigor cycles of DSR within a single program [2, 6, 17]. This dual contribution is what makes CR particularly attractive for DS at scale. We next illustrate these concepts through the EDC case, following the structure of the CR method adopted in an enterprise-grade open source project.

3 Case Study: Eclipse Dataspace Components

3.1 Research Domain and Setting

The EDC case is situated in the domain of data ecosystems and trusted data sharing, where a dataspace is defined as *"a trust context and supporting services to enable the sharing of data through an agreed set of policies, semantic models, protocols and processes"* [38]. Dataspaces strive to provide solutions for complex inter-organizational data sharing practices and the required integration of socio-technical capabilities and governance mechanisms to function effectively [39–42]. The strategic goal is to treat data as asset that can fuel new services and efficiency across value chains, under conditions of trust, compliance, and control [41, 43]. Achieving this requires interoperable capabilities in data governance, connectivity, identity management, data transfer, and more, which are often beyond the scope of any single firm [40, 43]. Thus, the domain knowledge for dataspaces is highly distributed. On the academic side, there were research contributions on dataspace fundamentals and architectures [44–46] and their modern approaches fostering data sovereignty and an inter-organizational perspective [40, 47]. On the practitioner side, various consortia (e.g., Catena-X or Eona-X) and industry associations (e.g., EF, International Data Space Association) had started formulating requirements, reference models, and prototypes. An active community of practice was emerging through working groups, open source communities, and pilot projects in different sectors [48]. However, differing stakeholder perspectives and inconsistent scoping have led to the emergence of competing architectural models, which in turn hampers consolidation and clarity in the existing knowledge base and limits the diffusion and scalable adoption of dataspaces. In short, the problem context was ripe for a coordinated design effort to create a common solution architecture.

Within this landscape, EDC was initiated as a collaborative open source project to develop a framework for dataspaces. The EDC would provide the core services needed to share data assets between organizations with fine-grained control (e.g., data usage policies, licensing, observability). EDC represents a consortium with members from research and industry and an open source project, hosted by the EF as a neutral foundation with clear governance (project charter, IP management, quality processes) [49], which we presuppose for enterprise-grade open source initiatives. While formal governance mechanisms are necessary to support enterprise-grade open source development and active contribution, their absence does not categorically preclude the use of open source projects in enterprise settings. Rather than each company building or procuring its own proprietary solution, efforts were consolidated under an open source initiative striving for openness and transparency from the very beginning.

As [17] observe, developing reference models or platforms in such a context serves to accumulate design knowledge from multiple sources. In the EDC setting, this accumulation is evident, as the project built on prior concepts of the dataspace domain but aimed to extend and generalize them into a fully realized open artifact. The CR approach was employed to manage this complex design endeavor, ensuring that academic rigor and industry relevance were both maintained throughout.

3.2 Consortium and Role Assignment

At the core of EDC's consortium are industrial companies, brought together by the research partners. Table 1 provides an overview of the EDC consortium members, limited to the partners that contribute resources with a Committer role according to the EF handbook. As of January 2026, the EDC organization overall lists 66 members [50].

On average, the EDC research team comprises three to four research staff engaged, working alongside a larger pool of industry members. This composition is comparable to the existing CC CDQ cases, as best-practice examples from academic literature [6, 16, 17]. The academic members, some of whom act as Committers, play a dual role. One role was facilitating the research process in terms of methodological guidance, design, documentation, and evaluation. The other contributing actual technical content.

Table 1. EDC Consortium Overview

Organization	Industry	Role	From	To
Amadeus	Mobility	E	07/2021	now
Amazon AWS	ICT	A	06/2021	02/2025
BMW	Automotive	A/E	06/2021	now
Mercedes Benz	Automotive	E	06/2021	05/2023
Deutsche Telekom	ICT	A	06/2021	05/2023
Fraunhofer	Research	A/E	06/2021	now
Microsoft	ICT	A/E	06/2021	now
SAP	ICT	A	06/2021	11/2024
ZF Friedrichshafen	Automotive	E	06/2021	07/2023
Huawei	ICT	PL/A	02/2024	now

A = Architect; E = Engineer; PL = Project Lead.

The EF's governance model requires the project to have a defined Project Management Committee (PMC) and a set of Committers. This maps closely to the roles found in other CR cases [2]. They ensured the project's goals stayed aligned with consortium needs and resolved any inter-organizational issues. Each partner also provided software architects and engineers who actively contributed to design discussions and coding. Additionally, subject matter experts from partner firms were tapped for specific knowledge; for instance, a legal expert on data licensing might join a session to ensure the connector's policy enforcement feature met regulatory requirements.

Overall, the consortium structure provides clear entry points into each partner's knowledge base. The steering group represents an organizational perspective and could secure resources, the working members brought hands-on expertise, and the subject experts provided deep dives as needed. Importantly, many partners are simultaneously consumers of the EDC artifact, which naturally incentivize them to contribute vigorously to its development and success.

3.3 Phases and Activities

The *analysis phase* of the EDC project commenced in early 2021, triggered by a broadly recognized need for a common architecture to support emerging dataspaces. Initial ideas coalesced around the notion that an *"dataspace solution"* was required to embody strict data sovereignty requirements in inter-organizational data sharing. This vague concept was gradually refined through a series of preliminary meetings and workshops. During Q1 to Q2 2021, consortium members surveyed existing solutions, notably the prototype Dataspace Connector (DSC) developed by Fraunhofer ISST [51] to learn from prior approaches. This assessment identified strengths to emulate and gaps to address, effectively capturing "what worked and what did not" in current practice. In parallel, discussions with subject matter experts from member firms helped ground the research idea in real-world requirements from the start. For example, automotive supply chain experts described use cases like sharing parts traceability data across organizations, which imposed specific security and performance requirements on the prospective solution.

By mid-2021, the consortium had drafted a detailed project charter, the EDC. The project outline also specified clear objectives, for instance, to provide *"a comprehensive framework [...] that dataspace implementations can re-use and customize [...] and ensure interoperability by design"* [52]. In addition, the outline defined the project's modus operandi and initial resource commitments from each partner, analogous to the multi-day workshop series and cost-sharing agreements seen in earlier consortia [2, 6]. A formal kick-off workshop, held virtually in July 2021, which produced several tangible outcomes such as a consolidated requirements list, a shared understanding of high-level architectural principles, and a mutual agreement to conduct the project under EF rules. These results mirrored literature examples of CR case studies' kick-off workshop, which likewise narrowed down the research focus and established mutual agreements among the partners [2, 6, 17]. Notably, as the EDC initiative gained visibility, additional companies expressed interest and were onboarded throughout the years. Each new partner's entry started a brief revisit of requirements, essentially re-opening the analysis phase, to incorporate new perspectives. This reflects the anticipated iteration in CR projects. This approach ensured the consortium remained open and growing.

The *design phase* of EDC started from Q2 2021 onward, initiated by the successful public review of the project within the EF. Design activities were organized in iterations of 6-8-week cadence with priorities defined agile through results of evaluation phases. Foremost, the consortium conducted focus group workshops roughly every week between the EDC Committer team. Researchers ensured that design decisions and rationales were captured, sometimes mapping them to existing design theories or patterns injecting academic rigor. Open issues were triaged and required design decisions were debated and made collectively. Further, workshops with broader groups were conducted to align the framework's design with additional requirements from further domains or specific use cases.

For example, in October 2021, an EDC hackathon event happened in Munich, where the design of the catalog component was discussed [53]. Such sessions exemplified knowledge socialization and combination, as participants exchanged experiences with various technologies and merged them into the evolving design. However, most collaboration happened virtual and asynchronous during the design sprints. Coordinated through open discussions, shared issue trackers, and version control leveraging capabilities of the GitHub platform, inter-organizational agile teams were formed. All discussions, decisions, and code contributions were documented in issues or design documents accessible to the public. Exemplarily, main activities of knowledge transfer between researchers and practitioners over the CR phases are depicted in Fig. 2.

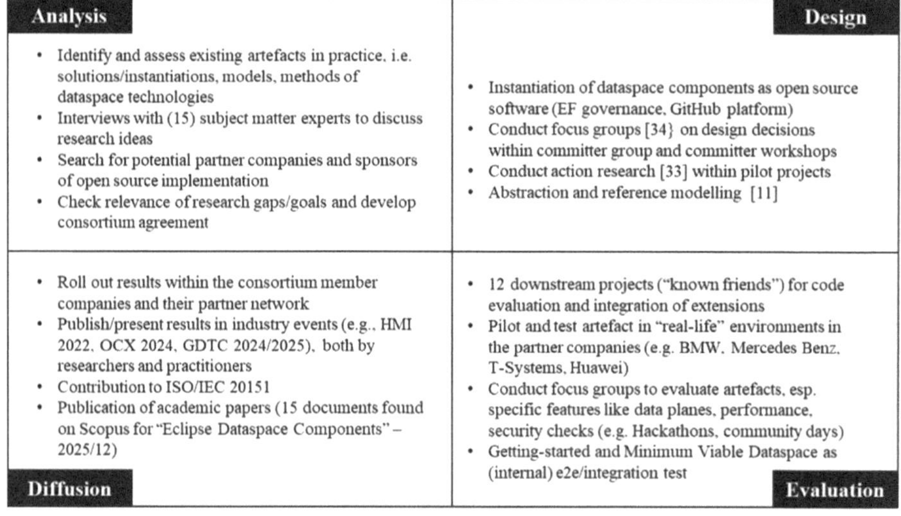

Fig. 2. Exchange of knowledge in EDC project

The *evaluation phase* largely took the form of pilot implementations and tests in practical setups, as recommended by the CR methodology [2, 9]. Each core industry partner integrated the early EDC builds into a local test environment and pilot cases. Practitioners tried out the artifact in real workflows, providing immediate feedback to the EDC Committer team. Researchers often helped facilitate these pilots, observing and analyzing usage issues. Just as an example of a CC CDQ consortium conducted action research in seven pilot projects to define objectives and evaluate artifact [2], the EDC consortium's pilots were essential for demonstrating and improving the design.

In the *diffusion phase*, results of the project where promoted. Examples are the "EDCCon 2022" with over 220 attendants [54] or the "Bergamo event" in 08/2025, focusing on efficient deployments within multi-cloud environments [55]. Academic publications took another important channel for diffusion. With the search term *"Eclipse Dataspace Components"*, Google Scholar shows over 150 hits, Scopus database around 20.

3.4 Results

The EDC consortium yielded several design artifacts and outcomes aligned with its goals. The primary artifact is the EDC framework as an open source implementation of core dataspace components. This artifact represents an instantiation in DSR terms, but, by providing a framework, it also embodies model characteristics. In fact, the EDC architecture itself has been documented as a reference architecture model defining key constructs and their relations, which in turn are based on agreed design principles. By the end of 2025, the EDC had reached a stable stage, with core features in place, tested in at least two domain contexts (automotive and mobility), and the project is in the process of moving from "incubation" to "mature" phase within the EF.

Thus, the consortium delivered both a concrete tool and a generalized architectural blueprint. Additionally, several supporting artifacts were produced. For example, formal protocol specifications were invented, submitted to ISO/IEC JTC1 PAS [56]. These specifications define dataspace communication and identity, thereby promoting consistency in terminology and foster interoperability. In total, the EDC consortium's outputs can be summarized in categories consistent with typical DSR contributions:

- **Instantiated Artifact:** The EDC, published under the Apache 2.0 license on GitHub, providing an extensible framework for dataspace components and runnable default extensions that any organization can deploy. Due to involvement of practitioners and their knowledge, the artifact achieved production-readiness and had been adopted by several dataspace initiatives like Catena-X and Eona-X.
- **Architecture Design:** The abstract architecture of a dataspace, derived from EDC's concepts, components, and interfaces. It generalizes those concepts, components, and relations beyond the specific code, offering a technology-independent abstraction for future dataspace implementations and expansions.
- **Methodical Artifacts:** Onboarding methodology, data usage policy templates, and a governance framework for operating a dataspace outlining roles and processes, derived from consortium discussions and evaluation throughout industry pilots. This includes lessons on technical governance, community building, and participant incentive alignment according to artifacts "fitness" [19] which contribute to the DSR knowledge base and the realm of engaged scholarship.
- **Empirical Insights:** While not artifacts per se, the consortium also generated knowledge about how to effectively use empirical data created in open source projects (issues, commit history, decision records) providing access to practical tacit knowledge.

All core partners took part in problem identification *(1)* and defining solution objectives *(2)*, reflecting the joint nature of analysis. Design and development *(3)* tasks were shared, with some companies contributing more heavily to certain components than others. Demonstration *(4)* occurred via pilot deployments. Evaluation *(5)* was likewise collaborative, with structured feedback coming from multiple organizations. Finally, communication *(6)* was performed by both researchers and practitioners. This confirms a pattern seen in prior CR application: the artifact development is truly a collective effort and each partner contributes to multiple DSR activities [2, 6].

In the EDC project, practical knowledge inputs were contributed by more than a dozen organizations, ensuring that the resulting design reflects genuinely inter-organizational expertise. The open source setting provided a transparent and inclusive environment in which contributions, design rationales, and implementation decisions were openly documented and continuously scrutinized. The open source governance model complemented CR's role structure by providing established practices for decision-making, contribution management, and intellectual property handling. This facilitated the incremental involvement of new partners without disrupting ongoing research activities. From a DS perspective, the openly accessible code base and issue histories constitutes a rich empirical dataset that enable traceable analysis of design iterations and outcomes (e.g., collections of decision records [57]).

Finally, adoption of EDC beyond the original consortium, including in adjacent domains such as energy data sharing, illustrates how open source dissemination reinforces the evaluation and diffusion phases of CR and supports the generalizability of the resulting design knowledge. In line with recent work by [17], the reference model and lessons from EDC serve to accumulate DS knowledge and turning practical consortium outputs into reusable knowledge artifacts for the IS field.

3.5 Challenges and Limitations

The EDC consortium case demonstrates the viability of CR in an enterprise-grade open source, multi-organizational context, but it also revealed certain challenges and limitations. Many of these are consistent with prior CR experiences, while others are particular to the open source nature of the project. Key issues observed include:

- **Personal and Organizational Discontinuity:** Over the project's duration (~5 years), several partner organizations saw changes in personnel assigned to EDC. For example, one company's lead architect on the project was reassigned internally, and another partner underwent a reorganization that shifted its priorities. These changes disrupted the continuity of knowledge flow and occasionally led to revised requirements midstream when new people came on board, similar to the personnel turnover problems noted in [2].
- **Expectation Management and Goal Alignment:** Partners sometimes differed in their expectations for short-term vs. long-term outcomes. Some industry participants pushed for immediate, tailor-made solutions to meet pressing project deadlines (e.g., Catena-X ecosystem releases), whereas the researchers and other partners emphasized rigorous design and generalizability which required more time and deliberation. This tension between "quick wins for my use-case" and "robust artifact for broad use" had to be managed.
- **Hidden Business Agendas and Strategic Sensitivities:** Although the project followed an open source approach, some partners encountered internal constraints when contributing certain components or evaluation results due to underlying strategic considerations. In particular, organizations needed to assess whether contributions might signal competitive positioning or conflict with ongoing commercial initiatives.

- **Project Management and Resource Load:** Running the EDC consortium required substantial coordination efforts and capabilities that are not traditionally prevalent in research teams, consistent with observations reported in prior CR projects [2]. The project management had to deal with multiple time zones, organizational cultures, and the complexities of open source community processes.
- **Data Volume and Documentation:** The collaborative development process generated a vast amount of data like design documents, meeting recordings, code commits, issue discussions, user feedback, etc. For the researchers aiming to analyze and derive insights, capturing and distilling this wealth of information was non-trivial. This resonates with the data collection challenge reported in earlier consortia [2] and reinforced methodologically by [9]. Not every discussion could be transcribed or formally coded for research purposes as the team had to balance effort vs. benefit according to "research pragmatism" as termed by [58].

While the EDC case validates CR in achieving a complex DSR outcome, it also underscores the operational difficulties of coordinating many partners' interests. Issues of continuity, expectation alignment, openness, management, and data handling must be actively mitigated. The CR methodology, with its explicit phases and roles, provided a helpful scaffolding to address some of these. For example, formal phase gates helped reset expectations, and defined roles helped ensure responsibilities were covered. However, some challenges, such as organizational turnover or differing short-term agendas, lie outside the method's direct control and require soft skills. Recognizing these challenges early and building trust among partners is critical.

4   Conclusion and Outlook

This study set out to examine how DSR at scale can be conducted through a consortium-based approach in an enterprise-grade open source project. Using the EDC project as a case, the paper demonstrated how the CR methodology can be operationalized in a multi-company, open source setting. The case confirms that CR combines with open source practices is an effective vehicle for bridging the gap between relevance and rigor in IS research. The project with its open source setup achieved its main objectives in line with CR instructions according to [9] (cf. Table 2), demonstrating that with careful management, the benefits of the combination of CR and open source outweigh challenges and limitations (cf. Sect. 3.5). The project delivered an artifact neither academia nor industry could likely have produced alone in the same timeframe, especially in dataspaces' dynamism, thereby exemplifying *"Design Science at scale"*.

A central contribution of the study is demonstrating how the CR cycle can be applied at scale in short, iterative cycles. In the EDC case, strategic goals were continuously aligned with socio-technical design areas and measurable outcomes, enabling incremental refinement of the artifact in response to evolving requirements while maintaining coherence across partners and design decisions.

The study contributes to the DSR knowledge base in two ways. First, the EDC artifact represents a rigorously evaluated, enterprise-grade instantiation of design principles for trusted data sharing with dataspaces. As an open source framework developed and

Table 2. Mapping CR and EDC (exemplarily representing open source) project

Consortium Research Characteristics	Enterprise-grade OS Project Setups
Research objectives are jointly defined by researchers and practitioners, who collectively assess progress and evaluate results throughout the project	Project objectives are collaboratively defined within the open source community; progress is continuously tracked through issue and pull-request management, version control systems, and code reviews, which also serve as ongoing evaluation mechanisms
Multiple partner organizations contribute domain expertise and grant academic researchers access to their practical knowledge bases	Multiple companies staff the project with experienced architects and engineers who contribute their expertise and share background knowledge in pursuit of a common development goal
Research outcomes take the form of artifacts designed to address relevant practical problems	Project outcomes consist of software artifacts, including source code, architectural designs, models, and accompanying documentation
Design activities are inherently iterative, spanning multiple cycles across the CR phases and involving several partner organizations	Development follows agile principles and is therefore inherently iterative, with recurring cycles of design and implementation involving multiple partner organizations
Partner companies evaluate developed artifacts through application and testing in their respective business environments	Project results are continuously tested in partners' operational environments, often complemented by feedback from a broader community experimenting with preliminary versions
Partner companies partially finance the research project through monetary or in-kind contributions	Enterprise open source projects are financed through partner involvement, primarily by allocating personnel re-sources and covering shared infrastructure costs (e.g., servers, hosting, community events)
Researchers and practitioners commit to the consortium project for a substantial, predefined period (typically around two years)	While no fixed duration is prescribed, partners typically assume Committer roles, implying sustained responsibility and engagement over a significant period
Research results are disseminated and made accessible in the public domain	Project artifacts are continuously available to the public; design processes, implementation progress, and iterative changes are transparently documented and accessible

tested across multiple organizations, EDC constitutes a concrete contribution to prescriptive IS knowledge. Documented architectural decisions and design rationales capture reusable principles and patterns. Second, the study provides methodological insights into consortium-based DSR by showing how open source projects can serve as platforms for DS with CR, extending prior work from CC contexts. Integrating open source practices enhanced CR by introducing transparency, open documentation of design discussions and code contributions, strengthening the rigor cycle through empirical material and lower entry barriers for onboarding new partners.

For researchers, the findings offer guidance on leveraging consortia and open source communities as research platforms. The case shows that CR enables the study of large-scale, inter-organizational design challenges beyond the scope of single-organization research. It highlights the importance of front-loading relevance through intensive practitioner engagement during analysis, as early alignment on problem framing and objectives proved critical for adoption and impact. Researchers must also be prepared to assume roles beyond traditional academic activities, including facilitation, coordination, and integration of diverse contributions.

From a practitioner perspective, the study underscores the value of adopting a DS orientation when pursuing consortium-based innovation. Treating a consortium initiative as a research endeavor rather than solely an engineering project encourages systematic problem exploration, iterative evaluation, and reflection on design decisions [18]. The CR framework provides structured support for harnessing collective expertise and validating solutions in real-world settings. The EDC case shows that openness and knowledge sharing can accelerate development and improve artifact quality, even among competing organizations, and thus serves as an exemplar for emerging consortia in domains such as finance, healthcare, and smart cities.

Beyond the specific case of CR, the findings also offer broader implications for multilateral DSR practice. They suggest that effective large-scale DSR requires methodological arrangements that explicitly address coordination, governance, and knowledge integration across organizational boundaries. Approaches that combine shared design artifacts, transparent collaboration infrastructures, mechanisms for cumulative learning, and structured documentation can help balance rigor and relevance in distributed, highly scaled settings. In this sense, the study informs not only consortium-based research, but also the design of future collaborative DSR initiatives in increasingly open, ecosystem-based innovation contexts.

Despite these contributions, the study has limitations. It reports on a single in-depth case in a specific context, limiting direct generalization. Future research should examine additional cases across industries to further evaluate and identify boundary conditions for the combination of CR and open source. Comparative studies could clarify when CR is most effective relative to alternative methodologies, while quantitative measures of artifact adoption and performance could complement the qualitative analysis. Further research should also examine the interplay between CR and open source projects without predefined governance as in case of EDC, particularly the influence on knowledge production and diffusion.

In conclusion, the paper demonstrates that DSR at scale can be achieved through embedding CR within enterprise-grade open source ecosystems. Leveraging this combination, researchers and practitioners can collaboratively address complex inter-organizational problems and produce artifacts that are both practically impactful and academically valuable. The findings point to a promising path for the generation of robust, generalizable, and relevant design knowledge in increasingly interconnected and dynamic research environments.

Disclosure of Interests. The authors have no competing interests to declare that are relevant to the content of this article.

References

1. Holmström, J., Ketokivi, M., Hameri, A.-P.: Bridging practice and theory: a design science approach. Decis. Sci. **40**, 65–87 (2009)
2. Otto, B., Österle, H.: Relevance through consortium research? Findings from an expert interview study winter. In: Zhao et al. (ed.) 2010 – Global Perspectives on Design Science, vol. 6105, pp. 16–30 (2010)
3. March, S.T., Smith, G.F.: Design and natural science research on information technology. Decis. Support. Syst. **15**, 251–266 (1995)
4. Hevner, A.R., March, S.T., Park, J., Ram, S.: Design science in information systems research. MIS Q. **28**, 75–106 (2004)
5. Peffers, K., Tuunanen, T., Rothenberger, M.A., Chatterjee, S.: A design science research methodology for information systems research. J. Manag. Inf. Syst. **24**, 45–77 (2007)
6. Pentek, T., Legner, C., Otto, B.: Towards a reference model for data management in the digital economy. In: Maedche, A., vom Brocke, J., Hevner, A. (eds.) Designing the Digital Transformation: DESRIST 2017 Research in Progress Proceedings of the 12th International Conference on Design Science Research in Information Systems and Technology, pp. 51–66. Karlsruher Institut für Technologie (KIT), Karlsruhe, Germany (2017)
7. Starkey, K., Madan, P.: Bridging the relevance gap: aligning stakeholders in the future of management research. Br. J. Manag. **12** (2001)
8. Kampourakis, K., McCain, K.: Is scientific rigor declining? In: Kampourakis, K., McCain, K. (eds.) Uncertainty: How It Makes Science Advance, pp. 217–242. Oxford University Press, New York, NY, USA (2019)
9. Österle, H., Otto, B.: Consortium research. Bus. Inf. Syst. Eng. **2**, 283–293 (2010)
10. van de Ven, A.H.: Engaged Scholarship. Oxford University Press, Oxford (2007)
11. Reason, P., Bradbury, H.: The SAGE Handbook of Action Research. SAGE Publications Ltd, London (2008)
12. Sein, M.K., Henfridsson, O., Purao, S., Rossi, M., Lindgren, R.: Action design research. MIS Q. **35**, 37–56 (2011)
13. Schuler, D., Namioka, A. (eds.): Participatory Design. Principles and Practices, CRC Press (2017)
14. Niitamo, V.-P., Kulkki, S., Eriksson, M., Hribernik, K.A.: State-of-the-art and good practice in the field of living labs. In: 2006 IEEE International Technology Management Conference (ICE), pp. 1–8. IEEE (2006)
15. Chesbrough, H.: Open Innovation. The New Imperative for Creating and Profiting from Technology. Harvard Business School Press, Boston, Massachusetts (2003)
16. Pentek, T., Legner, C.: Konsortialforschung zur Entwicklung von Referenzmodellen für die Digitalisierung von Unternehmen – Erfahrungen aus dem Datenmanagement. HMD **57**, 296–309 (2020)
17. Legner, C., Pentek, T., Otto, B.: Accumulating design knowledge with reference models: insights from 12 years' research into data management. JAIS **21**, 735–770 (2020)
18. Engström, E., Storey, M.-A., Runeson, P., Höst, M., Baldassarre, M.T.: How software engineering research aligns with design science: a review. Empir. Softw. Eng. **25**, 2630–2660 (2020)
19. Gill, T.G., Hevner, A.R.: A fitness-utility model for design science research. ACM Trans. Manage. Inf. Syst. **4**, 1–24 (2013)

20. Doyle, C., Luczak-Roesch, M., Mittal, A.: We need the open artefact: design science as a pathway to open science in information systems research. In: Tulu, B., Djamasbi, S., Leroy, G. (eds.) Extending the Boundaries of Design Science Theory and Practice. LNCS, vol. 11491, pp. 46–60. Springer International Publishing, Cham (2019)
21. Eclipse Foundation: Eclipse Foundation Annual Community Report 2025 (2025). https://www.eclipse.org/org/foundation/annual-reports/2025/#projects
22. Kautz, K.: Participatory Design Activities and Agile Software Development, vol. 318, pp. 303–316 (2010)
23. Oliveira, M.I.S., Barros Lima, G.D.F., Farias Lóscio, B.: Investigations into data ecosystems: a systematic mapping study. Knowl. Inf. Syst. **61**, 589–630 (2019)
24. Catena-X Automotive Network e.V.: About Us — Catena-X: Open and Collaborative Data Ecosystem for the Automotive Industry (2025). https://catena-x.net/about-us/
25. EONA-X: About — EONA-X: European Data Space for Logistic, Mobility and Tourism (2025). https://eona-x.eu/about/
26. Pfenninger, S., DeCarolis, J., Hirth, L., Quoilin, S., Staffell, I.: The importance of open data and software: is energy research lagging behind? Energy Policy **101**, 211–215 (2017)
27. Deshpande, A., Riehle, D.: The total growth of open source, vol. 275, pp. 197–209 (2008)
28. Otto, B., Österle, H.: Corporate data quality: prerequisite for successful business models (2015)
29. Brockhoff, K.: Forschung und Entwicklung. Oldenbourg Wissenschaftsverlag, Berlin (1999)
30. Fasnacht, D.: Open innovation ecosystems, pp. 131–172. https://doi.org/10.1007/978-3-319-76394-1_5
31. Linåker, J., Rempel, P., Regnell, B., Mäder, P.: How firms adapt and interact in open source ecosystems: analyzing stakeholder influence and collaboration patterns. In: Daneva, M., Pastor, O. (eds.) Requirements Engineering: Foundation for Software Quality. Lecture Notes in Computer Science, vol. 9619. Springer, Cham, Switzerland (2016)
32. Leydesdorff, L., Meyer, M.: The Triple Helix of University-Industry-Government relations. Scientometrics **58**, 191–203 (2003). https://doi.org/10.1023/A:1026276308287
33. Bartunek, J.M., Rynes, S.L., Daft, R.L.: Across the great divide: knowledge creation and transfer between practitioners and academics. Acad. Manag. J. **44**, 340–355 (2001)
34. Back, A., von Krogh, G., Enkel, E.: The CC model as organizational design striving to combine relevance and rigor. Syst. Pract. Action Res. **20**, 91–103 (2007)
35. Olle, T.W., Sol, H.G., MacDonald, I.G.: Information Systems Methodologies: A Framework for Understanding. Addison-Wesley Longman Publishing Co., Inc., USA (1991)
36. Brinkkemper, S.: Method engineering: engineering of information systems development methods and tools. Inf. Softw. Technol. **38**, 275–280 (1996)
37. Morgan, D.L., Krueger, R.A.: When to use focus groups and why. In: Morgan, D.L. (ed.) Successful Focus Groups: Advancing the State of the Art, pp. 3–9. Sage Publications, Newbury Park, CA, USA (1993)
38. ISO/IEC DIS 20151: Information technology - Cloud computing and distributed platforms - Dataspace concepts and characteristics (2025). https://www.iso.org/standard/86589.html
39. Zrenner, J., Möller, F.O., Jung, C., Eitel, A., Otto, B.: Usage control architecture options for data sovereignty in business ecosystems. JEIM **32**, 477–495 (2019)
40. Jarke, M., Otto, B., Ram, S.: Data sovereignty and data space ecosystems. Bus. Inf. Syst. Eng. **61**, 549–550 (2019)
41. Fassnacht, M., Leimstoll, J., Benz, C., Heinz, D., Satzger, G.: Data sharing practices: the interplay of data, organizational structures, and network dynamics. Electron. Markets **34** (2024)
42. Möller, F., et al.: Data ecosystems in IS research: the road so far, where we are now, and the road ahead. Electron. Markets **35** (2025)

43. Möller, F., et al.: Industrial data ecosystems and data spaces. Electron. Markets **34** (2024)
44. Franklin, M., Halevy, A., Maier, D.: From databases to dataspaces. SIGMOD Rec. **34**, 27–33 (2005)
45. Halevy, A.Y., Franklin, M.J., Maier, D.: Dataspaces: a new abstraction for information management. In: Hutchison, D., et al. (eds.) Database Systems for Advanced Applications. Lecture Notes in Computer Science, vol. 3882, pp. 1–2. Springer, Heidelberg (2006)
46. Franklin, M.J.: Dataspaces: progress and prospects. In: Sexton, A.P. (ed.) Dataspace: The Final Frontier. Lecture Notes in Computer Science, vol. 5588, pp. 1–3. Springer, Heidelberg (2009)
47. Scherenberg, F. von, Hellmeier, M., Otto, B.: Data sovereignty in information systems. Electron. Markets **34** (2024)
48. Otto, B., ten Hompel, M., Wrobel, S.: Designing Data Spaces. Springer International Publishing, Cham (2022)
49. Eclipse Foundation: Project Handbook (2025). https://www.eclipse.org/projects/handbook/
50. Eclipse Foundation: EDC – Members (2025). https://github.com/orgs/eclipse-edc/people
51. Pampus, J., Jahnke, B.-F., Quensel, R.: Evolving data space technologies: lessons learned from an IDS connector reference implementation. In: Margaria, T., Steffen, B. (eds.) Leveraging Applications of Formal Methods, Verification and Validation. Practice. LNCS, vol. 13704, pp. 366–381. Springer Nature Switzerland, Cham (2022)
52. Spiekermann: EDC – Creation Review (2021). https://projects.eclipse.org/projects/technology.edc/reviews/creation-review
53. Eclipse Foundation: EDC Hackathon – Munich (2021). https://github.com/eclipse-edc/Collateral/Events/Hackathons/2021-11
54. Marino, J. and Spiekermann, M.: EDC Conceptual Overview and Architecture (2022). https://www.youtube.com/watch?v=IGd4oafLyAg
55. Metaform Systems: Bergamo 2025 — Overview (Documentation) (2025). https://github.com/Metaform/content/en/documentation/overview/bergamo-2025
56. Eclipse Foundation: EDWG Advances Two Open Protocols Toward Global ISO/IEC Standardisation (2025). https://newsroom.eclipse.org/news/announcements/eclipse-dataspace-working-group-edwg-advances-two-open-protocols-toward-global
57. Eclipse Foundation: EDC – Decision Records (2025). https://github.com/eclipse-edc/Connector/tree/main/docs/developer/decision-records
58. Strübing, J.: Grounded Theory. Springer Fachmedien Wiesbaden, Wiesbaden (2021)

Developing Design Principles: Navigating the Design Knowledge Space with a Mode-Based and Abstraction-Aligned Framework

Timo Strohmann[1]([✉]) [iD] and Robert Winter[2] [iD]

[1] University of Münster, Münster, Germany
`timo.strohmann@uni-muenster.de`
[2] Institute of Information Systems and Digital Business, University of St. Gallen, St. Gallen, Switzerland
`robert.winter@unisg.ch`

Abstract. Design principles (DPs) are a central vehicle for prescriptive design knowledge in design science research (DSR), yet researchers still struggle to develop DPs that are both actionable and projectable. We propose a conceptual scaffold for understanding DP development as navigation in a design knowledge space. It integrates (1) a mode-based framework distinguishing modes of framing, reflection, and synthesis, (2) an abstraction-alignment model showing why design requirements, DPs, and design features must align at compatible abstraction levels, and (3) navigation moves that characterize recurring epistemic actions involved in shifting across abstraction levels and relating problem and solution knowledge. We illustrate the scaffold by reconstructing a project on virtual companionship, showing how a candidate DP evolved through feature abstraction from an existing system and how alignment stabilized the DP. Overall, the paper offers orienting guidance for DP development by helping researchers make abstraction choices, conceptual alignment, and reasoning moves more explicit, thereby supporting transparent and cumulative design knowledge construction.

Keywords: Design Science Research · Design Principles · Design Knowledge · Abstraction · Synthesis · Design Features

1 Introduction

Design Science Research (DSR) seeks to create innovative artifacts while generating reusable design knowledge that informs future solutions across contexts [1]. Design principles (DPs) have become a central means for articulating such knowledge because they express prescriptive insights that connect problem understanding with solution design [2]. Research on DPs has accelerated considerably in recent years across a wide range of domains, indicating a strong demand for prescriptive design knowledge and its systematic articulation [3]. At the same time, the growing prevalence of DPs has surfaced open questions about how they should be developed, framed, and abstracted.

© The Author(s), under exclusive license to Springer Nature Switzerland AG 2026
J. vom Brocke et al. (Eds.): DESRIST 2026, LNCS 16606, pp. 365–382, 2026.
https://doi.org/10.1007/978-3-032-28313-9_21

In recent years, several contributions have improved our understanding of how to construct and present DPs. Möller et al. [4] propose a method for DP development that distinguishes between a supportive approach, in which DPs are developed ex ante on the basis of meta-requirements and justificatory knowledge, and a reflective approach, in which DPs are abstracted ex post from an artifact and its design process. Gregor et al. [2] develop a conceptual schema for specifying DPs that includes elements such as a title, aim, context, mechanisms and enactors, and rationale, thereby strengthening the anatomy and communicability of DPs. Broader discussions of design knowledge emphasize the relationships between problem space and solution space, and how design knowledge evolves [5]. Complementary work has highlighted the importance and challenges of abstraction. Studies show that DPs can be formulated at multiple abstraction levels, each with different implications for generalizability and usefulness [6, 7].

Together, these streams provide a rich conceptual foundation but also reveal important gaps. Existing approaches often focus either on activity sequences for DP development or on the structural form of the final DP. Less attention has been given to how researchers actually navigate between problem and solution insights during DP creation and how they move across abstraction levels to arrive at a DP that is neither too specific nor too general. Current literature therefore offers limited support for understanding how requirements, candidate DPs, and design features (DFs) interact during development and how these elements can be aligned conceptually and abstracted appropriately.

This paper addresses these gaps by proposing a conceptual scaffold for understanding how DPs emerge through navigation in the design knowledge space. We build on and extend prior work on design knowledge, DPs, and abstraction to introduce three complementary elements:

First, a *mode-based framework* that conceptualizes DP development as a dynamic interplay between framing, reflection, and synthesis rather than a fixed sequence of steps.

Second, an *abstraction alignment model* that explains how design requirements (DRs), DPs, and DFs may exist at multiple abstraction levels and why robust DPs depend on their relative alignment.

Third, a *set of navigation moves* that represents recurring epistemic actions through which researchers shift across abstraction levels and relate problem and solution insights as DPs take shape.

Together, these elements provide a navigational scaffold for describing, reflecting on, and more deliberately navigating DP development. They sensitize researchers to the reasoning modes, abstraction choices, and alignment challenges involved in constructing DPs, without imposing rigid stepwise procedures.

To anchor this aim, we investigate the following research question (RQ):

RQ: How can DP development be conceptualized as navigation across modes of reasoning and abstraction levels in the design knowledge space?

To illustrate the usefulness of the proposed framework, we provide an illustrative reconstruction of DP development in a longitudinal DSR project on virtual companionship. The remainder of the paper is structured as follows. Section 2 presents background literature on design knowledge, abstraction, and existing approaches to DP development. Section 3 introduces the conceptual framework including modes, abstraction alignment, and navigation moves. Section 4 provides a demonstration. Section 5 discusses contributions, implications, and limitations.

2 Background

2.1 Design Knowledge

DSR seeks to address relevant real-world problems through the creation and evaluation of artifacts while simultaneously generating reusable design knowledge that can inform future research and practice [1, 8]. Design knowledge captures prescriptive insights about how classes of problems can be addressed through classes of solutions and is articulated at varying levels of abstraction. Rather than being confined to a single artifact instantiation, design knowledge is abstracted, formalized, and accumulated to support transferability and cumulative theorizing across projects and domains [5].

Prior literature distinguishes several interrelated constructs that together structure design knowledge in DSR. At a high level, requirements articulate what a solution should achieve for a given problem or problem class. These requirements are often informed by empirical insights, stakeholder needs, or kernel theories drawn from reference disciplines [1, 9]. Moving beyond individual problem instances, requirements can be formulated at a more general level to describe goals and needs that characterize a broader class of problems, thereby guiding the exploration of solution spaces [8, 10].

DPs represent a central form of prescriptive design knowledge in DSR. DPs express abstract guidance that links means and ends by specifying how certain design actions or mechanisms are expected to produce desired outcomes in a given context [2]. As such, DPs are often discussed as a bridging form of prescriptive design knowledge between problem-oriented requirements and concrete solution realizations, although they may themselves be articulated at different levels of abstraction [2, 6, 7]. They are more general than specific solution artifacts, yet more actionable than explanatory statements, making them particularly suitable for reuse and adaptation across contexts [3, 5].

To operationalize DPs in form of concrete artifacts, researchers often rely on more fine-grained constructs that specify how abstract prescriptions are realized in practice. Prior work highlights DFs as tangible, solution-oriented elements that translate abstract design knowledge into implementable characteristics of an artifact [4, 6, 11]. DFs thus serve as a bridging construct between DPs and instantiated artifacts by clarifying how prescriptive guidance materializes in concrete functionalities, processes, or interventions. This bridging role supports traceability from requirements to DPs and onward to instantiations, while also enabling iterative refinement and reuse of design knowledge across projects [12].

At the level of instantiation, artifacts such as software systems, prototypes, methods, or organizational interventions embody preceding forms of design knowledge in concrete settings [1, 8]. Instantiations serve both as vehicles for addressing practical problems and as sources of empirical feedback that inform the evaluation and refinement of requirements, DPs, and DFs. Through repeated cycles of building, intervention, and evaluation, insights derived from instantiations contribute to the evolution and accumulation of design knowledge over time [5, 8].

Although these constructs differ in their primary role within DSR, they should not be understood as each residing at a single fixed level of abstraction [7]. Rather, requirements, DPs, and DFs may each be formulated more concretely or more abstractly depending on the problem class, design scope, and stage of knowledge development [6, 7]. This makes abstraction itself a central challenge in DP development, which we address in the next section. To establish consistent terminology for the remainder of the paper, Table 1 summarizes the types of design knowledge constructs used and their role in DSR. We include meta-requirements here primarily to distinguish them from design requirements and to make explicit that the two are often conflated in the DSR literature (see also [13]). Where applicable, we indicate alternative terms used in prior literature and clarify how these relate to our terminology. In the remainder of this paper, we consistently use these constructs and terms to analyze abstraction, navigation, and alignment in DP development.

Table 1. Types of Design Knowledge Constructs

DSR Construct	Definition	Key References
Kernel Theory	Explanatory or justificatory knowledge from reference disciplines that informs problem framing, abstraction, and design decisions	[9, 10]
Meta-requirement (MR)	An abstract requirement that characterizes a class of problems by specifying the fundamental needs, goals, or conditions that motivate design, independent of any specific solution concept *Also referred to as general requirements or class-level requirements*	[9, 10, 14]
Design Requirement (DR)	A requirement that specifies what a class of solutions must be capable of in order to address a given problem class, taking into account relevant boundary conditions and design constraints *Also referred to as requirements or conflated with meta-requirements*	[4, 13]
Design Principle (DP)	A prescriptive statement linking design means to desired ends for addressing a defined problem class	[2]
Design Feature (DF)	A solution-oriented characteristic that operationalizes one or more DPs independent of a specific instantiation	[12]
Situated Requirement (R)	A context-specific expression of a (user) need, goal, or constraint derived from a concrete problem instance	[1]
Situated Feature (F)	A context-specific realization or implementation of a DF within a concrete artifact instance	[1, 8]

(continued)

Table 1. (*continued*)

DSR Construct	Definition	Key References
Instantiation	A realized artifact instantiated in a specific context that embodies design knowledge and enables evaluation. *Sometimes referred to as prototype*	[1, 8]

2.2 Abstraction in Design Science Research

Abstraction plays a central role in DSR because its primary objective is not to address isolated problem instances, but to develop prescriptive knowledge that is applicable to a broader class of problems [1, 8]. In contrast to routine problem solving, which typically produces situated solutions tailored to specific contexts, DSR aims to generate design knowledge that can be projected beyond the original design setting [7]. This aspiration requires researchers to work deliberately across multiple levels of abstraction in both the problem space and the solution space.

Prior work emphasizes that requirements, DPs, and DFs all exist at multiple levels of abstraction. Requirements may range from highly situated expressions of needs in a specific context to more general formulations that characterize a problem class [9, 10]. Similarly, DPs can be articulated at varying abstraction levels, from broad, highly general prescriptions to more domain-specific guidance [2, 6]. DFs, while often closer to instantiation, also span a continuum from relatively abstract operational concepts to highly specific, technology-bound specifications, as shown in prior analyses of DF formulations [12].

Because these elements do not reside on a single abstraction level, DP development necessarily involves navigation across abstraction levels. Researchers typically move from situated problem instances and concrete DFs toward more abstract requirements and DPs through processes of generalization and abstraction, while also moving in the opposite direction when instantiating and evaluating design knowledge in concrete settings [7, 8]. Effective DPs therefore emerge not from a fixed abstraction level, but from iterative movement across levels, converging on a formulation that is sufficiently general to support reuse while remaining concrete enough to guide design action.

A recurring challenge in this process is identifying an appropriate level of abstraction for DPs. Prior studies report two common failure modes. First, DPs may remain too close to specific solution instances, resulting in narrowly framed heuristics that lack transferability beyond the original context [6]. Second, DPs may be formulated at such a high level of abstraction that they lose actionable guidance and provide little support for actual design decisions [2]. These issues highlight that abstraction is not merely a matter of increasing generality, but of aligning abstraction levels across requirements, DPs, and DFs.

To conceptualize such alignment, Winter and Albani [7] draw on the notion of abstraction hierarchies, which describe how artifacts, problems, and solutions can be related through generalization and specialization relationships rather than simple aggregation or decomposition. Within such hierarchies, designs at higher abstraction levels are intended to be applicable to broader problem classes, whereas designs at lower levels address more narrowly defined contexts. Importantly, DSR projects often operate across several intermediate abstraction levels rather than a single abstract and a single instance level. Navigating these hierarchies requires deliberate abstraction and specialization activities to ensure that problem formulations and solution proposals remain compatible.

The concept of projectability further sharpens the role of abstraction in DSR. Baskerville and Pries-Heje [15] argue that traditional notions of generalizability, which are largely backward-looking and rooted in descriptive research, are insufficient for prescriptive design knowledge. Instead, projectability captures the forward-looking quality of DPs and design theories, emphasizing their capacity to operate meaningfully in future and alternative contexts. Projectability depends critically on abstraction choices. DPs that are formulated with overly specific contextual assumptions are difficult to project to new settings, while DPs that are formulated at an excessively abstract level may fail to provide guidance for concrete instantiations [15].

2.3 Limitations of Conceptual Approaches for DP Development

Prior research has made substantial progress in conceptualizing DPs and in providing guidance for their development. Foundational work has clarified the structure, components, and prescriptive logic of DPs [2, 10] and highlighted their central role in accumulating prescriptive design knowledge in DSR. More recent studies have proposed methods, taxonomies, and empirical insights to support the development of DPs in practice [4, 16, 17]. Despite these advances, existing approaches exhibit several limitations that complicate systematic and transparent DP development.

First, existing approaches differ substantially in where and how DPs are developed within the design process. Some studies emphasize reflective derivation of DPs after or during artifact construction, as commonly observed in action design research and inductive DSR projects [16, 18]. Other approaches advocate more supportive or theory-driven derivation of DPs prior to artifact instantiation, often grounded in literature, kernel theories, or conceptual reasoning [4, 10]. While this plurality reflects the richness of DSR practice, it also leads to heterogeneous and sometimes implicit development paths that are difficult to compare, replicate, or deliberately choose from, especially for novice researchers.

Second, although prior work acknowledges that DPs operate at different levels of abstraction, explicit guidance on navigating abstraction levels during DP development remains limited. Conceptual analyses often describe DPs as a bridging form of prescriptive design knowledge that connects requirements and DFs [2, 11], and empirical studies show that researchers move back and forth between problem understanding, solution exploration, and abstraction [16]. However, most approaches treat abstraction implicitly as an outcome rather than as a deliberate and traceable activity. As a result, DPs are often presented without making explicit how abstraction choices were made, how they relate to underlying requirements or DFs, or how alternative abstraction levels were considered.

Third, existing approaches provide limited support for aligning abstraction levels across different design knowledge elements. Prior studies typically focus on one dominant construct, such as DPs as prescriptive statements [2] or DFs as operationalized solution elements [17], but rarely explicate how requirements, DPs, and DFs are co-developed and mutually adjusted across abstraction levels. This lack of alignment can result in DPs that are either tightly coupled to specific solution features or detached from the problem class they are intended to address. While taxonomies and solution spaces help classify forms of prescriptive knowledge [17], they do not provide process-level guidance on how researchers move between these forms during DP development.

Fourth, empirical analyses of DP development strategies highlight a high degree of situatedness and path dependency. Schoormann et al. [16] identify multiple strategies for developing DPs that differ in their entry points, theorizing modes, and timing of abstraction. While these strategies offer valuable descriptive insight into how DPs are developed in practice, they also reveal that development paths are often shaped by project contingencies, collaboration settings, or methodological preferences rather than by explicit methodological guidance. Consequently, researchers may struggle to justify why a particular abstraction level was chosen or how alternative formulations were systematically explored and ruled out.

Taken together, existing approaches provide rich conceptual foundations and valuable empirical insights into DP development, but they offer limited methodological support for systematically navigating and aligning abstraction levels across requirements, DPs, and DFs. In particular, there is a lack of integrative guidance that helps researchers make abstraction choices explicit, relate these choices to projectability and reuse, and transparently document how DPs emerge through iterative movement in the design knowledge space. Addressing these limitations requires a framework that foregrounds abstraction navigation and alignment as central activities in DP development, which we propose in the following section.

2.4 Empirical DP Development Across DSR Boilerplates

Empirical DP development is often embedded in broader boilerplates for structuring DSR projects. Widely used or widely discussed examples include DSR methodology (DSRM) [19], action design research (ADR) [18], iterative DSR process models such as Kuechler and Vaishnavi [20], and more recent approaches such as echeloned DSR (eDSR) [21]. These boilerplates do not merely structure projects differently; they also foreground different moments and mechanisms through which design knowledge, including DPs, is expected to emerge. DSRM, for example, frames DSR as a nominal sequence from problem identification and objective definition to design, demonstration, and evaluation, thereby foregrounding the early derivation and later revision of prescriptive knowledge [19]. By contrast, Kuechler and Vaishnavi [20] place stronger emphasis on the iterative refinement of design and kernel theory through development and evaluation, making prescriptive knowledge development more explicitly theory-refining.

To illustrate how such project logics may shape DP development in practice, we briefly consider one representative study for each. In Seidel et al. [22], informed by DSRM, initial DPs grounded in prior literature are revised through three rounds of developing, demonstrating, and evaluating a prototypical implementation. In Strohmann et al. [23], following the adapted process model by Kuechler and Vaishnavi [20], DPs are first derived theoretically and then further refined through instantiation, evaluation, analysis of an existing system, and the derivation of DFs. In Herath Pathirannehelage et al. [24], using ADR, the study develops actionable DPs through an iterative process of artefact design, deployment, evaluation, and subsequent systematization of design knowledge. This is consistent with ADR more broadly, where DPs are shaped through build–intervene–evaluate cycles, identified and refined in reflection and learning, and fully articulated in the formalization of learning stage. In Ghanbari et al. [25], drawing on eDSR, DPs evolve across multiple interconnected design echelons over the course of a five-year project. This reflects the underlying eDSR logic, which emphasizes the accumulation of design knowledge across self-contained echelons that each contribute partial but validated knowledge outputs. These exemplary studies thus illustrate different empirical paths of DP development, while also suggesting that such paths are partly shaped by the organizing logic of the underlying boilerplate.

3   Conceptualization

3.1   A Mode-Based Framework for DP Development

The mode-based framework for DP development (Fig. 1) conceptualizes DP development as an iterative and non-linear process of reasoning across different design knowledge elements. The framework does not prescribe a sequence of activities or a preferred entry point. Instead, it distinguishes modes of reasoning that can be enacted in parallel and revisited throughout DP development.

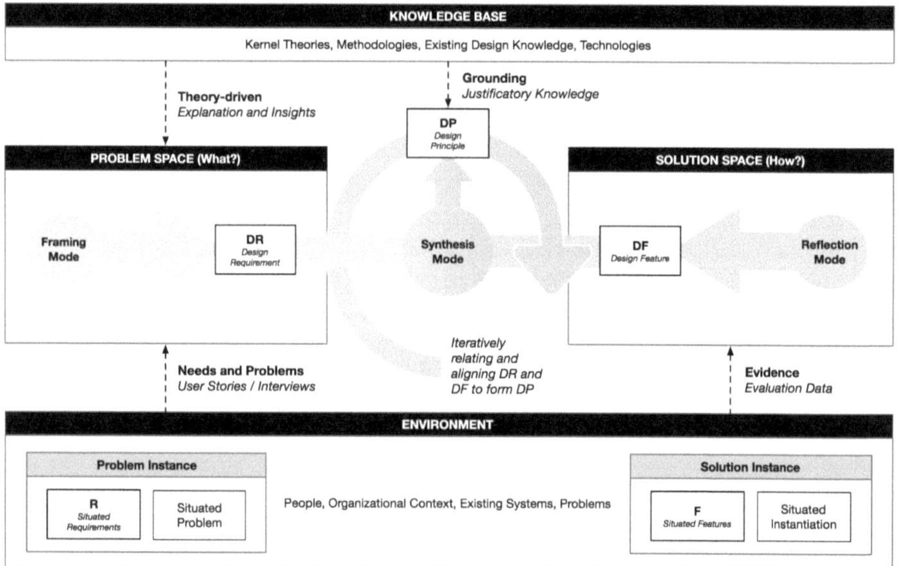

Fig. 1. A Mode-Based Framework for Developing DPs

The framework differentiates three modes: *Framing Mode*, *Reflection Mode*, and *Synthesis Mode*. Each mode is characterized by a dominant way of working with design knowledge, while DP development itself emerges through iteratively moving between these modes rather than within a single mode alone.

In the *Framing Mode*, DP development is driven by the construction and refinement of DR. In this mode, researchers engage in framing activities that articulate and delimit what a solution should be capable of, given the design context and boundary conditions. Framing does not result in DPs directly. Instead, it stabilizes DRs as a reference point against which emerging prescriptive insights can later be assessed.

In the *Reflection Mode*, DP development is driven by abstraction from concrete solution realizations. Researchers start from instantiations and reflect on their DFs to abstract recurring solution characteristics beyond a single artifact. This mode foregrounds learning from design practice and enables the articulation of DFs at a level suitable for comparison and generalization.

The Synthesis Mode constitutes the integrative reasoning dynamic at the center of the framework. In this mode, researchers actively relate and align DRs from the Framing Mode with DFs emerging from the Reflection Mode. DP development is understood as a process of matching and negotiating what a solution should achieve with how solutions have been realized or could be realized. Through this alignment, tensions and complementarities between DRs and DFs are resolved in the formulation of DPs. It is not a single final act of integration, but an iterative and non-linear process in which problem-side and solution-side insights are repeatedly brought together, compared, and refined. One could understand this conceptualization as a specialization of the three cycle model of DSR [26] for designing DPs.

3.2 The Abstraction Alignment Model

The abstraction alignment model (Fig. 2) complements the mode-based framework by explicating how DR, DP, and DF must be positioned relative to each other in the design knowledge space for robust DP development. The model draws on the theory of hierarchical systems [27] and its application in DSR, which conceptualizes design knowledge as organized across multiple levels of granularity and emphasizes the importance of relating elements at compatible levels [21]. Against this background, the abstraction alignment model focuses on how prescriptive design knowledge emerges through the alignment of requirements and features at appropriate abstraction levels.

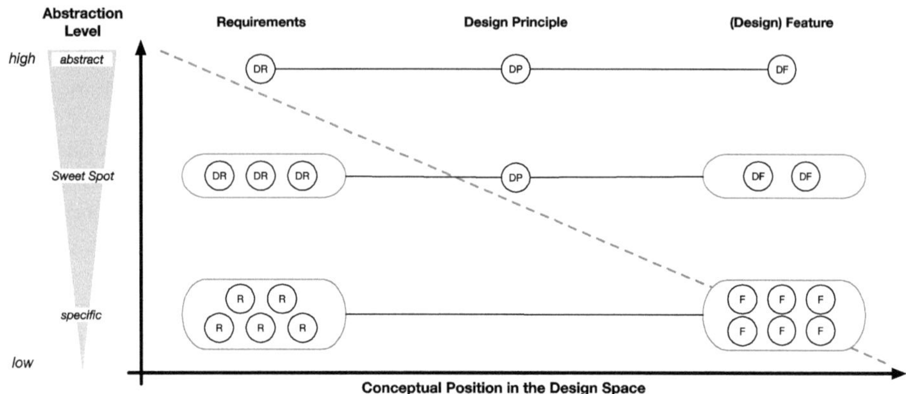

Fig. 2. The Abstraction Alignment Model

The model conceptualizes the design knowledge space along a vertical abstraction dimension ranging from specific, situated expressions at the lower end to highly abstract formulations at the upper end. DR, DP, and DF can each be formulated at different abstraction levels, and DP development is understood as the outcome of aligning these elements at compatible levels of abstraction. Importantly, the model does not assume a fixed or inherently correct abstraction level for any construct in isolation. Instead, it highlights that the relative positioning between DRs, DPs, and DFs is decisive.

At the center of the model lies a conceptual sweet spot, where DRs, DPs, and DFs intersect at compatible abstraction levels. In this region, DRs are sufficiently specific to provide orientation for solution development, DFs are sufficiently abstract to transcend individual instantiations, and DPs can articulate prescriptive means–ends relationships that are both actionable and projectable. DPs formulated in this region balance generality and specificity and are thus more likely to remain stable across contexts while still informing concrete design decisions.

The model also makes explicit several misalignment patterns that commonly occur during DP development. First, DRs may be framed at a very high level of abstraction, reflecting broad problem classes, while DFs remain closely tied to specific instantiations. In such cases, candidate DPs tend to become vague and underspecified, as the gap between what a solution should achieve and how solutions are realized is too large to support meaningful prescriptive reasoning. Second, DRs may be overly specific, reflecting narrow contexts or idiosyncratic constraints, while DFs are abstracted to a higher level. This configuration often results in DPs that collapse into local heuristics with limited transferability. Third, DPs themselves may be articulated at abstraction levels that are not supported by either DRs or DFs, leading to DPs that appear theoretically appealing but lack grounding in requirements or solution experience.

Within the overall framework, the abstraction alignment model functions as the conceptual lens that explains how this integration is achieved across modes. It captures how emerging DRs, DFs, and DPs are repeatedly brought into relation and adjusted toward compatible abstraction levels. Alignment does not imply forcing constructs to a single level, but rather negotiating their relative abstraction positions until prescriptive coherence is achieved. In this sense, Synthesis Mode marks the point at which such alignment becomes most explicit, but it is prepared through framing moves that refine DRs and reflecting moves that abstract or consolidate DFs. By making abstraction alignment explicit, the model provides a diagnostic and generative lens for DP development. It enables researchers to reason about why certain candidate DPs remain unstable, overly abstract, or overly context-bound, and to deliberately adjust abstraction levels to resolve these issues. In doing so, the abstraction alignment model operationalizes the reasoning logic introduced in Sect. 3.1 and offers an analytical lens for interpreting how researchers navigate the design knowledge space during DP development.

3.3 Navigation Moves in the Design Knowledge Space

Building on the mode-based framework and the abstraction alignment model, we conceptualize DP development as a process of navigation through the design knowledge space. This navigation is enacted through a set of recurring navigation moves that describe how researchers deliberately shift, relate, materialize, and stabilize design knowledge elements during DP development. These moves do not constitute a method or a prescribed sequence of steps. Instead, they capture recurrent epistemic actions that can be combined, repeated, and revisited across different reasoning situations. Table 2 summarizes the navigation moves, their dominant direction in the design knowledge space, and their purpose.

Table 2. Navigation Moves in the Design Knowledge Space

Move	Direction	Purpose
1. Abstraction *Generalize-Upward*	Low → Middle / High (R → DR; F → DF; DF → DP)	Abstract from situated or lower-level design knowledge to derive more general and reusable problem formulations, solution characteristics, or DPs
2. Specialization *Refine-Downward*	High / Broad → More Specific (DR → DR′; DF → DF′; DP → DP′)	Narrow scope, clarify boundary conditions, and sharpen intent to stabilize design knowledge at a more specific level
3. Instantiation *Materialize*	Middle → Low (DR / DP → DF → INS)	Translate abstract requirements or DPs into concrete, context-sensitive solution realizations that can be built and evaluated

(continued)

Table 2. (*continued*)

Move	Direction	Purpose
4. Alignment *Match DR$_i$ ↔ DF$_i$*	Horizontal across abstraction levels (DR ↔ DF ↔ DP)	Align what a solution should achieve with how solutions are realized at compatible abstraction levels to enable coherent DP formulation
5. Stabilization *Stabilize*	Within abstraction level (DR, DF, or DP)	Strengthen grounding, explicate mechanisms, clarify articulation, and consolidate empirical and theoretical support without changing abstraction level

The first move, *Abstraction*, captures upward navigation across abstraction levels. Through abstraction, researchers generalize from situated or lower-level design knowledge to derive more reusable forms. This includes abstracting from situated requirements to DRs, from situated features to DFs, and from DFs to candidate DPs. Abstraction supports learning from empirical material, existing solutions, and design experience by elevating situated insights beyond a single context.

The second move, *Specialization*, captures downward navigation across abstraction levels. Specialization involves narrowing scope, clarifying boundary conditions, and sharpening intent to concretize design knowledge at a more specific level. Importantly, specialization is not limited to requirements. Researchers may specialize DRs, DFs, or emerging DPs in order to reduce ambiguity and improve applicability without yet committing to a concrete instantiation.

The third move, *Instantiation*, represents a special form of specification that bridges abstract design knowledge to concrete solution realizations. Through instantiation, DRs or DPs are translated into DFs and realized in a specific artifact instance. Instantiation enables empirical evaluation and generates the solution material required for subsequent abstraction and reflection. While instantiation involves downward movement, it is distinct from specification because it crosses the boundary from abstract design knowledge into situated artifacts.

The fourth move, *Alignment*, operates horizontally across abstraction levels. Alignment relates what a solution should achieve, as articulated in DRs, with how solutions are realized or could be realized, as articulated in DFs. Through alignment, researchers assess whether requirements and features are expressed at compatible abstraction levels and whether their relationship supports coherent prescriptive reasoning. Alignment is central to DP development, as misalignment often results in DPs that are either overly abstract or overly tied to specific solutions.

The fifth move, *Stabilization*, supports the stabilization of design knowledge without necessarily changing its abstraction level. Stabilization may be applied to DRs, DFs, or DPs and involves strengthening grounding, explicating mechanisms, clarifying articulation, and consolidating empirical and theoretical support. Unlike abstraction or specialization, refinement does not imply directional movement in the design knowledge space, but rather consolidation and clarification of existing formulations.

Taken together, these navigation moves provide an analytical lens and sensitizing vocabulary for understanding how DP development unfolds as researchers move through the design knowledge space. By making these moves explicit, the framework supports systematic reflection on how DPs emerge, why misalignments occur, and how researchers may interpret and articulate the development of robust and projectable prescriptive design knowledge.

4   Demonstration

To make the proposed conceptualization tangible, we provide an illustrative reconstruction based on a prior DSR project on virtual companionship [23]. This illustration shows how the concepts of *Framing*, *Reflection*, and *Synthesis Mode*, the abstraction-alignment model, and the navigation moves can be used analytically to interpret the evolution of a DP over time. In that project, design knowledge was developed by deriving DRs from theory, translating them into DPs, and evaluating them through instantiations and empirical analysis. This demonstration illustrates how DP development becomes traceable as navigation between DRs, DFs, and DPs, enacted through *Framing Mode, Reflection Mode*, and *Synthesis Mode*.

We focus on one DP thread from the original publication, namely DP5 (Principle of relationship), which addresses the challenge of moving from transactional assistance toward sustained companionship. In the early stages of the project, DP development was dominated by *Framing Mode* and relied almost exclusively on theory from interpersonal relationships and the human need to belong. This resulted in a candidate DP that articulated a strong normative aspiration, but was derived without systematic reflection on technological realizability:

Candidate DP: *Establish a warm, positive and long-term relationship in order to ensure constant reuse and thus make and maintain friendship and form interpersonal attachment to satisfy the user's need for belonging.*

When attempting to instantiate this DP, it became evident that creating a conversational agent that genuinely supports long-term relationships is non-trivial from a technological and interaction-design perspective. In particular, it remained unclear which concrete system properties and interaction mechanisms would operationalize such an abstract relational goal. This motivated a shift toward *Reflection Mode*, in which the project team analyzed an existing application, Replika, and conducted a longitudinal study incorporating qualitative user feedback and chat interaction data. The goal of this move was to abstract DFs that appeared to contribute to perceived relationship continuity in practice. Table 3 reconstructs how this process can be understood as navigation in the design knowledge space and makes it explicit how its anatomical components become progressively articulated across iterations. The DP anatomy status column captures this progression in compact form by indicating which anatomical components [2] of the focal DP are already explicit at each stage and which only partially exist or begin to emerge.

Table 3. Illustrating DP Development through Navigation in the Design Knowledge Space

Iteration snapshot	Framing Mode output (DR)	Reflection Mode output (DF)	Synthesis Mode outcome (DP)	DP anatomy status
Initial framing	The companion should enable a warm, positive, and long-term relationship with the user to stimulate companionship	No concrete solution evidence yet. Argued primarily based on interpersonal relationship theory and the need to belong	Candidate DP expresses aspirational intent but remains weakly actionable	A, partial R
Abstraction (from existing system and evidence)	The companion should support relationship continuity through repeated interaction and a collaborative and friendly relationship logic	Abstracted DFs from Replika and Sarah include continuity across interactions, memory, proactive engagement and follow-up, relational framing, and reciprocal interaction patterns	Relationship-oriented DRs become linked to generalizable interaction mechanisms, enabling DP stabilization	A, emerging M
Alignment (stabilizing DP formulation)	The companion should be capable of sustaining relationship continuity through re-use and relationship-oriented interaction mechanisms	Instantiation evidence shows that companion-oriented interaction design supports perceived companionship and sustained usage compared to assistant-style interaction	Published DP5 with explicit aim, mechanism, and rationale grounded in friendship, collaboration, and belonging	A, M, R
Stabilization (improving articulation and grounding)	Unchanged	Consolidated DF bundle emphasizing continuity, proactive relational engagement, reciprocity, and shared conversational or collaborative activities	Iterated DP with explicit context, designer agency, refined mechanism articulation, and improved grounding through CASA	A, M, R, C, DA, BC

A = aim; M = mechanism; R = rationale; C = context; DA = designer agency; BC = boundary conditions.

First, in *Framing Mode*, the problem space was articulated through DRs describing what a virtual companion should be capable of in order to support long-term relationships. Second, in *Reflection Mode*, solution knowledge was abstracted into DFs based on the analysis of Replika and the companion-oriented interaction design of Sarah, including continuity across interactions, proactive engagement, relational framing, and reciprocal exchange. Third, in *Synthesis Mode*, DRs and DFs were matched at compatible abstraction levels, resulting in a stabilized DP that was published as DP5 in [23]:

Published DP: *To establish a warm, positive, and long-term relationship and thus stimulate and maintain companionship between human and virtual companion, ensure regular re-use and follow the principles of friendship and collaboration, because human beings are fundamentally and pervasively motivated by a need to belong, which results in a strong desire to form and maintain enduring interpersonal attachments.*

Across the snapshots, the project alternates between abstraction (deriving reusable DFs from evidence), specialization (sharpening the DR toward relationship continuity), instantiation (building and evaluating Sarah), alignment (matching DRs with DFs to stabilize the DP), and stabilization (improving the DP articulation and grounding). The published DP already reflects substantial progress compared to the initial candidate formulation, as it explicitly introduces mechanisms and justificatory grounding. However, when viewed through the abstraction-alignment logic of the proposed framework, it still remains partially underspecified with respect to agency, boundary conditions, and the sociotechnical rationale explaining why such mechanisms can succeed in human-machine interaction. Applying the framework retrospectively therefore enables a further refinement, not by changing the substantive intent of the DP, but by improving how the design knowledge is communicated at an appropriate abstraction level. In this final iteration, the DP is sharpened by making explicit the context of repeated interaction, the role of the designer, and an improved grounding that integrates the computers are social actors (CASA) paradigm [28] as the sociotechnical bridge between human relationship needs and machine interaction:

Iterated DP: *For users interacting repeatedly with a conversational agent over time, in contexts where interaction extends beyond isolated, transactional tasks, designers should design the companion to actively sustain relationship continuity by enabling regular re-use and implementing relationship-oriented interaction mechanisms that ensure continuity across interactions, proactive relational engagement, reciprocal exchange, and shared conversational or collaborative activities, because humans are fundamentally motivated by a need to belong and, consistent with the CASA paradigm, tend to apply social expectations and relational norms to interactive systems, making such interaction patterns capable of eliciting perceived companionship rather than mere task support.*

Overall, this illustration shows how DP development can be interpreted as navigation across framing, reflecting, and synthesizing, and how the proposed conceptualization helps make the evolution of prescriptive design knowledge more explicit and discussable.

5   Discussion and Conclusion

This paper contributes to an ongoing discussion in design science research on how to develop DPs that are both actionable and projectable. DSR has made important progress in clarifying what constitutes a well-formed DP as a knowledge artifact, for example through anatomy-oriented guidance that specifies key elements such as aim, context, mechanism, and justificatory rationale [2]. At the same time, researchers continue to report recurring quality issues in DP sets, including overly abstract formulations that resist instantiation, overly specific heuristics that do not travel, and unclear relationships between requirements, features, and DPs [3, 17, 29]. Our contribution builds on these developments by offering a complementary perspective that explains how such quality issues emerge during DP development and how they can be addressed through deliberate navigation and alignment.

First, this paper advances the **methodological understanding** of DP development by explicating the underlying modes of reasoning through which DPs are constructed. Existing work provides concrete procedures for DP development, for example through method proposals that guide researchers from empirical insights and justificatory knowledge toward DP formulations [4]. Our framework complements such methodical guidance by clarifying the epistemic logic that DP development must manage, namely shifts between framing DRs, reflecting on and abstracting DFs from instantiations or existing solutions, and synthesizing both sides through repeated alignment. By conceptualizing these modes as repeatedly enacted rather than sequential, the framework helps explain why DP development often oscillates between theory-led framing and solution-led reflection, and why DPs can remain unstable when these activities are not aligned.

Second, the abstraction-alignment model contributes to ongoing debates about **generalization and projectability** in DSR [6, 7, 14]. Prior discussions distinguish problem-driven and solution-driven strategies and highlight that different research strategies imply different forms of abstraction and theorizing [30]. Our framework does not privilege either strategy. Instead, it highlights that DP quality depends on whether DRs and DFs are expressed at compatible abstraction levels. This alignment perspective provides a conceptual explanation for persistent weaknesses observed in DP development practice, including DPs that remain aspirational because requirements are framed too broadly relative to available feature evidence, or DPs that remain narrow because DF statements are too situated. In this sense, the abstraction-alignment model provides a missing connective tissue between procedural DP development guidance [4] and anatomy-oriented expectations for the final DP articulation [2].

Third, the **demonstration** makes the sensitizing value of the conceptualization tangible. By reconstructing the evolution of a DP from a longitudinal project, the illustration shows how theory-driven framing can produce candidate DPs that are difficult to operationalize, how reflection on instantiations and existing systems can surface feature evidence, and how iterative synthesis through alignment can help explain the stabilization of DPs at a level that supports both grounding and projectability. Importantly, the demonstration is not an evaluation of a method but an analytical illustration that renders the proposed concepts empirically intelligible.

Fourth, the paper also speaks to **practice-facing** concerns about how DPs are used beyond academic codification. Prior work suggests that practitioners use DPs less as strict prescriptions than as flexible orientation devices [31]. Our framework supports such use by making more explicit how design intentions, requirements, and features can be related and aligned, thereby helping translate abstract prescriptions into discussable and actionable design guidance without collapsing into implementation detail.

Overall, the discussion highlights that improving DP quality requires both careful articulation and better conceptual understanding of how DPs are developed. By complementing anatomy-oriented expectations [2] and process-focused DP development guidance [4] with a mode-based and alignment-centered explanation, the proposed framework contributes a sensitizing conceptualization that offers orienting guidance for making DP development more transparent and cumulative in DSR.

References

1. Bichler, M.: Design science in information systems research. Wirtschaftsinformatik **48**(2), 133–135 (2006). https://doi.org/10.1007/s11576-006-0028-8
2. Gregor, S., Kruse, L.C., Seidel, S.: Research perspectives: the anatomy of a design principle. J. Assoc. Inf. Syst. **21**, 1622–1652 (2020)
3. Strohmann, T., Siemon, D., Elshan, E., Gnewuch, U.: Design principles in information systems research: trends in construction and formulation. In: AMCIS 2023 Proceedings (2023)
4. Möller, F., Guggenberger, T.M., Otto, B.: Towards a method for design principle development in information systems. In: Hofmann, S., Müller, O., Rossi, M. (eds.) Designing for Digital Transformation. Co-Creating Services with Citizens and Industry, pp. 208–220. Springer International Publishing, Cham (2020)
5. vom Brocke, J., Winter, R., Hevner, A., Maedche, A.: Special issue editorial – accumulation and evolution of design knowledge in design science research: a journey through time and space. J. Assoc. Inf. Syst. **21**, 520–544 (2020)
6. Wache, H., Möller, F., Schoormann, T., Strobel, G., Petrik, D.: Exploring the abstraction levels of design principles: the case of chatbots. In: Wirtschaftsinformatik 2022 Proceedings (2022)
7. Winter, R., Albani, A.: Abstraction and abstraction levels in design science research. In: Winter, R. (ed.) Designing the Information Systems Artefact: Typology, Architecture, Abstraction, Collaborative Evolution and Design Patterns, pp. 81–100. Springer Nature Switzerland, Cham (2025)
8. Gregor, S., Hevner, A.R.: Positioning and presenting design science research for maximum impact. MIS Q. **37**, 337–355 (2013)
9. Walls, J.G., Widmeyer, G.R., El Sawy, O.A.: Building an information system design theory for vigilant EIS. Inf. Syst. Res. **3**, 36–59 (1992)
10. Gregor, S., Jones, D.: The anatomy of a design theory. J. Assoc. Inf. Syst. **8**, 312–335 (2007)
11. Meth, H., Mueller, B., Maedche, A.: Designing a requirement mining system. J. Assoc. Inf. Syst. **16**, 799–837 (2015)
12. Strohmann, T., Khosrawi-Rad, B.: The relevance of design features: from abstract knowledge to practical implementation. In: Chatterjee, S., vom Brocke, J., Anderson, R. (eds.) Local Solutions for Global Challenges, pp. 116–134. Springer Nature Switzerland, Cham (2025)
13. Iivari, J.: Editorial: a critical look at theories in design science research. J. Assoc. Inf. Syst. **21**, 502–519 (2020)
14. Baskerville, R., Pries-Heje, J.: Explanatory design theory. Bus. Inf. Syst. Eng. **2**, 271–282 (2010)
15. Baskerville, R., Pries-Heje, J.: Projectability in design science research. J. Inf. Technol. Theory Appl. (JITTA) **20**, 53–76 (2019)
16. Schoormann, T., Möller, F., Kruse, L.C.: Uncovering strategies of design principle development. Presented at the 17th International Conference on Design Science Research in Information Systems and Technology (2022)
17. Möller, F., Hansen, M., Schoormann, T.: Synthesizing a solution space for prescriptive design knowledge codification. Scand. J. Inf. Syst. **34**, 3–38 (2022)
18. Sein, M.K., Henfridsson, O., Purao, S., Rossi, M., Lindgren, R.: Action design research. MIS Q. **35**, 37–56 (2011)

19. Peffers, K., Tuunanen, T., Rothenberger, M.A., Chatterjee, S.: A design science research methodology for information systems research. J. Manag. Inf. Syst. **24**, 45–77 (2007)
20. Kuechler, B., Vaishnavi, V.: On theory development in design science research: anatomy of a research project. Eur. J. Inf. Syst. **17**, 489–504 (2008)
21. Tuunanen, T., Winter, R., vom Brocke, J.: Dealing with complexity in design science research: a methodology using design echelons. Manag. Inf. Syst. Q. **48**, 427–458 (2024)
22. Seidel, S., Chandra Kruse, L., Székely, N., Gau, M., Stieger, D.: Design principles for sensemaking support systems in environmental sustainability transformations (2018)
23. Strohmann, T., Siemon, D., Khosrawi-Rad, B., Robra-Bissantz, S.: Toward a design theory for virtual companionship. Hum.-Comput. Interact. **38**, 194–234 (2023)
24. Herath Pathirannehelage, S., Shrestha, Y.R., von Krogh, G.: Design principles for artificial intelligence-augmented decision making: an action design research study. Eur. J. Inf. Syst. **34**, 207–229 (2025)
25. Ghanbari, H., Tuunanen, T., Kazan, E.: Towards competition and collaboration: a mid-range design theory for designing coopetitive news platforms. Eur. J. Inf. Syst. **35**, 26–53 (2026)
26. Hevner, A.: A three cycle view of design science research. Scand. J. Inf. Syst. **19**, 87–92 (2007)
27. Mesarović, M.D., Macko, D., Takahara, Y.: Theory of Hierarchical, Multilevel. Academic Press, Systems (1970)
28. Nass, C., Moon, Y.: Machines and mindlessness: social responses to computers. J. Soc. Issues **56**, 81–103 (2000)
29. Khosrawi-Rad, B., Grogorick, L., Strohmann, T., Robra-Bissantz, S.: Toward a method for design science research meta-studies to improve the reusability of design principles. In: Mandviwalla, M., Söllner, M., Tuunanen, T. (eds.) Design Science Research for a Resilient Future, pp. 182–196. Springer Nature Switzerland, Cham (2024)
30. Iivari, J.: Distinguishing and contrasting two strategies for design science research. Eur. J. Inf. Syst. **24**, 107–115 (2015)
31. Chandra Kruse, L., Purao, S., Seidel, S.: How designers use design principles: design behaviors and application modes. J. Assoc. Inf. Syst. **23**, 1235–1270 (2022)

Design Science Research in an Era of Generative AI—Challenges and Theoretical Guidelines

Philipp zur Heiden[1(✉)] , Daniel Beverungen[1] , Christian Bartelheimer[2] , and Christoph Breidbach[3]

[1] Paderborn University, Paderborn 33098, Germany
{philip.zur.heiden,daniel.beverungen}@uni-paderborn.de
[2] Georg-August-Universität Göttingen, Göttingen 37073, Germany
christian.bartelheimer@uni-goettingen.de
[3] Business School, University of Queensland, Brisbane, Australia
c.breidbach@business.uq.edu.au

Abstract. Information systems (IS) research is increasingly exploring the potential of generative artificial intelligence (GenAI), such as large language models (LLMs). For design science research (DSR), such technologies foster entirely new vistas for the design of IT artifacts that make use of their generative capabilities, but also influence DSR methodology. This shift is much more profound than it has been discussed so far. To identify existing implications of GenAI for design-oriented research in IS, we report results from an integrative literature review of recent DSR publications in leading IS outlets. Thereby, we synthesize five major theoretical challenges that arise when using GenAI in DSR projects: (1) an obscure composition of the artifact, (2) an opaque contextualization of the LLM, (3) a fragile internal consistency of the artifact, (4) a rapid erosion of prescriptive knowledge, and (5) missing methodological guidance. We investigate these challenges and conceptualize a set of three guidelines that inform DSR in the rising era of GenAI. These guidelines support researchers in designing and justifying GenAI-related DSR processes and in precisely articulating the theoretical grounding of their design decisions and evaluation strategies.

Keywords: Design Science Research · Generative Artificial Intelligence · Large Language Model · Fit and Misfit · Guidelines

1 Introduction

Generative Artificial Intelligence (GenAI), and especially Large Language Models (LLMs), represent the foundational technology for generating seemingly meaningful texts [18] that has started to disruptively revolutionize businesses and society [52]. Up to 80% of organizations have explored adopting GenAI into their organizational processes and information systems, although the vast

J. vom Brocke et al. (Eds.): DESRIST 2026, LNCS 16606, pp. 383–400, 2026.
https://doi.org/10.1007/978-3-032-28313-9_22

majority of adoption projects failed [11]. Additionally, these systems evolve at high speed, leading to more tasks than they can perform [1]. Hence, the Information Systems (IS) discipline is at a pivotal position to study LLMs and support organizations in their efforts to design and use LLMs in a value-adding way.

As one profound research stream in the IS discipline, design science research (DSR) relates to a pragmatic philosophy and focuses on the design and evaluation of IT artifacts to contribute theories for design and action [20]. The DSR paradigm is design-oriented, aiming to solve important business problems while enhancing theory [27,50]. Design must achieve fit between two entities: The artifact (form) and its context [3]. Since either of the two—mostly both—entities can be adapted to increase the fit between both and designers face a kind of double contingency [39], reconciling form and context has no clear starting point. Hence, designers experience ample degrees of freedom, while the outcome of the design process is non-deterministic and contingent on their design decisions. Hence, while "design science attempts to create things that serve human purposes" [42], multiple design outcomes can potentially solve a specific problem. Or, as framed by Simon [51], "design is a search process".

When designing IT artifacts that integrate LLMs (or other general-purpose GenAI applications), these artifacts become highly complex. LLM complexity is driven by, for example, a lack of explainability of LLM outputs, opaque data used to train an LLM, and uncertainty about the truthfulness of LLM outputs, e.g., indicated by hallucinations [30]. Notwithstanding these challenges, recent DSR studies on LLM-enabled artifacts do not account for the complexity of LLMs and often black-box these properties to reduce complexity. Hence, if an LLM becomes the major part of an IT artifact that cannot or only be partially designed or customized by IS researchers or teams, the number of possible solution paths [51] for designers of LLM-enabled artifacts decreases. This observation results in the questions of what is left to the design of IT artifacts, when LLMs improve even more; do we even need DSR in the future or can LLMs solve problems that IS researchers previously designed IT artifacts for; is prompt-engineering, i.e., interacting with an existing LLM [49], already DSR or where can we position the boundary between designing and customizing LLM-based information systems?

From a designer's perspective, we see that these questions are not to be answered in one single study but have to be tackled across multiple papers and from perspectives of multiple experts from the IS domain. While research has started to identify and solve problems of design-oriented research for LLMs [1], in this study, our objectives are to (1) assess the current state of DSR publications that design LLM-enabled artifacts[1], and (2) spark the discussion on the future of designing LLM-enabled artifacts in IS research. We first conducted an integrative literature review [17], analyzing existing papers that apply DSR (with or without explicitly stating it) to design LLM-enabled artifacts. To account for the latest

---

[1] In the sense of IS research, we view DSR as a means to design socio-technical systems [27], targeting the interplay of humans and LLMs, and refrain from focusing on a computer science perspective that would, e.g., strive to improve LLM algorithms and their accuracy.

trend of DSR-based research on LLM-enabled artifacts, we scanned all high-quality IS conference publications in 2025 and identified 62 articles. Out of these papers, 53 papers blackbox the LLM-parts of the IT artifacts, while only 11 papers report on the functionality and characteristics of the LLM in detail. Further, only 21 papers contextualize their LLM applications instead of relying on the pretrained, un-contextualized models.

Throughout analyzing the papers, we identified five central challenges of designing LLM-enabled artifacts: (1) an obscure composition of the artifact, (2) an opaque contextualization of the LLM, (3) fragile internal consistency of the artifact, (4) rapid erosion of prescriptive knowledge, and (5) missing methodological guidance. We start the discussion on the future of DSR in a GenAI-world by proposing three guidelines: (1) differentiating between design and non-design, (2) contextualizing the LLM enabling the artifact, and (3) communicating boundary conditions. We theorize the results using a 2×2 matrix, consisting of form and context on the one side and analysis and synthesis on the other side. This matrix allows to visualize the traditional DSR process, consisting of (1) analysis of the context, (2) synthesis of the artifact, (3) synthesis of the context, and (4) once again analysis of the context.

While the analyzed studies from the integrative literature review align with the traditional DSR process, we expect two further steps to white-box the complexity of the integrated LLMs that follow the analysis of the context: First, we suggest an analysis of the artifact prior to designing it, focusing on analyzing the LLM's capabilities. Second, we recommend either a further synthesis of the context through fine-tuning or contextualization of the LLM. Alternatively, researcher should reason why this step is not necessary. We contribute a future path for DSR, specifically for designing LLM-enabled artifacts. Researchers can continue this necessary discussion in the IS and DSR communities, or use our guidelines to reasonably design LLM-enabled artifacts.

Our paper is structured as follows. We start with identifying the foundations of DSR and GenAI systems in Sect. 2. After presenting our application of the integrative literature review as our research method in Sect. 3, we present its results in Sect. 4. In Sect. 5, we discuss five theoretical challenges for designing IT artifacts in a GenAI world and develop three theoretical guidelines. We conclude the paper in Sect. 6.

2   Theoretical Background

2.1   Design Science Research as a Quest for Fit Between Artifact and Context

Contrasting natural phenomena with no human control, designers develop artifacts purposefully to serve specific needs and imitate appearances in natural things [51]. Artifacts depict the interface between their internal environment—the artifact itself—and their surrounding—its context [51]. In IS research, in particular, IT artifacts are intended to solve relevant problems effectively and efficiently and are considered useful as long as they are superior to the performance of pre-existing (rival) artifacts [27,42]. IT artifacts comprise four types: constructs, models, methods, and instantiations [42]. Such artifacts are defined as objects, entities, or a combination of both, designed to benefit their users when applied to a particular context [46,59].

Context has to play a crucial role in shaping an artifact's form and function, defining requirements, boundaries, and—ultimately—the utility of an artifact [3,27,40,51]. Utility is generally conceptualized as fit between form and context. While fit between form and context cannot be precisely assessed, because the list of possible requirements from the context is endless, it is rather conceptualized as the absence of misfit [3]. The importance of recognizing context in design has since been inscribed into many methods that constitute the engineering sciences, including requirements engineering's purpose to identify features to be inscribed into an artifact [13].

Design-oriented research, following the DSR paradigm, aims to solve problems that arise from a specific context [27]. While the results have to improve the specific context, researchers applying the DSR paradigm aim to abstract the results to develop theories for design and action, portraying guidance on how an artifact ought to be designed to serve a more general purpose [20]. For DSR, context is an integral part [27]—especially considering the origins of the sciences of the artificial [3,51]—laying focus not on artifacts as forms, but on ensembles of form and context. As DSR stems from pragmatic philosophy, it favors utility over truth [2,27,29]. This pragmatic account indicates that a form has to be able to influence—i.e., *change*—a context in a way that is advantageous from a designer's and/or user's point of view. Thus, the "artifact is a vehicle for research and practice impacts" [6, p. 368]. The goal of DSR can thus also be framed as providing a working way to change certain properties of a context—e.g., improving health conditions of diabetes patients [12], lowering unemployment [34], and maintaining a continuous energy flow [37].

Popular methods for applying the DSR paradigm [36,47,55, for example] are made up of multiple steps that directly involve the context and the artifact. All involved activities, including problem analysis, design, demonstration, and evaluation, can also be framed as either analysis or synthesis of form and context. While analysis targets the detailed examination by dividing an object into its entities, synthesis is concerned with combining entities to a whole—described as the core of design [3]. Traditional DSR methods start first with an analysis of the context, including the formation of requirements or design objectives. Second, designers synthesize the form by combining existing technologies and actors to a new whole framed as the artifact. Third, the artifact is put into its envisioned context to demonstrate its functionality and evaluate its usefulness. This third step, thus, is a synthesis of the context. Fourth and last, the context is analyzed (again), and designers evaluate whether an artifact was able to successfully transform it. Combining these two perspectives—i.e., differentiating between activities of analysis and those of synthesis, and understanding design as an interplay of artifact and context—we can visualize the described process steps of DSR. The resulting 2×2 matrix, presented in Fig. 1, aligns with the central design methodologies applying the DSR paradigm.

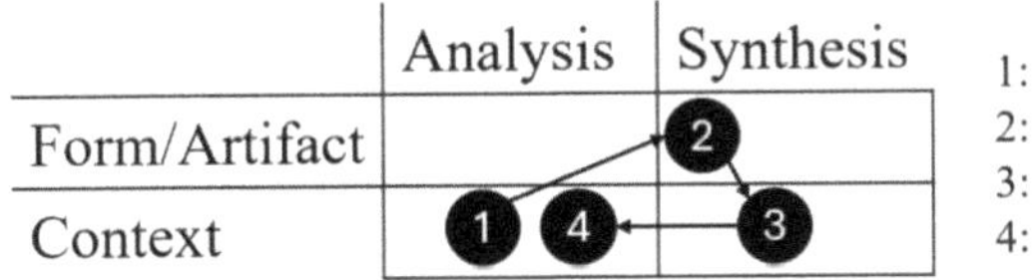

Fig. 1. Phases of DSR mapped to the steps of DSR methodology [47].

2.2   Generative Artificial Intelligence

Artificial Intelligence (AI) is defined differently depending on the research context [32]. Generally, however, âĂIJAIâĂİ refers to machines that embody intelligence comparable to humans [28]. Thus, AI is capable of âĂIJknowing, learning, perceiving, sensing, acting, planning, communicating and reasoningâĂİ [41, p. 206], enabling it to interpret and react to complex activities. Unlike general information technology, AI is able to learn and self-learn and can, thus, adapt its behavior, although the extend of these properties can vary [28]. Within this broader landscape, GenAI marks a transformative advance from discriminative (non-generative) AI. GenAI refers to a class of AI that is capable of autonomously creating novel and meaningful content in the form of text, images, audio, video, or code [18]. Leveraging deep generative models and advanced algorithms of machine learning, GenAI systems generate realistic and creative results by combining patterns learned from extensive training datasets with user-provided prompts [5]. One prominent technology enabling text-based GenAI systems are Large Language Models (LLMs) [4]. These models are the foundation of popular GenAI systems, such as OpenAI's Chat-GPT, Google's Gemini, and Microsoft Copilot, which LLMs can be fine-tuned in different ways to enable contextualized outputs [4].

GenAI can be described as a general purpose technology. General purpose technologies are characterized by being pervasive, improving over time, and allowing for complementary innovation and change [9, 10]. AI in general already fits these criteria [10], and we see strong signs of GenAI to also fit these criteria and even exceed the innovation capabilities of discriminative (non-generative) AI. This general purpose characteristics of GenAI can become a problem for design researchers, as the technology itself is already capable of solving multiple problems without explicitly designing this technology.

Based on the high impact of GenAI and especially LLMs on businesses and society, IS research is also strongly involving with this trend. For example, researchers have investigated the management of AI systems [8], the influence of GenAI and LLMs on knowledge and creative work [7], and reflecting on how research can benefit from and is endangered by these systems [15, 21, 45]. Additionally, researchers have started to design and evaluate IT artifacts that use LLMs as their main components. Exemplary designs include LLM-based hate speech detection [58], LLM-based agents for process automation [31], and tutoring systems for legal writing [56]. We posit that the design of general purpose technologies, such as GenAI and LLMs, calls for specifically respecting and considering the context to which the artifact must fit to implement complementary innovation and change [9, 10]—apart from other factors that make designing LLM-enabled artifacts that complex, such as agency, opacity, and their probabilistic nature.

Of course, LLMs are not only an object of design, but they can also enable the design of artifacts. For example, LLMs can be used to analyze the context of the research through knowledge-based search and review, generate interactive demonstrations, and assist in analyzing evaluation data [19].

3   Research Method

The two outlined objectives of our study can be further detailed, resulting in three aims of this study: (1) Identify and analyze current theoretical challenges of design-oriented papers in IS in following traditional DSR methods when designing LLM-based artifacts, and (2) condensate and discuss theoretical challenges in the backdrop to existing DSR literature that limit researchers' ability to transparently design reproducible artifacts, and (3) spark the discussion on the future of designing LLM-enabled artifacts in IS research. We therefore, conducted an integrative literature review [17], and utilize the results to theorize the insights and derive guidelines for future researchers designing LLM-enabled artifacts.

Integrative literature reviews are defined as "reviews of the literature that move beyond description of a body of evidence to derive new insights through integration and/or critique" [16, p. 2]. While this type of literature review is thus far rarely used in IS research, it can be seen as a combination of a theoretical review (synthesizing prior literature to derive, analyze, and synthesize theory) [48] and a critical review (summarizing and critically evaluating knowledge to provide directions for future studies) [48]. Conducting integrative literature reviews enables researchers, among others, to identify major trending themes and progress the knowledge bases on theses emerging research topics [17, 54]. In our case, the design of LLM-based artifacts is a relatively new topic that has mostly started with the rise of popular LLM APIs, such as OpenAI's ChatGPT API[2] and Google's Gemini API[3]. Therefore, we aim to identify the state of the art of LLM-based artifact design.

In general, in integrative literature reviews, there are no fixed arguments on which literature to select, but the literature itself should comprehensively show what is needed to drive future research [17]. In our case, we focus on design-oriented papers—either explicitly stating DSR as the underlying research

---

[2] https://openai.com/de-DE/api/.
[3] https://ai.google.dev/gemini-api/docs?hl=de.

paradigm or implicitly adhering to the DSR guidelines—in IS that aim to design LLM-enabled artifacts and view our integrative literature review as a home base for discussing challenges and guidelines for the future of desinging LLM-enabled artifacts in IS research.

In alignment with the DSR process, integrative literature reviews combine analysis and synthesis steps [17]. The analysis of the extant literature aligns with traditional literature review types [48,57]. Synthesis in integrative literature reviews is defined as integrating "existing ideas with new ideas to create a new formulation of the topic or issue" [53]. The output of the synthesis in integrative literature reviews can either be a conceptual framework or a theoretical framework [17]. In this paper, we provide a conceptual framework on future design-oriented research develops LLM-enabled artifacts.

For the application of the integrative literature review, we focus on papers that design LLM-based artifacts in the context of IS research. Due to the relative novelty of the topic in combination with long publishing cycles, we decided to focus on conference publications. In detail, we scanned all top conference publications in the IS discipline published in 2025 (according to the German VHB publication media rating[4], comprising the International Conference on Information Systems (ICIS), European Conference on Information Systems (ECIS), Advanced Information Systems Engineering (CAiSE), Conceptual Modeling (ER), Wirtschaftsinformatik (WI), Hawaii International Conference on System Sciences (HICSS), International Conference on Business Process Modeling (BPM), and International Conference on Design Science Research in Information Systems and Technology (DESRIST). As there are multiple LLM applications, sometimes not framed as LLMs but rather as AI or GenAI systems, we started by searching for papers that at least once mention "design" in their paper, yielding a result of 298 papers. We then analyzed whether these papers design AI-based applications, reducing the number of relevant papers to 87. Narrowing down the relevant papers to the design of LLM-based artifacts, our final sample consisted of 64 papers.

For assessing the current state of DSR publications that design LLM-enabled artifacts, we started by inductively scanning the identified papers. After approximately 25% of the papers were scanned, we derived categories and common themes—i.e., foundational research methods, blackboxed and detailed perspectives, contextualization of the LLMs. While analyzing the remaining papers for these constructs, we checked for further constructs, but did not identify further categories or common themes.

4 Descriptive Results

We report insights from analyzing all 64 publications identified in our review. While we do have all papers at hand, we decided not to reference specific papers in the following paragraphs. Our intention is by no means to criticize authors for the way in which they developed or presented their research. Instead, we

---

[4] https://www.vhbonline.org/en/services/vhb-rating-2024.

constrain our review to identifying properties that we perceive to be problematic in terms of developing IT artifacts based on LLMs and deriving prescriptive knowledge that informs IS research. The summarized results from the integrative literature review are summarized in Table 1.

First, considering the description of the basic LLM used to develop specific IT artifacts, we identified 53 papers that did not feature a description of any details of the LLM system that was used. The authors did not mention nor discuss the LLM's functionality, reasoning, and behavior. We term this abstraction from the implementation details as *blackboxing the design features of the LLM*. In five further papers, the authors also blackboxed the functionality, reasoning, and behavior of the LLM, but described how they improved the LLM system used—i.e., at least partially whiteboxing the LLM. Only in three publications, the authors explicitly described the LLM's core functionality, reasoning, and behavior. Only in one publication, the authors presented the design features of their LLM in detail. Two papers also present the LLM design in detail by outlining the process of their self-trained LLM models.

Second, we analyzed the degree to which LLMs were adapted to fit a specific application context encountered by an organization or in an industry sector. Authors of two publications trained an LLM themselves, displaying the highest degree of contextualization. On the other side, we identified 39 papers that integrated an LLM only by prompting, indicating no contextualization of the IT artifact that goes beyond pure utilization. Five more papers did not contextualize the LLM, but used multiple agents (also called nodes) of LLMs; thus, they used prompting to assign their LLM instances different perspectives or roles, still constrained by prompting. Eleven papers used retrieval-augmented generation (RAG)—a technique relating to LLMs that identifies documents relevant to a user query to output either documents or parts of these documents to answer specific questions [33,38]—or RAG based on graphs, i.e., GraphRAG [24]. Since these techniques are especially suited for discovering expert knowledge, (Graph)RAG is key for extending default LLMs by contextualized knowledge. Three papers discovered in our study used fine-tuning to contextualize their LLMs, whereas one additional paper used knowledge editing to put contextual knowledge into the LLM. Three other papers used detailed contextualization processes that combined multiple of the mentioned elements.

Third, we analyzed the identified papers for their attempts to generalize prescriptive knowledge from designing LLM-enabled artifacts. In 39 papers, the authors made no attempts for knowledge generalization, i.e., they did not abstract their insights to identify design principles [22], nor did they otherwise formalize design knowledge. However, some of these papers were not reporting completed research, yet, but presented intermediate results. For this reason, we acknowledge that the design projects might not have reached sufficient maturity to specify abstracted prescriptive knowledge. The other 25 papers specified design principles [22]. Two papers formulate two design principles, eight papers propose three design principles, four papers present four design principles, three

Table 1. Descriptive results of our integrative literature review.

Category	Characteristic	# papers
Description of the design features of the LLM	blackboxed	53
	blackboxed, but description of LLM improvement	5
	whiteboxed LLM functionality, reasoning, or behavior	3
	detailed description	1
	outlined process of self-trained LLM	2
LLM contextualization	prompting only (no contextualization)	39
	multiple LLM agents	5
	(Graph)RAG	11
	fine-tuned LLM	3
	knowledge editing of LLM	1
	combination of contextualization activities	3
	self-trained LLM	2
Knowledge generalization	No knowledge generalization	39
	Deriving design principles	25
Main methodological	No guidelines presented	17
	Peffers et al. (2007)	19
	Hevner et al. (2004)	5
	Kuechler & Vaishnavi (2008)	4
	Tuunanen et al. (2024)	3
	Kuechler & Vaishnavi (2012), Hevner (2007), Mullarkey & Hevner (2018), Sein et al. (2011)	2 ea
	Johannesson & Perjons (2021), Lee et al. (2011), Schoormann et al. (2024), Sonnenberg & vom Brocke (2012), Yang et al. (2023), Peffers et al. (2014), Vaishnavi & Kuechler (2015)	1 ea
	Multiple methodological guidelines	1

papers outline five design principles, and four papers show six design principles. Single papers even proposed seven, 12, 13, or even 29 design principles.

Fourth, we reviewed the papers' main methodological guideline, process, or advisory in the research papers. Out of the 64 papers, 17 papers do not state a research method at all. Nineteen papers referenced the general DSR methodology proposed by Peffers et al. [47]. Five papers justified their approaches even more generally, referencing the seminal DSR paper by Hevner et al. [27]. Further, four papers cite Kuechler & Vaishnavi [35], three papers performed design echelons (eDSR) [55], and two papers each were based on Kuechler & Vaishnavi [36], Hevner [26], Mullarkey & Hevner [44], or Action Design Research [50]. Seven further methodological guidelines were only referenced in one paper each. One paper referenced multiple methodological guidelines, however, it was unclear what guidelines were actually used.

5 Challenges and Guidelines for Design-Oriented Research Involving LLM-Enabled Artifacts

From the descriptive insights discovered in our literature review, we derive five challenges and propose three guidelines to inform design science research on LLM-enabled artifacts.

Challenge 1: Obscure Composition of the Artifact. As evidenced by our literature review, the boundaries between the IT artifacts that were originally designed by the researchers and the basic technology on which these artifacts were built—in most cases this was an LLM like ChatGPT—were blurred. The missing description obscures the composition of the IT artifact, i.e., its architectural design. Most of the conference publications that focused on LLM-enabled artifact design did not clearly describe what had been designed "on top" of exiting LLMs and which functionalities were provided by the underlying LLM as a general-purpose technology. In some cases, this blurring was so strong that it resembles an igon value problem [1], i.e., authors appear to be just superficially knowledgeable on AI and LLMs, thus, stating (partially) wrong technical details without providing the necessary grounding. In most papers, referring to the first two categories of our analysis, we see a severe lack of describing the perspectives that were taken. For example, authors could be interested in three different cases: (1) analyzing whether a given LLM was able to solve a specific problem encountered in the field; (2) identifying whether the LLM had to be adapted or customized to solve a specific problem, e.g., by designing a CustomGPT on top of the regular functionality; or (3) designing a specific IT artifact that was based on but still profoundly extends an LLM, for instance, by using an LLM only for background computation. While option (1) is a valid approach focusing on the evaluation of an artifact, options (2) and (3) refer to design and evaluation in the sense of DSR. We posit that not articulating which option is being pursued obscures the use of LLMs in a DSR study, which could severely blur the IT artifact's composition. The problem with a blurred composition is that readers will remain unable to understand what IT artifact exactly has been designed, to what extent it goes beyond the design of the underlying technology, and how the new properties of the artifact interplay with the existing LLM.

Challenge 2: Opaque Contextualization of the LLM. The majority of research papers we encountered reported no significant attempts to contextualize the LLMs used to solve a specific problem encountered in an organization or industry—or at least, no such attempt was explicitly reported. The authors used LLMs in their native forms as a general purpose technology, resorting to prompt engineering only. We posit that resorting to prompting is critical from a DSR standpoint, since prompt engineering is only one way to adapt an LLM to its context [43], focusing on the artifact's *use* instead of its *design* in a classical sense. A much stronger approach is context engineering, comprising multi-agent LLMs with RAG, memory systems, tool-integrated reasoning, as well as multiple ways to incorporate context knowledge [43]. Thus, there are multiple possibilities to contextualize an LLM and authors should make attempts to explicitly consider, reject or select these options. Additionally, context engineering allows to specify the general purpose character of LLMs to provide innovative, specialized solutions for complementary innovation [9,10]. Ultimately, we submit that researchers following the DSR paradigm in designing LLM-enabled artifacts should aspire to design and evaluate artifacts that are able to solve specific problems in context, pointing beyond the built-in functionality inscribed into— even highly advanced—off-the-shelf software such as LLMs.

Challenge 3: Fragile Internal Consistency of the Artifact. We observed that many authors resorted to prompt engineering to "design" their LLMs, while refraining from reporting their prompts, limiting the transparency of the research process. Also, only a part of the papers specified system prompts that actually changed the behavior of the LLM, while most resorted to prompts specified by users. We posit that referring to "prompting" as the only activity of design might cause multiple problems. First, the output provided by LLMs is inherently non-deterministic, i.e., the same prompts frequently lead to different outputs, such that the results depend on opaque contextual nuances. Second, resulting from this problem, framing prompt engineering as *design* impedes the reproducibility of DSR studies, whereas reproducibility is a crucial property of scientific inquiry. Third, readers need to know system prompts in detail to identify whether the authors narrowed the scope of an LLMs to fit a specific context, or if the native version of the LLM was used. Combined, we conclude that the non-deterministic output of LLMs, obscure (system) prompts, and a lack of fit between general purpose LLMs and their context can impede an IT artifact's internal consistency.

Challenge 4: Rapid Erosion of Prescriptive Knowledge. Our review identified that multiple papers refrained from reporting significant efforts to identify prescriptive knowledge that is generalizable. While we admit that this shortcoming might also reflect the papers' still immature status—many papers were still research-in-progress and/or might be developed further before being submitted to journals—this might still indicate a more profound problem. While identifying knowledge that generalizes beyond a specific problem instance is a core tenet of DSR, doing so appears particularly challenging for IT artifacts that are built on LLMs. Beyond the often obscure composition and fragile nature of the IT artifact itself, most artifacts based on LLM technology use third-party models that are subject to profound changes over time. For instance, a chatbot designed based on the OpenAI GPT4.0 model could change substantially as soon as other models such as GPT5.0 are introduced. The resulting changes might not only have drastic effects on the artifact itself, but also on the context in which the artifact is (to be) used. While new models keep being announced and differ substantially among LLMs, it is possible that design knowledge presented in a research paper is outdated even at the time a paper is published, which we refer to as rapid erosion of prescriptive knowledge. To avoid this effect, authors must take action to ensure that their results remain (as) stable (as possible), acknowledging that the underlying LLM is evolving.

Challenge 5: Missing Methodological Guidance. When comparing the papers' research methods, we identified that some papers refer to properties of the general DSR paradigm [25] and some refer to specific methods available for DSR [47,55], whereas many papers do not reference any specific methodology. Clearly, not employing specific DSR methods and not justifying once choice of a research method are profound deficiencies in a research process. Still, however, we did not find a DSR method that is specifically suited for designing LLM-enabled artifacts. Thus, we frame the fifth challenge as a lack of specific DSR guidelines to inform the design and evaluation of LLM-enabled artifacts. We trace this issue mainly back to the fact that current DSR methods primarily address the design of form and function of an IT artifact to fit a specific context. Meanwhile, however, first observations and anecdotal evidence on LLM-enabled artifact design suggest that often the ensemble of form and function is only designed to a limited amount, while the quest for utility depends on how far the context—including actors, resources, structures, and processes—can (be) adapted to fit the artifact.

Based on the five challenges, we propose a set of guidelines that can inform the design of LLM-enabled artifacts.

Guideline 1: Clarify the Composition of the IT Artifact vs. Its Underlying Technology: First, we call for distinguishing *customization* and *contextualization* from other *design* tasks. We urge design scientists to clearly identify the IT artifact designed in relation to their re-use or customization of the underlying LLM. Authors who aspire to design an artifact consisting at least partially of an LLM should clarify whether they want (1) to explore if/how well a given LLM can solve a particular problem (focusing on evaluation rather than design), (2) to improve an LLM by contextualization or by integrating it with other tools to solve a particular problem in a given context, or (3) to employ a given LLM to solve a problem in a context where, thus far, LLMs have not been (successfully) applied. In the light of this classification, readers could more easily identify the boundary between the artifact and a general-purpose LLM alongside any changes made to the artifact. Still, we consider that additional scenarios might evolve, such as designing a completely new LLM, which seems to be beyond single researchers' abilities at this time. We posit that differentiating between (see 2) improvement, and (see 3) exaptation types of DSR, dating back to DSR guidelines [23], remains relevant for the evaluation of DSR papers in a GenAI world. For DSR of the improvement type, we recommend evaluating the contextualized LLM against its general purpose version, to identify if the design process yielded an artifact that outperforms the third-party LLM. In the exaptation case, we strongly recommend to evaluate the resulting artifact in its natural context, to demonstrate that the artifact can cause the desired implications.

This first guideline also revolves around the differences among prompt engineering, context engineering, and self-developed LLMs. While we acknowledge that prompt engineering was once the only way to adapt given LLMs, context engineering now enables new possibilities and might be the preferred way to contextualize a given LLM. We anticipate that very soon new developments might require further, different, or even less activities to contextualize an LLM. From our point of view, this observation even bolsters the need for authors to clearly describe what exactly they designed and where they built on existing, pre-trained, or even pre-contextualized artifacts.

Guideline 2: Contextualize the LLM to Fit a Specific Problem: When DSR researchers present their results, it is important to clarify how an LLM was contextualized. We propose that authors disclose the instructions and the type of data used to customize an LLM. Authors may also state that they solely relied on a given, pre-trained and non-contextualized LLM, as long as this fits their research goal (cf. Guideline 1). A description of the contextualization should also be the starting point for the evaluation, i.e., whether the LLM could be compared against the native LLM. In such cases, we expect the designed artifact to surpass the results of a native LLM, else there would have been no need to design a new artifact.

Guideline 3: Specify Boundary Conditions of an IT Artifact's Contextual Design: The problem from a designer's perspective with general-purpose technologies such as LLMs is that they can be applied to a multitude of contexts without need for adaptation. We therefore call on designers of artifacts that are LLM-enabled to identify the boundary conditions set by the artifact's context, i.e., specify what contextual properties guide their design Framed differently, authors could describe in which contexts their designed artifact would not adequately solve the identified problem. These boundary conditions might include contextual knowledge, such that a native LLM might lack key insights of a domain, cultural background, or organizational processes. Clarifying these boundary conditions also allows readers to improve their understand of the relationship between the (designed) artifact and the context of the study. While this guideline is valid for all DSR publications, it is even more important for LLM-enabled artifacts.

With these three guidelines, we also expect a change in the future role of analysis and synthesis in DSR, i.e., two new possible steps. First, we see a need for an analysis of the form of the artifact, i.e., the native LLM. This new step should comprise analyzing existing LLM capabilities, scanning existing LLMs, and presenting or reasoning why an LLM is expected to be helpful in the problem space, i.e., the context. This step, titled α in Fig. 2, should follow the original first step of the DSR process. Second, as described above, the used LLM has to be contextualized to the domain by using different techniques and methods, e.g., RAG, GraphRAG, and others, bundled under the context engineering term

[43]. We frame this contextualization as a synthesis of the context (into the artifact), and visualize it in 2 using β. This β step can also be skipped, for example, if the analysis of the form (the α step) has already shown that the output of the artifact to be designed can be of general notion, i.e., does not require deep contextual knowledge. The β step should either happen after the α step or as part of the second step, i.e., the design and development. Looking forward, these two new steps provide a starting point to improve existing DSR guidelines for designing and evaluating LLM-enabled artifacts, aligning with our fifth proclaimed challenge.

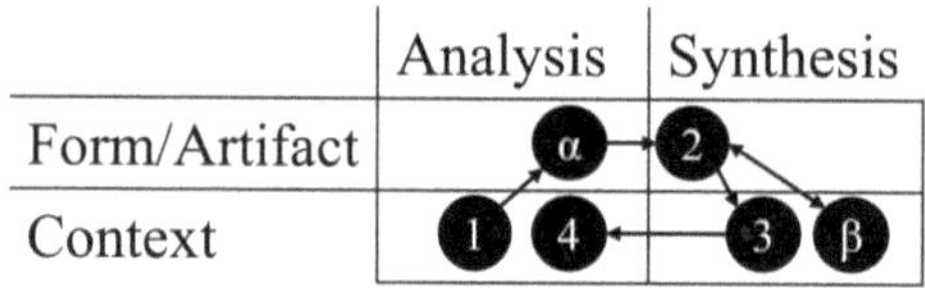

Fig. 2. Proposed update to the phases of the DSR methodology.

6   Conclusion

With our integrative literature review and the derived challenges and guidelines for designing LLM-enabled artifacts, we contribute the following to the body of knowledge on DSR: First, we scanned the literature for papers that apply the DSR paradigm to design LLM-enabled artifacts and reviewed the paper to find five challenges, including (1) blurred boundaries between design and non-design, (2) an opaque contextualization of the LLM, (3) fragile internal consistency of artifacts, (4) a lack of generalized design knowledge, and (5) a lack of DSR guidance. We abstracted the knowledge to derive three guidelines for designing LLM-enabled IT artifacts, covering (1) the distinction between design and non-design, (2) contextualization of given LLMs, and (3) the statement of boundary conditions for when the designed artifact no longer solves the problem in the context.

By abstracting the knowledge to a general DSR process, we provide a 2×2 matrix for analysis and synthesis of form and context. This typology serves as an initial step for a theory building process [14]. Through the outlined current practices of designing LLM-enabled artifacts, we see a need to understand how the interplay of artifact and context has changed due to fewer degrees of freedom in the design of LLM-enabled artifacts.

Clearly, our study is not without limitations. First, we only analyzed conference publications in our literature review. While integrative literature reviews are generally more open to the selection criteria of papers [17], we opted to build our analysis of conference papers published in 2025. Thus, in future studies, we aim to revisit journal publications designing LLM-enabled artifacts. Second, our paper is a starting point for the discussion on how DSR guidelines and methodologies have to be adapted to adequately allow for the design of LLM-based artifacts. We hope to spark a discussion and continue to show the value of DSR for providing high quality IS research. Third, we provided an initial version of guidelines that might be valuable to inform future DSR. Time will tell if these guidelines will make design-oriented research processes more transparent, reproducible, and improve the design and value of LLM-enabled artifacts. Future research could incorporate these guidelines into a specialized methodology for DSR. Additionally, we see further potential to in-depth analyze the usage of design principles in the identified papers, e.g., targeting overlaps between papers, different types of LLM-enabled artifacts, and literature relation.

Disclosure of Interests. The authors have no competing interests to declare.

References

1. Abbasi, A., Parsons, J., Pant, G., Sheng, O.R.L., Sarker, S.: Pathways for design research on artificial intelligence. Inf. Syst. Res. **35**(2), 441–459 (2024). https://doi.org/10.1287/isre.2024.editorial.v35.n2, http://dx.doi.org/10.1287/isre.2024.editorial.v35.n2
2. Aboulafia, M.: Philosophy, social theory, and the thought of George Herbert mead. SUNY series in the Philosophy of the Social Sciences, Albany, NY (1991)
3. Alexander, C.: Notes on the Synthesis of Form. Harvard Univ. Press, Cambridge, Mass (1964)
4. Ampel, B., Yang, C.H., Hu, J., Chen, H.: Large language models for conducting advanced text analytics information systems research. ACM Trans. Manag. Inf. Syst. **16**(1), 1–27 (2025). https://doi.org/10.1145/3682069, http://dx.doi.org/10.1145/3682069
5. Banh, L., Strobel, G.: Generative artificial intelligence. Electr. Markets **33**(1) (2023). https://doi.org/10.1007/s12525-023-00680-1
6. Baskerville, R., Baiyere, A., Gergor, S., Hevner, A., Rossi, M.: Design science research contributions: finding a balance between artifact and theory. J. Assoc. Inf. Syst. **19**(5), 358–376 (2018). https://doi.org/10.17705/1jais.00495
7. Benbya, H., Strich, F., Tamm, T.: Navigating generative artificial intelligence promises and perils for knowledge and creative work. J. Assoc. Inf. Syst. **25**(1), 23–36 (2024). https://doi.org/10.17705/1jais.00861
8. Berente, N., Gu, B., Recker, J., Santhanam, R.: Managing artificial intelligence. MIS Q. **45**(3), 1433–1450 (2021). https://doi.org/10.25300/misq/2021/16274
9. Bresnahan, T.F., Trajtenberg, M.: General purpose technologies 'engines of growth'? J. Econometrics **65**(1), 83–108 (1995). https://doi.org/10.1016/0304-4076(94)01598-t
10. Brynjolfsson, E., Rock, D., Syverson, C.: The productivity j-curve: how intangibles complement general purpose technologies. Am. Econ. J. Macroecon. **13**(1), 333–372 (2021). https://doi.org/10.1257/mac.20180386
11. Challapally, A., Pease, C., Raskar, R., Chari, P.: The GenAI Divide-State of AI in Business 2025. Project NANDA (2025). https://mlq.ai/media/quarterly_decks/v0.1_State_of_AI_in_Business_2025_Report.pdf

12. Chatterjee, S., Byun, J., Dutta, K., Pedersen, R.U., Pottathil, A., Xie, H.Q.: Designing an internet-of-things (iot) and sensor-based in-home monitoring system for assisting diabetes patients: iterative learning from two case studies. Eur. J. Inf. Syst. **27**(6), 670–685 (2018). https://doi.org/10.1080/0960085X.2018.1485619

13. Cheng, B.H.C., Atlee, J.M.: Research directions in requirements engineering. In: 2007 Future of Software Engineering, FOSE 2007, pp. 285–303 (2007)

14. Doty, D.H., Glick, W.H.: Typologies as a unique form of theory building: toward improved understanding and modeling. Acad. Manag. Rev. **19**(2), 230 (1994). https://doi.org/10.2307/258704

15. Drori, I., Teeni, D.: Human-in-the-loop ai reviewing: Feasibility, opportunities, and risks. J. Associat. Inform. Syst. **25**(1), 98–109 (2024). https://doi.org/10.17705/1jais.00867

16. Elsbach, K.D., van Knippenberg, D.: The academy of management annals: Looking back, looking forward. Acad. Manag. Ann. **12**(1), 1–4 (2018). https://doi.org/10.5465/annals.2016.0167, http://dx.doi.org/10.5465/annals.2016.0167

17. Elsbach, K.D., van Knippenberg, D.: Creating high-impact literature reviews: an argument for 'integrative reviews'. J. Manage. Stud. **57**(6), 1277–1289 (2020). https://doi.org/10.1111/joms.12581

18. Feuerriegel, S., Hartmann, J., Janiesch, C., Zschech, P.: Generative ai. Bus. Inform. Syst. Eng. **66**(1), 111–126 (2023). https://doi.org/10.1007/s12599-023-00834-7

19. Gau, M., Kretzer, F., Maedche, A., vom Brocke, J.: AI-based design science research: an exploratory framework for leveraging artificial intelligence in design science research, p. 18–31. Springer Nature Switzerland (2025). https://doi.org/10.1007/978-3-031-93976-1_2

20. Gregor, S.: The nature of theory in information systems. MIS Q. **30**(3), 611–642 (2006)

21. Gregor, S.: Responsible artificial intelligence and journal publishing. J. Associat. Inform. Syst. **25**(1), 48–60 (2024). https://doi.org/10.17705/1jais.00863

22. Gregor, S., Chandra Kruse, L., Seidel, S.: The anatomy of a design principle. J. AIS **21**(6) (2020). https://doi.org/10.17705/1jais.00649

23. Gregor, S., Hevner, A.R.: Positioning and presenting design science research for maximum impact. MIS Q. **32**(2), 337–355 (2013)

24. Han, H., et al.: Retrieval-augmented generation with graphs (graphrag) (2025). https://doi.org/10.48550/ARXIV.2501.00309

25. Hevner, A.R., March, S.: The information systems research cycle. Computer **36**(11), 111–113 (2003). https://doi.org/10.1109/MC.2003.1244541

26. Hevner, A.R.: A three cycle view of design science research. Scand. J. Inf. Syst. **19**(2) (2007)

27. Hevner, A.R., March, S.T., Park, J., Ram, S.: Design science in information systems research. MIS Q. **28**(1), 75–105 (2004)

28. Huang, M.H., Rust, R.T.: Engaged to a robot? the role of ai in service. J. Serv. Res. **24**(1), 30–41 (2020). https://doi.org/10.1177/1094670520902266

29. Iivari, J.: Distinguishing and contrasting two strategies for design science research. Eur. J. Inf. Syst. **24**(1), 107–115 (2015)

30. Ji, Z., et al.: Survey of hallucination in natural language generation. ACM Comput. Surv. **55**(12), 1–38 (2023). https://doi.org/10.1145/3571730

31. Kaltenpoth, S., Skolik, A., Müller, O., Beverungen, D.: A Step Towards Cognitive Automation: Integrating LLM Agents with Process Rules, p. 308–324. Springer Nature Switzerland (Aug 2025). https://doi.org/10.1007/978-3-032-02867-9_19

32. Kelly, S., Kaye, S.A., Oviedo-Trespalacios, O.: What factors contribute to the acceptance of artificial intelligence? a systematic review. Telematics Inform. **77**, 101925 (2023). https://doi.org/10.1016/j.tele.2022.101925

33. Klesel, M., Wittmann, H.F.: Retrieval-augmented generation (rag). Bus. Inform. Syst. Eng. **67**(4), 551–561 (2025). https://doi.org/10.1007/s12599-025-00945-3

34. Klier, J., Klier, M., Thiel, L., Agarwal, R.: Power of mobile peer groups: a design-oriented approach to address youth unemployment. J. Manag. Inf. Syst. **36**(1), 158–193 (2019). https://doi.org/10.1080/07421222.2018.1550557

35. Kuechler, B., Vaishnavi, V.: On theory development in design science research: anatomy of a research project. Eur. J. Inf. Syst. **17**(5), 489–504 (2008)

36. Kuechler, W., Vaishnavi, V.: A framework for theory development in design science research: multiple perspectives. J. AIS **13**(6), 395–423 (2012)

37. Landwehr, J.P., Kühl, N., Walk, J., Gnädig, M.: Design knowledge for deep-learning-enabled image-based decision support systems. Bus. Inform. Syst. Eng. (2022). https://doi.org/10.1007/s12599-022-00745-z

38. Lewis, P., et al.: Retrieval-augmented generation for knowledge-intensive nlp tasks (2020). https://doi.org/10.48550/ARXIV.2005.11401

39. Luhmann, N.: Social Systems (J. Bednarz & D. Baecker, Trans.). Stanford University, Stanford, California (1995)

40. Maedche, A., Gregor, S., Morana, S., Feine, J.: Conceptualization of the problem space in design science research. In: DESRIST 2019 (2019)

41. Manser Payne, E.H., Dahl, A.J., Peltier, J.: Digital servitization value co-creation framework for ai services: a research agenda for digital transformation in financial service ecosystems. J. Res. Interact. Mark. **15**(2), 200–222 (2021). https://doi.org/10.1108/jrim-12-2020-0252

42. March, S.T., Smith, G.F.: Design and natural science research on information technology. Decis. Support Syst. **15**(4), 251–266 (1995)

43. Mei, L., et al.: A survey of context engineering for large language models (2025). https://doi.org/10.48550/ARXIV.2507.13334

44. Mullarkey, M.T., Hevner, A.R.: An elaborated action design research process model. Eur. J. Inf. Syst. **28**(1), 6–20 (2018). https://doi.org/10.1080/0960085x.2018.1451811

45. Ngwenyama, O., Rowe, F.: Should we collaborate with ai to conduct literature reviews? changing epistemic values in a flattening world. J. Associat. Inform. Syst. **25**(1), 122–136 (2024). http://dx.doi.org/10.17705/1jais.00869

46. Orlikowski, W.J., Iacono, S.: Research commentary: desperately seeking the "it" in it research - a call to theorizing the it artifact. Inf. Syst. Res. **12**, 121–134 (2001)

47. Peffers, K., Tuunanen, T., Rothenberger, M.A., Chatterjee, S.: A design science research methodology for information systems research. J. Manag. Inf. Syst. **24**(3), 45–77 (2007)

48. Schryen, G., Wagner, G., Benlian, A., Paré, G.: A knowledge development perspective on literature reviews: validation of a new typology in the is field. Commun. Associat. Inform. Syst. **49**(1), 134–186 (2021). https://doi.org/10.17705/1cais.04607

49. Schulhoff, S., et al.: The prompt report: A systematic survey of prompt engineering techniques (2024). https://doi.org/10.48550/ARXIV.2406.06608

50. Sein, M.K., Henfridsson, O., Purao, S., Rossi, M., Lindgren, R.: Action Design Research. MIS Q. **35**, 37–56 (2011)

51. Simon, H.A.: The sciences of the artificial, 3rd edn. The MIT Press, MIT Press, London, England (1996)

52. Storey, V.C., Yue, W.T., Zhao, J.L., Lukyanenko, R.: Generative artificial intelligence: evolving technology, growing societal impact, and opportunities for information systems research. Inf. Syst. Front. **27**(5), 2081–2102 (2025). https://doi.org/10.1007/s10796-025-10581-7
53. Torraco, R.J.: Writing integrative literature reviews: guidelines and examples. Hum. Resour. Dev. Rev. **4**(3), 356–367 (2005). https://doi.org/10.1177/1534484305278283
54. Torraco, R.J.: Writing integrative literature reviews: Using the past and present to explore the future. Hum. Resour. Dev. Rev. **15**(4), 404–428 (2016). https://doi.org/10.1177/1534484316671606
55. Tuunanen, T., Winter, R., Brocke, J.V.: Dealing with complexity in design science research: a methodology using design echelons. MIS Q. **48**(2), 427–458 (2024). https://doi.org/10.25300/misq/2023/16700
56. Weber, F., Neshaei, S.P., Wambsganss, T., Soellner, M.: Intelligent tutoring for law courses: Design and evaluation of an llm-based system. In: ICIS 2025 Proceedings (2025)
57. Webster, J., Watson, R.: Analyzing the past to prepare for the future: writing a literature review. MIS Q. **26** (2002)
58. Wei, D., Chau, M., Li, Z.L.: Mitigating bias in hate speech detection with a small number of expert annotations: a prompt-based learning approach. MIS Q. **49**(4), 1483–1512 (2025). https://doi.org/10.25300/misq/2025/18416
59. Zhang, P., Scialdone, M., Ku, M.C.: IT artifacts and the state of IS research. In: Proceedings of the International Conference on Information Systems (2011)

Future of Ecosystems for Design Science Research

Testbed Research – Practitioners and Researchers as Architects of Digital Ecosystems

Simon Hiller[✉] [iD], Patrick Weber [iD], Maximilian Werling [iD], and Heiner Lasi

Ferdinand-Steinbeis-Institut, Bildungscampus 9, Heilbronn, Germany
{simon.hiller,patrick.weber,maximilian.werling,
heiner.lasi}@ferdinand-steinbeis-institut.de

Abstract. This paper addresses the critical challenges faced by organizations in designing and managing digital ecosystems within the ongoing digital transformation. Previous research has made notable progress in tackling technical and infrastructural concerns yet practical implementation, value creation, the integration of diverse partners remain underexplored and difficult to operationalize. Existing design-oriented research methods, such as Action Design Research (ADR), provide a strong foundation but lack a stepwise, process-oriented approach that fully recognizes the active roles of researchers as facilitators, knowledge providers, and trust anchors in the context of digital ecosystems. Moreover, current methods do not sufficiently accommodate the heterogeneity of ecosystem partners and the emergence of scientific artifacts during ecosystem formation. To bridge these gaps, we propose the Testbed Research approach, an adaptation of ADR specifically tailored for the complex realities of digital ecosystem development. Drawing on empirical evidence from 30 ecosystem initiatives conducted between 2016 and 2026, we demonstrate the methodological innovations and practical benefits of Testbed Research. Our findings contribute to both theory and practice by offering a robust framework that supports sustainable value creation and the effective orchestration of digital ecosystems, ultimately bridging the divide between academic insight and organizational practice.

Keywords: Action Design Research · Design Science Research · Design-oriented IS

1 Introduction

The design and management of digital ecosystems represent one of the core challenges in the era of digital transformation [8, 29, 31]. While scientific discourse has recently made significant progress, especially regarding technical and infrastructural issues, the practical implementation of and active participation in digital ecosystems remains a complex endeavor for companies [3, 7]. In particular, the impacts on value creation and the integration of diverse partners are still insufficiently researched and are often difficult to operationalize in real-world settings [3]. Organizations face numerous challenges

J. vom Brocke et al. (Eds.): DESRIST 2026, LNCS 16606, pp. 403–416, 2026.
https://doi.org/10.1007/978-3-032-28313-9_23

when attempting to initiate and shape their own ecosystems. Establishing such networks not only demands technological infrastructure but also requires the active involvement of a wide range of stakeholders, along with the fostering of trust and shared objectives [8, 30].

Design-oriented research methods, such as Action Design Research (ADR) indeed offer a robust methodological foundation (e.g. [10]) though there is a need when it comes to the dynamic formation and management of digital ecosystems [26]. In our understanding these approaches lack a stepwise, process-oriented view of ecosystem development and do not sufficiently consider the active role of researchers as facilitators, knowledge providers, and trust anchors as well as the contribution in the form of artifacts from different research fields. Furthermore, the heterogeneity of the partners involved and the emergence of scientific artifacts in the context of ecosystem formation have so far only been partly considered. Given these limitations, there is a need for an adapted research method that can meet the complexity and specific demands of ecosystems.

Thus, our approach positions itself as an elaboration of ADR specifically tailored towards the focus and process of the design of digital ecosystems. The impetus for Testbed Research arises primarily from the practical difficulties encountered by non-digital enterprises in establishing and sustaining such ecosystems. Drawing on the experience of actively conducting 30 ecosystem initiatives using Testbed Research between 2016 and 2026. The developed Testbed Research approach aims to generate scientific insights into future-oriented value creation within ecosystems and empowers the involved partners to actively shape such structures. By integrating research and practical application within a controlled test environment, Testbed Research opens new perspectives for bridging the gap between theory and practice and supports the sustainable strengthening of innovation within business ecosystems.

This paper is structured as follows: we first situate our work within the broader context of digital ecosystems, design science research and the gap that necessitates the development of Testbed Research. Next, we provide a structural description of the Testbed Research methodology, detailing its generic schema and stages. This is followed by one real-world application. We conclude with a discussion of the broader implications for research and practice, and an outlook on future directions for digital ecosystems.

2 Research Background

2.1 Digital Ecosystems

In this paper, the notion of digital ecosystems is employed to describe a specific mode of coordinated value creation among autonomous yet interdependent actors. Rather than advancing a novel ecosystem typology, the concept functions as an analytical shorthand for purpose-driven forms of inter-organizational collaboration that cannot be adequately captured through market, hierarchy, or dyadic partnership models alone [5, 14, 17]. The emphasis lies on how collective value creation is organized, stabilized, and sustained across organizational boundaries under conditions of mutual dependence. [2].

Digital ecosystems are understood as bounded constellations of heterogeneous actors that coalesce around a shared, predominantly business-oriented purpose [1]. This purpose provides the primary orientation for coordination and serves as the organizing reference point for participation, role allocation, and interaction. Ecosystem formation is thus not triggered by the mere availability of digital technologies or data assets, but by the recognition of a joint value-creation opportunity that exceeds the capabilities of any single actor [15]. Purpose, rather than technology, constitutes the starting point of collective alignment.

Participation within such ecosystems is deliberately selective. Actor constellations remain limited in size and composition, forming gated interaction spaces in which participants engage as practice partners rather than as anonymous contributors. This boundedness enables intensive coordination, repeated interaction, and mutual adjustment, which are necessary for integrating distributed activities and managing interdependencies over time. Digital ecosystems in this sense differ from digital platform ecosystems [11] or large-scale data ecosystems [20], where participation is loosely coupled and coordination is primarily rule-based.

Value creation within ecosystems arises from the recombination of complementary capabilities distributed across participating organizations [14]. These capabilities encompass not only data and information resources, but also domain-specific expertise, operational skills, and organizational capacities. Data exchange plays an enabling role by supporting coordination and integration across tasks, yet it does not constitute the focal object of value creation. What matters analytically is the alignment and interweaving of activities across organizational boundaries.

Finally, ecosystem coordination is socio-technically embedded [16, 28]. Digital technologies support and stabilize collaboration by structuring interactions, enabling information flow, and facilitating task integration. At the same time, these technologies remain embedded in broader organizational arrangements, governance structures, and institutional contexts [27]. The ecosystem is therefore not reducible to its technical infrastructure, but emerges from the interplay of purpose, bounded participation, complementary capabilities, and supportive technological systems.

2.2 Design Science Research Genres

The ongoing debate between rigor and relevance has shaped a broad spectrum of research genres, with significant progress already achieved well beyond the field of information systems [22]. Peffers et al. (2018) give a well-structured overview of different kinds of design science research genres by their characteristics and attributes [24]. Next to the genres mentioned *IS design theory* [9], *Design science research methodology* [23], *Design-oriented IS research* [22, 33], *Explanatory design theory* [4, 19] and *Action design research* [25]. *Consortium Research* [21] is another noticeable mention in the context of cooperation of researchers and practitioners. Looking at the characteristics of the different genres as well as the desired artifacts, ADR is the best fit due to its focus of designing a problem-solving artifact for the practitioners, a research artifact addressing a class of problems, the active participation by the researchers and its iterative sequential stages with researchers and practitioners that can work in parallel.

That argument gets supported by various recent publications by, among others, Guggenberger et al. (2025), Hiller et al. (2023) or Inoue et al. (2023) where ADR is used in the context of ecosystem research [10, 12, 13]. However, when taking a closer look at these publications it becomes clear that ADR is adapted or extended to fit the scope of doing research within digital ecosystems.

2.3 Need for a Research Subgenre When Designing Ecosystems

ADR is developed for clearly defined organizational problems in which a focal company works together with a homogeneous user environment and jointly develops artifacts iteratively with researchers [25]. Extensions and adjustments to ADR have been proposed among others by Mullarkey and Hevner (2018) [18]. However, digital ecosystems differ from this setting: they are complex, dynamic, multi-actor-driven, and have contradictory challenges [1]. These special characteristics exceed the original assumptions of ADR. Therefore, there is a need to expand ADR with a specific subgenre that meets the requirements of ecosystems.

The first key difference concerns the problem area. While ADR assumes that a single company has a clearly defined problem that is addressed by an artifact development process [25], challenges in ecosystems are characterized by heterogeneity and interdependencies. No single actor possesses the necessary resources or capabilities to solve the problem alone. Rather, there is a need for interaction between several partners. Problem definitions are rarely clear-cut and often even contradictory, as the organizations involved have different goals, perspectives, and incentive structures. A subgenre should therefore be able to deal with the existence of multiple actors, problems and diverging value logics [32].

The team composition also differs fundamentally. ADR envisages a bilateral or at least clearly structured relationship between researchers and a single organizational unit [25]. Ecosystems, on the other hand, inevitably operate in multi-actor constellations in which various stakeholder groups from several companies are involved in parallel. These groups must not only be informed, but also actively involved in the research and development process. A subgenre would therefore have to define mechanisms for jointly designing, moderating, and synchronizing heterogeneous stakeholder groups.

The decision-making structures also differ in the ecosystem context from the classic ADR setting. While ADR reflects decisions made by the partner company [25], ecosystems are based on cooperative value propositions and shared decision-making logic [1]. Decisions are often made through negotiation and participation and rely on trust. In addition, many data ecosystems require a neutral role or a so-called "trust anchor" that enables coordination, moderation, and governance [32]. ADR does not yet systematically take these intermediary roles into account.

Another difference can be seen in the artifacts and their contribution. ADR focuses primarily on software or ensemble artifacts that address a clearly defined problem [25]. In ecosystems, however, artifacts from different kinds and different disciplines emerge, such as governance models, technical interoperability mechanisms, cooperation agreements, or business model components. These artifacts do not have to function in isolation, but they must interact with each other to generate added value in practice. This not only increases complexity but also requires a much broader definition of what an "artifact" can be in the research process. At the same time, the form of scientific contribution is changing, extending beyond technical solutions to include social, organizational, and institutional innovations.

Finally, the role of researchers is also changing significantly. While ADR assumes that researchers are active interveners in a clearly defined organizational field [25], researchers in ecosystems act as orchestrators, as moderators of complex negotiation processes, and as actors who help shape, observe, and simultaneously stabilize structures. This role requires a more differentiated view of researcher activity, which is more focused on coordination, mediation, and interorganizational governance [30].

3 Testbed Research

The term testbed is used for an environment that provides the possibility to experiment and test new innovations and technologies. Different industry organizations use the term for their enablement for e.g. technologies such as the Digital Twin Consortium [6]. We follow this train of thought and create a rigorous research approach by elaborating ADR. Testbed Research aims to obtain scientific insights into future-oriented value creation of digital ecosystems and to enable participating partners to shape such digital ecosystems. Building upon the generic schema and the stages of ADR [25] we developed Testbed Research (see overview Fig. 1). We present the findings along four analytical dimensions: 1) Participants of Testbed Research, 2) Stages of Testbed Research, 3) Responsibilities, and 4) the Research Perspective embedded within the Testbed setting. This categorization provides a clear framework for understanding how actors, activities, and viewpoints interact throughout the research process. The accompanying summary figure synthesizes these elements and illustrates their interrelations in a consolidated overview.

3.1 Participants of Testbed Research

Starting with the two categories of participants which are divided into three groups. The research team consists of researchers that provide a form of guardrail for the whole project. The research discipline can differ and can be interdisciplinary depending on which kind of abstract problem and research question is followed. The research team should consist of two to max. five people.

The practitioners include participants from approximately three – required to establish a functioning multi-actor ecosystem – up to a maximum of ten companies. This number ensures that the effort needed to manage collaboration and identify a cooperative value proposition remains manageable. These companies together constitute the intended ecosystem. They form two different groups, the business task group which consists of the decision makers of the companies they are part of the project from the beginning to the end. The second group, the implementation task group, forms at a later stage of the project, consisting of technical experts from the companies which are part of the ecosystem.

3.2 Stage of Testbed Research

The initial stage of Testbed Research is characterized by the identification of a cooperative business opportunity, primarily originating from the practitioner side. This opportunity must inherently require an ecosystem-based approach, as it cannot be addressed by a single organization acting in isolation.

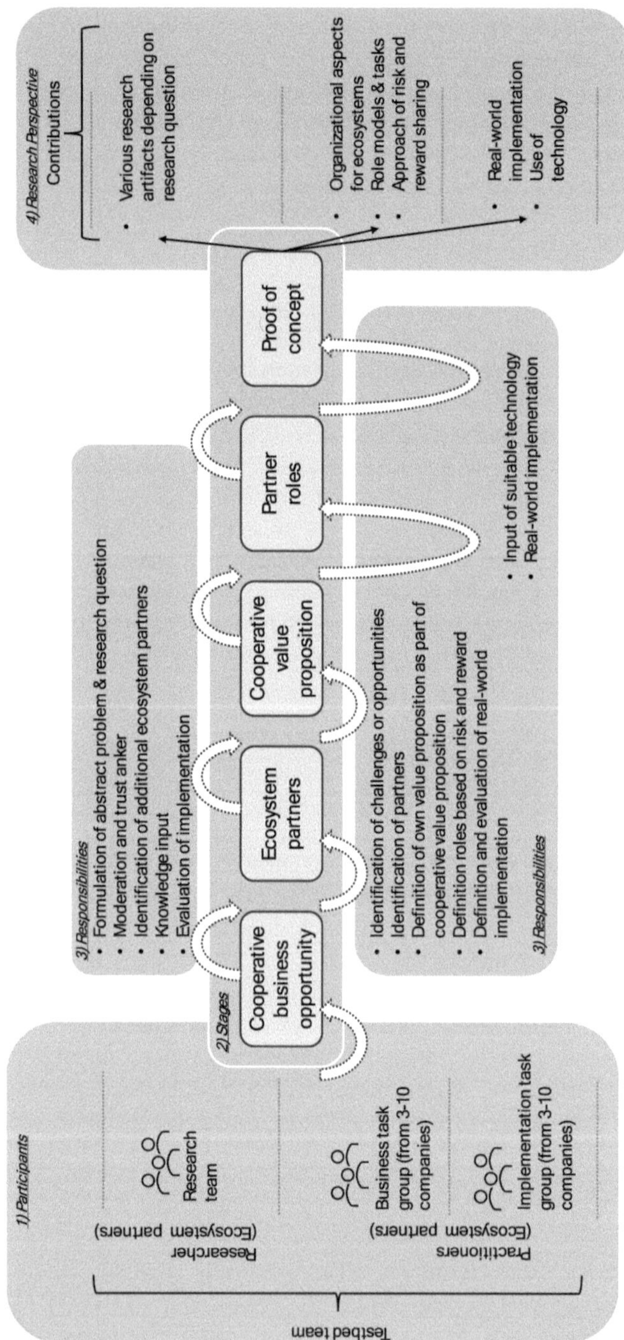

Fig. 1. Testbed Research Overview

Building on this, the second stage involves the selection and integration of ecosystem partners. The specific nature of the cooperative business opportunity informs the invitation of additional participants, ensuring that the ecosystem is composed of actors whose capabilities and interests align with the collaborative goal.

The third stage centers on the articulation of the cooperative value proposition. Here, the initial business opportunity is refined and consolidated into a value proposition that delivers benefits to all ecosystem partners. It is essential that each participant derives clear added value from this collective proposition, thereby reinforcing commitment and alignment within the ecosystem.

In the fourth stage, partner roles are defined in direct relation to the cooperative value proposition. These roles are determined by the distinct capabilities and resources that each organization contributes to the ecosystem. The delineation of roles is closely linked to the assessment and distribution of associated risks and rewards, ensuring that both are equitably managed among partners.

The fifth and final stage is the proof of concept, wherein the cooperative value proposition along with the defined roles are operationalized through the development of implementable software and hardware artifacts by the implementation task group, as well as through the establishment of organizational structures, tasks, processes, and mechanisms for risk and reward sharing.

Notably, the progression through these stages is iterative; for example, the ongoing refinement of partner roles may necessitate the integration of additional ecosystem participants as new requirements or opportunities emerge.

3.3 Responsibilities in Testbed Research

Within Testbed Research, the research team assumes several critical roles and responsibilities that shape and guide the entire project. First, the team is responsible for the formulation of the abstract problem and research question, ensuring that the research is grounded in a real-world challenge relevant to the ecosystem context. This task involves synthesizing interdisciplinary perspectives and providing a clear direction for the project, which serves as a guardrail for all subsequent activities.

A key function of the research team is moderation and acting as a trust anchor among participants. As orchestrators and moderators, researchers facilitate complex negotiation processes between ecosystem partners, fostering open communication and building trust across organizational boundaries. By mediating interactions and ensuring transparency, the team helps maintain a collaborative environment necessary for innovation and problem-solving.

The research team also lead the identification of additional ecosystem partners as the project evolves. Based on the cooperative business opportunity and emerging needs, the team assesses which organizations or stakeholders could provide valuable contributions, thus expanding the ecosystem and strengthening its capacity to deliver a cooperative value proposition.

Throughout the process, the research team provides knowledge input, drawing on disciplinary expertise and research methodologies to inform decision-making and support the development of both technical and organizational artifacts. Their interdisciplinary insights help bridge gaps between theory and practice, ensuring that solutions are both innovative and applicable.

Finally, the team is responsible for the evaluation of implementation. This involves assessing the effectiveness of the proof of concept and the realized artifacts – whether software, hardware, or organizational models – against the defined research objectives and the cooperative value proposition. The research team continuously accompanies the project, iteratively refining both the process and outcomes to maximize value for all ecosystem partners.

In summary, the research team's roles span from problem formulation and partner identification to moderation, knowledge contribution, and evaluation, all while providing structure and coordination throughout the iterative stages of Testbed Research. This multifaceted involvement ensures that both scientific rigor and practical relevance are maintained, supporting successful ecosystem formation and artifact development.

The primary responsibility of the business task group is centered on the identification and articulation of challenges or opportunities that can only be addressed through a cooperative, ecosystem-driven approach. By leveraging their deep understanding of market dynamics, organizational needs, and sector-specific pain points, these practitioners define the initial business opportunity that catalyzes the Testbed Research process. Their insights serve as a foundation for subsequent activities, ensuring that the project is grounded in practical relevance and aligned with the strategic interests of all stakeholders.

Partner selection is a critical function of the business task group, who identify and invite ecosystem participants based on existing business relationships, complementary capabilities, and the potential for mutual benefit. This process is inherently iterative, as the definition of the cooperative business opportunity may reveal the need for additional partners with specific expertise or resources. The business task group, in close coordination with the research team, evaluates potential partners not only for their technical or operational fit but also for their ability to contribute to the overall value proposition of the ecosystem.

A further responsibility involves defining the group's own value proposition within the broader cooperative value proposition. The business task group articulates the specific benefits, contributions, and expectations of their respective organizations, ensuring that the interests of each partner are clearly represented. This process requires careful negotiation and alignment, facilitated by the research team, to balance individual organizational goals with collective ecosystem value.

In determining roles and responsibilities, the business task group assesses and negotiates the allocation of risks and rewards among ecosystem partners. Drawing upon their understanding of organizational capabilities and strategic priorities, they define roles that reflect both the contributions and the associated risks for each participant. This task is closely linked to the iterative nature of Testbed Research, as evolving project requirements or emerging challenges may necessitate the reassignment or redefinition of roles over time.

Finally, the business task group plays an active role in defining and evaluating real-world implementations of the cooperative value proposition. They are responsible for setting criteria for success, establishing performance metrics, and participating in the assessment of proof-of-concept artifacts – whether these are technical solutions, organizational models, or new business processes. Throughout this process, the business task group collaborates with the research team and the implementation task group, whose complementary expertise in implementing and evaluation methodologies and interdisciplinary synthesis ensures that implementations are both innovative and practically viable.

The implementation task group is primarily responsible for translating research insights and business requirements into tangible, real-world solutions. Drawing on their technical expertise, these practitioners identify and contribute suitable technologies, methods, and tools that align with the cooperative value proposition and the evolving needs of the ecosystem. Their input ensures that the selection and integration of technologies are both feasible and scalable within the operational context of all partners involved.

In parallel, the implementation task group lead the realization of proof-of-concept artifacts, managing the deployment and adaptation of solutions in real-world settings. This includes overseeing pilot implementations, facilitating user engagement, and monitoring technical performance to ensure that developed artifacts address the identified challenges or opportunities. The group's hands-on involvement bridges the gap between conceptual design and operational execution, providing critical feedback to both the research and business task groups for iterative refinement.

3.4 Research Perspective in Testbed Research

The research team's primary contribution within Testbed Research is the production of rigorous research artifacts tailored to the specific research questions posed by the ecosystem initiative. These artifacts may include theoretical frameworks, methodological guidelines, and empirical analyses that inform both the design and evaluation of technical and organizational solutions. By integrating disciplinary expertise and research methodologies for data-collection and data-analysis, the research team ensures that the project maintains scientific rigor while remaining responsive to the evolving needs of the ecosystem. Their iterative involvement supports the translation of abstract concepts into actionable knowledge, which underpins the development of innovative and applicable artifacts across multiple domains.

The business task group's contributions center on the organizational dimensions essential for successful ecosystem formation and sustainability. This group develops role models and defines organizational tasks that clarify the responsibilities and expectations for all partners, ensuring that each participant's strategic interests are represented and aligned. In addition, the business task group is instrumental in establishing mechanisms for risk and reward sharing, negotiating value propositions, and facilitating agreements that balance individual organizational goals with collective ecosystem value. This approach not only fosters trust and transparency among stakeholders but also creates a solid foundation for long-term collaboration and the scalable adoption of cooperative business models.

The implementation task group's core contribution lies in the real-world realization of research and business insights through the deployment of technological solutions within operational environments. Drawing on technical expertise, this group identifies, adapts, and integrates appropriate technologies, methods, and tools that are both feasible and scalable for all ecosystem partners. Their hands-on role encompasses pilot implementations, user engagement, and ongoing performance monitoring, ensuring that developed artifacts effectively address the identified challenges or opportunities. By bridging the gap between conceptual design and tangible application, the implementation task group transforms theoretical and organizational advances into practical innovations that deliver measurable value to the ecosystem.

Testbed Research is fundamentally about fostering long-term collaboration among diverse partners, with a particular emphasis on integrating practical industry experience and academic expertise. By bringing together practitioners and researchers, this approach enables the co-development of innovative solutions that are both scientifically rigorous and operationally viable. The sustained partnership between practice and science ensures that ecosystem-driven initiatives not only address real-world challenges but also contribute to the advancement of theoretical knowledge.

4   Testbed Research in Use

Building on Testbed Research, we conducted more than 30 real-world ecosystem projects between 2016 and 2026. All projects consist of an ecosystem of partners accompanied by a research team. The project mode was workshops with the aim of a proof of concept in 12–18 months. The number of workshops is dependent on the number of ecosystem participants and the scope of the cooperative value proposition and is around 8 to 15 with additional in-between meetings. Some projects even further developed into spin-offs and own business units. One notable example is presented below and shows the concrete application of Testbed Research.

4.1   Participants

Recognizing a business opportunity, an original equipment manufacturer (OEM) explored the implementation of a pay-per-part (PpP) model within one of its assembly lines. Through a series of eight workshops – including two in-person sessions held at the researchers' conference facilities and six virtual meetings – a collaborative, ecosystem-driven PpP approach was systematically developed in partnership with all relevant stakeholders. Consisting of the OEM (represented by the chief engineering officer), a bank (represented by a managing director), an industrial service provider (represented by a managing director and CIO) as well as a mechanical engineering company (represented by the CEO).

4.2   Stages and Responsibilities

Ensuring that all ecosystem participants derived added value from the implementation of the PpP model was a key priority. For the original equipment manufacturer (OEM), the primary value lay in transitioning from capital expenditure to operational expenditure, enabling greater flexibility in response to volatile market conditions. The bank sought to leverage the PpP model to establish itself as a strategic partner for industrial enterprises and to expand its business portfolio with innovative financial solutions. The industrial service provider aimed to strengthen customer loyalty, grow its digital business segment, and assume the role of assembly line operator. Meanwhile, the mechanical engineering company pursued new business opportunities by gaining deeper insights into machinery performance in operational settings, thereby informing the development of next-generation equipment.

The project was conducted between January 2021 and May 2022. Next to the workshops supplementary shorter meetings were scheduled between the main workshops to focus on technical implementation tasks, carried out by an implementation task group. Within the automotive project, several essential roles were identified to effectively realize the anticipated added value:

- Bank: asset owner, risk manager, financier, and payment provider
- OEM: responsible for product and process specifications, risk management, asset operation, and connectivity provision
- Industrial Service Provider: risk manager, asset maintenance, and connectivity provision
- Mechanical Engineering Company: responsible for machinery and process specifications, risk management, and connectivity provision

The implementation task group was responsible for implementing the requirements specified by the decision makers and provided regular progress updates. Transparency regarding the assembly line machinery was achieved through its digital representation. Information needs were systematically gathered from each participant's perspective, and the relevant data and contextual requirements were defined accordingly. Initially, data on parts produced per hour was sourced from the OEM's Manufacturing Execution System and made accessible to all ecosystem participants via a cooperative data space. Subsequently, the approach evolved to collect data directly from the machinery, independent of the OEM's IT infrastructure.

The role of the research team within the project included the moderation, preparation and follow-up of every workshop. Due to the neutrality of the research team, they built trust amongst the participants. This trust became evident when the researchers introduced the bank as a new ecosystem partner as well as the knowledge input for the formulation of the cooperative value proposition as well as knowledge for the technical implementation of the proof of concept. Neutrality in the sense of moderation, the cooperation value proposition and the added value for each ecosystem partner were crucial in this project, as risks and rewards were highly controversial.

4.3 Research Perspective

The research team also formulated their abstract research problems and research questions they wanted to answer with this project. The goal was to get a blueprint of PpP ecosystems with a cooperative value proposition as well as the design-principle for PpP. The research team activities can be described as giving the project guardrails by actively providing input.

The following Table 1 gives an overview of the contributions regarding the different groups of the Testbed team within the PpP project.

Table 1. Contributions within the Pay-per-Part Project

Group	Contributions
Researcher	• PpP design principles [12] • Blueprint for creating PpP ecosystems
Business Task Group	• Cooperative PpP value proposition • Role model for PpP • Understanding of risks and reward in PpP ecosystem • Information requirements for leaders for a PpP project
Implementation Task Group	• Information requirements for PpP implementation • PpP cooperative data space • Cross-company implementation

5 Conclusion and Outlook

Testbed Research is positioned as a complementary approach within Design Science Research, specifically as an addition and refinement to the established ADR. It does not seek to supplant ADR or other DSR genres but rather to offer an environment that supports iterative experimentation, real-world validation, and the extension of theoretical frameworks. Importantly, Testbed Research is not itself a methodology; instead, it serves as a structured context for the application of various research methods, enabling nuanced insights into the interplay between innovation, implementation, and value creation within digital ecosystems.

Testbed Research extends the established ADR approach by refining its focus and process while maintaining the original roles of theory development and evaluation as outlined by Sein et al. (2011) and Peffers et al. (2018) [24, 25]. Specifically, Testbed Research focuses on digital ecosystems, emphasizing the dynamic interaction between practitioners and researchers. For practitioners, the primary outcome is the creation of artifacts that capture the business, organizational, and technical dimensions of digital ecosystems. Researchers, in turn, contribute insights shaped by their disciplinary perspectives and the interdisciplinary nature of the research team.

The Testbed Research process is characterized by its iterative structure and the active engagement of both researchers and diverse groups of practitioners. This collaborative model facilitates a productive interplay that supports innovation and value creation within digital ecosystems.

Looking ahead, several avenues for future research emerge. One critical area involves examining the impact of different funding models, such as government grants, single-company sponsorship, or multi-company collaborations, on project outcomes and stakeholder dynamics. Additionally, expanding the application of Testbed Research across various research institutions and increasing the number of projects conducted would further strengthen its empirical foundation. Finally, systematically exploring the suitability, benefits, and limitations of different research methods within the Testbed Research is essential for guiding researchers in effectively leveraging this approach.

By positioning Testbed Research as a complementary addition to the broader DSR ecosystem, this paper highlights its potential to facilitate iterative experimentation, real-world validation, and the extension of theoretical frameworks, ultimately advancing both academic knowledge and practical implementation in digital ecosystems.

References

1. Adner, R.: Ecosystem as structure. J. Manag. **43**(1), 39–58 (2017). https://doi.org/10.1177/0149206316678451
2. Adner, R., Kapoor, R.: Value creation in innovation ecosystems: how the structure of technological interdependence affects firm performance in new technology generations. Strat. Mgmt. J. **31**(3), 306–333 (2010). https://doi.org/10.1002/smj.821
3. Azkan, C., Möller, F., Ebel, M., Iqbal, T., Otto, B., Poeppelbuss, J.: Hunting the treasure: modeling data ecosystem value co-creation. In: ICIS 2022 Proceedings (2022)
4. Baskerville, R., Pries-Heje, J.: Explanatory design theory. Bus. Inf. Syst. Eng. **2**(5), 271–282 (2010). https://doi.org/10.1007/s12599-010-0118-4
5. Baumann, S., Leerhoff, M.: Networks, platforms, and digital business ecosystems. mapping the development of a field. In: Baumann, S. (ed.) Handbook on Digital Business Ecosystems. Strategies, platforms, technologies, governance and societal challenges. Research handbooks in business and management series, pp. 11–24. Edward Elgar Publishing, Cheltenham, UK, Northampton, MA (2022)
6. DTC: Digital Twin Testbed Program. https://www.digitaltwinconsortium.org/initiatives/digital-twin-testbeds/. Accessed 23 Jan 2026
7. Eustache, L., Brousseau, E., Toledano, J.: The economics of data-sharing: an empirical investigation of data sharing ecosystems. In: ICIS 2025 Proceedings (2025)
8. Fassnacht, M., Benz, C., Heinz, D., Leimstoll, J., Satzger, G.: Barriers to data sharing among private sector organizations. In: Bui, T. (ed.) Proceedings of the 56th Hawaii International Conference on System Sciences (2023). https://doi.org/10.24251/HICSS.2023.453
9. Gregor, S., Jones, D.: The anatomy of a design theory. J. Assoc. Inf. Syst. **8**(5), 312–355 (2007)
10. Guggenberger, T.M., Schlueter Langdon, C., Otto, B.: Data spaces as meta-organisations. Eur. J. Inf. Syst. **34**(5), 822–842 (2025). https://doi.org/10.1080/0960085X.2025.2451250
11. Hein, A., et al.: Digital platform ecosystems. Electron. Markets **30**(1), 87–98 (2020). https://doi.org/10.1007/s12525-019-00377-4
12. Hiller, S., Weber, P., Lasi, H.: Design principles for creating a pay-per-part value proposition in data ecosystems. In: ICIS 2023 Proceedings (2023)
13. Inoue, Y., Takenaka, T., Kasasaku, T., Tamegai, T., Arai, R.: How to design platform ecosystems by intrapreneurs: implications from action design research on IoT-based platform. Electron. Markets **33**(1) (2023). https://doi.org/10.1007/s12525-023-00618-7
14. Jacobides, M.G., Cennamo, C., Gawer, A.: Towards a theory of ecosystems. Strat. Mgmt. J. **39**(8), 2255–2276 (2018). https://doi.org/10.1002/smj.2904
15. Lingens, B., Miehé, L., Gassmann, O.: The ecosystem blueprint: how firms shape the design of an ecosystem according to the surrounding conditions. Long Range Plan. **54**(2), 102043 (2021). https://doi.org/10.1016/j.lrp.2020.102043
16. Lusch, R.F., Nambisan, S.: Service innovation: a service-dominant logic perspective1. MIS Q. **39**(1), 155–175 (2015). https://doi.org/10.25300/MISQ/2015/39.1.07
17. Moore, J.F.: Predators and prey: a new ecology of competition. Harv. Bus. Rev. **71**(3), 75–86 (1993)

18. Mullarkey, M.T., Hevner, A.R.: An elaborated action design research process model. Eur. J. Inf. Syst. **28**(1), 6–20 (2019). https://doi.org/10.1080/0960085X.2018.1451811
19. Niehaves, B., Ortbach, K.: The inner and the outer model in explanatory design theory: the case of designing electronic feedback systems. Eur. J. Inf. Syst. **25**(4), 303–316 (2016). https://doi.org/10.1057/ejis.2016.3
20. Oliveira, M.I.S., Lóscio, B.F.: What is a data ecosystem? In: Janssen, M., Chun, S.A., Weerakkody, V., Zuiderwijk, A., Hinnant, C.C. (eds.) Proceedings of the 19th Annual International Conference on Digital Government Research: Governance in the Data Age.dg.o 2018: 19th Annual International Conference on Digital Government Research, Delft The Netherlands, 30 May 2018–01 June 2018, pp. 1–9. ACM, New York, NY, USA (2018). https://doi.org/10.1145/3209281.3209335
21. Österle, H., Otto, B.: Consortium research. Bus. Syst. Eng. **2**(5), 283–293 (2010). https://doi.org/10.1007/s12599-010-0119-3
22. Österle, H., et al.: Memorandum on design-oriented information systems research. Eur. J. Inf. Syst. **20**(1), 7 (2011). https://doi.org/10.1057/ejis.2010.55
23. Peffers, K., Tuunanen, T., Rothenberger, M.A., Chatterjee, S.: A design science research methodology for information systems research. J. Manag. Inf. Syst. **24**(3), 45–77 (2007)
24. Peffers, K., Tuunanen, T., Niehaves, B.: Design science research genres: introduction to the special issue on exemplars and criteria for applicable design science research. Eur. J. Inf. Syst. **27**(2), 129–139 (2018). https://doi.org/10.1080/0960085X.2018.1458066
25. Sein, M.K., Henfridsson, O., Purao, S., Rossi, M., Lindgren, R.: Action design research. MIS Q. **35**(1), 37 (2011). https://doi.org/10.2307/23043488
26. Senyo, P.K., Liu, K., Effah, J.: Digital business ecosystem: literature review and a framework for future research. Int. J. Inf. Manage. **47**, 52–64 (2019). https://doi.org/10.1016/j.ijinfomgt.2019.01.002
27. Star, S.L., Ruhleder, K.: Steps toward an ecology of infrastructure: design and access for large information spaces. Inf. Syst. Res. **7**(1), 111–134 (1996). https://doi.org/10.1287/isre.7.1.111
28. Vargo, S.L., Lusch, R.F.: Institutions and axioms: an extension and update of service-dominant logic. J. Acad. Mark. Sci. **44**(1), 5–23 (2016). https://doi.org/10.1007/s11747-015-0456-3
29. Weber, P., Hiller, S., Lasi, H.: Dual scientific research framework – generating real world impact and scientific progress in internet of things ecosystems. In: PACIS 2021 Proceedings (2021)
30. Weber, P., Hiller, S., Lasi, H.: Impact based research institute-rethinking established research structures in the context of data ecosystems. In: ECIS 2025 Proceedings (2025)
31. Weill, P., Woerner, S.L.: Thriving in an increasingly digital ecosystem. MIT Sloan Manag. Rev. **56**(4), 27–34 (2015)
32. Werling, M., Werth, D., Lasi, H.: Towards a framework for building trust and transparency in collaborative data-driven use cases – learnings from a mobility case study. In: Bui, T. (ed.) Proceedings of the 57th Hawaii International Conference on System Sciences (2025). https://doi.org/10.24251/HICSS.2025.031
33. Winter, R.: Design science research in Europe. Eur. J. Inf. Syst. **17**(5), 470–475 (2008). https://doi.org/10.1057/ejis.2008.44

Collective Action Planning: A Method to Plan and Implement Circular Ecosystems

Anna Margolis[✉] [iD] and Fenna Blomsma [iD]

University of Hamburg, Von-Melle-Park 9, 20146 Hamburg, Germany
circulanna@gmail.com

Visual Abstract.

COLLECTIVE ACTION PLANNING (CAP)
A method to translate complex thought into simple action

J. vom Brocke et al. (Eds.): DESRIST 2026, LNCS 16606, pp. 417–429, 2026.
https://doi.org/10.1007/978-3-032-28313-9_24

Abstract

Motivation: Addressing today's social, environmental, and technological challenges requires not only strong strategies but also approaches that coordinate stakeholder activities across ecosystems. While many tools help multi-stakeholder partnerships analyze the past and envision desirable futures, stakeholders often struggle to translate those visions into actionable steps because their goals and values in the present are misaligned. This misalignment leads to planning paralysis or fragmented efforts.

The Collective Action Planning (CAP) method: CAP is a facilitation method that integrates diverse stakeholder goals and perspectives to create complementary, actionable solutions. Grounded in systems thinking and pragmatism – particularly the concept of simplexity, which balances complex understanding with simple action – CAP connects requirements, constraints, and activities across ecosystems, emphasizing how pilot experiments interact with existing structures.

Research Design: Developed through an echeloned Design Science Research (eDSR) process involving sixteen validation cycles in seminars, trainings, and projects, CAP now comprises five steps.

Practitioner benefits: We illustrate CAP use through the case of building a circular ecosystem for reusable to-go cups. CAP enhances sensemaking and coordination in multi-stakeholder partnerships, helping actors move from shared vision to collective action – in short, it is a method for acting together.

Keywords: circular economy · complexity · collective innovation · cross-sector partnerships · ecosystems · desirable futures · multi-stakeholder collaboration · orchestration · stakeholder dialogue

1 Introduction

Addressing the social, environmental, and technological challenges of today's world requires not merely a good strategy and effective stakeholder management from individual businesses, but also multi-stakeholder collaboration to develop novel ecosystems [1, 2]. Several methods and approaches support ecosystem-wide collaboration across sectoral and value chain boundaries. Strategic analysis and systems dynamics can help us engage in stakeholder dialogue, interpret past events, and understand why a problem persists in the present [3, 4]. Strategic foresight, future-making, and design approaches point us to desirable solutions for the future [5, 6].

Yet, while different stakeholders can often agree on a vision for a distant future, they struggle with developing actionable bridges from today into this future [7, 8]. Stakeholder goals, perspectives, and values in the present are often misaligned, leading to equivocality [9]. While the distant vision is clear, the present implementation appears complex and multi-directional as multi-stakeholder groups struggle to define common near-future priorities. That misalignment hinders working together on concrete plans and activities. As a result, multi-stakeholder initiatives often experience analysis paralysis due to an overload of data or tensions in decision-making, as happened in the case of a cross-sectoral partnership for sustainable and circular packaging [10].

However, the alternative – not to collaborate – is also not a viable solution when working on novel ecosystems, as a lack of collaboration would result in ineffective, uncoordinated and competing efforts. For example, companies developing AI solutions face uncertainty because they are uncertain how to interpret the EU AI Act; a closer collaboration between policy-makers and businesses could improve the situation [11]. Similarly, regenerative solutions – such as local food production and distribution networks – can only function sustainably if the actors across an ecosystem coordinate their actions [12]. Collaboration across sectors and the value chain is critical to establish effective new ecosystems.

Thus, we need more effective approaches to support action planning in multi-stakeholder collaborations, especially when developing novel ecosystems. These approaches must understand the diversity of actors as an advantage rather than a weakness and harness the equivocality to develop more systemic yet aligned implementation plans. Developing such an approach was the goal of the five-year design research project presented in this paper. We ask:

How can multi-stakeholder partnerships develop effective action plans that integrate diverse perspectives?

Answering that question is vital to overcoming analysis paralysis and decision-making tensions and moving towards the collective goal of a multi-stakeholder partnership. We address the research question through echeloned Design Science Research, an approach that enables us to co-develop a solution grounded in theory alongside practitioners [13]. The resulting method – Collective Action Planning – has been iteratively developed by moving between reviewing theoretical literature and developing and validating the method with practitioners in seminars, trainings, and projects.

The Collective Action Planning (CAP) method is grounded in systems thinking and pragmatism. Theoretically, we rely on the notions of.

(1) **Enabling simplexity**: A decision-making approach which enables decision-making by interweaving complexity in thought with simplicity in action [14];
(2) **Integrating perspectives**: The notion that deliberating diverse perspectives in a constructive and supportive manner can lead to the emergence of more viable and resilient solutions for all participating actors [15];
(3) **Contextualizing innovation**: A framework that helps us to link a multiplicity of constraints to actionable solutions through identifying appropriate innovation modes [16].

Practically, that results in a five-step method that can support collaboration in multi-stakeholder and cross-sectoral partnerships, just as across departments within a company. The CAP method can be used for alignment workshops either as a one-time session or as part of an ongoing process for transformation projects.

2 Problem Statement: Bridging the Present and the Future in Collective Action Planning

Collective action planning in multi-stakeholder initiatives is challenging across social, environmental, and technological fields, as it requires alignment among diverse actors. Decision-makers face ongoing tensions between.

(1) global demands and local constraints,
(2) existing structures and the need for innovation,
(3) creating the new without discarding the old, and
(4) detailed analysis and the bigger picture [21].

These tensions cannot be resolved through analysis alone and instead require learning through action [14]. However, defining what to learn and how is difficult, and groups risk falling into analysis paralysis or overvaluing dominant voices [9, 10, 22]. Therefore, methods are needed to support more constructive and inclusive deliberation and to develop viable, desirable action plans for all stakeholders involved.

3 Theoretical Background: Enabling, Integrating, and Contextualizing Collective Action

To address the challenge of bridging the gap between the present and the future in collective decision-making, we draw on three related streams of literature. While the three streams are distinct from each other, they share a systems perspective grounded in pragmatism, which makes them compatible. The first literature stream focuses on enabling decisions in a complex world. The second addresses the necessity of integrating different perspectives to advance towards viable and desirable solutions. The third focuses on the importance of contextualizing decision-making in order to choose the right approach to action. Each literature stream informs a design principle for developing the CAP method.

3.1 Enabling Decision-Making: From Complex Thought to Simple Action

In stable environments, decisions can rely on past experience, data, and expert judgment because conditions remain predictable, allowing prior knowledge to guide outcomes [14]. However, in unstable and fast-changing contexts, past experience alone is insufficient as new dynamics emerge, requiring a balance of complex thinking and simple action—referred to as simplexity [14]. In such situations, groups must learn through iterative action and reflection, creating new knowledge from real outcomes rather than assumptions. This evolutionary learning process helps reduce uncertainty, align diverse perspectives, and strengthen collaboration in multi-stakeholder settings [21, 23]. Thus, our first design principle is:

Design principle 1: *To support sensemaking in multi-stakeholder collaborations, combine experience sharing with learning-by-doing.*

3.2 Integrating Perspectives: Emerging Innovation Through Collective Creativity

It is not enough to simply act; actions in multi-stakeholder settings should emerge from collective deliberation. Such actions reflect shared imagination, producing outcomes that individuals could not have anticipated alone, and go beyond compromise or partial satisfaction. Instead, integrated actions arise from creatively combining diverse perspectives, turning equivocality into a source of insight and innovation rather than tension or paralysis [15]. For example, in a flat glass recycling project, participants initially struggled to agree on key constraints and solutions, but through dialogue recognised that their individual approaches were complementary and could create value across the value chain. Thus, our second design principle is:

Design principle 2: When facilitating multi-stakeholder collaborations, foster deliberative dialogue and integrate emerging insights to create more desirable and complementary solutions for all involved.

3.3 Contextualizing Innovation: Choosing the Right Approach to Action

Building on the previous principles, different contexts require different approaches to innovation, and diverse groups can generate better outcomes if they deliberate constructively (Design Principles 1 and 2). The key question is how such groups choose the right approach—when to rely on past knowledge and when to learn through action.

Complexity theory helps address this by distinguishing four innovation modes [16, 22, 24]:

(1) clear—stable contexts with known solutions and best practices;
(2) complicated—stable but requiring expert analysis to choose among options;
(3) complex—uncertain contexts requiring learning by doing through experiments;
(4) chaos—crisis situations requiring immediate action without time for analysis.

The first two modes apply to ordered environments where outcomes are predictable, while the latter two apply to unstable contexts where action is necessary to generate understanding. Overreliance on past solutions in changing environments can lead to failure. Thus, we define the third design principle as:

Design principle 3: To plan collective activities within an emerging ecosystem, a multi-stakeholder partnership must understand the context across the value chain and match it to an appropriate innovation mode.

3.4 Synthesis

The three design principles above are all grounded in a pragmatist and systems perspective on collective decision-making under complexity. They illuminate different angles of the same problem: the difficulty of agreeing on a shared course of action to bridge from the present towards the future vision. Together, the three design principles represent an action recipe of how multi-stakeholder partnerships can address that problem.

4 Research Design

The CAP method was developed through an echeloned Design Science Research approach, which allows to develop methods and tools through an iterative, cyclical design approach and accounts for uncertainties and unexpected findings [13]. Our research was situated in the context of developing a toolkit to support circular ecosystem development, with CAP being one part of this toolkit. CAP was validated in 16 instantiations. Seven demonstrations confirmed its clarity and logic in seminars with students and practitioners, while nine evaluations showed its usefulness in supporting collective action planning within multi-stakeholder partnerships. Of these nine evaluations, six were trainings or workshops with experts and three were interventions in multi-stakeholder projects (see Fig. 1). After each instantiation, we evaluated the received feedback and used it to improve the usability and usefulness of the method. To do so, we alternated between reviewing literature and validating the method until the three design principles and their practical applications iteratively crystallized.

Fig. 1. Expert workshop at the Social Circular Economy Research Week, Center for Sustainable Entrepreneurship, Odisee University of Applied Sciences, Brussels, March 2025

5   Results: The Collective Action Planning (CAP) Method

The CAP method translates the three design principles into a five-step action recipe (see Table 1). It assumes that the group already agrees on a solution or shared vision, typically developed using other systems thinking or future-making tools, such as systems mapping or future imaginaries. In this sense, CAP functions as a 'plug-in' method within a broader process, with the specific value of turning a vision into concrete action.

CAP can be applied in two ways. The preferred approach is a facilitated stakeholder workshop, usually lasting four to eight hours and led by experienced facilitators, conducted either in person using a system map or online with digital boards. If convening stakeholders is not feasible, an alternative is to gather inputs through interviews and document analysis, and then develop visual maps based on these insights. While less interactive, this approach can still reveal gaps—such as a lack of action-based learning—and prompt discussion on next steps.

To illustrate the five steps, we will use the example of establishing an ecosystem for a reusable cup-to-go from a start-up perspective.

Table 1. Steps in Collective Action Planning

#	Step	Guiding questions	Objectives
1	Identify requirements	What needs to happen in different parts of the ecosystem?	Integrating perspectives on how to establish a new ecosystem.
2	Assess Constraints	Overarching: What is keeping us from addressing these requirements? What must we consider? Additional prompts: • Which barriers exist? • What are risks and unknowns? • Are there tensions between the ecosystem requirements?	Moving towards an integrated perspective on ecosystem problems and challenges.
3	Define actions and actors	Actions: What do we need to do to address these constraints? Actors: Who needs to be involved? Addressing barriers: What if we did… to address…? Addressing unknowns/risks: What if we tried… to learn if it works. Addressing tensions: What if we did things differently? We could…	1. Activating collective creativity 2. Aligning on the need for action 3. Identifying important actors
4	Match the actions to innovation modes	Do these actions require the • clear (best practice), • complicated (good practice), or • complex (emergent practice) approach to innovation?	Choosing the right approach to project management by understanding the contextual conditions.
5	Prioritize actions	What are the top 3-5 action items? Why? What do we expect as the outcome of each? Who should lead that action? Who should be involved? How will these actions inform each other?	Developing a collective action plan.

5.1 Preparing the Collective Action Planning Workshop

Before starting a CAP workshop, facilitators will need three things: (1) a map of their ecosystem, (2) a collective idea for a future solution, and (3) sticky notes in three different colours. The ecosystem map can be produced by applying systems mapping methods [25]. The collective idea for a future solution is usually the result of previous stakeholder dialogue or even the explicit goal of a multi-stakeholder partnership. Sticky notes can be physical or digital, depending on your workshop format. For optimal exchange, a CAP dialogue should include three to eight participants, ideally representing different perspectives. For larger groups, we recommend forming breakout groups and then presenting each group's results in the plenum.

5.2 Step 1: Identify Ecosystem Requirements

The process begins with a group that already has a solution in mind – such as a reusable to-go cup system – and needs to align on next steps. We start by exploring the ecosystem's requirements: *What needs to happen in different parts of the ecosystem?*

In our example of a reusable to-go cup system, requirements include selecting suitable materials, engaging cafés as partners, encouraging consumers to adopt and return the cups, and organizing reverse logistics. These are mapped using the Circularity Compass, which fits this circular use case [23]. Different value chain actors often hold differing views on requirements. Therefore, agreeing on shared ecosystem requirements is a critical first step to integrating perspectives and enabling coordinated action.

5.3 Step 2: Assess Ecosystem Constraints

In the next step, we ask for each requirement: *What is keeping us from implementation? What must we consider?* This involves identifying barriers, risks, unknowns, and tensions. In general, this means examining regulatory or organisational constraints, anticipating uncertainties, and recognising trade-offs that may affect implementation.

In our example, this includes developing environmental and hygiene criteria aligned with existing regulations, understanding how customers and partners may respond, and addressing tensions such as lowering entry barriers while ensuring cups are returned. In group settings, stakeholders will bring diverse perspectives based on their roles and interests, leading to different views on constraints. The aim is to integrate these into a shared system map, even if the discussion becomes more problem-focused and less solution-oriented. Although this can create frustration, it is a necessary step to move from an abstract vision to a realistic and collectively supported action plan.

5.4 Step 3: Define Actions and Actors

The objective of this step is to move from a problem focus towards a solution and action focus. So, in this step the group moves from an analytical and critical mode towards a more creative and solution-oriented mode. We ask the group two questions:

(1) *What do we need to do to address these constraints?*
(2) *Who needs to be involved?*

Answering these two questions requires the group to develop solutions. Some may be fairly standard and well-known. Others may be ideas or guesses. It is important that each constraint from Step 2 is associated with a number of actions that may alleviate it. Additionally, each of these actions should be assigned to actors capable of making them happen. It is helpful at this stage to ask "what if…?" questions to trigger the group's creativity (see examples in Table 1).

5.5 Step 4: Match Actions to Appropriate Innovation Modes

In Step 4, each action identified in Step 3 is assigned to an appropriate innovation mode based on its context, as well as the clarity of its goal and pathway (see Table 2). In general, this classification helps determine whether an action can rely on existing best practices, requires expert input, or demands experimentation and learning.

Table 2. Overview of innovation modes

Innovation mode	Definition	Conditions: When to apply	Examples: How to apply
Clear, following existing *best practice*	There is a best practice you can follow for attaining your goal.	- context: well-known and stable - the goal to be attained is clearly defined; - project implementation can follow pre-defined milestones	- follow industry guideline; - copy competitor; - follow standardized management best practices, such as total quality management
Complicated, following existing *good practice*	There are different approaches to attaining your goal. So, you require expertise to evaluate options.	- context: stable; - the goal to be attained and the pathway to achieve it can be defined through expertise-based assessment of facts and figures; - project implementation can follow pre-defined milestones	- hire experts - bring in external consultants - model/calculate and compare different solutions - establish milestone-oriented project controlling
Complex, by probing and learning through *emergent practice*	There is no clear process to attaining your overarching objective and your goals keep moving. You can only learn by taking small steps and learning from the emerging effects.	- context: novel or unstable; - the goal to be attained is not yet clearly defined and can only be explored through action; - the outcome of a decision cannot be predicted based on experience or data analysis; - implementation pathway contains many uncertainties and unknowns	- experiments; - small-scale pilots; - other probing techniques

The *chaos* innovation mode was excluded due to limited relevance to the planning process in the multi-stakeholder partnerships that we have observed.

In our example, selecting materials and colours falls under the *clear* mode, as guidelines and best practices already exist. Meeting hygiene requirements is *complicated*, as it requires expert knowledge and structured implementation. Addressing uncertainties—such as partner and consumer reactions—falls under the *complex* mode, requiring pilots and iterative learning. Similarly, resolving *tensions* often requires complex, creative approaches. For instance, *RECUP* prioritised ease of adoption with a low deposit, while *Vytal* used an app with reminders and penalties to encourage returns. These different approaches illustrate how balancing competing goals often depends on experimentation and collective creativity.

Classifying actions is a critical step in Collective Action Planning, as it brings together the three design principles. Although often implicit, decision-makers tend to favor certain innovation modes based on their background—for example, start-up founders may lean towards the *complex* mode, while corporate and policy actors often prefer *complicated* or *clear* modes. The aim of this step is to help the group recognize that the appropriate mode depends on the context of each action, not individual preferences. At the same time, actions should remain sufficiently specific to enable small-scale pilots and iterative learning.

With this, even decision-makers who dislike the uncertainty of the *complex* innovation mode may become more open to it, as small-scale pilots feel planable and measurable. In this way, Step 4 creates the conditions to move from complex thinking to simple action in Step 5.

5.6 Step 5: Align on an Action Plan

In the final step, the group agrees on next steps by addressing four questions:

1. *What are the top 3–5 action items? Why?*

2. 2. *What do you expect as the outcome of each?*
3. 3. *Who should lead that action? Who should be involved?*
4. 4. *How will these actions inform each other?*

Answering these questions enables the group to develop a collective action plan for the coming weeks or months, reflecting shared priorities and increasing both desirability and resilience. Crucially, the plan should balance *complex* actions (learning-by-doing) with more planable *clear* and *complicated* actions. While *clear* and *complicated* actions typically lead to tangible outputs—such as defined material or hygiene requirements—*complex* actions generate learning, reduce uncertainties, and produce insights that may influence other parts of the ecosystem. Recognizing these interdependencies is essential for adapting and coordinating actions over time.

6 Implications: How Practitioners Can Leverage the CAP Method

The Collective Action Planning (CAP) method has been developed with and for practitioners in order to address the problem of bridging from a collective future vision to an effective action plan. The CAP method is grounded in three design principles: (1) enabling decision-making, (2) integrating perspectives, and (3) contextualizing innovation. The CAP method operationalizes these three design principles in a method that can be applied by facilitators, managers, policy-makers, and other actors involved in multi-stakeholder partnerships. The main implications for these actor groups are presented below.

6.1 Implications for Facilitators and Intermediaries

Facilitators and intermediaries often face the challenge that, despite many available tools, alignment on collective action in multi-stakeholder partnerships remains difficult [26]. The CAP method addresses this by providing a structured approach to integrating diverse perspectives. In practice, facilitators report that CAP helps uncover hidden challenges, supports constructive dialogue on how to address them, emphasises learning-by-doing, and clarifies expected learning outcomes. It also enables groups to explore relationships between challenges and actions, leading to more complementary solutions.

In applying CAP, two usage patterns emerge. Some groups follow the five steps closely, resulting in a comprehensive understanding of the ecosystem and clear links between challenges and actions. Others use the prompts more flexibly to spark open, deliberative discussions around "what if…?" questions and shared learning goals. While the former approach strengthens the overall system perspective, the latter often generates more creative, out-of-the-box solutions. Facilitators can adapt CAP to suit the needs and dynamics of each group.

6.2 Implications for Managers

Managers can apply CAP in two ways: to support multi-stakeholder collaboration and within their own organisations. While the previous section focused on the former, CAP can also be used inside firms to align perspectives across teams and departments. It is particularly useful in contexts such as product innovation, digital transformation, sustainability initiatives, and strategic planning.

6.3 Implications for Policy-Makers

Policy-makers can apply CAP in policy labs and stakeholder dialogue. In policy labs, CAP helps address the limits of linear theories of change by distinguishing between *complicated* and *complex* innovation modes, revealing overly simplistic assumptions and highlighting where learning-by-doing is needed [22, 27]. In stakeholder dialogue, CAP integrates diverse perspectives on constraints and solutions, enabling more deliberative and context-sensitive policy-making. Combined, these applications allow policy-makers to co-create and test policy experiments with citizens, businesses, and civil society organisations.

7 Limitations, Boundary Conditions, and Outlook

CAP has been developed in the context of circular ecosystems. While we assume that actors in other contexts can equally benefit from it, this has not been empirically validated. Also, the group participating in a CAP workshop should be somewhat open to systems thinking approaches in order to engage in a constructive dialogue. CAP requires facilitators skilled in facilitating group discussions in a participative and open manner. We recommend piloting the method in a small group of volunteers before launching it in larger multi-stakeholder workshops. CAP was validated across different European geographies. Applying CAP outside Europe may uncover additional insights.

8 Conclusion

The CAP Method supports multi-stakeholder partnerships in agreeing on a collective action plan and pursuing learning-by-doing. CAP also helps to uncover hidden assumptions and challenges across an ecosystem as it facilitates a constructive discussion among the members of the multi-stakeholder partnerships. CAP has been developed with and for facilitators and intermediaries in multi-stakeholder partnerships but can also be applied by managers and policy-makers to understand the context of the people who surround them and develop action.

Acknowledgements. The CAP method has been validated with the help of 255 researchers, practitioners, and students. From the practitioner side, we thank the participants of the Systems Mapping and Co-Design Lab, the Flat Glass Recycling Initiative, the bergisch.circular Initiative for Circular Cities, the Slovenia Deep Demonstration initiative, and the Circularity Thinking trainings for their valuable feedback on earlier versions of the CAP method. In particular, we would like to explicitly acknowledge those who have been intensively involved as intermediaries, facilitators, or project leads: Richard Bubb, Tove Margrethe Dyblie, Aleksandra Goldys, Rickard Nygren, Simon Siedlaczek, Oskar Storm, Milan Veselinov, Susanne Volz, and Karin Wannerberg. From the research side, we would like to thank the participants of the CenSE Research Week 2025, the bergisch.circular Initiative for Circular Cities, EGOS Conferences 2024 and 2025, and seminars at the University of Hamburg and Montpellier Business School, in particular, Maike Demandt, Domenico Dentoni, Elsa Dingkuhn, Tulin Dzhengiz, Philippe Eiselein, Franziska Erbe, and Charis Luedtke.

AI Use Statement. Generative AI (ChatGPT and Grammarly) was used solely for language editing. All ideas, analysis, and interpretations are the authors' original work.

Funding. The first author has received a doctoral scholarship from the Foundation of German Business (Stiftung der deutschen Wirtschaft, sdw). The second author has received third party funding from Onto-DESIDE financed under Horizon Europe (ID: 101058682). Further, projects where we have collected data for this research were funded by third parties. This includes:

- EIT Climate-KIC Deep Demonstration financed under Horizon Europe
- bergisch.circular financed by the The German Federal Ministry of Education, Technology, Space and Research (BMTRF), formerly known as the Federal Ministry of Education and Research (BMBF)

The funding organizations had no influence on the content of this article.

References

1. Stadtler, L., et al.: Cross-sector partnerships to address societal grand challenges: systematizing differences in scholarly analysis. J. Manag. Stud., 1–31 (2024). https://doi.org/10.1111/joms.13053
2. de Bakker, F.G.A., Rasche, A., Ponte, S.: Multi-stakeholder initiatives on sustainability: a cross-disciplinary review and research agenda for business ethics. Bus. Ethics Q. **29**, 343–383 (2019). https://doi.org/10.1017/beq.2019.10
3. Grant, R.M.: Contemporary Strategy Analysis. John Wiley & Sons (2021)
4. Senge, P.: The Fifth Discipline. Doubleday (1990)
5. Bühring, J., Liedtka, J.: Embracing systematic futures thinking at the intersection of Strategic Planning, Foresight and Design (2018)
6. Wenzel, M.: Taking the future more seriously: from corporate foresight to "future-making." AMP **36**, 845–850 (2022). https://doi.org/10.5465/amp.2020.0126
7. Crumbaugh, L.: Bridge the strategy gap. https://www.forrestconsult.com/blog/xzzg13igrfld jx6jdd45179u23ldqb. Accessed 21 Oct 2025
8. Lembi, R., Wentworth, C., Hodbod, J.: Recipe for a scenario: moving from vision to actionable pathways towards sustainable futures. Progress Environ. Geography. **3**, 89–114 (2024). https://doi.org/10.1177/27539687241253616
9. Williams, A., Parker, J.N., Kennedy, S., Whiteman, G.: A process study of evolving paradoxes and cross-sector goals: a partnership to accelerate global sustainability. J. Manag., 01492063241278803 (2024). https://doi.org/10.1177/01492063241278803
10. Kuhlmann, M., Meuer, J., Bening, C.R.: Interorganizational sensemaking of the transition toward a circular value chain. Organ. Environ., 1–31 (2023). https://doi.org/10.1177/108602 66231162057
11. Deloitte Survey: Scepticism towards EU AI Act. https://www.deloitte.com/dl/en/services/legal/research/umfrage-eu-ai-act-2024.html. Accessed 21 Oct 2025
12. Gualandris, J., et al.: Unchaining supply chains: transformative leaps toward regenerating social–ecological systems. J. Supply Chain Manag. **60**, 53–67 (2024). https://doi.org/10.1111/jscm.12314

13. Tuunanen, T., Winter, R., vom Brocke, J.: Dealing with complexity in design science research: a methodology using design echelons. Manag. Inf. Syst. Q. **48**, 427–458 (2024)

14. Colville, I., Brown, A.D., Pye, A.: Simplexity: sensemaking, organizing and storytelling for our time. Hum. Relations. **65**, 5–15 (2011). https://doi.org/10.1177/0018726711425617

15. Follett, M.P.: Creative Experience. Green and Co., New York, Logmans (1924)

16. Snowden, D., Boone, M.: A leader's framework for decision making. Harv. Bus. Rev. **07**, 68–76 (2007)

17. Bansal, P., Birkinshaw, J.: Why You Need Systems Thinking Now. Harvard Business Review (2025)

18. Jackson, M.C.: Critical Systems Thinking and the Management of Complexity: Responsible Leadership for a Complex World. Wiley (2019)

19. Maessen, C.D.: Probing futures, acting today: unlocking the interplay between imagining alternative futures and future-making practices (2025). https://doi.org/10.54195/9789465150154

20. Whyte, J., Mosca, L., Comi, A., Liu, L.X.: Project leadership for future making. Proj. Manag. J. **56**, 173–181 (2025). https://doi.org/10.1177/87569728251322703

21. Ansell, C.K.: Pragmatist Democracy: Evolutionary Learning as Public Philosophy. Oxford University Press, Oxford (2011)

22. van Tulder, R., Keen, N.: Capturing collaborative challenges: designing complexity-sensitive theories of change for cross-sector partnerships. J. Bus. Ethics **150**, 315–332 (2018). https://doi.org/10.1007/s10551-018-3857-7

23. Blomsma, F., Tennant, M., Ozaki, R.: Making sense of circular economy: understanding the progression from idea to action. Bus. Strateg. Environ. **32**, 1059–1084 (2023). https://doi.org/10.1002/bse.3107

24. Snowden, D.: Cynefin: a tale that grew in the telling. In: Greenberg, R., Bertsch, B., Goh, Z., Blignaut, S. (eds.) Cynefin. Cognitive Edge (2021)

25. Dentoni, D., Cucchi, C., Roglic, M., Lubberink, R., Bender-Salazar, R., Manyise, T.: Systems thinking, mapping and change in food and agriculture. In: BAE. 11, 277–301 (2023). https://doi.org/10.36253/bae-13930

26. Velter, M., Bitzer, V., Bocken, N., Kemp, R.: Boundary work for collaborative sustainable business model innovation: the journey of a Dutch SME. J. Bus. Models **9**, 36–66 (2021). https://doi.org/10.5278/JBM.V9I4.6267

27. Olejniczak, K., Borkowska-Waszak, S., Domaradzka-Widła, A., Park, Y.: Policy labs: the next frontier of policy design and evaluation? Policy Polit. (2020). https://doi.org/10.1332/030557319X15579230420108

Beyond the Golden Record: Toward a Design Theory for Trustworthy Master Data Management with Self-sovereign Identity

Niklas Schulte[1,3]([envelope]) [ORCID], Isaac Henderson Johnson Jeyakumar[2] [ORCID], Michael Kubach[2] [ORCID], and Christian Janiesch[1,3] [ORCID]

[1] Fraunhofer ISST, Dortmund, Germany
niklas.schulte@isst.fraunhofer.de
[2] Fraunhofer IAO, Stuttgart, Germany
{isaac-henderson.johnson-jeyakumar,
michael.kubach}@iao.fraunhofer.de
[3] TU Dortmund University, Dortmund, Germany
christian.janiesch@tu-dortmund.de

Abstract. Ensuring the timeliness and reliability of master data remains a persistent challenge for many organizations. To mitigate these quality deficits, organizations frequently rely on commercial data brokers. However, this practice creates strategic dependencies and poses significant business risks, particularly as providers typically disclaim liability for the accuracy of the supplied data. In contrast, modern data ecosystems enable the trusted sharing of data assets with strong data sovereignty. In this paper, we address this paradigm shift by deriving a nascent design theory for trustworthy master data management based on self-sovereign identity. The theory is grounded through a hermeneutic literature review combined with industry expert interviews and instantiated through integration into a reference architecture for data spaces. Following an evaluation through additional industry expert interviews, our work provides a framework for a trustworthy master data management in data ecosystems that is reliable, sovereign, and accountable.

Keywords: Master Data Management · Self-Sovereign Identity · Data Ecosystem · Data Space · Data Sovereignty

1 Introduction

The industrial landscape is currently undergoing a paradigm shift towards collaborative, cross-sector data sharing initiatives such as Gaia-X [1] and Catena-X [2]. In these socio-technical data ecosystems, stakeholders are moving away from centralized data platforms toward sovereign data sharing, leveraging interoperable, decentralized architectures and data usage control mechanisms. However, current Master Data Management (MDM) practices are not adhering to this paradigm shift. Organizations often rely on commercial data brokers to improve their master data quality [3, 4], which introduces

J. vom Brocke et al. (Eds.): DESRIST 2026, LNCS 16606, pp. 430–447, 2026.
https://doi.org/10.1007/978-3-032-28313-9_25

strategic dependencies and liability risks, as these data brokers are structurally unable to guarantee the validity or timeliness of the supplied data[1]. The business consequences are significant. Erroneous master data directly causes supply chain disruptions, failed regulatory reporting, and costly manual reconciliation efforts [5–7]. Moreover, as regulations such as GDPR, the Data Act, and eIDAS 2.0 impose stricter requirements on data provenance and accountability, reliance on unverifiable third-party master data increasingly constitutes a compliance risk. This practice places organizations in a precarious position, as they remain dependent on externally supplied master data whose validity is unverifiable, and no provider accountability can be assumed. In contrast to this, modern data ecosystems allow the accuracy, timeliness, and accountability of data to be attested directly by the data providers themselves, without any central intermediaries. Yet, this transition presents a critical challenge for current MDM practices, on which companies rely for regulatory compliance, process integration, and business relations [3, 6, 8].

Thus, in this paper, we explore the potential of Self-Sovereign Identity (SSI) for a decentralized MDM approach. While SSI is widely recognized as a trust-enhancing technology in modern data sharing environments, its application has been largely restricted to providing evidence for access control or compliance purposes, but not for the management and exchange of master data records [9–11]. We identified a significant research gap between the two domains: traditional MDM does not account for sovereign, decentralized data exchange, while current SSI applications lack the semantic rigor and integration capabilities required for the processing of master data records. To this end, we apply a Design Science Research (DSR) approach to derive a nascent design theory for trustworthy MDM with SSI. We address the following research question: *How can cross-organizational master data management be designed to ensure trustworthiness in decentralized data sharing environments?*

The remainder of this paper is structured as follows: Sect. 2 provides the background on MDM, data ecosystems, and SSI, followed by our DSR methodology in Sect. 3. Section 4 grounds the research through a literature review and expert interviews, which inform the design principles and features derived in Sect. 5. We demonstrate the theory's applicability in Sect. 6 and evaluate it via expert interviews in Sect. 7. Lastly, Sects. 8 and 8.2 present our discussion and conclusion, reflecting on the implications of our design theory for MDM practice and research, as well as its limitations and areas for future work.

2   Research Background

Our research is positioned at the interface between the traditional discipline of MDM and the emerging field of decentralized data ecosystems, which typically leverage the paradigm of SSI to establish digital trust between participants. Although existing research addresses solutions for decentralized sharing, the implications of these technologies for current MDM practices remain underexplored. Specifically, the shift away from a reliance on central data brokers for data quality improvements and the move from

---

[1] This is reflected in the terms of use of commercial providers such as North Data GmbH and Dun & Bradstreet, which offer data correction mechanisms rather than guarantees of accuracy [6,7].

centralized data governance of "Golden Records" towards distributed models represents a significant architectural challenge that has yet to be fully reconciled with the principles of data sovereignty.

2.1 Master Data Management and the "Golden Record"

Traditionally, MDM comprises methods and tools to ensure high data quality and reusability across organizations' business processes [12]. The central objective of traditional MDM is the establishment of a "Golden Record" to guarantee a single, authoritative source of truth that consolidates duplicate or conflicting data records into a unique, reliable representation, defined as "analytical MDM" by Otto et al. [3]. Insufficient master data management leads to inaccurate and incomplete information, which results in flawed stakeholder decision-making and potential financial losses for organizations [13].

In practice, master data is often collected company-internal in centralized architectures. As described by Loshin [14], MDM relies on central hubs or registries to harmonize data from various sources across organizations. This reliance on centralized systems extends beyond internal systems to modern cross-organizational data ecosystems. A prominent example of a central infrastructure for MDM is the Cofinity-X Golden Record Service (GRS) [15]. Currently operating in the Catena-X ecosystem, the GRS functions as a centralized intermediary that aggregates business partner data to perform duplicate management, error correction, and manual data enrichment. While this is an effective way to establish data quality, such centralized master data aggregations pose risks to data breaches and create unwanted central dependencies in decentralized data-sharing environments.

2.2 Self-sovereign Identities and Data Ecosystems

Self-Sovereign Identity (SSI) represents a paradigm shift in digital identity management, away from centralized control and governance of identity information towards the creation of a common identity layer for the internet [16]. The goal of SSI is to give users an independent digital existence and full control over their digital identities [16, 17]. Following the W3C recommendation for Verifiable Credentials [18], SSI mainly involves three roles: issuers, holders, and verifiers. Issuers issue identity claims as Verifiable Credentials (VCs), holders manage these credentials in digital wallets, and verifiers request and validate presented credentials from holders. Its adoption promises privacy, data security, and trust in digital ecosystems [10].

In data ecosystems, SSI-based digital identity management serves as a critical element for facilitating secure and sovereign data sharing across organizations [19]. For example, Gaia-X uses SSI concepts to establish trust not only in organizations and people, but also in services, data assets, and technical components, which receive verifiable self-descriptions linked to their identities. These self-descriptions, expressed as VCs or attestations, enable dynamic trust assessment across federated ecosystems. Although sovereign data exchange should ideally occur directly between two participants, current data space implementations often rely on intermediaries like clearing houses or brokers to establish initial trust and mediate trustworthy transactions [20].

Consequently, the move toward self-sovereign data exchange necessitates a strategic alignment with intra-organizational MDM practices. While SSI integrations in data ecosystems manage external trust using globally unique Decentralized Identifiers (DIDs), MDM systems are required to map these external identities to internal "Golden Records". By leveraging this approach, organizations can treat data ecosystems as a high-trust source system for inter-organizational master data exchange. Hence, incoming VCs containing validated business partner data can automatically update internal master data records. Following this approach, we resolve a disconnect between external data sovereignty and internal master data processing, ensuring that the trust established in the data ecosystem directly translates to automated master data quality maintenance.

3 Research Method

We ground our methodological approach in the DSR process model defined by Peffers et al. [21] as illustrated in Fig. 1. To ensure the accumulation of design knowledge, we adhere to the guidelines of vom Brocke et al. [22] regarding grounding, positioning, aligning, and advancing our contribution within the existing knowledge base.

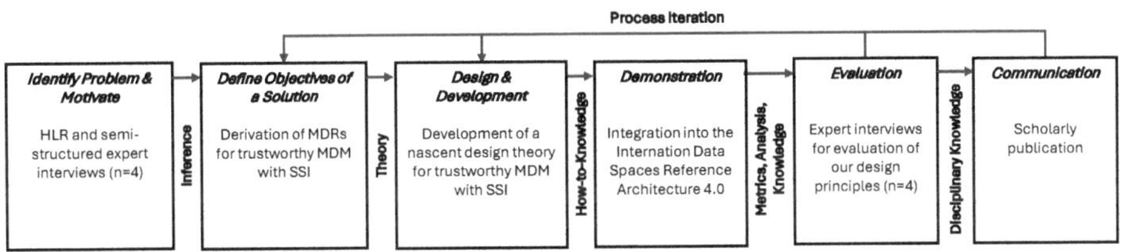

Fig. 1. DSR process for theory development based on Peffers et al. [21].

We employed a mixed-methods approach, bridging rigor and relevance cycles as defined by Hevner et al. [23] for problem identification. We first conducted a Hermeneutic Literature Review (HLR) following Boell and Cecez-Kecmanovic [24], an approach that treats the literature review as alternating cycles of "search and acquisition" and "analysis and interpretation." Through this, we ensure scientific rigor by grounding our work in established theories. To ensure practical relevance, we enriched these theoretical findings with semi-structured expert interviews to derive robust design requirements. We consider our problem identification as a holistic hermeneutic understanding process, combining literature review and interviews.

Based on this problem understanding, we derive a nascent information systems design theory as our primary DSR artifact. To systematically develop our design theory, we follow the hierarchical derivation approach of Herm et al. [25]. This method structures the development process into four logical levels: Meta Design Requirements (MDRs), Design Requirements (DRs), Design Principles (DPs), and Design Features (DFs). This hierarchy ensures traceability from abstract design requirements to concrete technical features. At first, the "purpose and scope" component of Gregor and Jones [26] is operationalized by defining MDRs. These MDRs delineate the class of goals our design theory addresses. Subsequently, we refine these MDRs into concrete DRs and, ultimately, into actionable "design principles of form and function". To ensure these DPs are actionable and effective, we follow the approach of Chandra et al. [27] and Gregor et al. [28] to provide a clear rationale for each principle. Lastly, we provide a mapping from our DPs to DFs to visualize how our DPs can be instantiated by concrete technologies [25].

Continuing our DSR approach, we developed a reference architecture showcasing an integration of decentralized MDM into the International Data Space Association (IDSA) Reference Architecture Model 4.0 [29] based on the derived DPs. Through this, we demonstrate the technical feasibility of our design theory and illustrate how it can be translated into a coherent system architecture. Subsequently, we evaluate our design theory by following the Framework for Evaluation in Design Science (FEDS) proposed by Venable et al. [30]. Given the abstract nature of the design artifact, we performed an ex-ante evaluation following the "Technical Risk & Efficacy Strategy" of FEDS. This evaluation strategy allows us to assess the efficacy and logical completeness of our DPs in an artificial setting. Hence, we conducted semi-structured expert interviews to validate our DPs. Following the approach of Janiesch et al. [31], we apply the metrics of "onto-logical expressiveness" to guide our interviews for evaluation. This formative evaluation strategy maximizes learning and improvement by directly identifying practical barriers to applying the DPs.

4 Problem Identification

Following Boell and Cecez-Kecmanovic [24], our HLR proceeded in iterative cycles across three databases, Scopus, ACM Digital Library, and AISeL, supplemented by forward and backward citation search. In Iteration 1, we conducted a broad search for MDM literature on ACM Digital Library and AIS eLibrary with the query (*"master data"*). For Scopus, we restricted our search term further by adding *AND ("governance" OR "data quality" OR "golden record")* to keep the search results manageable. After screening titles and abstracts for relevance to organizational MDM practices, 19 papers were retained after filtering, enriched by 5 papers through forward and backward citation search, resulting in a total of 24 papers. In Iteration 2, we extended the search to the use of SSI and MDM in decentralized data sharing environments using the query (*"master data" OR "self-sovereign identity") AND ("data space" OR "data ecosystem"*). Across all three databases, this yielded 27 results, of which 10 were retained after applying the same relevance criterion, enriched by 3 papers through citation search, leading to a total of 13 papers. Table 1 visualizes the paper selection process.

Table 1. HLR paper selection process.

I#	Scopus	ACM DL	AISeL	Filtering and Selection	Citation Search	Σ
I1	262	53	36	−332	+5	24
I2	22	2	3	−17	+3	13

4.1 Iteration 1: Traditional Master Data Management

Traditional MDM typically aims towards a centralized collection of data to provide a "single source of truth" within organizations. To this end, Raharjo et al. [32] identified technical solutions to support master data collection and proper data governance as critical success factors for MDM. However, Silvola et al. [4] note that organizations frequently suffer from inadequate data ownership and incoherent data management processes. Vilminko-Heikkinen and Pekkola [12] demonstrate that successful MDM requires strictly defined data owners with explicit authorities to make binding decisions. Following Keith and Seymour [6], this requirement is difficult to enforce in practice, as organizations constantly struggle with "data silos" and "fragmented infrastructures."

To address these governance challenges, Otto and Ofner [3] include the definition of a context-dependent "Nucleus" and the integration of commercial master data providers. Buffenoir and Bourdon [33] characterize this centralized governance model as the "Panopticon Paradigm", where data quality is enforced through centralized visibility and disciplinary power of the overarching organization. Technically, this is typically realized through central registries designed to support transparent access to a unique representation of master data [14].

Despite these frameworks, centralized models face inherent limitations in cross-organizational settings. Otto and Ofner [3] further identify a "lack of downstream visibility", indicating that central authorities cannot oversee how data is used at the edge. Although Otto et al. [34] acknowledge that there is a need for external communication for MDM, their reference model treats it as an output of the internal quality processes, assuming external partners will inherently trust it. However, in fully decentralized data sharing environments, inherent trust cannot be assumed, and the authoritative power to enforce it is omitted.

4.2 Iteration 2: Master Data Management in Data Ecosystems

Considering modern, decentralized data sharing solutions for master data exchange, the focus shifts from company-internal data quality optimizations towards the management of identities, interoperability, and trust relationships across organizational boundaries. In contrast to traditional MDM, the collaborative nature of data ecosystems requires mechanisms for unique identification and verification without a central intermediary.

A central hindrance to data sharing in data ecosystems is the heterogeneity of data sources. Datta et al. [35] recommend a reference architecture that harmonizes heterogeneous data sources to enforce rule-based compliance. However, Altendeitering and Guggenberger [36] emphasize that this is particularly critical for relational master data records, which serve as the backbone of business processes and require dedicated quality analysis tools. To enable a clear understanding across boundaries, semantic models are inevitable. Bader et al. [37] demonstrate how semantic models can be used to define not only data resources, but also the actors involved and their connectors in a machine-readable format. Furthermore, Azkan et al. [38] emphasize that defining master data attributes requires a clear classification of ecosystem roles to determine value creation.

A further fundamental prerequisite for decentralized MDM is the establishment of trustworthy identities. Gelhaar and Otto [39] identify trust building as a primary cooperative challenge, arguing that it has direct implications for managing partner relationships.

To address this, Babel et al. [10] describe the leveraging of SSI for data ecosystems. In addition, Barclay et al. [40] demonstrate how this concept extends to data accountability: they propose using VCs to create cryptographic "Bills of Materials" (BOMs). These BOMs provide a transparent, tamper-proof supply chain record, allowing consumers to scrutinize the origin and integrity of shared data assets.

4.3 Iteration 3: Stakeholder Interviews

To complement our theoretical findings with practical perspectives, we conducted four semi-structured expert interviews with practitioners engaged in data space implementations and SSI infrastructure development. We employed a purposive sampling strategy, selecting participants across the primary stakeholder roles of data space ecosystems: infrastructure providers, governance bodies, and domain-specific end-users. Selection criteria were: (1) active involvement in a multi-organizational data exchange project, (2) a minimum of 2 years' experience in either SSI or MDM, and (3) decision-making authority within their respective project (Architect, Board Member, or Product Owner). The purposive selection ensures coverage across these primary roles, and in alignment with DSR methodology, the interviews serve to inform design requirements rather than achieve statistical generalizability [21, 23]. Theoretical saturation was considered reached as no new themes emerged after the fourth interview.

Participants represented diverse organizational contexts: a chief architect for SSI solutions at a major enterprise software provider (P1), a board member of a European identity cooperative (P2), a research associate working on healthcare data spaces (P3), and a product owner for MDM in the automotive domain (P4), ensuring broad coverage across technical implementation, identity infrastructure, and domain-specific MDM applications. Table 2 provides further demographics. We prepared an interview guideline with 14 questions across 6 categories derived from the HLR findings, opening each interview with a shared understanding of MDM before exploring its significance for data spaces. All interviews were recorded, transcribed, and analyzed by the authors.

Table 2. Interview demographics for DSR problem identification.

P#	Role	Domain	Background in SSI?	Experience	Duration
P1	Chief Software Architect	IT Consulting	yes	22 years	22min
P2	Digital Identity Expert	Digital Identity	yes	15 years	47min
P3	Research Associate	Healthcare	no	4 years	27min
P4	Product Owner MDM	Automotive	no	2 years	42min
Σ					138 min

A recurring theme across all interviews was the challenge of maintaining current and accurate master data. P2 cited a current real-world example for this. Organizations maintain extensive datasets of business partner information, but often lack mechanisms to verify whether this data remains valid over time. For example, when contact people leave organizations without notification, often no updates are reported, which creates significant compliance risks. P2 further noted that changes to official registries can take multiple months to process, creating problematic gaps where outgoing executives retain signing authority while incoming leadership cannot exercise legitimate authority. Current approaches using commercial data brokers were identified as fundamentally problematic from a liability perspective.

P3 emphasized that services aggregating publicly available information explicitly disclaim responsibility for data validity, creating unacceptable risk exposure for business-critical decisions. P3 also introduced a different perspective, especially interesting for sensitive data sharing contexts, noting that Verifiable Presentations (VPs) enable answering specific queries without disclosing underlying data, which is essential for healthcare applications where privacy and confidentiality must be preserved. On semantic interoperability, P3 offered that rather than enforcing a single uniform data model, translation tables between established formats may prove more achievable, acknowledging that global consensus on standards in the healthcare domain remains elusive.

P4 emphasized the importance of system activation. Despite backing from major manufacturers and explicit membership targets, adoption in Catena-X remained below expectations. In addition, P2 highlighted significant potential for SSI in master data governance, describing, for example, bank account verification through VCs could eliminate multi-person approval processes currently required to prevent fraud, noting "the efficiency gain is enormous."

The expert interviews surfaced several requirements complementing our literature-derived findings. Inter-organizational master data solutions must accommodate temporal gaps between operational efficiency and official registry updates. Accountability for master data should be technically enforced through cryptographic signatures and ideally directly attested by the data owner. Identity architectures must support hierarchical relationships reflecting actual business structures. Lastly, practical adoption depends critically on demonstrating clear value propositions of the system, justifying initial investment for data ecosystem participation.

5 Design Theory for Decentralized MDM with SSI

In the following section, we present our nascent design theory for decentralized MDM with SSI. Figure 2 provides an overview of the derived theory, including refinements made following our evaluation phase. While DIDs and VCs are established building blocks, their systematic composition for MDM-specific requirements constitutes the novel contribution of this work. The following Meta Design Requirements (MDRs) are derived directly from the deficits of centralized MDM identified in HLR Iteration 1 and the specific interoperability and accountability challenges revealed in Iterations 2 and 3.

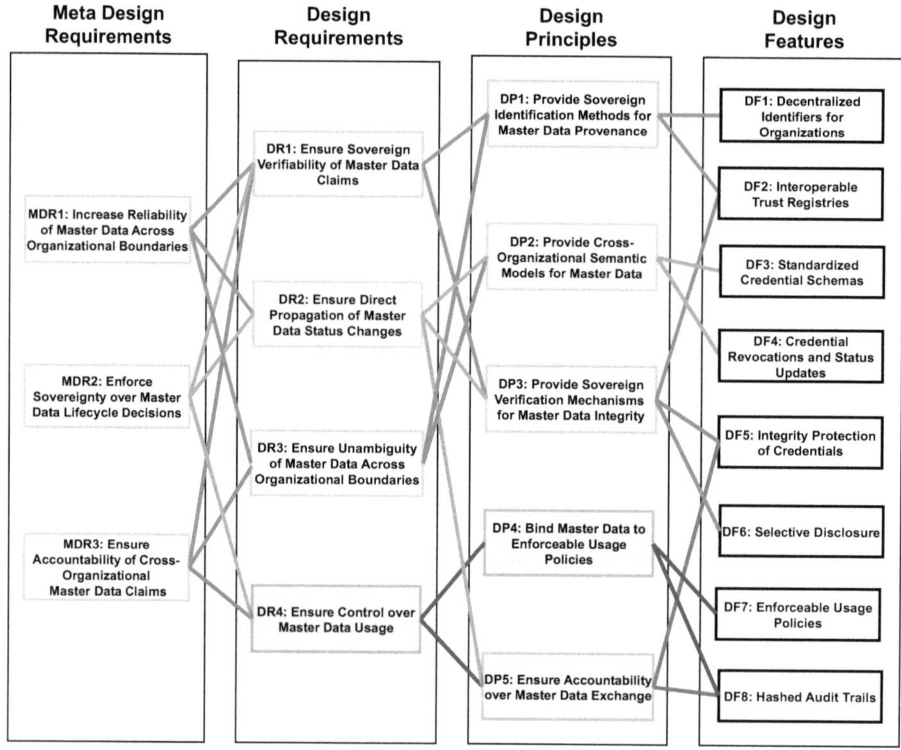

Fig. 2. Design theory for trustworthy MDM with SSI.

MDR1: Increase Reliability of Master Data Across Organizational Boundaries. Uncertainty about the status of master data is a major issue for organizations in practice. Often this is mitigated through the purchase of data from commercial data brokers [3]. While traditional MDM focuses on creating an organization's internal "Golden Record," data ecosystems require mechanisms that ensure reliability beyond organizational borders. Addressing the problematic missing updates, identified in our expert interviews (Sect. 4.3), MDR1 captures that inter-organizational MDM approaches need to have a similar reliability as organization-internal "Golden Records" [34]. This reliability needs to ensure the correctness, timeliness, and verifiability of master data originating from external organizations.

MDR2: Enforce Sovereignty over Master Data Lifecycle Decisions. In cross-organizational data ecosystems, master data assets are frequently created, shared, updated, and revoked. To overcome the "Panopticon Paradigm" of centralized governance identified in Iteration 1 (4.1) and leverage the decentralized control mechanisms of data spaces found in Iteration 2, data providers require sovereignty over master data lifecycle decisions such as issuance, modification, revocation, and usage even after data has been shared with external organizations [41, 42]. This is particularly critical for master data, as non-propagated changes can propagate inconsistencies across data ecosystems.

Therefore, MDR2 captures inter-organizational MDM approaches that must preserve the organization's sovereignty over master data lifecycle decisions.

MDR3: Ensure Accountability of Cross-Organizational Master Data Claims. When master data is shared across organizations, the receiving organization must be able to rely on it. Prior research on data governance emphasizes that effective inter-organizational data sharing requires clear accountability structures that allow actors to attribute data-related decisions and outcomes to identifiable parties [12]. In the context of MDM, accountability is particularly critical because master data often serves as a foundation for regulatory compliance, contractual relationships, and operational decision-making across organizational boundaries [34]. Directly responding to the lack of liability assumed by commercial data brokers identified in Iteration 3 (Sect. 4.3) and the "lack of downstream visibility" noted in Iteration 1 (Sect. 4.1), the receiving organization must be able to rely on shared data. Therefore, MDR3 states that inter-organizational MDM approaches must ensure accountability of master data claims to determine who issued, updated, or revoked specific master data.

On this basis, we operationalize the MDRs by deriving more granular DRs, which provide specifications that facilitate the practical instantiation of the design [25]. These DRs are subsequently used as the foundation to derive DPs.

DR1: Ensure Sovereign Verifiability of Master Data Claims. In contrast to centralized authorities that guarantee reliability in traditional MDM environments, for decentralized environments, we require the data itself to be verifiable. Drawing from the requirements of reliability (MDR1), sovereignty over lifecycle decisions (MDR2), and accountability for claims (MDR3). DR1 aims to improve trust between organizations in data ecosystems through direct verifiability of master data records as a key component for sovereign and cross-organizational data sharing.

DR2: Ensure Sovereign Direct Propagation of Master Data Status Changes. Master data frequently gets outdated or potentially even needs to be revoked by the data owner. These lifecycle decisions should be propagated in a sovereign way (MDR2) and thus increase the reliability of master data across organizational boundaries (MDR1). DR2 captures this requirement by ensuring that these changes are directly propagated by the organization that owns the master data.

DR3: Ensure Unambiguity of Master Data Across Organizational Boundaries. To eliminate interpretive ambiguity during inter-organizational exchange, master data records must be governed by deterministic definitions that ensure semantic alignment. DR3 directly increases the reliability of master data across organizational boundaries (MDR1) and enables accountability for master data (MDR3) by ensuring that all parties operate under an identical, objective understanding of the data's meaning and context.

DR4: Enforce Control over Master Data Usage. Organizations are often hesitant to share master data due to a lack of clarity about usage scenarios. DR4 directly addresses sovereignty over master data lifecycle decisions (MDR2) and sets a baseline for the accountability of the master data exchange (MDR3). This enforcement is critical, as only the master data owner can ultimately guarantee its reliability and thus also account for it.

Based on derived DRs, we formulate our DPs following the guidelines of Chandra et al. [27] to keep our DPs actionable and effective. In addition to our DPs, we further detail their content by providing additional DFs. These DFs demonstrate how our DPs can be instantiated by concrete technical features [25].

DP1: Provide Sovereign Identification Methods for Master Data Provenance. Provide the system with sovereign identification methods for master data providers in order for users to unambiguously assign master data claims, given that master data provenance needs to be verified across organizational boundaries. DP1 increases verifiability of master data provenance (DR1) through a clear identification of the master data providers and ensures the unambiguity of master data records across organizations (DR3).

DF1: Decentralized Identifiers for Organizations (W3C Decentralized Identifiers)

DF2: Interoperable Trust Registries (Trust Frameworks, e.g., Gaia-X).

DP2: Provide Cross-Organizational Semantic Models for Master Data. Provide the system with cross-organizationally defined semantic models for master data in order for users to unambiguously interpret shared master data, given that internal semantic schemas vary across organizational boundaries. DP2 enables the direct propagation of master data status changes (DR2) and ensures the unambiguity of master data across organizational boundaries (DR3).

DF3: Standardized Credential Schemas (W3C Verifiable Credentials).

DF4: Credential Revocations and Status Updates (W3C Bitstring Status Lists).

DP3: Provide Sovereign Master Data Verification Methods for Master Data Integrity. Provide the system with sovereign data verification mechanisms in order for users to assess the timeliness and integrity of the master data at the time of use, given that master data frequently needs to be updated or revoked. DP3 directly ensures the verifiability of master data (DR1) and ensures the direct propagation of status changes (DR2), which would lead to a failed validation on outdated data.

DF5: Integrity Protection of Credentials (Cryptographic Signatures, e.g., Ed25519)

DF6: Selective Disclosure (Selective Disclosure for JSON Web Tokens).

DP4: Bind Master Data Records to Enforceable Usage Policies. Provide the system with machine-readable usage policies in order for users to exercise granular control over master data dissemination, given that organizations lose physical control over their data usage once it is shared across organizational boundaries. DP4 ensures control over master data usage (DR4) by empowering the provider to explicitly formulate master data usage conditions and leverage policy-enforcement technologies.

DF7: Enforceable Usage Policies (W3C Open Digital Rights Language).

DP5: Ensure Accountability over Master Data Exchange. Provide the system with hashed audit trails in order for users to provide evidence over their shared master data, given that the exchange of master data should be accountable. DP5 ensures the system verifies the occurrence and integrity of these exchanges without revealing the actual data content through hashed audit trails. Moreover, it ensures that all lifecycle changes are observed (DR2) and reinforces the requirement for sovereign control over master data usage (DR4). In cases where cryptographic accountability alone is insufficient for dispute resolution, such as conflicting master data claims across jurisdictions, governance frameworks and legally recognized registries must serve as complementary arbitration mechanisms.

DF8: Hashed Audit Trails (Merkle Trees).

6   Reference Architecture for Sovereign MDM in Data Spaces

To demonstrate the applicability of our derived DPs, we present a reference architecture instantiating them within the IDSA Data Space Reference Architecture Model 4.0 [29]. As illustrated in Fig. 3, the architecture comprises four layers and one vertical service layer. The Identity Layer establishes a decentralized root of trust by integrating SSI technologies and thus removing reliance on central identity providers. Building on this, the MDM Services Layer secures master data provenance (DP1) by permanently binding records to DIDs, while embedding them in VCs to guarantee integrity and enable revocation (DP3). The Data Space Layer serves as the interoperability bridge between organizations, hosting dataspace-wide credential schemas to bridge internal semantic models into a shared vocabulary (DP2). Data catalogs enable asset discovery, while participant agent services and contract negotiation automate policy agreement prior to transfer. The Governance Layer maintains trust lists, governance frameworks, and machine-readable usage policies that govern contract negotiation (DP4). Finally, the Vertical Services Layer provides cross-cutting functionalities, including onboarding services, identity provisioning, and brokerage services that generate tamper-proof audit trails for system-wide accountability (DP5).

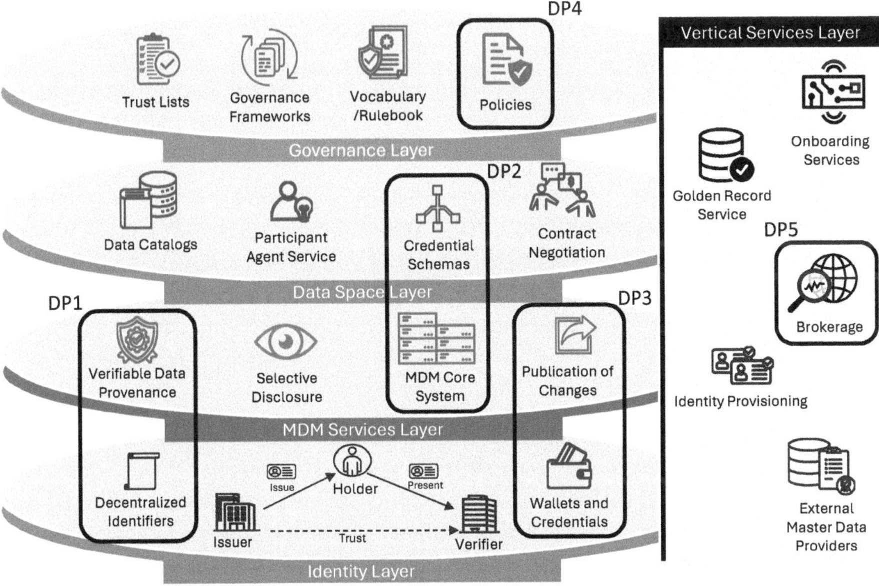

Fig. 3. Reference architecture for trustworthy MDM with SSI in data spaces.

7 Evaluation

Following the same purposive sampling strategy as in our problem identification interviews 4.3, we evaluated the nascent design theory through four expert interviews (E1–E4) targeting practitioners with and without SSI backgrounds across relevant domains. Overall, most experts confirmed the utility of the design theory, specifically highlighting the clear identification of organizations, semantic interoperability, and the integration of usage policies as helpful tools for building trust in cross-organizational master data exchange. However, the evaluation also revealed specific friction points regarding deficiency, redundancy, overload, and access to the design theory. Table 3 visualizes the demographics of our interview partners for evaluation.

Table 3. Interview demographics for DSR evaluation.

E#	Role	Domain	Background in SSI?	Experience	Duration
E1	Project Director	Automotive	yes	7 years	52 min
E2	Innovation Manager	IT-Security	yes	6 years	31 min
E3	Data Governance Manager	Energy	no	10 years	37 min
E4	Digital Transformation Lead	Mobility	no	20 years	35 min
Σ					154 min

Deficiency. The interviews highlighted a gap regarding legal enforceability and cross-jurisdictional trust. E1 emphasized that "a trade register enjoys public faith" and that emerging EU regulations (Company Law, EU Business Wallet) will establish legally binding identity infrastructures by 2027/28, noting "if there are already legally higher-value sources [...] they should also be used" (E1). E2 similarly noted that "decentralizing master data means probably going across jurisdictions" as a "common pitfall" (E2).

Redundancy. Experts identified semantic overlaps between DP1 ("Ensure Unambiguous Interpretability of Master Data") and DP5 ("Tamper-Proof Evidence of Master Data Exchange"). E2 observed that DP2 and DP3 could be combined, since technologies like VCs address both simultaneously (E2). E3 noted that "tamper-proof evidence [...] is essentially also master data provenance" (E3). We resolved this by shifting the focus of DP3 from general verifiability to master data integrity protection and DP5 to accountability of the master data exchange transaction.

Overload. Multiple experts noted that identification and semantic interoperability should not be combined within a single principle. E1 stated that "the identifiability of legal persons [...] has the potential to be explicitly listed" separately, while E3 reinforced that "semantic uniformity of master data" and provider identification serve distinct purposes. We addressed this by splitting the original DP1 into the current DP1 for identification of data provenance and DP2 for cross-organizational semantic interoperability. Regarding DP4, E1 distinguished between publicly available master data, where defining usage policies "means work […] for hundreds of thousands of business partners," and sensitive master data, where such investment is justified. We nonetheless retained the enforceability claim in DP4 given its importance across interviews, despite its acknowledged technical limitations.

Excess. Experts noted that DP4 and DP5 might constitute technical excess for certain data types. E1 explicitly questioned whether "traceable data exchange" is "really necessary for public data" (E1), though ultimately confirmed relevance for most cases. E4 further suggested that continuous access to master data with local storage would potentially reduce the need for extensive audit trails (E4).

8 Discussion, Limitations, and Future Work

8.1 Theoretical Contribution and Practical Relevance

In this paper, we obtained a nascent design theory for trustworthy MDM with SSI. Our research contributes to the scientific knowledge base by addressing the intersection of traditional MDM and decentralized SSI architectures. Existing MDM literature predominantly relies on centralized data governance models, where central authorities enforce data quality. We challenge this assumption by presenting a nascent design theory that enables high-quality master data exchange in decentralized data sharing environments without a central "Golden Record." Furthermore, we broaden the application scope of SSI with our contribution. While SSI research typically restricts its focus to the provisioning of static identity claims or access control mechanisms [9–11], our artifact demonstrates how DIDs and VCs can also be leveraged to directly transfer master data records. By deriving DPs, we provide a blueprint for managing dynamic master data assets effectively in decentralized environments.

Practically, our design theory offers a concrete solution to resolve the tension between the operational efficiency necessary for master data exchange and digital sovereignty in emerging data ecosystems like Gaia-X or Catena-X. A primary obstacle for MDM identified in our expert interviews is an unclear status of master data assets, where organizations suffer from a lack of reliable updates on their partners' data changes. Our design theory addresses this by introducing mechanisms for the automated, real-time verification of master data validity and provenance. Moreover, by leveraging SSI-based trust anchors, organizations can automate the labor-intensive process of data provenance verification and data quality assurance, directly reducing the costs resulting from low master data quality. Moreover, our artifact provides a sovereign integration solution for MDM into ecosystems like Catena-X, effectively reducing dependencies on central services for master data quality improvements like the Cofinity-X GRS.

Our design is also aligned with relevant regulatory frameworks: the GDPR's data minimization and purpose limitation principles are directly supported by selective disclosure in DP2, the Data Act's requirements for non-discriminatory data access are addressed through sovereign, policy-controlled sharing in DP1 and DP3, and eIDAS 2.0's trust framework for legal entities provides a natural governance layer for anchoring organizational identities used in master data exchange.

8.2 Limitations and Future Work

It is important to note that decentralized MDM still needs to overcome a couple of adoption barriers. Centralized MDM registries offer well-understood governance structures, lower verification overhead for consumers, and mature tooling [34]. The advantage of our approach lies not in decentralization per se, but in its ability to preserve digital sovereignty while maintaining data quality assurance. This is a combination that centralized registries structurally cannot provide. SSI-based MDM also offers concrete advantages over alternative decentralized approaches such as federated APIs. It enables cryptographically verifiable provenance without requiring shared infrastructure, selective disclosure of master data attributes, and the ability to integrate with established trust frameworks like eIDAS 2.0 without introducing new intermediaries.

Beyond this technical trade-off, several adoption barriers require future investigation. Incentives for organizations to become credential issuers are non-trivial, as they need to bear the operational cost of credential issuance, while API-based alternatives may appear less costly in the short term. Thus, future work should explore governance models and incentive structures that make SSI-based issuance economically attractive. Also, migration from existing "Golden Record" systems and bootstrapping the critical mass of issuers and verifiers in ecosystems like Catena-X present further practical challenges that hybrid architectures and governance anchor institutions should address.

Beyond functional applicability, non-functional requirements also need to be considered for a successful adoption. Regarding scalability, credential issuance and verification are computationally lightweight operations, and the absence of a central bottleneck allows the architecture to scale horizontally across participants. Moreover, the overhead for key management represents a practical concern whereby organizations must maintain DID documents and credential lifecycle operations, which increases operational complexity compared to centralized alternatives.

This paper presents a first complete DSR cycle, focusing on derivation and formative, ex ante validation of the design theory. Our evaluation relied primarily on experts familiar with decentralized data ecosystems and SSI, which was necessary for validating technical feasibility but limits generalizability regarding broader business adoption. Future DSR iterations should therefore broaden stakeholder involvement to include MDM practitioners beyond the SSI domain, exploring adoption incentives, migration pathways, and government-backed trust anchors such as the EU Business Wallet as complementary governance infrastructure.

9 Conclusion

In this paper, we presented a nascent design theory for trustworthy MDM in decentralized data sharing environments, comprising three MDRs, five DPs, and eight DFs, instantiated through an integration into data space architectures. Our findings demonstrate that SSI provides a viable technical foundation for reliable, sovereign, and accountable cross-organizational master data exchange, without reliance on a central "Golden Records." Our design aligns with key regulatory frameworks, including GDPR, the Data Act, and eIDAS 2.0, and offers a practical path toward reducing dependencies on central services in ecosystems like Catena-X. Future work should pursue subsequent DSR cycles to address these open challenges and validate the design theory in real-world deployments.

Acknowledgments. This work was supported by the Cluster of Excellence Cognitive Internet Technologies CCIT, which is funded by the Fraunhofer-Gesellschaft zur Förderung der angewandten Forschung e.V.

Disclosure of Interests. The authors declare that the research was conducted in the absence of any commercial or financial relationships that could represent a potential conflict of interest.

References

1. Gaia-X European Association for Data and Cloud AISBL: Gaia-X. https://www.gaia-x.eu. Accessed 22 Jan 2026
2. Catena-X Automotive Network e.V.: Catena-X: The First Open and Collaborative Data Ecosystem. https://catena-x.net/. Accessed 22 Jan 2026
3. Otto, B., Ofner, M.: Strategic business requirements for master data management systems. In: Americas Conference on Information Systems (AMCIS), pp. 936–947 (2011)
4. Silvola, R., Jaaskelainen, O., Kropsu-Vehkapera, H., Haapasalo, H.: Managing one master data - challenges and preconditions. Ind. Manage. Data Sys. **111**, 146–162 (2011). https://doi.org/10.1108/02635571111099776
5. Otto, B., Ebner, V., Hüner, K.: Measuring master data quality: findings from a case study. In: AMCIS 2010 Proceedings (2010)
6. Keith, K., Seymour, L.: Precursors of master data quality issues across enterprise systems. In: UK Academy for Information Systems Conference Proceedings 2025 (2025)
7. Baghi, E., Otto, B., Oesterle, H.: Controlling customer master data quality: findings from a case study. In: CONF-IRM 2013 Proceedings (2013)
8. Roth, H., Mönch, S., Schäffer, T.: Towards augmented MDM: overview of design and function areas – a literature review. In: AMCIS 2022 Proceedings (2022)
9. Laatikainen, G., Kolehmainen, T., Abrahamsson, P.: Self-sovereign identity ecosystems: benefits and challenges. 12th Scandinavian Conference on Information Systems (2021)
10. Babel, M., et al.: Self-sovereign identity and digital wallets. Electron. Markets **35**, 28 (2025). https://doi.org/10.1007/s12525-025-00772-0
11. Schäfer, F., Rosen, J., Zimmermann, C., Wortmann, F.: Unleashing the potential of data ecosystems: establishing digital trust through trust-enhancing technologies. In: European Conference on Information Systems (ECIS) (2023)
12. Vilminko-Heikkinen, R., Pekkola, S.: Changes in roles, responsibilities and ownership in organizing master data management. Int. J. Inf. Manage. **47**, 76–87 (2019). https://doi.org/10.1016/j.ijinfomgt.2018.12.017
13. Hikmawati, S., Santosa, P.I., Hidayah, I.: Improving data quality and data governance using master data management: a review. IJITEE **5**, 90 (2021). https://doi.org/10.22146/ijitee.66307
14. Loshin, D.: Master Data Management. Elsevier Inc. (2009). https://doi.org/10.1016/B978-0-12-374225-4.X0001-X
15. Cofinity-X: Golden Record Service. https://www.cofinity-x.com/golden-record. Accessed 8 Dec 2025
16. Tobin, A., Reed, D., Windley, F.P.J., Foundation, S.: The inevitable rise of self-sovereign identity (2017)
17. Richter, D., Anke, J.: Self-sovereign identity: a conceptual framework and research agenda. Electron. Markets **36**, 17 (2026). https://doi.org/10.1007/s12525-025-00867-8

18. W3C: W3C Recommendation - Verifiable Credentials Data Model. https://www.w3.org/TR/vc-data-model-2.0/
19. Laatikainen, G., Mustak, M., Hickman, N.: Self-sovereign identity adoption: Antecedents and potential outcomes. Technol. Soc. **82** (2025). https://doi.org/10.1016/j.techsoc.2025.102859
20. Jeyakumar, I.H.J., Kubach, M.: A trust implementation model for cross-domain decentralized identity ecosystems: architecture, use case, and implementation. Procedia Comput. Sci. **254**, 10–19 (2025). https://doi.org/10.1016/j.procs.2025.02.059
21. Peffers, K., Tuunanen, T., Rothenberger, M.A., Chatterjee, S.: A design science research methodology for information systems research. J. Manag. Inf. Syst. **24**, 45–77 (2007). https://doi.org/10.2753/MIS0742-1222240302
22. vom Brocke, J., Winter, R., Hevner, A., Maedche, A.: Special issue editorial – accumulation and evolution of design knowledge in design science research: a journey through time and space. J. Assoc. Inf. Syst. **21** (2020). https://doi.org/10.17705/1jais.00611
23. Hevner, A.R., March, S.T., Park, J., Ram, S.: Design science in information systems research1. MIS Q. **28**, 75–106 (2004). https://doi.org/10.2307/25148625
24. Boell, S.K., Cecez-Kecmanovic, D.: A hermeneutic approach for conducting literature reviews and literature searches. CAIS **34** (2014). https://doi.org/10.17705/1CAIS.03412
25. Herm, L.-V., Steinbach, T., Wanner, J., Janiesch, C.: A nascent design theory for explainable intelligent systems. Electron. Markets **32**, 2185–2205 (2022). https://doi.org/10.1007/s12525-022-00606-3
26. Jones, D., Gregor, S.: The anatomy of a design theory. J. Assoc. Inf. Syst. **8** (2007). https://doi.org/10.17705/1jais.00129
27. Chandra, L., Seidel, S., Gregor, S.: Prescriptive knowledge in IS research: conceptualizing design principles in terms of materiality, action, and boundary conditions. In: Hawaii International Conference on System Sciences (HICSS). pp. 4039–4048. IEEE Computer Society, USA (2015). https://doi.org/10.1109/HICSS.2015.485
28. Gregor, S., Kruse, L.C., Seidel, S.: Research perspectives: the anatomy of a design principle. J. Assoc. Inf. Syst. **21** (2020). https://doi.org/10.17705/1jais.00649
29. International Data Space Association: International Data Space Reference Architecture Model 4.0. https://internationaldataspaces.org/offers/reference-architecture/. Accessed 26 Jan 2026
30. Venable, J., Pries-Heje, J., Baskerville, R.: FEDS: a framework for evaluation in design science research. Eur. J. Inf. Syst. **25**, 77–89 (2016). https://doi.org/10.1057/ejis.2014.36
31. Janiesch, C., Rosenkranz, C., Scholten, U.: An information systems design theory for service network effects. J. Assoc. Inf. Syst. **21** (2020). https://doi.org/10.17705/1jais.00642
32. Raharjo, T., Abdurrahman, M.H., Yossy, E.H.: A model of critical success factors for master data management development projects using analytic hierarchy process (AHP): an insight from Indonesia. In: International Conference on Management Science and Industrial Engineering, Chiang Mai, Thailand, pp. 17–22 (2023). https://doi.org/10.1145/3603955.3603959
33. Buffenoir, E., Bourdon, I.: Reconciling complex organizations and data management: the panopticon paradigm. In: Pacific Asia Conference on Information Systems (PACIS) (2013)
34. Otto, B., Hüner, K.M., Österle, H.: Toward a functional reference model for master data quality management. Inf. Syst. e-Bus. Manage. **10**, 395–425 (2012). https://doi.org/10.1007/s10257-011-0178-0
35. Datta, S.K., Bokan, T., Resman, L.: A reference architecture for agricultural data spaces: case study from DIVINE project. In: 2025 International Wireless Communications and Mobile Computing (IWCMC), pp. 8–13 (2025). https://doi.org/10.1109/IWCMC65282.2025.11059474
36. Altendeitering, M., Guggenberger, T.M.: Data quality tools: towards a software reference architecture. In: Hawaii International Conference on System Sciences 2024 (HICSS-57) (2024)

37. Bader, S., et al.: The international data spaces information model – an ontology for sovereign exchange of digital content. Presented at the Lecture Notes in Computer Science (2020). https://doi.org/10.1007/978-3-030-62466-8_12

38. Azkan, C., Möller, F., Ebel, M., Iqbal, T., Otto, B., Poeppelbuss, J.: Hunting the treasure: modeling data ecosystem value co-creation. In: International Conference on Information Systems (ICIS) (2022)

39. Gelhaar, J., Otto, B.: Challenges in the emergence of data ecosystems. In: Pacific Asia Conference on Information Systems (PACIS) (2020)

40. Barclay, I., Preece, A., Taylor, I., Radha, S.K., Nabrzyski, J.: Providing assurance and scrutability on shared data and machine learning models with verifiable credentials. Concurr. Comput. Pract. Exper. **35** (2023). https://doi.org/10.1002/cpe.6997

41. Jarke, M., Otto, B., Ram, S.: Data sovereignty and data space ecosystems. Bus. Inf. Syst. Eng. **61**, 549–550 (2019)

42. Weber, K., Otto, B., Oesterle, H.: One size does not fit all—a contingency approach to data governance. ACM J. Data Inf. Q. **1** (2009). Article 4. https://doi.org/10.1145/1515693.151 5696

Author Index

J. vom Brocke et al. (Eds.): DESRIST 2026, LNCS 16606, pp. 449–450, 2026.
https://doi.org/10.1007/978-3-032-28313-9

MIX
Papier aus verantwortungsvollen Quellen
Paper from responsible sources
FSC® C105338

If you have any concerns about our products,
you can contact us on
ProductSafety@springernature.com

In case Publisher is established outside the EU,
the EU authorized representative is:
Springer Nature Customer Service Center GmbH
Europaplatz 3, 69115 Heidelberg, Germany

Printed by Libri Plureos GmbH
in Hamburg, Germany